THE NEW TESTAMENT

THE NEW TESTAMENT

ITS HISTORY
AND THEOLOGY

James L. Price

Duke University

MACMILLAN PUBLISHING COMPANY
New York

COLLIER MACMILLAN PUBLISHERS
London

225.6
P945n
1987

Earlier editions entitled *Interpreting the New Testament* copyright © 1961, 1971, by Holt, Rinehart and Winston.

Macmillan Publishing Company
866 Third Avenue, New York, New York 10022

Collier Macmillan Canada, Inc.

Library of Congress Cataloging-in-Publication Data

Price, James L. (James Ligon)
  The New Testament.

  Rev. ed. of: Interpreting the New Testament.
2nd ed. 1971.
  Bibliography: p.
  Includes index.
  1. Bible. N.T.—Introductions. I. Price, James L.
(James Ligon), 1915– . Interpreting the New
Testament. II. Title.
BS2330.2.P7 1987   225.6   86-5381
ISBN 0-02-396610-6

ACKNOWLEDGMENTS

Permission has been granted to quote from the following publications:

The Scripture quotations contained herein, unless otherwise noted, are from the Revised Standard Version of the Bible, copyrighted 1946, 1952, 1971 by the Division of Christian Education of the National Council of the Churches of Christ in the U.S.A., and are used by permission. All rights reserved.

H. J. Cadbury, *The Book of Acts in History*, New York: Harper & Row, 1955.

James Robinson, ed., *The Nag Hammadi Library in English*. New York: Harper & Row, 1977.

P. R. Ackroyd and C. F. Evans, eds., *The Cambridge History of the Bible, Vol. 1, From the Beginnings to Jerome*. Cambridge University Press, 1970.

Jacob Neusner, *From Politics to Piety: The Emergence of Pharisaic Judaism*. Englewood Cliffs, NJ: Prentice-Hall, 1973.

M. Hengel, *Acts and the History of Earliest Chritianity*. Philadelphia: Fortress Press, 1980. Rights to the English translation held by the translator, John Bowden, Director SCM Press, London.

W. G. Kümmel, *Introduction to the New Testament*. English translation copyright, Abingdon Press, 1975.

W. D. Davies, *Invitation to the New Testament: A Guide to Its Main Witnesses*. Garden City, NY: Doubleday, 1966.

R. E. Brown, *The Birth of the Messiah: A Commentary on the Infancy Narratives in Matthew and Luke*. Garden City, NY: Doubleday, 1977.

Printing: 1 2 3 4 5 6 7   Year: 7 8 9 0 1 2 3

ISBN 0-02-396610-6

Preface

IN introducing *The New Testament*, I am reminded of the "scribe" described by Jesus as one who, in his training for the kingdom, like a householder "brings out of his treasure what is new and what is old" (Matthew 13:52). For more than three decades of teaching—college and university students for the most part—I have endeavored to keep abreast of the exciting advances in New Testament scholarship resulting from the discoveries of new primary source materials and experimentation with new approaches. Also during this time I have come to a greater appreciation of the work of some not-so-recent scholars whose contributions have stood the test of time and whose insights have not been invalidated or superceded. Accordingly, this book surveys a broad spectrum of opinion concerning the issues of New Testament interpretation and seeks to avoid a restriction of interest to the currently popular modes of research or "schools" of interpretation. That is to say, its purpose is to bring out of the treasure of knowledge "what is new and what is old."

This is a new book, although not entirely so since it retains some materials published in the first and second editions of my *Interpreting the New Testament*. The revisions, however, have been sufficiently extensive to justify giving the text a new name. A few similarities and differences are noted here.

The most evident similarity is the continuation of a distinctive feature of the previous books. A first reading from the New Testament is the early chapters of the Acts of the Apostles. In Chapter 2 a rationale is offered for beginning with Acts instead of the Gospels, which are in some sense accounts of Jesus' life and teaching, and instead of the epistles of Paul, commonly believed to be the earliest Christian writings. Suffice it here to say that although not the oldest source, the Acts provides a singularly important narrative context, establishing a perspective on the Gospel's records of Jesus' ministry in their forms and content. The early chapters of Acts also offer the reader a background for the controversies arising from the inauguration of Christian missions to the Gentiles and from the attendant reservations and resistance of Jewish Christians to these missions. Relating the Paul of Acts to the Paul of his letters is not without difficulties, yet the Acts narrative of Christian beginnings is indispensable to the student of the Apostle's life and thought.

Another feature of the earlier books is retained; each New Testament writing is examined as a literary whole, and an exposition of its text is the main objective. The use that these texts may have for historical reconstruction is a secondary consideration. To assist the reader in viewing each book as a literary unit, the earlier editions proposed outlines, placing them at the introduction to each book. In this edition, comprehensive outlines are omitted, except in the exposition of the shortest writings. Instead, the larger texts are divided according to the successive stages in the development of their narratives, argumentative discourse, and so on. These parts of the whole are accompanied by a mini-commentary. In no instance is this commentary exhaustive. Its purpose is to join closely text and interpretation, to invite reflection upon a portion of the text in its literary context. The reader is asked: Do you see what I see in this text? Or better, do you see in it what others have seen, others who are specialists and whose training and research merit our attention?

A new feature of this book is the inclusion of "extended notes" that appear in the margins and serve in a variety of ways to provoke further discussion of related issues, questions of origin, perennial concerns of New Testament criticism, and so on. These marginal notes can be left aside by the reader without a noticeable disturbance in the flow of the primary exposition, but the information they contain may excite and increase one's understanding of the texts having these notes. In seminars or small discussion groups, the notes may be a catalyst in stimulating a movement of thought from what the text meant (to its writer and first readers) to what the text means in a contemporary context.

The reader is informed that the position taken in this book regarding the Acts of the Apostles is more positive than many contemporary scholars will support. While I acknowledge that the writer of Luke–Acts was motivated by theological (and, perhaps, political) interests that have affected his "objectivity," recent criticism has underestimated the historical worth of Luke's two volumes, especially the book of Acts.

Another conviction of the author is that *Interpreting the New Testament* did less than justice to the significance of the relationships between Judaism and Christianity as major factors in the development of Christian institutions, theology, ethics, and apologetics. Many New Testament scholars share the belief that these writings can best be understood as various expressions of a heightening of tension between the synagogue and the church in the First Century. This is not to overlook the evidence for Graeco-Roman influences, yet the accumulated evidence for this Hellenistic conditioning, so to speak, indicates that it was mediated to Christians in Palestine and in the Diaspora through Hellenistic-Jewish agencies.

I am especially indebted to Professor Eric Meyers of Duke University for his guidance in the selection of pertinent material on developments within Judaism in the Second Temple Period, and also to a former, esteemed colleague, Professor W. D. Davies, for reading the section on Jesus and the Torah scholars and for his critical views concerning this subject. I wish to acknowledge here, with hearty thanks, the contribution of Professor Raymond Brown to my revision of the sections in this book on the Gospel and Epistles of John, and for his kindness to me during a term's residence at Union Theological Seminary in New York.

I wish to thank my editors at Macmillan: Helen McInnis, executive editor; and Wendy Polhemus, production editor, for her careful preparation of the manuscript.

Rollie Grams, an advanced graduate student in New Testament at Duke, helpfully assisted me in editing this text and in preparing the Bibliography.

J. L. P.

Contents

PART III
CONFLICT AND CONSOLIDATION IN THE POSTAPOSTOLIC AGE

Chapter 17 Writings from the Pauline Circle   *381*

Chapter 18 Five "Open Letters" to Christians   *398*

Maps and Charts

THE NEW TESTAMENT

INTRODUCTION

<table>
<tr><td>

Interpreting the
New Testament

</td><td>

Chapter
1

</td></tr>
</table>

WHAT is the New Testament? It may be instructive to answer that question by referring to two important functions served by this collection of twenty-seven writings. On the one hand, the New Testament is the primary source book for knowledge of the Christian movement in its earliest period. On the other hand, it is Christianity's normative guidebook, containing fundamental statements and interpretations of the Christian faith. This twofold definition acknowledges that the subject matter of the New Testament is both historical and theological and suggests that its readers are prompted by somewhat disparate interests or approaches. This separation is not called for and, indeed, should not be encouraged.

THE HISTORICAL ASPECT

Consider first the New Testament as the primary source for knowledge of the origins of Christianity. What bearing has the nature of this source book upon the determination of suitable approaches to it?

A better understanding of the New Testament is obtained if its readers apply to its writings literary and historical criticism. Please note that to be critical of the Bible does not mean finding fault. Criticism is the formation of judgments based on publicly accessible evidence and commonly accepted principles of investigation. The term *exegesis* is ordinarily used with reference to biblical criticism. Exegesis is a word borrowed from Greek, the verb form meaning "to lead out." An exegetical exercise attempts to locate and to state the meaning or meanings of a text. A synonym for exegesis is exposition. The objective is to recover the historical context or setting of a text, the circumstances that occasioned its composition, its author's intended meaning or point of view, and its first reader's perceptions. An exegesis of Paul's Letter to the Galatians, for example, aims at gaining access to the meaning of the Apostle's words. What did he write? Why did he write what he did to these Christians? What was the situation?

It may seem that the importance or the necessity of an historical approach to the New Testament is being belabored here, for it probably is obvious to a modern reader that in order to understand an ancient text some things about its origin must be known. The books of the New Testament, no less than other writings from late antiquity, can and should be understood in their historical setting.

THE ADVANCE OF CRITICISM: A STRUGGLE FOR LEGITIMACY

The idea and practice of applying the ordinary interests and tools of historical research to the exegesis of "sacred scripture" is a modern development. It was a major intellectual product of the late seventeenth-century cultural revolution commonly known as the Enlightenment. Still, the historical-critical approach to biblical texts became widely accepted only in the nineteenth century, and then in the face of enormous resistance. Even today it is not uncommon in conservative religious circles to find sharp opposition to biblical criticism, or at least a vague sense of its impropriety or danger. This apprehension cannot be dismissed as merely reactionary. Some influential scholars of the modern period, identified as "historians of early Christianity," proposed radical revisions of traditional views of Christian beginnings. Some of this scholarship lacked the objectivity claimed for it; their results have not infrequently been discredited. Yet in spite of noteworthy errors and excesses (which the critics' own methods have tended to correct), there can be no turning back to a nonhistorical or precritical approach in undertaking a serious reading of the Bible. As a record of Christian origins, the New Testament should be understood historically. The investigative procedures of professional historians and literary critics afford valid approaches to the New Testament writings.[1]

THE THEOLOGICAL ASPECT

We shall return to a consideration of the proper role of historical criticism in New Testament exegesis, but for the moment consider the other function served by the New Testament: its normative or constitutive role for Christian faith and theology. Are other than historical approaches and methods needed to gain a religious or theological understanding of the New Testament?

Some New Testament scholars have espoused a "theological exegesis" of its texts; that is, their exegesis seeks to recover the theology or theologies of the New Testament writings. This effort is sometimes faulted as treating historical criticism as dispensable or merely preliminary. While such disparagement of historical criticism is not defensible, it is certainly quite legitimate, indeed inevitable, that interest in the New Testament should not be limited to historical reconstruction and description. Since these writings have functioned (and for many persons continue to function) as sacred scripture, historical understanding is often valued as a means to an end. The texts of the New Testament are not primarily grist for the historian's mill, but positive expressions of a community's faith, and as such they function today as the classical statement of the faith of countless millions, a faith that is renewed by a return to its source.

HERMENEUTICS: AN OLD WORD WITH A NEW MEANING

The threat of a widening breach between the aims of historians of the Bible, on the one hand, and of biblical theologians, on the other, has awakened a lively interest in a subject called "hermeneutics." Again we have a word borrowed from Greek: *hermeneuein,* meaning "to interpret." The term was first applied to the scriptures by seventeenth-century Christian scholars to refer to a systematic analysis of the principles and methods of Bible study, to a disciplined reflection on the exegetical process. While the earlier Christian use of the term has been retained, its modern meaning has been broadened to encompass the theory and practice of the art and science of interpretation.

As was noted above, the ascendency and domination of historical-critical methods during the nineteenth century tended to limit the purpose of exegesis to historical description. The goal of contemporary hermeneutics is to understand New Testament texts in terms of past and present meanings: the movement in thought from what a text probably *meant* to what it may *mean.* The process by which understanding is achieved is itself hermeneutics.

A HERMENEUTICAL DIAGRAM

It may be helpful to consider briefly the dynamic dimensions of the exegetical process by reference to a simple diagram:

The point designated "author" focuses upon questions concerning the origin and purpose of a given text. What is known about the author, his sources and the circumstances that occasioned his writing? What is known about the persons being addressed, about their life-world? These are, as has been noted, the concerns of historical criticism aimed at understanding the original meaning of a text.

EVIDENCE: BOTH INTERNAL AND EXTERNAL

The separation of points (a) and (c) is not absolute; indeed, the text itself provides primary evidence concerning the author, his purpose, and so forth. But this internal evidence, which is often indirect, is assessed by the historian along with the external evidence, evidence gleaned from contemporary literary sources—Jewish and pagan documents, other Christian writings, archeological data, and so forth. The operations of exegesis thus directed to this point primarily seek answers to the question, *What lies behind the text, or what is known or plausibly can be inferred about the environment of the author and his intended readers that sheds light upon the meaning of the text?*

The value of the introduction of this evidence depends not only upon the collection and correlation of relevant data, but upon the personal judgments and the critical acumen of the exegete. And so attention is drawn to point (b) of the diagram.

The focus at this point is upon "the reader," the person doing the exegesis, the assumptions, interests, and experiences that make up the life-world of the serious reader of the New Testament. The questions here are, *What influences and interests provide the frame of reference for the reader's placement of the text*, and what ideological presuppositions, what specific cultural assumptions constitute an angle of vision for interpretation?

THE IMPOSSIBILITY OF EXEGESIS WITHOUT PRESUPPOSITIONS

In doing an exegesis the reader is not a neutral observer; he or she is as much a product of one's personal beliefs and cultural heritage as was the first-century author and readers. Modern hermeneutics stresses the importance of this subjective factor in determining the outcome of an exegesis. It is easy to demonstrate how either strong, antireligious prejudice or theological dogmatism forecloses the likelihood that exegesis can be a learning experience. It is not easy, however, to assess the effects of one's own or another critic's presuppositions upon exegesis. In many cases an exegesis does not reflect explicitly the exegete's ideology, but only the exegetical "conclusions" that have gained scholars' consensus and a wide dissemination. In any case it is not possible to exclude all prior assumptions in doing an exegesis. However, premature judgments that coerce results and force the evidence can be avoided.

TESTING ONE'S OWN PRESUPPOSITIONS

The problem with prior assumptions is not that the reader of the New Testament has them—they promote an interest in the text to begin with. The crucial question is whether the reader is sufficiently aware of his or her particular assumptions and is willing to test these against evidence provided by the text. A reader's "correction" of his or her own or another reader's interpretation is not a deduction from "better" presuppositions, but from "better" marshaling of evidence provided by the text. The ideal might be stated in this way: hold in hypothetical status what you think a text says and means until it can be determined whether that meaning is confirmed, modified, or left unsupported by careful exegesis. We are thus brought to the final point in the diagram designated "Text" (c).

The focus here is an acknowledgment that the reading of the text is more basic to understanding than a knowledge of its origin, its authorship, sources, and composition. Meaning is derived from a first-hand experience of viewing a text as a finished product, yet in being guided by its author to an ever greater clarification of its distinctive point of view. The primary exegetical question here is this: *What shows itself in the text; what does it tell?* Assenting to or dissenting from a text should be resisted until it has been read; looking into it for answers to your own questions should be avoided until you have sought to understand the questions and answers that concern the author.

The reader's encounter with a text of the New Testament, however, is often indirect and mediated. By separately focusing on (c) and (a) we recognize another important factor in the exegetical process. We attend to the fact that many texts of the New Testament signify more than their historically conditioned original meaning.

THE EXTENDED MEANING OF SOME NEW TESTAMENT TEXTS

Significant texts often generate and acquire extended meanings as they are applied to situations other than those that occasioned their composition; their original meanings become separated from the putative intentions of their authors (a not uncommon phenomenon with regard to classic texts, as literary critics often note). This "after-life," so to speak, refers to the meaning that texts acquire subsequent to their composition, as they are applied to situations other than those that occasioned their writing, situations that have been perceived by exegetes to be analogous and therefore illuminated by these texts.

This extended meaning of texts can be positioned between (b) and (c) in the diagram, for the exceptionally productive after-life of many New Testament texts serves as a screen or, perhaps better, a lens through which the reader focuses upon their meanings.

THE TENSION BETWEEN SCRIPTURE AND TRADITION

This consideration introduces the problem of the relation between scripture and tradition, which has been variously assessed by Christian churches. Suffice it here to say that the history of hermeneutics in Eastern Orthodox, Roman Catholic, and Protestant theologies reveals a sensitivity to the dangers of individualism growing out of a natural tendency in humans to generate idiosyncratic interpretations of scripture. More subtle is the influence of the great traditions—Augustinian, Thomistic, Calvinistic, Wesleyan—upon scholars nurtured in them. Yet from time to time voices have been raised affirming the normative particularity of the Bible's text as a "rule" of Christian faith and the need to be open to its teaching, its claims of truth. For Christians these claims are perceived not as mute objects preserved in literary monuments at one's disposal, but rather as proclamations of a living subject: God's personal address to his human creatures.

CONCLUSION

The simple diagram used here may illustrate the dynamic interplay of factors in the exegetical process and may support the view that one does not need to opt for mutually exclusive approaches in seeking to understand either a text's history and literary design or its theological content. Of course, any exegete's particular interests may focus on one or the other, but to do so is not without risk of obtaining a distorted or at least a partial vision of the text's meaning.

A few words remain concerning the positive role of historical criticism in a contemporary appropriation of the messages of the New Testament. The present writer is convinced that in the process of taking seriously the historical life-situations revealed in its texts, a genuine encounter with their present meanings may occur. Thus, contemporary understanding may arise out of (not apart from) a clearer comprehension of the situations that occasioned the text's form and content.

Not all historical criticism establishes a dynamic dialectic between past and present meanings. (Historical criticism can be quite antiquarian.) But by adopting an openness to the claims of the texts of the New Testament one is in a position to give responsible assent to or dissent from them.

Finally, in some concrete ways historical criticism exercises an adversarial role in the interest of achieving positive objectives. Criticism will be directed against anything that can obstruct understanding. It will be leveled against occasional distortions of the text resulting from copyist's mistakes and other linguistic errors accompanying its transmission (the objectives of the science of textual criticism). It will be directed against deformation of a text's meaning resulting from overiding biases and faulty assumptions tending to alter a text or place it in an artificial or anachronistic context. And not least in importance, historical criticism prompts the interpreter to self-criticism and may serve as a restraint upon an all too private or sectarian interpretation of texts. Historical criticism also curbs impatient demands for a text's instant relevance.

As this book will demonstrate, historical criticism, far from being a destructive or diversionary dead end, can put in place those necessary foundations for a more adequate understanding of the New Testament and of its spiritual values in today's world.

NOTE

1. For the most part *historical criticism* is used here in a wide sense, including philological, rhetorical, and other types of literary criticism; textual criticism; and archeological and sociohistorical criticism. M. Hengel wrote: "the 'historical-critical method' simply represents a necessary collection of the 'tools' for opening up past events; that is, it is not a single, clearly defined procedure, but rather a mixture of sometimes very different methods of working." (*Acts and the History of Earliest Christianity* [Philadelphia: Fortress Press, 1980], p. 54. See also the valuable appendix, Pt. III, pp. 127ff.)

Adopting a Point of Departure: New Testament Chronology	Chapter 2

T HE arrangement and order of books in the New Testament canon poses a basic problem. What point of departure should the reader adopt? Among a variety of approaches, which is to be commended? And how is one to proceed, once a beginning has been decided upon?

FOUR APPROACHES TO THE NEW TESTAMENT

From first to last, according to the order of the New Testament: Each book is a significant whole and can be studied profitably as a unit. Many "introductions to the New Testament" recognize this fact and follow its traditional literary arrangement. Beginning with The Gospel according to Matthew, each book is viewed in terms of its origin and other special problems relating to its content. Such questions as the following carry forward the discussion: Who wrote this book? When and from what place? For whom was it written and for what purpose?

At first sight this plan of study seems logical. Yet a number of difficulties face the reader starting with Matthew and working straight through to Revelation. It is known that the books in the canon nearest the front were not the earliest written. For example, most scholars agree that Mark was written before Matthew, Galatians before Romans, and so on. Moreover, the present arrangement of books does not provide the reader with a consecutive development of events. For example, 1 and 2 Thessalonians, the thirteenth and fourteenth books, reflect situations in the life of Paul and the Church that are earlier than those presupposed by the Apostle's letter to the Romans (the sixth book).

From first to last, according to dates of composition: Some books that introduce the New Testament have been organized on a strictly chronological plan. It is proposed that the students begin with the earliest books, that is, with the letters of the Apostle Paul and, a few persons would add, the Letter of James. The development of the Christian Church is then traced according to its primary documents considered in the order of their writing.

Aside from the fact that there are uncertainties about the dates of these books, there are serious weaknesses in this approach. This method obscures some obvious truths. For example, Paul's career followed that of Jesus and the establishment of the Christian Church. We know from his own writings that Paul takes for granted his readers' acquaintance with the main facts about Jesus. Also it can easily be shown that Paul's missions presuppose the existence of earlier Christian communities. Paul's gospel rests upon the testimony of Christians before his conversion. This is true whatever we may say about Paul's independence or about his reinterpretation of the traditional faith. It is hazardous, therefore, to overlook Christianity before Paul and to give no consideration to its possible influence upon him. A serious reader ought to fill in the background as clearly as possible before tackling Paul's letters. They are never easy to understand, but they are especially difficult if one starts with them.

From the career of Jesus to the latest book concerning him: It is perhaps the most common practice to introduce a systematic study of the New Testament with the life and teachings of Jesus, as they may be recovered from the Gospels. Obviously there are good reasons for beginning with Jesus. Christianity originated as an interpretation of Jesus' ministry, and still draws its inspiration from this original source. But this approach, as ordinarily followed, presents some real problems. The fact is that the New Testament contains no biography of Jesus written during his career or even shortly thereafter. At the appropriate place we shall consider how the Gospels came to be written and what their distinguishing characteristics are. It is sufficient now to affirm that they were made up from fragments of the oral and written tradition relating to various aspects of Jesus' work and teachings and were composed by men who selected and treated these materials according to their own theological interests and motives. Before the stories of Jesus were written down they had been employed in the preaching, teaching, worship, and defense of the earliest Christian communities. Thus the Gospels, like all other New Testament writings, are the products of the life and thought of various Christians. It is Jesus as he is remembered by the earliest Christians and experienced in their fellowship whom we meet in the Gospels. If the Gospels of the New Testament are interwoven with the life and thought of the earliest Christians, it is important that we consider what is known about these communities transmitting the stories of Jesus.

From the early Church through the Gospels to Jesus, thence to Paul, his letters, and the remainder of the New Testament books: This fourth alternative approach to the study of the New Testament has been adopted for this book. Consideration will first be given to The Acts of the Apostles, the one New Testament writing that proposes to record the experiences, the faith, and the characteristic activities of the earliest Christians.

Does this seem to be a case of putting the cart before the horse, to begin with a sketch of primitive Christianity and not with the life of Jesus? At the risk of belaboring a point, let it be said again that in spite of its apparent reasonableness, the alternative of beginning with the ministry of Jesus is beset with grave difficulties, particularly for the nonspecialist. The desire to get back to the "real Jesus," to get behind the testimony of the Gospels, can be a worthwhile endeavor. Indeed, it can be a scientific study and, at the same time, can be prompted by the highest religious motives. "The quest of the historical Jesus" has engaged New Testament scholars for over a century. It is unlikely that it will be eclipsed by other interests in the years ahead, at least for very long. But it is questionable whether in an introduction of this sort the reader should be encouraged to begin with a matter of such very great complexity and importance.

The logic of the approach that is being adopted here has been stated by H. J. Cadbury:

> The recent study of the Gospels is making clear to us how important for our understanding of them it would be to know thoroughly the apostolic age. They are not merely uncolored accounts of Jesus' words and deeds but they have included the interests, motives and ideas of the generation through which the story had already been handed down—largely in a fluid state of oral tradition. They are at once a witness to that early Christianity and they themselves are in need of being corrected or discounted by that Christianity if the facts and the figure behind them are to be surely known. *Now the book of Acts is our principal narrative source for knowledge of that exact period in which these influences on the Gospel material were active.*[1]

The first half of the Acts narrative, chapters 1 through 12, provides a point of departure in tracing the fascinating history of the gospel tradition. Upon a completion of a study of the origin of the earliest Gospels and their distinguishing characteristics, a sketch of some major aspects of Jesus' ministry will be attempted.

After the study of Jesus we shall return to Acts and follow its narrative from chapter 13 to the end. A narrative of Paul's career would be practically impossible without Acts. A few of Paul's experiences can be gleaned from his letters, but no one has satisfactorily ordered these fragments without having recourse to the Acts narrative. After studying the New Testament source for our knowledge of Paul's missionary journeys, we shall then consider the letters of Paul in what appears to be their order of composition.

The concluding section of the book will study the remaining texts of the New Testament. The early Church had no historian to portray its fortunes in the latter part of the first and the early part of the second century. If the writer of Acts ever planned a third volume, as some scholars suppose, there is no evidence that he wrote it. Even the most skeptical critic of the historical value of Luke-Acts will realize the appropriateness of the adage, "You never miss the water till the well runs dry."

It is hoped that the approach of this book will commend itself as an historical one.[2] It was the dynamic development of a particular religious community, under certain known conditions, in a given period of world history, that produced the books of the New Testament. It is hoped that the relevance of these texts to your own life and time will be better understood as you study the vital interplay of life and literature in Christianity's first century. In the words of Albert Schweitzer: "In spite of all innovations of doctrine, present or future, it will always remain the true ideal that our faith should return to the richness and vitality of the primitive-Christian faith."[3]

THE EARLY CHURCH AND THE LITERATURE OF THE NEW TESTAMENT

In the first century of its existence, Christianity manifested two stages of development: a period of rapid expansion, ca. 30–65 C.E. followed by one of intensified conflict and the need for consolidation, ca. 65–150 C.E.[4]

The year of Jesus' death is usually reckoned to be 30 C.E. Within a single generation, Christian communities were established in nearly all of the eastern provinces of the Roman Empire as well as in Italy and in Rome itself. This early expansion is partially narrated in the Acts of the Apostles. This book was probably not composed until late in the first century; however, it is the most primitive narrative source of Christian beginnings. This period of rapid expansion is most clearly reflected in the letters of Paul, the earliest literary documents of Christianity. According to the great majority of modern scholars, the New Testament contains nine genuine letters of the Apostle. Six of these were almost certainly written between the years 50 and 60 C.E.: 1 and 2 Thessalonians; 1 and 2 Corinthians; The Letter of Paul to the Galatians; and another to the Romans. The origin of Galatians—the place where it was written, the date, and destination—is variously described. Three other letters, known as *the Prison (or Captivity) Epistles,* are also assigned various dates and places: the letters of Paul to Philemon; to the Philippians; and another, to the Colossians. The Letter to the Colossians is sometimes attributed to a follower of Paul, not to the Apostle. The same judgment also pertains to a tenth writing traditionally attributed to Paul, the Letter to the Ephesians. The identification of the genuine letters of Paul and of the occasions for their composition will be discussed in some detail in Part II of this book. The points to be grasped now are these: in spite of uncertainty about the precise number of and occasions for Paul's genuine letters, the New Testament contains a great treasure in its "Pauline corpus." These books reflect the great Apostle's interpretation of Christianity. From them it is possible to trace the main lines of Paul's theology. Few men in antiquity are known as intimately as Paul is known through his writings. His letters disclose the main lines of the early development of Christianity, the amazingly vigorous thrust and penetration of Christian missions northwest from Jerusalem into Asia Minor, Greece, and Italy within a single generation. They illustrate conditions existing within the young churches in these regions, their internal affairs, and some of the typical attitudes of outsiders.

The end of the first stage can be fixed at the point at which the steady advance of Christianity was momentarily halted. In the winter of 64–65 there was a disastrous fire in Rome. The rumor spread that the Emperor Nero (54–68) had set the city afire in order to further his building plans for a greater capital. According to Tacitus, Nero put the blame for the fire upon the followers of a "mischievous superstition."[5] The emperor turned upon Christians as a minority group within the city and made scapegoats of them. Christianity was outlawed and, as Tacitus reported, those who were thus victimized suffered terrible brutalities.

Just how long Christianity had been established at Rome and what had been the early fortunes of the Church there are subjects for conjecture. The Roman writer Suetonius, in his *Lives of the Twelve Caesars,* said that Claudius (41–

Dates	New Testament Writings	Events	Herods	Roman Governors	Roman Emperors	Dates
				Caponius	9	
				M. Ambibulus	Augustus	
				A. Rufus 12	14	
					15	
−20			Herod Antipas	V. Gratus		−20
					26 Tiberius	
−30		Ministry of John the Baptist	Philip	Pontius Pilate		−30
		Ministry of Jesus; Crucifixion/Resurrection				
		Pentecost				
		Persecution of "Hellenists;" Stephen is executed				
		Conversion of Paul	d. 34	Marcellus? 36	36	
		Beginning of Gentile Missions	Herod Agrippa I	Marullus?	37 Gaius	
−40					41	−40
		Martyrdom of James, son of Zebedee	39			
			d. 44	C. Fadus		
				T. Alexander 46	Claudius	
		Apostolic Conference in Jerusalem		V. Cumanus 48	48	
−50	1, 2 Thessalonians	Paul in Corinth				−50
	1, 2 Corinthians			ca. 52		
	Galatians	Paul in Ephesus			54	
	Philippians?					
	Romans			C. Felix		
		Arrest of Paul in Jerusalem				
		Imprisonment of Paul in Caesarea		ca. 60	Nero	
−60	Colossians	Journey to Rome				−60
	Philemon	Martyrdom of James, the Lord's brother		P. Festus		
	Ephesians?			Albinus	64	
		Martyrdoms of Peter and Paul		G. Florus		
				66	66 Galba Otho Vitellius } 68	
		Flight of Christians from Jerusalem to Pella;	Herod Agrippa II			
		of Yohanan ben Zakkai to Yavneh				
−70	Mark	Destruction of Jerusalem				−70
		Fall of Masada				
					Vespasian	
	Hebrews?				79	
−80	Luke				Titus	−80
	Acts				81	
	Matthew					
	1 Peter?		ca. 86		Domitian	
	James?					
−90	Revelation					−90
	John					
	1, 2 Timothy, Titus					
	1, 2, 3 John				96	
					Nerva	
	Jude?				Trajan	
100					100	
	2 Peter				117	

Left margin vertical labels: APOSTOLIC AGE (upper), POSTAPOSTOLIC AGE (lower)

13

54) expelled the Jews from Rome for continual rioting "at the instigation of Chrestus."[6] Many scholars take this comment to refer to troubles between Jews and Christians. If this identification is correct, Christianity had reached Rome and attracted the attention of the government within two decades after Jesus' death.

In the years following 65, the beginning of the period of conflict and consolidation, Christians in the Empire must have been painfully aware of their hazardous position. There is no evidence that they were continually persecuted by government authorities. Still, the ever-present possibility of persecution must have called for courage and endurance. It should not be supposed that during the years of the rapid expansion of Christianity the followers of Jesus enjoyed an immunity from suffering. Various kinds of opposition and conflict were experienced, mostly arising from the Jewish synagogues and the authorities of the temple in Jerusalem. But the conflict of Christians with the Roman government dates from the period now under review.

The typical mood of the New Testament books written at the close of the apostolic age is one of tension. Christians are warned to be on the alert, to stand ready to sacrifice themselves. The reader also senses in these books a wistful longing for a better life beyond the crises of the time and an intensification of hope that the promise of the new age will soon be fulfilled, mixed with some perplexity that the time is delayed. Ancient Church tradition has it that both Peter and Paul were martyred at Rome during Nero's persecution. These tragedies are not reported in the New Testament but there are no good reasons for doubting that they happened. The thinning of the ranks of eyewitnesses to Jesus' historic Ministry aroused the churches to a need for perpetuating their recollections of Jesus.

The first composition of a connected account of the Ministry, so far as is known, was The Gospel according to Mark. The troubled conditions that existed in Nero's Rome may provide a factual basis for the Evangelist's concern. Mark emphasized the example of Christ's sufferings as the precondition of his glory. Martyrdoms ordered by Nero may have occasioned this Gospel's warning that his disciples must take up their crosses, led to an emphasis upon Jesus' sayings concerning the near advent of "the Son of man," and the vindication and victory of those persons who confess him in and through their sufferings.

Within the next two critical decades other Gospels appeared. The one entitled The Gospel according to Matthew has been aptly described as a revised and enlarged edition of Mark. The new material in Matthew includes, among other things, the teachings of Jesus concerning "the higher righteousness of the kingdom of heaven." The Gospel according to Luke is the first part of a two-volume work dedicated to one who is addressed "most excellent Theophilus." The second volume is the book of Acts. These companion books, which fittingly can be designated Luke-Acts, are dominated by a strong emphasis on the outreach of the church to the Gentiles.

Other writings commonly assigned to the early part of the postapostolic period are The First Letter of Peter; The Letter to the Hebrews; and The Revelation to John. Several scholars have held that these three writings are best understood as relating to three phases of a single crisis growing out of the stiffening opposition of Rome to the Christian movement. The fact is that there are large elements of conjecture with respect to the origin of these books and their relationship, if any, to each other. Anyone seeking to trace the changing fortunes of Christianity in the Roman Empire, the attitudes of various emperors and other authorities toward the Christian religion, enters a darkened tunnel. Not until the turn of the century does one emerge from this darkness and begin to see the problems with greater clarity. But it is probable that during the last three decades of the first century, Christians in various parts of the Roman Empire had faced stern opposition. In some cases they had suffered martyrdom. Other Christians had become indifferent. Some had renounced their faith. A letter from Pliny, the governor of Bithynia, to the Emperor Trajan (ca. C.E. 112) reports that some of the persons he had questioned in his province, who were loyalty risks, had testified that they had abandoned their Christian faith many years before.[7]

The latest writings of the New Testament are dated within the last years of the first century to the middle of the second century. They indicate that there were dangers confronting Christianity at this time which were more insidious than was the open hostility of some Jewish synagogues or Caesar's agents. The "heroic age" had passed in which powerful forces for unity had been felt. For one thing, the hope that Jesus the Messiah would soon return seems to have waned. There is some evidence that the validity of this hope was being denied by some Christians. At any rate, aggressive leadership and efficient organization were needed if the churches were to survive in the indeterminate future. Most important of all, the integrity of the rank-and-file membership had to be secured. Christian literature of this time is much concerned with the promotion of order and discipline and shows an acute sensitivity to irregularity of belief in the Christian churches.[8]

This final stage in the development of the Church of the New Testament has been known as an age of consolidation. The word, through its military usage, suggests the strengthening of a position that has been gained by costly struggle and some losses, through reorganization or retrenchment. The Letter to Titus, and The First and Second Letters to Timothy, commonly referred to as "the Pastoral Epistles," were written for this purpose, to consolidate the discipline and doctrine of Christianity. Several letters known as "the General (or Catholic) Epistles" also seem to fit into this period and contribute to our knowledge of it. Among these are The First, Second, and Third Letters of John, and The Letter of Jude. It is probable, too, that The Letter of James dates from this period. The book called The Second Letter of Peter is probably the last of the New Testament books to have been written.

No mention has been made thus far of The Gospel according to John. There are sufficient reasons for dating this important book within a few years on either side of 90 C.E. The other writings of the New Testament that belong to this time afford some help in understanding the contemporary significance of "John's Gospel." Yet there remain many perplexing problems concerning its origin. Ancient Church tradition and the evidence of the Gospel itself are not decisive. Scholars recently have ransacked non-Christian literature of the period in the hope of uncovering the particular needs that John in his Gospel sought to satisfy. Scholars have hoped in this way also to identify the source of the specific thought-forms that are employed in this Gospel.

The origin and environment of the Fourth Gospel is an exceedingly complex study, more interesting to some readers than to others. But whatever a student's interest in these historical questions, it will be readily acknowledged that the book has had a pervasive influence upon the life and thought of the Church from the late second century to the present time. John presents a fresh interpretation of Jesus and his ministry, in some ways different from the other three Gospels. It is probable that he told his story in order that the Church might be enabled to bear witness to those Jews and Greeks possessed of a particular type of mentality, to the end that both understand the gospel and believe it. At any rate, whatever his immediate intention, the Fourth Evangelist created a language for the Church that has spoken to the human situation in every age. For many persons this book mediates the gospel of Jesus Christ with an unparalleled directness and power.

The two charts that follow exhibit the margins of uncertainty concerning the dating of several of the books of the New Testament. Some of the letters attributed in Ancient Church tradition to the principal Apostles, for example, Colossians and the Pastorals to Paul, 1 Peter and James to the Apostles bearing

THE DATING OF THE NEW TESTAMENT BOOKS
[and Early Writings of the Apostolic Fathers]

1–30 C.E. The Time of Jesus	30–70 C.E. Apostolic Age (The great apostles—Peter, Paul, and James died in the 60s)		70–100 C.E. Postapostolic Age	After 100 C.E.
	Christian Writings Incorporating Reflection on Church Problems			
Public Ministry ca. 28–30 C.E.	**30–50** / P E R I O D O F P R E A C H I N G	**50s** ¹₂⎤ Thessalonians ¹₂⎤ Corinthians Galatians Romans Philippians ▬▶	**60s** Letters from Prison: Colossians ▬ ▬ ▬ ▶ Philemon Ephesians ▬ ▬ ▬ ▶ Patoral Letters:* 1, 2 Timothy ▬ ▬ ▬ ▶ Titus Hebrews ▬ ▬ ▬ ▬ ▶ ▬ ▬ ▶ 1 Peter ▬ ▬ ▬ ▬ ▶ ▬ ▬ ▶ James ▬ ▬ ▬ ▬ ▬ ▶ ▬ ▬ ▶ Jude ▬ ▬ ▬ ▬ ▬ ▶ ▬ ▬ ▶	**70** Acts	**70s–80s**	**90s** 1, 2, 3 John Apocalypse (Revelation to John) [1 Clement] [Didache] ▬ ▬ ▬ ▬ ▶	**100–** 2 Peter [Letters of Ignatius of Antioch] ▬ ▬ ▬ ▬ ▶
	Christian Writings Witnessing to the Words and Deeds of Jesus (Gospels)			
	P R E A C H I N G	Oral tradition; and pre-Gospel writings (now lost)	Mark	Matthew Luke	John	[Apocryphal Gospels]

*only 1, 2 Timothy and Titus are "Pastoral Letters"

CHRONOLOGY OF NEW TESTAMENT WRITINGS

	Kümmel*		Robinson†		The Present Writer	
			ca. 47–48	James		
A	50–51	1, 2 Thessalonians	50–51	1, 2 Thessalonians	50–51	1, 2 Thessalonians
P	53–56	Galatians,				
O		Philippians,	Spring 55	1 Corinthians	55 or 56	1 Corinthians
S		1, 2 Corinthians	Autumn 55	1 Timothy	56	2 Corinthians
T	56–58	Romans,	early 56	2 Corinthians	56	Philippians
O		Colossians,	early 57	Romans		
L		Philemon	Spring 57	Titus	56 or	
I					early 57	Romans
C			Spring 58	Philippians	56–58	Colossians,
			Summer 58	Philemon		Philemon,
A			Summer 58	Colossians		Philippians
G			late 58	Ephesians		
E			late 58	2 Timothy		
			ca. 45…60	Mark		
			ca. 40…60+	Matthew		
			−57…60+	Luke		
			61–62	Jude		
			61–62	2 Peter		
			−57…62+	Acts		
			ca. 60–65	1, 2, 3 John		
			Spring 65	1 Peter		
			ca. −40–65+	John		
			ca. 67	Hebrews	64–69	Mark
	ca. 70	Mark	late 68(−70)	Revelation		
P	70–90	Luke				
O	80–90	Acts,			80–85	Matthew
S		Hebrews			80–85	Luke
T	80–100	Matthew,			85–90	Acts
A		Ephesians			80–90	Hebrews
P	90–95	1 Peter,			ca. 90	Ephesians
O		Revelation			90+	Revelation
S	90–100	John			90+	1 Peter
T	90–110	1, 2, 3 John			90±	John
O	−100	James			90–110	1, 2 Timothy, Titus
L	ca. 100	Jude			ca. 100	Jude
I	100+	1, 2 Timothy, Titus			−100	James
C	100–150	2 Peter			100+	1, 2, 3 John
					100+	2 Peter
A						
G						
E						

* INT[2]

†J.A.T. Robinson, *Redating the New Testament*, Philadelphia: Westminster Press, 1976, p. 352. Omitting Robinson's references to the Apostolic Fathers.

these names, are frequently assigned by scholars to situations after their deaths. The origins of other writings are recognized by all as being difficult to locate, e.g., the anonymous Letter to the Hebrews, or the letters attributed to Jude and Peter (2 Peter).

Some scholars hold that all or nearly all of the New Testament writings are to be dated before 70 C.E., i.e., before the close of the Apostolic Age or the Fall of Jerusalem. J. A. T. Robinson, whose chronology is given in the second chart, vigorously defends this hypothesis. Opposed to this position, namely that most of the books of the New Testament date from the 50s or 60s, is the usual view that, for the most part, the evidence points to their origin in the 80s or 90s.

The different positions have a bearing on questions concerning the development of doctrine, orders of ministry, and the institutions of the Early Church.

Some persons seem to consider that questions relating to the integrity and authority of certain writings are at stake.

THE COMMON FAITH AND HOPE OF THE EARLY CHURCH

The above sketch provides a temporal or circumstantial setting in the early history of Christianity for all twenty-seven books of the New Testament, and may stand as a prospectus for this book. The origin of each writing must be studied as we come to it, without preconceived solutions. But the margin of uncertainty should not be exaggerated. Most of the books of the New Testament are more easily understood—their authors' intentions as well as their present applications—through a search for their specific setting in the ongoing development of the witnessing Church.

The above survey may help the reader to appreciate the fundamental unity that underlies the rich variety of the New Testament. While the analysis of each book must be mainly concerned with its particular circumstances and its distinctive teachings, the process of dividing and dissecting the New Testament can go so far as to obscure the intrinsic unity of the whole. The historical continuity of the witnessing, expanding community of Christians supports and carries forward the oral traditions, as well as the written records, out of which the New Testament was composed. This cavalcade of people and events marking the rapid expansion, defense, and consolidation of the Christian movement provides a dynamic and unified background against which one can view the varieties of thought and experience found within the New Testament.

The claim has been made that no religion becomes a distinctive phenomenon until it has produced a community, a fellowship of persons bound together by common ideas and experiences. Judged by this standard, Christianity in New Testament times emerges as a distinctive phenomenon in history. Christianity is not so much distinguished by its common ideas and distinctive practices as by the attachment of its members to the person of Jesus. The New Testament reflects a central and controlling perspective because everything is focused upon this one person. As different as these books are in their form and verbal expression, they all bear witness to Jesus as one who acted, taught, and suffered as the Messiah, as the Christ. Moreover, the writers and the communities they represent stand united in a common loyalty to Jesus; not only to the Christ who had come, but also to One acknowledged to be the living Lord of life. Every book reflects the impact of the person of Jesus upon men in the present, as well as in the recent past. And finally, throughout the New Testament there is also manifested a confidence that the leadership of Jesus Christ as Lord is destined in the future to become worldwide, unto the glory of God and the fulfillment of His purposes for all humankind.

NOTES

1. H. J. Cadbury, *The Book of Acts in History* (New York: Harper & Row, 1955) pp. 122–123. Italics mine.

2. "The proper historical approach to the study of the New Testament . . . is by way of church history, viz. in its earliest period." F. C. Grant, *The Gospels: Their Origin and Their Growth* (New York: Harper & Row, 1957), p. 17.

3. A. Schweitzer, *The Mysticism of Paul the Apostle,* trans. W. Montgomery (London: A & C Black, Ltd., 1931), pp. 384–384.

4. C.E. = Common Era, a designation employed by Jewish and Christian scholars instead of Christendom's. A.D. = the year of the Lord. B.C.E. = Before the Common Era.

5. Tacitus, *Annals* xv. 44. See Chapter 6, pp. 383–384.

6. Suetonius, "Claudius," xxv. *Lives of the Twelve Caesars.*

7. Pliny, *Letters* xcvi–xcvii.

8. "The catchword propounded by the Pastorals, 'sound doctrine,' . . . is something like the common denominator which can be found in most of the New Testament writings of the postapostolic period." In E. Käsemann, L. E. Keck and J. L. Martyn, eds., *Studies in Luke-Acts* (1966), p. 290.

PART I

THE RECOVERY OF CHRISTIAN ORIGINS

Reconstructing the World of Jesus and His First Followers

JESUS and his disciples were Palestinian Jews who lived in the Hellenistic Age. Strictly speaking, the Hellenistic Age extended from the death of Alexander the Great (323 B.C.E.), to the demise of the Hellenistic kingdoms and the establishment of the Roman Empire (30 B.C.E.), and therefore ended before the lifetime of Jesus. Yet Greek influences outlasted the political domination of the Macedonians and permeated the societies of eastern and western peoples for many years. "New Testament Times" therefore fall within "Hellenistic" or "Graeco-Roman" boundaries. Jewish scholars frequently date the origins of Christianity within the "Late Second Temple Period."

What does the reader of the New Testament need to know about Jesus' homeland in order to understand the world in which he lived? This is a difficult question to answer without offering too little or too much. It is obvious, however, that if one is to be oriented historically one must possess basic information about the political socioeconomic, and religious conditions that establish the contours of Jesus' life and public ministry, for Jesus did not withdraw from the world but, according to the Gospels, ministered to persons within it, knowing the external factors that circumscribed their lives, as well as being sensitive to their inner personal concerns.

The various developments within the Graeco-Roman world affecting Judaism and Christianity will be described in two installments. In this chapter attention will be focused upon Judaism in Palestine during the Period of the Second Temple, before and during the time of Jesus and the establishment of the earliest churches. Chapter 12 presents a second installment where consideration is given to that broader geographical and cultural environment beyond Palestine in which communities of Christians were established.[1]

THE CONQUESTS OF ALEXANDER THE GREAT
(334–323 B.C.E.)

Alexander was twenty years old when his father, Philip of Macedon, was assassinated. Philip had added to his dominion the city-states of Thrace and

Sculpture of Alexander the Great, the youthful Macedonian monarch and world conqueror, 334–323 C.E. *(Courtesy of the Trustees of the British Museum.)*

central Greece and had turned his attention to the East, for Greece had been threatened by two Persian offensives in the fifth century. Alexander quickly mounted a war of vengeance against the Persians. His armies crossed the Hellespont and pushed through the Cilician Gate into Syria. After beseiging the coastal cities of Tyre and Gaza, the Macedonians marched into Egypt. The Persian garrison at Memphis surrendered without a fight.

Josephus recorded that Alexander turned toward Jerusalem after conquering Gaza. His objective was abandoned when a large entourage of priests came to meet him. Alexander accorded the people of Judea special privileges and the right to live according to their ancestral laws.[2] Josephus also reported that the Samaritans sought Alexander's favor, "feigning" themselves to be Jews. In return for an offer of 8,000 soldiers, Alexander gave his approval for the construction of a temple on Mount Gerizim.

Alexander marched his victorious armies as far east as the region that is now Pakistan. Here his troops balked and Alexander was forced to establish his court in Babylon. He died in Babylon just before his thirty-third birthday.

Did Alexander dream of one world mastered by Greek culture? It might be more correct to say that he believed that the gods had destined him to rule over a single state made up of peoples from east and west participating in its governance.

EXCURSUS A

A NOTE CONCERNING THE LITERARY SOURCES

Before surveying the conditions in the lands of the Jews under the rule of the Hellenistic kingdoms and later the Roman empire, a brief description of major literary sources is necessary.

A principal source for knowledge of the four decades beginning with the Maccabean wars of liberation and ending with the death of the last of the Maccabean brothers, Simon, ca. 175–134 B.C.E. is the book 1 Maccabees. This history, modeled upon the historical books of the scriptures and written in Hebrew ca. 100 B.C.E., was preserved in a Greek version and placed in a Christian collection of Jewish writings known from ancient times as *The Apocrypha*.

A second source entitled 2 Maccabees, which is also in the Apocrypha, was written in Greek in Egypt also ca. 100. Except for a preface consisting of two letters, the book is an abbreviation of five volumes composed by Jason of Cyrene. The narrative of 2 Maccabees parallels the events reported in 1 Maccabees 1:1–7:50 and reaches an emotional climax in the report of the final, major victory of Judas Maccabeus over the Syrians a year before his death (160 B.C.E.).

The principal purpose of the author of 1 Maccabees seems to have been to affirm the legitimacy and religious fervor of the House of Mattathias as "the family . . . through whom deliverance was given to Israel" (5:62–64). The author roundly condemned the Gentile oppressors, but also the Hellenizers, "the lawless and wicked men" in Israel.

2 Maccabees belongs to the genre of Greek literature known as "pathetic" history, which sought to arouse the reader's emotions. Among the Hasmoneans only Judas is praised; instead, Onias III, the ousted high priest and the true Zadokite, is glorified. This narrative is replete with mysterious signs and miraculous interventions of the angels (such portents are lacking in 1 Maccabees). While passive resistance and martyrdom are viewed as weakness by the author of 1 Maccabees, the writer of 2 Maccabees assured faithful martyrs a resurrection and enduring fame.

In our sketch and in the secondary sources, both books are used with an awareness of their polemical biases. As a general rule 1 Maccabees is preferred, but 2 Maccabees provides valuable supplements, especially in reconstructing the period immediately preceding the revolt.

A few words are in order about the collection to which both Maccabean histories belong, the Apocrypha. The creation of a Greek version of the Hebrew scriptures was an event of great significance for Diaspora Judaism and the Christian Church.* The Latin title of this Greek version, "Septuagint," and the symbol used to identify it, LXX, are derived from the legend that seventy Jewish scholars in Alexandria collaborated in this translation in the third century B.C.E. Some books were later added to the LXX, including 1 and 2 Maccabees, so that after 100 C.E. the LXX contained more than a dozen writings not included in the Hebrew scriptures commonly venerated by Torah scholars in Palestine. These extra books, included in copies of the LXX but excluded from the canon of the Hebrew scriptures, form the collection known as The Apocrypha of the Old Testament.

*Diaspora is a Greek word referring to the dispersed Jews living in places other than the Holy Land.

The modern Revised Standard Version of the Apocrypha contains the following books: I Esdras, 2 Esdras, Tobit, Judith, Additions to the Book of Esther, The Wisdom of Solomon, Ecclesiasticus (or the Wisdom of Jesus the Son of Sirach), Baruch, The Letter of Jeremiah, The Prayer Azariah and The Song of the Three Young Men, Susanna, Bel and the Dragon, The Prayer of Manasseh, I Maccabees, 2 Maccabees. (The Old Latin translation of the LXX included 2 Esdras, written after 70 C.E., and not in the Greek version.)

Besides the Apocrypha and the special collection known as the Dead Sea Scrolls many other Jewish writings dating from the Second Temple Period have survived in various states of preservation. Some of these writings contain Christian interpolations and supplements. It is customary to refer to these writings as the *Pseudepigrapha,* a term used as early as the time of Jerome to identify writings falsely attributed to an ancient personage.

The English edition of the *Pseudepigrapha* edited by R. H. Charles is an early twentieth-century classic (1913). Scholars are presently preparing new editions of the *Pseudepigrapha* that more than triple the number of writings in the Charles' edition, which contains the following sixteen books: Jubilees, Letters of Aristeas, Book of Adam and Eve, Martyrdom of Isaiah, I Enoch, Testament of the Twelve Patriarchs, Sibylline Oracles, Assumption of Moses, 2 Enoch, 2 Baruch, 4 Ezra (the same as the apocryphal 2 Esdras), Psalms of Solomon, 4 Maccabees (Charles assigned 3 Maccabees to the Apocrypha), Pirke Aboth (Sayings of the Fathers—a tractate of the Mishnah), Story of Ahikar, and Fragments of a Zadokite Work (the Cairo-Damascus Document, a Dead Sea Scroll).

To some degree after the first war of the Jews against Rome, 66–74 C.E., and more certainly after 135 C.E., these writings were disparaged by the rabbis as "not defiling the hands" (that is, as lacking holiness), and banned as fraudulent. Had not some of these writings aroused false hopes and bloody insurrections? Only in ancient Christian churches did these writings survive.

Consideration of literary sources must include the writings of the Jewish historian Josephus, for he provides the narrative for the Roman-Herodian Era that will be presented as our sketch continues. We have, however, already drawn upon Josephus to supplement the Maccabean books which, indeed, he used and amplified.

Josephus was born in Jerusalem in 37 or 38 C.E. The date of his death is not known, but he outlived Herod Agrippa II, for Josephus records his death in 100 C.E. Josephus claimed descent from the Hasmoneans. As a young man he identified himself with the Pharisees. During the procuratorship of Felix (ca. 52–60 C.E.), Josephus went to Rome to obtain the release of some priests who had been arrested. Shortly after his return the Jewish war began. Perhaps the impressions of Roman military might led Josephus to attempt to thwart the foolish rebellion, but he was swept into the maelstrom as a partisan and given a military post in Galilee. After Roman victories in this region and his arrest, Josephus sought to mediate between the warring groups. Josephus thus was able to observe the conflict in Judea and the triumphal procession of Titus in Rome. Josephus lived in the imperial capital until his death, writing his defenses.

Four works of Josephus survived because of their popularity with early Christian writers. The first, *The Jewish War* (seven books), was written ca. 75 C.E. primarily for Jews in Babylon, to discourage insurrection, and is a history of Jewish nationalism from ca. 175 B.C.E. to 70 C.E. The second, *The Antiquities of the Jews* (twenty books), was written ca. 95 C.E. for Gentiles to refute the slander that Judaism was an insignificant, ephemeral cult. It is a history of the Jews from the creation to the beginning of 66 C.E. The third book, a *Life*, was written as a sequel to *The Antiquities* and is a defense of the career of Josephus and of his histories. The fourth book, a treatise *Against Apion* (two volumes), is a reply to further criticism of himself and of the Jewish people.

The patent apologetic motives of Josephus coupled with the patronage of Roman officials account for the distortions and willful omissions in his writings. For example, he describes various Jewish sects as though they were philosophical schools; he claims that the insurrections against the Romans were instigated by self-seeking, violent "brigands" and secular-minded nationalists; he almost turns a blind eye to messianic uprisings; and he is given to gross exaggerations. Yet in spite of these and other limitations, the works of Josephus must be judged according to the standards of his time and on the basis of the quality of his sources. Without the writings of Josephus a connected narrative of Jewish history in New Testament times would be impossible. Few would deny him a place among the most important historians of the ancient world.

THE HELLENISTIC KINGDOMS AND THE JEWS

After the death of Alexander the Great there was no man to succeed him who was his equal. It is doubtful that even Alexander's personal magnetism could have kept his sprawling empire intact. Two decades of fighting among his generals led to inevitable ruptures.

In the East, Asia Minor came under the control of Antigonus, who, with his soldier son Demetrius, attempted to rule as king over Alexander's entire realm, appointing his generals to rule in specified territories. But Ptolemy and Seleucus claimed for themselves independent kingdoms: Ptolemy founded a dynasty in Egypt; Seleucus assumed control in Babylon. Both claimed Coele-Syria and Phoenicia, but these regions were first governed by Ptolemy. Seleucus established his capitol on the Orontes, naming it Antioch.

Inevitably Judea was affected by these political events in the late fourth century. Once again, as in earlier periods of their history, Judeans were positioned between two great powers, one on the Nile, the other on the Euphrates. As stated earlier, Judea initially was ruled by the Ptolemaic kingdom, a control that was maintained for more than a century. Greek city-states *(poleis)* were established in the outlying territories—more than thirty in Palestine—within or near ancient settlements. These cities served chiefly as fortresses and commercial centers but also to further Greek customs and institutions.*

During the Ptolemaic rule of Palestine the influence of the hereditary office of the high priest greatly increased. The first steps were taken toward political independence in that the high priest "assumed the aspect of a petty monarch."[3]

THE HELLENIZATION OF JUDEA AND THE MACCABEAN WARS OF LIBERATION

In the year 199 B.C.E., the Syrians ruled by Antiochus III ("the Great") were able to wrest control of Judea from the Ptolemies. The leadership in Jerusalem

* Rich discoveries of papyri have shed light upon Ptolemy's bureaucratic rule in Egypt and Palestine during the first half of the 3rd century B.C.E. Reference in the Zenon papyri to "the land of Tobiah" and to "Tobiah's

men" is of special interest because of this family's later involvement in Judean politics. Tcherikover, ed., *World History of the Jewish People*, (1964), Vol. 6, pp. 68–76, 87ff.

welcomed this change with enthusiasm in the persons of the high priest, Simon II ("the Just") and members of the Council. Antiochus responded by giving the Jerusalemites permission to live according to their ancestral laws. (Before considering the major crisis that was to alter drastically this situation, attention must be given to several internal developments within Judea. To anticipate the story, and to emphasize its importance, it must be said that Hellenism was not introduced into Judea by overzealous Hellenistic kings, but by rich and powerful persons within the Judean populace who became enamored of Hellenistic modes of life and who found it to their great personal advantage to move in a more cosmopolitan society than was possible within the traditions of their native culture.)

By the early second century the priests were the strongest and wealthiest class among the peoples of Judea. The temple served as a bank of deposit, and the control of this treasury provided a solid financial basis for their power. The secular, land-owning aristocrats were the most powerful class after the priests. Many no doubt were connected with priestly families, such as the Tobiads. A third class in Judean society was composed of scribes or interpreters of the Torah and their followers. As many of the priests became wealthy or moved in the circles of the wealthy landowners, they were separated from the lives of the masses. There arose a company of sages who gained the respect of fellow citizens because of their earnest effort to apply the Torah to every sphere of private and public life. The Hasidim (devout ones) are first mentioned in Jewish writings as representatives of the segment of Jewish society that took up the banners of the Maccabees,[4] but it is clear that the Hasidim were an element in society before this. As the detested reforms of the Hellenizers from within the ranks of the priests and nobles were instituted, the Hasidim were driven to become a sectarian movement.

It is understandable that rivalries would develop among the rich and powerful priests and nobles as they sought to curry or maintain favor with the Hellenistic kings vying for political control of Judea. While still subject to the Ptolemies, Jerusalem's high priest, Onias II, calculated the rising power of the Seleucids and refused to pay Ptolemy III the customary tribute (ca. 242 B.C.E.). Joseph, a Tobiad (noted earlier as the semi-independent owners of large tracts of land) put himself forward as conciliator. He succeeded not only in assuaging Ptolemy's anger but also in having himself appointed tax collector, becoming in effect Jerusalem's representative to the king. Joseph's power base subsequently expanded and he became collector of taxes "from all Coele-Syria, Phoenicia, Judea, and Samaria."[5] Josephus summarizes the political activities of Joseph with the eulogy that he "brought the Jewish people from poverty and a state of weakness to more splendid opportunities of life. . . ."

"Splendid opportunities" for personal gain were surely sought by "the sons of Tobias" in the years after the conquest of Judea by Antiochus III (199 B.C.E.). One such opportunity was provided early in the second century by a power struggle between the high priest Onias III and a priest named Simon. Both sides sought support from the governor of Coele-Syria and Phoenicia. Meanwhile, Seleucus IV died or was murdered. He was succeeded not by his son but, in a power play, by a brother, Antiochus IV Epiphanes. The high priest Onias was ousted, also by a brother, Joshua, who changed his name to the Greek "Jason."

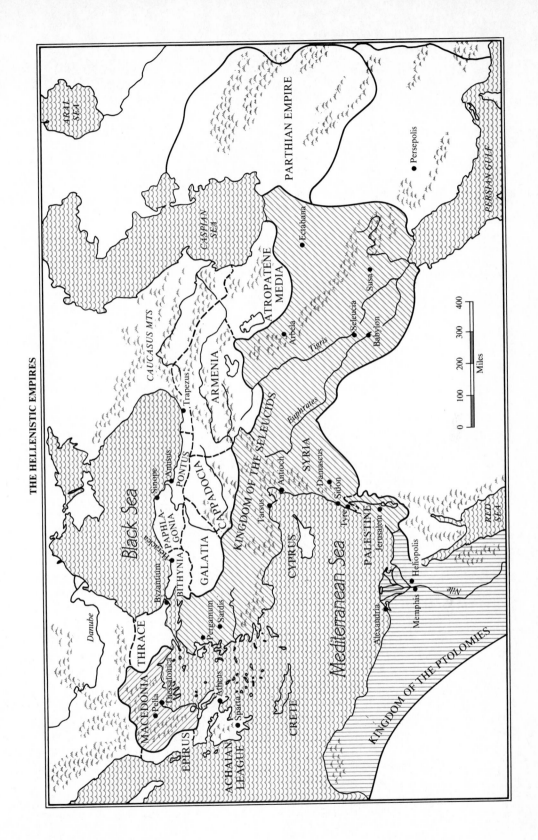

THE HELLENISTIC EMPIRES

ARAL SEA

PARTHIAN EMPIRE

• Persepolis

PERSIAN GULF

CASPIAN SEA

ATROPATENE MEDIA

• Ecbatana

CAUCASUS MTS

• Susa

• Seleucia
• Babylon

ARMENIA

• Arbela

Tigris

KINGDOM OF THE SELEUCIDS

Euphrates

• Trapezus

Sinope •

PONTUS

PAPHLA-
GONIA

• Amisus

CAPPADOCIA

SYRIA

• Antioch

• Damascus

GALATIA

• Tarsus

• Sidon

Heraclea •

BITHYNIA

• Tyre

Black Sea

Byzantium •

CYPRUS

PALESTINE

• Jerusalem

Pergamum •

• Sardis

THRACE

Danube

Mediterranean Sea

RED SEA

Nile

MACEDONIA

• Alexandria

• Pella

• Memphis

• Heliopolis

Thessalonica •

EPIRUS

• Athens

Sparta •

ACHAIAN
LEAGUE

CRETE

KINGDOM OF THE PTOLOMIES

400

300

200

100

0

Miles

29

HELLENISTIC RULERS

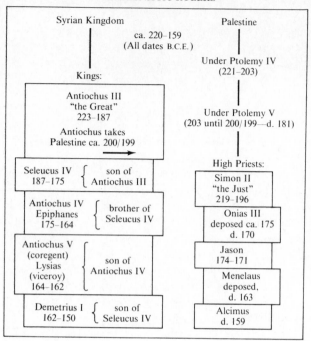

Syrian Kingdom	Palestine
ca. 220–159 (All dates B.C.E.)	Under Ptolemy IV (221–203)
Kings:	Under Ptolemy V (203 until 200/199—d. 181)
Antiochus III "the Great" 223–187 Antiochus takes Palestine ca. 200/199 →	High Priests:
Seleucus IV 187–175 { son of Antiochus III	Simon II "the Just" 219–196
Antiochus IV Epiphanes 175–164 { brother of Seleucus IV	Onias III deposed ca. 175 d. 170
Antiochus V (coregent) Lysias (viceroy) 164–162 { son of Antiochus IV	Jason 174–171 Menelaus deposed, d. 163
Demetrius I 162–150 { son of Seleucus IV	Alcimus d. 159

Jason's candidacy was supported by the Tobiads, but the cost of Jason's elevation was enormous.[6]

The cause of the Hellenistic reformers in Jerusalem was materially advanced. Jason gained permission from the Seleucid king "to establish a gymnasium and a body of youth for it, and to enroll the men of Jerusalem as citizens of Antioch."[7] Accordingly, Jason "shifted his countrymen over to the Greek way of life" and "destroyed the lawful ways of living and introduced new customs contrary to the law."

Jason's power was envied by the Tobiads, so they selected a successor named Menelaus. Early in 171 Menelaus purchased from Antiochus his office of high priest, and Jason was forced to flee to lands beyond the Jordan. Late in the year 169 B.C.E. Antiochus visited Jerusalem after an imperial adventure in Egypt, having been warned by the Romans to desist. On this occasion Antiochus looted and desecrated the temple.[8] Pro-Ptolemaic sentiment spread rapidly among the noncitizen Jews. Only the Tobiads and the citizens of Antioch in Jerusalem remained loyal to the king. Shortly afterward, a rumor spread that Antiochus had been slain. Jason left his Transjordan hiding place and, with about a thousand men, attacked Jerusalem. There is some confusion in the sources over what happened, but it is probable that a people's revolt repulsed Jason's conquest and also forced Menelaus to take refuge in the citadel.[9] Antiochus sent Apollonius on a punitive expedition in defense of the Antiochenes in Jerusalem. A bloody battle on the Sabbath left many of the Hasidim slain in the streets. Apollonius then proceeded to fortify the city and to construct a strong fortress with barracks for Syrian soldiers. The location of the fortress, or *Akra,* is obscure, but it was large enough to become a refuge for Jewish Antiochenes.[10] Many noncitizens fled the city in terror.

It is probable that the Hasidim were able to gain control of the city, except the Akra; in any event, the situation seemed sufficiently critical for Antiochus to adopt a desperate strategem. If devotion to the Mosaic Law had become the rallying point of the insurgents, then the Law must be done away with by any means necessary.*

According to the decree of Antiochus, the observance of all the Jewish ordinances, in particular those relating to the Sabbath and circumcision, was prohibited; their continuance would lead to punishment by death.[11] In every town of Judea sacrifice was to be made to foreign deities. On the 25th of Kislev (December) 167 B.C.E., a "desolating sacrilege" was erected upon the great altar in Jerusalem's temple.

Despite the violence that followed, the numbers of the Hasidim increased. To make firm their determination to resist, an unknown writer penned an apocalypse under the pseudonym of Daniel. Stories of heroic loyalists of an earlier time were told to fire their descendents' zeal in defense of the Law. The author confidently foretold of an imminent divine judgment upon past and present heathen oppressors and the establishment of an everlasting world dominion ruled by "the devout."[12] This apocalypse doubtless inspired a spirit of stubborn resistance, but the defiance of one Judean family sounded the call to arms.

When the king's men came to the village of Modein to enforce the life-or-death decrees, an aged priest named Mattathias, supported by his five sons, refused to obey the command to sacrifice a ceremonially unclean animal upon an altar. When a renegade came forward to comply, Mattathias slew him, and in the ensuing affray, some of the king's officers were also killed. The priest and his sons fled to the wilderness.[13] The Hasidim rallied behind these fearless loyalists who quickly mustered troops for an offensive against the Syrians, vowing unremitting warfare, even on Sabbath days, in defense of their religion.

At the time of his death, within a year of these events, Mattathias singled out for leadership one of his sons, Simon, and another son, Judas "the Maccabee" to be commander of the army.**

Judas's first battles were in defense of Judea against invasion from the north and northeast. In these rugged territories the enemy's movements could be observed by Judas's guerilla forces, which were able to repulse the overly confident Syrians with surprise attacks.

It has been noted that with the persistence of the rebellion during the next two years the Syrians responded with the direct involvement of progressively higher echelons of administration. First, the regional officer in Jerusalem was ordered to put down the uprising. Then the governor of Coele-Syria and Phoenicia was ordered to quell the revolution. Next, Antiochus's viceroy, Lysias, deployed a strong force under two commanders; and, finally, Lysias himself advanced upon Jerusalem from the south in two campaigns; in the second accompanied by the king and the bulk of the Syrian army.[14]

In between these encounters, all of which (prior to the campaigns of Lysias) ended in a rout of the Syrians, Judas was able to liberate Jews living in predominantly non-Jewish towns in bordering regions, sometimes evacuating them to Judea. But his most significant action was his provision of a security force in

*During the years 188–176 B.C.E., he had been a hostage in Rome where he had come to admire Rome's governmental policies. Rome extended citizenship to non-Roman towns and formed new self-governing towns. In all such cases Rome defended its citizen's rights, including their freedom to fulfill their religious obligations even when such conflicted with the laws of the subjugated communities. In commanding Jason to enroll Antiochenes in Jerusalem, Antiochus pursued a Roman policy. J. Goldstein, 1 *Maccabees* (1976).

**The etymology of Judas's (or Judah's) surname is uncertain: Maccabee = hammer. If given earlier as a nickname, it may have been suggested by a distinguishing physical feature, but it could have been given to him to mean hammer (for God), or one who pursued a strategy of inflicting hammerlike blows upon the enemy. It was applied to the family otherwise known as the Hasmoneans, which is also a designation of uncertain origin. Possibly Hasmoneus was an ancestor (*Jos. Antiq.* XVI. vii. 1; XX. vii. 2) or the term was honorific, signifying "princes."

*It may not be possible to identify this "desolating sacrilege" ("the abomination of desolation": 1 Macc. 1:54; 2 Macc. 6:2, 5; Dan. 11;31; 12:11). The restorations of the priests in removing the "defiled stones" from the altar (1 Macc. 4:42), may support the theory that meteorites had been placed to represent male and female deities of the Syro-Phoenicians. (2 Macc. 6:7).

Jerusalem, which enabled priests from among "the devout" to challenge Menelaus's control of the temple and to purify its precincts. All signs of its desecration were removed, the "desolating sacrilege" was destroyed, and the altar of burnt offerings rebuilt. On Kislev (December) 25, 164 B.C.E. an eight-day festival was begun, celebrating the rededication of the temple to the worship of Israel's God.*

We return now to the military and political crises in 164 and 163 B.C.E. resulting from the invasions masterminded by the Syrian viceroy, Lysias. In 165, Antiochus IV had launched a military expedition in the eastern region of his kingdom (modern Iran). He made his young son, Antiochus V, coregent and appointed Lysias as his son's guardian and chief administrator of affairs in the western portion of the realm.

The first campaign of Lysias (164 B.C.E.) resulted in heavy losses among the Hasmoneans, and a negotiated peace was required. Meanwhile, early in 164 B.C.E., Antiochus IV died and Lysias's position was threatened at home. Judas took this opportunity to besiege the Akra in Jerusalem. Lacking the necessary

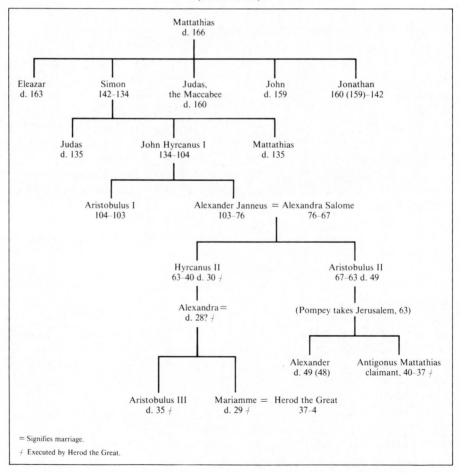

THE HOUSE OF THE MACCABEES (HASMONEANS)
(All dates B.C.E.)

= Signifies marriage.
+ Executed by Herod the Great.

means—siege engines, ramps, and so on—it is doubtful that he could have been successful. However, the news of Lysias's armies again in the south made it necessary to lift the siege. In a costly, pitched battle the Syrians were victorious. Eleazer, one of the Maccabean brothers, was slain, and Judas's men barely escaped to the mountains. Antiochus V deposed Menelaus and appointed Alcimus high priest.

Further dynastic strife in Syria during the year 162 B.C.E. relieved Judea of invading armies, but Demetrius, son of Seleucus IV, emerged from his exile and seized the Syrian throne; killed his cousin Antiochus V and Lysias. Demetrius I confirmed Alcimus as high priest and, in response to a request, sent his armies to stop the fighting among the Jews. In a second of two expeditions, staged at Elasa, Judas was killed (160 B.C.E.). Within a year Alcimus died, and the office of high priest was left vacant. Religious freedom had been restored, but politically and militarily Syria was again in control.

Jonathan was chosen by the demoralized warriors to succeed his slain brother, Judas. After several indecisive battles, the Syrians' strategy shifted to the establishment of strong fortifications in Jerusalem and its surrounding towns. Leaving behind substantial garrisons of soldiers, the invading army departed.[15]

The Establishment of an Independent Jewish State (141–63 B.C.E.)

Beginning in 153 B.C.E., the Syrian throne was occupied by a succession of "kings-for-a-day," each attaining power by a palace revolution and murder, inviting the unwelcome attentions of Ptolemy VI as well as of Rome. Rival claimants to the throne attempted to outdo one another in offering concessions to the Hasmoneans in return for their support.[16] Jonathan was not only allowed to establish himself in Jerusalem and to assume the office of high priest, but subsequently he was installed as governor of Judea. He was able to annex border territories and to gain Jewish control of seaports on the Mediterranean. "Jonathan was outstanding in his grasp of the political situation and in his uncanny ability to exploit the situation to his advantage."[17] The ultimate aim of Jonathan and of his brother Simon (the last surviving sons of Mattathias) clearly was the complete severance of Judea from the Seleucid kingdom and its establishment as an enlarged and independent Jewish state.

This aim was apparent to the Syrian army officer Tryphon, who seized power in 143 B.C.E. Jonathan was a victim of trickery, being arrested and executed within the year.[18] But Simon, who succeeded Jonathan, brought the dream to reality.

One of Simon's first acts was to send a delegation to Demetrius II, who was struggling to regain the Syrian throne. Although Demetrius was in no position to recognize Jewish independence, the report reads (according to the Syrian calendar): "in the one hundred and seventieth year [i.e., 141 B.C.E.] the yoke of the Gentiles was removed from Israel, and the people began to write in their documents and contracts, 'In the first year of Simon the great high priest and commander and leader of the people.' "[19]

Simon's chief accomplishments were the acquisition of Joppa, Judea's natural seaport; the conquest of Gazara; and the expulsion of "the lawless men" from the Akra in Jerusalem.[20] His crowning achievement, however, was Simon's procurement by the expressed will of priests and people of dynastic succession. It was declared that he "should be their leader and high priest forever [i.e., through his heirs], until a trustworthy prophet should arise"[21] Legitimization of Simon's offices by the people was soon followed by a resolution to that effect of the Roman Senate.*

Although Simon and his subjects enjoyed a much celebrated "established peace," like all his brothers the prince was destined to die a violent death. His son-in-law, Ptolemy, had Simon and two sons, Judas and Mattathias, and their mother murdered.

Simon's sole surviving son, John Hyrcanus, became the lawful successor in 134 B.C.E. His rule began inauspiciously but the defeat and death of Antiochus VII in wars with the Parthians (129 B.C.E.) gave Hyrcanus the opportunity to undertake bold wars of aggression in all directions around Judea. To obtain sufficient manpower, mercenaries were needed. Samaria was destroyed, as was the Samaritan fortress, Shechem.[22] Under the command of Hyrcanus, and later under his sons, many Hellenistic *poleis* were beseiged and their male inhabitants forcibly circumcised. Resistance to Judaization could lead to severe reprisals.[23] Some strategically located cities were repopulated by Jews, and longstanding commercial monopolies thereby broken up.**

Hyrcanus ruled from 134 to 104 B.C.E. His son, Judas Aristobulus, ruled for one year only, 104–103; another son, Alexander Janneus, ruled from 103 to 76 B.C.E.

The regimes of Hyrcanus and his sons were marked by mixed reactions of the populace to their priest-kings. Military exploits and territorial expansion were doubtless applauded by Jewish patriots and the moneyed class—the priests and nobles who stood to gain by an increase in wealth and commerce. But the autocratic actions of the Hasmonean princes were offensive to "the devout." Whether intentionally or not, the rulers of Judea came to resemble the Hellenistic tyrants in their ambitions and attitudes to their subject-slaves. Janneus laid heavy tax burdens upon his Jewish subjects as well as his captives. Increasingly large sums of money were needed for his wars of conquest. The populace found the person and conduct of their priest-king increasingly offensive.[24] So serious were their grievances that they urged the Syrian king to invade Judea and joined their enemies in fighting against their monarch. This popular rebellion led Janneus to order the crucifixion of 800 of "the king's enemies," and to force the flight of 8,000 of "the hostile faction." In all probability these enemies of Janneus were members of a party identified by Josephus as "the Pharisees."

It is difficult to determine what led these "Pharisees" to take up arms against Janneus and to assess the extent of their influence in stirring up an insurrection. In his writing, *The Jewish War*,[25] Josephus cited a source that depicted the Pharisees as political opportunists. They rose to power in the reign of Janneus's successor, his wife Salome Alexandra (76–67 B.C.E.). Taking advantage of a pious queen who, Josephus reported, listened to the Pharisees "with too great deference," these politicians became "the real administrators of the state." However, in his *Antiquities*, written twenty years later (ca. 95 C.E.), Josephus gave a revised version of the rise to power of the Pharisees after their persecution under Janneus: "in place of a credulous queen, we have a supine one; in place of conniving Pharisees, we have powerful leaders of the whole nation . . .

*"The people," as distinct from priests, who participated in this action (1 Macc. 14:28) consisted of scholars of the Law, representatives of distinguished and wealthy families, and the elders of the clans. See the important essay (A. Schalit, in Tcherikover, *Jewish People*, Vol. 6, pp. 256ff.) describing Simon's contribution to the development of representative or "republican" governing bodies, or "courts" (from the time of Hyrcanus known by the Hebraicized Greek term *Sanhedrin*).

**[the Syrian king's deputy protested to Simon] ". . . you have done great damage in the land and taken possession of many places in my kingdom . . ." [the deputy therefore demanded reparation] "but Simon gave this reply: we have neither taken foreign land nor seized foreign property but only the inheritance of our fathers, which at one time had been taken by our enemies. Now that we have opportunity we are firmly holding the inheritance of our fathers . . ." A. Schalit, in A. Toynbee, ed., *The Crucible of Christianity* (1969), pp. 68f.

the mass slaughter of *War,* in which the Pharisees killed anyone they wanted, is shaded into a mild persecution of the Pharisees' opposition.'' (It is likely that in the later version Josephus was serving as a broker for the Pharisees at Yavneh who, at the time of his writing, were negotiating with the Romans. The tenor of Josephus's comment is that any government wanting peace in Palestine had better gain the support of the Pharisees, who in turn enjoy the strong support of the masses, as their history attests.)[26]

Unable herself to fulfill the role of the high priest, Salome Alexandra appointed her older son, Hyrcanus II to this office. No official position was tendered to the younger son, Aristobulus II. During the queen's last illness Aristobulus gathered his father's war cronies and seized some of the most strategic Judean fortresses. When the queen died, the army of Aristobulus drove Hyrcanus from Jerusalem. A fratricidal war erupted, leading to the defeat of the appointed priest. Apparently his removal from office was not traumatic; as Josephus reported, the disposition of Hyrcanus II "was too lethargic to be troubled about public affairs."

EXCURSUS B

THE EARLY HISTORY OF SOME FIRST-CENTURY JEWISH SECTS

Some knowledge of Jewish sects in the Late Second Temple Period will shed light upon important developments within Judaism as well as upon the social environment of early Christians. Jesus and his first disciples lived among Pharisees, Sadducees, Essenes, Samaritans, disciples of John the Baptist, and other less clearly identified groups. The emergence of Jewish and Jewish-Christian sects helps to explain the messianic tensions and ferment of the times in which Christianity flourished.*

THE SADDUCEES

Recall that the Hellenization of Judea reached its apogee in the reforms promoted by Jason and his wealthy aristocratic supporters. After the revolt, and under the first Maccabees (Judas, Jonathan, and Simon), these leaders were removed from the scene.

Yet the influence of the priestly aristocracy was by no means totally diminished. Purged of the extreme Hellenophiles among them, the priests and nobles continued to wield political power, and their social position and values continued to foster a laxity toward strict observance of the Mosaic Law. They knew that "the Jewish state could only survive if it adopted the technical achievements of the Hellenistic world, especially in matters of administration, warfare, and economics."[27] During Simon's regime their power was not obtrusively exercised. In the reigns of Simon's successors, however, their influence exceeded that of all others. The expansionist policies of Hyrcanus and his sons depended upon this political basis of support.[28]

Josephus referred to this faction of priests and nobles as *the Sadducees* for the first time in his account of Jonathan's high priesthood, and distinguished their views from those held by other sectaries: the Pharisees and the Essenes.[29] Like the earlier Hasmoneans, the natural sympathies of Hyrcanus were with

* The term *sect* is used here as designating a minority group within an organized religion whose adherents conform to special standards of teaching and practice and who are more or less active in seeking to establish their standards as the politically dominant ones in their religion and society. Various strategies are employed by sectaries to counter the opposition or indifference of elements in their society and to ensure the conformity of "the faithful."

* The common though not undisputed view is that the Sadducees derived their name from Zadok (Saddouk, LXX), that is, they traced their origin through the priestly line of Zadok who served in Solomon's temple, and whose successors formed the main body of the priesthood in the postexilic age. Because many of the priestly aristocracy in the Second Temple Period belonged to this family, they and their supporters were known as *Saddoukaioi* (Greek), Sadducees.

the spiritual heirs of the Hasidim, but in the end Hyrcanus became a Sadducee, and during Janneus's wars of aggression the Sadducees clearly were the king's counsellors, forming an elite privy council.*

Given their sociopolitical orientation, the scattered, disparaging references of Josephus to the Sadducees form a coherent picture of the sect. They "were persons of the highest reputation," yet they were "influential only with the wealthy," and "had no following among the populace."[30] In their relationship to each other, the Sadducees were "rather boorish in their behavior," in their relations with their countrymen, "as rude as with aliens."[31]

One could hardly expect religious idealism to flourish among the Sadducees; theirs was the pragmatic stance of expediency. Driven to make the most of bad bargains, they maintained that human choices are free and responsible. They held "that all things lie within our own power."[32] The Sadducees stood for the old dogma: God is responsible for the good; humans are responsible for their misfortunes. "As for the persistence of the soul after death, penalties in Hades and rewards," Josephus recorded that the Sadducees "will have none of them."[33]

One statement of Josephus highlights a fundamental difference in principle between the Sadducees and other contemporary sects: they did not "regard the observation of anything besides what the Law enjoins them."[34] The Sadducees "refused to be bound by the achievements of the previous few centuries in regard to both the interpretation of the Torah and the development of religious views. Their conservative and autocratic tendencies on the one hand and their secular culture on the other, inclined them to hold as either superfluous or unacceptable the progressive religious ideas of the Pharisees."[35]

THE PHARISEES

We have noted that the Hasidim emerged as an identifiable community of Jews in reaction to the Hellenistic reforms of the early second century B.C.E. When the Maccabeans revolted, "the devout" rallied behind them, becoming the principal component of the armies defending the Torah and "the traditions of the fathers." They may have wished only to restore the legal position adopted by Antiochus III: the enjoyment of religious freedom under Seleucid sovereignty. The Hasmoneans were increasingly convinced, however, that tolerance of the Jewish faith could not be expected from a Hellenistic monarchy in Antioch and that political independence was necessary.

In spite of this divergence of aims, the Maccabean family and the Hasidim fought together during the first stage of the crisis in Judea, but the pursuit of nationhood under the sons of Simon divided the Maccabeans from their former allies. A gulf widened between the priest-kings and the sons of the Hasidim, many of whom became known as "the Pharisees," according to Josephus, as early as the time of Jonathan's priesthood.**

** Some scholars deny that the term "sect" is appropriate since Pharisaism represents quintessential Judaism, but in the

Events that led to an open breach in the relations between the Hasmoneans and the Pharisees occurred in the time of John Hyrcanus and are preserved in two versions of a legend. Extremist spokesmen demanded that the priest-king renounce his priesthood and retain only the crown.[36] In the ensuing bad relationships, Hyrcanus is said to have abolished "rulings" introduced by the Pharisees "according to the tradition of the fathers." For six years Alexander Janneus, Hyrcanus's successor, turned his mercenaries upon his own subjects.[37]

It is not surprising that after the death of Alexander Janneus Queen Alexandra sued for peace, not only because of her personal preference for the Pharisees but in order to preserve the nation. The rulings of the Pharisees that were abolished by Hyrcanus were restored, and the sectaries came to dominate the domestic affairs of Jewish public life. (Certain inconsistencies in the narratives of Josephus concerning this course of events and the role of the Pharisees throughout have been discussed earlier.)[38]

As in the case of the Sadducees, we can summarize the depiction of the Pharisees by Josephus. They held the reputation "of excelling the rest of their nation in the observance of religion, and as exact exponents of the laws." In the same account Josephus stated that the Pharisees were considered "the most accurate interpreters of the law," and were "the leading sect."[39] It is clear that their observance included obedience to the traditional scribal interpretation as well as to the letter of the Torah. The Pharisees "imposed on the people many laws from the tradition of the fathers not written in the law of Moses."[40]

Two such developments in doctrine were apparent. First, the Pharisees believed that human souls "possess an immortal power and that under the earth there are rewards and punishments for those who in life have given themselves over to virtue or vice, and that eternal imprisonment is destined to some, but to others an easy passage to a new life."[41] By contrast, as noted above, the Sadducees denied resurrection, believing that souls perish together with bodies.[42]

Another view distinguishing the Pharisees is somewhat obscured by the effort of Josephus to relate to philosophical tenets familiar to his readers, but it comes to this: the Pharisees believed that everything that happens comes about through God's providence; therefore, it must be assumed that God cooperates in human actions both good and bad.[43] While for the Sadducees the human factor in all actions was stressed, and for Essenes belief in divine predestination predominated, the Pharisees affirmed divine omnipotence and providence, but also human freedom and responsibility.[44]

When the Pharisees are introduced by Josephus they are involved, as we have seen, in Hasmonean politics, It would be a mistake to infer from this that throughout its history the sect was essentially a political party. The Pharisees assessed their civic responsibilities from first one and then another scriptural standpoint. Given their belief in divine providence, they leaned toward the view that "God gave power to the Gentiles over his people in order to punish them for their transgressions." The righteous must therefore submit willingly to this divine chastisement, and even endure harsh rulers as long as the observance of the Torah was not thereby impeded. But given their belief in Israel's divine election, the yoke of Gentile rule could be, and sometimes was, perceived as a usurpation of divine sovereignty: only to God or to his "anointed" belonged the kingdom and the power.[45] Since unlike some Essenes the Pharisees did not withdraw from society and live apart, it was inevitable that from time to time their zeal for the Torah would turn them from their peaceful pursuits to political activism.

Period of the Second Temple the Pharisees were a minority group distinguishable from the rest chiefly because of greater strictness in their interpretation of and allegiance to the Torah and its scribal supplementation, the so-called "oral Law." Schürer, *History of the Jewish People*, Vol. 2, pp. 395–399. M. Smith, in M. Davis, ed., *Israel: Its Role in Civilization*, (1976), pp. 67–81; Cf. E. Rivkin, *A Hidden Revolution* (1978), pp. 316–318.

THE ESSENES

* In his most detailed description of the Jewish sects (*B.J.* II. viii. 1ff.), Josephus gave most space to the Essenes, yet he provided no information directly concerning their origin or early history. Neither did Philo, the 1st century Alexandrine Jewish apologist; nor Pliny the Elder nor Dio (Roman authors); nor the Christians, Hippolytus or Eusebius. All of the above made incidental references to the Essenes.

Josephus first mentioned the Essenes together with the Pharisees and Sadducees in his account of Jonathan's rule. It is probable that the Essenes, like the Pharisees, considered themselves spiritual descendents of the Hasidim.* The writer of the Damascus document discovered in Cairo (very likely an Essene writing), takes the revolt of the devout against Antiochus Epiphanes as a point of departure in referring to the founder of the sectarian community, "the Teacher of Righteousness."[47] Twenty years after the revolt against the Hellenization of Judea, "the Teacher of Righteousness," a Zadokite priest, protested against Jonathan's assumption of the high priest's role (151 or 152 B.C.E.). Henceforth Jonathan was referred to by the Teacher and his followers as "the Wicked Priest."[48] Simon, Jonathan's elder brother and successor, was likewise condemned. It is possible that Simon's installation, narrated so glowingly in 1 Maccabees, was accompanied by a warning directed to the Teacher, among other hostile dissenters: "and none of the people or *priests* shall be permitted to nullify any of these decisions or to oppose what he [Simon] says, etc."[49]

In any event, the Teacher and his sectaries withdrew to a place of exile during the reign of Jonathan or Simon. Possibly this place was Qumran, for archeological evidence found at the site reveals that a settlement there can be dated ca. 140–130 B.C.E.[50] In a Qumran-Essene commentary on the prophecies of Habakkuk, allusion is made to a visit of the Wicked Priest to the wilderness retreat of the sectaries on the Day of Atonement, at which time the Teacher's life was threatened. The subsequent violent death of the Wicked Priest was viewed by the Qumran Essenes as a divine punishment.[51] Hyrcanus and his sons were intensely hated by the sect, particularly Alexander Janneus, to whom reference is made as "the furious young lion."[52]

We shall have occasion later to observe the responses of the Qumran Essenes to public events in Roman-Herodian Palestine. (In the account of the Essenes' community life and teaching that follows, attention will first be drawn to the classical sources, following the procedure used in describing the other major sects. Some similarities and differences between these Essenes and the Qumran sectaries will then be noted.)

According to both Josephus and Philo, there were more than 4,000 Essenes in the early years of the first century C.E. Josephus reported that they lived in many of the small villages. Philo's reference to their self-contained societies, and Pliny's note concerning their settlement on the west side of the Dead Sea, imply the establishment of isolated communities.[53] Their domiciles were asylums for the sick and the aged but also for traveling brothers.[54] Only adults belonged to the Essenes, but children were received at their centers for training.[55] Each community was headed by "superiors" to whom all members gave unconditional obedience.[56] The chief occupations of the Essenes seem to have been in agriculture.[57]

Candidates for membership in the sect were given a year's probation, and worthy persons admitted then to "the waters of purification." Two additional years were required before admittance to full membership into the council of the community. The "tremendous vows" of initiation included an oath of obedience to the standards of piety prescribed by the sect, submission "to their elders, and to the majority," preservation of the secrets and books of the order, and so on.[58]

The Wadi Qumran, the Sectarian Settlement, and the Dead Sea *(above). (Courtesy of John Allegro.)*

Pere de Vaux *(below)*, principal archeologist of the Qumran ruins, standing at the opening of Cave 1 where the first Dead Sea Scrolls were found. *(Courtesy of James Charlesworth, Princeton Theological Seminary.)*

Philo was cited by Eusebius as the authority for the view that the Essenes were celibate. Josephus wrote that they were distrustful of women and "disdained marriage," but he also reported that some Essenes did marry, not "for self-indulgence but for the procreation of children."[59]

The daily life of the Essenes was ordered according to the Torah and the traditions of the sect. Josephus declared that "after God" the Essenes hold most in awe the name of the lawgiver [Moses], any blasphemer of whom is punished with death."[60] They were especially scrupulous in observing the Sabbath.

Josephus described several distinctive manifestations of Essene piety, such as prayers toward the rising sun, their ritual baths and white garments, the sanctity and silence of their meals in a common refectory, the scruple against anointing with oil, spitting, and the modesty of members in disposing of excrement.

The report of Josephus concerning the attitude of the Essenes to the temple is ambiguous: "and when they send what they have dedicated to God into the temple, they do not offer sacrifices, because they have different rites of purification; on which account they are excluded from the common court of the temple, but offer their sacrifices themselves [at another place?]." This question can be answered in the negative if Philo's comment is our guide: "they have shown themselves especially devout in the service of God, not by offering sacrifices of animals, but by resolving to sanctify their minds."[61]

Josephus took note of the fatalism of the Essenes and of their doctrine of the future life and its states. The Essenes believed more firmly in God's predestination of all things than did the Pharisees. He likened the Essenes' belief in perishable bodies and immortal souls to Greek conceptions: Essenes "maintained that for virtuous souls there is reserved an abode beyond the ocean . . . refreshed by the ever gentle breath of the west wind . . . while they relegate base souls to a murky and tempestous dungeon, big with never ending punishments."[62]

*Four scrolls recovered from Cave One are especially important as primary sources for knowledge of the organization, doctrines, and customs of the Qumran Essenes: the Manual of Discipline, or Community Rule (1QS); the Messianic Rule (1QS$_a$); a Hymn Scroll (1QH); and a War Scroll (1QM).

Several of the Dead Sea Scrolls are primary sources of information about the organization, religious teaching, and practices of the sect.* The community at Qumran claimed to be the true Israel and contained both priests and Levites and a lay component, representing the twelve tribes.[63] "The sons of Zadok" (or of Aaron) governed the community through a "Council" but were the final judges in all matters.[64] Even the smallest cell of ten members was presided over by a priest to see that all of the practices of the sect were observed. An overseer, presumably also a priest, attended to admissions, instruction, and other practical matters, such as the community finances.[65]

All houses and settlements of the sect were under the guardianship of a priest-superintendent.[66] In the ultimate phase of the community's life, at the end of the days, its head is to be a prince or royal Messiah.[67]

The Community Rule described in detail the procedures of admission to the wilderness settlement, beginning with "entry into the covenant" accompanied by an oath to obey all the laws of Moses according to the interpretation of the priests of the sect. Thus, there were probationary "members of the covenant" in the camps undergoing a period of instruction and examination for more than two years.[68] Punishments, including expulsion, were specified for major and minor infractions. Full membership included voting and the sharing of property.

The sectarian scrolls are unclear concerning attitudes toward celibacy and marriage. The Cairo-Damascus document refers to married members and children,[69] and they are present in the eschatological community,[70] but in the final war of the sons of light against the sons of darkness, women and children are excluded from the camps.[71]

Members of the sect gathered for a general assembly once a year, the Feast for the Renewal of the Covenant (Pentecost); other solemn meetings were at meals, when bread and "juice of the grape" were blessed by the presiding priest.[72]

The hymns of the sect celebrated the knowledge and grace of God in revealing to the Elect the divine mysteries and leading them into the ways of holiness. The laws of purification were scrupulously followed.[73] One passage in the Community Rule possibly alludes to a ritual bath of cleansing in connection with "entry into the Covenant."[74]

If our description of the early history of the Qumran Essenes and their quarrel with the Hasmonean priest-kings is correct, then the attitude of the sectaries to the Temple revealed in the scrolls is understandable: its priests were wicked, its precincts polluted, and the liturgical calendar unlawful. The sect looked forward to the restoration of the temple at the end of the days.[75]

Other aspects of the eschatology of the Qumran Essenes will be treated in Chapter 4. It should be noted here, however, that although the resurrection of the dead was not a prominent doctrine of the sect, there are numerous references in the scrolls to the eternal life that the Sons of Light will inherit in company with the Sons of Heaven.[76]

Perhaps readers have been reaching their own conclusions based on close similarities between the description of the Essenes in the classical sources and of the sectaries revealed in the scrolls. Arguments favoring their identification are strong. Qumran would appear to be the location of the principal settlement of the Essenes alluded to by Pliny; Essenes flourished, according to Josephus, between the time of Jonathan and the first Jewish war with Rome; the occupation of the Qumran site is dated by archeologists during the same period.[77]

There are undeniable differences. There is no mention in the secondary sources of the Teacher of Righteousness, no reference to Essene belief that the sectaries were the true Israel, the community of the new covenant, and the Sons of Light. It is debatable whether or not the Dead Sea Scrolls support the emphasis in the classical sources on the common ownership of property, on celibacy, or on pacifism; however, most of these differences can be explained. Not every group of Essenes was alike at every stage of the sect's existence.

Against the few significant differences there is the striking amount of agreement concerning the organization, doctrines, and practices of the sectaries in the two sets of sources. The equation of the Qumran sectaries with Essenes merits the highest degree of probability.

ROMAN CONQUEST AND THE DECLINE OF THE HASMONEANS
(63–37 B.C.E.)

After the death of Queen Alexandra Salome the debilitating struggle for supremacy between her two sons gave Rome the opportunity to intervene and eventually to annex Judea as an eastern province of its far-flung empire.

Josephus may have misinterpreted the peaceable temperment and indecisiveness of Hyrcanus, Alexandra's elder son and successor to the high priesthood and kingship, as a lack of ambition. Hyrcanus was able to mount a threatening counterattack upon his younger brother, Aristobulus, after the latter had driven him from Jerusalem, and he persisted in his effort to retain his appointed offices. In this purpose he was prompted by a fear that his life was endangered. A warning of this was voiced by Antipater, a wealthy Idumean nobleman, who had been confirmed in his office as governor of Idumea by Hyrcanus I and his sons. Antipater was responsible for securing the military aid of Aretas, king of the Nabateans,* in seeking the defeat of Aristobulus.[78] Antipater's power was subtle but effectively exercised.

While fratricidal struggle was being intensified in Judea, Pompey and his formidable Roman legions were pressing eastward. Having secured the submission of Pontus and Armenia, the Roman armies marched into Syria, occupying Antioch and then Damascus. Upon the appearance of the Roman army, in advance of Pompey, both Hasmonean rivals appealed to Pompey's general, offering large sums of money in exchange for support. At first Aristobulus was favored, and Hyrcanus and his confederate, King Aretas, were forced to withdraw from Jerusalem. But by the Spring of 63 B.C.E. Pompey himself arrived at Damascus and the Judean question was subject to review. Three groups appeared before Pompey: Aristobulus supported by his Sadducean followers; Hyrcanus and his supporters; and a third group who desired the end of the Hasmonean dynasty and a restoration of the legitimate priestly line. Some Pharisees were probably among the supporters of Hyrcanus, but others may have sided with those repudiating both brothers. Antipater accused Aristobulus of being the sworn enemy of the Greek cities bordering Judea (whose peoples hated this son of Janneus), and of acts of piracy along the shores of the Mediterranean. Both actions discredited Aristobulus, but Pompey delayed a decision pending the completion of his campaign against the Nabateans, and took Aristobulus with him.

As the armies marched southward it was noticed that Aristobulus was absent without leave. Pompey's suspicion led him to pursue Aristobulus, to arrest him, and advance upon Jerusalem. The warriors of Aristobulus secured themselves upon the temple mount.[79] After a three-month siege, on the Day of Atonement, 63 B.C.E., a breach was made in the wall. Rome's occupation of the city and temple resulted in a massacre of 12,000. Pompey banished Aristobulus and his sons to Rome, and confirmed Hyrcanus as high priest without royal title. The eldest son of Aristobulus, Alexander, escaped on the journey to Rome.

Pompey liberated the Hellenized cities that had been conquered by the Hasmoneans. Nine cities in the Transjordan, together with Scythopolis, were now confederated as the Decapolis.[80] What was left of the Hasmonean state was made tributary to Rome. Antipater was appointed governor of Judea and charged with keeping law and order.

When Julius Caesar came to Judea in 47 B.C.E., Antigonus demanded that he should be appointed ruler because of his family's loyalty. The brash young Hasmonean failed to supplant Antipater in Caesar's esteem. To consolidate his control, Antipater appointed his two sons, Phasael and Herod, to be the rulers of Jerusalem and Galilee, respectively.

*The *Nabateans* were originally a nomadic Arab people who began to occupy Edomite territory during the 6th century B.C.E. Their kingdom was founded upon agricultural and commercial interests, as modern excavations of their chief city, Petra, reveal. *Idumea*, the region immediately south of Judea, was settled by Edomite refugees after the Nabatean influx. John Hyrcanus conquered Idumea and forcibly circumcised its male inhabitants. (Jos. *Antiq.* XIII. ix. 1; Jos. *B.J.* I. ii. 6.) The Idumeans, as a part of Judea, fought with the Jews against Rome in "the great rebellion," 66–70 C.E.

HEROD THE GREAT AND HIS SUCCESSORS

According to a modern biographer, Herod's first acts were warning signs to the leaders in Jerusalem of the presence of a military and political genius whose power would totally eclipse their own.[81] Herod rounded up and executed without trial a large number of "bandits" who were attacking Syrian villages believed to contain collaborators with Rome. The "bandits" were probably members of a resistance movement.[82] The Jerusalem Sanhedrin was incensed upon hearing of this high-handed action, and summoned Herod to be tried. The high priest was warned by the governor of Syria that no harm should befall Herod. Knowing this, Herod presented himself arrogantly arrayed in royal purple. The court was intimidated. One Pharisee named Sameas, identified by Josephus in another context as a fearless defender of the Law, insisted that the trial be conducted, but Hyrcanus dismissed the case and actually assisted Herod in his escape.

Herod's rise to power was a stunning accomplishment. After the assassination of Julius Caesar (44 B.C.E.), which touched off civil war in Rome, the opponents of the House of Antipater hoped to provoke a political revolution in Judea by assassinating Antipater. The Idumean was poisoned, but his sons exacted their revenge without giving rise to public disturbances. In overcoming opposition, Herod's ruthlessness was tempered by one restraint: the risk of his subject's open revolt. When Cassius came to Syria after conspiring in the mur-

THE HERODIANS

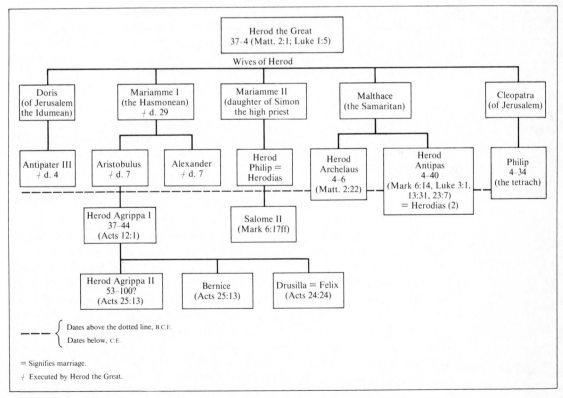

der of Caesar, and again when Mark Anthony came East after his victories in 42 B.C.E., the administrations of Phasael and Herod were reconfirmed.

In the year 40 B.C.E. the Parthians overran Syria. Antigonus, the Hasmonean, seized this opportunity to attack Jerusalem. His uncle, Hyrcanus, Phasael, and Herod fortified themselves in the Hasmonean palace. A Parthian army arrived under the king's cupbearer and called for peace negotiations at the Parthian camp in Galilee. Despite Herod's warning and refusal to meet the Parthians, Phasael and Hyrcanus were victims of the ruse. Phasael was killed and Hyrcanus was mutilated, which disqualified him for priesthood. The Hasmonean prince was taken into exile to Parthia.

Herod was able to escape with members of his family and the family of his fiancee, Mariamme.* Leaving his entourage with a guard at the Masada fortress, Herod hastened to Rome to seek Anthony's help. In the year 40 B.C.E. the Roman senate, acting upon the triumvir's advice, declared Herod "king, ally, and friend of the Roman people." Herod's realm, consisting of Judea, Galilee, and Idumea, was enlarged to include Samaria and a portion of the Transjordan, Perea.

For three years Herod was unable, without Anthony's military aid, to defeat Antigonus, but after the Parthian threat was successfully repulsed, Anthony dispatched a large army to assist Herod. In 37 B.C.E., just before the fall of Jerusalem, Herod celebrated his marriage to Mariamme in Samaria, turning then to the capture of his capitol. Antigonus was taken captive and beheaded. As incredible as it may seem, the death agony of the Hasmonean dynasty was prolonged until 31 B.C.E. A sister of Antigonus withdrew to the fortress Hyrcania with hard core opponents of the House of Antipater. The defeat of Mark Anthony, Herod's Roman patron, in the Battle of Actium may have been a portent of Herod's downfall. But in 31 B.C.E. (as in 47, after Caesar's overthrow of Pompey) the victor, this time Octavian (subsequently Emperor, Augustus Caesar) forgave Herod for supporting his rival and retained him as Rome's obedient servant. In the following year Octavian confirmed Herod as king and restored to him territories ceded to Cleopatra by Mark Anthony.

It is now apparent that the House of Antipater was able to survive mainly because of the "clearsightedness of the successive masters of the Roman Empire in appreciating the facts that Judea was an exceptionally difficult country for Rome to control and that Antipater and Herod were indispensable local instruments of Roman policy. They were indispensable because they were both political realists and effective men of action."[83]

Herod's policies were at all times shaped by this political realism, by his determination to ensure absolute subservience of his Jewish subjects to Rome, and by his readiness to adopt any means to eliminate subversive elements within his palace and within his realm. Suspects were arrested by Herod's secret police; the properties of the wealthy were confiscated; and prisoners disappeared without a trace.[84] The shedding of blood extended to members of the king's family suspected of conspiracy. Herod's agents drowned Aristobulus III, the younger brother of Mariamme and high priest for less than a year; the beloved Mariamme herself was executed, as was her grandfather, Hyrcanus II, whom Herod ransomed from Parthian exile. Mariamme's mother, Alexandra; Herod's two sons by Mariamme, Alexander and Aristobulus; and Antipater III, Herod's

*Mariamme was the daughter of Alexandra, and Alexander the son of Aristobulus (see the Hasmonean family tree). Her marriage was a political arrangement to strengthen the bond between the houses of Hyrcanus and Antipater, but Herod was passionately in love with the Hasmonean princess. The match proved to be calamitous for all concerned.

Caesar Augustus (Gaius Julius Caesar Octavianus), first Roman emperor, 27 B.C.E.–14 C.E. The marble sculpture *(top left)* displays his manly beauty, which was praised by Suetonius *(Divus Augustus, 79)*. *(Courtesy of the Trustees of the British Museum.)* The coin of Augustus *(top right)* portrays the youthful face of his granduncle, the deified Julius Caesar. The terra-cotta medallion bearing the image of Augustus *(bottom right)*, like the coin, was found in the agora excavations in Athens. *(Courtesy of the American School of Classical Studies, Athens.)*

only son by his first wife Doris were also executed. The Emperor Augustus, upon hearing of these killings, is said to have remarked that he had sooner be Herod's swine (huis) than his son (huios).

HEROD'S IMAGE: HIS OWN AND THAT OF HIS SUBJECTS

While palace intrigue and a reign of terror marred the declining years of Herod's rule, this dark picture ought not to obscure the outward splendor of

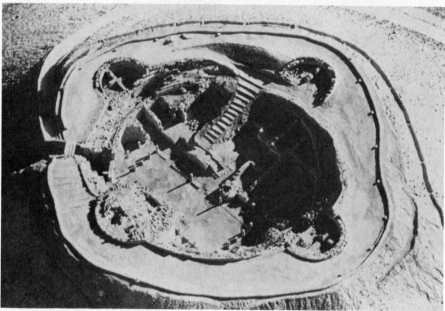

Herod the Great hewed out of a Judean mountain a palace-fortress for security from invaders *(above)*. He also may have wished to provide for himself a grandiloquent mausoleum. Known as Herodion, this fortress was used in the wars with Rome, 66–70 and 133–135 C.E. The aerial photograph *(below)* shows the fortress from the northwest. *(Courtesy of Pictorial Archive.)*

the middle period of Herod's reign. With the establishment of the principate of Octavian in 27 B.C.E. and the formal restoration of the republic and senatorial powers, a relatively stable situation was attained. Octavian was given control of the more difficult provinces and the title "Augustus." In friendly alliance with Augustus, Herod was able to manifest an impressive array of the benefits of the new order. Historians, supported by massive archeological evidence, have

View of the southeastern wall of old Jerusalem, adjacent to the temple area, showing the joining of Herodian construction *(above)* to a portion of an earlier wall. *(Courtesy of James Charlesworth, who stands at the juncture.)* The author's picture *(below)* of the Western, or "Wailing" wall, showing a section of original Herodian masonry built ca. 20 B.C.E. to support the temple platform. We view the throngs who gather here on Tishah b'ab, the day of "lamentation" that the temple no longer belongs to the Jews.

marvelled at Herod's achievements as a builder and beautifier of cities. Jerusalem became a celebrated capitol of the East, furnished with a royal palace, a theater, and other public edifices; the ancient citadel at the northern wall of the temple was rebuilt and renamed Antonia; and the rebuilding of the temple was begun in 20 or 19 B.C.E. Fortresses were constructed throughout the countryside, and ancient bulwarks, notably Masada, were equipped with fine buildings. Outside Jerusalem, Herod's supreme architectural achievements were the construction of Caesarea, on the site of Strato's Tower, and the rebuilding of Samaria, which Herod renamed Sebaste (a Greek version of Augustus' name). Both of these cities were peopled with non-Jews for the most part.

Josephus concluded that a desire for fame inspired the magnificence of Herod's building program,[85] but the king also may have wished to overcome the isolation and national exclusiveness of his realm, "to open the doors to foreign cultural influences and to mutual understanding . . . to integrate the Jews in the Hellenistic-Roman *oikoumene* as one of the many peoples which made their contribution to the common welfare—a welfare which was also their own."[86]

Whatever might have been Herod's expectations concerning the response of his subjects to these benefactions, as well as to his tax cuts and relief funds, the Indumean monarch was hated intensely as being transparently an agent of Rome in a total subjugation of Judea. Such a despot could have little regard for "the traditions of the fathers," surrounding himself with Greek advisors and artists, appointing high priests without regard to their legitimacy, packing the Sanhedrin with "friends of the king." It is doubtful that the Sadducees were at this time involved in anti-Roman activities, although in the early years of Herod's rule many of their number lost their wealth, their land, and their lives.[87] The Qumran Essenes interpreted the Roman-Herodian conquest as the fulfillment of the prophets' and their sectarian teacher's words concerning "the Kittim" as agents of divine judgment upon an apostate priesthood and people.*

Some Pharisees also may have considered the scourge of Herod as God's punishment for the nation's sins.[88] It is, however, difficult to describe the position of these sectaries to Herod's rule. Josephus reported that twice Pharisees refused to take an oath of loyalty, and for the second time over 6,000 were fined and some were put to death.[89] In the year of Herod's death two Pharisees emboldened a band of youths to demolish a golden eagle that Herod had placed over the temple's entrance.[90] Forty of the vandals were put to death by burning.

Two famous Jewish sages were contemporaries of Herod: Hillel the Elder and Shammai the Elder. Hillel's aim was to pursue peace through social justice in obedience to the teachings of the Torah. Shammai, known for his greater strictness, appears also to have been preoccupied with cultivating sectarian piety. Perhaps the Pharisees functioned as a religious sect for most of Herod's reign but became politically involved near its close.[91]

Shortly before the aged Herod died, a baby born in Bethlehem was given the name Jesus.

Herod's kingdom was shaken upon the news of his death by a convulsion of violence, the expression of the pent-up hatred and bitterness of his subjects. Only the hasty action of the governor of Syria brought the rioting under control.** The last of Herod's many wills decreed that his kingdom should be

*During Herod's reign the Essene settlement at Qumran seems to have been abandoned. A terrible earthquake in 31 B.C.E. (Jos. *Antiq.* XV. v. 2; Jos. *B.J.* I. xix. 3) may account for this, but the co-existence of Herod's palace at Jericho and of this puritanical sect just seven miles away may have become intolerable. What would Herod have thought of the Qumran War Scroll (1QM)?

**"It would be a mistake to see in

To assist in visualizing Jerusalem as it was in the First Century, archeologists have built a model of the ancient city. The point in time was the year 66 C.E., four years before the city was destroyed by the Romans. The chief archeologist was Professor Avi-Yonah of Hebrew University, Jerusalem. The model is constructed on the property of the Holy Land Hotel; the scale is 1/4 inch = 1 foot. *Above,* "Herod's Temple"; *below,* his palace.

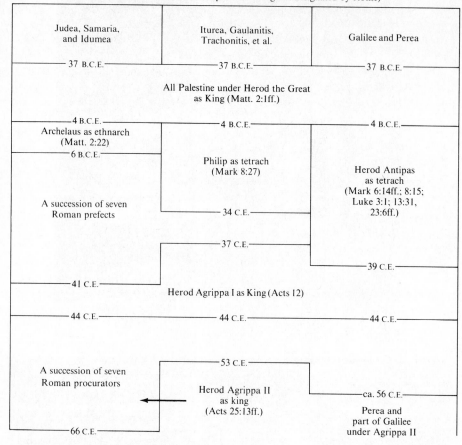

Herod only a bloody ruthless tyrant. Herod was first and foremost a statesman, and as such we cannot but acknowledge the acumen of his political insight and judgment . . . in trying to establish a secure place for his kingdom and the Jewish people within the framework of the Augustan Roman Empire . . . he was deeply convinced . . . that there was no room for national independence . . . and that the only way to exist in a tolerable, nay even an honourable way, was to come to terms with Roman power. . . . Schalit, in Toynbee, *The Crucible*, p. 72.

Rome's Provisions for the Government of Palestine from the Accession of Herod the Great to the First War of the Jews Against Rome*

(The three vertical columns represent the regions designated by Rome)

Judea, Samaria, and Idumea	Iturea, Gaulanitis, Trachonitis, et al.	Galilee and Perea
37 B.C.E.	37 B.C.E.	37 B.C.E.
All Palestine under Herod the Great as King (Matt. 2:1ff.)		
4 B.C.E.	4 B.C.E.	4 B.C.E.
Archelaus as ethnarch (Matt. 2:22)		
6 B.C.E.	Philip as tetrarch (Mark 8:27)	Herod Antipas as tetrarch (Mark 6:14ff.; 8:15; Luke 3:1; 13:31, 23:6ff.)
A succession of seven Roman prefects	34 C.E.	
	37 C.E.	
		39 C.E.
41 C.E.		
Herod Agrippa I as King (Acts 12)		
44 C.E.	44 C.E.	44 C.E.
A succession of seven Roman procurators	53 C.E.	
	Herod Agrippa II as king (Acts 25:13ff.)	ca. 56 C.E.
		Perea and part of Galilee under Agrippa II
66 C.E.		

◄ Authorized to supervise the temple and appoint the high priest.

*Adapted from a table in B. M. Metzger, *The New Testament, its Background, Growth, and Content*, Nashville: Abingdon Press, 1965, p. 29

divided among three of his surviving sons: Herod Antipas was to receive Galilee and Perea, and the title "tetrarch"; Philip, the territories northeast of the Sea of Galilee, and the same title; and Archelaus was to be given Samaria, Judea, and Idumea and the title "king." Augustus approved these bequests except that he reduced the rank of Archelaus from king to ethnarch, in effect putting Archelaus on probation. After several years of civil strife in which Archelaus was forced to use his troops to quell the rioting, a delegation appealed directly to Caesar, and Archelaus was exiled to Gaul (6 C.E.). He was replaced by a governor of equestrian rank, a *praefectus* named Coponius, and Judea became a Roman province.*

* Under Augustus and Tiberius the usual title for governors in the third rank was *praefectus,* "prefect." An inscription found

Little is known of Herod's son Philip, but he seems to have been an able ruler of his region. Herod Antipas was the most capable of the three, a favorite of the Emperor Tiberius. Like his father, Antipas was a builder. A new capitol, named for his mentor, Tiberias, was established on the shores of the Sea of

Galilee. Because it was built on an ancient burial site, Jews were not forced to live there. Apparently Antipas did not wish to offend his Jewish subjects (e.g., his coins bore no images), and since he was able to rule until 39 C.E. he must have been fairly successful. Jewish sources reported that Antipas was a shrewdly clever man; Jesus, according to Luke's Gospel, likened him to a "fox."[92]

The downfall of Antipas resulted from the ambitious schemes of his wife, Herodias, and of her kinsman, Herod Agrippa. Herodias was first the wife of a half-brother of Antipas, Herod Philip, a son of Mariamme II. Herodias accepted the proposal of Antipas to marry him, but in order to effect this marriage Antipas needed to divorce his wife, a daughter of the Nabatean king, Aretas. This divorce led to a punitive expedition in which Antipas was defeated. This marriage also led to a public condemnation of the king by a popular prophet, John the Baptist.[93] Josephus recorded that Antipas was threatened by John the Baptist, that the prophet was arrested, imprisoned at Machaerus, and killed.[94]

Upon the death of Philip the tetrarch in 34 C.E., the Emperor Gaius (Caligula) arranged to assign this territory to Agrippa, his friend in Rome of an earlier day. In one of his first acts upon becoming Emperor, Gaius gave Philip's tetrarchy to Agrippa and made him a king. The envy of his sister Herodias was aroused, and she urged her husband Antipas to petition for a royal title for himself. Agrippa's report to Gaius was unfavorable, and reference was made to a large arsenal being amassed by Antipas. The Emperor's suspicions were aroused and Antipas was exiled to Gaul where he died.

JUDEA UNDER THE RULE OF PREFECTS (6–41 C.E.)

After the deportation of Archelaus and the establishment of Judea as a Roman province ruled by the prefect Coponius, the Emperor sent Quirinius, the legate of Syria, to take a census so that taxes could be levied. A "Galilean" named Judas incited his countrymen to revolt, "upbraiding them as cowards for consenting to pay tribute to the Romans and tolerating mortal masters after having God for their Lord." Josephus commented: "this man was a sophist who founded a sect of his own, having nothing in common with the others."*

Little is reported in Jewish or Roman sources of the governorships of the next three prefects, just as Christian sources are nearly silent concerning these years in which Jesus grew to maturity. The period of Pilate's rule in Judea is, however, illuminated by non-Christian records as well as by the Gospels, and will be noted in the context of Jesus' arrest, trials, and execution.

An alarming incident occurred in the years of the last prefect, whose term coincided with the years of the Emperor Gaius (Caligula), 37–41 C.E. The egotistical, mentally deranged Emperor came to believe that his subjects should worship him as divine and that refusal was proof of their rebellion. Persons within the large colony of Jews in Alexandria were the first to refuse. "Patriotic" mobs were provoked to violent antisemitism and the governor of Egypt offered no protection.[95] Upon hearing of Jewish resistance to Emperor worship in Alexandria and elsewhere, Gaius ordered that a statue of his likeness be set up in the temple at Jerusalem, and that the governor of Syria enforce this decree with half of his army.[96] Massive demonstrations of Jews sought to pre-

at Caesarea in 1961 is evidence that Pontius Pilate bore this title. From the time of Claudius, the title *procurator* came into use for governors of this type. Their official residence, the *praetorium*, was in Caesarea. Persons appointed as prefects to govern Judea were: Coponius, 6–9 C.E., Marcus Ambibulus, 9–12, Annius Rufus, 12–15, Valerius Gratus, 15–26, Pontius Pilate, 26–36, (?)Marcellus, 36, (?)Marullus, 37–41.

*Josephus wished to identify Judas and his followers as constituting a sect that, from the year 6–7 C.E., grew in numbers and influence and was a root cause of the first war with Rome, 66–73 C.E.. This is doubtful, although many modern historians seem to accept it. Josephus provided no evidence of continuing armed resistance motivated by Judas's ideology. The sect known as "the

Sculptured portrait of the emperor Claudius (41–54 C.E.). Although many of his contemporaries considered him a weak, eccentric cripple, Claudius ranks as an outstanding emperor. Christian missions were aided by his extention of the Pax Romana to the eastern provinces. His friendship with King Herod Agrippa I led him to seek to pacify his Judean subjects, but rioting in Rome led Claudius to expel all Jews from the capital, probably in 49 C.E. Acts 18:1f.; Suetonius, "Claudius," xxv., *Lives of the Twelve Caesars.* *(Courtesy of the Trustees of the British Museum.)*

Zealots" was formed in the Winter of 67–68 C.E. See D. Rhoads, *Israel in Revolution,* pp. 47ff.

vent this vile profanation of the temple. Agrippa, visiting in Rome, was horrified to learn of the Emperor's order and pled with his friend to rescind it. Gaius withdrew the decree but commanded that altars and temples be built to him outside of Jerusalem. Only Gaius's assassination in 41 C.E. averted an open revolt in Judea.

King Agrippa remained in Rome and probably had some role in securing the imperial throne for Claudius. At any rate, for some favor he was confirmed in his royal domain by the Roman senate, and Judea and Samaria were added to his possessions. Thus ended rule by the prefects in Judea, and Herod Agrippa I inherited the whole of his grandfather's kingdom.

A Brief Calm Before the Storm

Agrippa's life is an enigma. As a young man living in Rome, he was self-indulgent and profligate. We have noted his misrepresentation to Caligula of his brother-in-law, Antipas, and the latter's exile. Yet as king of the Jews, Agrippa was a model of piety. "It was his pleasure to reside continually in Jerusalem," wrote Josephus, "and he meticulously observed the precepts of his fathers. He neglected no rite of purification and not a day passed without its appointed sacrifice."[97] Hellenophile away; devout Jew at home. One consistent thread runs through Agrippa's adventure-filled life. He had a winsome personality. Because of his popularity with his subjects, Rome kept a watchful eye for signs of movement toward independence.

This adulation of his Jewish subjects may have prompted him to two acts that were reported by Josephus and by the Christian writer of The Acts of the Apostles. To please his Jewish supporters who were opposed to Jesus' followers, Agrippa arrested and put to death a disciple of Jesus, James, one of the sons of Zebedee; to please himself, Agrippa appeared before his adoring public arrayed in splendid robes, and permitted their obeisance as before a god. Subsequently he died of some sort of seizure.[98]

The Roman Procurators (44–66 C.E.)

The son of Agrippa was seventeen years old and living in Rome when his father died. Because he was a protege of the Emperor, Claudius wished to make him his father's successor, but Claudius's advisors were suspicious of the young man's ambition. Instead, the whole of Palestine was given provincial status and procurators were sent to maintain law and order. These fiscal officials of low rank seemed to be conscious of little besides the arbitrary power that they exercised; the religious sensibilities of their subjects were objects of contempt.* The first two procurators, "by abstaining from all interference with the customs of the country," were able at least to keep "the nation at peace."[99] But serious troubles began in the time of Cumanus. This procurator permitted his soldiers to perpetrate gross acts that were highly offensive to the devout, and then used violence to disperse the protestors. As more and more lawless acts were allowed without appropriate discipline (e.g., the destruction of a Torah scroll) counter-violence erupted.

Disorder spread to the countryside during the procuratorship of Felix, a man who was neither officially nor personally qualified for his sensitive post. Tacitus wrote that "in practising every kind of cruelty and lust, [Felix] wielded royal power with the instincts of a slave."[100] During his tenure a band of assassins was formed known as *sicarii* because they carried concealed daggers (*sicae*).[101] Their practice was to mingle among the crowds to avoid detection and to strike down Romans and Jews suspected of collaboration with the Romans.

In the time of Feli, there also appeared on the scene "the Egyptian," a Jewish prophet who gathered a popular following, intending to assemble them on the Mount of Olives. He predicted that the walls of Jerusalem would collapse at his order and allow his people to assume control of the city. Felix precluded this

*The final series of Roman governors in New Testament times, reported by Josephus; the *Annals* and *Histories* of Tacitus provide some supplementation (all dates C.E.): Cuspius Fadus, 44–(?)46; Tiberius Alexander, (?)46–48; Ventidius Cumanus, 48– ca 52.; T. Claudius Felix, ca. 52–60(?) (Acts 23:24–24:26); Porcius Festus, (?)60–62 (Acts 24:27–26:32); Albinus, 62–64; Gessius Florus, 64–66.

miraculous event by a massacre. "The Egyptian" escaped; doubtless some supposed a miraculous deliverance and return.[102] The imprisonment of the Apostle Paul occurred during the last two years of the procuratorship of Felix.

The new governor, Porcius Festus, seems to have been a well-intentioned man but he was quite unable to overcome the animosity provoked by his predecessor. When Festus came to Palestine ca. 60 C.E., King Herod Agrippa II and his notorious sister, Bernice, hastened to welcome him. Before this visit, "the chief priests and the principal men of the Jews informed Festus against Paul."[103] To pacify them Festus seemed ready to order that Paul be tried in Jerusalem, but the apostle exercised his right as a Roman citizen and appealed to Caesar. Festus took advantage of the state visit of King Agrippa to stage a hearing. Paul defended himself eloquently but Agrippa resisted involvement.*

On occasions of insurgency, Festus, like the previous procurators, resorted to severe measures of pacification, outraging the masses and thereby encouraging their support of the Jewish militants.

In the interval between the death of Festus in 62 C.E. and the arrival of his successor, Albinus, total anarchy reigned in Jerusalem. According to Josephus, it was during this interval that the Sadducean high priest, Annas (the son of Annas of the passion narrative) had James, the brother of Jesus, and other Jewish Christians, put to death because of alleged violations of the Torah. Some Torah scholars (probably Pharisees) protested to both King Herod Agrippa II and Albinus on his way from Alexandria and secured the dismissal of Annas.[104]

The new procurator seemed only concerned with exploiting the disorder, accepting bribes from the contending factions for personal gain. Yet, according to Josephus, Albinus was a "righteous man" in comparison with the last procurator, Gessius Florus, who flaunted his greed, plundering not only the holdings of individuals but whole cities.[105] Agrippa's defense of the authority of Florus ended the king's moderating influence.

When Florus robbed the temple treasury there was a public uproar that was silenced only by the governor's selective scourgings and crucifixions. In the summer of 66 C.E., a motley group of peasants, lower-class priests, and other malcontents banded together, united by their implacable hatred of Florus. Led by the temple captain, Eleazer, son of the high priest Annas, these "Zealots" banned all temple offerings from Gentiles, including the twice-daily sacrifice on behalf of the emperor. This act was tantamount to a declaration of war. Josephus wrote that "the principal citizens assembled with the chief priests [Sadducees] and the most notable Pharisees . . . now that they were faced with what seemed irreparable disaster."[106] Being unable to reason with Eleazer and the Zealots who had occupied the lower city, the moderates sought to prevent the insurrection from spreading to the upper city. In the struggle that followed the Zealots were assisted by the *sicarii* under the leadership of a certain Manahem. Several buildings were burned and the Roman troops stationed in Jerusalem surrendered and were slaughtered. When Manahem approached the temple dressed in royal robes he was slain by Eleazer's partisans for this messianic presumption.[107]

Cestius Gallus, governor of Syria, marched to Jerusalem with a large army to put down the rebellion. His assault upon the temple mount failed and his surprising retreat turned into a rout. Much needed military equipment was

*Acts 25:13ff. Procurators ruled Judea until the first war of the Jews with Rome, but Claudius gradually assigned Palestinian territories to Agrippa's son. He held the right to appoint the high priests (Jos. *Antiq.* XX. v. 2; vii. 1; viii. 4, 8). When the great rebellion began, Agrippa attempted to restore order but he was banished from Jerusalem (Jos. *B.J.* II. xvii. 1). Agrippa supported the Romans throughout the war. His reign ended ca. 86 C.E.

captured by the Jews. On his approach to Jerusalem, Gallus was attacked from the rear by a revolutionary band headed by Simon bar Giora, one of the many groups in the countryside plundering the wealthy suspected of pro-Roman sympathies.[108]*

So great was the impact of the rout of Gallus that the spokesmen for peace were forced to remain silent and the pro-Romans to flee for their lives. A provisional government was formed, controlled by chief priests and Pharisees, to organize the defense effort. Perhaps leaders from both sects were encouraged by events in the larger world. There was a ground swell of dissatisfaction with Nero's rule; a war between Rome and Parthia seemed imminent, and help in Jerusalem from Jews who lived under the Parthians in Babylon as well as the support of Alexandrian Jews was a likely prospect.[109] But events were not to turn out as some moderates probably hoped, and the despair of the masses led them to look for other leadership. Infighting among contending groups slowly drained the means if not the will for a successful revolution.

For the defense of the homeland each region was assigned to a commander. Galilee was assigned to Josephus (the future historian), who was the son of an aristocrat named Matthias. In the description of his preparations for defense, Josephus introduced, with a scurrilous attack, John of Gischala. John grew suspicious of Josephus's reliability and plotted his murder. John subsequently was captured by the Romans, but he escaped to assume a leadership role in the provisional government in Jerusalem.[110] John's move from defeat in Galilee to Jerusalem's defense apparently was based on his conviction that the city's defenders "could never fear capture, since the city was God's."[111] In the last desperate defense of Jerusalem, John vied with Simon for leadership but the two warriors fought alongside one another at the end.

*Annas the high priest sought to force the brigands to give up their weapons, but Simon and his revolutionaries fled to Masada. In the Spring of 69, when John of Gischla (see p. 56) was tyranizing the Jerusalemites, the chief priests and Idumeans threw their lot in with Simon (Jos. *B.J.* II. ix. 11f).

THE DEFEAT OF THE JEWS AND THE DESTRUCTION OF JERUSALEM

When Nero heard of the rout of the armies of Gallus, the emperor assigned an experienced general, Vespasian, the task of subduing the Jewish revolt. Over 60,000 soldiers were placed under Vespasian's command. Galilee was the first region to be conquered. Despite efforts of Josephus's comrades-in-arms to thwart his purpose, Josephus surrendered to the Romans. Brought before Vespasian he prophesied the general's future elevation to the imperial throne.[112] Although kept in fetters, Josephus was treated with respect. By the summer of 68 C.E., Vespasian succeeded in conquering the entire country with the exception of Jerusalem and its environs.

In the city, the Zealots attributed these losses to a lack of passion for liberty on the part of the nation's leadership. Some prominent persons were imprisoned, others murdered, and the Zealots installed their own high priest, who was chosen by lot.[113] In turn, efforts were made by the provisional government to expel the Zealots, but the revolutionaries were re-enforced by John of Gischala and his followers and by Idumean warriors. This coalition toppled the government and occupied the temple mount as their stronghold. The Idumeans withdrew but the Zealots were able to establish their own "democratic" regime. Their occupation of the temple was in part religiously motivated. Zeal for the

Sculptures of the head of Vespasian (69–79 C.E.), and of his son and successor, Titus (79–81 C.E.). Portrayers of the Flavian emperors gave more attention to the personal qualities of their subjects than did the artists who sculptured their predecessors, the Julio-Claudian emperors. *(Courtesy of the Trustees of the British Museum.)*

temple's purity would, they believed, ensure God's favor and defense. The Zealots maintained their identity as revolutionaries throughout the war, but factionalism and anarchy seriously reduced their contribution to Jerusalem's defense.

After Nero's death in 68 C.E. there was a year of uncertainty over the succession. In July, 69 C.E., Vespasian was proclaimed emperor in Egypt; a few days later the Palestinian and Syrian legions followed suit. Vespasian entrusted to his son, Titus, the continuation of the Jewish war. During these delays the strife in Jerusalem intensified. Large stores of grain were burned by one faction to prevent the other's access to it.[114]

Titus began his siege of Jerusalem a few days before Passover, 70 C.E. The siege lasted for about five months and ended in total disaster. Refusing to surrender after scornfully receiving an impassioned plea by Josephus, the defenders of the city, under Simon's command, were butchered. Only the lives of the most handsome warriors as well as of John and Simon were spared so that they could be humiliated in the victory march of Titus in returning to Rome. (Simon was later executed in the Roman Forum; John imprisoned for life.[115] "Herod's Temple" was demolished, and all of Jerusalem lay in ruins; Herod's towers were preserved as security for an occupying force.*

Sometime before the conquest of Jerusalem, the doomed city was abandoned

*"It might have been . . . If the Roman

The Arch of Titus *(above)*, erected in the Forum Romanum by the Senate (ca. 100 C.E.) to commemorate the war with the Jews, which Titus brought to a devastating end with the destruction of Jerusalem and its outlying fortresses. Bas relief from the Arch of Titus *(below)*, depicting the procession of Jewish captives. Among the sacred objects looted from the temple in Jerusalem was the seven-branched menorah. *(Courtesy of Ali-nari/Art Resource, New York.)*

procurators had concentrated less on exterminating the militant minority (thus gaining sympathy for them among the masses) and instead sought to understand the religious motives underlying this insurgency . . . if they had sought effective contacts with the Pharisees, who were (at least by Herod's time) depoliticized . . . the terrible war

by representatives of two groups. When the provisional government of the moderates was overthrown by the coalition formed by the Zealots, if not earlier, Jewish Christians left Jerusalem in obedience to "divine guidance" and fled to Pella, one of the Gentile cities of the Decapolis.[116] Shortly afterwards, probably in 68 C.E., a Torah scholar, Yohanan ben Zakkai, made his way to Vespasian's camp and requested that the Jerusalem Sanhedrin be allowed to move to Yavneh (Jamnia). The request was subsequently granted and the foundations for "the classical form" of Judaism (rabbinic Judaism) were laid at this town on the coastal plain (from ca. 70 to 125 C.E.). Much of the pre-70 Pharisaic tradition was preserved as the rabbis of Yavneh developed the legal traditions, later to be redacted in the Mishnah of Judah the Patriarch (ca. 200 C.E.). The rabbis of Yavneh are also credited with the final canonization of the Hebrew scriptures and for composing the main petitions of the Jewish Prayerbook. (See Chapter 10.)

(Left) A fault in a stairway in the Qumran settlement probably is evidence of the earthquake, 31 B.C.E., which led to the abandonment of the site. Some members of this Essene sect took part in the war with Rome and were among those warriors who fled to Masada. *(Right)*, The last encampment holding out against the Roman legions 70–72 C.E. This massive rock fortress had been elaborately furnished by Herod the Great. The aerial view of Masada is to the north with the Dead Sea in the background. *(Courtesy of Pictorial Archive.)*

The first war with Rome marked the end of the Sadducees, Herodians, Essenes, and other sects that flourished earlier in the century.

FROM THE DESTRUCTION OF JERUSALEM TO THE DOWNFALL OF BAR KOKHBA (135 C.E.)

The rallying slogan of the Jewish patriots—"no lord but God"—was not yet only a melancholy memory. The fortresses of Herodium, Machaerus, and Masada were still occupied by Jewish revolutionaries. The first two were easily taken by the forces of the senatorial governor, but Masada was held by the sicarii until 73 C.E. When all hope for the 960 people who were living in the fortress was gone, the defenders first killed their families and then each other.[117] The Romans' appetite for slaughter after the long siege was frustrated.

During the years 115–117 C.E., the military and economic resources of the Roman Empire were severely strained by the Emperor Trajan's war of aggression beyond the Euphrates. Jewish revolts erupted on the island of Cyprus, in Egypt, and in Cyrenaica, and were subdued with great difficulty.

The vigorous suppression by Rome of the revolts in the Jewish Diaspora and the accession of Hadrian as emperor may have only postponed a revolt for which careful preparations had been made as Palestine recovered from its desolation. The signal was given for this revolt when Hadrian began to implement his plan to build a Hellenistic city on the ruins of Jerusalem to be called Aelia Capitolina; this, together with the prohibition of circumcision, was one minor (to Hadrian) item in his Hellenizing program. Under united leadership—Rabbi Akiba as head of the Sanhedrin, and "the prince," Simon ben Kosiba, as commander of a disciplined army—the Roman legion of the governor of Judea and Syria was defeated and Jerusalem taken. Hadrian's response was swift and determined.*

External conditions favoring revolt were much worse than in the time of Nero, but Hadrian's forces, under the command of Julius Severus, took two and a half years to subdue the Jewish revolutionaries. Roman losses were heavy, but hundreds of thousands of Jews fell with their leader in battle or died of hunger. Tens of thousands were sold as slaves. The rest scattered to the four winds of the earth. Jews were forbidden to enter Jerusalem and the name Judea was suppressed. The province was renamed Syria Palaestina. Some Christians evidently returned, but only Gentile followers of Jesus. Eusebius noted that for the first time Jerusalem's bishop was not a Jewish Christian.

A CONCLUDING NOTE

The above sketch is a political history for the most part. This is because the authors of the principal narrative sources were manifestly limited in their interests and influenced by the contemporary models of historiography. The writers of the books of the Maccabees and the historian Josephus, were not only epitomists of earlier, fuller accounts, but those authors and the writers of their sources were often indifferent to matters of great importance for historical reconstruction. Jewish historians in the Second Temple Period, like their pagan

might have been averted.

And yet, "Israel kept its national identity (the one nation in antiquity to do so). . . . This is due in no small measure to the warriors who lost two wars against Rome. The desperate undertakings of the Zealots thus appear in a positive light, however much one may regret the amount of suffering . . ." M. Avi-Yonah, *The Jews of Palestine*, (1976) pp. 13f.

*Manuscripts found near Murabba'at in 1952 establish that the warrior's name was "Simon ben Kosiba." His name was punned by Akiba who hailed Simon as Messiah (Bar Kokhba = son of a star; cf. Num. 24:17). A letter written by Simon reads: "From Simon ben Kosiba to Yeshua ben Gilgola, to the men of the stronghold, greeting. . . ." The letter threatens Yeshua with punishment if he does not break away from certain Galileans he has been protecting.

contemporaries, were chiefly interested in great cities, forms of government, wars, public disturbances, and ineluctable Fate.[118] Other important interests to ancient historians were the fortunes of prominant members of the upper classes, individual generals, politicians, and the like. There was, of course, some concern to include "ethnographic and religious information," but usually historians failed to note "the situation of the ordinary population, the manual workers and slaves, the proletariat in the city and the peasant and tax farmers in the country, in short everything that is of particular interest today under the heading of 'social history.' When it came to this kind of thing, the ancient historian at best raised the question with slave rebellions and other social unrest, with famines and severe 'natural' catastrophes."[119] Because of the conspicuous absence of information in the classical narrative sources concerning the socioeconomic conditions and cultural developments of particular persons and groups, especially among the lower classes, special attention is drawn to other than historical writings as well as to nonliterary sources, e.g., the evidence provided by archeology, inscriptions, and the papyri.

Of chief value among the additional literary sources are the rabbinic writings. The Torah scholars were often quite indifferent to chronology and other historical interests. Their tradition is therefore severely limited as a source for locating a sequence of "external" events, but it is of great value as a disclosure of the "internal" history of the Jewish people in the Late Second Temple Period. These rabbinical writings reflect the impact of external political events upon the religious consciousness, upon the beliefs and hopes held by individuals and groups, and upon the institutions that gave meaning to their personal and corporate existences.

The Apocrypha and Pseudepigrapha also are valuable supplements, and they have come to possess greater significance, for some of these documents are now identifiable as sectarian writings (e.g., Jubilees was especially important to the Qumran Essenes).

These literary and nonliterary sources, which enhance our knowledge of Jewish beliefs and practices during the time of Christian origins, will be drawn upon at appropriate points in relation to the ministry of Jesus, and the witness of his first followers.

NOTES

1. This two-installment scheme may seem an unnecessary fragmentation, yet a comprehensive survey of the historical setting of the entire New Testament suggests that the environment of Jesus and the earliest Christians was more complex than in fact it was. When one seeks to understand Christian writings and institutions after the movement had spread beyond Palestine it becomes necessary to explore the wider world.

2. Flavius Josephus, a first-century C.E. historian (see pp. 26f). A legendary account, but it is unlikely that the Jerusalemites ignored Alexander after his conquests along the coast. A delegation probably went to meet him (Josephus *Antiquities of the Jews* XI. viii, 5 [hereinafter cited as Jos. *Antiq.*]). V. Tcherikover, *Hellenistic Civilization and the Jews* (1959), pp. 42ff. Jewish rabbis in the Middle Ages elaborated upon this event, perhaps rationalizing the momentous character of the advent of Hellenism.

3. Tcherikover, *Hellenistic Civilization*, p. 59.

4. 1 Macc. 2:4.

5. Jos. *Antiq.* XII. iv, 10.

6. Heretofore foreign rulers granted or withheld approval of an hereditary candidate; henceforth the high priest became a royal official dependent on the king's favor.

7. 2 Macc. 4:9.

8. 1 Macc. 1:20ff.

9. Tcherikover, *Hellenistic Civilization*, pp. 187ff.; Jonathan A. Goldstein, *1 Maccabees*, Anchor Bible (1976), pp. 122f. For a discussion of the confused chronology and different resolutions, see E. Schürer, *History of the Jewish People in the Age of Jesus Christ* (1973) Vol. 1, pp. 150ff.

10. 1 Macc. 1:33–36.

11. The reader is encouraged to examine the accounts of this crisis in 1 and 2 Maccabees: 1 Macc. 1:41ff., and 2 Macc. 6:1ff. Cf. Jos. *Antiq.* XII. v. 4.

12. Apposite to this crisis are Dan. 7–11, which can be read with profit, especially if the text is annotated.

13. 1 Macc. 2:1–48; 2 Macc. 6:11; Jos. *Antiq.* XII, vi. 2.

14. M. Avi-Yonah, in Tcherikover, ed., *World History of the Jewish People* (1964), Vol. 6, pp. 147ff. For a series of charts depicting the maneuvers and battles of the Syrians and Hasmoneans, see Y. Aharoni and M. Avi-Yonah, eds., *The Macmillan Bible Atlas* (New York: Macmillan, 1977), charts 185–213.

15. 1 Macc. 9:50–53.

16. 1 Macc. 11–12.

17. J. Klausner, in Tcherikover, *Jewish People*, Vol. 6, p. 183.

18. 1 Macc. 12:41–48; Jos. *Antiq.* XIII, vi. 1–2.

19. 1 Macc. 13:36–42; Jos. *Antiq.* XIII, vi. 7.

20. The Akra was occupied by Hellenizers—"Macedonians," Syrians, as well as Jewish "Antiochenes"—for twenty-six years.

21. 1 Macc. 14:41.

22. G. E. Wright, *Shechem, the Biography of a Biblical City* (1965), pp. 183f.

23. Jos. *Antiq.* XIII. xv. 4.

24. A. Schalit, in Tcherikover, *Jewish People*, Vol. 6, pp. 285–288. According to the psalmist in Ps. of Sol. 17:33, Israel's ideal priest-king, the messiah, "will not multiply to himself gold and silver for war."

25. Jos. *B.J.* I. v. 2.

26. J. Neusner, *From Politics to Piety* (1973) p. 63. Cf. Neusner's thesis with that of E. Rivkin, *A Hidden Revolution* (1978). The latter's contention is that "the Scribes-Pharisees sat in Moses' seat *during* the Hasmonean Revolt . . . *throughout* the years of the Hasmonean dynasty, and *under* Herod, the procurators, and King Agrippa." See pp. 363ff.

27. M. Avi-Yonah, *The Jews of Palestine* (1976), p. 4.

28. Schalit, in Tcherikover, *Jewish People*, Vol. 6, pp. 270–273; Schürer, *History of the Jewish People*, Vol. 2 (1979) pp. 412f.

29. Jos. *Antiq.* XIII. v. 9.

30. Jos. *Antiq.* XIII. x. 5f.; cf. Jos. *Antiq.* XVIII. i. 4.

31. Jos. *B.J.* II. viii. 14.

32. Jos. *Antiq.* XIII. v. 9.

33. Jos. *B.J.* II. viii. 14.

34. Jos. *Antiq.* XVIII. i. 4.

35. Schürer, *History of the Jewish People*, Vol. 2, p. 413.

36. Jos. *Antiq.* XIII. x. 5f. For a "parallel" version in the Babylon Talmud, Qiddushin 66a, see Schalit, in Tcherikover, *Jewish People*, Vol. 6, pp. 271ff.

37. Jos. *Antiq.* XIII. xiii. 5.

38. Cf. Jos. *B.J.* I. v. 2 and Jos. *Antiq.* XIII. xvi. 2.

39. Cf. Jos. *B.J.* 1. v. 2; II. vii. 14, and Jos. *Antiq.* XVII. ii. 4; and the New Testament passages, Phil. 3:5f; Acts 22:3; 26:5.

40. Jos. *Antiq.* XIII. x. 6.

41. Jos. *Antiq.* XVIII. i. 3f.; Jos. *B.J.* II. viii. 14.

42. The statement in Acts 23:8 that the Pharisees believed in the existence of angels and demonic spirits is not attested explicitly elsewhere but was probably derived, like their belief in a general resurrection and a last judgment, from the development of apocalyptic cosmology.

43. Jos. *B.J.* II. viii. 14; Jos. *Antiq.* XIII. v. 9; XVIII. i. 3.

44. Schürer, *History of the Jewish People*, Vol. 2, pp. 392–394.

45. *Ibid.*, pp. 394–395.

46. Jos. *Antiq.* XIII. v. 9.

47. "The Cairo-Damascus document" (CD) was found in the late 19th century. Numerous features of this document resemble Dead Sea Scrolls discovered in the years 1947–1956, especially the so-called Community Rule, or Manual of Discipline. Eight copies of the CD were found in the Qumran caves.

48. Some scholars propose that the Wicked Priest was Menelaus, whose purchase of the high priesthood scandalized the Teacher (172 B.C.E.). Others propose Simon (143–134). F. M. Cross argues for the latter alternative in *The Ancient Library of Qumran* (1961) pp. 137ff. Arguments for the major proposals are examined by J. A. Sanders, "The Dead Sea Scrolls—A Quarter Century of Study," *The Biblical Archeologist*, 36 (1973): 110–148. For a daring but not improbable synthesis of the pertinent data, see J. Murphy-O'Connor, "The Essenes in Palestine," *BA* 40 (1977): 100ff.

49. 1 Macc. 14:44ff.

50. R. de Vaux, *Archeology and the Dead Sea Scrolls* (1973) pp. 5, 18.

51. 1Q$_p$Hab 11:4–8; 9:2, 9–12. The meanings of symbols commonly used in identifying the Dead Sea Scrolls: 1 = cave number, Q = Qumran, Hab = Habakkuk (or the appropriate abbreviation of a biblical text being interpreted), $_p$ = pesher, the type of commentary explaining the fulfilment of the scripture in the life of the sect, the numbers indicate the column and the line(s) of the texts.

52. In 4Q Testimonia (a collection of scripture texts) reference is made to two brothers who are "instruments of violence": Jonathan and Simon? 4Q$_p$ Nah 1:5 refers to "the furious young lion."

53. Jos. *B.J.* II. vii. 2; an excerpt from Philo's work, "Apology for the Jews" in Eusebius *Praeparatio Evangelica* VII. 11.; Pliny (the Elder), *Natural History* 73. For the Essene's population, see Jos. *Antiq.* XVIII. i. 5; Philo, *Quod omnis probus liber sit*, 12.

54. Jos. *B.J.* II. viii. 4.

55. Jos. *B.J.* II. viii. 2.

56. Jos. *B.J.* II. viii. 6.

57. Jos. *Antiq.* XVIII. i. 5.

58. Jos. *B.J.* II. viii. 7, 9.

59. Eusebius *Praeparatio Evangelica* XIII: "no one of the Essenes marries a wife." Cf. Jos. *Antiq.* I. v. and Jos. *B.J.* II. viii. 13.

60. Jos. *B.J.* II. viii. 9.

61. Jos. *Antiq.* XVIII. i. 5; Philo *Quod omnis probus.* XII.

62. Jos. *Antiq.* XVIII. i. 5; Jos. *B.J.* II. viii. 11.

63. 1QS 8:5–9; 1QM 2:1–3.

64. 1QS 5:2; 9:7.

65. 1QS 6:2–5; 13–23; CD 13:7–16; Schürer, *History of the Jewish People*, Vol. 2, 575ff. The author is indebted to the editors of the revision of Schürer for this section and its documentation.
66. CD 14:6–12. Earlier the same source provides for a body of ten judges, four priests and Levites and six laymen, elected for limited terms, CD 10:4–10.
67. 1QM 5:1; 1QSa 2:14, 20.
68. 1QS 1:16ff., 5:1–11, 6:13ff.
69. CD 7:6–7.
70. 1QS$_a$ 1:4.
71. 1QM 7:4–5. Whereas the main cemetary at Qumran yielded (with one exception) male skeletons, the secondary cemeteries held the remains of women and children. Schürer, *History of the Jewish People*, Vol. 2, p. 578.
72. 1QS 6:4–5; 1QSa 2:17–21.
73. CD 10:10–13; 1QM 14:2–3; 1QS 3:4–5.
74. 1QS 5:13.
75. 1QM 2:5–6. 4Q Florilegium 1:1–7. 11Q Temple 3–47. The third scroll cited here, the longest of all the Dead Sea Scrolls, contains a description of the proper functions of priests and Levites. The reasoning for its many innovations seems to be an eschatological "restoration" of the temple and its legitimate Zadokite priesthood. Y. Yadin, "Temple Scroll," *Encyclopedia Judaica Yearbook, 1977/1978* (1979) pp. 361ff.
76. 1QS 11:5–9; 1QH 11:10–14 and others.
77. Paleographical as well as archeological evidence supports this fact. The scripts of the scrolls reveal that the nonsectarian scrolls, especially the biblical manuscripts, begin in quantity ca. 150 B.C.E.; manuscripts that were composed as well as copied by the sectarian community begin about the middle of the Hasmonean period, i.e., ca. 100 B.C.E.; finally, there is a relatively large corpus of Herodian manuscripts dating between 30 B.C.E. and 70 C.E. F. M. Cross, "Early History of the Qumran Community," in D. N. Freedman and J. C. Greenfield, eds., *New Directions in Biblical Archeology* (1969), pp. 65–67.
78. Jos. *B.J.* I. vi. 2; Jos. *Antiq.* XIV. i. 3f.
79. Jos. *Antiq.* XIV. iv. 1f.; Jos. *B.J.* I. vi. 6f.; vii. 2.
80. Jos. *Antiq.* XIV. iv. 4; Jos. *B.J.* I. vi. 7.
81. A. Schalit, in A. Toynbee, ed., *The Crucible of Christianity* (1969) pp. 70f. Schalit's definitive biography of Herod has not been translated from German.
82. These "bandits" were led by Hezekiah, whose son, Judas, led a popular uprising at Sepphoris in Galilee after the death of Herod in 4 B.C.E. (Jos. *B.J.* II. iv. 2). Josephus is not clear whether Judas is to be identified with "the Galilean" revolutionary name Judas.
83. Schalit, in Toynbee, *The Crucible*, p. 71.
84. Jos. *Antiq.* XV. x. 4.
85. Jos. *Antiq.* XVI. v. 4.
86. Schalit, in Toynbee, *The Crucible*, pp. 72f.
87. Some scholars argue that the high priest Joazar in 6 C.E. represented a Sadducean resistance, but see D. M. Rhoads, *Israel in Revolution* (1976), pp. 41f. Avi-Yonah used the term *Neo-Sadducees* to distinguish Roman-Herodian priests and aristocrats from the sectaries of the Hasmonean era. *The Jews of Palestine*, p. 9. Some old Sadducees still favored the beleaguered Hasmonean dynasty.
88. See Asmp. M. 6:2–7, belonging to the collection of writings known as the Pseudepigrapha. According to R. H. Charles, this writing was composed by a Pharisee. See also Jos. *Antiq.* XV. i. 1.
89. Jos. *Antiq.* XVII. ii. 4.
90. Jos. *Antiq.* XVII. vi. 2f.; Jos. *B.J.* I. xxxiii. 1–4.

91. Rhoads, *Israel in Revolution*, pp. 36–39; Neusner, *From Politics to Piety* (1971), pp. 90f. Cf. G. Alon, "The Attitude of the Pharisees to Roman Rule and the House of Herod," in *Jews, Judaism and the Classical World* (1977), pp. 18–47.
92. Luke 13:32.
93. Mark 6:14ff.
94. For more on the prophet John the Baptist, see Chapter 10.
95. Schürer, *History of the Jewish People*, Vol. I, pp. 388ff. Cf. the works of Philo, *In Flaccum* and *Legatio*.
96. Jos. *Antiq.* XVIII. viii. 2.
97. Jos. *Antiq.* XIX. vii. 3.
98. Jos. *Antiq.* XIX. viii. 2; XX. ix. 1; Acts 12:1ff. Peter was also arrested but escaped death by a miraculous deliverance.
99. Jos. *B.J.* II. xi. 6.
100. Tacitus, *Histories* V. 9.
101. Jos. *Antiq.* XX. viii. 10.
102. Jos. *B.J.* II. xiii. 4f.; Acts 21:38.
103. Acts 25:1ff.
104. Jos. *Antiq.* XX. ix. 1.
105. Jos. *B.J.* II. xiv. 2.
106. Jos. *B.J.* II. xvii. 3.
107. Jos. *B.J.* II. xvii. 9.
108. Jos. *B.J.* II. xix. 2.
109. See Rhoads, *Israel in Revolution*, pp. 150f.; Avi-Yonah, *The Jews of Palestine*, p. 11.
110. Jos. *B.J.* IV. iii. 13.
111. Jos. *B.J.* VI. ii. 1.
112. Jos. *B.J.* III. viii. 9.
113. Jos. *B.J.* IV. iii. 6–8.
114. Jos. *B.J.* V. i. 1–5.
115. Jos. *B.J.* VII. v. 6.
116. Eusebius *Historia ecclesiastica* III. v. 2–3.
117. Jos. *B.J.* VII. viii. 1–3.
118. M. Hengel, *Acts and the History of Earliest Christianity* (1980), pp. 13f.
119. *Ibid.*, p. 14.

A Narrative of Christian Beginnings: Acts 1–12

THE Acts of the Apostles is the second part of a two-volume work. The "first book" is the Gospel according to Luke. The two writings are joined by their prefaces or prologues: Luke 1:1–4, and Acts 1:1ff. Both books are dedicated to a person addressed in the first as "the most excellent Theophilus." Unless Acts was written as an afterthought (with a purpose unrelated to the Gospel, which seems unlikely), it can be concluded that the author of "Luke-Acts," following a common literary convention of Hellenistic writers, intended his principal preface to set forth an aim served by the two volumes.

In Chapter 1 of this book the position was defended that it is important to learn what one can about the origin of a canonical text, to identify the occasion of its composition, its author's purpose. This is not only necessary for accurate historical reconstruction, but is conducive to locating a text's meaning, its hermeneutical function for a modern reader. Now it seems we are presented with a dilemma. On the one hand, some well-founded perception of the meaning and purpose of Luke-Acts as a whole provides the proper orientation for an exegesis of any part of either book. On the other hand, this perception is a consequence of tracing and combining "conclusions" accumulated from wide-ranging lines of evidence: for example, a comparison and contrast of Luke's Gospel with others like it (Matthew and Mark), and a determination of the relation of Luke's portrayal of Paul to Paul the Apostle (revealed in his own letters). Anyone searching for the author's purpose needs to sort out an astonishing number of clues.

How then can this dilemma be resolved? Perhaps the way ahead is to give attention to the author's prefaces, and to the particular part of his narrative that has been selected for reading, and to learn what one can about Luke's interests and concerns. This evidence will be gathered step by step. Accordingly, one does well to defer a definition of the purpose or purposes of the writer to Theophilus until one has first-hand acquaintance with his entire narrative. For some books of the New Testament—for example, the Revelation to John—a rather comprehensive grasp of the form and purpose of the whole work is a necessary preparation for interpreting its parts. For Luke-Acts, however, there are so many considerations involved that a case can be made for proceeding inductively.

THE PREFACES OF LUKE-ACTS

Luke's reference in 1:1 to "narratives" compiled by many has led some exegetes to conclude that this preface applied to the Gospel only, for although Luke's knowledge of other Gospels is highly probable, there is no evidence that other books like Acts had been written. Yet verses 2 through 4 may apply to both the Gospel and Acts and state Luke's claim that he was in possession of reliable knowledge: first, concerning Jesus, having received it from "those who from the beginning were eyewitnesses and servants of the word"; second, concerning some of the events relating to Paul, having himself been an observer. H. J. Cadbury, a major contributor to studies on Luke-Acts, has contended that the verb "having followed" was not used in earlier and contemporary writings to mean "having investigated" (i.e., through inquiries or research). Rather, the verb connoted "having observed, been in close touch with, or having participated in events." *

If in Luke 1:1 "narrative" applied to sources of various kinds, and "the things which have been accomplished among us" referred to deeds of Jesus *and* of his apostles, then Luke may have intended his preface to the Gospel to apply also to Acts, and three stages in the development of the tradition are implied: the events→the observers→the account. With respect to the Gospel and the early part of Acts, Luke's witness would represent stage 3; with respect to significant passages of the concluding part of Acts, stages 2 and 3.

Who was Theophilus and what was his problem? Nothing is known of either except that which can be inferred from Luke-Acts. The author assumed that Theophilus needed and might welcome reliable knowledge concerning Christian origins. The verb translated "have been informed" in the RSV and NEB, reads in some other English versions, "have been instructed" (KJV, JerB). This latter reading lends support to the view that Theophilus was a Christian. Perhaps he knew some of the earlier narratives concerning Jesus' words and deeds to which Luke alluded. Why would such a person, who was already a believer, need what Luke undertook to supply? Did his faith need re-enforcement, greater assurance? The answer is not given here, but is to to be found in Luke's narratives?

If the final verb is alternatively translated, and Theophilus had only been "informed" concerning these things, this may mean that he was not a Christian. Perhaps his previous knowledge of Christian origins was a mix of fact, rumor, and hearsay. (For this connotation of the verb, "to be (mis-) informed," cf. Acts 21:21, 24.) In any case, whatever the nature of the information Theophilus had received, he had retained an open mind, and by accepting books dedicated to him, he manifested a desire to obtain accurate knowledge.

The secular terminology of the preface, and the form of address, "most excellent Theophilus," may support the view that Luke's "patron" was not a Christian. **

The secondary preface, Acts 1:1ff., treated only indirectly the need of Theophilus and the purpose of Luke-Acts. Its contribution depends on the determination of its limits. Acts 1:1–2 summarizes the content of "the first book." This is followed by a report of Jesus' conversation with and charge to his apostles "during forty days" (3–5). Then Jesus' oracle concerning "the kingdom"

* Josephus wrote (*Apion* I. 10): "It is the duty of one who promises to present his readers with actual facts first to obtain exact knowledge of them himself, either *through having been in close touch with the events* [the same verb used in Luke 1:3], or by inquiry [note the contrast] from those who know of them." See H. J. Cadbury, " 'We' and 'I' Passages in Luke-Acts," *NTS* 3 (1956): 130f.

** Only persons of equestrian rank are addressed in this manner elsewhere in Luke-Acts: Felix and Festus, by Paul in deference to their

is reported, and his prophecy of the universal outreach of the apostles' witness (6–8).

Possibly the preface ended with verse 5, but it is probable that verses 6 through 8 constitute its climax. If Theophilus was a Christian, verse 6 may express a difficulty he was having maintaining belief in the imminence of the kingdom of God in view of the church's ignorance of the time of its coming. In this case verses 7 and 8 may signal Luke's solution: the church's ignorance is rendered tolerable by its reception of the Spirit and its imperative of a universal mission.[1]

Alternatively, if the preponderant evidence suggests that Theophilus was a well-disposed unbeliever, verses 6 and 7 may have quashed for him a rumor that Jesus had encouraged Jewish nationalism; and verse 8 may have been an impressive confirmation of the Gospel's salvific power, since Luke's narrative reported the fulfilment of Jesus' prophecy that the Gospel would reach "to the end of the earth" (Rome? Ps. of Sol. 8:16; or Gentiles? Cf. Acts 13:46f.)

Perhaps it is now clear that a satisfactory hypothesis concerning Luke's purpose or purposes cannot be derived solely from an exegesis of the prefaces. We must allow Luke's narratives to be the commentary that hopefully will elucidate his aim and locate the principal value that the work may have for us.

offices as procurator (Acts 24:2; 26:25 [23:26]). Luke's books were probably not written for Theophilus alone. Did Luke know that the concerns of Theophilus via-à-vis the church were shared by others in his society? Did Luke recognize Theophilus as the patron of his work? A not unreasonable conjecture given the "literary" character of Luke's ambitious undertaking.

ACTS 1–5

A. Introduction: Days of Preparation for Witness, 1:1–26
    1. Secondary preface, 1:1–8
    2. Jesus' ascension, 1:9–11

It may be instructive to read the ending of Luke's Gospel, especially 24:36–52, and Acts 1:9–11. Certain discrepancies are apparent. For example, according to the Gospel narrative the ascension took place on the day of resurrection; according to Acts, on the Mount of Olives forty days later.[2] It is probable that this is initial evidence for us that Luke's primary concern (to be illustrated elsewhere as well) was not to write up the traditional accounts so that Theophilus could know what actually happened. Rather, by the double form of the narratives Luke may have intended to emphasize that the ascension was the end of the story of Jesus' earthly ministry, but also the beginning of the Church's mission.*

In all of the New Testament writings, the time that follows the resurrection—whether perceived as short or long—was understood to be in some sense the End (or the beginning of the End), the last chapter in the series of God's redemptive acts in human history. As we shall see, for Mark (perhaps also for Paul) "the stress lies on the adjective *last*. For Luke the stress lies in the fact that the last chapter is a *new* chapter. Christ is the End; but (and this is how Luke prefers to think of Him) because He is the End He is also the Beginning . . . the starting point of a new kind of history, Church History, whose horizons are indefinitely remote.[3]

A. 3. The twelfth apostle is enrolled, 1:12–26

*Significant parallels between the narratives, Luke 24 and Acts 1:1–12, have been noted. Luke's selection of materials for his narratives, and their compositional patterns, may have been influenced by stylistic principles of duplication and balance that were typical of Hellenistic forms of narrative. See C. H. Talbert, *Literary Patterns, Theological Themes, and the Genre of Luke-Acts* (1974). For Luke 24–Acts 1, pp. 58–61, 112–116. See also J. Dupont, *The Salvation of the Gentiles* (1967), pp. 13–19.

*Cf., however Acts 14:14. Luke was not the originator of the idea of *twelve* apostles. Earlier, Paul attested to their existence and importance (1 Cor. 15:5,11). *Unique to Luke is this criterion of apostleship*. Possibly he exaggerated the influence of the Twelve. One does not get the impression from Paul that all of the Twelve exercised leadership in the Jerusalem church (cf. Gal. 1:17; 2:9).

**Note the "scriptural" formula of Luke's introduction: "when the day of Pentecost was fulfilled." Other critical moments in Luke-Acts are introduced in this way (Luke 2:6f): "when the days were fulfilled for [Mary] . . . she gave birth to her first-born son;" (Luke 9:51): "when the days were fulfilled for [Jesus] to be received up, he set his face to go to Jerusalem." Cf. Luke 1:1.

†In the Gospel of John another tradition is

In the secondary preface to Luke-Acts, the indispensable role of Jesus' eleven remaining apostles is given prominence. It was to them that Jesus "presented himself alive after his passion by many proofs"; the reader is reminded that these men were his "chosen" witnesses. Among the writers of the Gospels, Luke most clearly distinguished the twelve "apostles" as an exclusive, inner circle of Jesus' followers (6:13; 9:10; 11:49; 17:5; 22:14, 28–30; 24:10, 33ff. Contrast the one reference in Mark to "the apostles," 6:30). They were not the only persons to whom the risen Christ appeared (Luke 24:33), but the apostle's testimony was viewed by our author as essential to the progress of the gospel. To them the gift of the Holy Spirit was promised (Luke 24:46–49; Acts 1:4f., 8). As witnesses of the earthly life of Jesus, from the baptism of John to the ascension, they became the guarantors of the gospel tradition (Acts 1:21f.; 10:37–43; 13:24f., 30f.; Luke 1:2). Only from this standpoint can one explain why Luke denied to his "hero," Paul, the status of an apostle, which Paul so adamantly claimed!*

For Luke the ostensible reason for the enrollment of Matthias was that since one of the Twelve had defected, someone must be chosen by the Lord to take his place. Support for this was found in the scriptures. It is probable that Luke held in mind a saying of Jesus that he reported in his Gospel: "You [my apostles] are those who have continued with me in my trials, and I assign to you, as my Father assigned to me, a kingdom, that you may eat and drink at my table in my kingdom, *and sit on thrones judging the twelve tribes of Israel*" (Luke 22:[14], 28–30. Cf. Matt. 19:28.) It is noteworthy that when James was martyred (12:1f.), no replacement was sought. "Unlike Judas, he was faithful unto death, and might hope to reign with Christ in resurrection, if not (as he had once expected, Mark 10:35ff.) in this present life."[4]

B. The Inspired Witness of the Apostles to the Gathered Jewish Community in Jerusalem, 2:1–47
   1. At Pentecost, the Lord gives the Spirit, 2:1–13

Pentecost held momentous significance for Luke.** Efforts have failed to identify a written source for his narrative.[5] Its basis was probably a historical tradition that the public proclamation of the gospel by the apostles began in earnest (as one might say), with the coming of the next Jewish festival, the day of Pentecost, celebrated on the fiftieth day reckoned from "the morrow after the [Passover] Sabbath" (Lev. 23.15ff.).†

Jewish traditions, cultic and exegetical, shed light upon the sign character of Luke's narrative. First of all, Pentecost, originally a harvest festival, came in time to be associated with the giving of the Law at Sinai. Philo interpreted the tongues of fire to have been "tongues" of speech. Palestinian rabbis taught that by means of this fiery breath God created "in the souls of each and all another kind of hearing of the ears." God had spoken the Torah in seventy languages (corresponding to the seventy nations of the world), but only Israel had hearkened and obeyed. Luke emphasized, however, that on the day of Pentecost the hearers of the gospel were Jews, devout ones (Hasidim), all dwellers in Jerusalem, including those whose origin had been in one of the many communities of the Diaspora (Acts 2:5, 14, 22, 36, 39; also 3:25f.). The conversion of Gentiles was to be a later work of the Spirit, in large measure resulting from the missions of Paul and his colleagues (Acts 8:1, 4:25; 9:15; 10:44f; 11:19–21; Chs. 13–28).* Attention also may be called to "a parallel to Pentecost" later in Luke's story, marking the first conversion of a Gentile, the "devout" Roman centurion, Cornelius (Acts 10:1ff.; see especially 10:44–46). Although Luke reported that the ecstatic speech of the apostles and their company was comprehensible to many, it is interesting that others heard only a garbled raving, suggesting drunkenness. The emotional outbursts of those possessed by the Spirit did not bring others to faith, rather to bewilderment; it was Peter's proclamation of the gospel that won 3,000 converts!

B. 2. Peter's Pentecost speech, 2:14–40

A reading now of Acts 2:14 to 4:4 will enable one to observe two literary conventions employed by Luke to interpret Pentecost and the events that followed: first, the interlarding of the narrative with speeches delivered by principal persons in the story (in this case, Peter) or by persons with supporting roles; and second, the composition of summary statements linking its various episodes. Whatever the sources available to Luke, the speeches and summaries were composed by him. These literary techniques were commonplace in historical and biographical writings of the Hellenistic Age, and were often taken as evidence of the rhetorical skills of their authors. Their interest for us lies in their disclosure of Luke's theology.[6]

The "missionary speeches" recorded in the early chapters of Acts merit special attention. The first two are attributed to Peter, which we have just read (2:14–40 and 3:12–26): two others are also attributed to Peter (4:8–12 and 10:34–43); and a fifth is attributed to Paul (13:16–41). Although these speeches are suited to the occasions of their delivery, striking similarities in their structure and content have been noted.[7]

The exegesis of these speeches has led to opposing conclusions. On the one hand, it is argued that they reproduce in outline form what was actually said by the apostles; on the other hand, it is contended that the speeches record the gospel preached in the churches of Luke's time, in the 80s of the first century.

Defenders of "the historicity" of the speeches appeal to internal evidence supporting Luke's use of early Aramaic sources. They also point to parallels in the content of the gospel preached by the apostles in Acts with statements in Paul's letters concerning the traditional gospel that he preached and that (he contended) was not different from the gospel proclaimed by those who were apostles before him.[8] Those who argue that the speeches in Acts reflect late first-century Hellenistic Christianity, claim that the Christology of the speeches is Lucan. They also contend that traditions concerning the apostles were not preserved, that Luke's use of early sources cannot be demonstrated, and that his knowledge of the earliest period was severely limited.[9]

Both views are probably untenable extremes. That the speeches were composed by Luke in Greek is undeniable. Scriptural "proofs" are taken from the LXX. There are, however, elements in the speeches that are not typically Lucan. For example, the resurrection and ascension are not separate events in the speeches, as they certainly are in Luke's understanding. Also, Peter's descrip-

reported, that on the evening of the day of resurrection Jesus had "breathed" on [his disciples], "and said to them, 'Receive the Holy Spirit.'" Yet his disciples did not immediately become witnesses to the risen Christ (John 20:21f. Note 20:26; also 21:1, 14). The words of Jesus in the Fourth Gospel concerning the Father's sending of the Spirit, may reflect the alternative tradition (John 14:25f.; 15:26f.).

*Undeniably the universality of the gospel was a major conviction of the "writer to Theophilus." Codex Sinaiticus omits the word "Jews" in 2:5, thus allowing the mistaken idea that the Pentecost audience was international. The context makes this reading unacceptable. Luke reported that only native Judeans and Diaspora Jews were witnesses to the Spirit's activity on the day of Pentecost.

tion of Jesus' reception of the Spirit in Acts 2:33 and 36 does not agree with Luke 4:1,18 and 9:35. Luke probably worked over earlier traditions, but not merely to recover the form of the earliest gospel. Rather, his interest was to convince Theophilus and other readers that the Church's gospel is the gospel that the risen Lord had commanded his apostles to preach, a gospel still powerful to save.[10]

Undoubtedly the gospel was expressed and applied in manifold ways, according to the needs of individuals and groups and the special concerns of those who proclaimed and interpreted it. But allowing for diversity, the "missionary speeches" in Acts may be examined on the assumption that they contain summaries of a traditional gospel, proclaimed at Pentecost and afterwards.

* Kērygma, a word borrowed from the Greek word *kērys-sein*, "to proclaim" as a "herald" *(kēryx)*. Kērygma = "proclamation" is a semi-technical term often used instead of "preaching" which, in English versions of the New Testament, is a somewhat misleading translation. Kērygma connotes "the *active* sense of proclaiming, see, e.g., 1 Cor. 15:14, 2:4, but also what is proclaimed, "the *content-sense*, the preaching about Christ," e.g., I Cor. 15:1–3; Rom. 16:25.

Kērygma, the noun, occurs only once in Luke-Acts—Luke 11:32, but the verb *kērys-sein* is used nine times in the Gospel, eight in Acts (e.g., the active sense, Luke 4:44; 8:1; Acts 10:42; the content sense, Luke 4:19, 21; 9:2; Acts 8:4, 14, 25 and 9:21).

THE EARLY CHRISTIAN GOSPEL OR KERYGMA *

The "proclamation" of the apostles was that

1. The day of fulfilment has dawned with the coming of the Messiah (2:16; 3:18,24; 10:43; 13:32f).
2. The Messiah is Jesus, who was born of David's lineage (2:30f; cf. 13:23). His ministry was accompanied with signs and wonders (2:22; cf. 10:38) He was unjustly crucified, but his death was God's will for His anointed (2:23, 36; 3:13f; cf. 4:10; 5:30; 10:39; 13:27–29).

    He was raised from death, in accordance with the scriptures (2:32; 3:15; cf. 4:10; 5:30–32; 13:30–35).
3. By his resurrection Jesus was not only exalted by God's right hand (i.e., by His mighty power, 2:33), but seated at God's right hand, to reign over all humankind: God has made Jesus "Lord" as well as "Messiah" (2:34–36; 3:13; cf. 4:11; 10:42, 13:38).
4. The time of God's hoped-for salvation of his people is here, "whoever calls upon the name of the Lord shall be saved" (2:21). Repent, and be baptized in the name of Jesus the Christ for the forgiveness of sins, so as to receive the gift of the Holy Spirit (2:38f.; 3:19; cf. 4:12; 10:43; 13:38).
5. God's present offer of final blessedness, his present final judgment, will be followed by his sending yet again the Messiah Jesus, "whom heaven must receive until the time for establishing all that God spoke by the mouth of the holy prophets from of old" (3:20f; cf. 10:42. Note 1:6).

In proclaiming the gospel to "the house of Israel," the apostles appealed to the scriptures containing some elements of the messianic speculation of Judaism's Second Temple period. The claim of Peter was that "all the prophets who have spoken from Samuel, and those who came afterwards, also proclaimed these days. . . . God having raised up his servant [Jesus] sent him first to you [the sons of the prophets and of the covenant] to bless you. . . ." (2:36; 3:25f.; cf. 10:42).

B. 3. First major summary: results of the proclamation, 2:41–47

Attention has been called to the general summaries that punctuate Luke's narrative. These are his compositions and, along with the kerygmatic speeches in the early chapters, provide valuable clues to Luke's special interests and interpretation. The major summaries in Acts 1–5 are 2:41–47; 4:32–35; and 5:11–16. Minor summaries are 4:4 and 5:42.

Ernst Haenchen reported the efforts of several scholars who, in his view, were unsuccessful in linking these passages with early traditions. "The summaries," he concluded, "appear to flow entirely from the pen of Luke."[11] Coupled with this conclusion is Haenchen's view that few stories of the activities of the apostles and their converts were preserved in the early church. Belief in the imminence of the return of the Lord Jesus precluded the development of such biographical material. Luke has written his legend-colored traditions in such a way as to illustrate effectively those ideals and norms of church life that he held to be apostolic, views that are given general statement in 2:41–47 and in subsequent summaries. Actually, the facts were otherwise. Haenchen claims, "in the quiet life of the primitive community there were no mass assemblies such as Luke places at the outset of the Christian mission, therefore no conflicts with the Sadducees arising from them."[12]

Undoubtedly Luke did employ the technique of summary to fill in gaps, to convey the impression of uninterrupted developments. The motif of the Spirit's (or Word's) unimpeded progress is a prominent Lucan theme.[13] But Haenchen's view that in the early church there was no interest in the deeds of the apostles and their converts, and hence no surviving tradition for Luke's employment, needs to be questioned in the light of evidence from Paul's letters.[14] 1 Thessalonians is especially important, for in this letter Paul expressed his conviction concerning the imminence of the Day of the Lord. Yet he wrote to recent converts: ". . . you received the word in much affliction, with joy inspired by the Holy Spirit, so that you became an example to all believers . . . for not only has the word of the Lord sounded forth from you . . . but your faith in God has gone forth everywhere [in which is reported] how you turned to God . . ." Note also Paul's reference to the Thessalonian Christians' knowledge of the persecutions endured by "the churches in Judea."[15] "So far from conditions being unfavorable to the formation of a tradition of the apostolic period, accounts of the apostles and the faith of the communities had their place in the preaching from the beginning." Luke was not the first to believe that the radical changes in human behavior, which were the effects of the kerygma, witnessed to the power of the risen Christ and the presence of the Spirit.[16]

The descriptions in Acts of pneumatic phenomena in the early Church may be puzzling to the modern reader.* Luke's major interest should not be overlooked. He was more impressed with other signs of spirituality than "tongues of fire," or sounds "like the rush of a mighty wind." The practitioner's techniques in miracles of healing are barely noticed. But he delighted in reporting the amazing moral achievements of the first followers of Jesus: their boldness in declaring and defending their beliefs and actions, their self-effacing acts of mercy, their practical concern for the well-being of all who belonged to their group.

It is highly improbable that Luke imposed this strong consciousness of community upon the primitive traditions, even though he may have idealized it. In ancient Judaism the hope of the manifestation of the Spirit in the Age to Come reflected a persistent social reference. By means of his Spirit, God would create in the last days a people—usually conceived as a reconstituted Israel—to inherit

* *Pneumatic phenomena, pneumatism:* terms derived from the Greek word *pneuma,* "spirit." In Christian doctrine pneumatology refers to beliefs and teaching concerning the activity of the Holy Spirit.

the blessings of the new age. Where such ideas were held, a corollary of faith in the coming of a messiah was belief in the emergence in history of the eschatological congregation.[17]

Pneumatism in early Christianity can best be understood in the light of these ancient Jewish conceptions. Possibly the beliefs and practices of the Essenes brought into sharp focus this communal aspect of Jewish eschatology. The followers of Jesus were, like these sectaries (and unlike the associations of the Pharisees and other parties within Judaism), conscious that they were already the eschatological congregation, the community of the last days. Nevertheless, the gift of the Holy Spirit is only anticipated in Essenism, while the early Christians believed that the eschatological events were taking place. With the coming of the Messiah, now risen from the dead, they were being called out of Israel to become the people of God who would soon inherit His glorious kingdom.

Luke reports that some early Christians "sold their possessions and goods and distributed them to all, as any had need" (2:45; 4:36f.). It would be wrong to assume that the earliest Christians developed a communistic society. There was no organized communal production among them and the common purse was made up of voluntary offerings.[18] The obligation of the Church to provide for the material needs of all its members is exemplified in this early impulse toward the voluntary sharing.

Unlike the devotees of the many Hellenistic religions, the first Christians did not cultivate the Spirit; that is to say, they did not seek to induce states of ecstasy leading to the suspension of consciousness or of rationality. When we consider Paul's missions, we shall learn that many religions of the Hellenistic age tended to relieve the individual of his or her responsibilities toward society. The spirituality of individuals in the church at Corinth, influenced by popular religious conceptions, tended to be void of social responsibility. From its earliest days, however, the Christian Church fostered and sustained a strong sense of community among its members.

Still more important for the future was the fact that the leaders of the early Church were men who had known Jesus personally. In him whom they worshiped as the bearer of the divine Spirit they had a concrete standard by which to judge the workings of the Holy Spirit in themselves and in their community.

C. Further Witnessing in Jerusalem: Successes in Spite of Intimidation, 3:1–5:42
   1. Peter heals a lame man, 3:1–11
   2. Peter's speech in the temple, 3:12–26
   3. The arrest of Peter and John, 4:1–3
   4. Summary, 4:4
   5. The apostles' arraignment before the council, 4:5–7
   6. Peter's speech before the council, 4:8–12
   7. The apostles are threatened and released, 4:13–22
   8. Prayers of gratitude bring a fresh outpouring of the Holy Spirit, 4:23–31
   9. Second major summary: the practice of sharing; the example of Barnabas, 4:32–37
   10. The deception of Ananias and Sapphira, 5:1–10
   11. Third major summary: signs and wonders, 5:11–16

The first believers in Jesus the Christ wrought miracles of healing. Such events were understood as "signs and wonders," either manifesting the Holy Spirit in the Messianic Age or evidencing the power of the risen Christ.[19]

Some scholars have discounted these miracle stories. Luke's writings reveal a personal fondness for miracles, especially for miracles of healing, which has contributed to his uncritical use of popular "wonder stories." Yet according to the earliest Gospels the disciples believed healing of the sick a part of their mission as well as of Jesus' ministry. The Gospels also report that the power of "the name " of Jesus, in dealing with the demon-possessed, had led persons outside of the disciple band to employ it.[20] Moreover, like Peter in Acts, Paul testifies in his letters that miracles of healing were wrought among his converts. He also attributes them to the power of the risen Christ, or the Spirit.[21] It seems reasonable, therefore, to conclude that Luke is here reporting early traditions. That he should have magnified the miraculous elements in the narrative is of course more understandable than that he should have treated them skeptically. At the same time, it is noteworthy that very little notice is taken of this aspect of the Holy Spirit's work in the later letters of Paul and in the New Testament books after his time.[22] Such evidence represents the reduction of an emphasis that was prominent in the earliest days. Belief in miracles of healing was an inevitable accompaniment of the initial outbursts of Christian enthusiasm. Such miracles happened again where they were expected. That the disciples believed that Jesus could and did heal through them can scarcely be doubted.

The first conflict with Jewish authorities followed the healing of the lame man at the gate of the temple (3:1ff.). Luke reports that "the priests and the captain of the temple and the Sadducees" arrested Peter and John, held them overnight, and, at a hearing the next morning, forbade them "to speak or teach at all in the name of Jesus." The apostles were released and resumed their teaching and healing "in Solomon's Portico" (5:12; cf. 3:11). Following a repetitive emphasis on the unity of the church and the freedom from want of all of its members, Luke reported a second arrest of the apostles. The sequence of events closely resembles the circumstances of the previous arrest (as our proposed outline notes).

> C. 12. The arrest and arraignment of the apostles, 5:17–27 (cf. 4:1–7)
>   13. Peter's speech in defense, 5:28–32 (cf. 4:8–12, 19f.)
>   14. The council deliberates; Gamaliel's speech, 5:33–39 (cf. 4:13–17)
>   15. The apostles are beaten, and released, 5:40–42 (cf. 4:18, 21–23)

Various explanations of this parallelism have been offered. Proponents of multiple-source theories see evidence here of variant accounts of the same events. Perhaps Luke failed to see this, or recognizing that two of his sources contained this parallelism, recognized also that each account contained significant details. Moreover, he may have needed narrative material to fill up a relatively long period about which he had little information. Other scholars who believe the evidence is insufficient to support the theory that Luke possessed written sources for the early period are inclined to Haenchen's view that Luke freely composed these narratives out of independent units of oral tradition, and that this parallelism reflects the influence of contemporary literary forms upon Luke's style of narration.[23]

It is not surprising that some exegetes have questioned the authenticity of these trial scenes. Not only their form but their content raises questions. Such clashes with Jewish authorities are seen as being inconsistent with Luke's summaries, which declared that the early Christians stood well in the estimation of the Jews in Jerusalem. Sadducees might have regarded the rapidly growing Christian community as a threat to the peace. They may have investigated the situation, but it unlikely that any official repressive measures were taken. The peace enjoyed by the Christians in Jerusalem was first broken by Stephen and his sympathizers. After their departure persecution ceased. Herod's martyrdom of James and the miraculous escape of Peter are overlaid with legend. According to these critics, it is not possible to disentangle from this story anything that can be called historical, aside from the fact that James was an early martyr and Peter narrowly escaped death in Jerusalem. That James's death would have "pleased the Jews" is scarcely credible.[24]

This skepticism with regard to Acts is ordinarily rejected as going too far. The Sadducees rather than the Pharisees would have had cause to fear the possible political consequences of the movement. Yet so long as Jesus' followers did not cry for vengeance, or oppose the temple, there was no need for violent repressive action. Moreover, under the Roman procurators it would have been difficult to devise an effective method of persecution, even with the aid of the Pharisees. But the Pharisees had no reasons for such persecution and many reasons for cautious tolerance. Most of the early Christians were zealous for the Torah and Jewish traditions, and some of the Pharisees had become identified with the movement.

Luke's information may have been meager for this part of his narrative, yet it seems highly probable that the author knew that the apostles had been arrested and threatened, and that the learned sage, Gamaliel, had counselled toleration of the Galileans.[25] For his narrative concerning "the seven" and Stephen's martyrdom, Luke was more fortunately furnished, yet the following developments are not without difficulties.

ACTS 6–12

D. The Witness of the Hellenists in Judea and Samaria, 6:1–8:40
    1. Appointment of the seven, 6:1–6
    2. Summary: numerous converts, including "a great many priests," 6:7

Accompanying the growth of the church in Jerusalem, tensions developed between members whose difference was most apparent in their divergent languages and cultural origins. A specific grievance of a minority group, cited by Luke, was quickly remedied by action initiated by "the Twelve"; however, the sequence of events may reveal that the particular complaint was symptomatic of a more serious division involving the church's gospel and mission. Anticipating these events to follow, it can be concluded that Luke drew a direct line between the appointment of "the seven" and the eventual deliberate evangelization of Gentiles by the group they represented (8:1, 4–8; 11:19f.). But Luke's account of the expansion of the Christian movement is not without the dramatic involvement of Luke's principal heroes, "the apostles" (8:14–25; 9:32–11:18), and Paul (8:1a; 9:1–30; 11:25f.).

At the outset Luke identified this innovative minority in the church as "the Hellenists." The usual view (which is likely to be correct) is that by this term Luke intended Greek-speaking Jews whose native connections were with the Diaspora rather than Palestine, but who had settled in Jerusalem and established there synagogues of their own. (Of course, the Hellenists of 6:1 were converts to Christianity, but probably those "who disputed with Stephen" [6:9], belonging to "the synagogue of the Freedmen," were also Hellenists, although Luke does not use the term with reference to these Jews.) "The Hebrews" then would identify the majority in the Jerusalem church, those Aramaic-speaking Jewish Christians, including the apostles, mostly natives of Palestine, who had custody of the community's assets (4:31, 37; 5:2 [6:1, Codex D]).

It is a bit strange that nothing more is reported about "the seven" in the discharge of their appointed task. Attention focuses on Stephen's preaching and healing ministry (which must have left him little time "to serve tables," 6:8–8:3). Philip leaves the Hellenist widows behind, conducting a mission to the Samaritans (8:5–25), converting an Ethiopian (8:26–40), and finally appearing in Caesarea, where he is known as "the evangelist" (21:8). Little wonder it is that some scholars surmise that Luke drew upon two or more written sources concerning Stephen, which he was not able to combine harmoniously. The familiar technique of a summary (6:7) may have been employed to join 6:1–6 to a separate account of Stephen's martyrdom (but in such a way as to acknowledge Stephen's ordination by the apostles to his ministry?)[26]

> D. 3. A campaign against Stephen by Diaspora Jews leads to his arrest, 6:8–7:1
>   4. Stephen's speech, 7:2–53
>   5. Stephen's martyrdom and the scattering of the Hellenists, 7:54–8:3 [Saul's outraged reaction, 8:1, 3]

A reading of Acts 6:8–15 followed by 7:54–60 provides evidence for a persistent question: Was Stephen lynched by an angry mob? It does seem that Stephen's radiant face (6:15) anticipates his heavenly vision (7:54f), but a perusal of 7:1–53 suggests that Stephen's death was a consequence of a judicial procedure in which the accused was permitted a lengthy self-defense. Has Luke used and combined two disparate sources? That he worked over an early tradition is likely; he would not have freely composed this narrative, given his convictions, one, that the apostles were those best qualified to proclaim and defend the church's gospel; and, two, that it was the Sadducees who took the initiative in using violence against the Christians in Jerusalem. There was nothing to oblige Luke to introduce Stephen's defense of the gospel, in a speech of unparalled length, in the face of an aggressive attack by Hellenistic Jews of the Diaspora, "unless there was a tradition he could not ignore."[27]

It is unlikely that Luke saw any discrepancy in the tradition between the Sanhedrin's participation and the murderous action of a mob. Luke's previous references to the Council (which no doubt reflected his own feeling) depicted it "as an assembly capable of any act of violence and carried away, unchecked, by passion" (5:33; cf. 23:1–10).[28] The major problem in this part of the narrative is Stephen's speech.

Does Stephen answer the charges that led to his arraignment? For those persons who judge that the speech (or a large part of it) is irrelevant to the trial scene, the question becomes: What purpose might have led Luke to compose this lengthy historical survey or edit one associated in some way with traditions concerning the martyr Stephen?[29] There are others, however, who do not consider the speech in its trial setting to be irrelevant.[30]

Haenchen's exegesis affords an excellent example of the first position. He assumes that 7:2–53 is a Lucan adaptation of a "neutral" presentation of sacred history (Dibelius). Verse 25 introduces the polemical element and, along with verses 35, 37, 39–43 and 48–53, appear to be Lucan additions. In this way Luke "cleverly combined a synagogue sermon about the destiny of Israel with passionate complaints against Israel." These "complaints" reflect an attitude current in Luke's church vis-à-vis Diaspora synagogues in the late-first century.[31]

Alternatively, many exegetes have held that Luke's composition (7:2–53) probably reported *the general sense* of Stephen's defense of the gospel before the Sanhedrin (and in the Hellenist synagogues?). This exegesis supposes that Luke drew elements of the speech, and possibly—at least in part—its wording, from an early source. Against the view that the speech voices only Lucan or traditional theology is the fact that a more sharply negative attitude toward the Jews is reflected in it from that found in the missionary speeches (reported before and after Chapter 7 in Acts) attributed to Peter and to Paul, a posture toward the synagogue that Luke surely considered the normative Christian attitude.

The frequency with which scholars have noted the development of two major themes in Stephen's speech leads one to suspect that the oft-repeated assertion of its irrelevance and absence of consistency may deserve re-examination. The first of these themes is enunciated at the beginning of the speech and is reasserted at its ending. God's revelations to his people have never been restricted to one land or one holy place. Major events in Israel's history have taken place outside of Palestine: Abraham's call "while he was in Mesopotamia;" Joseph's and Moses' preparations to become Israel's saviors occurred in Egypt; God gave his law through Moses while his people were wanderers in the wilderness. Likewise, while "in the wilderness of Mount Sinai," God had provided his people a tent or tabernacle, a moveable shrine witnessing to His presence, which subsequently in David's reign was "pitched" on the hill of Zion. It was Solomon who "built a house" for God to dwell in—a fixed, holy place that, Israel's prophets had affirmed, was contrary to the divine will.

This shocking climax to Stephen's speech, which opposes the tabernacle to the temple (with its clear implication that the latter's establishment was an act of apostasy), links the first theme with a second: the rejection by all elements of the Jewish nation (6:12) of the proclamation of witnesses to "the coming of the Righteous One," was all of a piece with the attitude of their fathers in times past. The corruption of true worship in Jerusalem's temple from Solomon to the present, was the historical sequel to Israel's worship of the golden calf, and of Moloch and Rephan, during the forty-year sojourn in the wilderness, when

Moses' leadership was more than once "thrust aside." Earlier still, the patriarch, Joseph, had been "sold into Egypt" by his brethren.

Through Joseph, Moses, David, and the prophets, God had provided for the salvation of his people. Before they possessed the land of their "inheritance," when they were in Egypt, living in exile (while separated from Palestine among the Diaspora?), Israelites were never bereft of God's presence, symbolized from the time of the Exodus by the moveable "tent of witness." But God's salvific acts and Torah had been repudiated time and again, under the leadership of the temple's priests.

If this speech ascribed to Stephen is taken to represent his personal views, as it seems one should, the conclusion follows that his opponent's accusations were in part true. Certainly Stephen did not "speak blasphemous words against Moses and God" nor deny the divine origin of the Torah, but he did speak against the temple, which was sanctioned by the law. Stephen's understanding of the teaching of Jesus apparently provided him with a new perspective upon Israel's institutions, the law as well as the temple. Belief in Jesus as Lord as well as Messiah did indeed effect a radical change in the status "of the customs which Moses delivered" to the people of God, for their authority was now superceded by the person and teaching of Jesus, God's eschatological revelation, the mediator of a new covenant.*

*Some of Jesus' actions and words appear to warrant Stephen's exposition of the Christian kerygma, a revolutionary aspect of the gospel that was concealed by the adherence of "the Hebrews" in the church to the Torah, and their continued participation in Temple worship. In important ways Stephen anticipated Paul; perhaps more directly, the teaching of the Letter to the Hebrews and the Gospel of John.

D. 6. Philip proclaims Christ to the Samaritans, 8:4–13
   7. The apostles confirm the Hellenist's missions, 8:14–25
   8. Philip and the Ethiopian, 8:26–40
[E. *The First Account of the Conversion of Saul-Paul, 9:1–31 (22:3ff.;26:1ff.)*
   1. *Saul's vision of Christ near Damascus, 9:20–30*
   2. *The ministry of Ananias, 9:10–19*
   3. *Saul preaches, escapes arrest, in Damascus, 9:20–30]*
   4. Summary: the church's growth, 9:31
F. First Witnessing to Gentiles, 9:32–11:30
   1. Peter at Lydda and Joppa, 9:32–43
   2. Conversion of the Roman centurion, Cornelius, 10:1–11:18
   3. A church is founded and flourishes at Antioch, 11:19–21
   [4. *Barnabas is sent to Antioch from Jerusalem, 11:22–24*
   5. *Barnabas fetches Saul from Tarsus, 11:25f.*
   6. *Agabus prophesies a famine; relief is sent to Jerusalem, 11:27–30]*
G. Herod's Persecution of the Church in Jerusalem, 12:1–25
   1. The martyrdom of James; Peter's arrest, escape, and departure "to another place," 12:1–9
   2. The death of Herod, 12:20–23
   3. Summary: marking the progress of Christianity, and of the Acts' narrative, 12:24f.

Significant segments of the narrative outlined above (and set apart by brackets) are devoted to the conversion of Saul-Paul, to his preparation for his missions to the Gentiles. Perhaps the best place to give consideration to these developments is in connection with a later reading of Acts 13–28. In thus leaving aside for the present 9:1–31 and 11:22–30, it may seem that violence is being done to the text. This is not so, for although Luke was bound to locate Saul's conversion in its historical setting, he clearly wished to do two things before giving over his narrative almost completely to the accomplishments of Paul: to credit the Hellenists with their innovative missions in Judea and Samaria (fulfilling the Lord's command, 1:8); and also to report God's provision that Peter be the instrument of the Spirit in leading the first Gentiles "to repentance unto life" (11:18–20; cf. 9:15, 20, 28f.; 11:25).

The stories in Acts 8–10 concerning the Hellenist, Philip, and of Peter's activities in Lydda, Joppa, and Caesarea, have the outward form of popular folk tradition. One is reminded of the Old Testament stories reporting the wonder-working powers of the ecstatic prophets, Elijah and Elisha, which are different in kind from the historical narrative in which they are embedded. The modern reader's inclination may be to esteem lightly such "fanciful" accounts. A cautionary word of Martin Hengel may be cited. The modern historian

> cannot give either a prompt and over-hasty "yes" or an emphatic "no" to the question whether a particular [early Christian] narrative has historical value. Even legends with a miraculous character may well have a valuable historical nucleus, whereas allegedly eye-witness accounts and original documents could well be forgeries. Accounts of miracles keep cropping up in "secular" historiography from ancient times, since the way in which reality was understood in this period by the narrator . . . was substantially different from our own. Even when we doubt the historicity of a particular account, we must look for its historical nucleus, or ask why it was produced in the first place.[32]

Philip's own testimony may have furnished Luke with material for his accounts of the Hellenist's missions (8:4–40) following the expulsion of "the seven" and their sympathizers from Jerusalem.

Acts 8 may contain traditions of unequal value, yet the substantial historicity of missions among the Samaritans and of the apostles' subsequent participation may be maintained. Pro-Samaritan and anti-Samaritan traditions in the four Gospels not only confirm an early Christian mission, but imply that apostles had labored in this region.[33] However much they may have shared the antipathies of Palestinian Jews toward these "apostates," Jesus' example and concern for outcasts and marginal folk led the apostles to support Philip's ministry in Samaria.[34] It is not likely that Luke understood the apostle's imposition of hands as a prerequisite for the conferral of the Spirit (note 10:44), nor as an apostolic legitimization of Philip's (provisional) labors. Since the Judean-Samaritan relations were so strained, it may be that some such dramatic evidence of God's approval needed to be an experience shared by the new converts and the apostles.[35]

Some interesting textual variants appear in the story of Philip and the Ethiopian official.* In the following passage we may confidently speak of the "Western text" (italicized) as scribal alteration, but in some other cases one may judge that a superior reading has been preserved in this text type:

> 8: 35. Then Philip opened his mouth, and beginning with this scripture [Isa. 53:7f.] he told him the good news of Jesus.
> 36. And as they went along the road they came to some water, and the eunuch said, 'See, here is water! What is to prevent my being baptized?' *(37). And Philip said, 'If you believe with all your heart, you may.' And he replied, 'I believe that Jesus Christ is the Son of God.'* (RSV mg)
> 38. And he commanded the chariot to stop. . . .
> 39. And when they came up out of the water, *the Spirit of the Lord fell*

*Two major forms of the text of Acts have been preserved, both dating from the 2nd century—the Alexandrian: B, alpha, A, C, p[45], p[74]; and the Western: D, E, p[38], p[41], p[48], some ancient versions and patristic citations. The Western text is approximately a tenth longer

upon the eunuch, and the angel of the Lord snatched Philip away. (cf. RSV)

The Western addition, verse 37, and emendation, verse 39, are probably to be attributed to a conviction that no one is baptized without a confession of faith, or goes "on [one's] way rejoicing" without having received the gift of the Spirit.

Possibly as many as three sources provided Luke with materials for his narrative of Peter's conversion of Cornelius, an event that obviously held great significance for him.

One source may have contained the story of Peter's vision on the housetop of Simon the tanner (10:9–16, recounted in 11:5–10). Apart from the connections (10:17, 28), Peter's vision is not directly related to the narrative of the conversion of Cornelius. From Paul's letter to the Galatians we learn that the impact of the gospel upon Jewish ceremonial laws concerning "clean" and "unclean foods" did not become an acute issue until the missions to Gentiles were well underway, and until in mixed congregations there were occasions for table-fellowship among Jewish Christians and Gentile converts. Also, according to Acts 15:20, 29, it appears that Jewish Christians in Jerusalem were never persuaded that the food laws of the Torah were completely abrogated. Perhaps the original setting for Peter's story of his liberating vision was this later controversy. It is plausible that the story of Cornelius was preserved in an independent source consisting of 10:1–8, 17–24, 30–48, 11:2f., 18. It is not likely that either Peter or the Jerusalem disciples grasped fully the logical connections implied by the Lucan narrative, which only gained acceptance after much controversy: God has revealed to Christ's followers that no foods are "unclean" (ceremonially forbidden), therefore Jews who are believers may eat all foods; therefore one may have meal-fellowship with Gentiles as well as Jews; therefore one should seek to bring all persons, Gentiles as well as Jews, into an inclusive fellowship of equals under the Lordship of Christ.[36]

Luke's emphasis upon the hesitations and lack of full comprehension on the part of Peter and "the apostles and brethren in Judea," with respect to the implications of their "actions," is a corollary of his prominent stress upon the divine initiative and direction in the course of events. The "exceptionally high incidence of divine directions and interventions" that can be observed in Luke's story of Philip and the Ethiopian reaches an apogee in the so-called "Gentile Pentecost," which occurs during Peter's preaching in the house of Cornelius. Neither conversion resulted from the persuasion or zeal of Philip or Peter; the first conversions of Gentiles were not the work of men but of God.[37]

An event of far-reaching consequence took place when some of the "scattered brethren" came to Antioch and "spoke to the Greeks" (11:20). Antioch was the seat of the imperial legate of the province of Syria and Cilicia and, as such, ranked as the capital of the East. According to Josephus, Antioch was the third city of the Empire, in importance exceeded only by Rome and Alexandria. The population was predominantly Gentile and hence the language and culture of the city were Greek. There was a large Jewish colony in Antioch. From its foundation the city's Christian community was composed of both Jews and Greeks.

The reader's first impression may be that Luke was very casual in noting the establishment of Christianity in this strategic city and the beginning of a Chris-

than the Alexandrian. Most of the significant variations appear in Acts 13–28. C. K. Barrett, *New Testament Essays*, pp. 102–104.

tian mission to Gentiles. But the concluding sentence reporting this event should be noted (11:26). For the first time the followers of Jesus were designated *Christians* (Christ-followers). Those who coined this nickname were outsiders.[38] For such persons, Christ would be considered a personal name, not a title. Yet, although the religious nature of the attachment of the followers of Christ to him was not understood by people in Antioch, they sensed that these men stood apart from the various Jewish parties and sects of the city. The Acts narrative subsequently makes it clear that Luke considered the Gentile mission of the Church a vigorous offspring of the community at Antioch.[39]

Luke's report of the sending of Barnabas from Jerusalem to Antioch further supports this view that the development in Antioch was a significant departure (11:22–24). The choice of Barnabas, rather than Peter or one of the "the Twelve," may have been caused by the latter's absence from Jerusalem. Whatever the reason, the selection of Barnabas was fortunate. Peter, whose actions prior to the Cornelius story indicate that he shared the narrow outlook of most of the Jewish Christians, may not have received readily and joyfully the Gentile Christians at Antioch (11:23). The conservatism of Peter, however, should not be contrasted too sharply with the enlightenment of Barnabas. Peter was pliable to the Spirit's direction, and Barnabas later aligned himself with the reactionary Jewish Christians at Antioch. Neither Peter nor Barnabas was destined to become the champion of Gentile Christianity. The greatest service that Barnabas rendered the early Church was his introduction of Saul-Paul to "the Christians" at Antioch.*

*Apart from expressed indications of the will of God concerning individuals—the Ethiopian and Cornelius — Jewish Christians, some Hellenists as well as Hebrews, "spoke to none except Jews" (11:19). This limitation of vision and outreach of Jewish Christian missions before Paul accounts in large measure for the widespread opposition to Paul. It also explains why so much of the gospel tradition preserved in the earliest churches relate Jesus' teaching to Judaism and the Torah.

The cause for the murder of James by Herod Agrippa I, and of the reaction of the Jews in Jerusalem to this deed, is at first sight not clear (12:1–3). Did he recognize that popular Jewish opinion in Jerusalem was disturbed by the fact that the Hellenists, Samaritans, and perhaps Essenes were being received into the local community, and that uncircumcised Gentiles were being admitted elsewhere? Herod's eagerness to be recognized as a zealous advocate of Judaism could have prompted him to "lay violent hands" upon those Christian leaders responsible for permitting such serious deviations. If this was the cause of Herod's action, many pious Jews of Jerusalem would have felt it was justified. The short duration of this persecution may have been due not only to Herod's death (44 C.E.), but also to the fact that leadership of the Christian community passed into the hands of that other James who adhered strictly to the Torah and traditions of Judaism.

With the exception of two brief periods of violence, the earliest Christians enjoyed some immunity from official interference. They were free to bear witness to the gospel in the temple area and in various synagogues of Jerusalem, and to meet together within the walls of the city. Immunity from persecution did not mean freedom from controversy with the Jews. Far from it. It was not easy for the early Christians—who felt themselves bound to expose the guilt of those who had consented to Jesus' death—to maintain a close relationship with the Jews in the hope of winning their acceptance of the gospel. A Jewish Christian community with a mission to the Jews existed in Jerusalem at least until the first Jewish war with Rome. The existence and influence of this mother church was destined to be short-lived. Nevertheless, its impress is stamped upon the surviving traditions about Jesus, and the career of Paul is inextricably related to the church in Jerusalem and to its leaders, who never understood him.

AN EXCURSUS: ANCIENT JEWISH ESCHATOLOGIES AND MESSIANIC HOPES

Eschatology is a term that modern readers of the New Testament should understand and use, not because it is "trendy" in twentieth-century scholarship, but because eschatology refers to an important aspect of the religion of the Bible in its Old Testament, but more especially its New Testament expression. Derived from the term *eschaton* (Greek "end"; plural "last things") eschatology has, in systematic Christian theology, treated such topics as death, the intermediate state, the general resurrection, and the last judgment. But when biblical writers refer to the "last" or "end" of the days, the reference is not limited to views concerning death, resurrection, judgment, and so forth. Their position is that the last event, or series of events, discloses the meaning or purpose of the entire series leading to a divinely appointed end or goal. The Eschaton may be conceived as the ultimate End, the end of this age, or else penultimate goals may be envisioned; for example, Israel's conquest of "the land of promise," and the establishment of the united kingdom.

The eschatology of the Bible is rooted in Israel's faith that history is the arena of God's activity, that his purposes are accomplished in and through the historical processes. Almost from the beginning, the Hebrews believed that their nation had been destined to serve the divine purpose in a special way. This was Israel's doctrine of election. The pre-exilic prophets assert this faith with special clarity and force. In the nation's early history pivotal events had occurred that were understood as God's mighty acts. Viewed in retrospect, these represented the successive stages in the working out of God's purposes for his world.

A corollary of this perception of a directing providence was the prophets' clear recognition of the existence of evil in history. They were acutely aware of the terrible rebellions of God's chosen people in the past and in their own generations. They witnessed the rise of rulers who defied God and usurped powers that belonged to Him alone. They saw that empires, established upon unrighteousness, collapsed, and they considered this the judgment of God upon pride. When the prophets pondered man's capacity for evil, they were grim pessimists. But when they considered the power and mercy of God they were convinced that He continued to direct the course of history toward some ultimate purpose, which would not only reveal the glory of God but bring to fulfillment Israel's high calling.

Most of the prophets, from the eighth century B.C.E. on, looked forward to the consummation of "the Day of the Lord" and grounded the validity of their religious interpretations of history upon the realization of this hope. They were confident that the ultimate issues of history must be understood in the light of this divine purpose or goal. In the eighth century B.C.E., the popular idea was that "the Day of the Lord" would be a good time for Israel. The prophets argued that the coming day would be a time for the triumph of God and thus only of the righteous in Israel.

The beginning of what is commonly known as Israel's messianic hope may be reflected in the prophecies of Isaiah of Jerusalem and his contemporary, Micah. According to these prophets, the future deliverer of Israel will be an ideal king, like David.[40] The actual kings of Judah in succeeding generations seriously declined from this prototype, yet later prophets, Jeremiah and Ezekiel, kept alive the Davidic ideal.[41]

Some scholars have detected in Ezekiel's oracles the beginning of a separation of Israel's messianic hope from the Davidic dynasty. Whether or not this is the case, Ezekiel did seem to be more interested in the restoration of the temple than the monarchy. Possibly the prophet was responsible for giving impetus to an alternative type of messianism, involving a priest rather than a king. With the editing of the priestly tradition of the Law during the Babylonian exile, which provided for the consecration of the priest by anointing, the way was prepared for a transference of the title *messiah* to the ruling priest.[42]

After the restoration of the Jews from their Babylonian captivity, the hope of the good time coming revived. When a descendant of the Davidic house was restored to power in Jerusalem, patriotic prophets revived the older type of messianism.[43] In eschatological passages attributed to the latest of the prophets, however, the Davidic hope is often conspicuous by its absence. At the same time, the earlier prophets' faith that the coming day would bring a divine judgment upon evil was explicitly reaffirmed.

200–63 B.C.E.

Let us consider now various eschatologies that were being offered the Jews in New Testament times. Ecclesiasticus reflects the broadly humanitarian spirit of the Jewish sage, Jesus the son of Sirach. Yet one passage presents his vision of the great day coming, and reflects not only his nationalistic fervor but the persistence of several strands of the prophetic eschatology of the Old Testament.

> And the Lord will not delay,
>   neither will he be patient with them,
> till he crushes the loins of the unmerciful
>   and repays vengeance on the nations;
> till he takes away the multitude of the insolent,
>   and breaks the scepters of the unrighteous. . . .
>
> Hasten the day, and remember the appointed
>   time,
>   and let people recount thy mighty deeds. . . .
> Gather all the tribes of Jacob,
>   and give them their inheritance, as at the
>   beginning,
> Have mercy, O Lord, upon the people called
>   by thy name,
>   upon Israel, whom thou hast likened to a
>   first-born son.
> Have pity on the city of thy sanctuary,
>   Jerusalem, the place of thy rest.
> Fill Zion with the celebration of thy wondrous
>   deeds,
>   and thy temple with thy glory.
> Bear witness to those whom thou
>   didst create in the beginning,

and fulfil the prophecies spoken
in thy name.
Reward those who wait for thee,
and let thy prophets be found
trustworthy. . . .[44]

Other passages in Ecclesiasticus speak of the restoration of the house or kingdom of David, and allude to the coming of Elijah the prophet before the judgment.[45]

Owing to its contents and purpose, there is little eschatology in 1 Maccabees. In this writer's time Israel's great day might seem to some persons to have come. Yet at his death, Mattathias voiced the traditional hope of the restoration of the dynasty of David.[46]

The Book of Judith contains the following gruesome dirge.

Woe to the nations that rise up
against my people!
The Lord Almighty will take
vengeance on them in the day
of judgment;
fire and worms he will give to their
flesh;
they shall weep in pain for ever.[47]

Tobit's song of thanksgiving echoed the more positive element in traditional eschatology: the peace, security, and joy of Jerusalem,[48] the ingathering of exiled Jews, and the conversion of the nations.[49] The poet of 1 Baruch also gloried in Jerusalem's good time to come. He exulted in the gathering of the dispersed Jews, in language reminiscent of 2 Isaiah.[50]

In these writings dating from the period 200 to 100 B.C.E. the "day" that is coming remains an event within history. But alongside these one must set books that describe "the coming age," or "the end of the days," in other ways. These writings are known as apocalypses, and the descriptions of the end that they contain, apocalyptic eschatology. The term *apocalypse* is derived from the Greek word *apocalypsis*, meaning revelation.* Some readers of this book have been introduced to Jewish apocalyptic by a study of Old Testament literature dating from the postexilic period. The best way to learn what an apocalypse is like is to read some of these books; however, it may be helpful to list some of their distinguishing characteristics.

Pseudonymity: Since it was believed that the age of authentic prophecy had ended, Jewish seers in New Testament times deliberately took for pen names Enoch, Moses, Daniel, Ezra, and so on. It is doubtful that anyone purposed to deceive, or that the reader assumed that such books were really ancient.[51]

Secrecy: An apocalypse is commonly represented as something that had been or ought to be kept secret.[52] This air of mystery relates to the conception that the book contains a prevision by men in the long ago.

The division of history into periods: The vision of the end in an apocalypse is usually preceded by a historical survey. But it is strangely

*P. D. Hanson wisely urges that distinctions be recognized between "apocalypticism," "apocalyptic eschatology," and the literary genre, "an apocalypse." (See the valuable article in *IBDS*, pp. 28ff.) Apocalypticism is "a system of thought produced by visionary movements" composed of persons who together have experienced alienation from their society and who identify with an alternative "symbolic universe." This new world is conceived to be the real world of the future. "Revelations" of it are partially reminiscent of the eschatologies of Israel's prophets, but reflect Jewish ideological developments of the Second Temple Period.

telescoped history, divided into eras of special length and possessing special characteristics.[53]

Determinism: All the events of history have been divinely predetermined. There are so many kings and empires before the coming of the end; so many and no more.[54] The periods of history rush on toward their appointed goal.

Belief in the nearness of the end: The last judgment will soon take place; the golden age is near.

The other-wordly or cosmic dimension: Unlike the eschatology of the earlier prophets in Israel, the apocalyptist's vision of the end is not an event like those experienced in the past or present times: a new heaven and a new earth will be created. The Age to Come is not the extension or reformation of existing conditions, but a new series of events belonging to another order of existence.

Dualism: Existing evils are caused by the influence of supernatural demonic powers, a problem that requires for its solution more than human arms and intellect. God and his angels must intervene to destroy these sinister powers.

Pessimism: Apocalyptic eschatology depicts a pessimism concerning human nature and human remedies for the existing situation. Yet in one sense its writers are stubbornly optimistic and idealistic, for they believe that God rules over the kingdoms of humankind: the darkest hour precedes the dawn; the labor pains bring forth the new creation.[55]

Mythological symbolism: Apocalyptic visions "are frequently unvisualizable" for they represent their writers' effort to describe the unexperienced, the unknown.[56] Interpreters of these bizarre, impressionistic images must allow for poetic license, and a logical or chronological order should not be imposed upon them.

Several writings of this type are commonly dated in the time of the Hasmonean dynasty. The persecutions of Antiochus Epiphanes provided a setting in life for apocalyptic visions. For the writer of Daniel, this crisis demanded a vindication of divine justice, which would soon take place, a judgment that forshadowed the triumph of "the saints of the Most High." The righteous are to experience a resurrection from the dead, and they "shall shine . . . like stars for ever and ever."[57]

The oldest sections of 1 Enoch portray the coming judgment as the accompaniment of the advent of "the holy and great One," of cosmic upheavals, and terrible distress upon the earth.[58] A destruction of the wicked is depicted, of wicked angels as well as of humans, and the coming age is described as one of spiritual well-being, peace, and justice.[59] In the final chapters the traditional hope of an altogether terrestrial good time is given in a vision of the "new Jerusalem."[60] In what may also be early material, the figure of a messiah appears, "the white bull with large horns." This image does not describe a superhuman being. His righteousness is magnified, but only as that of a first among equals.[61]

Other writings that express the eschatology of the Hasmonean period are Jubilees, the Testaments of the Twelve Patriarchs, and very probably, the Qumran Manual of Discipline. None of these books can be classed an apocalypse, but they contain apocalyptic eschatology. Jubilees makes no mention of an individual messiah descended from the house of David, unless he is referred to in the passage concerning "a prince" of Judah "over the sons of Jacob." At any rate, this author saw "princes and judges and chiefs" coming forth in the end time from Levi.[62] In the Testaments and the Manual the coming of several eschatological leaders is also predicted; among them a messiah arising from the house of Aaron.

Although the Testaments contain both Jewish and Christian materials, differing widely in their date of origin, and set forth ethical injunctions for the most part, prophecies from the Hasmonean times concerning the Age to Come are found in some of them. In the Testament of Levi we find a "little apocalypse." After the rule of corrupt priests, God will "raise up . . . a new priest, to whom all the words of God shall be revealed; and he shall execute a righteous judgment upon the earth for a multitude of days."[63] In the Testament of Judah, the crown of the priesthood is given to Levi, but the crown of civil rule to Judah "until the salvation of Israel (and of repentant Gentiles) shall come."[64] At "the end of the days" each tribe is blessed by angelic powers, but God himself blesses Levi. In the Testaments, "Beliar" [Belial] has become a personification of all evil, and at the end the "spirits of deceit" are cast into "the fire of gehenna."[65] The righteous arise to receive the reward for their deeds, in the bliss of a new Jerusalem, and glorify the Lord forever.[66]

According to the Manual of Discipline (1QS), the members of the sect "shall be ruled by the first laws with which the men of the community began to be disciplined until the coming of a prophet and the anointed ones of Aaron and Israel."[67] The messiah of Aaron is clearly a priestly messiah, while the messiah of Israel may refer to a lay figure.[68] In the Qumran Manual there appear the divisions of time characteristic of the apocalyptic writings, and the conviction of predetermined seasons and of the final period or end, at which time Beliar is cast into "eternal fire." The righteous are promised eternal felicity, not merely as God's chosen people, but individually as "sons of light."[69]

CA. 63–1 B.C.E.

Of the documents commonly assigned to the first half-century of Roman rule in Palestine the following are of special interest: the Psalms of Solomon, the Similitudes of Enoch, the Qumran Habakkuk scroll (1QpHab), and the Cairo-Damascus document (CD). In these writings one sees an increased interest in the personality of a coming messiah. This may have been a repudiation of the Maccabean kings as messiahs. Chapter 17 of the Psalms of Solomon is evidently an indictment of the Hasmonean usurpers, as well as of Rome the oppressor:

> Behold O Lord, and raise up from them their king,
>   The son of David
> Against the time which thou, O God, chooseth for him
> To begin his reign over Israel thy servant,
> And gird him with strength to shatter unrighteous rulers,
> And to purge Jerusalem from Gentiles that trample her
>   Down to destruction. . . .[70]

This messiah's triumph inaugurates the new Age in which Jerusalem becomes the center of the world. Gentiles serve under the messiah's yoke; the

Jewish exiles are gathered in; Palestine is redivided among the tribes. Yet there is hardly a trace of interest in material prosperity. The rule of righteousness is the theme of the poet. The only discipline that will be needed in the new Israel is the power of the spirit exercised by the Davidic king-messiah who will be "instructed by God." What a travesty upon this hope were the Herods whose military discipline was soon to be felt throughout the land. Elsewhere in the Psalms of Solomon there is reference to the resurrection of the righteous unto eternal life, and to the wicked who are doomed to perish.[71]

In the Similitudes of Enoch a personal messiah stands in the center of the Messianic Age. He is designated "the righteous one" or the "elect one." When he appears, mighty kings are to be destroyed or else handed over to the righteous.[72] Heaven and earth will be transformed for the dwelling of the elect.[73] In chapter 46 we have a reworking of the vision of Daniel 7. The coming of "the son of man" is described. He will "raise up mighty kings from their seats, and the strong from their thrones." He will "break the teeth of sinners . . . darkness will be their dwelling, and worms will be their bed." Is this "son of man" in Enoch a collective figure for Israel, as in Daniel, or a messiah? Scholars are divided on this question. In either case the manifestation of the son of man is associated with the glory of Israel, as well as with the enlightenment of Gentiles. In the Similitudes, the Messianic Age is described as a time when nature will be transformed and the dead will be raised. Whether this resurrection was considered a universal one is not explicitly indicated, but emphasis is placed upon the future of "the righteous and holy" who, in that day, will learn from a messiah "the secrets of wisdom."[74] Later chapters describe the severe troubles leading up to the end: the sending forth of "the angels of punishment" and the binding in chains of the wicked, and their imprisonment in the place of destruction.

In the Cairo-Damascus document there is but one messianic figure, the "Messiah of Aaron and Israel."[75] The argument that the sect represented by this document expected the resurrection and return of the "Teacher of Righteousness" as the Messiah falls short of being convincing. It is more probable that the Teacher became for his followers a prototype of the Messiah, or that he was considered to be one whose mission foreshadowed certain functions to be fulfilled by a messiah. Several references in the Damascus document and the Qumran Habakkuk commentary suggest that the sect believed that the invasion of the Kittim (Romans?) represented the tribulations at "the end of the days"; that the wealth and spoil of the last priests of Jerusalem would soon be delivered into their hands; and that the elect of Israel, "the sons of Zadok," would stand "in that day."[76] Here also is the thought of periods of fixed time decreed by God. The judgment is by fire of brimstone that will become a purging of all worshippers of idols, of all wicked from the earth.[77] There is also the idea that, by the elect, God will judge and chastise all the nations. But God's mercy will be shown "unto thousands to them that love him, and them that wait for him unto a thousand generations."[78]

1–70 C.E.

The two Jewish writings to be discussed in this section were probably written during Jesus' lifetime but before the earliest Gospels were compiled. This was the period of the rule of Herod's sons and of the procurators. These were the years of mounting tension leading up to the Great Rebellion against Rome. At one time it was thought surprising that so few apocalyptic writings from this time had survived. The discovery of the apocalyptic literature of the Qumran sect has filled this lacuna. We now know that early apocalyptic writings were still being copied and read and that new ones were being composed. Fragments of Jubilees, the Testaments of the Twelve Patriarchs, Daniel, and other known and unknown apocalypses have been found in the Dead Sea caves. It is evident that these writings constituted the literature of the Qumran sect up to the time of their abandonment around 64 C.E.

The writer of the Assumption of Moses, the first-century document in the Pseudepigrapha, employs the common stock of apocalyptic images and ideas, especially those of Daniel and 1 Enoch. Moses relates to Joshua the history of Israel down to the beginning of the reigns of Herod's sons.[79] At this point the history breaks off, for the writer believes that the end has come.

A Levite, Taxo, is urged to withdraw to a cave with his seven sons and die at the hands of the wicked rather than transgress the Torah. Yet God will avenge their deaths, for

> *His kingdom shall appear throughout all creation,*
> *And then Satan shall be no more,*
> *And sorrow shall depart with him.*
> *Then shall be filled the hands of the angel who*
> *   stands on high [Michael]*
> *And he shall forthwith avenge them of their enemies,*
> *For the heavenly one will arise from his royal throne . . .*
> *   and the earth shall tremble, to its end shall it*
> *   be shaken . . .*
> *Then thou, O Israel, shalt be happy!*
> *And thou shalt mount upon the neck and wings of the eagle*
> *And (his days) shall be ended.*
> *And God will exalt thee, and cause thee to reach*
> *   to the heaven of the stars,*
> *To the place of their habitation. . . .*[80]

Is this coming victory of God to be realized on earth? Or is it to be beyond history? This much is clear: it is God, not humans, who will establish this kingdom. It has been suggested that since there is no thought of a general resurrection, the writer's vision closes with a glimpse of the eternal blessedness of the righteous in the heavenly world. Others hold that the figures of Israel's exaltation are conventional ones depicting the restoration of the Jewish nation to power and glory. Taxo's heroism is reminiscent of that of Mattathias. Did some "left-wing" Pharisee (or militant Essene or Zealot) grossly miscalculate the power of Rome? Was he convinced that heroic faith in God would enable the Jews to throw off the yoke of the Herods in the same way the yoke of the Seleucids had been removed? Did he call upon Taxo and his sons to take up the Maccabean banners? This victory day, whether on earth or in heaven, is a projection of the deep hatreds and nationalistic aspirations shared by many Jews of the period.

The same questions of interpretation are raised by the reader of the Qumran scroll, the War of the Sons of Light Against the Sons of Darkness (1QM). This curious writing ostensibly contains instructions for the eschatological campaign against the army of "Belial and the men of his lot." It also prescribes the correct ceremonial procedures and equipment for the warring priests, so that they may avoid defilement in the forthcoming slaughter. The whole piece is shot through with apocalyptic sentiments, and the document ends with a war poem, followed by blessings and curses.[81] It is possible that the "mighty man . . . the man of glory" in the war chant of this scroll is to be identified with the sect's "Messiah of Israel," for by his side stands his superior, the high priest. The military scroll speaks with confidence that God "will send eternal help to the lot he has redeemed by the power of the angel . . . Michael," to exalt "the dominion of Israel over all flesh."[82]

AFTER 70 C.E.—EARLY SECOND CENTURY

There have survived two apocalypses that most scholars believe to have been written after the fall of Jerusalem in 70 C.E.: "the Ezra apocalypse" (2 Esdras or 4 Ezra), and "the apocalypse of Baruch" (2, or Syriac, Baruch). It is commonly agreed that one of the two writers has imitated the other, but no agreement has been reached about their relationship. The differences in the writers' attitude to the Torah is a subject of great interest. The author of 2 Esdras succumbed to the deepest pessimism of the apocalyptists. The law had proved to be a standard almost impossible to attain. It is therefore Israel's condemnation. 2 Baruch exulted in the Law. Like Hillel and like the rabbis at Jamnia, the author saw obedience to the Torah as a practical program, Israel's greatest joy and hope.[83]

The eschatology of Esdras is not reducible to a single pattern of thought. The indebtedness of the writer to earlier apocalypses is everywhere present. The first vision declares the end to be near at hand. It is to be heralded by desolations in the earth and heavenly portents, and by the rule of an unexpected one (who is not identified).[84] A second vision presents premonitory signs: the opening of the book of judgment, the blast of the trumpet warning of the end.[85] A third vision portrays the new Jerusalem. The Messiah will be revealed to those who have not died. He will remain on earth for four hundred years, after which there will be a universal death and seven years of silence. Then comes the general resurrection and the great judgment, at which time men will be delivered to gehenna or to paradise.[86] The fourth vision concerns a woman who appears to be desolate and sorrowful; she is transformed into a woman of surpassing beauty. The figure represents the transformation of Jerusalem, which is in ruins, into the city that is to come.[87] Visions six and seven are original adaptations of imagery drawn from Daniel. There is a symbolic sketch of history leading up to the prediction. The three-headed eagle may well be a transparent symbol of Rome. The destroying lion is declared to be the Davidic Messiah, who delivers the righteous.[88] Daniel's "son of man" image is also introduced as a personification of the Messiah. He consumes those who war against him "with the breath of his mouth." Here the Messiah appears to be a transcendent, a more than human, figure. The militant, nationalistic spirit of the earlier visions has quite evaporated.[89]

It has been said that 2 Baruch more closely than any other apocalypse sets forth messianic hopes resembling "those in the earliest parts of the Talmud and Midrash."[90] The end is preceded by twelve periods producing great terrors and torments. Little interest is shown by this writer in the person of a messiah. He is both a man of war and of peace. But the glories of the Messianic Age are vividly described. Nature will produce unimagined marvels, and great peace shall prevail. The heavenly Jerusalem will indeed descend to earth and endure "until the time is fulfilled." Then the Messiah returns to heaven (there is no mention of his death), and "all who have fallen asleep in hope of him shall rise again."[91] In this unending new world, the people Israel, inclusive of proselytes, will shine in brightness as the stars and have the face of angels. Yet this change in personal appearance will not prevent recognition. In this blissful state there will be neither toil nor sorrow.[92]

The writings and rabbinic traditions after 70 C.E. make clear the following fact: Although stunned and disillusioned by the tragic outcome of the war with Rome, Israel maintained its confidence in God and in the imminence of the Messianic Age. With the rebirth of hope there seems to have arisen a new zeal for the nation's destiny, a longing for the redemption of Israel, a scanning of the horizon for the appearance of a messiah.[93]

We have reached the end of New Testament times and, looking backwards, observe a fact of great importance for understanding the eschatology of Jesus and of the early Church. There had not emerged in ancient Judaism a uniform or consistent hope for the future. To speak of "the messianic hope" of the Jews is misleading, since no single solution for the ills of the present prevailed. There was no fixed utopian dream that brought satisfaction to all people. Hence unresolved tensions are evidenced between hope for the nation and its historical destiny, and hope for the achievement of individual blessedness in some other world, perhaps discontinuous with the present one.

This diversity of ideas is clearly evidenced in the uncertainty over the manner of God's redemption of his people. Would He act directly, or through angelic or human agency; through a messiah, or through anointed ones? If through a man, then what Israelite ideal or ideals of rulership would that man fulfill? Moreover, what would be achieved at "the end of the days"? National prosperity, or the universal triumph of righteousness? Would Israelites be vindicated and the heathen punished, or would idolatry and corruption be overcome everywhere? Would Gentiles turn to God and learn his truth and experience his mercies? And, finally, what would be the sequence of these last days? Would the age of the messiah be coterminous with the Age to Come? Or would the messiah's time be an extension of the present age, a kind of intermediate period of good times for the Jews, before the end?

Questions of this sort are given no definitive answers. Yet, through all of the diversity and perplexity of religious and political aspiration, there persisted this faith: God must act; He will deliver those who trust in Him; His purposes will be accomplished! The Christian movement arose out of this inchoate medley of hopes for a better day, those crosscurrents of pessimism and optimism, of nationalistic fervor and broader sympathies, of this-worldly hopes and other-worldly dreams. Eschatological images and symbols achieved a tremendous power to move the spirit of humans. They become the vehicle for expressing the faith and hope of the earliest Christians. This potent imagery was reformulated in the creative intuitions of Jesus and of the earliest interpreters of his person and mission.

NOTES

1. S. Brown, "The Role of the Prologues in Determining the Purpose of Luke-Acts," in C. H. Talbert, ed., *Perspectives on Luke-Acts*, (1978), p. 109.
2. See Kümmel's dismissal of various theories of a secondary alteration of the beginning of Acts, W. G. Kümmel, *Introduction to the New Testament* Revised English Edition (New York: Abingdon, 1975), pp. 157f. E. Haenchen notes that the twice-told story of the ascension is a first example of Luke's typical repetitive style. Cf. especially the three differing accounts of Paul's conversion. *The Acts of the Apostles* (1971), pp. 146f.
3. C. K. Barrett, *Luke the Historian in Recent Study* (London: Epworth Press, 1961) (1970), pp. 53–58. "Indefinite," yes; but does the term "remote" accurately report Luke's perspective? See p. 140. J. Dupont, *The Salvation of the Gentiles* (1979), pp. 16–19.
4. F. F. Bruce, *Commentary on the Book of Acts* (1956), p. 52. Note Rev. 21:14.
5. Concerning the various hypotheses that for Acts 1–15, Luke used written sources, see Kümmel, *INT*², pp. 174–177. The difficulty with identifying sources, assuming that he had some, is that Lk "is not satisfied with transcribing his sources, he re-writes the text by putting the imprint of his vocabulary and style everywhere." J. Dupont, *The Sources of Acts* (1964), p. 166.
6. "It is only the summary narratives and the speeches that can be used with methodological certainty in determining the theological ideas of the author of Acts that dominate his account." Kümmel, *INT*², p. 170.
7. E. Schweizer, "Concerning the Speeches in Acts, in L. Keck and J. L. Martyn, eds., *Studies in Luke-Acts* (1980), pp. 208ff.
8. C. H. Dodd, *The Apostolic Preaching and its Developments* (1936).
9. Haenchen, *Acts of the Apostles*, pp. 185–188; Kümmel, *INT*², pp. 167–169.
10. G. N. Stanton, *Jesus of Nazareth in New Testament Preaching* (1974), pp. 67–85. See, now, the judicious comment of J. A. Fitzmyer, "The Gospel According to Luke, I–IX," in *Anchor Bible Commentary* (1981). While the kerygma in Acts may represent "the Christian preaching of Luke's own day, we still have to attend to the substantial similarity of what is proclaimed there to what is regarded as the Pauline kerygma. . . ." pp. 159–161. 1 Cor. 15:1–11; Gal. 1:6f. Cf. Heb. 2:1–4; 1 Pet. 1:10–12.
11. Haenchen, *Acts of the Apostles*, pp. 193–196.
12. *Ibid.*, p. 258. Cf. M. Hengel, *Acts and the History of Earliest Christianity* (1980), pp. 73f.
13. Cf. 2:47 and 28:30f., and numerous passages in between, 5:42; 6:1, 7; 8:4, and others.
14. J. Jervell, "The Problem of Traditions in Acts," *Luke and the People of God* (1972).
15. 1 Thess. 1:6–10, 2:1–16 (some consider this passage an interpolation, see p. 140). Cf. 2 Thess. 1:4; Rom. 1:3.
16. A. J. B. Higgins, "The Preface to Luke and the Kerygma in Acts," in W. W. Gasque and R. P. Martin, eds. *Apostolic History and the Gospel* (1970), pp. 85ff. Some of the gospel tradition is not without significance also, e.g., Mk. 14:9.
17. R. Bultmann, *Theology of the New Testament*, Vol. 1 (1951, 1952), pp. 37f.
18. The action of Ananias and Sapphira was morally reprehensible, not because they

retained some of their property, but because of their deception in pretending to give everything they owned, 5:1–11.

19. Acts 3:11, 4:21, 5:12, 8:4–13.
20. Mk 10:1, 9:38ff, Mt. 7:22.
21. Gal. 3:5; 1 Cor. 12:10; Rom. 15:19.
22. W. L. Knox, *The Acts of the Apostles* (1948), pp. 88ff.
23. C. H. Talbert, *Literary Patterns, Theological Themes, and the Genre of Luke-Acts* (1974), pp. 35–39.
24. M. Goguel, *The Birth of Christianity* (1953), pp. 454ff. Haenchen, *Acts of the Apostles*, pp. 220ff and 254ff and literature cited.
25. *IB*, Vol. 9, p. 81; W. L. Knox, *The Acts of the Apostles*, pp. 21ff; B. Reicke, *The New Testament Era* (1968), pp. 188ff.; Hengel, *Acts and Earliest Christianity*, pp. 73f., 96f., 112.
26. ". . . 6:1–6 and 6:8ff represent two different Stephen traditions, which are juxtaposed but unrelated, neither explaining or being explained by the other. . . . F. D. Gealy, "Stephen," *IDB*, 4:442; J. Dupont, *Sources*, pp. 51ff.
27. Haenchen, *Acts of the Apostles*, p. 273.
28. *Ibid.*
29. M. Dibelius, "The Speeches in Acts and Ancient Historiography," *Studies in the Acts of the Apostles* (1951), pp. 167–170; Haenchen, *Acts of the Apostles*, pp. 286f.; C. K. Barrett, *New Testament Essays* (1972), pp. 108–112.
30. C. S. C. Williams, *Commentary on the Acts of the Apostles* (New York: Harper & Row, 1957), pp. 100ff.; F. F. Bruce, *Commentary on Acts*, pp. 141ff.; M. Simon, *St. Stephen and the Hellenists in the Primitive Church* (1958), pp. 39ff.; W. Manson, "Stephen and the World Mission of Christianity," in *Epistle to the Hebrews* (1951); Hengel, *Acts and Earliest Christianity*, pp. 72–74.
31. Haenchen, *Acts and Earliest Christianity*, pp. 288–290; also Haenchen, "The Book of Acts as Source Material for a History of Early Christianity," in L. Keck and J. L. Martyn eds., *Studies in Luke-Acts*, p. 264.
32. M. Hengel, "History Writing in Antiquity and in Earliest Christianity," *Acts and Earliest Christianity*, pp. 12f.
33. Luke 9:51–56; 10:29–37; 17:11–19. Cf. John 4. Cf. Mt. 10:5.
34. Cf. Lk. 9:54 and Acts 8:14–17.
35. F. F. Bruce, *Commentary on Acts*, pp. 182f.
36. Cf. Mk. 7:14–23, Barrett, *New Testament Essays* (1972), pp. 112f.; M. Dibelius in *Studies in the Acts* (1956), p. 12ff. The possibility of a source underlying Peter's speech, 10:36ff., has been noted. The syntax of verses 36–38 and the scriptural citations are arguments against "a complete Lucan composition." J. Fitzmyer, *JBC*, Acts 45:58.
37. Haenchen, *Acts of the Apostles*, pp. 314–317, 362f.
38. Bickerman, "The Name of Christians," pp. 109ff. It is not likely that followers of Jesus gave this name to themselves (*contra.* Bickerman), Acts 11:26 and 26:23 imply its use by outsiders.
39. See p. 278.
40. Isa. 7:10ff.; 9:1ff.; 11:1ff., Mic. 5:2ff.
41. Jer. 23:5f.; Ezek. 34:23f.
42. For a discussion of this exilic and postexilic eschatology, detached from any specific messianic elements, see R. H. Fuller, *The Foundations of New Testament Christology* (1965), pp. 26ff.
43. Hag. 2:23ff.; Zech. 3:8ff., 4:7ff., 6:9ff.
44. Sir. 35:18ff., 36:1ff., 47:11.
45. *Ibid.*, 45:25, 48:10 (cf. Mil. 4:5f.).

46. I Macc. 2:57. Note that the expectation of "the prophet" indicates that the present days are an interim before the coming of the messianic age, 4:46, 14:41.
47. Jdt. 16:17.
48. Tob. 13:9–12.
49. *Ibid.* 14:5–7.
50. Bar. 4:36f.
51. H. H. Rowley, *The Relevance of Apocalyptic* (1955), pp. 35f. See also D. S. Russell, *The Message and Method of Jewish Apocalyptic* (1964), pp. 104ff.
52. Dan. 8:26; Asmp M. 1:18; I Enoch 1:2.
53. Unfulfilled OT prophesies sometimes provided mystical numbers and symbols for plotting these divisions. Dan. 9:1ff.; I Enoch 89:59.
54. Dan. 7:21f.; Asmp M. 12:4ff.
55. Rowley, *Relevance*, pp. 153ff. For an alternative description of "conceptual presuppositions" derived from apocalyptic eschatologies, see H. C. Kee, *The Community of the New Age* (1977), pp. 70–74.
56. A. N. Wilder, *Eschatology and Ethics in the Teaching of Jesus* (1950), p. 30. G. F. Moore, *Judaism in the First Centuries of the Christian Era*, Vol 1. (1927–1930), p. 343.
57. Dan. 7:9–18, 12:2f. The apocryphal books 1 and 2 Macc. record the historical occasion for the Daniel apocalypse. 2 Macc. also offers the hope of resurrection as an incentive to heroism and martyrdom.
58. I Enoch 1:1–7.
59. *Ibid.* 80:3ff., 99:4ff. Also 1:3ff., 19:1df., 25:3ff.
60. J. Klausner, *The Messianic Idea in Israel* (1955), pp. 277, 283f. I Enoch 90:17ff.
61. Did the hope persist in the early years of Maccabean rule that divine deliverance would be achieved by a righteous warrior?
62. Jub. 31:13ff. Note also 23:25ff.
63. Test. of Levi 18:2ff. The Qumran scholar, J. T. Milik, dates the XII P in the first or second century C.E., *Ten Years of Discovery in the Wilderness of Judaea* (1959), pp. 34f. Cf. R. H. Charles' dating: 109–106 B.C.E.
64. Test. of Judah 21–25. Cf. Test. of Simeon 7:1–3; Zech. 4:12–14.
65. Test. of Levi 18:2; Test. of Judah 25:3; Test. of Reuben 2:1f.
66. Test. of Dan. 5:9–13.
67. 1QS 10 f. Cf. reference to a Cave 4 fragment in F. F. Bruce, *Second Thoughts On the Dead Sea Scrolls* (1956), pp. 77f., in which the same three figures appear.
68. 1QSa ii. 11ff. Cf. 1QS vi, 5ff; CD (A) vii, 20, xi, 9.
69. 1QS i, 18, ii, 8, 17f., iii, 13f.
70. Pss. of Sol. 17:21ff. J. H. Charlesworth, "The Messiah in the Pseudepigrapha," in *Aufstieg und niedergang der römischen Welt* (1979), pp. 197ff.
71. Pss. of Sol. 3:16, 13:10, 15:15.
72. 1 Enoch 38:1ff. The "Similitudes" may be the writing of a first- or second-century author. Note their absence among the Qumran fragments. Milik, *Ten Years of Discovery* (1959), pp. 33f.
73. 1 Enoch 45:4–6.
74. 1 Enoch 50–51.
75. CD ii 10, viii 2, ix 10(B), 29(B), xv 4, xviii 8. R. H. Charles edition. See K. G. Kuhn, "The Two Messiahs of Aaron and Israel," in K. Stendahl ed., *The Scrolls and the New Testament* (1957), pp. 54ff.
76. CD v 7–vi 9; 1QpHab. ii 6.
77. CD ii 1–8, ix 10–20, ix 40–49 (B text).
78. CD v 1ff., ix 10, 29, xviii 8.
79. Asmp M. 6:7–9. Cf. Jos. Antiq. XVIII x 2.

80. Asmp M. 10:1–9. T. W. Manson, *The Servant-Messiah a Study in the Public Ministry of Jesus* (Cambridge: the University Press, 1953), pp. 31f.
81. 1QM xii 10ff.
82. 1QM xvii 5ff.
83. R. H. Charles, *Religious Development between the Old and New Testaments* (1914), pp. 250f.
84. 2 Esd. 4:44f. J. H. Charlesworth, *The Messiah*, in *Aufstieg und niedergang* (1979), pp. 202–206.
85. 2 Esd. 6:11ff. Cf. Rev. 5:1ff.
86. 2 Esd. 7:26ff.
87. 2 Esd. 9:38ff.
88. 2 Esd. 11:iff.
89. 2 Esd. 13:1ff.
90. J. Klausner, *Messianic Idea*, pp. 331ff.
91. 2 Bar. 25:1ff. Cf. 70:1ff. Charlesworth, "The Messiah," in *Aufstieg und niedergang* (1979), pp. 200ff.
92. 2 Bar. 29:4f., 48:50, 50:2ff., 73:1ff.
93. J. Klausner, *Messianic Idea*, pp. 394–403; H. H. Rowley, *The Relevance*, pp. 105ff.

Chapter 5

Early Oral and Written Traditions Concerning Jesus

THE early Christian Church expanded by boldly proclaiming Jesus the Messiah, ordering the common life of its membership, and withstanding various threats to unity and survival both from within and without.

The first followers of Jesus in Judea understood themselves to be the Israel of the Age to Come. Their spiritual fervor, which found expression in ecstatic speaking and healings, tended to distinguish them outwardly from their fellows. Yet in many respects they appeared pious and loyal Jews; so they wished to remain. They were regarded for some while as another sectarian movement within Judaism; however, within a brief span of ten to fifteen years the community had a phenomenal growth unparalleled by any other separate synogogue or Jewish community in Palestine. Greek-speaking Jews and proselytes, natives of other regions of the Roman empire living in Judea, as well as Samaritans, joined the movement. At Antioch in Syria, Greeks were numbered among "the Christians." At its growing edge, the primitive Church broke free of its provincial beginnings and became an inclusive fellowship. Meanwhile, the original community in Jerusalem was confronted with one crisis after another.

A view of the spread of Christianity could focus attention, as Luke does in Acts 13, upon the missions of the Apostle Paul. Instead, one can turn from Acts and consider the three earliest Gospels of the New Testament—Mark, Luke, and Matthew. In all probability, Paul proclaimed the Christian gospel in the regions reported in Acts 13–28 and composed his letters to the churches before any Gospels were written. Nevertheless, the Gospels preserve traditions concerning Jesus' ministry that for the most part, had taken shape in the churches of Palestine and Syria during the first two decades of the Christian movement. It is quite possible that by the time Paul was brought to Antioch by Barnabas, and his great missions were begun, essential traditions concerning Jesus' ministry had become well established.[1]

The stories of Jesus that the earliest Gospels contain are those which the first Christians cherished and passed on to others. These were the traditions perceived to be those most useful in declaring, confirming, and defending the Christian *kerygma*; in instructing converts in the rites, discipline, and way of life of the Christian communities; and in inspiring believers to endure suffering and maintain hope. The Church's memory of Jesus is, at every point, intimately related to the life and thought of the earliest Christians, and the communities described in the Acts were among those which provided the historical matrix of the gospel tradition. Whatever else the Gospels of the New Testament may be, they are the literary deposit of the oral preaching, teaching, and worship of the primitive churches. Having just concluded a study of the exact period in which these formative influences were active, we deem it appropriate to trace the history of the gospel tradition. In this way one can move forward from the early Church to the origin of the three earliest Gospels, then, through the eyes of these writers, view the ministry of Jesus and seek to understand his actions and his teaching.

EARLIEST TRADITIONS
THE PASSION AND RESURRECTION

The proclamation and defense of the *kerygma* called for repeated references to the ministry of Jesus, especially to its closing days. It was essential to show that events in Jerusalem confirmed rather than denied the claim that the Messiah who is to come had been manifested. The manner of Jesus' death and his appearances afterward to chosen witnesses above all else confirmed for the Christians the gospel they professed: God had revealed the Messiah in his sufferings unto death and in his resurrection.

There can be little doubt which part of this testimony most seriously offended both Jews and Greeks. Writing to the Corinthians, Paul acknowledged that "the word of the Cross" was a "stumbling-block to the Jews and folly to the Gentiles."[2] For the Apostle this "word" was the message of the resurrection of the crucified Jesus. Thus it is not difficult to see why the Jews took offense at the cross of this man. To affirm God's resurrection of one who had been judged a blasphemer and crucified was, for the Jews, a scandal indeed.

As we have seen, the earliest Christians viewed Jesus' death as a treacherous murder. Yet connected with this idea was the belief that Jesus' rejection had not frustrated but, instead, accomplished the will of God.[3] At once the question was raised: How is one to validate these unheard-of claims? Rational arguments would not suffice for the Jews. The only way to relate the crucifixion of Jesus to the divine purpose concerning God's Messiah was to appeal to his former revelation in law and prophecy. But alongside this proclamation of the necessity of the cross, its divine foreordination, there was also the deeper problem of the meaning of the cross, a question which, in any event, Jewish Christians would have pressed upon themselves. "Precisely because of Jesus' resurrection the question had to arise as to why Jesus had to go the way of suffering to the cross . . . If subsequently God was to manifest in the resurrection his divine power, why did God permit Jesus' rejection by the Jews?"[4] Thus for the purpose of "clarifying its own understanding of the momentous events out of which it emerged, and also for the purpose of making its gospel intelligible to the outside public," the earliest Church had to demonstrate that in the course of Jesus' ministry specific scriptures had been fulfilled.[5]

The early Christians were also compelled to answer another question: Had

Jesus been a criminal and blasphemer, as his enemies maintained, or a blameless person, as the disciples declared? The innocence of Jesus and the determination of responsibility for his death could have been established only by stating the circumstances of his arrest, trial, and crucifixion.[6]

It is unlikely that the earliest witnesses felt a need for a connected narrative following the burial of Jesus. They thought it sufficient to report that particular persons had visited the tomb and found it empty, and that Christ had appeared to individuals and to groups. Brief stories of appearances of Jesus to his disciples were offered as a confirmation of the summary statement in the early proclamations concerning the resurrection. The resurrection tradition in the Gospels bears the marks of the early oral and corporate witness of the Church.[7] The same motives that prompted the preservation of these stories led also to the early formulation of lists of specific persons who had seen the risen Christ after his death and burial. These too seem to have become an essential element of "the received tradition."[8] The longer, more detailed narratives in the Gospels of Christ's appearances and the circumstantial stories of the finding of the empty tomb bear the marks of more personal motives. Perhaps these stories were first offered as evidence of the resurrection in the worship of believers rather than in the Church's witness to outsiders. Some of them are associated with "the breaking of bread," which may point to their origin in the meal ceremonies of the earliest Christians.[9]

"The breaking of bread" in the household assemblies of the primitive Christians was a deliberate renewal of the Last Supper memories of the disciples in the light of their Easter experiences and their advent hope. It is unlikely that the rehearsal of Jesus' words and actions that gave meaning to this early Christian ceremony merely called to mind the events on that night "when Jesus was betrayed." The historical setting of the Last Supper, within the story of the passion which it interpreted, would have been provided. The worship, then, of the earliest Christians, as well as their proclamation to outsiders, influenced the formation of the passion narrative and the selection and preservation of various stories supporting faith in the resurrection.

STORIES CONCERNING JESUS AND JOHN THE BAPTIST

Interest in the relation of the missions of Jesus and of John the Baptist tended to fix in the memory of Jesus' disciples incidents dating from the beginning of his ministry. The early *kerygma* emphasized that Jesus' messiahship was heralded by the martyred prophet. Moreover, the similarities and differences between the baptismal rites of the disciples of John and the earliest followers of Jesus drew attention to the actions and the proclamations of the two men. Some of the gospel tradition concerning John was probably shaped by a rivalry that developed between Christians and the disciples of John. But the principal interest that led to the preservation of much important information about John and his relation to Jesus is doubtless reflected in the summaries in Acts of the early preaching: Jesus' messiahship was confirmed by the witness of the word of God spoken through the prophet John. The role of John was that of herald or forerunner of the Messiah.

GOD'S PROMISED SALVATION AND JESUS' MIGHTY WORKS

We have seen that the earliest witnesses called attention to "the signs and wonders" that God wrought in the ministry of Jesus the Messiah. In the description of Jewish apocalyptic eschatology notice was taken of the belief that when the new age dawned the power of Satan or Belial would be overcome by the power of God. As in former times, so at "the end of the days," God would reveal his power and saving purpose unto Israel by mighty acts and by his outstretched arm. For the earliest Christians, Jesus' mighty works were essential tokens that these last days were at hand. Doubtless, many incidents drawn from Jesus' healing ministry were recalled and reported again and again by the earliest preachers, and the form and content of these stories were influenced by the various scriptures associated with "the end of the days" in popular Jewish eschatology.

This perspective of the earliest witnesses makes improbable the view that the miracle stories were related merely to prove Jesus' supernatural power, or to support the authority of his teachings, or to illustrate his sympathetic and compassionate nature. The powers manifested in Jesus' ministry were proclaimed to awaken faith in the eschatological fulfillment of God's saving power, revealed for the redemption of Israel.[10]

EARLY INTEREST IN DECISIVE MOMENTS IN JESUS' MINISTRY

It is sometimes supposed that in the absence of any practical need for, or interest in, a connected story, the true course of events of Jesus' ministry was forgotten in the decades following Easter. Consequently the element of chronology in the Gospels is the result of the editorial joining of originally unconnected stories. The earliest preachers usually did not tell the story of Jesus' ministry from its beginning to its close, nor show how one incident followed upon another as cause and effect. If the detailed itinerary of Jesus' ministry had been given prominence in the preaching of the first generation of Christians, the outlines and plans of the Four Gospels would be more uniform than they are. In none of them is the sequential pattern of events unbroken. Yet it is very unlikely that there ever was a time in the early Church when all interest was lacking in the succession of events.[11] The passion story itself raised questions concerning previous phases of Jesus' ministry. What had Jesus done and said to provoke the hostility that confronted him when he came to Jerusalem? Was Jesus persuaded by others to visit the city, or did he go there of his own accord? Did his death come as a surprise? If he journeyed there voluntarily did he give his disciples any reason for doing so? In order to answer such questions, the earliest disciples would need to recall brief sequences of the ministry.

THE APOSTLES' TEACHING

According to Acts, the earliest converts "devoted themselves to the apostles' teaching."[12] What was the nature of this teaching that accompanied and followed upon the apostles' proclamation? According to some scholars, a clear distinction can be made between the *kerygma* and *didache* (teaching) of the early Church. Whereas the *kerygma* proclaimed the good news of God concerning Jesus the Messiah and had for its object the interpretation of his coming, the *didache* set forth the nature of one's response to the gospel and had for its object the interpretation of the moral demands of the new life of obedience to Jesus as Lord.[13] This distinction, if drawn too sharply, can hardly be maintained. The author of Acts associates the apostles' teaching with their *koinonia* (their "fellowship," or more probably, their "sharing" of all things), as also with the breaking of bread and the prayers. The early Christian teaching included instruction in the moral practices of the order, but the religious rites of the community must also have been subjects for teaching.

As a basis for the authority of their teaching, the apostles made repeated reference to sayings of Jesus. Moreover, in their disputes with fellow Jews, in their different interpretations of scriptures, appeal was made to pronouncements of Jesus.

Jesus' Parables and Other Sayings

According to the earliest Gospels, Jesus taught by parable. Also he employed vivid similitudes and aphorisms in his teaching. An example of the latter is his word concerning gifts to the poor: "sound no trumpet before you as the hypocrites do in the synagogues and the streets that they may be praised by men."[14] Or, scoring a point, he concluded with a terse paradox: "many that are first will be last and the last first."[15]

In order to establish or clarify the appropriateness of these parables and the other figurative language of Jesus, it is likely that a brief narrative setting for them in his ministry would be required. Some important information about Jesus was doubtless preserved indirectly in these narrative frames for his words. Yet it is evident from the different settings in which some words of Jesus are reported in the Gospels that other sayings were remembered without reference to their occasions for the simple reason that interest centered upon their application to new situations. Moreover, in their eagerness to appeal to Jesus it is quite possible that some early Christians ascribed to him words of uncertain origin. Thus the gospel tradition was expanded unintentionally.[16]

A recognition of these developments gives rise to a question of great importance: to what extent have the experiences of the early churches influenced the record of Jesus' actions and teaching? In other words, was a truly historical impression of Jesus' ministry preserved during the time between Easter and the earliest written sources?

The Method, Values, and Limitations of Form Criticism

Early in this century a critical method was developed for investigating the pre-literary stages in the growth of the gospel tradition. This method originated in Germany and was given the name *Formgeschichte* (form history). In English-speaking circles the method is commonly known as "form criticism."* The following assumptions mark four sequential steps in a form-critical analysis of the gospel tradition:

*Three European scholars set the agenda for form-crit-

Step 1   Stories and sayings of Jesus circulated initially as small independent units (pericopes). A reasonable basis for this assumption is apparent by taking note of the vague temporal and geographical connections that are easily detected in Mark, and that appear to be editorial (e.g., 2:23; 3:1, 7, 13; 4:1, etc.). The more skillful editing of Matthew and Luke obscures these sutures, yet the same pericopes are sometimes found in different settings in these Gospels, suggesting that the Evangelists are themselves responsible for their location (e.g., Matt. 8 and parallels; Luke 14 and parallels).

Most form critics agree that the narratives of Jesus' passion are exceptions to the first "rule" of form-critical analysis, that they were recounted as connected stories from the earliest days, for the reasons noted above.[17]

Step 2   These self-contained pericopes or paragraphs, separated from their "editorial introductions and conclusions," can be classified according to their literary *forms* or types. This assumption rests upon the observed fact that the oral traditions and literary expressions of a folk follow relatively fixed forms.*

Unfortunately the pioneer form critics proposed different classifications of these typical literary units characteristic of the gospel tradition. Some of their labels are derived from classical literature and are as unfamiliar in name as in the given structures they are intended to identify. Other labels proposed as descriptive of a literary form imply historical judgments. The advantage of a classification system proposed by Howard C. Kee is that standard English terms are used to identify the various forms, terms that are without prejudice to the historicity of the respective literary units.[18]

The Gospels preserve a tradition of reporting sayings of Jesus and also narratives of his Ministry.

The "main categories" within the "Sayings Tradition" are classified by Kee as "Aphorisms" (short, pithy sayings, maxims, proverbs, etc.), "Parables," and "Sayings Clusters." A few illustrations are:

1. Aphorisms: Mark 4:9, 25; 10:25, 43; Matt. 10:24, 39; Luke 13:30; 17:20f.
2. Parables: Mark 4:1–8, 30–32; Matt. 18:12f., 23–33; Luke 10:29–37; 14:15–23.
3. Sayings Clusters:
    a. Topical groupings: Mark 4:21–25 (seeing-hearing); Matt. 5:17–20 (Law); Luke 14:26–33 (discipleship).
    b. Formal groupings: Matt. 5:3–12 (Beatitudes); Luke 6:24–26 (Woes); parables of the kingdom, Mark 4; parables concerning the lost, Luke 15.

Kee's classification of the "Narrative Tradition" follows:

1. Anecdotes (brief, usually biographical, self-contained narratives revealing "some unusual feature of the person described"): Mark 1:23–26, 29–31; Matt. 11:2–6; Luke 5:1–11.
2. Aphoristic narratives (a brief account that "frames" an aphorism of Jesus): Mark 2:23–28; 3:1–5; Matt. 8:18–22; Luke 14:1–6.
3. Wonder stories (longer, more circumstantial narratives than the aphor-

ical studies of the Gospels through publications in the years 1919–1921: Karl Ludwig Schmidt, *Der Rahmen der Geschichte Jesu* (The Framework of the Story of Jesus); Martin Dibelius, *Die Formgeschichte des Evangeliums* (From Tradition to Gospel); and Rudolf Bultmann, *Die Geschichte der synoptischen Tradition* (The History of the Synoptic Tradition). A classical statement by Bultmann entitled "A New Approach to the Synoptic Gospels," was published in the *Rel* 5 (1926): 337ff. A modern introduction is Edgar V. McKnight, *What is Form Criticism?* (1969).

*One does not need to appeal to ancient cultures to demonstrate this phenomenon. The daily newspaper contains a variety of stereotypes: letters to the editor, obituary notices, human interest stories, comics, etc. "Each form has its specific characteristics: certain expressions or formulae and perhaps even a given structure." *The New Oxford Annotated Bible*, pp. 1519f.

istic and anecdotal forms; vivid, often dramatic detail, evoking amazement): Mark 5:1–20; 9:14–27; Luke 7:11–17.

4. Legends (*biographical*, focusing on the Christological significance of Jesus, often supported by testimonies from the Old Testament; and *cultic legends* providing "the background and therefore the authorization for the place of Jesus in the worship of the Christian community"):

   a. Biographical legends: the birth narratives, Matt. 1:18–25; Luke 2:1–20; Luke 2:21–40 (Presentation in the Temple); Mark 9:2–8 (Transfiguration).

   b. Cult legends: Mark 1:9–11 (Baptism of Jesus); Mark 14:22–25 (Lord's Supper).

5. Passion Narrative: Mark 14:1–16:8; Luke 21:1–24:11; John 18:1–20:29.

Step 3 Once the typical units are identified and their stylistic characteristics noted, the necessary foundation is laid for distinguishing early forms from their later amplifications. The origin and age of a pericope can be conjectured according to its shape, either as a "pure form" belonging to its type, or as a form bearing the marks of its development.*

* This stage of analysis is difficult and "one to be pursued with great caution" (Bultmann). Yet, by observing how Matthew and Luke revise Mark (assuming the priority of Mark) it is argued that one can deduce certain characteristics of their editing and extrapolate the same "laws" as operative in the transmission of the oral, precanonical tradition.

The "parable form" in the "sayings tradition" may exemplify this third step in form-critical analysis. In the course of its oral transmission, the details of a traditional parable were embellished; some parables addressed by Jesus to his opponents or to a crowd were applied to the Christian community; a parable with an eschatological intent was sometimes given a general, hortatory application. Before their placement in one or more of the Gospels, parables that were alike were probably assembled into collections or, possibly in some instances, fused. If these and other "laws of transformation" are taken into account, an earlier form of a parable can be recovered.[19]

Step 4 The final step in a form-critical analysis of the gospel tradition is the search for the *Sitz im Leben* (the setting in life, or life-situation) of each pericope within the traceable stages of its formation. The assumption here is that both the "Sayings" and "Narrative Tradition" were shaped by the particular functions that they served in the earliest Christian churches.

In this placement procedure, two steps can be followed separately or concurrently: one can start with a reconstructed, precanonical literary unit and conjecture what church interests occasioned this unit's form and content; or, one can start with the early church's *kerygma*, corporate life, problems, aspirations, and so forth (such as are manifested in Paul's letters and the early chapters of Acts) and account for the shape of the particular gospel traditions corresponding to these interests, needs, and activities.

So much for the assumptions, aims, and procedures of form criticism. A few words should be written about its values.

Form criticism has demonstrated that each unit of the gospel tradition links Jesus' deeds and words with the faith and life of his followers. The witness of the early Church was not merely oriented toward the past history of a man who was dead, but to a present experience and to a belief in the continuing importance of Jesus' work and words. Thus it was considered more important to obey Jesus than to retain in memory the precise words that he taught on any specific occasion. It was more important to appreciate the meaning of the Christian meal rite for the participant than to record precisely the proceedings of Jesus' Last Supper.

At no point did the preservers of the gospel tradition adopt the "detached view" of the historian or biographer who labors so that the things of the past may be remembered. Nor did early Christian curiosity dwell upon aspects of Jesus' personality that were of no importance to faith; for example, the color of his eyes and hair, the sound of his voice, or characteristic gestures when teaching. Form criticism reminds us that the earliest Christians never indulged "in scene painting for its own sake."[20] Neither did they base the validity of Jesus' teaching upon the verbal infallibility of their reports.[21]

Form critics have recognized that since each unit of the gospel tradition served some concrete religious interest, a definition of its setting in the life of the early Church defines the modern situation in which these stories are apt to be appreciated in their meaning and power. For example, Jesus' teaching on almsgiving is most germane when you give alms; the teaching on prayer, when you pray.[22]

Form critics have emphasized that the Gospels are a social possession. The traditions they contain are not the recollection of a few individuals, but represent the corporate testimony of a witnessing and worshipping community. Thus the possibility of fabrication by several persons of limited intelligence and comprehension is completely ruled out. But the point has more important implications. Personal reminiscences cherished by friends are often quite different from the corporate testimony that a group gives to its leader. In the latter instance the most valuable traditions are selected, culled, supported, and verified through constant repetition, and shaped into their most useful forms.[23]

Form criticism has demonstrated that the Gospels are valuable sources for knowledge of the earliest Christian churches. From a study of the various units in the Gospels, many interests and problems of the Palestinian communities, as well as the history of later developments, can be inferred. These results sometimes supplement and correct the data afforded by Acts and Paul's letters.[24]

These values are of considerable importance. At the same time, form-critical analyses have exposed the serious limitations of the method.

Form critics have gone too far in ruling out all interest in the early Church in the course of events in Jesus' ministry or in the strategy of his actions. It is not clear why the first generation of Christians should have been completely disinterested in an outline of Jesus' ministry, whereas the second generation of believers felt a need for one. Granted that the thinning of the ranks of eyewitnesses and the geographical expansion of the Church afforded an impulse for Gospel writing, it is unlikely that the eyewitnesses left behind them only vivid recollections of particular happenings and isolated sayings, apart from any information concerning their setting. The broad outline of Jesus' ministry must have become the common property of a large number of Christian teachers and communities.[25]

Form critics have frequently overlooked the influence of "eyewitnesses and ministers of the word" (Luke 1:2). Some writers claim that the gospel was a product of unconscious "social processes" at work in anonymous Christian communities. But it is positively misleading to imply that the traditions concerning Jesus were left to the mercy of an anonymous, relatively illiterate people who were not aware that the events they had witnessed were epoch-making. "Clearly defined 'personalities' can be found at the beginning of earliest Christianity . . . the transmission and formation of the oral tradition about Jesus certainly did not bypass the leading figures of the first community."[26] Some of Jesus' disciples visited the Palestinian and Syrian churches in which the gospel traditions were being "shaped"; their witness would have prevented the radical displacement of events, for example, of Peter's confession of Jesus as the Christ, which one form critic places after Easter.[27] Besides this, Jesus' sayings are cast in forms easy to remember. It is not improbable that some were retained simply because he had spoken them, not just for their utility. Form critics have too radically rejected the view, as ancient as Justin Martyr, that the canonical Gospels preserved for the Church "recollections (or reminiscences) of the apostles and those who followed them."[28]

Form critics have tended to assign to unknown Christians the responsibility for "creating" more of the stories and sayings of the Gospels than is credible. It is one thing to ask what motive the early church might have had for reporting a particular deed or saying of Jesus; quite another to assume that this motive accounts for its invention. More probable is the position that the interests of early Christians led them to select, interpret, and apply the gospel tradition, than that the same interests led them to formulate pericopae whose historical kernels (if there are any) are beyond recovery. If a significant part of the gospel tradition was created by communities *lacking historical perspective* and prompted by their own interests, one would expect to find Jesus and his disciples "speaking in tongues," or engaging in disputes concerning Gentile entitlements in eschatological Israel.

Two other reservations may be noted. Questions concerning the precanonical history of a traditional form are sometimes confused with others having to do with its historicity. Form critics have used terms (e.g., "myth") suggestive of a judgment concerning substance rather than form. The tendency to pass from one to the other is especially evident in form-critical analysis of the miracle stories of the Gospels. Honest criticism may lead one to ask whether or not a particular miracle occurred, but an answer depends upon broader considerations than a literary analysis of miracle-story forms.[29]

Finally, early form critics have been faulted for their arbitrary, artificial descriptions of the *Sitze im Leben* of some of the gospel traditions; e.g., their sharp distinctions between "Palestinian" (early) and "Hellenistic" (later) are untenable. Fundamental questions concerning the sociocultural settings of the gospel pericopae were insufficiently investigated. One should ask what kind of community would have transmitted such a tradition? What function did the tradition serve in the community within which and for which it was written?[30]

In summary, we can say that "despite difficulties and disagreements about forms and corresponding 'life-situations' . . . the broad lines of the picture form criticism presents of the circumstances surrounding the transmission of the traditions of Jesus stand forth clearly enough. The concrete conditions and urgent practical requirements of the Christian community, and not any straight historical interest as such, determined not only what traditions were preserved but also how they were preserved, modified, and renewed.[31]

THE BEGINNING OF WRITTEN ACCOUNTS

Luke's Gospel begins with the declaration that "many have undertaken to compile a narrative of the things which have been accomplished among us . . ." (1:1). We have no way of knowing the number of such writings in existence at the time (ca. 80–85 C.E.?) nor when the traditions concerning Jesus were first committed to writing. For more than a century scholars have been convinced that the measure of agreement among Matthew, Mark, and Luke can be explained only as the result of some literary interdependence. These three Gospels have come to be known as the *Synoptic Gospels* because it has been judged that the three Evangelists "view together" the ministry of Jesus. The evidence upon which this assumption rests may be readily seen by placing the three Gospels in parallel columns, forming a synopsis or "harmony." Comparative study reveals striking differences as well as similarities among them. Thus "the synoptic problem" is: how can these similarities and differences be explained most satisfactorily?

During the course of the nineteenth century every conceivable relation between the Gospels was explored, some scholars working together, others independently. By the turn of the twentieth century a "scientific solution" to the synoptic problem seemed in sight. It was called "the two-document hypothesis." This theory declares (1) that Mark was the first of the Gospels to be written, and that Mark's narrative was used by the writers of Matthew and Luke as a source; (2) that Matthew and Luke also used a second document, which may be described as a compendium of Jesus' teaching. This second document is commonly referred to by the symbol Q (*Quelle* is German for "source").

The so-called "two-document hypothesis" is the most widely held "solution" to the synoptic problem, and seems to the present writer to be basically correct. The fact that other possible "solutions" are advanced by specialists indicates, however, that the hypothesis has not been proven, and that not all the evidence is thereby explained with full satisfaction.[32] A major alternative "solution" will be noted later, but because of its greater probability the "two-document hypothesis" is explained in some detail. (At various points the reader is directed to books and articles that question the following reading of the texts).[33]

The Priority of Mark   Several considerations provide a cumulative case supporting the priority of Mark:

1. Common subject matter. The Greek text of Mark contains 661 verses. Of these, 601 are found in Matthew and in Luke. Matthew reproduces 90 percent of the subject matter of Mark; Luke better than half of it. Only three of Mark's 88 paragraphs are missing from the other two.[34]

2. Common outline. The sequence of Mark's narrative is supported either by Matthew or by Luke. In the earlier portions of his Gospel, Luke adheres to Mark's order; in the latter portions of Matthew, agreement with Mark's outline is noteworthy. Where either departs from Mark, the other is usually found supporting him, and there is no case where Matthew and Luke agree together against Mark in a point of arrangement. It is also noteworthy that the parallelism in the order of Matthew and Luke begins where Mark begins and ends where Mark ends.[35]

3. Common order extends to words and sentences. In spite of the fact that Matthew frequently abbreviates the source material derived from Mark, a characteristic to be discussed below, it has been estimated that Matthew employs 51 percent of the actual words of Mark.[36] Although Luke revises the rough style of Mark more extensively than does Matthew, it is significant that many of Mark's details, omitted by Matthew, are found in Luke. As a result, where it appears that Luke is dependent upon Mark, slightly over 50 percent of Mark's words are reproduced. The proportion of verbal agreement of Luke with Mark rises to 69 percent when words of Jesus are quoted.[37]

4. Concurrence in the use of unusual words. The fact that rare words and rough constructions found in Mark reappear in Matthew and Luke calls for special attention. This linguistic data can be appreciated only when viewed in a Greek synopsis, but its importance cannot fail to be noticed by anyone. It is not likely that these rare words and harsh constructions were transmitted to three independent writers through an oral tradition that was subject to the transformations noted in the foregoing discussion of factors present in this period, nor is it likely that Mark "butchered" the grammatical constructions of Matthew and Luke.

5. The meager amount of agreement between Matthew and Luke. Alongside the data listed above should be placed facts such as the following: Although Luke's agreement with Mark is over 50 percent, his agreement with Matthew in the same sections declines to 42 percent. Luke's agreement with Matthew against Mark is less than 6 percent.[38]

Such evidence has led a majority to conclude that Matthew and Luke made use of Mark. It is sometimes declared that their copies of Mark must have been different from the text of modern editions upon which these comparisons are based. If the common source used by Matthew and Luke was our present Mark, then we may ask what explanation is provided, first, for their omission of whole sections of Mark's text, and second, for the minor agreements of Matthew and Luke against our present Mark. One answer to these questions is based on the assumption that an earlier edition of Mark ("Ur-Marcus," or Proto-Mark) was used by the late evangelists. This theory has failed to commend itself to most source critics. The omissions of Mark can be explained upon other assumptions, and the minor agreements may be attributable either to accidental concurrence because of the evangelists' improvements of Mark's diction, or to a reflection of similar theological views or influences. It is also probable that there occurred some accidental assimilation between the text of Matthew and Luke in the process of copying.[39]

The Probability of Q   Remove the Markan passages from Matthew and Luke, and approximately two hundred verses remain that parallel one another closely. On the basis of the criteria listed above it has been argued that a second source was employed by the First and Third evangelists. As noted above, this source has been designated by the symbol Q. The existence of Q cannot be other than hypothetical since it is not extant, and can be recovered only from Matthew and Luke.

The difficulties of reconstructing this lost writing can be appreciated when we consider the use of Mark. A reconstruction of Mark out of identical passages in Matthew and Luke would result in a Gospel three fourths the length of its present text. Moreover, the order in which Matthew and Luke use their common, non-Markan material is very different, as can be seen in the outline on page 106. Even though it is probable that Luke has ordinarily preserved the original order of his sources, it can never be more than a probability that this was the case in his use of Q.

It is not surprising that there should be wide differences of opinion concerning the nature of Q. Some scholars use the symbol merely to refer to that collection of stereotyped tradition used by Matthew and Luke in addition to Mark, and hold that part of this tradition may well have reached the synoptists through independent channels of oral traditions. There are others who are willing to dispense altogether with the hypothesis of a written source. This is surely going too far. Yet it is a natural reaction against the subjectivity of some who have claimed that Q was originally a "Gospel."[40]

Perhaps Q should be used as a symbol designating only those verbal parallels in Matthew and Luke that were not derived from Mark. It is not mere fancy, however, which supposes that the content of Q may have extended beyond the limits of these parallels. Since Matthew and Luke omitted some things from Mark, is it not likely that they were also selective in their use of a second source? Some passages found only in the First or Third Gospel are embedded in a complex of the Q tradition and resemble it in style and thought. It is reasonable to hold that such material originally belonged to the Q source. Moreover, it is easier to explain the absence of some of these sayings from one Gospel as omissions from Q than to suppose that their location in the other Gospel is merely editorial.[41]

It is sometimes supposed that Q was used in the composition of Mark. Passages in Mark that echo sayings in Q are the Beelzebub controversy (3:22–30), sayings of Jesus on the responsibilities of witnesses (4:21–25), teaching in connection with a mission of the Twelve (6:7–11), sayings concerning discipleship (9:35–37, 41–50), and condemnation of the Pharisees (12:38–40). A theory of literary dependence is neither a necessary nor a probable explanation for these resemblances. At least some of the sayings of Jesus collected in Q must have circulated apart from this source, in the oral tradition of the Church.

The outline of Q that is given on page 106 is speculative but conservative. Several passages found in other reconstructions have been omitted where there is considerable debate.[42] This outline may enable the reader to visualize the content and arrangement of the document, as well as the different order of its sections in the two Gospels.

Upon the assumption that Q was a written source, various views concerning its origin have been advanced. Several scholars have conjectured that Q was originally a compendium of Jesus' teaching composed in Aramaic by Matthew the disciple of Jesus. This theory, and the fragment of second-century tradition upon which it rests, will be noted in Chapter 8. Suffice it here to say that the hypothesis is unconvincing. Concerning the date and place of origin of Q, one can only appeal to inferences from its content and from its use by Matthew and Luke. The fact that Q contains so little controversial matter—90 percent of it

An Outline of the Sayings Source

	Luke	Matthew
A. John the Baptist and Jesus:		
1. The proclamation of John	3:7b–9, 16b–17	3:7b–12
2. The temptations of Jesus	4:1b–12	4:1–10
3. Jesus' teaching	6:20–49	(cf. parallels 5–7; 10:24f; 12:33–35; 15:14)
4. Response to Jesus' proclamation		
a. Centurion's faith	7:6b–9	8:8–10
b. Emissaries from John	7:19, 22f, 24b–28, 31–35	11:3–11, 16–19
B. Jesus and his disciples:		
5. Two applicants	9:57b–60	8:19–22
6. Mission charge	10:2f, 5, 12	9:37f; 10:11, 15–16a
7. Woe to Chorazin, etc.	10:13–15	11:21–23
8. Privileges of discipleship	10:21b–24	11:25–27; 13:16f
	11:9–13	7:7–11
C. Jesus and his opponents:		
9. The Beelzebub controversy	11:17–18a, 19f, 20–23	12:25–28, 30
10. The return of the Evil Spirit	11:24–26	12:43–45
11. The sign for this generation	11:29b–32	12:39f; 42, 41
12. Concerning the light	11:34	7:22–23a
13. Against the Pharisees	11:39, 42f, 49–51	23:25, 23, 6, 34–36
14. Fearless confession	12:5–9	10:28b–33
D. The future:		
15. Cares and the coming kingdom	12:22b–31, 34	6:25–33, 21
16. Watchfulness and faithfulness	12:39–40, 42–46	24:43–51a
17. Parables of mustard seed and leaven	13:18f, 21	13:31b–33
18. The table fellowship in the kingdom	13:28f	8:11f
19. Lament over Jerusalem	13:34f	23:37–39
20. Discipleship in the time of crisis	16:13, 16–18	6:24; 11:12f; 5:18, 32
21. The day of the Son of man	17:24, 26f, 30, 37b	24:27, 37–39, 28

is positive teaching—has led many to conclude that it was composed as a manual of instruction for converts. Its teaching was probably intended for Gentile Christians. Antioch has been considered the most likely place for its origin. "Probably a date between A.D. 50 and 60 would command most general assent for the writing of Q."[43]

AN ALTERNATIVE "SOLUTION" TO THE SYNOPTIC PROBLEM

The most popular alternative to the "two-document 'solution' " to the synoptic problem is known as the *Griesbach*, or *Griesbach-Farmer hypothesis*. An essential element in the theory, the priority of Matthew's Gospel, combined with the subsequent publication of Luke's Gospel, and the view that Mark is a conflation of Matthew and of Luke, was set forth by Johann J. Griesbach (1745–1812) in publications during the years 1789–1794. This "solution" to the synoptic problem, which was eclipsed by a growing consensus favoring the "two-document hypothesis," was reintroduced into modern scholarly debate concerning the literary relations among the synoptic gospels by William R. Farmer in 1964. In addition to arguments supporting Matthew's priority, Farmer sought to substantiate the conclusion that Luke was dependent upon Matthew. In briefest statement the Griesbach-Farmer "solution" is: Matthew was first, Luke used Matthew; Mark used both.[44]

This theory of literary dependence runs as follows: After Matthew composed his Gospel, Luke, using Matthew as one primary source, composed his narrative, drastically reordering the accounts according to his own views, especially taking the teaching material and putting much of it into his new travel section in the middle of the Gospel. Other substantial alterations of Matthew were introduced into Luke's framework. Then Mark wrote his Gospel, using both Matthew and Luke as his primary sources and very little else. Making sure to put into his account nearly every pericope that appeared in the same order in his two major sources, Mark then interspersed material from each as it suited his purposes, in general following Matthew's order after his first five chapters.

Most students of the synoptic Gospels remain unpersuaded that the arguments of "Farmer's School" have established a modified version of the Griesbach hypothesis; however, exegeses of particular passages have exposed the weakness of some of the "proofs" for the priority of Mark and the probability of Q, and have compelled those who accept the two-document hypothesis to demonstrate its tenability pericope by pericope."[45] Perhaps neither of the major theories, relying on arguments for *literary* dependence, pay sufficient attention

THE GOSPELS OF MATTHEW AND OF LUKE: A SOURCE THEORY

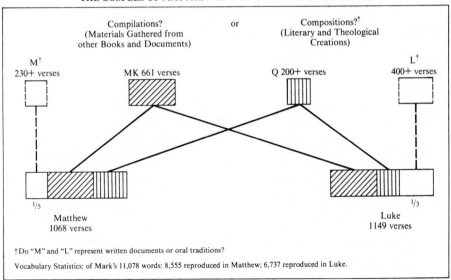

		or	
	Compilations? (Materials Gathered from other Books and Documents)		Compositions?[†] (Literary and Theological Creations)

M[†]
230+ verses

MK 661 verses

Q 200+ verses

L[†]
400+ verses

1/5

Matthew
1068 verses

1/3

Luke
1149 verses

†Do "M" and "L" represent written documents or oral traditions?

Vocabulary Statistics: of Mark's 11,078 words: 8,555 reproduced in Matthew; 6,737 reproduced in Luke.

to the likelihood that oral traditions continued in circulation alongside near-parallels in written form and were accessible to the evangelists.[46]

The present writer agrees with the following statement of the case: "the Two Document Theory has outlived all its major rivals, and there is no good reason for now deserting it as a fundamental working hypothesis. But it is certainly an oversimplification of the evidence and requires modification."[47] In favoring a documentary "solution" to the synoptic problem, early source critics tended to reject evidence for the existence of independent reservoirs of oral tradition; the Gospels were viewed as compilations of materials gathered from books or fragmentary *written* sources. The some 230 verses unique to Matthew and the more than 400 unique to Luke were thought to reproduce substantially the contents of additional documents. Form critical studies have tended to identify, *as the evangelist's selection from oral tradition,* the special "source" of Matthew (M, or Special Mt.), which probably overlapped at some points with Q, and the special "source" of Luke (L, or Special Lk.), which may have overlapped with Mark and Q. (See the diagram on page 107. The broken lines indicate the probability of oral traditions.)

NOTES

1. The tradition was formulated "during the first twenty years of the Christian movement, and appears to have been largely accomplished by the time of Paul, who seems to regard the tradition as already fixed." A. M. Perry, "The Growth of the Gospels," *IB*, vol. 7 (1951), p. 73; Luke 1:2. Perry's Statement has substantial validity, although the history of the synoptic tradition reveals persistence into the second century "of a living, free tradition of sayings of Jesus, out of which the Gospels have come," and which "did not come to an end with the writing of the Gospels." N. Perrin, *Rediscovering the Teaching of Jesus* (1976), p. 34.

2. 1 Cor. 1:23.

3. Lk. 24:25ff.; Acts 2:23–31; 3:18; 10:43; 13:27, 29, 32ff.; 1 Thess. 2:14f.; 1 Cor. 15:3f.

4. W. Pannenberg, *Jesus—God and Man* (1968), p. 246.

5. C. H. Dodd, *According to the Scriptures* (1952), p. 13–16; M. Goguel, *The Birth of Christianity* (1953), p. 103; R. Bultmann, *The History of the Synoptic Tradition* (1963), pp. 280ff.; Pannenberg, *Jesus—God and Man*, pp. 246f.; B. Lindars, *New Testament Apologetic* (Philadelphia: Westminster, 1961), pp. 75f. M. Hengel, *Acts and Earliest Christianity*, pp. 43–46.

6. Weiss, *Earliest Christianity*, vol. 1 (1937), p. 189; V. Taylor, *The Formation of The Gospel Tradition* (London: Macmillan, 1935), pp. 44ff. While Paul Winter (*On the Trial of Jesus*, Berlin: W. deGruyter, 1961)) too sharply separates religious and historical interests, he demonstrates that complex factors contributed to the growth of the passion traditions of the early Church.

7. E.g., Mt. 22:8ff.; 28:16ff.; Jn. 20:19–21. C. H. Dodd, "The Appearances of the Risen Christ," in D.H. Nineham, *Studies in the Gospels* (1955), pp. 9ff.; Taylor, *Gospel Tradition*, pp. 59ff.

8. 1 Cor. 15:1ff.; cf. Lk. 24:33f.

9. E.g., Lk. 24:13–35; John 21:1–14. Dodd, "Appearances of the Risen Christ," pp. 13ff. Cf. Bultmann, *Synoptic Tradition*, pp. 284ff.; H. Anderson, *Jesus and Christian Origins* (1964), pp. 192ff.; Pannenberg, *Jesus—God and Man*, pp. 88ff.

10. T. W. Manson, *Jesus the Messiah* (1946), pp. 56ff.; A. Richardson, *The Miracle-Stories of the Gospels* (1941), pp. 16ff. Note Acts 3:1–16; R. H. Fuller, *Interpreting the Miracles* (1963), pp. 46ff; H. C. Kee, "Aretalogy and Gospel," *JBL* 92 (1973): 416ff.

11. O. Piper, "The Origin of the Gospel Pattern", *JBL* 78 Pt. 2 (1959), pp. 115f. V. Taylor, *Gospel Tradition*, pp. 238ff., 174f. C. H. Dodd, "Framework of the Gospel narrative," in *New Testament Studies* (Manchester University Press, 1952), pp. 1–11. R. H. Fuller, *The Mission and Achievement of Jesus* (Chicago: Alec R. Allenson, 1954), pp. 51ff. H. Riesenfeld, "The Gospel Tradition and its Beginnings," *Studia Evangelica* 73, pp. 61ff.

12. Acts 2:42.

13. C. H. Dodd, *Gospel and Law* (Columbia and Cambridge University Presses, 1951), pp. 10ff. R. Heard, *An Introduction to the New Testament* (New York: Harper and Brothers, 1950), pp. 31f.

14. Mt. 6:2.

15. Mk. 10:31; cf. Mt. 10:39, 23:12.

16. Christian prophets and scribes very probably contributed to the expansion of the gospel tradition. Their words, aptly suited to life situations in early churches, carried authority corresponding to the remembered words of Jesus because (it was believed) they were spoken under the inspiration of the Spirit of Jesus. Acts 2:18, 11:27; Mt. 18:18–20, 13:51f.; Rev. 22:6, 16. W. R. Farmer, "Jesus and the Gospel Tradition: A Form-Critical and Theological Essay," *Perkins* 28, 2, (1975), pp. 15–18.

17. The conclusion should not be drawn that the story of Jesus, once established in oral tradition, was handed on without change. P. Winter, *Trial of Jesus* (1961), pp. 5f. J. R. Donahue, "From Passion Tradition to Passion Narrative," in W. H. Kelber ed., *The Passion in Mark* (1976), pp. 1–20.

18. H. C. Kee, *Jesus in History: An Approach to the Study of the Gospels* (1977), pp. 301–306.

19. J. Jeremias, *The Parables of Jesus* (1962), pp. 23ff.

20. R. H. Lightfoot, *The Gospel Message of St. Mark* (1958 ed.), pp. 102–104. P. Minear, "Form Criticism and Faith," *RLife* 15, n. 1 (1945), pp. 46ff.

21. Minear, "Form Criticism," p. 48.

22. "The Church not only remembered and reported facts. It lived them. If we have understood this, we are near to the secret of the Gospels." C. H. Dodd, *About the Gospels* (1950), p. 22.

23. F. C. Grant, *The Gospels* (1957), pp. 1f. A. M. Perry, "The Growth of the Gospels," *IB* Vol. 7, p. 71.

24. K. Kundsin, "Primitive Christianity in the Light of Gospel Research," in F. C. Grant ed., *Form Criticism* (New York: Harper & Row, 1962), pp. 79ff. R. Bultmann, *Theology of the New Testament*, Vol. I (New York: Charles Scribner's Sons, 1951), pp. 33–62.

25. M. Hengel, *Acts and Earliest Christianity*, pp. 19f.; P. Benoit, "Reflections on Formgeschichtliche Methode," in *Jesus and the Gospel*, Vol. I (1972), pp. 31–33; G. B. Caird, "The Study of the Gospels: II, Form Criticism," *ExpT* 87, 5, (1976), pp. 138ff.

26. M. Hengel, *Acts and Earliest Christianity*, pp. 25–27.

27. Mk. 8:27ff., and parallels. R. Bultmann, *Synoptic Tradition*, pp. 257ff., 427. Doubtless theological motives prompted the Sitze-im-Leben of some pericopae so that original settings are problematic. But anecdotes and teaching in poetic forms are more readily retained in memory than chronological data.

28. N. A. Dahl, "Memory and Commemoration in Early Christianity," in *Jesus in the Memory of the Early Church* (1976), pp. 11–29. M. Hengel, *Acts and Earliest*

Christianity, pp. 25–29. See Justin Martyr, *Dial.* 103.8, also 100.4, 101.3, and others.

29. P. Benoit discusses the effect of antisupernatural philosophical presuppositions upon the exegesis of form critics. In this connection recall the comments concerning prior assumptions and their role in exegesis in chapter I.

30. H. C. Kee, *Jesus in History*, pp. 29–31.

31. H. Anderson, *The Gospel of Mark* (1976), p. 14.

32. R. H. Fuller, "The Synoptic Problem After Ten Years," *Perkins* 28 (1975), pp. 63–68.

33. A detailed statement of the case is presented by B. H. Streeter, *The Four Gospels* (1924), pp. 151ff.; A. M. Perry, "The Growth of the Gospels," pp. 61ff.; Kümmel, *INT*[2], pp. 56ff.; J. A. Fitzmyer, "The Priority of Mark and the Q Source in Luke," *PRS* 2 (1970), pp. 130–170.

34. On the assumption that Mk. used Mt., is it credible that he would have omitted so much while padding his own narrative with vivid but often inconsequential details? Mk. takes 194 words to tell the story of the feeding of the five thousand, Mt.'s story has 157.

35. Streeter, *The Four Gospels*, pp. 151, 161f. Cf. E. P. Sanders, "The Argument from Order and the Relationship between Matthew and Luke," *NTS* 15 (1968), 249–261.

36. *Oxford Studies in the Synoptic Problem*, ed., W. Sanday (Oxford: Clarendon Press, 1911), pp. 85ff.

37. Streeter, *The Four Gospels*, p. 160; A. M. Perry, *Growth of the Gospels*, pp. 62ff.

38. Implausible is the view of some scholars that Lk. used Mt. as one source for this would imply that Lk. separated Jesus' sayings from their Matthean context, relocating them and removing traces of Mt's interpretations. Cf. R. T. Simpson, "The Major Agreements of Matthew and Luke Against Mark," *NTS* 12 (1966), pp. 273ff.

39. Streeter, *The Four Gospels*, pp. 168ff. Cf. J. P. Brown, "An Early Revision of the Gospel of Mark," *JBL* 78, Pt. 3 (1959), pp. 215ff. Kümmel, *INT*[2], pp. 61–63; F. Nierynck, *The Synoptic Problem*, *IDBS* (1976), pp. 715ff.

40. Kümmel, *INT*[2], pp. 63–76; H. C. Kee, *Jesus in History*, pp. 76ff.

41. Note Lk. 9:60b–62 (cf. Mt. 8:19–22); also Lk. 9:57–60. F. C. Grant, *The Gospels*, pp. 45f.

42. A. Harnack, *Sayings of Jesus* (London: Williams & Norgate, 1908), pp. 253ff.; T. W. Manson, *The Sayings of Jesus* (London: SCM Press, 1949), pp. 15–20, 39ff. Cf. H. C. Kee's "formal classification of Q material," and "the thematic interests of Q," *Jesus in History*, pp. 84–89.

43. Heard, *Introduction*, p. 52; T. W. Manson, *Sayings*, p. 20; Kümmel, *INT*[2], pp. 67ff.; Kee, *Jesus in History*, pp. 83, 117ff.; R. A. Edwards, *A Theology of Q: Eschatology, Prophecy and Wisdom* (1976); R. D. Worden, "Redaction Criticism of Q: A Survey," *JBL*, 94, 4 (1975), 532–546. G. Stanton, "On the Christology of Q," in *Christ and Spirit in the New Testament*, eds. B. Lindars and S. Smalley (1973), pp. 38–42.

44. B. Orchard and T. R. W. Longstaff, *J. J. Griesbach: Synoptic and Text-critical Studies* (1978); W. R. Farmer, *The Synoptic Problem* (1964); also, "Modern Developments of Griesbach's Hypothesis," *NTS*, 23 (1977), 275–295; D. L. Dungan, "Mark—the Abridgment of Matthew and Luke," *PRS*, (1970), 51–97. In a lengthy essay, Farmer has set forth his reconstruction of the history of the synoptic tradition (see note 16, above), hypothesizing the sociological and theological *Sitz im Leben* of Mt., Lk., and Mk. according to his "solution" of the synoptic problem.

45. R. H. Fuller, "The Synoptic Problem," p. 67. Note the following exchange in articles appearing in the *JBL*: H. Talbert and E. V. McKnight, "Can the Griesbach

Hypothesis Be Falsified?" (91 [1972], 338–368), and G. W. Buchanan, "Has the Griesbach Hypothesis Been Falsified?" (93 [1974], 550–572).

46. Xavier Leon-Dufour de-emphasizes the literary relation among the Gospels and hypothesizes the influence of oral tradition upon each. *Introduction to the New Testament*, eds. A. Robert and A. Feuillet, pp. 140f.

47. G. B. Caird, "The Study of the Gospels," p. 103; also 102. "What is called for . . . is to replace a rigidly literary method of sorting out sources by an approach which takes more fully into account the creativity of the Evangelists," Kee, "Mark's Gospel in Recent Research," *Int*, 32, 4 (1978), 361.

Chapter 6

The Gospel of Mark

T HE Synoptic Gospels preserve fragments of an oral and written tradition concerning Jesus that are in large measure shaped by other than historical-biographical interests. Yet these texts may not rightly be viewed as mosaics, haphazardly formed from surviving bits and pieces of an irretrievably shattered image of Jesus. The gospel tradition conceivably might have so disintegrated had it not been for the constructive work of the Four Evangelists (as well as some of their predecessors), and the actions of ancient churches in canonizing their narratives.[1]

A consequence of the establishment of the fourfold Gospel has been that the impressions of Jesus, which Christians have treasured through the ages, are a composite of traits and features drawn from all four Gospels. This persisting tendency to harmonize the Gospels reflects a theologically sound instinct; no single Gospel does full justice to the person of the Christ; in them all the one Lord is proclaimed. At the same time this tendency to treat the four Gospels as one source (supplying mutually supplementary details), has had the effect of obscuring the distinctive witness to Christ of each Gospel. A proper recognition of the essential coherence of the portrayal of the person of Jesus, manifested in the four-dimensional Gospel canon, will neither deny nor minimize the individuality of and the differences among the separated Gospels. While this plurality of Gospels has sometimes been viewed as a serious historical and theological problem, the four-fold canon has served to enrich the Church's Christological reflection, and, from time to time, to prevent the absolutizing of partial aspects of the Gospel tradition.[2]

The aim of this chapter, and of the two that follow, is to identify the occasions for the composition of the Gospels of Mark, Luke, and Matthew and to describe the distinguishing features of each. A basic assumption is that the Evangelists were influenced by the theological and social issues that were being addressed in their Christian communities or in those for which their Gospels were written. Employing form-critical terminology, our objective is to identify the *Sitze im Leben*, the "life-situations," that occasioned the composition of these Gospels. Accordingly, attention is focused on the latest, most explicit level of meaning: the respective Evangelist's interpretation of Jesus' words and works. (Neither the *Sitze im Leben* of the oral, largely anonymous witnesses nor the original *Sitze im Leben* of Jesus' teaching and actions will be treated in Chapters 6, 7, and 8. A sketch of the ministry of Jesus is undertaken in Chapters 10 and 11.)

No names of authors or dates were attached to the Gospels when they were written and first circulated. As long as the Gospels were not treated as "scripture," questions of their origin and individuality were of no special significance. But, by the later half of the second century questions had arisen concerning their authority, difference, and relative value. The following statement, written around 180 C.E. and attributed to Irenaeus, Bishop of Gaul, reports the tradition in the church at that time:

> Matthew published a written Gospel among the Hebrews in their own language, while Peter and Paul were preaching and founding the Church in Rome. After their decease, Mark, the disciple and interpreter of Peter—he also transmitted to us in writing those things which Peter had preached; and Luke, the attendant of Paul, recorded in a book the Gospel which Paul had declared. . . .[3]

The comparative study of the Synoptic Gospels in the modern period has cast shadows of doubt upon the truth of these traditions. The evidence set forth in the preceding chapter justifies a consideration of Mark before Luke or Matthew, notwithstanding the order reported by Irenaeus.

THE GOSPEL OF MARK

THE PAPIAS TRADITION CONCERNING MARK

There is a church tradition concerning Mark's origin that is earlier than Irenaeus. Around 140 C.E., Papias, Bishop of Phrygia, wrote a work entitled "Expositions of the Words of The Lord." From this work the following statement is cited:

> And the elder said this also: Mark, having become the interpreter of Peter, wrote accurately everything he remembered, without however recording in order what was either said or done by Christ. For neither did he hear the Lord, nor did he follow him; but afterwards, as I said, [attended] Peter, who adapted his instructions to the needs [of his hearer] but had no design of giving a connected account of the Lord's oracles. So then Mark made no mistake, while he thus wrote down some things as he remembered them; for he made it his own care not to omit anything that he heard, or to set down any false statement therein.[4]

It is possible that this is the source of the tradition reported by Irenaeus, for Irenaeus knew the book by Papias. But reference of Irenaeus to the date of Mark may represent an independent tradition. The value of these second-century reports concerning Mark cannot be decided until the Gospel itself has been closely examined.

THE SOURCES AND PLAN OF MARK

In the modern period, interest in the sources Mark may have used in composing his Gospel has been prompted by a variety of concerns.[5] With the ascendancy of "the two-document solution" of the synoptic problem, the view (at least as old as Augustine) that Mark was an abridgment of Matthew was abandoned. Belief in the priority of Mark was accompanied by a conviction that the earliest Gospel was the most reliable. When read alongside Matthew and Luke and when compared with John, Mark seemed "the least theological" and therefore "the most objective." Biographers of Jesus in the late nineteenth century often assumed that Peter and other early witnesses to Jesus' ministry furnished Mark his information, facts that warranted the recognition of Mark as the basic "history" of Jesus.*

One result of form criticism as applied to the Gospels was a radical shift in perspective concerning Mark. "The traditions of Jesus which the Evangelist had at his disposal would not have come to him, direct, intact, or untouched from the time of Jesus, either as straightforward reports of separate past events or as integral pieces in a continuous life story."[6] Form critics held that Mark's separate pericopes had their *Sitz im Leben* in early Christian communities, and the plot of his Gospel (at least leading up to the Passion) was a construction of the Evangelist. Yet neither Dibelius nor Bultmann were particularly interested in investigating Mark's editorial activity: the Evangelist was "not sufficiently master of his material to be able to venture on a systematic construction himself."[7]

Paramount interest in Mark as author and theologian developed from the introduction in the 1950s of the youngest member of the family of critical methodologies in Gospel research, *Redaktionsgeschichte*. "Redaction Criticism" is a discipline that aims to locate "the theological motivation of an author as this is revealed in the collection, arrangement, editing, and modification of traditional materials, and in the composition of new materials or the creation of new forms within the traditions of early Christianity."**

Redaction (or composition) criticism of Mark's Gospel has produced a wide variety of opinions concerning the earliest Evangelist's "theological motivation." Methodological questions remain in debate.[8] Evidence derived from the Gospel needs to be correlated with relevant external evidence, and the whole with ancient church tradition.

Some scholars have sought to identify Hellenistic literary models (Jewish and pagan), to which Mark's "gospel form" corresponds, and whose purposes are sufficiently established to shed light upon Mark's aim in clothing his Christology in a conventional genre.[9] Other scholars claim to have found in the first-century church, or in the cultural milieu of Hellenistic society, the protagonists of theological or social views that aroused Mark's opposition. Such studies present the Evangelist's conception of his work as a dialogue with, or a counter attack upon, these opponents. Although quite speculative in their reconstructions of the Evangelist's historical situation, proponents of this approach do "move away from bondage to the distinction between [pre-Markan] tradition and redaction as the only gateway to Mark's theology."[10] Given the present status of the art of criticism, one must acknowledge that a determination of the *Sitz im Leben* of Mark's Gospel entails substantial inference drawn from slight evidence. Accordingly, a variety of approaches to the subject is needed.

* In the development of the two-document solution, some source critics postulated an earlier edition of Mark (*Ur-Marcus* or primitive Mark) to explain omissions in Matthew and Luke of several passages, as well as minor agreements of the later Evangelists against Mark. Efforts to recover "primitive Mark" (or for that matter any *written* sources employed by Mark) are handicapped because of the difficulty in establishing critical criteria for identifying such sources. The unity of Mark's style is also an obstacle to the demarcation of sources.

** N. Perrin, *What is Redaction Criticism?* (1969). Early publications based on source and form critical "conclusions" pursued the aim set forth in the first part of this definition: An Evangelist's theology was to be found in his alteration of sources. This research was (not surprisingly) more successful in treating Matthew and Luke, on the assumption that both used Mark.

NOTES ON THE NARRATIVE OF MARK

A. Introduction: The Beginning of the Good News of Jesus Christ, the Son of God, 1:1–15
    1. The scriptures are fulfilled; the way is prepared, 1:1–8
    2. The anointing and ordeal of the beloved Son, 1:9–13
    3. Transitional summary: Jesus proclaims the nearness of the kingdom of God, 1:14f.

By title (1:1), and by reporting the designation of Jesus at his baptism (1:11), the earliest Evangelist discloses the identity of the one whose story he tells. The man named Jesus is "the Son of God" who came from Nazareth of Galilee to be baptized by John and who, in returning to the same region, "came . . . preaching the gospel of God." As we shall see, Mark reports that this disclosure and this identity were kept secret from human participants in the story until, as Son of man, Jesus suffered many things, was rejected, and killed."[11] But readers of Mark are challenged at the outset to believe (or not believe) that through the good news that Jesus brought and the good news proclaimed by the church about Jesus, God's kingdom comes.

For Mark, John the baptizer was the long-awaited Elijah whose coming signaled the beginning of this divine reign in the End time.[12] Mark is little interested in depicting John's person as a type of holy man; his appointed, prophetic role was to be the precursor of Jesus, to "prepare the way of the Lord." The term *way* appears in the two prophecies Mark cited, one from Isaiah, the other (without acknowledgment) from Malachi. Quite possibly for Mark these oracles signified another dimension of John's role as precursor of Jesus: in the final analysis, John's significance was to be found in a martyr's fate that he shared with Jesus.[13] "The way" of John (as of Jesus and of his disciples), in preparing for the coming of God's kingdom, was not merely characterized as bold proclamation and the administration of baptism, but as a readiness to be "delivered up" to death in faithful acknowledgment of and witness to God's sovereignty.[14] According to Mark, the end of the "way" for Jesus was foreshadowed in his baptism and temptation in the wilderness. Psalm 2:7 (possibly, Gen. 22:2) and Isaiah 42:1 are combined to interpret God's purpose for his "beloved Son": he is not only destined to suffer many things, and be rejected, but he is to be "delivered" into the hands of his enemies to be killed.[15] In his wilderness ordeal God's Son/Servant was not deterred from his resolve to follow in this "way," to accept this divinely appointed ministry.

Mark's introduction is concluded with the sudden appearance in Galilee of the Stronger One (to whom the Baptist had pointed), emerging victorious from his initial contest with Satan, and heralding the good news that God's kingdom is "at hand."[16]

> B. Jesus' First Activity in Galilee: His Authoritative Word and Work Provoke the Pharisee's "Hardness of Heart," 1:16–3:12
>   1. The call of the disciples, 1:16–20
>   2. Manifestations of Jesus' power over demons, illness, sin, and the Mosaic law, 1:21–3:5
>   3. The determination of the Pharisees and Herodians to "destroy" Jesus, 3:6
>   4. Transitional summary: Jesus heals many who come to him from far and wide, 3:7–12

Not only this first narrative section (1:16ff.) but the next two as well (3:13ff., and 6:7ff.) open with a delineation of the role of Jesus' disciples (represented by "the Twelve"), who are challenged to share in Jesus' ministry.[17] Mark 1:16–20 reports the calling of a pair of disciples on two occasions: Peter and Andrew "left their nets," typifying perhaps disciples of Jesus who abandon their livelihood or renounce their possessions (cf. 2:13f.; 10:21); James and John, who "left their father," are others who forsake their families to follow Jesus (cf., 10:29).

In introducing Jesus' public ministry, Mark emphasized his activity as a teacher (1:21f). Subsequently in the Gospel Jesus is so described eleven times; sixteen times it is noted that he taught. Yet the content of Jesus' teaching is sparsely reported in the earliest Gospel (principally Chs. 4, 7, and 13). At the outset Mark seems concerned to claim that Jesus' God-given authority as teacher was attested by his power to heal the sick. On account of these mighty works, his "fame" as an authoritative teacher spread abroad (3:7f). Into some of these narratives Mark introduced Jesus' injunction to secrecy, as though this ministry of healing was not the most crucial activity in revealing his mission as Son of God. In summary statements the Evangelist comments that while Jesus "healed many who were sick with various diseases and cast out many demons . . . he would not permit the demons to speak *because they knew him* (1:34; cf. 3:11f.).

Since the publication in 1901 of a major book authored by William Wrede, it has been widely recognized that Jesus' injunction to secrecy (the messianic self-concealment) constitutes a leitmotif of Mark's gospel tradition and provides an essential clue to the Evangelist's theology.* The significance of this motif—which is not as pervasive or all-inclusive as Wrede contended—can best be seen in its dominant expression later in the Gospel, that is, in those passages in which there is revealed to the disciples (but not comprehended by them) "the mystery" surrounding Jesus' imminent death and the relation of this apparent defeat to the coming of the kingdom of God. Suffice it here to note that it is this "secret" that probably accounts for the charge of Jesus to the demons that they not disclose his true identity (in the passages just cited, 1:34; 3:11f.), and his command to others that his miraculous acts not be publicized (1:44; 7:36).** Mark's point does not seem to be that Jesus' miracles were or should be kept secret. Rather that it is only in the light of the passion and resurrection that Jesus' true identity can be seen or the nature of true discipleship revealed.

Mark 2:1–3:5 contains five stories (probably a pre-Markan complex) reporting Jesus' controversies with "scribes" of the sect of the Pharisees (2:6, 16 [18], 24). The center of interest in these pericopes has shifted from Jesus' healing ministry to his teaching and action vis-à-vis the Mosaic Law, but the issue of Jesus' authority is thereby extended. Jesus is presented as himself offering a sinner forgiveness, as having table fellowship with other sinners, as working on the Sabbath—all actions in contravention of the Torah as interpreted by the Pharisees. Mark's summary (3:6) shows that, for the Evangelist, this notice of the conspiracy to destroy Jesus foreshadows his passion.

*Wrede's book, *The Messianic Secret* (Eng. trans.), is mainly concerned with the historical question of the origin of the secrecy motif rather than its function in Mark's narrative. W. C. Robinson, Jr., "The Quest for Wrede's Secret Messiah," *Interpretation*, 27 (1973): 10ff.; H. C. Kee, *Community of the New Age* (1977), pp. 167ff.

**Jesus' stern commands in Mark's exorcism stories (1:23–26; 9:14–29; 4:36–41; 8:33), his word—"be silent!"—is not intended to curb publicity, it is in itself an attack upon a demonic stronghold. Several references to Jesus' withdrawals from crowds (e.g., 6:31; 7:24; 9:30) probably were occasions for renewal (cf. 1:12f, 1Kgs. 19).

C. Jesus' Ministry Around the Sea of Galilee: Jesus' Authoritative Word and Work Provoke the Separation of "Outsiders" from the Disciples Who are "with" Jesus, or "Around" Him, 3:13–6:6
   1. Jesus' appointment of the twelve "to be with him," 3:13–19
   2. Parables: of the house divided; of the kingdom of God, 3:20–4:34
   3. Additional mighty works: fear versus faith (nonrecognition/recognition), 4:35–5:43
   4. Rejection of Jesus by his countrymen and kinsfolk, 6:1–6a
   5. Transitional summary: Jesus goes among the villages teaching, 6:6b

As in 1:16 so again in 3:13 the reader of Mark learns that a disciple of Jesus is, first of all, one whom he chooses and calls. Not all who "come" to Jesus or who "follow" him are privileged to be his disciples, not all are willing to follow in *his way*. In this section a sharp distinction is drawn between those who are "with" Jesus, and those who are "outsiders."

The sequence of the narrative (3:19–35) exhibits Mark's technique of fitting one story into another. Into a report that Jesus' family sought to "seize" him, on the supposition that he was "out of his mind," Mark inserted the report of the Beelzebub controversy. After this, Mark resumes the homecoming scene. By this technique, called *intercalation*, Mark dramatized the intensification of Jesus' opposition.* Members of the physical family of Jesus, in their acquiescence before the calumny of the scribes, stand among those who are "outside" (3:31). Only those who are "around" Jesus (32, 34) insofar as they "do the will of God," constitute Jesus' true family.[18] Those who know Jesus best, or should (his immediate family), and those who should be best able to discern the will of God (Jerusalem's scribes), are the very persons who reject Jesus—he was "without honor" in "his own country, and among his own kin, and in his own house" (6:4).

Mark treated Jesus' parable of the sower (4:1ff.) as a key to understanding all of his parables (4:11–13). "The secret of the kingdom of God" is probably taken by Mark to refer to the private instruction given to his disciples. Only the parable of the sower is provided a semi-allegorical interpretation but, in view of 4:34, the explanation of 4:14–20 was probably understood by the Evangelist as illustrative of Jesus' practice in training the Twelve.** According to Mark, Jesus also communicated privately to his disciples in ways other than parable interpretation: by clarifying an enigmatic saying (7:14–23), or a prophecy (13:1ff.), or by accounting for a mighty work (9:28f.).

Beginning with 4:35–41, the stories in Mark "differ in style and motif from the preceding miracle stories." The Evangelist probably drew upon a pre-Markan complex consisting of two parallel cycles of gospel tradition, each beginning with a report of an epiphany of Jesus (a mysterious appearance or disclosure) in the midst of a storm at sea, followed by a sequence of healing miracles, and ending with a feeding of the multitudes.[19] Mark's narrative of a succession of boat trips taken at Jesus' initiative, consisting of journeys from Jewish to largely Gentile territories (3:7–10; 4:35; 5:1, 21; 6:32–34, 45, 53–56) and concluding with an extension of Jesus' ministry to regions beyond Galilee (7:24, 31), possibly portrays a major interest of the Evangelist. The proclamation *of* Jesus concerning the kingdom to Jews and Gentiles alike legitimates the proclamation of the Gospel of God (the Church's proclamation *about* Jesus) to all humankind.[20] It is plausible that Mark may have wished to loosen the traditional association of the Eucharist with Jesus' Galilean epiphanies, especially with regard to the feeding stories. At any rate, in Mark's Gospel the Eucharist is instituted by Jesus at the *last* passover meal commemorated with his disciples. The sacramental bread that is broken is his body; the cup, his "blood of the covenant" (14:22–25).[21]

D. The Expanding Ministry: the Epiphanies of Jesus (even to the Gentiles) as Lord over Demons, Sickness, and Death; His Own Disciple's Lack of Understanding, 6:7–8:26

*Intercalation is an interruption of a narrative by the insertion of another between its beginning and its end. Others in Mark are 5:21–24 [25–34] 35–43; 6:7–13 [14–29] 30–32; 11:12–14 [15–19] 20–26; 14:1–2 [3–9] 10–11; 14:2–16 [17–21] 22–25; 14:54 [55–65] 66–72. In each instance the framework and the insertions interpret each other.

**The reader may ask, does "the hardening theory" of Mark 4:11f. present Mark's conclusion that Jesus' parables were esoteric and intended for a select few? Mark reports that all were invited to listen and question (4:1–3; cf. 7:14), and the disciples' lack of understanding is also reproved as the hardening of their hearts. Jesus' instruction of the Twelve in response to their enquiry is given so that the Christian community may benefit from the disciples' employment of Jesus' parables (4:21–25).

1. The sending of the Twelve; the beheading of John the baptizer; the disciples' return, 6:7–31
2. The epiphanies of Jesus: signs given, and signs sought, 6:32–8:13
3. The hardening of the disciples' hearts, 8:14–21 (6:52)
4. Transitional pericope: the progressive opening of the eyes of the blind, 8:22–26

Employing the typical device of intercalation, Mark stressed the equivocal results of the apostles' calling and mission (6:7–31). Sent on their journey by Jesus, and solely accountable to him, they share in his salvific ministry. But they must recognize that as they give their "testimony" their reception will also be mixed, their lives will be at risk, and they could share the fate of John the baptizer (6:14–29).

In spite of the fact that they have been with Jesus, his epiphanies led them not to recognize him but to "utter astonishment" for, Mark reported, "their hearts were hardened" (6:51f; for the harshness of this phrase, cf. 3:5). The questions of Jesus (8:17–21) are intended to recall the description of those who are "outsiders"; Jesus' own disciples are counted among these for their eyes do not yet perceive (cf. 4:11f.)

E. Teaching Concerning God's Destined Way for Jesus and His Disciples, 8:27–10:52
   1. First prediction of the suffering, death, and resurrection of the Son of man; the disciple's messianism discredited; Jesus' cross and resurrection afford the paradigm of discipleship, 8:31–9:1
   2. Proleptic glorification of the Son of man; Elijah's eschatological role, 9:2–13
   3. Healing of the epileptic boy: ineffectual and effectual faith, 9:14–29
   4. Second prediction of the suffering, death, and resurrection of the Son of man; the disciples' lack of understanding and fear; Jesus teaches that authentic discipleship may be hidden in lowly service, in costly self-discipline, 9:30–50
   5. Discipleship and the Torah: paradoxically the child, not the earnest legalist, "enters the kingdom of God," 10:1–31
   6. Third prediction of the imminent suffering, death, and ressurrection of the Son of man; the disciples' ambitious presumption prompts the depiction of the servant-paradigm, 10:32–45
   7. Transitional pericope: the disciple whose eyes are opened follows Jesus "on the way," 10:46–52

The middle section of Mark's narrative, (8:22–10:52), contains important clues to major theological concerns of the Evangelist. He portrays faithfully Jesus' self-understanding (Mark's Christological purpose), together with Jesus' teaching concerning those whom he calls to follow him "on the way" (Mark's discipleship theme). The location of two transitional pericopes (8:22–26 and 10:46–52) probably functions as an *inclusio,* an editorial device employed by Hellenistic authors to designate a literary unit. If so, then Mark presents Jesus' action with respect to his disciples' incomprehension (of what he says about himself and about his true followers) as the cure of blindness. Only those disciples whose eyes have been opened to the mystery of Jesus' person and of their relation to him, and the implications of both for the coming of God's kingdom, are able to follow "on the way." (Cf. 10:35–38 and 10:51f; note repeated references to "the way," 8:27; 9:33, 10:17, 32.)

Within this narrative unit a threefold pattern, thrice repeated, can be observed: (1) Jesus' announcement concerning the necessity of his passion, is (2) received by his disciples as incomprehensible and resisted, which (3) becomes the occasion for Jesus' teaching concerning the nature of true discipleship. (Examine the passages designated 1, 4, and 6 in the above outline.) According to Mark, no one can understand Jesus or follow him without acknowledging that the suffering of the Son of man and of his followers is the necessary prelude to entering into glory, to the coming of God's kingdom in power. Only in the light of his cross and resurrection is Jesus' historic ministry rightly understood, the meaning of true discipleship comprehended. For the present, the disciple is called to follow the Master through the reality of suffering in the hope of experiencing the surpassing reality of the glory that the faithful will share with him at his (second) coming.[22]

F. Jesus' Journey to Jerusalem; His Actions in the Temple, and Related Teaching, 11:1–13:37
1. The ironies of Jesus' triumphal entry, 11:1–11
2. The fate of the unfruitful fig tree a sign of the temple's fate, 11:12–25
3. A third visit to the temple; Jesus' teaching; his avoidance of entrapments, 11:27–12:27
4. A scribe and a widow endorse Jesus' temple teaching, 12:28–44
5. Prediction of the temple's destruction, 13:1f.: Jesus dissociates the hope of the coming kingdom from this catastrophe, 13:3–23; proclaims the imminent but undatable coming of the Son of man, and urges watchfulness, 13:24–37

Mark's depiction of the approach of Jesus and his followers to Jerusalem is fraught with irony. The same lack of understanding is exhibited here that the disciples of Jesus displayed in their earlier responses. The procession of pilgrims celebrates the imminent establishment of the Davidic kingdom on Mount Zion.[23] Jesus' followers mistakenly suppose that he enters Jerusalem to establish the eschatological kingdom in power and glory; Jesus enters the city to be "rejected by the elders and the chief priests and scribes, and be killed," to be hailed, derisively, "the king of the Jews," hanging on a cross. For Mark the regal authority of Jesus, the Son of God, was manifested in this moment of humiliation and agony, acknowledged first of all not by "the Twelve," not by the wider circle of Jesus' disciples, but by a Roman centurion participating in the mock execution of "the king of Israel" (15:22–39).

Mark's account of "the cleansing of the temple" so-called is enclosed in typical fashion by two parts of the story of "the cursing of the fig tree" (11:12–25). By this juxtaposition Mark interprets the meaning of Jesus' action in the temple. The fig tree, Israel,[24] which has not borne proper fruit and which is therefore cursed by Jesus, is symbolic of the temple's barrenness, which prompted the malediction of Jesus and his prophecy of its imminent destruction (13:2). By so framing the story of the temple's "cleansing," Mark portrays Jesus' action as prophetic of God's judgment upon that lack of faith manifested by the custodians of the temple in their violent resistance to Jesus' teaching, and upon their failure to declare the temple "a house of prayer for all nations." Does Mark imply that with Jesus "the right time" *(kairos)* had arrived for the replacement of the temple, a national institution, with a new and universal form of worship: faith in the gospel, an openness to what God is ready to give, a faith which, assured of God's forgiveness, is forgiving (11:22–25. Cf. 14:57f)?[25]

Features of the story of the challenge of Jesus' authority by the temple authorities (11:27–33), and the parable that follows, spoken against its custodians (12:1–12), reflect the influence of early Christian conflicts with Judaism.[26] But it was Mark who framed these pericopes with notes concerning the response of the temple authorities: they scorned and feared the multitudes attending to Jesus' teaching and they actively sought to arrest and destroy him (11:18; 12:12, 6–8). Christians perceived that by his resurrection Jesus had become the "cornerstone" of the new temple, the Christian community (12:10f). Those "tenants" of the old temple who "left Jesus and went away" were in effect discrediting themselves and giving place to others who are appointed to care for God's people (12:9).

Mark reports that further attacks of members of the Jerusalem Sanhedrin upon Jesus, within the temple precincts, were futile. They were not able to draw him into controversial debate with represenatives of Jewish sects (12:13–17, 18–27). The upshot was that Jesus seized the initiative. An admiring scribe's question enabled Jesus to locate the heart of his teaching, concerning the reality of God's reign, in Israel's fundamental creed: "Hear, Israel, the Lord our God, the Lord is one" (12:29; Deut. 6:4f.). Yet in the context of Mark's narrative this citation of the *Shema* extends the theme of Jesus' criticism of the temple: the oneness of God implies the unity of all the nations that the existing temple ritual did not recognize. But what is worth more than "all whole burnt offerings and sacrifices" is the double commandment of love, which, if taken with full seriousness, is creative of a new community transcending all national identities. Jesus' invitation to Mark's readers is this: anyone who acknowledges this Torah standard to be "first of all" is "not far from the kingdom of God" and may enter it by becoming his disciple.

The ministry of Jesus in Jerusalem's temple is climaxed by his prophecy of its imminent, total destruction. Mark's location of this discourse of Jesus—a discourse of unusual length—and especially its introduction (13:1–5a), bring into sharp relief the Evangelist's anti-temple posture. Cast in the form of a last will and testament and delivered on the Mount of Olives "opposite the temple," Jesus' discourse directly relates problems concerning expectations of the coming of the Messiah and of other events associated with the End, to the devastation of Jerusalem.*

An *inclusio* (13:5f., 21f.) brackets the initial segment of this discourse (verses 5b–23). Mark's readers are warned that the succession of catastrophes described in verses 7–20 will give rise to premature, false claims that the Christ has come for a final time, that his Parousia has already taken place.

In the next segment (verses 24–27), Mark writes that when "the Son of man" does in fact return the signs will be unmistakable, evident to all (verses 24–26), especially to the elect (verse 27). Nevertheless, while the Evangelist warns against premature anticipations of the End, he declares that it will come

*Various views concerning the origin of Mark 13 are that it is (1) a farewell discourse of Jesus; or (2) a Jewish pamphlet occasioned by Caligula's threat to place his image in Jerusalem's temple (40 C.E.), preserved perhaps in

in the near future. Temporary delays must not lead one to assume falsely that the End is to be delayed indefinitely or may not come at all.

The discourse is concluded with an urgent statement of the one theme that is consistently developed within Mark 13: readers of the Gospel are cautioned to be ever on the alert; this time, for the coming of "the Son of man in great power and glory" (verses 32–37: cf. verses 5, 9, 23). Because none can reckon in advance the time of the Parousia, watchfulness is mandated.

The development in Mark 13 of a theme important to the Evangelist (most impressively set forth, as we have seen in 8:27–10:52) is noteworthy: Christ's disciples may not hope to escape the fate of their crucified Lord. They too will be persecuted by Jews and Gentiles (verse 9), hated for his "name's sake" (verse 13). Nevertheless, their preaching of the gospel to all nations is essential to the fulfilment of the eschatological scenario (verse 10). The threatening aspects of Mark's apocalypse are overshadowed by wondrous promises. Note the absence of judgment in the Parousia scene. The sole emphasis is upon the universal gathering of the elect (verses 24–27). "He who endures to the end will be saved" (verse 13; cf. 4:14–20; 10:28–31).

Much attention has been given to 13:14, which refers to an event causing sufferings of incomparable intensity. Beyond doubt Daniel 9:27, 11:31, and 12:11 provided the imagery, which identifies the incident as a desecration of Jerusalem's temple. But the question is: To what first-century events does this crisis refer?

The "desolating sacrilege" is identified by some historians as "a coded reference" to the Roman general Titus who commanded the final assault on the temple ("where *he* should not be"). The great "tribulation" identifies the terrible carnage and the agonies endured during the Roman-Jewish war, 66–70 C.E.[27]

Others, however, have argued for a pre-70 dating. "The lack of precision in the prophetic description of the fate of Jerusalem in Mark 13, while not conclusive evidence, points to its having been written prior to the events which it depicts . . . The imminence of catastrophe and the sure expectation of deliverance following the doom of the city of Jerusalem confirms this impression." The present writer agrees with this latter position: the whole of Mark was probably composed in the late 60s.[28] While the evidence is nonexplicit and can be interpreted either way, a date for Mark's Gospel can be fixed "within quite narrow limits."[29]

The antitemple teaching of Jesus is, in either event, applied by Mark to his own generation. The temple was "cursed," and whether at the time of the Evangelist it still stood or lay in ruins, it had fallen into the hands of evil powers. The temple's desecration and destruction should occasion no surprise or alarm for Mark's readers because Jesus in his actions and teaching sealed its doom, became himself the cornerstone of a new temple to be founded (the Markan community formed its nucleus), and dissociated Jerusalem's tragedy from his Parousia.

G. The Passion and Resurrection of the Son of Man, 14:1–16:8
    1. The plot against Jesus, 14:1f. / Matt. 26: [1] 2 [3–4a] 4b–5
    2. The anointing at Bethany, 14:3–9 / Matt. 26:6–13

a text adapted by pre-Markan Christians to meet a later crisis; (3) a creation of Christian prophets constrained by an outbreak of apocalyptic fanaticism to utter this "word of the Lord" (Jesus); or (4) Mark's own composition based on scattered sayings of Jesus addressed to his community shortly before or after 70 C.E. G. R. Beasley-Murray, *Jesus and the Future* (1954); L. Gaston, *No Stone on Another* (1970); Kee, *Community of the New Age*, pp. 43–45.

3. Summary: the treachery of Judas, 14:10f. / Matt. 26:14–16
4. The Passover Meal, 14:12–31/ Matt. 26:17–24 [25] 26–35
5. Gethsemane, 14:32–42 / Matt. 26:36–46
6. Betrayal and arrest; the flight of the disciples, 14:43–52 / Matt. 26:47–51 [52–54] 55–56
7. The priests's hearing and condemnation of Jesus, 14:53–65 / Matt. 26:57–68
8. Peter's denial, 14:66–72 / Matt. 26:69–75
9. Trial before Pilate, 15:1–15 / Matt. 27:lf. [3–10] 11–18 [19] 20–23 [24–25] 26
10. The crucifixion, 15:16–36 / Matt. 27:27–49
11. God's Son revealed in dying, 15:37–39 / Matt. 27:50–51a [51b–53] 54
12. Summary: the attending women, 14:40f. / Matt. 27:55f.
13. The burial, 15:42–47 / Matt. 27:57–61
14. Visit of the women to an empty tomb, 16:1–8 / Matt. [27:62–66] 28:1–10

Redaction criticism of Mark's Gospel has demonstrated that the Evangelist's editorial work is evident in his account of Jesus' passion, as in the earlier parts of his narrative. This judgment takes exception to the opinion of pioneers in form-critical analysis, which was that the content of the passion narrative was essentially established in pre-Markan tradition.[30] It is unlikely that Markan contributions can be identified with precision, but several themes have attracted the notice of special students of Mark and can be mentioned. Mark's witness to the failure of Jesus' disciples is repeated with poignant sharpness in the passion narrative (14:10, 18–24, 27–31, 37–46, 50, 66–72).[31] Also, Mark's emphasis upon Jesus' anti-temple teaching—a pervasive theme from chapter 11 forward—reaches its climax in Jesus' trial by "the chief priests and scribes." Jesus' opposition to the temple led to his arrest, but at his trial he is portrayed as one who would "build another not made with hands" (14:55–61). As a reference to Jerusalem's temple the confused testimony was "false," but as a reference to Mark's Christian readers, who formed the new temple, the word was a fulfilled prophecy.

A third prominent Markan motif is also exhibited in the Gospel's account of Jesus' trial before the Sanhedrin: the self-identification of Jesus as Son of man. The earlier critical response of Jesus to the title "Christ," as others applied it to him, should be recalled (8:29ff.). Although Jesus did not then reject the title confessed by Peter, he enjoined silence and qualified its application to himself by speaking of the necessity of the suffering of the Son of man. At his trial Jesus accepts the title in public, but qualifies it in relation to the Son of man's heavenly session and future coming (14:61b, 62).

In the trial narrative the Evangelist brings together his essential Christological teaching, patterned as a divinely willed suffering followed by vindication, a hiddenness in which is unveiled the messianic secret.[32]

The trial of Jesus by the Sanhedrin prepares the way for Mark's portrayal of Jesus' crucifixion as the enthronement of Christ as "Son of God." The Roman governor, Pilate, is the first to refer to Jesus as "king"; 15:2.[33] Thereafter the crowd that clamored to have Jesus crucified hails him as king (verse 12); the soldiers, mocking Jesus, salute him as king (verses 16–20); the temple authorities ridicule him as king, (verse 31f.). In Mark's passion narrative the perpetrators of Jesus' death thus confer royalty upon him. Ironically, Jesus' crucifixion is a coronation event: "the inscription of the charge against him, fastened to his cross, read, "the King of the Jews" (verse 26).

Two immediate consequences of Jesus' death are reported in Mark: the temple's curtain was torn in two "from top to bottom" (verse 38), and a Roman centurion perceived Jesus to be "Son of God" (verse 39). "By dying a death instigated by the temple authorities, Jesus precipitates the demise of the authorities traditional place of power." In his own death, Godforsaken and seemingly powerless, Jesus, the herald of the coming kingdom of God, is acknowledged by an outsider to be God's Son—an unlikely witness, but "the only true confession made by a human being in the Gospel." According to Mark, the messianic secret was impenetrable during the lifetime of Jesus. For this reason none of Jesus' disciples, absent from the scene of his cross, understood the significance of Jesus' person—until there were witnesses to his resurrection.*

Is it credible that Mark ended his Gospel with the episode recorded in 16:1–8? The present writer now agrees with those who hold that his "conclusion" is the original one. The earliest and best manuscripts support this judgment, and the wide divergence of Matthew and Luke at this point indicate that their copies of the Gospel ended here. Moreover, this conclusion is consonant with interests and concerns of the earliest Evangelist.**

Mark 16:1–8 "makes the essential point of Jesus' resurrection with all necessary emphasis, and shows, in the reaction of the women the amazement and holy awe which the news of the resurrection must always arouse in those who really understand its import."[34] We have seen that Mark presents Jesus' rejection as resulting from the ambiguity of his personal history. Perhaps in conclusion he wished to witness to the ambiguous relation of Jesus to his disciples—even as their risen Lord: only the Parousia will clear away the mystery of his person—for all who heed Jesus' admonition: "and what I say to you I say to all: watch" (13:37).

DATE, AUTHORSHIP, AND LOCATION OF MARK'S GOSPEL

As noted above, the present writer's view is that Mark should be dated in the mid-60s, perhaps just before the outbreak of the Jewish war with Rome.[35] Recall now the second-century traditions concerning the writing of Mark. According to Papias, someone named Mark, an interpreter of Peter, compiled this Gospel. This ascription has been widely accepted, for Mark was neither an apostle nor a person otherwise sufficiently prominent in the Church to have a purely anonymous writing attributed to him. But who was Mark? The answer to this question in the second century possibly rested upon an inference drawn from I Peter 5:13. Mark had assisted Peter in "Babylon," that is, in Rome.[36] I Peter attests the currency of the belief—in the early years of the second century at the latest—that Peter and Mark were in Rome together. The tradition of Papias and Irenaeus may also presuppose a belief that Rome was the place of Peter's martyrdom. This martyrdom tradition finds support in a writing dating from the last decade of the first century, 1 Clement.[37] Since there is a tendency in ancient church tradition to bring together references to all persons of the same

*Kelber, *Mark's Story of Jesus,* pp 82:

Mark's portrayal of Jesus' disciples, "the Twelve," is complex. The claim seems to be unfounded that the Evangelist wrote his Gospel to depict the disciples as representatives of a Christological "heresy" current in Mark's church (T. W. Weeden, *Mark —Traditions in Conflict*). Yet the disciples' failure probably serves Mark's Christology: they did not receive Jesus' word concerning his suffering and death, therefore they could not understand his teaching concerning his person and fate. P. Achtemeier, *Mark,* p. 100. E. Best, "The Role of the Disciples in Mark," *NTS,* 23 (1977): 377ff. R. C. Tannehill, "The Disciples in Mark," *JRel,* 57 (1977): 386ff.

**Arguments for a "lost ending" are that Mark 8:31; 9:9, 31; 10:34 lead one to expect a narrative of one or more post-resurrection appearances;

Mark 14:28 looks forward to Jesus' meeting with disciples in Galilee, and the mention of Peter (16:7) anticipates a restoration of the disciple who denied his Lord.

name, it is uncertain whether the author of the Second Gospel should be identified with the "John whose surname was Mark" who appears in Acts and in letters of Paul.[38] Form-critical analysis has demonstrated that Mark's narrative was based on a community tradition, and although some of it doubtless originated in Peter's testimony and that of other eyewitnesses, this derivation could not have been direct. In this connection it may be observed that uncertainty concerning the author's identification and the tracking of his sources in no way detracts from this Gospel's authority as "gospel."

Various places have been suggested for the writing of Mark's Gospel: Alexandria, Antioch, Galilee, Rome. Rome remains the most likely location. We have observed many references in the Gospel to the necessity of suffering and persecution for Jesus' disciples. Their *Sitz im leben* may be the threatening situation facing the church in Rome at the time of the Neronic persecutions.

The "Annals" of the Roman historian Tacitus provide an important source of knowledge of the situation facing Christians in Rome in the 60s of the first century. It was rumored that the great fire that broke out there in the winter 64–65 C.E. had been started by Nero to make way for the enlargement of his palace complex and gardens. "Therefore," writes Tacitus,

> to dispel the report Nero made a scapegoat of others, and inflicted the most exquisite tortures upon a class hated for their abominations, whom the populace called Christians. The Christus from whom the name had its origin had been executed during the reign of Tiberius by the procurator Pontius Pilate. The mischievous superstition was thus checked for the moment, but was reviving again, not only in Judea, the original seat of the evil, but even in the capital, where all that is anywhere hideous or loathsome finds its center and flourishes. Accordingly some were first put on trial; they pleaded guilty, and upon the information gathered from them a large number were convicted, not so much on the charge of arson as because of their hatred of humanity. Wanton cruelty marked their execution. Covered with skins of wild beasts they were torn in pieces by dogs, and thus perished; many were crucified, or burned alive. . . .[39]

One is cautioned in providing for the Gospel this *Sitz im Leben*. Mark 13 implies widespread disturbances (verses 7f.), and there is no evidence to support the supposition that Nero's persecution of Christians spread beyond Rome. Perhaps the most that can be concluded is that the Gospel was written for a church predominately Gentile, located in an area outside of Palestine,[40] that was experiencing or expecting persecution for the sake of the gospel. The readers of this Gospel, then as now, are challenged to believe that they live between the announcement that with Jesus, God's kingdom dawns (1:14f.), and the promise of its final coming is fulfilled in his return in power and glory (14:62). It cannot be correct to say that Mark's purpose excludes biographical interest, yet his primary aim seems to have been to proclaim what the church's traditions concerning Jesus meant, and mean, to disciples who follow in "the way" of the Son of God who "goes before" them into the future.

NOTES

1. In referring to the composers of the Gospels as "evangelists," one acknowledges the judgment (both ancient and modern) that these authors were not merely editors of the Jesus tradition but proclaimers of the gospel in narrative form.

2. Readers who wish to probe the issues relating to the unity and diversity of the Gospel accounts concerning Jesus are referred to the October 1979 issue of *Int.* See also O. Cullmann, "Plurality of the Gospels as a Theological Problem," in A. J. B. Higgins, ed., *The Early Church* (1956), pp. 39ff.

3. Eusebius, *H.E.* v.8ff, citing Irenaeus, *Adv. Haer.* III. 1. i.

4. Eusebius, *H.E.* III. 39. 15.

5. H. C. Kee, "Mark's Gospel in Recent Research," *Int.* 32 (1978): 353ff.; N. Perrin, "The Interpretation of the Gospel of Mark," *Int.* 30 (1976): 115ff.

6. H. Anderson, *The Gospel of Mark* (1976), p. 14.

7. Bultmann, *The History of the Synoptic Tradition* (1963), pp. 347ff.; cf. M. Dibelius, *From Tradition to Gospel* (London: Ivor Nicholson, 1934), pp. 229–232.

8. R. H. Stein, "What is Redaktionsgeschichte? *JBL* 88 (1969): 45–56; and "The Proper Methodology for Ascertaining a Markan Redaction History," *NovT* 13 (1971): 181–198. N. Perrin, "The Interpretation of Mark," pp. 115ff.

9. M. Hadas and M. Smith, *Heroes and Gods: Spiritual Biographies in Antiquity* (1965); C. H. Talbert, *What is a Gospel?* (1977), Ch. 4. Cf. H. C. Kee, *Jesus in History*, 1970), pp. 136ff. Also, D. O. Via, *Kerygma and Comedy in the New Testament* (1975).

10. J. R. Donahue, "Introduction: From Passion Tradition to Passion Narrative," in W. H. Kelber, ed., *The Passion in Mark: Studies on Mark 14–16* (1976), pp. 17f. T. J. Weeden, *Mark—Traditions in Conflict* (1971); Kelber, *The Kingdom in Mark* (1974), pp. 129–147. Note E. Trocme's analysis of "the aversions displayed, and the causes defended by Mark," *The Formation of the Gospel According to Mark* (1975).

11. Mark 8:31; 14:60–62; 15:39. A distinctive feature of Mark's Christology is his deliberate use of "Son of man" to interpret the major titles "Son of God" and "Christ" (which some persons in Mark's community were applying to Jesus in misleading ways?). See further pp. 217f.

12. Implicitly, Mark 1:6; explicitly, 9:13.

13. Mark 6:14–29; 11:27–33. P. Achtemeier, "Mark as Interpreter of the Jesus Traditions," *Int.* (1978): 342.

14. Mark 1:14. The term translated "arrested," also "betrayed" (14:10f., 18, etc.), is the same word used in Mark 9:31, 10:33: to be delivered (up), or handed over, probably echoing Isa. 53:6, 12, as connoting divine ordination of the Servant's redemptive suffering. R. P. Martin, *Mark, Evangelist and Theologian* (1972), pp. 66–69. W. Wink, *John the Baptist in the Gospel Tradition* (1968). In Mark, "John's suffering as Elijah-incognito prepares the way for the fate of Jesus. . . ." p. 17.

15. Mark 15:23–39; 8:31; 9:31; 10:33f.

16. Mark 3:27. Note also 8:33: again God's way for Jesus is threatened by Satanic temptation. Doubtless Jesus' demon exorcisms were viewed by Mark as evidence of a continuing (successful) contest with Satan (1:21ff.; 5:1ff., etc.).

17. E. Schweizer comments that Mark does not limit Jesus' call of disciples to the Twelve. In 8:34f. Mark states explicitly that Jesus "called to him the multitude, with his disciples, and said to them, 'If any man would come after me, let him deny himself and take up his cross and follow me.' Cf. 4:10. "The Portrayal of the Life of Faith in the Gospel of Mark," *Int.* 32 (1978): 391.

18. P. Achtemeier, "Mark as Interpreter," pp. 342ff. Mark 10:28–31. For the significance of this redefinition of "family" for the Markan community's understanding of itself, see H. C. Kee, *Community of the New Age* (1977), pp. 89f.

19. P. Achtemeier, "The Origin and Function of the Pre-Marcan Miracle Catanae," *JBL* 91 (1972): 205ff.; E. J. Mally, "The Gospel According to Mark," *JBC* 42 (1968), 38ff.

20. W. H. Kelber, *Mark's Story of Jesus* (1979), pp. 30–42.

21. Achtemeier adduces evidence that Mark de-emphasized the eucharistic overtones of

the two feeding stories in his source. Thus Mark "was able to preserve the valuable material . . . about Jesus' career, while at the same time subordinating them to his own understanding of Jesus and the Eucharist." "Origin and Function," p. 221; V. Robbins, "Last Meal: Preparation, Betrayal, and Absence," in W. Kelber, ed., *The Passion in Mark* (1976), pp. 21ff.

22. R. H. Lightfoot, *History and Interpretation in the Gospels* (1934), pp. 76–80; N. Perrin, *What is Redaction Criticism* (1969), pp. 53–56; P. Achtemeier, "Mark as Interpreter," pp. 347f. The location in Mark's narrative of "the transfiguration" (9:2–8), provided a preview of the glory to come. Mark's conviction is thereby re-enforced that for Jesus, as well as for his uncomprehending disciples, there is no triumph without suffering and self-sacrifice. Kelber, *Mark's Story of Jesus*, pp. 53–55.

23. Amos 9:11; Jer. 23:5ff.; Isa. 8:6ff.

24. For example, Jer. 8:13; Hos. 9:10

25. Perhaps Mark's use of the same term, *kairos*, in 1:14 and 11:3 was intentionally ironic. For the temple authorities, and for Jesus' disciples, it was not the right time for fruiting, i.e., for the extension beyond Israel of God's kingly rule and its blessings to the gentiles (Isa. 56:7). The Evangelist affirmed that "the right time" was marked by the proclamation of Jesus at the outset of his ministry, in Galilee and beyond its borders. Yet in another sense, within the time frame of passion week, "the right time" was not yet, although it was fast approaching: the temple's judgment, and the mission of Jesus' disciples "to all nations" were a consequence of his death and resurrection. See Mark 15:37f; 13:10.

26. H. Anderson, *The Gospel of Mark*, pp. 269–271.

27. W. H. Kelber, *The Kingdom in Mark* (1974), pp. 111f; S. G. F. Brandon, "The Date of the Markan Gospel," NTS 7 (1961): 126ff.

28. Kee, *Community of the New Age*, pp. 100f.; H. Anderson, *The Gospel of Mark*, p. 26; J. A. T. Robinson, *Redating the New Testament* (1976), pp. 15–19.

29. D. E. Nineham, *The Gospel of St. Mark* (1962), pp. 41f. Note Kümmel's caution, INT², p. 98.

30. P. Achtemeier, *Mark*, pp. 82ff.; in Kelber, *The Passion in Mark*, pp. 153–159. Dibelius, Bultmann, and the English form critic, V. Taylor, agreed that the Markan passion narrative preserved an earlier consecutive account. See, e.g., M. Dibelius, *From Tradition to Gospel*, pp. 178–217.

31. "The picture of Jesus, bereft of the companionship of his disciples, going to his lonely death dramatically establishes . . . that the disciple is never above or equal to his Master but can only follow him in 'cross-bearing' at a distance (14:54; 15:40) and on the ground of what the Master has done on his own beforehand." H. Anderson, *The Gospel of Mark*, p. 303.

32. J. R. Donahue, *Are You the Christ? The Trial Narrative in the Gospel of Mark* (1973), pp. 178–181. The Messianic secret is "unveiled" in that Jesus as the suffering Son of man formally discloses in what sense he is "the Christ, the Son of the Blessed": yet only as the enthroned and coming Son of man will his "full identity" be revealed. See also "Temple, Trial, and Royal Christology," in Kelber, *The Passion in Mark*, p. 71.

33. It should be remembered, however, that the body of Jesus was anointed "beforehand for burying" (14:8) by a woman in Bethany. Did Mk. thereby wish to affirm that Jesus' coronation began with his death, being manifested before his resurrection?

34. D. Nineham, *The Gospel of St. Mark*, p. 441. See Lightfoot, *Gospel Message of St. Mark* (1963), pp. 190ff. Perhaps Mark purposed that the last word of the Gospel be God's word (brought by the angel his messenger), confirming the word of Jesus (cf. 16:7; 14:28), which rendered eloquent the women's astonished silence and holy fear.

35. See p. 121.

36. Rev. 14:8; 16:19, and others; 2 Bar. IX. 1; *Siby*. Or. V. 143.

37. Cullmann, *Peter* (1962), pp. 89ff. See also pp. 401f.

38. Acts 12:12, 25; 13:13; 15:36ff; Col. 4:10; Philem. 24 (2 Tim. 4:11).

39. E. T. Merrill's translation. Cited in A. E. J. Rawlinson, *St. Mark* (London: Methuen, 1942), pp. xvif.

40. Commentators note that Mark assumes that his readers were unfamiliar with Aramaic (5:41; 7:34; 15:34), and that the Evangelist betrays his unfamiliarity with Palestinian geography and regional customs.

<table>
<tr><td>

Chapter

7

</td><td>

The Gospel of Luke

</td></tr>
</table>

THE late-second-century tradition that Luke was the author of the Third Gospel has been reported above.[1] Possibly earlier, indirect support is provided by the dialogues of Justin Martyr. Justin refers to the Gospels as "the memoirs of the apostles," composed by them and by "those who followed them." This last clause may be a reference to Mark and Luke, respectively, as followers of Peter and Paul.[2] The Muratorian canon reports the convictions of the Church at Rome around 180–200 C.E.

> The third gospel according to Luke. After the ascension of Christ, Luke, whom Paul had taken with him as an expert in the way, wrote under his own name and according to his own understanding. He had not, of course, seen the Lord in the flesh, and therefore he begins to tell the story from the birth of John on, insofar as it was accessible to him.[3]

It is often said that a presumption favoring the Lucan authorship of the Third Gospel and Acts is that Luke was not a prominent person in the apostolic age or later. Is it likely, one is asked, that anonymous writings should have been ascribed to a person who was neither an apostle nor a follower of "the Twelve"? It might be answered that any evidence which the New Testament affords could have been observed by second-century Christians as well as by modern ones. The same data used to corroborate Lucan authorship today might have given rise to this tradition.

LUKE IN THE NEW TESTAMENT

In our examination of the prefaces to Luke-Acts it was noted that the "me" of Luke 1:3 may anticipate the author's use of "we" in Acts 16:10 and in certain other passages thereafter. These abrupt shifts from the third person to the first person plural (e.g., Acts 20:5–6; 21:7) have been explained as evidence that the author at such places used his own or someone's travel notes. The question therefore arises: Who was with Paul during the times and places noted in the "we" passages? For the answer one can turn to letters traditionally ascribed to Paul. Colossians is of special interest.[4] Some of Paul's companions mentioned in Colossians are ruled out, for they are distinguished by name from the diarist in the "we" sections. Furthermore, if the diarist was a Gentile Christian, as has been commonly inferred from his interests, the field of choice is narrowed. The most likely candidate becomes "Luke the beloved physician."[5]

A comparison of the language and style of the "we" sections and the rest of

Acts leads to the conclusion that if Luke was the diarist he was also the compiler of the whole of Acts.[6] Furthermore, if Luke was the author of Acts he was also the author of the Third Gospel, for the prefaces of the two books link them as parts of a single work. The "trump card" sometimes used by defenders of the ancient church tradition is that the medical language of Luke-Acts establishes that the author was a physician. This contention has met with vigorous, oft-cited objections.[7] Yet the medical interest of the writer of Luke-Acts cannot be denied, and his choice of terms is, at the least, compatible with the tradition.[8]

This brief summary may lead the reader to conclude that the witness of the ancient Church is strongly supported by evidence that the New Testament provides. But some argue that the case for the Lucan authorship is discredited by the discrepancies between the Paul of the Acts and the Paul of the epistles, both with respect to events of his life and his theology. Could Luke, Paul's occasional travel companion, have authored such discrepancies? Conclusions concerning the origin of Luke-Acts must again be deferred.[9]

THE SOURCES AND PLAN OF LUKE'S GOSPEL

We have seen that among the several theories concerning the composition of the Third Gospel, "the two-document solution" is the most widely held: Mark and Q were Luke's principal sources. In addition, Luke drew from other sources, written or oral or both, identified as "L" or "Special Luke."[10]

Luke preserves the order of Mark with remarkable fidelity. Of the 109 paragraphs before Luke 19, only three occupy a different position from parallels in Mark.[11] Up to the passion narrative, passages in Mark appear in the following sections: 4:31–44; 5:12–6:19; 8:4–9:50; 18:15–43. Luke's omissions from Mark, however, are noteworthy, especially the section Mark 6:45–8:26, commonly known as "Luke's great omission." It is not necessary or probable to account for these omissions by an appeal to some form of an Ur-Marcus theory. Several of them can be explained as Luke's avoidance of duplications.[12] Partial parallels to Mark in other sources are sometimes preferred.[13] Some of Mark's stories were thought misleading or unedifying to Gentile readers.[14] For the rest, we can assume that Luke needed room for non-Markan traditions that he favored.

Luke's revisions of Mark's language are more drastic than Matthew's, but probably some of the same motives prompted him to make them. Like Matthew, Luke abbreviated some of Mark's stories. Even Mark's meager report of Jesus' teaching is somewhat abridged in Luke.[15] He removed redundancies, rewrote some awkward passages, and replaced Mark's nonliterary expressions with elegant phrases. Moreover, doctrinal motives may have determineid several of Luke's revisions. Reverence for the person of "the Lord" is shown, and consideration for his disciples.[16]

Luke's editing procedures can be summarized as follows. He exercised the greatest freedom in revising the introductions and conclusions to Mark's stories; he is less free in revising the narratives themselves. The words of Jesus are quoted most exactly.[17] (The composition of Luke's passion narrative and its relation to Mark will be discussed later.)

Most of the Q tradition is either located in one short sequence, 6:20–8:3 (known as Luke's "lesser interpolation"), or in another, much longer section,

9:51–18:14 (commonly referred to as Luke's "greater interpolation"). Probably Luke held the order of Q, as well as that of Mark, in greater respect than did Matthew. The First Evangelist freely transposed, combined, and conflated his sources. Luke's practice is to select passages from one source and to follow it to the exclusion of another, and thus incorporate blocks of material from his sources.[18]

It is almost universally considered that Chapters 1 and 2 stand apart from the apostolic tradition contained in sources reporting Jesus' public ministry. The unity of the infancy narratives and their peculiar style and language distinguish them from the remainder of Luke's special sources. It is likely that this prologue to Jesus' ministry was composed by the Third Evangelist, based upon the LXX and various Jewish-Christian sources.[19]

The variety of the rest of "Special Luke" makes it difficult if not impossible to identify precanonical collections. Both narrative and discourse are included. Some of the narrative peculiar to Luke may have been used by him in place of their partial parallels in Mark.[20] Some narratives amplify or illustrate Mark's outline.[21] Yet other pericopes have no connection with the Markan traditions.

In his account of the passion of Jesus, Luke has transposed the order of Mark's narrative to an unparalleled extent. Two explanations for this are offered. One opinion is that the L tradition contained a passion narrative that provided the major source for the conclusion of the Third Gospel, into which have been interpolated some Markan contributions.[22] The alternative view is that Mark provided Luke with the foundation for the passion story, which he amplified with some details from his special source.[23]

These alternatives are often related to opposing accounts of the procedure followed by the Third Evangelist in writing his Gospel. Those who judge that his passion narrative was constructed upon a non-Markan framework with Markan insertions, hypothesize that Luke composed a first draft of the *entire* Gospel (excluding the infancy narratives) from Q and L material. Into this "proto-Luke," blocks of Mark were later inserted (when a copy of this Gospel came into his hands), and the whole was given a new preface, Luke 1–2. Alternatively, the proponents of the Markan hypothesis hold that Luke employed Mark's outline as the framework for his entire narrative, beginning with Chapter 3, into which he inserted material from his other sources, and for which he composed an introduction.

The importance of "the proto-Luke hypothesis" consists in its proponent's claim that Luke contains an independent narrative of Jesus' ministry, parts of which were written at least as early as Mark, and which confirms much of the latter's outline and substance. It is also said that the traditional view of the origin of the Third Gospel derives some support from this hypothesis: proto-Luke might have been written by a companion of Paul as early as 56 or 60 C.E. in Caesarea or Rome.

Although the proto-Luke hypothesis has these attractive features, it has not been supported by the majority of scholars, who espouse the alternative.[24] Several passages, crucial to a proto-Luke theory, probably represent the Evangelist's editing and enrichment of Mark from oral and written sources, rather than pericopes taken from an independent, non-Markan narrative. Concede this in a few if not all of the passages in question, and "the gospel-like document" called proto-Luke dissolves into an amorphous assortment of traditional materials.

THE DATE OF LUKE AND PLACE OF ORIGIN

There is some evidence in the Gospel that provides a clue to its date. The reference to Jerusalem, the "forsaken," (Luke 13:35) and a comparison of Luke 19:41–44 and 21:20–24, with their Markan parallels, suggest that Luke looked back upon the siege and destruction of Jerusalem.[25]

Two critical assumptions make the margin of uncertainty concerning the date of Luke very narrow indeed: the dependence of Luke upon Mark, and the writing of Acts before or during the last decade of the first century. The Third Gospel was probably completed within the period 80 to 85 C.E.. The absence of any evidence of Luke's use of Matthew, and vice versa, points to a date for Luke closely approximating that of the First Gospel.

The author's claim that he had been in touch with "eyewitnesses and ministers of the word," suggests that materials for the Gospel were gathered in Syria and in Palestine—whether by himself or others one cannot say; however, this internal evidence tallies well with the tradition that Luke had been with Paul in Antioch and in Syria. Scant data exist for locating the place where the Third Gospel was composed. Various inferences have been drawn from passages in Luke-Acts to defend or to discredit the second-century tradition that the author wrote in Achaia (Greece), but none of these arguments is conclusive.

For an interpretation of Luke, an identification of the writer's purpose or interests does not depend upon certain information concerning either its date or place of origin.

NOTES ON THE NARRATIVE OF LUKE

These notes on the Third Gospel presuppose the fundamental unity of Luke-Acts. The two narratives were conceived and written with common or at least complementary purposes. Exegesis of the Gospel discloses some of the same interests discerned in our reading of the early chapters of Acts, thereby broadening the base and quality of the internal evidence. A second methodological assumption has been argued above: for his Gospel, Luke employed Mark and Q, as well as a rich resource in his own special traditions. Observation of Luke's editorial activity therefore affords a major (although not the only) means for discovering his interpretation of Jesus' significance.[26]

    A. Preface, 1:1–4
    B. Luke's Infancy Gospel: Birth of the Prophet John, and of Jesus the Messiah, 1:5–2:40
        1. Annunciation to Zachariah of the birth of John, 1:5–25
        2. Annunciation to Mary of the birth of the Son of God, 1:26–38
        3. Greetings exchanged by the two mothers. The prophecy of Mary ("the Magnificat"), 1:39–56. The three principal canticles in Luke 1–2 are tradi-

tionally designated by titles derived from the first words of each in the Vulgate.

4. Birth, circumcision, naming of John. The prophecy of Zechariah ("the Benedictus"), 1:57–79
5. John, a remarkable child, 1:80
6. Birth, circumcision, naming of Jesus. Prophecies of Simeon ("Nunc Dimittis") and of Anna, 2:1–39
7. Jesus, a remarkable child, 2:40

In this reading of Luke, as of Mark, our aim is an understanding of the Evangelist's theology. As has been observed, redaction criticism brackets out questions concerning a tradition's factual basis. Also, interpretations of Jesus belonging to pre-Gospel sources are of primary interest only insofar as they provide clues to the Evangelist's theology as this is revealed in his editorial activity. In redaction criticism the focus is on the finished product.

It is difficult to adhere to this limited objective when one reads the early chapters of Luke's Gospel. The infancy narrative is perceived by many readers to be quite different from the rest of the gospel traditions, and is of such nature as to prompt questions concerning its historical origin and value.[27] Nevertheless, for the present, let this be our single aim: to discover the meanings that the gospel narratives had for the Third Evangelist.

We have seen that for Mark "the beginning of the gospel of Jesus Christ, the Son of God" was the historic mission of the prophet John; the first moment of Christological revelation, the baptism of Jesus by John. The Earliest Evangelist maintained, however, that although Jesus was already the Messiah/Son of God throughout his ministry (note also 9:2–8), he was not identified as such by a human witness until his death (15:39), and only proclaimed Son of God by the "apostles" after his resurrection.[28] Notice now that while Luke reports these traditional epiphanies—Jesus' baptism, his transfiguration, his resurrection—by prefacing his account of Jesus' ministry with a nativity narrative, Luke moves back the designation of Jesus as "Son of God" to the moment of his conception in the womb of the virgin Mary.[29]

The first two chapters of Luke's Gospel mark a transition from the story of Israel to the story of Jesus, from the time of expectation to the time of fulfilment. The Third Evangelist's depiction of Zechariah and Elizabeth are reminiscent of characters portrayed in the pages of the Hebrew scriptures—Israel's pious folk, constant in their observance of the Law of the Lord, and undaunted in their hope. And Mary, whose role in the fulfilment of that hope is celebrated by the Evangelist, voices the aspirations of the remnant of the nation, those "poor ones" who constitute God's servant people, Israel. In her response to the annunciation of the birth of the Son of God, Mary typifies an ideal Israelite, accepting the authority of the word of the Lord and believing that He is faithful respecting His promise to the fathers (1:45, 54f.). Indeed, all of the characters in Luke's nativity narrative celebrate in poetry and prophecy the new era inaugurated by the birth of John and of Jesus.*

The canonical Gospels preserve in different forms a Christian tradition that "the good news" began with the person of John the baptizer, and each bears witness to his subordination to Jesus (the Fourth Gospel most explicitly). Luke's construction of Chapters 1 and 2 was intended to show the almost parallel mis-

*A much debated question is whether in Luke's view John belongs to the time of Israel or the time of Jesus. H. Conzel-

sions of John and Jesus. Yet the subordination of John is maintained in that the miraculous element in the conception of Jesus (without a male parent) is portrayed by Luke as a far greater event than John's natural conception (albeit by aged parents). In Luke's Gospel no rivalry exists between John and Jesus. The same angel, Gabriel, announced both conceptions and their related but distinctive meanings (1:19; [13–17]; 26 [30–33]), and when the two happy women meet Elizabeth praises Mary "as the mother of my Lord," and the baby in Elizabeth's womb leaps for joy (1:41–44; cf. John 3:27–30).

It is sometimes argued that a traditional pre-Lucan story of the annunciation to Mary (1:26–38) did not contain the idea of a virginal conception, and that verses 34–35 were added (by Luke?) to introduce this notion, which is not explicit in the remainder of the narrative.[30]

Luke's intention is indeed to affirm the virginal conception of Jesus. This conviction is closely associated with his depiction of the child of destiny as the Davidic Messiah. While not directly designating Jesus "the Son of David," Gabriel's prophecies concerning the future of Mary's child echo 2 Samuel 7: 8–16. Note the crucial italicized phrases that follow:

> 2 Samuel 7:
> 9: *I shall make you* a great name . . .
> 13: *I shall establish* the throne of his kingdom forever.
> 14: *I shall be his father, and he will be my son* . . .
> 16: *And your* house *and your kingdom will be made sure* forever.

A messianic interpretation of this passage is given in a Qumran fragment, 4Q Florilegium 10–13:

> The "he" [2 Samuel 7:14] is the "shoot" of David [Isa. 11:1] who will arise with the Interpreter of the Law who (will rule) Zion in the last days. As it is written, "I shall raise up the fallen hut of David" [Amos 9:11] "The fallen hut of David is he who shall arise to save Israel."

In Gabriel's message to Mary, Jewish messianism gives place to Lucan Christology: Jesus is not to receive adoption as God's Son coincident with his coronation; rather, the Virgin's baby is to be called "holy, the son of God" because his existence derives from an intervention of God's creative Spirit. (There was no Jewish expectation that the messiah would be God's *son* in the sense of having been conceived without a male parent.)[31]

Consistent with the Lucan traditions concerning Mary is her response when confronted with her singular role "in the mysterious plan of God embodied in the person of her son."[32]

The centrality of the Spirit's activity in the nativity stories recalls the role of the Spirit in the origin of the church. Because the Spirit is the moving force, thrusting the early disciples of Jesus toward a universal mission in Acts, so it is "the Spirit-filled Simeon who makes the major forecast of this universalism in the nativity story."[33] The aged Simeon stands within the circle of "poor ones" ardently hoping for the ultimate "consolation of Israel," but, "inspired by the Spirit," he declares that "a light for revelation to the Gentiles" is incar-

mann in his seminal study (*The Theology of St Luke* [1961], pp. 82ff.) argues that John "belongs to the earlier of the two epochs," but only after rejecting Luke 1–2 as a source for the Evangelist's theology.

nate in the child Jesus. The "Nunc Dimittis" is reminiscent of Isaiah's prophecies that God's salvation includes Gentiles among his "people" (2:38).[34] "For
Luke, the mission to Gentiles was no aberration nor a desperate alternative for
the mission to Israel. Rather it had been God's plan from the beginning . . .
the opening chapters of the Gospel and of Acts portray many Jews as seeing
this and accepting Jesus"; but there were also Jews who did not acknowledge
the clear line of salvation history which, for Luke, connected Jesus to the history of Israel.[35]

    C.   Inauguration of the Messiah's Ministry, 2:41–4:30
        1. The witness of the boy Jesus in the Temple, 2:41–52
        2. The proclamation and witness of John the baptizer, 3:1–20
        3. The witness of Jesus' baptism, ancestry, temptation, and early teaching,
           3:31–4:15
        4. The inaugural sermon of Jesus in Nazareth's synagogue, 4:16–30

Luke's inclusion of a story from Jesus' boyhood served as a transition to the
narrative of his ministry.[36] Throughout the section that this pericope introduces
there is repeated emphasis on the witness to Jesus as God's "son": in the first
episode, his own witness to a filial consciousness is given, in the last (4:14–30),
Jesus inaugurates his mission as the anointed Son, and anticipates his people's
rejection.

Luke alone among the evangelists extended the Baptist's citation from Isaiah
40 to include the prophecy: "And all flesh shall see the salvation of God."[37]
Also only Luke records that "the multitudes" flocked to John and were exhorted by him. Does Luke suggest in this way a distinction between the true
people of God, receiving John's baptism or, at least, raising unanswered questions about the implications of his presence and the leaders of Israel who reject
John's proclamation?[38] The location of the genealogy of Jesus is probably intended to show that Jesus was Son of God by descent, as he had been by divine
choice, and by the anointment of the Spirit at his baptism. Unlike Matthew,
Luke carried Jesus' ancestry beyond Abraham the father of the Jews, to Adam
the progenitor of the human race. Perhaps Luke wished to affirm that the Son
of God's *human* origins "are shared by all who walk the face of the earth,
Gentile and Jew alike."[39] At any rate, Luke goes on to declare that the Son of
God was, like Adam, tempted by Satan to rebel against the divinely appointed
limits of his humanity.

Luke's tradition (before the Galilean ministry of Jesus) gives prominence, as
was noted above, to the work of the Holy Spirit; all persons participating in
the miracle of the Messiah's birth were "filled with the Holy Spirit." Luke read
in Mark that John the Baptist had predicted that Jesus would baptize with the
Holy Spirit. The coming of the Spirit therefore authenticated John and his proclamation. After Jesus had received baptism with water, "the Holy Spirit descended upon him in bodily form as a dove . . ."[40] "Full of the Holy Spirit,"
Jesus returned from the Jordan and "was led by the Spirit for forty days in the
wilderness."[41] The guidance of the Holy Spirit in the ministry of Jesus as well
as in the witness of his followers is a pervasive theme in Luke-Acts. While
praying, both Jesus and his disciples receive the direction of the divine Spirit.[42]

Luke omitted Mark's summary of the proclamation of Jesus at the beginning of his ministry, and substituted for it an illustration of his preaching at Nazareth.[43] The position and treatment of this section indicate clearly some of the interests of the Third Evangelist. Under the inspiration of the Spirit, Jesus declares the dawning of the age of promise. But Jesus reminds his hearers in the synagogue that God had benefited non-Jews through his servants the prophets. The murderous attack upon Jesus by the Galileans is predictive of his cross. But his rejection by Jews is followed by the extension of Jesus' message to the Gentile world.

In Luke's introduction of the ministry of Jesus he emphasizes, more emphatically than Mark, that the time of salvation is a present reality. He does not substitute for Mark's hope of an imminent coming of the kingdom a wholly different conception of fulfillment. But Luke's principal focus is upon the significance of the ministry of Jesus as the decisive time of salvation—time that also incorporates the Church's mission (Luke-Acts)—rather than upon the temporal nearness of the final coming of Christ.[44]

> D. The Messiah Teaches and Acts with Authority, 4:31–6:11
> 1. Teaching and healing in Galilee, 4:31–44
> 2. First disciples are given the sign of abundant fish, 5:1–11
> 3. Healing of a leper and a paralytic, 5:12–26
> 4. At Levi's feast, controversies with the Pharisees, 5:27–39
> 5. The authority of Jesus and Sabbath laws, 6:1–11

In this section Luke's pericopes are Markan and appear in the Markan order, with the exception of 5:1–11. Their pervasive theme is the unsurpassed "authority" and "power" of Jesus, themes present in the Markan source but rendered explicit by the editing of the Third Evangelist.[45] Also editorial is Luke's notice that the actions of Jesus were accompanied with prayer.[46]

Luke's choice of a non-Markan story of the call of disciples (5:1–11) may have been because of its symbolic features. "Implicit in Peter's cry, 'Lord,' is the messianic confession that only later comes to conscious expression. Likewise, Christ's response is the prelude to Peter's later commissions."[47]

Mark's narrative of Levi's call to discipleship was doubtless dear to Luke's heart. Further on he added a story from his own source (L) of Jesus befriending another tax collector, Zacchaeus (19:1–10). He also drew upon his special parables' source to accent this feature of Jesus' ministry (15:1ff). That Jesus should have gone "to be the guest of a man who is a sinner" was in itself an exceptional act, but his eating at the tables of such persons led to "murmurings" among the Pharisees and their scribes." Yet wherever Jesus' call of "sinners" led to their repentance, "salvation" came to that house, "for the Son of man came to seek and to save that which was lost" (19:9f.; 5:32; cf. Mark 2:17; 7:33f.).

> E. Further Acts of the Messiah, 6:12–8:3
> 1. The choice of "apostles" amidst "a great multitude" of disciples, 6:12–19
> 2. "The Sermon on the Plain," 6:20–49
> 3. Jesus heals the servant of a centurion and commends his faith, 7:1–10; he has compassion on a bereaved widow and raises her only son, 7:11–17

4. Questions of identity: John the Baptizer and Jesus, 7:18–35
5. Women in attendance upon Jesus: a penitent prostitute anoints his feet and receives forgiveness, 7:36–50; other women, whom Jesus healed, support his itinerant ministry, 8:1–3

In this section Luke departs from the Markan narrative, drawing upon Q and L to set forth the nature of the impending messianic "kingdom" and to depict the prerequisite traits of its recipients (Luke's "Lesser interpolation"). In proclaiming "the good news of the kingdom of God" Jesus announced a forthcoming deliverance to the penitent "poor," to Gentiles as well as Jews, to various afflicted and immoral persons, to the sorrowing and dying. But those who were hearing Jesus in those "days" were not told to await patiently a hoped-for redemption, and to "look for another" savior to deliver them (7:19; cf. 7:16, 28).[48] In Jesus, God had "visited his people!" But the response was mixed. On the one hand, the powerless and socially ostracized folk gratefully received the liberating message of Jesus (6:20; 7:2, 6–9; 7:22, 37–39, 47–50; 8:2); on the other hand, the self-satisfied rejected Jesus, either by actively opposing him or by maintaining their neutrality (6:24–26; 7:30–35, 44–47).

The response of Jesus to the centurion's faith is almost identical in Matthew and Luke, suggesting that the story was derived from the Q source. But in the narrative framework of Luke's version, his special interest is manifested. He identified the centurion as a "God-fearer" whose contact with "the Lord" was through Jewish elders and friends.[49] This centurion, like the centurion Cornelius in Acts, probably represented men like Theophilus, who had received the salvation of God through the Jews and their scriptures. The gospel was meant for all persons. It was received by those who had only God's mercy to fall back upon; for example, a bereaved widow and mother, and another woman who was a social and religious outcast. These are but two of the many women to whom, Luke tells us, Jesus had brought "good news of the kingdom of God."

F. The Messiah Widens the Scope of His Ministry, Teaching by Parables and Performing Mighty Works, 8:4–56
1. The parable of the sower, or the four soils, 8:4–18
2. The true family of Jesus, 8:19–21
3. Calming a storm at sea, 8:22–25
4. Healing a raging demoniac, 8:26–39
5. Raising the daughter of Jairus; healing a hemorrhaging woman, 8:40–56

Luke's editorial comment (8:1–3) may have been intentionally transitional. A notice that some (other) women were healed indicates that the compassion shown to "a woman of the city" was not exceptional; while emphasis upon the movements of Jesus indicates an acceleration and widening of the Messiah's activity, as well as that of "the Twelve." At this place he introduced another segment of the Markan narrative.[50] Also, a framework is provided for the Parable of the Four Soils (8:4–15). The Third Evangelist's interpretation probably concentrates upon the losses rather than the harvest's miraculous abundance, in keeping with Luke's "rejection motif." But there are those who hear "the word of God" in Jesus' teaching, who "believe" and are "saved."[51]

The "lighted lamp" saying of Jesus, (8:16–18) is also found in Matthew, but their differing applications probably reflect different interests: in Matthew the light is to give illumination to those already in the house; in Luke, the light enables those outside to find the door.[52]

Several of Luke's interests are manifested in his editing of this Markan sequence. For example, the Third Evangelist's appreciation of Jesus' sensitivity to the pathos of persons benefitted by his healing power is evident in minor details of his narratives. The little twelve-year-old girl who was dying was "an only daughter" of Jairus. When "her spirit returned," Jesus "directed that something should be given her to eat."[53] Also Luke's understanding of the human weaknesses of "the Twelve," and a softening of Mark's derogation of them, is reflected here.[54]

G. Confirmation and Rejection of the Messiah and His Mission, 9:1–50
  1. The sending of the Twelve "to preach the kingdom of God and to heal," 9:1–9
  2. The feeding of the multitude, 9:10–17
  3. Peter confesses Jesus' messiahship, 9:18–27
  4. The transfiguration, 9:28–36
  5. Failings of the disciples, 9:27–50

The mission of "the Twelve," or the sending of "the apostles" (perceived by Luke to be the authorized bearers of the Jesus tradition)[55] was, as we have seen, an extension of Jesus' own missions consisting of "preaching the kingdom and healing." This expanded program drew the unwelcome attention of Herod (Antipas), but, in the face of this threat, the activity of Jesus was not curtailed.[56] In these episodes from the Markan narrative, future successes and failures are foreshadowed. Until the death and resurrection of the Son of man, Jesus' disciples were severely limited in their understanding of the Messiah's role and of their own as his disciples (9:45–50). In the abbreviated form of his narrative of the close of the ministry in Galilee, Luke retains these prominent Markan themes.[57]

Luke expanded the middle section of Mark's Gospel by introducing a large amount of material, mostly Jesus' teaching (besides brief similitudes, more than twenty parables) drawn from Q and his special sources. This "greater interpolation" (9:51–18:14) accounts for nearly one third of the Gospel. Luke's narrative unfolds with five references to Jesus' movement toward Jerusalem (9:51; 13:22; 17:11; 18:31, and 19:28), but, as has been frequently observed, it was not the Evangelist's intention to compose a travelogue or chronological account (Jesus is no nearer Jerusalem at 17:11 than at 9:51–53). Rather, the repeated references to the journey provide a framework for developing the major theme: Jesus the Messiah who is divinely appointed to suffer, who must "accomplish" an "exodus" in Jerusalem (9:31; also 12:50; 13:33, and 18:31), teaches his disciples "the way" of their Lord, and warns his opponents of their liability to severe judgments in the future.

H. The Messiah, On His way to Suffer Shamefully and Be Killed, Prepares His Disciples for Their Witness, 9:51–19:27
  1. Hostile Samaritans; half-hearted disciples, 9:51–62

2. Mission of the seventy; the blessedness of those receiving the Messiah's revelation, 10:1–24
3. Question: Who inherits eternal life? The parable of the good Samaritan, 10:25–37
4. The incomparable importance of hearing Jesus' teaching, 10:38–42
5. Teaching concerning prayer, 11:1–13
6. Demon exorcism: a sign of the kingdom, 11:14–28
7. The sign of Jonah; the importance of "sound" eyes, 11:29–36
8. Alas for Pharisees, and lawyers, 11:37–54
9. Words of warning to disciples, and assurances, 12:1–48
10. Signs of the present time: divisions and approaching judgment, 12:49–13:9
11. Sabbath activity: healing and parabolic teaching, 13:10–21
12. Table talk: banquets, invitations, guests—included and excluded, 13:22–14:24
13. The cost of discipleship, 14:25–35
14. Three parables on God's joy in the recovery of the lost, 15:1–32
15. Teaching on the use and abuse of riches, 16:1–31
16. Teaching on causing sin; on forgiveness, and duty, 17:1–10
17. The grateful Samaritan leper, 17:11–19
18. Response to the anxious concerning the coming of the kingdom and the Son of man, 17:20–37
19. Two parables concerning prayer, 18:1–14
20. On entering the kingdom: the paradigm of the children; the inhibiting riches of the ruler; last of the three Markan passion predictions, 18:15–34 (Note 9:22 and 44)
21. Jesus in Jericho: a blind beggar receives his sight; the conversion of a rich tax collector, 18:35–19:10
22. Jesus in Jericho: the parable of a rejected king, 19:11–27

Luke's long section begins with a report of Jesus' presence in Samaria, and of the inhospitality of this people long held in contempt by their Jewish neighbors. Surely the Third Evangelist appreciated the significance of these contacts, as would Theophilus. Did they not show how Jesus sought to break down barriers of prejudice and national feeling? In this fact was the possibility and promise of a world mission that the apostles were destined to carry forward. Only Luke reports the mission charge of Jesus to "the seventy." In the Torah, seventy is the number of all the nations of the earth. Although this is not a Gentile mission, it is likely that Luke's readers would take it to be a mission among the Samaritans, and predictive of the wider mission that was to come.[58] Luke included two units that reveal Jesus commending Samaritans who put Jews to shame by their behavior. A Samaritan exemplifies the good-neighbor spirit, and, among the ten lepers who are healed, only the Samaritan returns to express gratitude to his benefactor.

It can be said that 10:1–24 is a single episode in three acts: mission instructions, 1–12 (cf. 9:1–5); woes upon the villagers rejecting the mission of Jesus and of those appointed by him, 13–16; the church's assurances of victory in the midst of manifest rejection, 17–24. We have noted that much of the teaching of Jesus collected in this section pertains to his instruction of disciples (10:38f;

11:1, 27f., 33–35, and others). Others addressed by Jesus are those who are hostile or unreceptive to his mission (11:14–26, 29–32, 37–54, and others). A dominant literary pattern presenting this teaching is the selection of an incident or saying from Jesus' ministry, followed by a parable, or pair of parables, explaining their meaning. Luke's grouping of material is sometimes indicated by a unity of time and place that is given to the whole, for example 14:1–24 (note verses 1, 7, 12, 15), or a common key word, 15:1–32 (note verses 4, 6, 8f., 24, 32).

Chapters 15–19 have been called "the gospel of the outcast." In this section there is "a great concentration of teaching, chiefly in the form of parables, the purpose of which is to demonstrate God's care for those whom men despise and condemn,"[59] and, one should add, to teach his rebuke of self-righteous pride. Luke gave more space than the other Evangelists to the traditions revealing Jesus' love for outcasts and sinners. The story of Jesus and Zacchaeus summarizes an important aspect of the Third Gospel: "For the Son of man came to seek and to save the lost." In reading this section of Luke's Gospel, Theophilus could not fail to see Jesus portrayed as a friend of humanity.

The very fact that Luke epitomizes Jesus' ministry as a "journey" may have some complementary relation to his depiction of the witnessing disciples as "those of the way."[60] Luke envisions God's purpose of salvation reaching its fulfillment *in this whole progression of events,* defined more broadly than the passion-resurrection of the Jewish Messiah. The conclusion of Jesus' ministry is unfolded by Luke as the death, resurrection, and ascension of the Christ; but also included is his gift of the Spirit to chosen witnesses, who are with him in "the way," and his final manifestation as universal Savior and Judge.

Luke picks up the thread of Mark's narrative at 18:15, containing references at this point to Jesus' approach to Jerusalem, his passage through Jericho; however, another interest may have prompted his selection of Mark 10:13–34: the aptness of its three pericopes to the teaching of Jesus concerning the question: Who are those who enter the kingdom of God (or inherit eternal life)? They are those persons who approach Jesus like trusting children (15–17); who (like Jesus' disciples) leave all to follow him and do not allow their possessions (unlike the rich ruler) to compromise their commitment (18–30), or who (like the blind beggar) have implicit faith in the mercy of Jesus (35–43).[61]

I. The Consummation of the Messiah's Ministry in Jerusalem, 19:28–24:53
    1. The triumphal procession; "the cleansing of the temple," 19:28–46
    2. Controversies with "the chief priests and the scribes and the principal men of the people," 19:47–20:26; with Sadducees concerning the resurrection, 20:27–40. Jesus rebuffs the scribes for their vainglory, 20:41–47; an example of true piety, 21:1–4
    3. Teaching in the temple concerning things to come, 21:5–38
    4. The plot to kill Jesus; preparations for Passover, 22:1–13
    5. Jesus' last supper with the apostles, 22:14–23
    6. A farewell discourse, 22:24–38
    7. Gethsemane: Jesus' prayer of consecration; betrayal; arrest, 22:39–53
    8. Jesus is denied by Peter, reviled by his guards, 22:54–65
    9. Hearing before the Council at dawn, 22:54–65

10. Jesus is tried by Pilate, examined by Herod (Antipas), 23:1–16 (17)
11. Pilate thrice declares the innocence of Jesus, but delivers him to those who clamor for his crucifixion, 23:18–25
12. The way to the cross, 23:26–32
13. Last words of the dying Messiah; the centurion's declaration of the innocence of Jesus, 23:33–49
14. The burial of Jesus, 23:50–56
15. Women discover the empty tomb, 24:1–11 (12)
16. The risen Messiah appears on the road to Emmaus, 24:13–35
17. Jesus appears to the eleven, and applies the scriptures to his death and resurrection, 24:36–49
18. Farewell and ascension, 24:50–53

Before turning to Luke's passion story, notice should be taken of his version of Mark's "little apocalypse." Luke's account roughly parallels Mark 13, but his rearrangements suggest that although he also believed the end would come suddenly, Luke wished to show that God had filled, with eschatological significance, the time beforehand.[62] It is hardly correct to conclude, as some have claimed, that Luke had completely given up the imminent expectation of the Christ of glory and has substituted the phenomenon of the Holy Spirit as a solution to the problem of delay. But it does seem to be true that for Luke the early realization of the Church's advent hope did not hold, as it did for Mark, an urgency of concern. The importance of the time of Jesus and of his Church is emphasized more strongly in the Third Gospel.*

In Luke's account of the trials and execution of Jesus his innocence is stressed. It is plausible that Luke sensed that his readers might not understand the disturbance in the temple, and abbreviated the story of the cleansing.[63] Yet for Luke, Jesus' daily presence and teaching in the temple held great significance. "It is in the temple that the final manifestation of who Jesus is, is now given in view of his imminent passion."[64] Passages from "special Luke" relating to Jesus' trial explicitly state that the charges brought against him were unfounded. Jesus had committed no violent or treasonable act. Especially noteworthy are the repeated statements of Pilate and the centurion's protest: "Certainly this man was innocent."[65] Luke noted that the pious Jewish councilman, Joseph, had not consented to the crime of the cross.

It is often declared that Luke emphasizes the guilt of the Jews while exonerating the Romans. Yet, with the possible exception of 23:13, the rulers and not the people oppose Jesus and clamor for his death.[66] Even though apologetic interests are found in the passion story they do not dominate the scene of Jesus' death. Luke portrayed the intensity of Jesus' sufferings and the anguished emotions of those who watched him die.[67] One of the robbers was converted by the sight of Jesus. Surely Luke witnessed, in and through his moving narrative, to the faith expressed by Paul: although the cross is "folly" to Gentiles, "it is the power and wisdom of God to those who are called, both Jews and Greeks."[68] In his story of Jesus' sufferings, Luke appealed to the conscience and the will of his reader.

As in the other three gospels, so in Luke the Easter story begins with the discovery of the empty tomb. But Luke has reworked the traditional materials at hand to emphasize that the fulfilment of the promises of God to Israel are

*For a lucid discussion of Luke's understanding of Jesus' teaching concerning the future, as Luke related it to a major issue in his church—the nonoccurrence of Jesus' *parousia* (final) "coming," see W. C. Robinson, Jr., "Luke, Gospel of," *IDBS*, 558–560. C. H. Talbert, "The Redaction Critical Quest for Luke the Theologian," in *Jesus and Man's Hope*, ed. D. Miller. Vol. 1 (1970), pp. 171–222.

"accomplished" in Jerusalem. Luke's ubiquitous interest in the fulfillment of scripture in Jesus' ministry is prominent in his special Easter story, the Road to Emmaus. "And beginning with Moses and all the prophets [the risen Jesus, present with his disciples yet hidden from them] interpreted to them in all the scriptures the goings concerning himself." It is clear that "Jesus occupies for Luke the center of the line of "sacred history," going back to Israel and forward to the epoch of the Church. The things concerning Jesus of Nazareth, which took place in Jerusalem in those days, are the culmination of God's history with Israel."[69] Thus Jerusalem, which in Jewish prophecy was the locus of the eschatological salvation for all nations, became the point of origin of the apostle's mission to the Gentiles.

The last words of Jesus reported in the Third Gospel anticipate Pentecost and the second part of the work written to Theophilus. Yet these words reach backward as well as forward: A Christian mission "to all the nations" was the declared purpose of God, foreshadowed in scripture and now brought to fulfillment in the ministry of Jesus and the witness of his disciples to Christ "the Lord."

NOTES

1. P. 118. The oldest Greek manuscript ascribing the Third Gospel to Luke is p. 75 (ca. 175–225 C.E.).
2. Justin Martyr, *Dial.* 103. 8, 19.
3. Kümmel, *INT²*, p. 147. The so-called "anti-Marcionite" prologue to the Gospel is of dubious origin. For its text see E. E. Ellis, *The Gospel of Luke* (London: Oliphants, 1974), pp. 40f.; J. A. Fitzmyer, *The Gospel According to Luke* (1981, 1985), pp. 37–41.
4. Col. 4:7–14. Also Philem. 24. See p. 368. Cf. 2 Tim. 4:10–12, which may contain a fragment of a genuine letter from Paul. See p. 389.
5. The issue of the Evangelist's ethnic origin is discussed on p. 303.
6. C. S. C. Williams, *The Acts of the Apostles* (1957), pp. 3–6. Cf. Kümmel, *INT²*, pp. 176–178.
7. *The Style and Literary Method of Luke* (1920). Fitzmyer, *Luke*, pp. 51–53.
8. G. B. Caird, *The Gospel of St. Luke* (1963), p. 17.
9. See p. 302.
10. As noted in Chapter 5, the Griesbach-Farmer hypothesis presents the most serious challenge to this source theory. See J. B. Tyson, "Source Criticism of the Gospel of Luke" in C. H. Talbert, ed. *Perspectives on Luke-Acts* (1978), pp. 24ff. Tyson states that redaction critics should "not simply concentrate on the editorial activity of Luke." Such questions as the following should be asked: "Why has Luke arranged his material in the way we have it here? What attention has he given to plot and characterization? . . . What kind of readership has he presumed?"
11. Lk. 3:19; 6:12–16; 8:19–21. The second of these passages introduces, and the third concludes a section in Lk. made up of non-Markan materials. See *Gospel Parallels: A Synopsis of the First Three Gospels*, ed. by B. H. Throckmorton, Jr., and others (New York: Thomas Nelson & Sons, 1967), pp. 54ff., 71.
12. Lk. 11:14–22, cf. Mt. 9:32–34; Lk. omits Mk. 3:22–27, cf. 12:22–30.
13. Note the placement in Lk. of Jesus' teaching concerning divorce: the Evangelist's report, Lk. 16:18 (cf. Mt. 9:32–34), and his omission of Mk. 10:1–12 at Lk. 18:15.

14. E.g., Mk. 7:24–30; 11:12–14, 20–25.

15. Lk. 8:4–18 (cf. Mk. 4:1–29); Lk. 9:10–17 (cf. Mk. 6:30–44).

16. Lk. 5:12 (cf. Mk. 1:40); Lk. 8:45 (cf. Mk. 5:31). Note Lk's omission of Mk. 14:50: "they all forsook him and fled," as well as the expansion of Mk. 14:37: Jesus "found them sleeping *for sorrow*," Lk. 22:45.

17. A noteworthy exception is Lk. 5:32 (cf. Mk. 2:17 and 9:13).

18. J.M. Creed, *The Gospel According to St. Luke* (1942), pp lxv f.; H.J. Cadbury, *The Making of Luke-Acts* (1968), pp. 101ff. The problem of recovering "the original Q" *should be recalled. See pp. 104–106.*

19. Kümmel, *INT²*, pp. 136f. R. E. Brown, *The Birth of the Messiah* (1977), pp. 244–250, 265–269, 346–355, 408ff. Fitzmyer, *Luke*, pp. 309–312.

20. E.g. Lk. 4:16–30, cf. Mk. 6:16–30; Lk. 7:26–50; Cf. Mk. 14:3–9.

21. E.g., in Mk. Jesus is accused of consorting with "tax collectors and sinners," but aside from the call of Levi, (2:13–17), no evidence is given of this.

22. A. M. Perry, *The Sources of Luke's Passion Narrative* (1920); B. H. Streeter, *The Four Gospels* (1924), pp. 202f.; V. Taylor, *Behind the Third Gospel* (1926); P. Winter, "The Treatment of His Sources by the Third Evangelist," *Studia Theologica*, 8 (1955): 138ff.; Caird, *St. Luke*, pp. 23–27.

23. Creed, *St. Luke*, p. lxiii f., S. McL. Gilmour, "A Critical Examination of Proto-Luke," *JBL* 67 (1948): 151ff.; Kümmel, *INT²* pp. 133–135.

24. It is claimed that the verdict one gives here makes a considerable difference to one's estimate of the historical value of the Gospel. For the Markan hypothesis "involves the corollary that Luke used wide editorial freedom in rewriting his sources." Caird, *St. Luke*, p. 23. For a summary of objections to the proto-Luke hypothesis, see, Fitzmyer, *Luke*, pp. 89–91.

25. This is likely even though it is argued that Luke's description echoes the IXX versions of previous Jerusalem disasters rather than the 70 C.E. siege. I. Marshall, *The Gospel of Luke* (1978) p. 35. E. E. Ellis (*Gospel of Luke*, pp. 55–60) reports that current scholars date Lk's Gospel in one of two periods, 60–65 C.E. or 70–90, and also favors a time of publication "during or shortly after the Jewish rebellion." Cf. Kümmel, *INT²* pp. 150f. Fitzmyer, *Luke*, pp. 53–57.

26. While it is probable that Mk. was the foundation document to which Lk. added Q and L, Mk. does not determine the structure of the whole. All sources can be regarded as "quarries from which the Evangelist selects and adapts material to serve his own end." Ellis, *Gospel of Luke*, p. 27. One must allow for Lucan "alterations *ad hoc*" and for "the fusing of different sources" whose nature and extent are indeterminate. *Ibid.*, p. 25. C. H. Talbert, "Shifting Sands: The Recent Study of the Gospel of Luke," Int. 30 (1976): 392–394.

27. "Scholarship and the Infancy Narratives," in Brown, *Birth of the Messiah*, pp. 25–41; Caird, *St. Luke*, pp. 29–31.

28. The crucial importance of the resurrection in establishing the divine sonship of Jesus is preserved in an early creedlike formula, Romans 1:3f.; cf. Acts 13:30–39.

29. The Fourth Evangelist reports another development of the church's Son of God Christology, affirming that Jesus pre-existed creation (John 1:1–18; 17:5,24). See p. 438. Second-century apologists were the first to combine Johannine and Lucan Christologies: the incarnation of a pre-existent deity in the womb of the virgin Mary. Ignatius, *Eph.* vii. 2; xviii. 2; Justin. *Apol.* I. xxi, xxxiii.

30. Brown argues cogently that the original annunciation tradition contained the idea of a virginal conception, and that Luke's composition of the scene always contained verses 34f. *Birth of the Messiah*, pp. 298–309. A.R.C. Leaney (*A Commentary on the Gospel According to St. Luke* [1958], pp. 20ff.) states that there are manifest inconsistencies in Lk's narratives that reflect disparate sources, but argues that Lk. did not perceive these inconsistencies to be of importance.

31. There is also no known non-Jewish tradition comparable to the Lucan (or Matthean) idea of a virginal conception. See Brown, *Birth of the Messiah,* pp. 522f.; Marshall, *The Gospel of Luke,* pp. 72–77.

32. Note Lk. 8:19–21 (cf. Mk. 3:20–35), and Acts 1:14, Brown, *Birth of the Messiah,* pp. 318, 499.

33. Acts 1:4f.; 2:1ff.; 4:31; 5:32; 10:44f., and others. H.H. Oliver, "The Lucan Birth Stories and the Purpose of Luke-Acts," *NTS,* 10 (1963): 224f. It is characteristic of Lk. to juxtapose Spirit and power.

34. Isa. 40:5; 42:13; 49:6; 52:9f.

35. While the blindness of many Jews did not cause the Gentile mission, which was impelled by the Holy Spirit according to Lk., it "offered an explanation as to why the mission to Israel was now no longer a major issue in the churches Luke knew." Brown, *Birth of the Messiah,* pp. 236f.

36. Jewish legends concerning Israel's child prodigies, e.g., Moses (Jos. *Antiq.* II. ix. 6; Philo, *Life of Moses* I. 5f.) and Samuel (Jos. *Antiq.* V. x. 4) may explain why Lk. would attach this pericope to an infancy narrative as an expanded preface to Jesus' ministry.

37. Lk. 3:4ff.; cf. Mk. 1:2f and Mt. 3:3.

38. Luke 3:7, 10, 15. (Cf. Mt. 3:7).; Lk. 20:1–8 (Mk. 11:27–33).

39. Brown, *Birth of the Messiah,* pp. 90f.; Marshall, *The Gospel of Luke,* p. 161.

40. Lk. 3:22. (Cf. Mk. 1:9–11; Mt. 3:16f).

41. Lk. 4:1, 14.

42. Lk. 4:19; 10:21 (cf. Mt. 11:25); 9:29; 21:36; 22:40–46; Acts 1:14; 2:42; 4:23–31, and others.

43. Lk. 4:14–30. (Cf. Mk. 1:14f., Matt. 4:12–17.) Fitzmyer, *Luke,* p. 529.

44. Cf. Lk. 4:28–30, Acts 28:28–31. No opposition frustrates the fulfilment of Isaiah's prophecies in the proclamations of Jesus and his witnesses—"without hindrance" (NEB). Concerning Lk's eschatology, see pp. 135, 140.

45. Lk. 4:14, 32, 36 (cf. Mk. 1:22, 27); 4:40 (cf. Mk. 1:34); 5:5; 5:17 (Mk. 2:2); 5:26 (Mk. 2:12). Note also Acts 10:37–39.

46. Lk. 5:15f. (cf. Mk. 1:45). Note also 3:21 (Mk. 1:9f.); 6:12 (Mk. 3:13); 9:18, 28 (Mk. 8:27, 9:2); 22:40–46, especially 43f. (Mk. 14:32ff).

47. Lk. 9:20; 22:32. Ellis, *The Gospel of Luke,* p. 102. Cf. Fitzmyer, *Luke,* pp. 562–564.

48. A. J. Hultgren ("Interpreting the Gospel of Luke," *Int* 30 [1976], p. 356) notes that in referring to times past the author of Luke-Acts frequently employs the term "day(s)." From the standpoint of the third generation Luke looks back upon the "days" of Jesus and the early church. In this context, Lk. 6:12. Note 9:51; 24:18; Acts 1:15, 22; 5:37, and others. Also, for more distant "days" past, Lk. 4:25; 17:26, 28; Acts 5:37; 7:45.

49. Lk. 7:1–10 (cf. Mt. 8:5–13.)

50. Lk. 8:4ff. (cf. Mk. 4:1ff.) Lk. 8:22, 26, 40; 9:1ff.

51. Cf. Lk. 8:15, also 12f., and Mk. 4:20, and 15, 17. Alternatively, Fitzmyer wrote that Luke's parable stresses the abundant success of God's message despite seeming failure and formidable opposition, *Luke,* pp. 701f.

52. Mt. 5:15. for another variant of this saying, see Lk. 11:33.

53. Lk. 8:42, 55 (cf. Mk. 5:23, 42). The tragedies involving other *only* children evoke the compassion of Jesus, Lk. 7:12f., 15; also 9:38, 41f. (cf. Mark. 9:17, 19).

54. Lk. 8:24f. (cf. Mk. 4:38–40); also 8:45f. (Mk. 5:30f.) Often cited is "Luke the physician's" omission of the derogatory reference to others of his profession, Lk. 8:43f. (cf. Mk. 5:25f.). Perhaps a physician's interest is reflected in 22:50f. (Mk. 14:47; Mt. 26:51.): a hapless victim's plight is not overlooked by Jesus in the affray leading to his own arrest.

55. Lk. 6:13. Recall Acts 1:15–26, and the note on p. 168.

56. Jesus did not go into hiding, Lk. 9:10f. (cf. 13:31–33). The movement to Bethsaida may have been understood as cautionary. An interesting hypothesis is that in re-writing Mk. 6:14–16, Lk. has Herod ask the crucial question growing out of Jesus' ministry in Galilee: "Who is this about whom I hear such things?" (9:7–9; cf. 8:25). Luke's editing of the Markan episodes that follow suggest that he found in them either explicit or implicit answers to Herod's question. J. A. Fitzmyer, "The Composition of Luke, Chapter 9," in Talbert, *Perspectives on Luke-Acts*, pp. 139ff.

57. Note the omission of Mark 6:45–8:26. Perhaps Luke considered that this miscella-neous material rendered less clear Mark's report of these essential developments at the end of the Galilean mission. Note that Luke omits a notice of the faith of the epileptic boy's father (Mark 9:23f.) and stresses the disciples' lack of faith (9:41) and the unbelief of the marveling crowd of bystanders (9:43).

58. The table of the nations (Gen. 10). Alternatively, "seventy" was a symbolic number designating representatives of the people Israel, participating in the ongoing life of the nation (Ex. 1:5; 24:1; Num. 11:24f.). Recall that the Jewish Sanhedrin con-sisted of seventy rulers of the nation. For the Samaritan mission, see Acts 8.

59. T. W. Manson, *The Sayings of Jesus as Recorded in the Gospels According to St. Matthew and St. Luke* (1950), p. 282.

60. W. C. Robinson, Jr., "The Theological Context of Luke's Travel Narrative" (9:51ff.) *JBL* 79 (1960): 20ff. Acts 9:2; 22:4; 24:14, 22.

61. Mark's story of the rich ruler's rejection of Jesus' challenge to distribute his wealth to the poor may have called to Luke's mind the story preserved in his special source: a rich tax collector who, when confronted by Jesus, gave half of his goods "to feed the poor" (18:22f., 19:2, 8). The Zacchaeus pericope epitomized for Luke a major concern of Jesus' ministry: his release of the outcast, salvation for the lost, a pro-gram announced at the outset of the ministry (4:14–30), and reiterated in Jesus' reply to John (7:18–23).

62. Luke 21:5–36 (cf. Mark 13:1–37; Matt. 24:32–40). Other pertinent passages are: Luke 12:32–40; 17:20–18:8; 19:11–27; 22:69. Also Acts 1:6–11; 2:32–36; 3:18–23; 10:40–43.

63. Luke 19:45f. (cf. Mark 11:15–17.)

64. H. Conzelmann, *Theology of St. Luke* (1963), p. 78. See Ellis's "special note on Jesus and the Temple," *Gospel of Luke*, pp. 230f. The continuity of Israel's cult with Christian worship was not broken by Jesus and his earliest followers, according to the Third Evangelist (Luke 1:13; 2:27, 49; 19:47–20:1; 21:37f. Note Luke's omission of the accusation that Jesus threatened the temple's destruction, cf. Mark 14:57–61 and Luke 22:54, 66–71. Also Luke 24:52f., and Acts 2:46; 3:1; 5:12, 25, 42). The continuity was broken by the corruption and hostility of the ruling priests (Luke 20:1f.; 22:52f.; Acts 4:1–3; 5:17). Cf., however, the attitude of the Hellen-ists (Christians), which came to prevail (Acts 7:44–50).

65. Luke 23:47 (cf. Mark 15:39); 23:4, 13–16, 20, 22.

66. This is ambiguous. Cf. Conzelmann, *Theology of St. Luke*, pp. 90ff.

67. Luke 22:63f.; 23:11, 27, 36, 39, 48.

68. 1 Cor. 1:23f.

69. Anderson, *Jesus and Christian Origins* (1964), p. 229; H. C. Kee, *Jesus in History* (1970), pp. 189–191. For Lk., Easter was "the denoument of past redemptive history and the determining event for future redemptive history: forthwith repentance and forgiveness of sins are to be preached in [Christ's] name to all nations." 24:46f; Acts 2:38; 5:30–32; 10:39–42; 13:38.

The Gospel of Matthew	Chapter 8

THE late-second-century tradition that Matthew, a disciple of Jesus, was the author of the First Gospel was cited at the beginning of Chapter 6. Again, as in the case of Mark, a quotation from a lost book by Papias furnishes the earliest reference to this tradition.

THE PAPIAS TRADITION CONCERNING MATTHEW

Following his notice of the comment of Papias concerning Mark, Eusebius wrote:

> But concerning Matthew the following statement is made: "so then Matthew composed the oracles [sayings] in the Hebrew language, and each one interpreted [translated?] them as he could . . ."[1]

It is probable that the second-century notes concerning the literary activity of Matthew were meant to refer to the First Gospel, or a preliminary version of the same, and not to one or another source underlying it.[2] Now it is evident to most students of Matthew's Gospel that literary criticism has seriously discredited the ancient tradition of direct apostolic authorship. On the assumption that Mark was a major source, it is difficult to believe that the disciple Matthew would have based his narrative upon that of another author who was not an apostle or an eyewitness of Jesus, rather than upon his own recollection of events. Moreover, it is clear that Matthew's Gospel is not a "translation" from a Semitic language (Aramaic), but was written in Greek, in dependence on Greek sources.[3]

THE SOURCES AND PLAN OF MATTHEW

The evidence upon which Matthew's use of Mark and Q has been hypothesized has been set forth. The characteristic tendencies in Matthew's adaptation of material drawn from these sources will be noted here. There remain some 230 verses in the First Gospel that are not derived from Mark and that have no parallel in Luke. This material is commonly referred to as "M" or "Special Matthew." It is unlikely that this material, which contains both narrative and discourse, was written in a single source. Indeed, "the most probable supposition" is that Matthew has used only oral tradition in addition to Mark and Q.[4]

The Gospel of Matthew is often referred to as "a revised and enlarged edition of Mark." Indeed we can use this description to summarize some of the editorial methods employed by the First Evangelist.

Matthew revised Mark by a partial rearrangement of the order of his source. A second characteristic of his revision is a compression of Mark's narratives. Thus, for example, the stories of the storm at sea, the Gadarene demoniac(s), Jairus's daughter and the woman with the hemorrhage, told in Mark in 821 words, are reduced to 357 in Matthew.[5] Doubtless the First Evangelist wished to make room for non-Markan material at his disposal and concluded that some of Mark's vivid detail was unedifying, or dispensable for other reasons. A third type of revision is an improvement of Mark's diction. He removed redundancies,[6] eliminated ambiguous statements,[7] and modified inelegant or irregular forms of speech.[8]

Other revisions seem to have been prompted by doctrinal motives. Thus, by means of editorial omissions or alterations, there is a safeguarding of Jesus' power and goodness against detraction.[9] The same motives apparently led Matthew to revise Mark's references to Jesus' disciples and to offer a defense of "the Twelve."[10] Other revisions of the substance of Mark's statements probably reflect doctrinal motives. Matthew increased the number of persons benefited by Jesus' mighty works.[11] As we shall see, he also conformed events more closely to Old Testament prophecies and made more explicit the apocalyptic utterances of Jesus in Mark.

Matthew's enlargements of Mark can now be summarized. First of all, Matthew added narratives at the beginning and end of his Gospel: the nativity stories, the extra incidents in the passion narrative, and the account of Christ's postresurrection appearances to chosen witnesses. Second, Matthew enlarged Mark by inserting at appropriate points Old Testament passages with his characteristic formula. Finally, Matthew enlarged Mark's outline by dovetailing into it five or possibly six discourses. On four occasions, Matthew started with a section of Mark as a nucleus and expanded it by non-Markan supplements, into a discourse or "sermon": Matthew 9:35–11:1 (Mark 6:7f.); Matthew 13 (Mark 4); Matthew 18:1–19:2 (Mark 9:33f.); and Matthew 24:1–26:2 (Mark 13). The first in order of Matthew's discourses, Chapters 5–7, is a unique composition. It is a collection of Jesus' teaching drawn from several sources and built into an outline provided by a sermon found in the Q source.

The Composition of Matthew 5–7

```
5:3–12   —The Sermon in Q (Luke 6:20–23)
    13–16 . . . . . . . . . . Q (Luke 14:34–35; 11:33)
    17–37—Special Mt. (25–26—Q cf. Luke 12:57–59)
    38–48—The Sermon in Q (Luke 6:29–30; 27–28; 32–36)
6:1– 8   —Special Mt.
    (9–13) . . . . . . . . . (cf. Luke 11:2–4)
    (14–15) Mark (cf. Mark 11:25–26)
    19–34 . . . . . . . . . Q
          (Mt. 6:19–21—Luke 12:33–34)
          (      22–23—        11:34–36)
```

```
          (           24—        16:13)
          (        25–34—        12:22–31)
7:1– 5   —The Sermon in Q (Luke 6:37–38, 41–42)
     6   —Special Mt.
   7–11 . . . . . . . . . . Q (Luke 11:9–13)
    12   —The Sermon in Q (Luke 6:31)
 13–14 . . . . . . . . . . Q (Luke 13:23–24)
 15–27—The Sermon in Q
                    (Luke  6:43–46)
                    (        13:26–27)
                    (         6:47–49)
```

In constructing these discourses, Matthew followed two literary conventions. One is known as the conflation of sources. At the outset it is evident that both Mark and Q contained versions of John's preaching. Matthew was therefore faced with the alternative, either of choosing one source and ignoring the other, or of drawing features from both, "conflating" his sources. Matthew followed the second of these alternatives. Chapters 5–7 provide good examples. A second literary convention employed by Matthew is a procedure termed "agglomeration," which consists in joining sayings variously placed in the sources to form larger units of tradition, thus developing a single subject or cognate themes. (Matthew 5–7 also illustrate this practice of the First Evangelist.)[12]

The above comments on Matthew's revisions and expansions direct attention to his literary habits and miscellaneous motives explaining these. In the notes that follow, however, further observation of the distinctive features of Matthew's editing may produce more directly personal concerns of the Evangelist and his perceptions of the needs of his readers. These observations disclose some important aspects of the purpose of this Gospel.

NOTES ON THE NARRATIVE OF MATTHEW

A. Prologue: the Person of Jesus the Christ, 1:1–4:16
1. The record of the birth of Jesus, the son of David, the son of Abraham, 1:1–17
2. The significance of persons and places associated with the birth of Jesus, God's son, 1:18–2:23
3. Preparation for the ministry of Jesus, the Son of God, 3:1–4:16 *(baptism by John, 3:1–17; temptations in the wilderness, 4:1–11; Capernaum; the first location of Jesus' ministry, 4:12–16)*

The basic theme of Matthew's "birth record" of Jesus is that as "the son of David" he fulfilled a dominant element in Jewish messianic expectations. This is patent in the genealogy, but also stressed in the narrative: in obedience to "an angel of the Lord," "Joseph, son of David," assumed public responsibility for Mary and her baby, and a father's right to name the child, thus accepting Jesus as his son and heir.[13]

To Matthew, the meaning that Jesus is also designated "the son of Abraham" is less certain; however, the First Evangelist probably wished to declare that Jesus not only brought to fulfilment God's promise to David, kept alive in Jewish messianism, but "his wider promise" to Abraham of blessings to the Gentiles.[14]

Reference to four women in Matthew's genealogy (atypical of such tables) was probably intended to show that, as in the case of Mary, there was something out of the ordinary in the union of these women with their partners, a union that, though it may have been scandalous even to outsiders, continued the lineage of the Messiah and so, providentially, foreshadowed his coming.[15]

A distinctive element in Matthew's nativity narrative (1:18–2; 23) is the introduction of five citations of scripture with a fulfilment formula (1:22f.; 2:5, 15, 17f., 23). We have observed that fourteen such notices appear in Matthew and are a major feature of the First Evangelist's expansion of Mark's narrative. Seven of the fourteen are cited in the Gospel's "prologue."[16] Unlike Luke, Matthew does not stress the virginal conception of Jesus as a miracle so much as the fulfilment of God's plan enunciated in Hebrew prophecy. Matthew saw in his adaptation of Isaiah 7:14 scriptural support for both Davidic and divine aspects: "the Who" and "the How" of Jesus' identity.[17] Isaiah's "sign" was addressed to "the House of David" (Isa. 7:13) and consisted of a virgin being with child and giving birth to a son. It is unlikely that Matthew's supplied interpretation of "Emmanuel" was offered as a name for Jesus (which nowhere appears in the First Gospel). Rather Matthew proclaimed that in Jesus God's presence was manifested finally, once-for-all, indeed, "to the close of the age" (Matt. 28:20).

In the composition of 1:18–2:23 Matthew combined a traditional narrative of an angel's annunciation of the birth of the Davidic Messiah (similar to an account employed by Luke in that both contained the affirmation that Jesus was begotten through the Holy Spirit) with a popular narrative concerning Joseph and the infant Jesus, modeled upon the adventures of the patriarch Joseph and the infant Moses. In fusing these narratives Matthew structured his stories around a series of scripture texts, and a sequence of dreams through which divine guidance was communicated.*

Brief attention must be given to principal motifs developed in Matthew 2. Verses 1–12 focus upon Bethlehem as the birthplace of Jesus; verses 13–23 upon the move from Bethlehem to Egypt as the place of asylum for the holy family, and finally their settlement in Nazareth and Capernaum. Why this sustained interest, one may ask, in places? Perhaps Matthew was concerned to meet the Jewish objection that since Jesus was from Galilee, neither a Davidic or divine origin could be claimed for him.[18] As a true son of David, Matthew contended, Jesus was born in Bethlehem. Moreover, it was not historical accident but the fulfilment of prophecies that God's son was called out of Egypt and came to be known as a Nazarene (2:15, 23).

Yet Matthew's primary goal was not apologetic but kerygmatic. Both canonical infancy narratives function as miniature "gospels": the proclamation of the good news establishes a crisis resulting either in joyous acceptance or in rejection and persecution.[19]

Matthew's nativity narrative probably reflects the situation in his own time and place: Jesus had been and was being proclaimed to Gentiles (Matt. 28:18),

*Matthew's infancy narratives call to mind several features of the Genesis stories of the patriarch Joseph and of Moses in Exodus. Both Josephs go down to Egypt. Matthew's Herod takes on the character of the Pharaoh "who did not know Joseph" (Exod. 1:8) and who sought to slay Israel's destined savior by killing male infants of the Israelites. Like Moses, Jesus escaped the monarch's pogrom. Yet, like Moses, Jesus

and large numbers of these alien "wise men" were receiving the blessings promised to Abraham (1:1; 8:11). But along with their fellows of Jewish origin, Gentile Christians are reminded that the church's kerygma can be understood adequately only in the light of the scriptures fulfilled in it.

was forced to live in exile until the wicked ruler's death.

The theme of the divine sonship of Jesus, implicit in 1:18–2:23, is affirmed by the voice of God at the moment of Jesus' baptism (3:17), and this identity is confirmed by the obedience and unwavering trust of Jesus (3:15, 4:1–11). The providentially ordered travels of Jesus end in Capernaum, which is located in the district designated "Galilee of the Gentiles" (4:12–16).[20] At its outset, the ministry of the King of the Jews was destined to bring "light" to Gentiles. The significance of this citation of scripture was undoubtedly not overlooked by Matthew's readers.

The conclusion of Matthew's prologue is for the most part constructed from Mark and Q. One can therefore expect to find clues to the First Evangelist's interpretation in his editing. It has often been noted that Matthew has assimilated the preaching of Jesus to the preaching of John (4:17; cf. 3:1f.).[21] Yet the scriptures cited ensure that a clear distinction is affirmed: 4:14–16 ensures that Jesus' message is the fulfilment of prophecy, while the scripture cited at 3:3 limits John's message to promise, or preparation. Consistent with this distinction is Matthew's notice that although John and Jesus call their hearers to "repentance," the gift of forgiveness of sins comes only from Jesus. "The story of the Baptist goes no further than confession."[22]

The narrative of Satan's confrontation, in the Judean wilderness, of Jesus in his capacity as the Son of God (reproduced from the Q source) probably served Matthew's apologetic and was a conscious extension of the parallelism, noted earlier, between Jesus and Moses.[23] Jesus is portrayed as triumphing over the temptations (tests) to which Israel, God's son (Exod. 4:22f.), had succumbed in the desert (Deut. 8:3; 6:16, 13), thus reliving in his person the history of Israel and proving himself a faithful Son of God, in perfect trust submitting himself to the Father's will.

B. Jesus' Proclamation in Galilee of "the Gospel of the Kingdom," 4:17–16:20
1. Call of disciples; an active ministry of "teaching, preaching, and healing" begins, 4:17–25 (9:35)
2. First Discourse: the higher righteousness of the kingdom ["the Sermon on the Mount"], 5:1–7:29 (introduction, 5:1f.; the blessings of disciples, and their relation to the world, 5:3–16; Jesus' teaching fulfils the Law, 5:17–20; is contrasted with the old, 5:21–48; inner piety, 6:1–18; other teaching and warnings, 6:19–7:23; concluding parable, 7:24–27; summary, 7:28f.)
3. The narrative resumed: Jesus' mighty works, 8:1–9:34: (descent from the mountain and three healings, 8:1–17; interlude: teachings concerning discipleship, 8:18–22; three manifestations of Jesus' power, 8:23–9:8; the independence of Jesus' disciples, 9:9–17; three miracles, 9:18–34)
4. Second Discourse: the perilous mission of Jesus' disciples and his charge to them, 9:35–11:1: (laborers being few, Jesus gives "the Twelve" authority for mission, 9:35–10:4; they are charged to go to "the lost sheep of the house of Israel," 10:5–15; they are forewarned of perils but assured of rewards for endurance, 10:16–11:1)
5. The narrative plot thickens: Jesus' rejection, by all groups in Israel, antici-

> pated, 11:2–12:50: (John questions whether Jesus is "the coming one," 11:2–15; Jesus' "generation" misconstrue his actions, 11:16–24; Jesus attributes his rejection to the Father's will, 11:25–30; Jesus is attacked as a law breaker, as an agent of demons, and a sign from him is demanded, 12:1–45; family ties do not suffice to distinguish Jesus' true disciples in "this evil generation," 12:46–50)

Beginning with 3:1, Matthew patterned his Gospel according to Mark and, in reporting the beginning of Jesus' ministry, he continued to be guided by his major source. However, after a summary statement, 4:23–25, Matthew dropped the Markan thread, offered an original account of Jesus' ministry in Galilee and did not return to the Markan outline until Chapter 12. Opinions differ widely over Matthew's reasons for thus abandoning the order of Mark, and it is probable that he exercised similar freedom with respect to his other sources.

An influential theory, popularized by B. W. Bacon, is based on the observation that with the conclusion of chapter 4 Matthew's account alternates between narrative and discourse, and the transition between a discourse and the resumption of narrative is the formula: "and when Jesus finished these sayings . . ." If Chapters 1 and 2 are judged to be prologue, and Chapters 26–28 epilogue, the remainder of the Gospel manifests the following pattern:

Book I:
 Narrative, 3:1–4:25
 Discourse, The Sermon on the Mount, 5:1–7:27
 Formula, 7:28f.

Book II:
 Narrative, 8:1–9:35
 Discourse, The Mission of the Twelve, 9:36–10:42
 Formula, 11:1

Book III:
 Narrative, 11:2–12:50
 Discourse, Parables of the Kingdom, 13:1–52
 Formula, 13:53

Book IV:
 Narrative, 13:54–17–21
 Discourse, Life in the Church, 17:22–18:35
 Formula, 19:1

Book V:
 Narrative, 19:2–25:46
 Discourse, Farewell; the End is Foretold, 23:1–25:46
 Formula, 26:1

According to Bacon, Matthew gathered Jesus' teaching into these five "books" after the fashion of the Mosaic Pentateuch to counter the danger of lawlessness in his church. Each of the discourses sets forth "the higher righteousness" that Jesus commanded (5:20). Each was prefaced by accounts of his marvelous deeds, just as, in the Pentateuch, narrative is interspersed with legislation, much of which celebrates the signs and wonders wrought by God in redeeming his people from their bondage. The first discourse in Matthew's Gospel establishes the Evangelist's aim: Jesus, the new Moses, gives the new Torah from a mountain, symbolic of a new Sinai.[24]

This interpretation of the structure of Matthew's Gospel can be faulted on a number of points. The infancy narrative should not be separated from the Gospel's story as though it served the Evangelist as a "preamble" only. More serious is the error of placing the passion and resurrection narratives outside the main structure of the Gospel. The absence of clear distinctions between narrative and discourse from Chapter 11 forward suggests that the identification of five "books" may be forced. The complete change of setting between Chapter 23 and Chapters 24–25 may indicate a sixth discourse.

For these and other reasons "the Pantateuchal Theory," developed from the five-fold formula, does not provide a pattern sufficiently comprehensive to discover in it Matthew's principal purpose. We have observed some traces of a "new Moses" typology in the infancy narrative, but it is doubtful that this feature of the Gospel is as pervasive as Bacon and others have contended.[25] "The Pentateuchal Theory" is often urged in support of the thesis that Matthew's Gospel is primarily a legislative manual, designed to be a catechetical instrument for the church of the Evangelist. If, however, due attention is given to themes treated in the "prologue" (1:1–4:16), themes that receive development throughout the Gospel, the conclusion seems warranted that Matthew's purpose may be more adequately described as Christological rather than catechetical.[26] While the First Gospel "certainly reflects ecclesiological concerns, it is the Christology of Matthew that has determined its character."[27]

What can be said in a more positive vein concerning Matthew's intentions, as revealed in his adaptation of traditional material relating to Jesus' ministry in Galilee? One exegete notes the following: "in Chapters 5–7 Matthew seeks to present Jesus as messiah in his message, in Chapters 8–9 as messiah in his ministry. The repetition at 9:35 of 4:23 frames "this two-part intent."[28]

In order to understand the purpose served by Chapter 10, it is important to note that the Q version of the sermon was followed by the story of Jesus' healing of a centurion's servant (Luke 7:1–10), and by the enquiry of the Baptist concerning the identity of Jesus (Luke 7:18–23). In response to John's query it was reported that Jesus cited his mighty works. It therefore seems that Matthew collected his nine healing stories, constituting Chapters 8–9, as concrete evidence supporting the reply of Jesus to John (11:4–6). Perhaps it is significant, however, that Matthew does not place this reply directly after the sequence of miracle pericopes: he first inserts Chapter 10 because he wants to make the point that the same authority to perform miracles is also given to the community. The response of Jesus to the disciples of the Baptist is also the response of Matthew and his church to those who are hesitant or doubtful.

Further sayings concerning the Baptist (11:7–19), and two pericopes concerning the eschatological crisis occasioned by Jesus' presence, conclude Matthew's independent account of the Galilean ministry. With Chapter 12 the First Evangelist resumes his close adherence to Mark's outline.

Perhaps the development of Matthew's interpretation of Jesus' Galilean ministry is further clarified if it is recognized that 4:17 to 11:30 (or 12:50?) is a major part of a longer section of his narrative extending from 4:17 to 16:20. Several students of Matthew's Gospel have observed that the verses 4:17 and 16:2 ("From that time Jesus began . . .") "function within the Gospel much as superscriptions."[29] Accordingly, it is urged, 1:1–4:16 present Jesus the messiah, most importantly in his personal significance as Son of God; 4:17–16:20 follow with a description of Jesus' proclamation in Galilee with emphasis on its characteristic features and its results; and, finally, 16:21–28:20 narrate the suffering, death, and resurrection of Jesus, the Son of God.[30]

From Mark, Matthew draws the stories that bring to a climax his narrative of the negative reactions of Jewish hearers to Jesus' proclamation of "the gospel of the kingdom" (12:1–50).

> B. 6. The third discourse: Jesus interprets to his disciples his parables, 13:1–53: *(seven parables of the kingdom, two of which are interpreted, 13:1–50; the skill of the scribe instructed in the kingdom, 13:51–53)*
> 7. The narrative of the Galilean ministry is continued, 13:54–16:20: *("crowds" witness Jesus' mighty works but do not accept him; the Nazarenes are offended, 13:54–58; Herod fears that the martyred prophet, John, has returned, 14:1–12; a multitude is fed and Peter's faith is challenged, 14:13–36; Matthew's close of the ministry in Galilee leading up to Peter's confession, 15:1–16:16; the blessing of Peter, 16:17–20)*

Since beginning with 12:1 Matthew follows closely the plot of Mark, it is to be expected that certain themes developed in his source or in the preceding chapters of his own Gospel would be repeated. Yet Matthew's special interests are revealed in his editing of Mark. Here as elsewhere, emphasis is placed upon Jesus' healing ministry (14:13f., 34–36; 15:29–31).[31] Evidence is taken from Mark of the growing hostility to Jesus; but, unlike Mark, Matthew excludes the disciples (and Jesus' family?) from those persons and groups who are uncomprehending. The disciples are portrayed as men exhibiting "little faith," but not unbelief; they are in need of Jesus' teaching, but their hearts are not hardened, nor are their eyes blinded to the true significance of his person. They are privileged to "know" the mysteries of the kingdom.[32]

It is unlikely that Matthew freely composed the account of Jesus' blessing of Peter (16:17–19). This tradition may have received its present form sometime after 70 C.E. when, as we have seen, Judaism organized itself under the authority of the rabbis at Yavneh. Perhaps to oppose them the (Syrian?) church declared that God, through the agency of Jesus, had granted to Peter the authority of "binding" and "loosing."[33]

Matthew interprets Jesus' injunction to silence (Mark 8:30) as his insistence that he not receive public recognition as "the Messiah" according to popular expectation.[34] The introduction of the formula at 16:21 indicates that Jesus' teaching concerning his fate in Jerusalem and his rebuke of Peter for rejecting it were not momentary events. They became the principal agenda for the rest of Jesus' life.

> C. Jesus the Messiah Leads His Disciples to Jerusalem; Predictions of His Passion and Resurrection, 16:21–25:46

1. The narrative of the Galilean ministry is concluded, 16:21–18:35 *(first pre-diction of Jesus concerning his suffering and glory; their consequence for his disciples, 16:21–28; a christophany: Jesus' "transfiguration" and a conversation about Elijah's coming, 17:1–13; the cure of an epileptic, 17:14–21; a second prediction of the Passion, 17:22f.; the issue of the temple tax, 17:24–27)*

2. A fourth discourse: interpersonal relations within the church, 18:1–35 *(sayings concerning children and "little ones," 18:1–14; the proper treat-ment of a sinning brother, 18:15–20; a parable: forgiveness "from the heart," 18:21–35)*

3. The narrative unfolds with controversy in a Judean setting, 19:1–23: (39?) *(marriage and divorce, 19:1–12; the blessing of children, 19:13–15; a young man's love of possessions, 19:16–26; rewards of discipleship, 19:27–30; a parable: of vineyard workers; 20:1–16; a third Passion prediction, 20:17–19; a mother's ambition, 20:20–28; the sight of two blind men is restored, 20:29–34; procession toward Jerusalem ending in the temple's "cleansing," and the cursing of the fig tree, 21:1–22; the issue of Jesus' authority, 21:23–27; three parables: the two sons, the evil vineyard workers, and the royal marriage feast, 21:28–22:14; the issue of tribute money, 22:15–22; the Sadducees' riddle, 22:23–33; the great commandment, 22:34–40; the Pharisees question about David's son, 22:41–46; [woes to the scribes and Pharisees, a fifth discourse (?), 23:1–39]; the temple's destruction, 24:1f.)*

The fact that Matthew's narrative of the Judean ministry of Jesus is almost verbally identical to Mark's makes the editing of the First Evangelist particu-larly interesting. A few points may be noted. Matthew's conviction that Jesus' teaching from this time forward was directed almost exclusively to his disciples dictated editorial changes (Cf. Mark 8:24 and Matthew 16:24; note also Mat-thew's alteration of Mark 10:1: Jesus' public ministry of healing is continued, but not of teaching, Matthew 19:1f.) Matthew's account of "the transfigura-tion" of Jesus is significant in this regard: the scope of his discipleship teaching is more broadly defined, not limited to forecasts of his imminent passion and resurrection.[35]

Matthew's editing of the story of the transfiguration (17:1–13) raises again the issue of the First Evangelist's "new Moses" typology. The command, "lis-ten to him" (17:5), "both looks backward to chapters 5–7 [and to 9:35–11:1 and chapter 13?] and forward to 17:5–18:35."[36] It is significant, however, that the disciple's response to the commanding voice ("they fell on their faces and were filled with awe," 17:6) suggests that Jesus' status was perceived by them to be more than that of a "Mosaic teacher." To them it was revealed that he was the beloved Son of God. (Note also Matthew's use of the term "Lord," 17:4, in place of Mark's "rabbi", 9:5). "The strictly Mosaic traits in the figure of the Matthean Christ . . . have been taken up into a deeper and higher context."[37] In his transfiguration Jesus is not depicted as Moses come as Mes-siah so much as Messiah, the Son of God, to whom is given divine authority to fulfil the Mosaic function, to impart "the torah" of God.[38]

It is often stated that among the synoptic Gospels Matthew most transpar-ently reflects life situations and interests of its author and the community he addresses. "At every point the question has been raised [by the First Evangelist] how does this apply to the contemporary church?"[39] The so-called "fourth discourse," placed between the second and third predictions of the Passion, is a clear illustration of this feature of Matthew's Gospel. The Evangelist is concerned to give support to "the little ones" in his community who believe in Jesus (18:6, 10) but who are weak, susceptible to sinning and, therefore, at risk of becoming lost. Matthew's deep concern to set forth strategies for reproving and winning back a fallen brother shows how seriously his community viewed moral lapses. Everything possible must be done to make sure the offender is aware of his fault and is given an opportunity to repent. And those in a position to discipline others must remember the gracious forgiveness of God, and the imperative to extend forgiveness to others whose debt, comparatively speaking, is infinitesimal.[40]

Matthew's narrative reporting the Pharisee's confrontation of Jesus upon his entering "the region of Judea" (19:1ff.) calls attention to one of the most complicated questions facing the interpreter of this Gospel, one that merits an excursus: How may one describe Matthew's understanding of the attitude of Jesus to the Mosaic Law and contemporary scribal interpretations?

Before noting the relevant pericopes in Chapter 19, a good beginning may be an examination of 5:17–48. According to an initial programmatic statement, Matthew understood that it was clearly not Jesus' intention to abolish the Mosaic Law (5:17). Indeed, on first reading, it would seem that Matthew believed that Jesus required of his disciples a more stringent obedience to the Torah than that demanded by "the scribes and Pharisees" (5:18–20). But what does one learn in turning to "the antitheses" that follow (5:21–48), ostensibly intended to explain this summary statement concerning Jesus and the Law of Moses? ("You have heard that it was said to men of old . . . But I say to you. . . .")

Interpreters of Matthew have not agreed concerning the implications of this Gospel's six antitheses. Some persons claim that Jesus is here represented as one who intensified and radicalized the intention of Mosaic Laws, not as one who was the proponent of a new Torah.[41] Others contend that this is not the full picture, that Matthew understood that some of the precepts of Jesus had the effect of rescinding the binding authority of the Torah.[42]

Perhaps agreement can be reached that the first and second antitheses, having to do with murder and adultery (5:21–30), only intensify the force of two of the so-called "ten commandments." Also the sixth antithesis, requiring love of one's enemy (5:43–48), may simply radicalize a command of Moses (cf. Lev. 19:18). But one is less sure of what Matthew intends in the third, fourth, and fifth antitheses.

In the fourth (5:33–37), Jesus revokes the Law's provisions concerning religious vows and oaths.[43] In the fifth (5:38–42), Jesus forbids his disciples retaliation when wrongs are suffered, although there is provision for such in the Law of Moses.[44]

The third antithesis in the Sermon on the Mount (5:31f.) relates directly to the passage Matthew 19:3–12 (which was the point of departure for this excursus on Jesus and the Law). Words of Jesus concerning divorce were found by Matthew in both of his major sources, Mark and Q, and probably also in his special tradition, M. According to Mark and Q, Jesus rescinded the Law's permission of divorce (allowed by Deut. 24:1–4), and annulled the command requiring "a certificate of divorce." Yet in Matthew's accounts—and in Matthew's only—Jesus allows for divorce in cases of "unchastity" (5:32 and 19:9).[45] Moreover, in answer to his disciples' objection that this proscription of divorce made it expedient not to marry (19:10ff. [M]), the Matthean Jesus declares that not all men can "receive" this and, by choice, adopt a celibate life.

In Matthew's "exceptive clauses" (5:32 and 19:9), and in the pericope that acknowledges that celibacy is a vocation for some only, one sees a tendency in Matthew's church toward a temporizing of Jesus' "counsels of perfection," a softening of his absolute precepts, and a recognition of individual differences with respect to the application of Jesus' demands concerning discipleship.[46]

Thus far the evidence in Matthew's Gospel leads to the conclusion that the Evangelist's view was that Jesus upheld the formal authority of the Mosaic Law and in his teaching penetrated to its full meaning. Nevertheless, on occasions he revoked the Torah and instead commanded a more radical obedience. In similar fashion Matthew understands Jesus' attitude toward the oral law, "the tradition of the elders": while recognizing its formal authority (23:2f., 23), Jesus taught that where obedience to tradition conflicted with the demands of love—love of God and neighbor—his disciples were loosed from its binding authority. The Law as interpreted by Israel's sages and prophets, oral and written, comes to its full expression in the commandment to love (7:12 and 22:34–40).

One can gather from all this that Matthew, responding to his church situation, opposed the position that for Christians the Mosaic Law had been abrogated. At the same time he was intent to set forth the difference between the church's understanding of what it means to do the will of God and the understanding that prevailed in contemporary Judaism (and among some Jewish Christians?). Perhaps Matthew believed that the Christian "scribe," "trained for the kingdom of heaven" under the tutelege of Jesus, "is like a householder who brings out of his treasure what is new and what is old," thereby teaching Jesus' disciples the true Torah.[47]

Now how does this portrayal of Matthew's understanding of Jesus' attitude to the Torah and its traditional interpretations square with Matthew 5:17–20? The conclusion seems correct that the law which remains in force "till heaven and earth pass away" is the law Jesus taught his disciples and church. "What is ultimately normative for the disciple is not the command of Moses but the word of Jesus. That word [as we have shown] may or may not coincide with the command of Moses, but its normative value in any case comes from its being the word of Jesus."[48] Until "the close of the age"—"until all is accomplished"—the church is commanded to "make disciples of all nations . . . teaching them to observe all that [Jesus] commanded . . .," (28:19f.).[49]

Before concluding these notes with a brief consideration of Matthew's passion narrative (26:1ff.), attention is directed to a sequence of three parables, (21:28–22:14) and to the final discourse in this Gospel (24:1–25:46) for the light these passages shed on Matthew's concerns.

The Markan parable of the vineyard and its wicked tenants is placed by Matthew within the frame of two from other sources:

$$\text{Mt. 21:28–32 (M)} \quad \left[\begin{array}{c} \text{21:33–46} \\ \text{cf. Mk. 12:1–12} \end{array} \right] \quad \text{22:1–14 (Q)}^?$$

The three parables are linked in that they develop and intensify Jesus' warning respecting the rejection of the Messiah, the Son of God, by Israel's leaders. According to Mark, an attack upon Jesus had been transformed into a trial in which the leaders of Israel were themselves examined (the issue of the authority of Jesus was left unresolved); Mark 11:27f., 33; cf. Matthew 21: 23, 27). Focusing upon the surprising outcome of Jesus' ministry, Matthew's parable of the two sons condemns Israel's leaders: tax-collectors and harlots—the nay sayers—believed in Jesus as they had in John the baptizer, while the yea-sayers to God's commandments were steadfastly unwilling to walk in the prophet's "way of righteousness" and consequently rejected the Messiah. The second parable sentences, those rejecting Jesus, again view his ministry from its end. It also anticipates the execution of that sentence as depicted in the third parable (21:41, 43; 22:7).

As a pendant to the whole complex, Matthew warns Christians that they will incur the same judgment if they act as Israel's leaders, if they are deaf to their calling to walk in "the way of righteousness" required of God's chosen ones (22:11–14; 5:20; 6:33; 21:32).[50]

> *C. 4.* A final discourse: Jesus' farewell; the end is foretold, 24:3–25:46 *(signs of the approaching End, 24:3–36; on preparedness, 24:37–44; three parables referring to the judgment, 24:45–25:30; the last judgment, 25:31–46.)*

Matthew's "eschatological discourse" closely parallels the Markan apocalypse (Mark 13). According to Mark, the troubles that are the signs of the final coming of Jesus, the Son of man, are derived from two sources: hatreds and killings arise from the synagogues and councils of the Jews but also from within the church itself (Mark 13:9–13). (Note that Matthew incorporated this passage into the earlier discourse containing instruction of disciples for their mission to Israel, 10:17–21.) In Matthew 24:9–12 the Evangelist distinguishes the Israel-inflicted suffering endured by Jesus and his disciples from the dreadful End-time tribulation that will result from the hatred "by all nations" of Jesus' disciples "for [his] name's sake." Matthew also emphasizes that the destructive activities involving fellow members of Christian families and churches are exacerbated by the presence of "false prophets" who "lead many astray."

In this passage (24:9–12), one may detect a reference to persons in Matthew's church advocating lawlessness, and to their "evil fruit" (7:15–23). Against this loveless refusal to recognize "law," Matthew teaches Jesus' higher righteousness, the law of love.

In these notes attention has been given to Matthew's portrayal of Jesus as, above all, "the Son of God." One writer has shown that this title in Matthew's usage is "confessional," for it conveys "the deepest mystery" of the person of Jesus, namely, that "it is in him that God has drawn near with his eschatological rule to dwell with his people."[51] It is important now to notice that the title "Son of man" is a Christological term in the First Gospel that nearly equals in importance that of "Son of God."

In the course of his public ministry Jesus refers to himself as the Son of man; this title serves to describe his significance in relation to the world—Israel first and then the Gentiles—and especially as he interacts with the crowds and his opponents (8:19–22; 9:2–8; 11:18f.; 12:1–8, 30–32). In his passion predictions Jesus foretells what malevolent men will do to the Son of man (16:13–21; 17:12, 22f.; 20:18f.; 26:2, 24f., 45). It is, however, in Matthew's depiction of the role of Jesus at "the close of the age" that all titles descriptive of Jesus' person are clearly subordinated to that of Son of man. As Son of man, Jesus, the risen, exalted Lord, raises up "sons of the kingdom" (13:37f.) and, at his parousia, judges the nations of the world, bestowing eternal life upon "the righteous" and consigning the accursed to unending sorrows and distress (10:22; 13:40–43; 16:28; 19:28; 24:29–31, 37–44; 25:31–46; 26:62–64).

MATTHEW'S PASSION/RESURRECTION NARRATIVE, 26:1–28:20

The outline and order within the Matthean and Markan passion narratives are, without exception, identical. (The slight variations within this basic narrative are displayed on pages 121f.; Matthew's additions to the Markan account, excluding stylistic corrections, are marked with brackets.) It is probable that one needs to suppose Matthew's indebtedness to extra-Markan traditions relating to Jesus' passion and resurrection to explain these variations, but it is not easy to distinguish between pre-Matthean material and Matthean redaction. For example, from whence came the extra notes concerning the fulfilment of scripture in Jesus' passion? Were they drawn from oral tradition, a testimony book, or are they ad hoc creations of the Evangelist? In any event, this feature of Matthew's passion narrative is further evidence of the Evangelist's (and his reader's) lively interest in the correspondence between prophecy and fulfilment.[52]

As in earlier passages in the narrative, so in Jesus' passion, Matthew proclaims that Jesus is the Son of God. In Gethsemane the Son is totally obedient to his father (26:39, 42); at the high priest's trial Jesus is asked whether he is "the Christ, the Son of God" (26:63).[53] Ironically it is as Son of God that Jesus is condemned to die, that he is blasphemed (27:39f.), and mocked (41–44). After supernatural portents, which are viewed as the father's attestation of Jesus' divine sonship, Gentile soldiers confess his true nature (22:51–54). Obediently and with perfect trust Jesus dies, accomplishing for humankind "the forgiveness of sins" (26:28; 1:21). The rending of the temple veil signifies the end of the early temple service and judgment upon Judaism.

In his account of the resurrection Matthew reflects a moment on the development of the church's apologetic, which emphasized the objective, evidential character of this event. The stories of the guard at Jesus' grave are naive Christian responses to the absurd calumny of some Jews that the resurrection of Jesus' body was a hoax (27:62–66; 28:11–15). It has been noted, however, that Matthew reflects the hesitancy characteristic of all New Testament writers to name witnesses to the raising of Jesus. Indeed, Matthew writes of Jesus as coming out of the sealed tomb while the guards are sleeping, but it is doubly noteworthy that the women, who observe everything else, do not see the risen Christ emerging from his tomb.[54] According to Matthew, no observable phenomenon, however remarkable, exhibited what had happened, only the word of God (the angel's message) led to understanding.

In these notes repeated reference has been made to the conclusion of Matthew's Gospel (28:16–20). After the postresurrection appearances of Jesus to "the eleven" he does not depart, as in Mark 16:19 or Luke 24:49 (Acts 1:9). Instead, Jesus remains with his disciples. Since all power and authority are now given to the Son of God, his disciples may always enjoy this support. At the same time, this presence of Jesus is not intended for passive enjoyment: Jesus' disciples are commanded to teach and to do everything that he taught them. This is, of course, not the last word of this Gospel: at "the close of the age" those who are chosen will inherit the enduring kingdom and eternal life (22:1–14; 24:30f., 45–25:31–46).

MATTHEW: THE AUTHOR, HIS TIME, PLACE, AND SITUATION

While it is highly unlikely that the First Evangelist should be identified as Matthew, one of the twelve apostles, it is possible that the ex-tax collector was at one time associated with the church that stands behind this Gospel, and was esteemed as a founder or "patron disciple." This would explain why the pericope in the First Gospel concerning the call of "Matthew" replaces Mark's story of the call of "Levi."[55] But what can be said in a positive way about the identity of the First Evangelist?

Some students of the Gospel hold that its author was a Gentile Christian. His use of the LXX; his tendency to "improve" the highly Semitic Greek of Mark; and his word-plays, which suggest that Greek was his native tongue— all have been noted. Also, Matthew's vigorous polemics against Pharisaism (3:7–10; 23:1–33) and Israel itself (21:43) have been noted. His universal outlook and his sympathy for the Gentile mission constitute further evidence.[56]

Yet the preponderant evidence favors the view that Matthew was a Christian of Jewish background. His respect for the authority of the Law (5:17–20), observance of the Sabbath (24:20), and tithing (23:23); his formal acknowledgement that the Pharisees "sit on Moses' seat" (23:2f.); his use of rabbinical modes of argumentation from scripture—all of these things, combined with his sharp hostility toward scribes and Pharisees who oppose Jesus (23:13, 29–33), make credible the view that the First Evangelist was formerly a scribe of the sect of the Pharisees. We ask again: Is Matthew's reference to the scribe "trained for the kingdom of heaven" who "brings out of his treasure what is new and what is old," an autobiographical note (13:52)? Matthew's universal outlook and undoubted support of the Gentile mission does not obscure his concern to affirm, not reject, his own and others' Jewish past. Moreover, he valued the Jewish-Christian traditions of Jesus' ministry that he had received, for, properly reinterpreted and understood, these traditions provided important supports for the church's appeal to Israel. While there is reason to believe that Matthew's church had become increasingly Gentile in composition, and tensions between the church and synagogue had intensified, it is unlikely that all missionary efforts on behalf of Jews had ceased (10:8–11:1; 23:34).

While full agreement has not been reached over whether Matthew was a Gentile Christian or a (Hellenistic?) Jewish Christian, scholars favor Syria as the location of Matthew's church. Christian settlements in this region, especially in Antioch, would contain many Greek-speaking Jews as well as Gentiles. There would be synagogues present, and in Syria "one could plausibly encounter a converted scribe who wrote in Greek and knew Hebrew."[57] The mention in the Gospel of pagan officials persecuting disciples of Jesus as a consequence of their preaching to "all nations," would suggest an area outside Judea or Galilee (10:18).

The relationship of Matthew to Mark, the allusion to the "burning" of Jerusalem (22:7), and the evidence of sharp polemics with the synagogue, make plausible a date for the composition of Matthew's Gospel in the 80s or 90s. Perhaps date in the early 90s is to be preferred if, as seems probable, Matthew's church had already separated from Judaism and a Gentile mission was flourishing, free from restraints concerning circumcision and the food laws. The knowledge of Matthean tradition reflected in letters of Ignatius (d. ca. 107 C.E.) supports a date for Matthew before the turn of the century.[58]

NOTES

1. Eusebius, *H.E.* III. 39. 16. In another section of his history of the Church Eusebius wrote, "Matthew, having first preached to the Hebrews, when he was about to go to others, compensated for the loss of his presence . . . by delivering to them in writing his Gospel in their native language." *H.E.* III. 24.
2. For an "interpretation" of the Papias tradition, see David Hill, *The Gospel of Matthew* (1972), pp. 23–27.
3. This judgment is shared by those who are not persuaded that an immediate literary dependence of Mt. upon Mk. is demonstrable. The LXX is usually cited in Mt. but this is not always the case; see R. Brown, *The Birth of the Messiah* (1977), pp. 143–153, 184–188. Kümmel, *INT²*, pp. 110ff.
4. Kümmel, *INT²*, pp. 108–112. D. Hill, *The Gospel of Matthew*, pp. 31–34. For a demonstration of the difficulty of separating pre-Matthean material from Matthew's redaction, see Brown, *The Birth of the Messiah*, pp. 96–121.
5. Cf. Mk. 4:35–5:43 and Mt. 8:18–9:26.
6. Cf. Mt. 8:16 and 26, and Mk. 1:32 and 4:39.
7. Mt. 13:58 (Mk. 6:5f.).
8. Greek texts supply the evidence, but cf. Mt. 4:1 and Mk. 1:12f. (RSV)
9. Mt. 3:13–15 cf. Mk. 1:9; Mt. 12:9–14 cf. Mk. 3:1–6; Mt. 13:55 cf. Mk. 6:3.
10. Mt. 20:20 cf. Mk. 10:35; Mt. 12:40 cf. Mk. 3:34. Several references in Mk. to the disciples' ignorance or bewilderment are omitted: cf. Mk. 9:5–7 and Mt. 17:4f. Others are toned down: cf. 8:14–21 and Mt. 16:5–12.
11. Two demoniacs, cf. Mt. 8:28–34 and Mk. 5:1–20. Two blind men, cf. 9:27–31 and Mk. 10:46–52.
12. B. W. Bacon, *Studies in Matthew* (1930), p. 17.
13. "The crucial point is legal recognition, not biological descent." E. Schweizer, *The Good News According to Matthew* (1975), p. 25.
14. To David—2 Sam. 7:8–16; to Abraham—Gen. 12:1–3; 22:15–18. R. E. Brown, *Birth of the Messiah*, p. 68.
15. Brown, *Birth of the Messiah*, pp. 73f. Or, again, to note that Jesus, the messiah of the Jews, was related by ancestry to Gentiles? Schweizer, *The Good News*, pp. 24f. An exegesis attributed to Luther.
16. Perhaps "the evangelist regarded the infancy as a section of Jesus' life still relatively unexplored in reference to the Old Testament. In this it might be contrasted to the passion that had been studied against an Old Testament backdrop from the beginning of Christian preaching." Brown, *Birth of the Messiah*, p. 99.

17. *Ibid.*, pp. 149f.
18. Note Jn. 1:45; 7:41f., 52.
19. Cf. Brown, *Birth of the Messiah*, pp. 180–183, 411f., 444f.
20. J. D. Kingsbury, *Matthew: Structure, Christology, Kingdom* (1975) pp. 7ff.; Kümmel, *INT²*, pp. 103, 105f.; cf. Brown, *Birth of the Messiah*, pp. 49f.
21. See also Mt. 7:19 (cf. 3:10); 13:30 (3:12); 12:33f. and 23:33 (3:7).
22. Schweizer, *The Good News*, pp. 47, 56. Note that in 3:6, Mt. follows Mk. 1:5 but omits 1:4 (retained by Lk. 3:3). Mt. also emphasizes the preparatory role of John by identifying him more closely with the expected Elijah who has come. Cf. Mt. 11:13f. and Lk. 16:16; Mt. 17:12f. and Lk. 9:13. W. Wink, *John the Baptist in the Gospel Tradition* (1968), pp. 33ff.
23. Cf. Mt. 4:2 and Exod. 34:28.
24. For a list of scholars adopting Bacon's outline, with variations, see Kingsbury, *Matthew: Structure, Christology, Kingdom*, pp. 2–4; also his "Form and Message of Matthew," *Int.*, 29 (1975): 13–15.
25. W. D. Davies, *The Sermon on the Mount* (1966), pp. 10–17; G. Barth, "Matthew's Understanding of the Law," G. Bornkamm, G. Barth, and J. J. Held, eds., *Tradition and Interpretation in Matthew* (1963), pp. 157–159.
26. Matthew's five-fold formula need not be discounted as a mere literary feature. It may call attention to the incomparable importance of the words of Jesus, which have the status of divine revelation. Considered together, Matthew's discourses offer a complete summary of Jesus' teaching. When last used Matthew's formula read: "when Jesus had finished *all* these sayings . . ." The so-called "antitheses" of the Sermon on the Mount (5:21f., 27f., 31f., 33f., 38f., 43–45) make the same point, as does the concluding parable of the sermon, 7:24–27.
27. Kingsbury, "Form and Message," p. 18.
28. Schweizer, *The Good News*, pp. 69f.
29. Kingsbury, "Form and Message," p. 18; *Matthew: Structure, Christology, Kingdom*, pp. 7ff. Cf. T. B. Slater, "Notes on Matthew's Structure," *JBL*, 99 (1980): 436.
30. These major divisions are followed in the outline proposed here, with the exception that 26:1–28:20 seem to constitute a concluding section (although the precise formula of 4:17 and 16:21 is missing). Note, however, that 26:1 seems to function as a superscription. Kümmel, *INT²*, pp. 103–106; D.P. Senior, *The Passion Narrative According to Matthew* (1975), pp. 12f., 27.
31. Although Mt. asserts explicitly that Jesus' ministry was directed to "the lost sheep of the house of Israel" (10:5ff.), and edits Mk. 7:24–30 accordingly, it is only Mt. who reports that Jesus commended the "Canaanite woman": "O woman, great is your faith!", Mt. 15:28 (viewed by Mt. as a challenge to those disciples of Jesus in Mt's church of "little faith"?) Note also Mt. 15:31; 12:15–21.
32. Cf. Mk. 6:45–52 and Mt. 14:22–33 (also Mk. 4:35–41 and Mt. 8:18–27); Mk. 8:14–21 and Mt. 16:5–12; Mk. 8:27–30 and Mt. 16:13–20; Mk. 4:10f. and Mt. 13:10–17.
33. Schweizer, *The Good News*, pp. 338f.
34. The only adequate confession, according to Mt.'s church, is that Jesus is "the Messiah, the Son of the living God," a title misunderstood by the public. Mt. 14:33; 26:63; 27:39–44.
35. Cf. Mt. 17:22f., and Mk. 9:30–32, Lk. 9:43b–45. Although Mt. recognizes the significance of Jesus' teaching concerning his passion, he "has so softened and shortened his reference to it (17:22f.) that he has robbed it of its total pre-eminence."
36. Davies, *The Sermon on the Mount*, pp. 23f.
37. *Ibid.*, p. 27.

38. Observe that "Matthew associates the setting of the 'mountain' exclusively with Jesus as the Son of God." Kingsbury, "Form and Message," p. 21. Mt. 4:3; 6:8; 14:23, 33; 28:16–19.

39. G. B. Caird, "The Study of the Gospels," *ExpT* 87 (1976): p. 169.

40. Space precludes doing justice in these notes to this pervasive interest of Mt. Not only "the great discourses" reflect an adaptation of the gospel tradition to post-Easter circumstances, but also the narrative-pericopes. Vivid examples of the latter are Mt.'s editing of two Markan "nature miracles," Mk. 4:35–41 and 6:45–52. Cf. Mt. 8:18–27 and 14:22–33. G. Bornkamm, "The Stilling of the Storm in Matthew," in Bornkamm, Barth, and Held, *Tradition and Interpretation*, pp. 52–57; also, H. J. Held, "Matthew as Interpreter of the Miracle Stories," in Bornkamm, Barth, and Held, *Tradition and Interpretation*, pp. 165ff., especially pp. 200–206.

41. See, e.g., Davies, *The Sermon on the Mount*, pp. 27–32.

42. J. P. Meier, *Law and History in Matthew's Gospel: A Redactional Study of Mt. 5:17–48* (1976), pp. 125–161; Kingsbury, *Matthew: Structure, Christology, Kingdom*, pp. 81–84.

43. Cf. Exod. 22:10f.; Lev. 19:12; Num. 5:11–31; Deut. 6:13; 23:21–23, and others.

44. E.g., Exod. 21:23–25; Lev. 24:19f.; Deut. 19:21, and others. Again, on the opposite side, Jesus does not in principle abrogate the Sabbath Law according to Mt. 12:1–14, and 24:20 may suggest that in Matthew's church the Sabbath was sanctified. It is not certain that in Mt. 15:10–20 Jesus is understood to rescind the dietary laws. Note Matthew's omission of Mk. 7:19b.

45. Some scholars understand the term rendered "unchastity" (R.S.V.) to refer to incestuous marriage within the degrees of consanguinity or affinity prohibited by Lev. 18:6–18. Meier, *Law and History*, pp. 140–150; Kingsbury, *Matthew: Structure, Christology, Kingdom*, p. 83. Cf. Schweizer, *The Good News*, pp. 122–126, who opts for "the usual interpretation" implying "continued infidelity."

46. See also Mt. 19:16–22; 5:48. Was the goal of perfection required only of the "heroic" disciple?

47. Mt. 13:52. Also 16:19; 18:18–20.

48. Meier, *Law and History*, p. 65. Mt. 24:35.

49. The apocalyptic language—the passing of heaven and earth, the accomplishment of all things, i.e., the coming to pass of prophesied events—possibly refers back to Jesus' death and resurrection as well as forward to his final coming, so that, as Meier suggests, Mt. 28:16ff. may aptly be termed "a proleptic parousia." For Matthew's church the binding force of the Mosaic Law "as an inviolable whole" has already passed away with the death and resurrection of the Messiah. Before this eschatological event, Jesus restricted himself to the people and the land of Israel (Mt. 10:7; 15:24) and showed himself faithful in principle to the Mosaic Law, but already within the ministry of Jesus he signalled, in word as in deed, the coming of the new age.

50. Possibly this "trial schema" is repeated in the following sequence: The disputations (22:15–46) may represent the *trial* of Israel; the series of woes (23:1–32), the *verdict*; 23:33–36 the *sentence*; and 23:37–24:2 its *execution*. "With Jesus, God himself leaves the city, as is visibly demonstrated by the destruction of the temple (an event already in the past for Matthew and his readers)." Schweizer, *The Good News*, p. 402.

51. Kingsbury, *Matthew: Structure, Christology, Kingdom*, p. 56.

52. Mt. also emphasizes (again, more strongly than Mk.) that in his passion Jesus' own word is fulfilled, 26:2; 28:66; 27:62f.

53. In place of Mk.'s "I am" (14:62), Jesus' response in Mt. is ambiguous. Perhaps this is Matthew's emphasis upon the continued ignorance of the high priest with respect

to the reality of Jesus' divine sonship. Kingsbury, *Matthew: Structure, Christology, Kingdom*, pp. 73f.

54. Cf. the apocryphal Gospel of Peter, 8:28–11:49, *New Testament Apocrypha*, Vol. 1, ed., Hennecke-Schneemelcher (1963), pp. 185f. Schweizer, *The Good News*, p. 525.

55. Cf. Mk. 2:14 and Lk. 5:27 with Mt. 9:9. Mk.'s list of Jesus' disciples corroborates this equation; cf. Mk. 3:18 and Lk. 6:15 with Mt. 10:3. Kingsbury, *Matthew: Structure, Christology, Kingdom*, p. 104.

56. Mt. 2:1f., 11; 4:12–16; 8:5–13; 12:21; 13:37f.; 24:14; 26:13; 28:16–20.

57. R. Brown, *Birth of the Messiah*, p. 47; Schweizer, *The Good News*, pp. 15–17.

58. Perhaps the major role given to Peter in this Gospel associates it with Antioch in Syria. A combination of notes, Acts 12:17 and Gal. 2:11ff., locates Peter in this church for a time. Schweizer notes an affinity between the concerns of Matthew and those of the writer of the Didache, the latter presumably reflecting the church in Syria "at a somewhat later stage of development." *The Good News*, p. 17.

| The Historical Jesus | Chapter 9 |

THE Gospels of the New Testament contain the memories of Jesus that the early Christians cherished and passed on to others; stories from his ministry, as well as his teaching, that were most useful in supporting and advancing the Christian kerygma and community. The application of form criticism to the study of the Gospels has gone far to validate this assumption. This is widely recognized, even by those who have serious reservations concerning some of the conclusions of individual form critics. The Gospels of the New Testament are a literary deposit of the preaching, teaching, and worship of the first generation of Christians, and it has been shown that those interests have left their impression upon the precanonical "sources," either oral or written or both.

But the Gospels are more than this. From a study of the structure of Mark and of the other Gospels and the editorial techniques employed in them, clues have been derived for a recovery of the distinctive theologies of the Evangelists or, at least, their theological tendencies.

These developments in synoptic criticism have unquestionably intensified the problematical nature of Jesus research. "Must we not recognize that Jesus is not only screened from us by the beliefs of early Christians, which have colored the oral tradition and written sources about Jesus, upon which the Gospel writers drew, but also by the minds of the Gospel writers themselves? Do not Matthew, Mark and Luke, as interpreters, cast their own mantles around Jesus so that he himself is hidden more and more from our eyes?"[1]

The force of these questions and of the acknowledgments they imply are not to be denied. It is now commonly conceded that the investigation of Jesus' history is a far more complex task than earlier historians seem to have recognized. While a more adequate understanding of the origin and nature of the Gospels has not led scholars to despair of these books as sources for knowledge of Jesus, it is apparent that the outcome of nineteenth-century research upon the Gospels, and the theological issues that were sharpened by this research, have had a sobering if not inhibiting effect upon recent scholarly attempts to describe Jesus.

THE QUEST OF THE HISTORICAL JESUS, OLD AND NEW

"The historical Jesus" denotes both the person of Jesus as an object of historical investigation, and the picture that is drawn of him, which is the result of this research. The phrase therefore may be said to refer to the historians' Jesus (not any particular historian's Jesus, but to the man who may be known and described by applying to the records of his life commonly accepted methods of historical criticism).

At the turn of the present century, Albert Schweitzer published a devastating criticism of the major "lives of Jesus" written by German and French scholars between 1778 and 1901 and based ostensibly on data that the Gospels provide. The English title of Schweitzer's book gave a popular name to this prodigious literary effort: "the quest of the historical Jesus." Schweitzer demonstrated that the confusing variety of biographies that he reviewed can be accounted for by the rationalistic or romantic biases of their authors, and by the psychological conjecture that they had foisted upon the data of the Gospels to make plausible their own descriptions of Jesus' personality.

It was left to other critics to point out that the failure of the nineteenth-century "quest" to discover "the real Jesus" was caused by a more basic error, an error that Schweitzer had failed to recognize and that also vitiated his own effort. These biographers, as well as their critic, had based their work on the presupposition that the overbearing influence of Christological dogma was the *only* serious obstacle to recovering the real Jesus. It was assumed that even from the days of the early Church, Jesus had been more or less misunderstood, so that the writers of the Gospels themselves, wittingly or unwittingly, had obscured the essence of what Jesus taught as well as the real meaning of his actions. But now, at long last, scientific historiography has enabled competent scholars to gain access to the true facts. Schweitzer's principal complaint was that those who had searched for the real Jesus in modern times had not been sufficiently objective. This fault Schweitzer himself sought to overcome.[2]

During the early decades of this century, when form criticism was leading the way to a more adequate understanding of the preliterary history of the Gospel tradition and exposing the arbitrary use of faulty source theories by the "objective" biographers of Jesus, two leading European theologians, Karl Barth and Rudolf Bultmann, were questioning seriously the legitimacy of this century-long quest. "Historicism" was the pejorative term used to condemn the methodology of these biographers of Jesus, a methodology that many philosophers of history and historians were repudiating. But more serious to these theologians was the conviction that the quest itself was invalid according to the Christian proclamation and faith.*

The impact of the objections raised by Bultmann upon subsequent developments was especially strong because the Marburg theologian had pioneered in applying the methods of form criticism to the New Testament and was in the process of publishing the successive editions of his *History of the Synoptic Tradition*. As early as 1929 Bultmann wrote:

> It is not permitted to go beyond the proclamation, using it as a source in order to reconstruct the historic Jesus with his messianic consciousness, his inwardness or his heroic character. This would be precisely the "Christ according to the flesh" [2 Cor. 5:16] who belongs to the past. It is not the historic Christ who is the Lord, but Jesus Christ as he is encountered in the proclamation.[3]

In Bultmann's later defense of his position, in answer to some of his students who sought to modify it, he reiterated that Christ of the *kerygma*, and not the

*Given the nature of the Gospels, they have a limited value as sources for historical reconstruction; they are primarily testimonies of faith. We probably possess no single word or account of an act of Jesus, no matter how incontestably genuine, that does not also reflect in some way the post-Easter faith of those preserving the Gospel traditions.

person of the historical Jesus, is the object of a Christian's faith. The person whom the *kerygma* addresses is neither able, as has been commonly supposed, "to free the picture of the historical Jesus from the dogmatic overlay that had concealed it in the primitive Christian message, nor may he inquire behind the kerygma for a legitimation offered by historical research." In his various responses to persons seeking to appraise or reappraise his position, Bultmann persisted in denying both the theological necessity and the historical possibility of knowing Jesus as he really was, how he lived, and what he taught before his crucifixion.[4]

Following Bultmann's major contributions, the course of Jesus research flowed into two main channels. On the one hand, the writings of some New Testament scholars in this country and abroad revealed that the unfulfilled expectations and methodological errors of their predecessors had not established the futility of "the quest of the historical Jesus." As one writer has observed, "the resilience of the historical approach" is a phenomenon to be taken into account in a survey of recent trends.[5] On the other hand, one can distinguish a group of scholars by the more direct influence of Bultmann's theology and form critical judgments upon their work. They began what has been called, "a new quest of the historical Jesus." This descriptive phrase, useful at the outset in identifying the special viewpoint and contributions of several major scholars, begs the question: How "new" is the new quest? "Post-Bultmannian" is a preferable identification since this term does not focus directly on this question of novelty, which can detract from other more material issues. "Post-Bultmannian" identifies the program of those scholars who acknowledge the seriousness of the issues that Bultmann raised, yet who seek to modify his position through the application of some basic insights and skills that Bultmann taught.[6]

One important conviction can be said to unite the great majority of scholars engaged today in Jesus research; however, they can be distinguished as groups or as individuals. Unlike Bultmann, they affirm the necessity and possibility of postulating a continuity and substantial agreement between "Jesus as he was" and the Christ to whom witness was borne in the Christian *kerygma* of New Testament times. They have seen that Bultmann's insistence on the theological irrelevance of knowing "Jesus as he was" threatens to reduce the Incarnation to a symbol of timeless truth, and encourages a revival of Christ-myth theories. They agree that there is no stability in a position that affirms Jesus' historicity as well as his full humanity, as Bultmann does, but denies the interest of faith in the "features and traits" of Jesus' personal life and in the actual teachings and happenings of his ministry. But to insist on the relevance of Jesus as he was leads at once to the problem: How can this knowledge be established? There is indeed "no logical connection between theological necessity and historical possibility."[7] If one must acknowledge the misguided attempts and failures of earlier generations, how is one to avert them and achieve a greater measure of success?

Because of the complexity of the sources and the meager results of research, it can be argued that "the quest of the historical Jesus" might well be abandoned, especially if the whole enterprise is theologically suspect. In response it can be said that since the person of Jesus continues to fascinate so many people and lead them, for various motives, to a recreation of his image, it is important that this research be done in a responsible way and not left to novelists and moviemakers. As for the issue of theological relevance, one can agree with Bultmann that to seek legitimation of the Gospels by historical research is to demand "signs," and is evidence of doubt, not faith. But a desire to know what Jesus was like need not be prompted by doubt but by a sincere wish to establish one's response to the Gospels upon an image of Jesus that is as objective as may be obtainable. Just as the second generation of Jesus' disciples "made themselves contemporaries" with the pre-Easter Jesus and his first disciples, so modern disciples may wish to respond in as unmediated a way as possible to the words and deeds *of* Jesus.[8]

MODEST CLAIMS AND A MORE RIGOROUS METHODOLOGY

It is not permissible today to minimize the difficulties of Jesus research. The dangers of subjectivity—the inevitable influence of ideological presuppositions—are especially perceptible here, if not in one's own work, then in that of others.[9] Add to this fact the observations made above concerning the nature of the sources at the historian's disposal: one can only find the history of Jesus within the fragmentary, "kerygmatized" material preserving the witness of the apostles and others within the early churches, and edited by the evangelists with their particular viewpoints. The conclusion follows that "only by methodologically pure and critical work can the received traditions be made useful for a historical description of Jesus."[10]

This section concludes with a report of methodological procedures used by many contemporary scholars as they have attempted to advance from an analysis of the Gospel tradition to a description of Jesus as he was. These procedures adopt three criteria: the criterion of dissimilarity; the criterion of multiple or cross-sectional attestation; and the criterion of coherence.[11]

The first two criteria have been considered especially useful in identifying "authentic sayings" of Jesus. The criterion of dissimilarity identifies teaching of Jesus that for various reasons cannot be derived from ancient Judaism or attributed to the early Church. Special attention can also be called to certain actions of Jesus that appear offensive, or at least startling, to foe and friend alike. An example of a saying of Jesus meeting this criterion is his use of "abba" ("father" or "my father") in addressing God. Jesus' baptism by John, signifying repentance of sins, is an example of an action of Jesus satisfying this criterion.

The criterion of dissimilarity is undeniably flawed. Rigorously applied, we not only set Jesus apart from his Jewish contemporaries and allegedly eliminate later Christian accretions in the Gospels, we exclude that material which could possibly be common either to Jesus and ancient Judaism, or to Jesus and the Church. If we place a saying or incident to the credit of Judaism or the Church are we obliged to debit it from our picture of Jesus? His most original teaching was perhaps not most characteristic. A non-Jewish Jesus, exhibiting no relationship in what he said and did to the testimony of the early disciples and Evangelists is a caricature. Finally, it can be observed that any explicit claims that Jesus might have made concerning his person would seem to be eliminated from his teaching by this principle, since it is at least probable that any such self-revelation would, in later Christian communities, be applied to the risen Lord.[12]

In spite of these limitations, the application of this criterion to the Gospels, if applied with care, can be useful. By means of it one possesses "only a critically assured minimum," however, and some readers would doubtless argue that one should begin with the whole or maximum of material and, when in doubt, favor the witness of tradition.[13]

The criterion of multiple or cross-sectional attestation identifies sayings of Jesus that either in their form or content or both are found in more than one of the sources underlying the Synoptic Gospels. By exercising this criterion, scholars have discovered Jesus' proclamation concerning the coming of the kingdom of God; his attitude toward the Torah, and especially, toward persons treated by others as society's outcasts—"the tax collectors and sinners" of the Gospels. Some scholars claim that this criterion rarely attests specific sayings of Jesus.[14] But by its application one can discover some things more important than isolated sayings, namely, authentic features and traits of Jesus, and thus be led to an understanding of his intention.[15]

The criterion of coherence examines and accepts as authentic Jesus tradition, which coheres or is harmonious with sayings or actions identified by other criteria, especially by the criterion of dissimilarity. Some persons would apply this criterion only to material found in the earliest sources or strata of the gospel tradition, but the possibility cannot be excluded that authentic sayings were preserved in secondary literary sources. Of course this criterion must be used with caution. Sayings that have "the ring of authenticity," or actions that are "characteristic of Jesus" appear differently to different persons.

The persisting quest of historians to learn what Jesus was really like has been compared with "the work of the archaeologist who attempts to restore an old monument of which only the foundation and a few scattered stones remain." As a scientist he will make one or more sketches in an attempt to picture the monument as it stood. No one will deny the usefulness of these archeological drawings. At the same time, the scholar will be expected to call attention to points in his sketch "where exact knowledge ends and his tutored imagination has taken over." When he has discovered the precise spot where a few of the stones originally lay, he will value this precious evidence far more than the total monument he has reconstructed by his inferential methods.

In a similar fashion, sketches of the historical Jesus will continue to be drawn in the absence of sufficient information to reconstruct his life after the order of a modern biography. Some of the sketches drawn by scientifically competent scholars have great value and, like the hypothetical reconstructions of great archeologists, become the impulse for further research and advance knowledge. Over an extended period, however, "an expansion of our exact knowledge of primitive Christianity and of Judaism in Jesus' time" may mean more for modern man's rediscovery of Jesus than many imaginative sketches portraying him as he probably was.[16]

NON-CHRISTIAN SOURCES AND THEIR VALUE

There is just enough information about Jesus in Jewish and pagan writings to anchor him in history. It is important that this evidence be reviewed. In an earlier critical period a few scholars argued that the Christ of the Gospels was a myth, or a symbol fortuitously associated with the life of a man who had never lived. More recently, radical form critical views have threatened to uproot the Christian Gospel from the solid earth of Jesus' unique historical existence.

The earliest Jewish testimony to Jesus is found in the *Antiquities* of Josephus. The following passage in Book XX is commonly considered genuine:

> Ananias called the Sanhedrin together, brought before it James, the brother of Jesus who was called the Christ, and certain others . . . and he caused them to be stoned.[17]

Another passage is found in Book XVIII. It describes Jesus as a teacher and a miracle worker, reports that "after his renunciation by our leading citizens, Pilate condemned him to be crucified," and that he was raised from the dead in fulfillment of prophecy. This passage is almost universally considered to be a Christian insertion, but whether in whole or in part is a matter of conjecture.[18]

It is impossible to believe that Josephus knew nothing about Christian origins. The explanation of his almost complete silence must be found in the historian's apologetic motives. Writing as a Pharisee and for the Romans, Josephus studiously avoided commenting upon messianic movements within Judaism. This explanation does not rest solely upon an argument from silence, for in telling of John the Baptist and his tragic fate, Josephus conceals from his readers the messianic import of John's proclamation and baptism.[19]

The references to Jesus and to his followers in the Talmud are designed to contradict the claims of the Christian gospel and are therefore of little independent value. Two plausible reasons have been given for the scarcity of references to Jesus and to Christianity in the Talmud. In the first place, events of the period are seldom noted; for example, no reference is made to the Maccabean Revolution! By the time of "the sages of the Talmud," the popular stories concerning Jesus "were turned into subjects of ridicule." The Jewish scholar Joseph Klausner summarizes the statements of the Tannaim about Jesus that are found in the Talmud. The founder of Christianity was remembered as a rabbi whose name was Jesus of Nazareth, who practiced sorcery and beguiled Israel, who mocked the words of the wise, who expounded scripture in the same manner as the Pharisees, who had five disciples, who said that he was not come to take away from the Law or to add to it, who was hanged as a false teacher and beguiler on the eve of the Passover that happened on the Sabbath, and whose disciples healed the sick in his name.[20]

The earliest Latin passage in which Christ is mentioned is found in the correspondence of Pliny the Younger (a governor of Bithynia, with the Emperor Trajan), noted in the second chapter of this book. In a letter, usually dated in 112 C.E., Pliny reports that his investigation had convinced him that the Christians were a crudely superstitious folk. On certain days they assembled before dawn and "sang hymns to Christ as to a God."[21] About the same time, Pliny's friend, Tacitus, recorded in his Annals the persecution of Christians under Nero. This passage, noted in connection with the study of Mark, reports that "Christ was put to death in the reign of Tiberius by the procurator Pontius Pilate."[22]

References in Roman literature to Christ and early Christianity are rare. This is not surprising. As late as the second century the whole movement was considered a "mischievous superstition," according to Tacitus. In Roman literary circles Christianity was just another contemptible Oriental cult. Why did it matter if its own account of its origin was real or fictitious?[23] Although the comments of Latin authors are of very little value to this study of the history of Jesus, it is interesting that Roman society became aware of Christ as "an object of worship and the historical founder of a religious community." The same twofold witness is given to Jesus throughout the New Testament.[24]

AGRAPHA AND THE APOCRYPHAL GOSPELS*

With the composition of the Gospels of the New Testament, the reservoir of Jesus tradition was not depleted. (Note the hyperbolic statement of the Fourth Evangelist, John 21:25.) This tradition was preserved in ancient Christian writings, some of which were unknown until recently.

Several "agrapha" of Jesus can be cited. A familiar agraphon is the word attributed to Jesus in Acts 20:35: "it is more blessed to give than to receive." Single manuscripts of a Gospel provide other agrapha. For example, in a sixth-century manuscript, Codex Bezae, the following incident is recorded after Luke 6:5

> On the same day, seeing someone working on the Sabbath, he [Jesus] said to him, "Man, if indeed you know what you are doing, you are blessed; but if you do not know, you are cursed and a transgressor of the Law."

In most cases agrapha of this type are easily identifiable as scribal additions. But the authenticity of a few, such as the one just cited, has been maintained.[25]

A third source of agrapha are the writings of the Church Fathers. Probably Bishop Papias was the first of the fathers to collect the sayings of Jesus not recorded in the Gospels. The results was five volumes entitled *Expositions of the Words of the Lord.* Unfortunately, Papias was not a very intelligent man, as Eusebius observed, and citations of agrapha from the collection of Papias suggest that the work was of little value. Agrapha in the works of Justin Martyr, Clement of Alexandria, Origen, and a few others deserve serious consideration. Take this passage from Origen, for example:

> I have read somewhere that the Saviour said . . . "He that is near me, is near the fire; he that is far from me, is far from the kingdom."[26]

Still another source of agrapha are the Egyptian papyri that have been found during the past century. Especially noteworthy are the Oxyrhynchus Papyri (P. Oxy.) in which one agraphon ordinarily follows another without context, introduced by the formula "Jesus says." An example reminiscent of Matthew 18:20 is:

> Jesus says: Wheresoever there are two, they are not without God, and where there is one alone, I say, I am with him. Lift up the stone, and there shalt thou find me; cleave the wood, and I am there.[27]

Did most of these agrapha originally stand in some gospel or are they isolated sayings taken from the oral tradition that persisted alongside of written gospels? Since the discovery of several "gospels" in the Coptic language in the vicinity of Nag Hammadi (Egypt) in 1945 or 1946, support is given to the former alternative.[28] At least it can be said that isolated sayings found their

*Agrapha, lit. "unwritten" — a term used to identify units of the Jesus tradition, mostly sayings, "not written" in the critically established texts of the canonical Gospels.

way into gospel manuscripts, from which they were cited by the Fathers of the Church.

The existence of extracanonical gospels is attested to in Christian literature of the second and third centuries. With the canonization of Matthew, Mark, Luke, and John, most of these rival gospels were destroyed or became the property of special groups who found them congenial to their doctrines. It is difficult to classify these "remains" chronologically and to identify the documents of which they were originally a part. In writings of the Church Fathers some of the same works may be referred to by different titles.

Two types of apocryphal gospel material can be distinguished. The first contains a pious "embroidery" upon some aspect of canonical tradition or upon traditions approximately parallel to those in the Gospels. The Protoevangelium of James provides an excellent example of this type.[29] It contains legends relating to Mary, Joseph, and Jesus' birth and childhood. The passion and resurrection narrative in an extant fragment of a Gospel of Peter also belongs to this type.[30] These traditions may preserve some early reminiscences. Tendentious gospels are a second type of apocryphal material. These contain traditions that were collected in sectarian groups to support the community's special interests. Examples of such writings are the Gospel of the Egyptians[31] and the Gospel of Basilides. Among the Nag Hammadi manuscripts are well-preserved specimens of apocryphal gospel traditions of the second type; for example, the Gospel of Thomas.

Until very recent times it was commonly held that in the apocryphal gospels the history of Jesus had been "irretrievably smothered beneath legend and fantasy." Here and there in the midst of "worthless rubbish" discoveries of a "priceless jewel" have been claimed.[32] The continuing discoveries of papyrus fragments stood as reminders that questions concerning the value of extracanonical traditions should not be foreclosed. The remarkable Nag Hammadi discoveries have led some to opine that the historian is now in possession of some agrapha that may be as authentic as sayings of Jesus in the Synoptic Gospels. Among these newly recovered Coptic documents, the Gospel of Thomas holds special interest for Jesus research. It contains no narrative but only sayings of Jesus, similar in form to the Oxyrhynchus Papyri, and parables that, in their content but not in their setting, resemble Matthew's Gospel. The question that is difficult to resolve is the relationship between Thomas and the Synoptic tradition. The evidence seems to favor their independence, and the view that the sayings of Jesus in Thomas "either are present in a more primitive form or are developments of a more primitive form of such sayings."[33]

It is, of course, possible that new discoveries will supplement our knowledge of Jesus in some important and valuable ways.[34] But it is probable that such materials will shed more light upon the Christian communities preserving extracanonical traditions than upon Jesus himself, and this to a much greater extent than is the case with the Gospels of the New Testament.

AN OUTLINE OF JESUS' MINISTRY

Reconstructions of the chronology of Jesus' history are bound to contain speculative elements, given the scant and apparently conflicting information provided by the Gospels.[35] Our reading of Mark disclosed that the first part of Jesus' ministry was centered in Galilee, the latter part in Judea. This division of the principal scenes of Jesus' activity reappears in Matthew and Luke, despite the differences in editorial aims and methods. That these areas were the principal foci of Jesus' ministry finds further support in the summary statements of the apostle's *kerygma* in the early chapters of Acts. Between the Galilean and Judean periods of the ministry in Mark, as well as in Matthew, Jesus traveled in regions to the north and northwest of Galilee. Luke's omission of some of Mark's episodes relating to this period obscures this area of the ministry in the Third Gospel. Yet it is unlikely that Luke offers a variant historical tradition. He has introduced stories that do not fit into the Markan framework, but he provides no clear itinerary of his own. The reader of Luke 9–18 learns that Jesus made a somewhat leisurely progress through the central districts of Palestine toward Jerusalem.[36]

Because the chronological connections are loosest in Mark 7–9, it is reasonable to suppose, as Luke seems to have done, that more time should be allowed for a ministry in Perea and Judea and, perhaps, in Jerusalem itself.

Reconstructions of the chronology of Jesus' ministry have ordinarily been based on one of two alternatives. The choice lies between a ministry of from one to two, or from two to three years' duration, depending on whether the primary value is given to the course of events in Mark or in John. On the one hand, defenders of the Johannine chronology have tended to follow its notations concerning a succession of Jewish feasts and have "harmonized" with this pattern references in the Synoptic Gospels. The most popular dates for the longer ministry are 26–29 or 27–30 C.E.[37] On the other hand, defenders of the primary value of Mark's outline have usually rejected the idea that John's Gospel is constructed upon a chronological scheme. They have contended that nothing in the Gospels suggests that the ministry of Jesus lasted more than one or two years.[38] Some exponents of this view have been willing to accept John's account of a longer ministry in Jerusalem than the synoptic outlines imply. Alternative dates for the shorter ministry are 27–29 or 28–30 C.E., depending chiefly upon how one determines "the fifteenth year of the reign of Tiberius Caesar" (Luke 3:1) and the relation of the beginning of Jesus' ministry to the mission of John the Baptist.

It is commonly held that the birth of Jesus occurred in the year 7–6 B.C.E.* The most significant aspect of the continuing debate on chronological problems concerns the date of Jesus' death.[39]

On the basis of these generalizations the main stages of Jesus' ministry and their approximate dates can now be conjectured:

27 C.E. *Fall–Winter:* The appearance and proclamation of John the Baptist; Jesus' baptism and temptation in the wilderness.[40]

28 C.E. *Early Spring:* After John's arrest Jesus begins his ministry in Galilee in the towns surrounding the Sea of Galilee; he preaches in the synagogues and heals; he also carries on his work in the open and by the lakeside; a popular following is gained but the hostility of the scribes of the Pharisees is provoked; an inner circle of disciples is drawn to Jesus.

* To speak of the birth of Jesus 7 or 6 years "before Christ," or B.C.E., is patently absurd. In the 525th year of the Era of Diocletian, Pope John I fixed the moveable date of Easter. Jesus' birth was dated Dec. 25, 754. On the authority of Pope John, 754–55 became "Anno Domini I." Since the older calendar dated Herod's death in 750, the new calendar dated it 4 B.C.

Early Summer: A mission of the disciples; a popular demonstration by the Sea of Galilee; the feeding of a multitude.

Summer: The suspicions of Herod Antipas are aroused; Jesus leaves Galilee and with his disciples wanders to the north; in the vicinity of Caesarea Philippi, Peter confesses that Jesus is the Christ.

Fall–Winter: Jesus goes to "the region of Judea and beyond the Jordan."[41]

29 C.E. *Spring:* Jesus makes his triumphal entry into Jerusalem and within the week is arrested, tried, and crucified.

There are elements of speculation in the above sketch. Yet in the main it is supported by the traditions, sufficiently well at any rate to provide a narrative framework for interpreting the history of Jesus.

Before this interpretation is attempted, we should give attention to some of the prominent themes that underlie Jesus' ministry and that give coherence to the story as a whole. This is the most hazardous step in the whole undertaking of historical reconstruction. Yet a recognition of this fact should not discourage us in the search for clues sufficiently comprehensive to provide an intelligible framework for the ministry. If such clues are not derived from the Gospels themselves, they will be introduced into the story by the reader, wittingly or unwittingly. We should not decide beforehand that clues for interpreting the history of Jesus are not a part of the history itself. All the relevant passages in the Gospels—understood in the light of their first-century Palestinian setting insofar as this is possible—provide the historical norms of interpretation.

The Coming of the Kingdom of God

There is an impressive agreement among students of the Gospels that Jesus' teaching concerning the kingdom of God is basic to an understanding of his ministry. According to the earliest Gospels, the coming of the kingdom of God was proclaimed by Jesus throughout his public life. "His teaching, his healings and exorcisms, the task of the Twelve, his whole campaign and even his death, all serve to make good this proclamation and the faith that inspires it."[42]

References in the Synoptic Gospels to Jesus' teaching concerning the kingdom may be grouped under four headings: statements explicitly proclaiming the coming of the kingdom of God; statements implying its coming; sayings of Jesus concerning the sorts of persons who are to receive or enter the kingdom; and the parables of the kingdom.

Proclaiming the Kingdom

Mark:

1. . . . Jesus came into Galilee, preaching the gospel of God, and saying, "The time is fulfilled, and the kingdom of God is at hand; repent, and believe in the gospel." Mark 1:14–15 (Matthew 4:17)

2. And he said to them [the disciples], "Truly, I say to you, there are some standing here who will not taste death before they see the kingdom of God come with power." Mark 9:1 (Matthew 16:28–Luke 9:27)

3. "Truly, I say to you [the disciples], I shall not drink again of the fruit

of the vine until that day when I drink it new in the kingdom of God."
Mark 14:25 (Matthew 26:29; cf. Luke 22:16, 18)

Q:

4. "I tell you, among those born of women none is greater than John
[the Baptist]; yet he who is least in the kingdom of God is greater than
he." Matthew 11:11–Luke 7:28

5. "Whenever you [the disciples] enter a town and they receive you, eat
what is set before you; heal the sick in it and say to them 'the kingdom
of God has come near to you' [Matthew: is at hand] . . ." Matthew
10:7–Luke 10:8, 9 (11)

6. "Thy kingdom come, thy will be done. . . ." Matthew 6:10–Luke
11:2

7. ". . . if it is by the Spirit [Luke: finger] of God that I cast out demons, then the kingdom of God has come upon you." Matthew 12:28–
Luke 11:20 (cf. Mark 3:22–27)

8. "I tell you, many will come from east and west and sit at table in the
kingdom of God, while the sons of the kingdom [Luke: "workers of in-
iquity"] will be thrown into outer darkness; there men will weep and
gnash their teeth." Matthew 8:11–12–Luke 13:28–29

9. "From the days of John the Baptist until now the kingdom of God
has suffered violence, and men of violence take it by force. The law and
the prophets were until John." Matthew 11:12–Luke 16:16[43]

"Special Luke":

10. Being asked by the Pharisees when the kingdom of God was coming,
he answered them, "The kingdom of God is not coming with signs to be
observed; nor will they say, 'Lo, here it is!' or 'There!' for behold, the
kingdom of God is in the midst of you." Luke 17:20

PROCLAIMING (BY IMPLICATION) THE KINGDOM

Mark:

11. And Jesus said to them [the people who asked why his disciples, unlike John's, did not fast] "Can the wedding guest fast while the bridegroom is with them? As long as they have the bridegroom with them
they cannot fast. The days will come, when the bridegroom is taken away
from them, and then they will fast in that day." Mark 2:19–20

Q:

12. And Jesus answered them [the disciples of John], "Go and tell John
what you hear and see [the signs and proclamation of the kingdom of
God?]: the blind receive their sight and the lame walk, lepers are cleansed
and the deaf hear, and the dead are raised up, and the poor have good
news preached to them. And blessed is he who takes no offense at me."
Matthew 11:4–6–Luke 7:22–23 (cf. saying No. 7)

13. "Blessed are the eyes which see what you see [the signs of the kingdom?]. For I tell you that many prophets and kings desired to see what
you see, and did not see it, and to hear what you hear [the proclamation
of the kingdom?], and did not hear it." Luke 10:23–24–Matthew 13:16–
17

14. "The queen of the South will arise at the judgment with the men of this generation and condemn them; for she came from the ends of the earth to hear the wisdom of Solomon, and behold, something greater [neuter adj., the kingdom of God?] than Solomon is here. The men of Nineveh will arise at the judgment with this generation and condemn it, for they repented at the preaching of Jonah, and behold, something [sic] greater than Jonah is here." Luke 11:31–32; Matthew 12:41–42

"Special Luke":

15. He [Jesus] opened the book [of Isaiah], and found the place where it was written, "The Spirit of the Lord is upon me, because he has anointed me to preach good news [of the kingdom?] to the poor . . . to proclaim the acceptable year of the Lord." Luke 4:17–19 (in place of Mark 1:15)

RECEIVING AND ENTERING THE KINGDOM OF GOD

Mark:

16. And he said to them [the twelve], "To you has been given the secret of the kingdom of God [Matthew; Luke: given to know the secrets of], but for those outside everything is in parables." Mark 4:11

17. ". . . if your eye causes you to sin, pluck it out; it is better to enter the kingdom of God with one eye than with two eyes to be thrown into hell. . . ." Mark 9:47

18. . . . and he said to them [the disciples], "Let the children come to me, do not hinder them; for to such belongs the kingdom of God. Truly, I say to you, whoever does not receive the kingdom of God like a child shall not enter it." Mark 10:14–15

19. . . . and Jesus looked around and said to his disciples, "How hard it will be [Luke: it is] for those who have riches to enter the kingdom of God! . . . It is easier for a camel to go through the eye of a needle than for a rich man to enter the kingdom of God." Mark 10:23, 25

20. And when Jesus saw that he [the scribe] answered wisely, he said to him, "You are not far from the kingdom of God." Mark 12:34

Q:

21. "Blessed are you poor [Matthew: poor in spirit], for yours is the kingdom of God [Matthew: heaven]." Matthew 5:3–Luke 6:20

22. ". . . seek first his kingdom, and these things [clothing, food, drink] shall be yours as well." Matthew 6:33–Luke 12:31[44]

"Special Matthew":

23. "Blessed are those who are persecuted for righteousness' sake, for theirs is the kingdom of heaven." Matthew 5:10

24. "Whoever then relaxes one of the least of these commandments and teaches men so, shall be called least in the kingdom of heaven; but he who does them and teaches them shall be called great in the kingdom of heaven. For I tell you, unless your righteousness exceeds that of the scribes and Pharisees, you will never enter the kingdom of heaven." Matthew 5:19–20

25. And he said to them [the disciples], ". . . every scribe who has been trained for the kingdom of heaven is like a householder who brings out of his treasure what is new and what is old." Matthew 13:52

26. "I will give you [Peter and the other disciples] the keys of the kingdom of heaven, and whatever you bind on earth shall be bound in heaven, and whatever you loose on earth shall be loosed in heaven." Matthew 16:19 (cf. Matthew 18:18)

27. "Whoever humbles himself like this child, he is the greatest in the kingdom of heaven." Matthew 18:4

28. ". . . and there are eunuchs who have made themselves eunuchs for the sake of the kingdom of heaven." Matthew 19:12b

29. Jesus said to them [the Pharisees?], "Truly I say to you, the tax-collectors and the harlots go into the kingdom of heaven before you!" (The tax-collectors and the harlots "believed John" [the Baptist]). Matthew 21:31b

30. ". . . I tell you [Pharisees?], the kingdom of God will be taken away from you and given to a nation producing the fruits of it." Matthew 21:43

31. "Then the king will say to those at his right hand, 'Come, O blessed of my Father, inherit the kingdom prepared for you from the foundation of the world. . . .' " Matthew 25:34

"Special Luke":

32. Jesus said to him [a candidate for discipleship], "No one who puts his hand to the plow and looks back is fit for the kingdom of God." Luke 9:62

33. "Fear not, little flock, for it is your Father's good pleasure to give you the kingdom." Luke 12:32

34. "You are those who have continued with me in my trials; as my Father appointed a kingdom for me, so do I appoint for you that you may eat and drink at my table in my kingdom, and sit on thrones judging the twelve tribes of Israel." Luke 22:28–30[45]

PARABLES OF THE KINGDOM

Mark:

35. And he said, "The kingdom of God is as if a man should scatter seed upon the ground . . ." Mark 4:26–29

36. And he said, "With what can we compare the kingdom of God, or what parable shall we use for it? It is like a grain of mustard seed . . ." Mark 4:30–32 (cf. No. 37 below)[46]

Q:

37. "It [the kingdom of God] is like a grain of mustard seed . . ." Matthew 13:31–32–Luke 13:18–19

38. "It [the kingdom of God] is like leaven . . ." Matthew 13:33–Luke 13:20–21

39. One of those who sat at table with him [Jesus] . . . said . . . "Blessed is he who shall eat bread in the kingdom of God!" But he said to him, "A man once made a great banquet and invited many . . ." Luke 14:15–24 (cf. Matthew 22:2–14)[47]

"Special Matthew":

40. ". . . the kingdom of heaven may be compared to a man who sowed good seed in his field; but . . . his enemy came and sowed weeds . . ." Matthew 13:24–30 (note also 13:36–43)[48]

41. "The kingdom of heaven is like treasure hidden in a field . . ." Matthew 13:44–46

42. "Again, the kingdom of heaven is like a net which was thrown into the sea . . ." Matthew 13:47–50

43. ". . . the kingdom of heaven may be compared to a king who wished to settle accounts with his servants . . ." Matthew 18:23–25

44. "For the kingdom of heaven is like a householder who went out early in the morning to hire laborers. . . ." Matthew 20:1–16

45. "Then the kingdom of heaven shall be compared to ten maidens who took their lamps and went to meet the bridegroom . . ." Matthew 25:1–13

Several conclusions widely held today are now given:

One, upon Jesus' lips, the phrase *kingdom of God* did not denote a territory or social order under the rule of God. At least this was not its primary reference. The Aramaic term that underlies the Greek of the Gospels means kingship rather than a kingdom or a domain. The term expressed the faith of Israel that God is king. Many would paraphrase the kingdom of God to read "the reign of God," for it connotes the sovereignty of His will in history.[49] Yet even the terms *reign* or *rule* are not adequate, if one thinks of them as abstract concepts. "The kingdom of God is the power of God expressed in deeds; it is what God does wherein it becomes evident that he is king . . . it is quite concretely the activity of God as king."[50]

Two, there is no difference in meaning between the kingdom of God and the kingdom of heaven, the latter phrase being that which Matthew prefers. "Heaven" was a pious periphrasis for the unspeakable Name.

Three, in proclaiming the coming of the kingdom, Jesus was not announcing a slowly evolving movement within history or an event that men could bring or "build" by adhering to the principles of Jesus' ethic. Whereas the parables of growth have been interpreted in this way, most scholars reject this reading of them on the basis of nonparabolic teaching concerning the kingdom.[51] Jesus believed that God manifested His rule in history in His own time and way.

Four, when Jesus spoke of the kingdom of God as "coming" he spoke of an eschatological hope. It is true that in ancient Judaism the phrase *kingdom of God* could refer to a present reality perceived by faith: God rules His world; He always has and He always will. It was possible to speak of this everlasting kingdom as an established reality whenever and wherever God's people acknowledge His supremacy and obey His will. But it is unlikely that any of the passages above can be properly understood in this way. In proclaiming the "coming" of the kingdom of God, Jesus testified to his generation that God would usher in that new Age to which the prophets and writers of apocalypse had looked forward. This day of judgment and of salvation was "at hand."

Beyond these areas of agreement, interpretations diverge over the meaning of Jesus' teaching. In the main, three viewpoints can be distinguished: Jesus taught that the coming of the kingdom was an imminent, altogether future event; Jesus taught that the kingdom of God had come in the course of his ministry; or Jesus taught that the future kingdom of God was already in some sense being manifested in his ministry. The first two viewpoints have the advantage of simplicity and logical consistency. The third may be suspect as representing a middle-of-the-road position. Expositions of this, as of paradoxical statements generally, can fall short of being convincing by reason of their vagueness. Yet the third viewpoint has this obvious advantage: It takes into account all of the above sayings concerning the kingdom that merit our confidence as reporting Jesus' teaching. For this reason it is a more widely accepted interpretation than either the first or the second.

The third viewpoint will be presented in the next chapter as reflecting the perspective of Jesus throughout his ministry. Representative statements of the first and the second alternative positions will be given here.

The view that Jesus was determined by a belief in the imminent coming of the kingdom of God, after the manner of Jewish apocalyptic expectations, has been forcefully maintained by Albert Schweitzer.[52]

According to Schweitzer, Jesus was obsessed by an apocalyptic vision. He was convinced that the birth pangs of the new Age were being experienced in his time. The final judgment of God would soon fall upon Satan and other invisible demonic powers. The day determined by God for the establishment of His kingdom was at hand. The Son of man would appear on the clouds as the agent of divine judgment and of salvation. The dead would be raised, and the deeds of men, both good and evil, would receive their reward. The condemned would be cast into a fiery pit, and the righteous would enter upon a life of unending bliss, living as angels and enjoying forever the presence of God.

After Jesus' contact with the Baptist, he expected these last things. At his baptism, Jesus became convinced that he was the Messiah-designate. Yet he did not make this belief a part of his public preaching. Indeed, since he identified himself with the apocalyptic Son of man who would come in clouds of glory, he made no personal claims in the brief period of his public teaching.[53] He offered his disciples no private instruction. His sole purpose was to set in motion the apocalyptic program of events. When Jesus sent out "the Twelve" on a mission in Galilee he expected the End to take place before they had completed their tour (Matt. 10:22–23). He did not expect to see them again in "this present Age." When this expectation was not realized, Jesus revised his forecast, as well as the conception of his personal role in relation to the End.[54] His death was to be the apocalyptic "tribulation" precipitating last things. The predestined kingdom of God was to be taken by violence. Jesus and his disciples became the penitent stormtroopers "engaged in forcing on and compelling the coming of the kingdom."[55] Thus Jesus' journey to Jerusalem was "the funeral march to victory." The Messiah of the coming kingdom

> lays hold of the wheel of the world to set it moving on that last revolution which is to bring all ordinary history to a close. It refuses to turn and he throws himself upon it. Then it does turn and crushes him. Instead of bringing in the eschatological conditions, he has destroyed them. The wheel rolls on, and the mangled body of the one immeasurably great Man, who was strong enough to think of himself as the spiritual ruler of mankind and to bend history to his purpose, is hanging on it still. That is his victory and that is his reign.[56]

According to Schweitzer, Jesus' eschatology and his ethical teaching form a consistent whole, His radical demands constitute the ethic of the interval, *In-*

terim-ethik, a heroic world-denying ideal appropriate to the last days. In his famous metaphor, Schweitzer affirmed that "the late-Jewish Messianic world view is the crater from which bursts forth the flame of the eternal religion of love."[57]

Let us consider now the position that represents the opposite pole of the theory just examined. Some scholars hold that, far from patterning his life upon the rigidly deterministic scheme of Jewish apocalypse, Jesus through his teaching reveals his radical break with this scheme. His announcement of the coming of the kingdom was indeed based upon current apocalyptic expectations. Yet, in employing the language and symbols of apocalypticism, Jesus gave them a quite original interpretation. It is not wise to assume, as does Schweitzer, that the content of the idea of the kingdom of God, as Jesus meant it, may be filled in from the speculation of apocalyptic writings. Neither in his action nor in his words does Jesus imply an early end of the world. Both are, in fact, inconsistent with such a belief. Jesus' proclamation "that the kingdom of God had already come dislocates the whole eschatological scheme . . . the eschaton has moved from the future to the present . . . from the sphere of expectation into that of realized experience."[58] At the same time, Jesus' thought remains "eschatological" in its orientation. The coming of the kingdom in his ministry is, as in prophecy and apocalyptic, the ultimate, decisive act of God in history.

This position, which opposes all futurist interpretations of Jesus' perspective, goes by the name of "realized eschatology." Its foremost representative in the English-speaking world is C. H. Dodd.[59] According to Dodd, Jesus came into Galilee proclaiming that the kingdom of God had come. Explicitly and by implication, Jesus announced that the eschatological Day is a present fact.[60] This view is given support and illustration in Jesus' parables, which depict in vivid and variable imagery "the arrival of a zero hour in human experience." The kingdom of God confronts men with a crisis and demands of them decisive action. Moreover, Jesus' miracles are tokens that "the powers of the kingdom of God were abroad."

Jesus' proclamation carried with it the implication that the Messiah had come. He chose the mysterious title "Son of man" to disclose to those who could hear it the "mystery of the kingdom of God." He used this symbol to reveal the truth that "in his own life of service and conflict, in suffering and in death, God was at work bringing in His kingdom and that beyond suffering and death lay eternal glory in which He should reign as the Lord of a redeemed humanity."[61]

Dodd does not overlook the predictive element in the Gospel tradition. He holds, however, that predictions of Jesus belong to different planes of thought that have been confused. While some of Jesus' words refer to forthcoming historical events, others refer to "events of a wholly supernatural order." Predictions concerning the fall of Jerusalem, his death, and the tribulations of his disciples belong to the former group. But sayings concerning the coming of the kingdom subsequent to Jesus' ministry speak of realities transcending history. It is probable that Jesus used the traditional apocalyptic language concerning "last things" to speak of ultimate truth, of the glories of a world beyond this. Yet "his future tenses are only an accommodation of language." "The kingdom of God in its full reality is not something which will happen after other things have happened. It is that to which men awake when this order of time and space no longer limits their vision."

There are passages in the Gospels that seem to foretell a period of waiting between Christ's resurrection and return. According to Dodd, it is not probable that these passages truly represent the teaching of Jesus. In this case it is not the intent of Jesus' words that has been misunderstood. Rather, his words have been reapplied to a new situation. A setting in the life of the Church has replaced the original setting in Jesus' ministry. An example of this is given in the so-called "eschatological parables" of Matthew. When these are studied in the light of Jesus' teaching, applying the principles of form criticism, the conclusion is reached that they are parables originally intended "to enforce his appeal to men to recognize that the kingdom was present." When the historic crisis with which Jesus confronted men had passed, these parables were adopted by the Church to enforce its appeal to men to prepare for the second and final crisis that the Church (through its understanding of Jesus' teaching) believed to be approaching.[62]

Dodd believes that the eternal significance of history was revealed in the ministry of Jesus, once and for all time. It is not necessary, nor indeed likely, that Jesus expected an imminent end of the world. Much of Jesus' teaching "implies that human life will go on, under much the same outward conditions, with the same temptations and moral problems, and the same need for forgiveness and grace, as well as of daily bread."[63] Accordingly, Jesus' commandments do not constitute an *Interim-ethik* but a moral ideal for men who have "received the kingdom of God" and who are henceforth living in the new age in which God's judgment and grace stand revealed.

The reader of Dodd's exposition of Jesus' teaching cannot but be impressed by the brilliance of this scholar whose writings form such a significant contribution to an appreciation of the New Testament. Dodd has dealt conscientiously and critically with all of the relevant passages of the Gospels. Yet it does not seem that this exposition of Jesus' perspective is fully adequate. The particular texts that stand in the way of accepting the thesis that Jesus uniformly taught a "realized eschatology" will be examined in the next chapter.

The attempts to order Jesus' teaching along the lines of either a "consistent" or a "realized" eschatology have failed to convince most scholars. Rather it is concluded that Jesus' thought centered around two foci, neither of which can be ignored or explained away. One focus of Jesus' teaching is "the eschatological crisis precipitated within the ministry . . . the other focus is the eschatological consummation which, within the framework of the ministry, remains a future event."[64] The message of Jesus can be understood only if it is recognized that he proclaimed both the coming of the kingdom in the future and its present reality. In some sense the coming kingdom was already making its presence felt; in another sense, it had not yet fully come. Such teaching cannot be regarded simply as a particular form of Jewish apocalyptic. At the same time, it cannot be completely detached from the historical context of apocalyptic thought.

Can such apparently paradoxical teaching be shown to form integral parts of a consistent whole? In the final analysis the question becomes: Can this perspective yield a sketch of Jesus' history that is more intrinsically probable than those that are offered by Schweitzer and Dodd?

NOTES

1. W. D. Davies, *Invitation to the New Testament* (1966), p. 132.

2. H. Anderson, *Jesus and Christian Origins* (1964), pp. 18f.

3. These lines are from an essay by R. Bultmann, quoted in S. Neill, *Interpretation of the New Testament* 1861–1961 (Oxford University Press, 1964), p. 271; the complete essay can be found in *Glauben und Verstehen*, vol. 1 (2d ed., 1954).

4. R. Bultmann, "The Primitive Christian Kerygma and the Historical Jesus," in C. E. Braaten and R. A. Harrisville, eds., *The Historical Jesus and the Kerygmatic Christ* (1964), pp. 15ff.

5. Anderson, *Jesus and Christian Origins*, pp. 56ff.

6. E.g., E. Käsemann, *New Testament Questions of Today* (1979), pp. 23ff.; G. Bornkamm, *Jesus of Nazareth*, (1960), pp. 9–26; H. Conzelmann, "Method of Life-of-Jesus Research," in Braaten and Harrisville, *Historical Jesus* (1964), pp. 54ff.

7. V. A. Harvey, "The Historical Jesus, the Kerygma, and Christian Faith," *RLife* 33 (1964): 433.

8. G. Bornkamm, *Jesus of Nazareth*, pp. 23f.

9. Anderson, *Jesus and Christian Origins*, pp. 97ff.; N.A. Dahl, "The Problem of the Historical Jesus," in C. Braaten and R. Harrisville, *Kerygma and History*, New York: Abingdon Press, (1962), pp. 150ff.

10. Dahl, "Historical Jesus," p. 151.

11. Perrin, *Rediscovering the Teaching of Jesus*, pp. 39ff.; H. K. McArthur, "Survey of Recent Gospel Research," *Int* 18 (1964): 39ff.; Anderson, *Jesus and Christian Origins*, pp. 99f.

12. M.D. Hooker details some "serious faults" in the logic of scholars who apply the criteria of dissimilarity and coherence to the Gospels' reports of Jesus' teaching, "Christology and Methodology," *NTS* 17 (1971): 480ff.

13. Oscar Cullmann's application of these criteria allows for a more extensive correspondence between Christian "community formulations" and authentic sayings of Jesus. "The Church . . . selected such genuine sayings of Jesus as accorded with its own tendencies . . ." *Salvation in History* (1967), pp. 189–193. I. H. Marshall, *The Gospel of Luke* (1978), p. 33.

14. Perrin, *Teaching of Jesus*, p. 46.

15. Anderson, *Jesus and Christian Origins*, p. 100. Major examples of the application of this criterion to the Gospels and of the material so identified can be found in C. H. Dodd, *History and the Gospel* (1938), and T. W. Manson, *The Teaching of Jesus* (1948).

16. Dahl, "Historical Jesus," p. 155. This emphasis on the great value of incremental "exact knowledge" may be related to the problem of methodology. Unfortunately, in viewing Jesus' teaching against the background either of first-century Judaism or the Church and its Christology, one is not comparing an unknown with other well knowns. It would perhaps "be a fairer statement of the situation to say that we are dealing with three unknowns, and that our knowledge of the other two is quite as tenuous and indirect as our knowledge of Jesus himself." Hooker, "Christology and Methodology," p. 482.

17. Jos. *Antiq.* XX. ix. 1.

18. Jos. *Antiq.* XVIII. iii. 3. For efforts to reconstruct the original text in Josephus, see M. Goguel, *The Life of Jesus* (1933), pp. 75ff.; J. Klausner, *Jesus of Nazareth* (1925), pp. 55ff.; cf. P. Winter, "Josephus on Jesus," *J Hist St*, 1 (1968): 289–302. S. Pines, *An Arabic Version of the Testamonium Flavianum and its Implications* (1971).

19. See p. 185.

20. Klausner, *Jesus of Nazareth*, p. 19; Davies, *Invitation to the New Testament*, pp. 66f. For identifications of the Talmudic literature and of the rabbis known as the Tannaim, see pp. 197f.

21. Pliny, *Letters* X. 96.
22. See p. 124. The passage in Suetonius, *Lives of the Twelve Caesars,* cited in Ch. 2 (Life of Claudius 25.4) should be noted. If "Chrestos" is a corruption of Christos, then Suetonius supposed that Christ had been in Rome ca. 49 C.E., so little was the historian interested in Christianity's account of its origin.
23. Cf. Herodotus, who fails to mention Zoroaster in writing of Persian religion; and Dio Cassius, who says nothing of Simon bar Kokhba in commenting on the Jewish revolt in Hadrian's time.
24. C. H. Dodd, "Life and Teachings of Jesus," in T.W. Manson, ed., *A Companion to the Bible* (1946), p. 367.
25. J. Jeremias, *Unknown Sayings of Jesus* (1957), pp. 49ff.; R. Dunkerley, *Beyond the Gospels* (1957), pp. 121ff.
26. Jeremias, *Unknown Sayings of Jesus,* p. 54. The same saying is found in the Coptic Gospel of Thomas, Saying 82, in J.M. Robinson, ed., *The Nag Hammadi Library in English* (1977), p. 127.
27. *P. Oxy,* 1, 4. In the Matthean word Jesus promises his presence to those who pray in his name; in this agraphon the promise is to those who labor.
28. See note 26.
29. E. Hennecke and W. Schneemelcher, ed., *New Testament Apocrypha,* Vol. 1 (1963), pp. 370ff. See also pp. 60–64.
30. *Ibid.,* pp. 179ff.
31. "The so-called Gospel of the Egyptians, existing in two versions among the tractates in the Nag Hammadi library, is not related to the well-known apocryphal Gospel of the Egyptians," A. Böhlig, in Robinson, *The Nag Hammadi Library,* p. 195. See Hennecke and Schneemelcher, *New Testament Apocrypha,* Vol. 1, pp. 166ff.
32. A.M. Hunter, *The Work and Words of Jesus* (1950), p. 16.
33. H. Koester, "The Gospel of Thomas," in Robinson, *The Nag Hammadi Library,* p. 117; O. Cullmann, "The Gospel of Thomas and the Problem of the Age of the Tradition Contained Therein," *Int* 16 (1962): 418ff. Cf. H. K. McArthur, "The Dependence of the Gospel of Thomas on the Synoptics," *Exp T* 71 (1960): 286ff.
34. Jeremias, *Unknown Sayings of Jesus,* p. 32; Dunkerley, *Beyond the Gospels,* pp. 15f., 163f.
35. G. B. Caird, "Chronology of the New Testament," *IDB* 1 (1962), 599–603; G. Ogg, *The Chronology of the Public Ministry of Jesus* (1940).
36. Luke's "great interpolation" (9:51–18:14) preserves traditions of Jesus' contact with the people of Samaria, which have left traces in John. While in the Fourth Gospel, Jesus' ministry alternates between the two districts, John 7:1f. marks a transition. After this there is no return to Galilee.
37. T. W. Manson, "The Cleansing of the Temple," *BJRL* 33 (1951); Dodd, in Manson, *Companion to the Bible,* pp. 371f. Cf. Goguel, *Life of Jesus,* pp. 271ff.
38. Caird, "Chronology of the New Testament," p. 603, proposes the dates 28–30 C.E.; Ogg, *Public Ministry of Jesus,* argues for a 2 to 3 year ministry, 29/30–33.
39. J. Jeremias, *The Eucharistic Words of Jesus,* (1955), pp. 1–60. See pp. 227f.
40. The Fourth Evangelist reports that Jesus worked for a short while alongside the Baptist (Jn. 3:22f.; 4:1). C. H. Dodd, *Historical Tradition in the Fourth Gospel* (1963), pp. 285–287, 300f.
41. The better part of a year may be implied by Mk.'s narrative, 6:39–14:1ff. Jn: 7:32ff. reports Jesus' presence in Jerusalem during the feasts of tabernacles and dedication (Sept.–Oct. and Dec.). Did Jesus retire from Jerusalem and labor in "the region of Judea and beyond the Jordan" (Mk. 10:1) until the final Passover? Several units of the synoptic tradition, contrary to Mark's plot, imply that Jesus had been in Jerusalem before his passion, e.g., Lk. 13:34, Mt. 23:37; Mk. 11:1–10. See further p. 224.

42. A. Wilder, *New Testament Faith for Today* (1955), p. 74; N. Perrin, *Teaching of Jesus*, p. 54.

43. For this emended text, see Kümmel, *Promise and Fulfilment* (1957), pp. 12f. Cf. N. Perrin, *The Kingdom of God in the Teaching of Jesus* (1963), pp. 171ff. The following passages are probably editorial additions: Lk. 4:43 (cf. Mk. 1:38); Lk. 9:11 (cf. Mk. 6:34); Lk. 9:60 (cf. Mt. 8:22); Lk. 21:31 (cf. Mk. 13:29); and Mt. 24:14 (cf. Mk. 13:10, 13b).

44. Mt. 7:21 is not listed here as belonging to the Q source. Cf. Lk. 6:46.

45. Lk. 18:29b appears to be an editorial addition. Cf. Mk. 10:29.

46. Mark's parable of the fig tree (13:28f.) may originally have been a parable of the kingdom. Cf. Lk. 21:31. Mark's parable of the vineyard may also be compared with the banquet parable, no. 39.

47. The Q parable of the cloud and the south wind may be a parable of the kingdom. Mt. 16:2f. and Lk. 12:54ff.

48. Mt. 13:19 is clearly an editorial gloss. Cf. Mk. 4:15.

49. "Thy kingdom come, Thy will be done . . ." Matt. 6:10.

50. Perrin, *Teaching of Jesus*, p. 55.

51. Sayings nos. 22–30 and 39–44. See the article "Basileus" (King) by K. L. Schmidt, K. G. Kuhn, G. von Rad, and H. Kleinknecht, in G. W. Bromiley, ed., *Theological Dictionary*, Vol. 1 (1964), pp. 564ff.

52. A. Schweitzer, *The Quest of the Historical Jesus* (1968), pp. 348ff.; idem., *The Mystery of the Kingdom of God* (1950). Whatever one's view of its details, Schweitzer's thesis that "consistent eschatology" provides the essential clue to Jesus' mission makes him the foremost representative of the futurist position. Schweitzer challenges his critics to render a more probable explanation of some of the most crucial texts in the Gospels. Schweitzer's foremost "disciple" is M. Werner, *The Formation of Christian Dogma* (1957). See Perrin, *The Kingdom of God*, pp. 37ff.; also G. Lundström, *The Kingdom of God in the Teaching of Jesus* (1963), pp. 77ff.

53. In this way Schweitzer explains the Messianic secret motif. "The eschatological solution . . . at one stroke raises the Markan account as it stands, with all its disconnectedness and inconsistencies, into genuine history." *Quest of the Historical Jesus*, p. 335.

54. "The fact which alone makes possible an understanding [of Jesus] is lacking in Mark (sic, cf. note 53.) . . . without Mt. 10–11, which is historical as a whole and down to the smallest detail, everything remains enigmatic . . ." Schweitzer, *Quest of the Historical Jesus*, pp. 358, 361. The decisive influence of Schweitzer's reading of Mt. 10 upon the development of his theory is stressed by Perrin, *The Kingdom of God*, pp. 32f.

55. Schweitzer, *Quest of the Historical Jesus*, p. 355. (See saying no. 9 above).

56. *Ibid.*, p. 369.

57. A. Schweitzer, *Out of My Life and Thought* (1933), p. 69. Schweitzer concluded that Jesus' actions and words are better than his apocalyptic "dogma." The latter belongs to an outmoded world view that Jesus himself destroyed by "forcing" the eschatological program into actual history. It is natural that moderns should place a high premium upon Schweitzer's reading of the Gospels since he exemplified in his own life so many of the traits of the man they portray. Yet Schweitzer's sketch must be examined with the same critical seriousness with which Schweitzer examines the "lives" written by others. See further, p. 190.

58. C. H. Dodd, *Parables of the Kingdom* (1936), p. 50.

59. Dodd in Manson, *Companion to the Bible*, pp. 373ff. A critical review of the evidence is set forth in Dodd, *Parables of the Kingdom*. See also Hunter, *Work and Words of Jesus*, pp. 68ff., 101ff.

60. Dodd considers the above sayings in the following order: 7, 1 (the phrase "at hand" is rendered "has come"), 12, 13, 11, and 9.
61. Dodd in Manson, *Companion to the Bible*, p. 374.
62. Some of Dodd's "disciples" have gone further, claiming that the apocalyptic sayings in the Gospels are the result of early misinterpretations and editorial distortions, e.g., Heard, *Introduction to the New Testament*, pp. 246ff. So also other scholars, F. C. Grant, *The Gospel of the Kingdom* (1940), and H. B. Sharman, *Son of Man and Kingdom of God* (1943). In *The Interpretation of the Fourth Gospel* (1953), p. 447, Dodd concedes that "realized eschatology" is a "not altogether felicitous term," and acknowledges with approval an alternative suggested by E. Haenchen, the untranslatable "sich realisierende Eschatologie" (an eschatology that is in process of realization?). See J. Jeremias, *Parables of Jesus* (1962), p. 230.
63. Manson, *Companion to the Bible*, p. 376. Dodd examines the relation of eschatology and ethics in the teaching of Jesus in *Gospel and Law* (1951), pp. 53ff.
64. C. K. Barrett, "New Testament Eschatology," *ScotJTh* 6 (1953): 231; Lundström, *The Kingdom of God*, pp. 232ff.; Perrin, *Kingdom of God*, pp. 159ff. Cf. Perrin, *Teaching of Jesus*, in which a sustained effort is made to interpret the words present and future as signifying experiential rather than temporal realities. See also Bornkamm, *Jesus of Nazareth*, p. 90ff.

Chapter 10

The Ministry of Jesus: In Galilee

THE earliest followers of Jesus proclaimed that his ministry had begun with John the Baptist. Historians must adopt this point of departure, for, in the preaching and baptism of John, Jesus received his first impulse to public action. No man exerted a greater influence over Jesus. For him, as for the apostles, John was the greatest of all the prophets. His career marked the boundary between the old age and the new.[1]

BEFORE THE MINISTRY

The facts relating to John's birth and early life are shrouded in legend. Luke 1–2 can hardly be used directly for historical reconstruction (see p. 132). Yet from this tradition one learns that John's parents were of priestly descent, and that he had lived in the wilderness of Judea before "the day of his manifestation to Israel."[2] While in this desolate region, John received his call. Since the discoveries at Qumran, some scholars have concluded that before his public life John was in contact with the sect of the scrolls. Perhaps John lived for a while at the Qumran settlement; he may have been orphaned (Luke 1:17) or sent there by his parents.[3] Josephus reported that Essenes "adopted other men's children" and "molded them in accordance with their own principles."[4] All speculation aside, it is noteworthy that the presence in the wilderness of both John and the dissident priests at Qumran was inspired by the summons from the prophecy of Isaiah: "In the wilderness prepare the way of the Lord . . ."[5] Both John and the Qumran priests believed that the last days were at hand; both demanded from their fellow Israelites a thoroughgoing repentance, and both practiced a ceremonial immersion in water.[6] Probably John knew of the Essenes; yet it is only a possibility that he had ever been a probationer in one of their settlements.

JOHN'S PROCLAMATION AND APPEAL

The following passages in the Synoptic Gospels describe the person and proclamation of John the Baptist: from the earliest Gospel (most of which is used

The great Isaiah Scroll found in Cave 1, Qumran. Isaiah 40:3 inspired the missions of the Dead Sea community and of John the Baptist, 1QS viii. 13–16; Mk. 1:3 and pars.

by Matthew and Luke)—Mark 1:2–8; from Q—Matthew 3:7–12, Luke 3:7–9 and 15–17; and from "Special Luke"—Luke 3:10–14.

Josephus also provides a description of John's mission:

> John, called the Baptist, . . . was a pious man who bade the Jews who practiced virtue and exercised righteousness toward each other and piety toward God, to come together for baptism. For thus, it seemed to him, would baptismal ablution be acceptable, if it were used not to beg off from sins committed, but for the purification of the body when the soul had previously been cleansed by righteous conduct . . .[7]

According to Christian sources, John heralded the imminent day of judgment. He forecast that God's retributive punishment would soon fall upon apostate Israel. The "wrath to come" was impending: the ax lay at the root of the unfruitful trees, corrupt men would flee the terrors of the coming judgment like vipers slithering before the burning stubble of the harvest field, the harvester held the winnowing fork in his hand to clear the threshing floor.[8] Besides, the synoptic Evangelists report that the prophet claimed to be the unworthy forerunner of one mightier than himself who would destroy the wicked with his fiery breath or spirit.

John appealed to the multitudes who came to hear him at the fords of the Jordan, urging them to repent while there was yet time. He required that their repentance be accompanied by a baptism in the river, and followed by moral actions appropriate to the new life to which God called them.

The account of Josephus differs widely from this description of John, but few would consider the *Antiquities* a more objective record. In accord with his tendency to relate Jewish teachings to Greek philosophy, Josephus transformed the fiery eschatological prophet into a preacher of virtue not unlike the Stoics, and John's baptism became a ritual washing like the neo-Pythagorean lustrations that signified a corresponding inward and outward purity. It is not surprising that Josephus obscured the messianic character of John's following.[9]

Much interest has centered on John's rite of baptism. Two problems can be distinguished: the question of John's originality, and the relation of John's proclamation to his form of baptism.

One need not look beyond Judaism for near parallels to John's baptism. It has been widely held that John's rite was modeled upon the practice of baptizing Gentile proselytes, although it cannot be proved that this custom antedates John.[10] Those who assume the currency of proselyte baptism emphasize that this water bath afforded John a suitable model for an initiation ceremony. Unlike other Jewish washings it was a once-for-all event. Perhaps John deliberately applied to "the children of Abraham" a rite devised by them to benefit pagans, thus declaring his conviction that the whole Jewish nation had gone astray and needed to be reconstituted as the people of God.[11]

John's references to the eschatological baptism by fire or the spirit or both parallel the expectations of the Qumran sect. Yet, unlike the Essene "purifying waters," and despite the implications of the comment of Josephus, John's baptism was a nonrecurring act.[12] Moreover, there is not the slightest evidence that John's candidates passed through a period of probation or were examined by a council, or that through baptism they were admitted into a community of discipline. John's public ministry was entirely independent of the priests at Qumran.[13]

It is a sound conclusion that the form of John's baptism was determined by the nature of his proclamation. John drew upon apocalyptic imagery, which frequently represented the inexorable divine judgment as a stream of fire, sometimes issuing from the throne of God or as the fiery breath of a messiah.[14] John's baptism may have been performed in the streams of the Jordan because running water was necessary to the symbolism of submersion in this river of fire. Repentant individuals were to enact in advance their acceptance of the eschatological judgment of God. Apparently it was John's conviction that by a humble submission before God in the present, one could be assured of divine forgiveness in the future judgment. The originality of John's baptism consists in the fact that it dramatized the substance of his eschatological proclamation.[15]

JOHN'S BAPTISM OF JESUS

When Jesus came from Galilee to hear the fiery prophet, he presented himself for baptism. Mark's notice (1:9) is clearly historical, for the early Church cannot have been responsible for originating the tradition that Jesus submitted to John's "baptism of repentance for the forgiveness of sins." Only Matthew provides an explanation (which must have arisen in the Jewish Christian community of the First Gospel) to guard against misunderstanding: Jesus' repentance was a positive act, the fulfillment of "all righteousness."[16]

Since the Gospels were written from the standpoint of faith and not primarily as biographies, it is probably fruitless to speculate upon the question of the

The river Jordan. *(Courtesy of the Israel Government Tourist Office.)*

meaning to Jesus of his baptism. Yet the question will arise: Were early Christians responsible for bringing together Psalm 2:7 and Isaiah 42:1, thus representing Jesus' baptism as his anointment to be the servant-Messiah, or did Jesus at some later time (in his training of the disciples) so interpret his calling? Mark 1:10f. implies an intensely private experience, but Matthew 3:17 and Luke 3:22 describe a public revelation. The Fourth Evangelist ascribes to the Baptist "a knowledge and awareness of Jesus' inner consciousness which he could not possibly, at this time, have possessed."[17]

John's Martyrdom and His Significance

The imprisonment and death of John are reported in Mark 6:17–29. These events were recorded also in the passage from Josephus cited earlier:

when everybody turned to John—for they were profoundly stirred by what he said—Herod feared . . . an uprising (for the people seemed likely to do everything he might counsel) he thought . . . it better to get John out of the way in advance, before an insurrection might develop, than . . . be sorry not to have acted once an insurrection had begun. So because of Herod's suspicion, John was sent as a prisoner to Machaerus . . . and there put to death. But the Jews believed that the destruction which overtook the army came as a punishment to Herod, God wishing to do him harm.[18]

Herod's arrest of John is credible. Not only would the ruler's suspicions have been aroused by John's popular following, but the prophet's moral exhortations might have given rise to criticism of Herod and to popular scorn. Christian sources clearly support John's influence over the masses. Yet the Markan account of John's arrest and martyrdom, like Luke's account of his birth, is probably legendary.[19]

The Q tradition reports that John sent from his prison a delegation to Jesus asking, "Are you he who is to come or shall we look for another?"[20] If John had previously identified Jesus as "the Mightier One," then his question could imply disillusionment, or at least uncertainty over the correctness of his earlier expectation. But John's question may reveal no more than the beginning of his active interest in the work done by his Nazarene convert.

Although John's prison walls cannot be penetrated to learn his final attitude toward Jesus, the Synoptic Gospels provide several glimpses of the significance that the Church attributed to John. Is it possible that one or more of the following passages reflect also Jesus' estimate of John's mission? Notice should be taken of Mark 9:11–13 (Matt. 17:10–13); Matthew 11:7–12; Luke 7:24–28; 16:16 (Q); Matthew 11:14f. (M). According to the Q passage, Jesus recognized John to be a true prophet. In this context his words, "and more than a prophet" suggest further the belief that John had been the one destined to herald the Age to Come. If these words go back to Jesus, then support is given to the view that he also identified John as the Elijah of traditional expectation, the messenger sent to prepare the way for the coming of the Lord. In Matthew 11:12, and its variant Luke 16:16, we may possess an authentic reminiscence of Jesus upon John's death. John had suffered that violence to which men are exposed who stand at the threshold of the coming Age and who are obedient to the call of God.[21]

JESUS' TEMPTATION IN THE WILDERNESS

In the Synoptic Gospels the baptism and temptation of Jesus are presented as two phases of one critical experience in the life of Jesus. The Spirit possessing him at the moment of his baptism "drove him" to seek the seclusion of the wilderness. The historical sequel to Jesus' baptism is reported in Mark 1:12f., and a narrative of this temptation was contained in the Q source.[22] Some scholars, with an eye to Mark's simple declaration that Jesus was "tempted by Satan," consider the Q account an impressive commentary, in parable form, on the entire course of Jesus' ministry. Some Christian teachers reflected upon the courses of action Jesus might have taken but had rejected at various stages of his career.[23] If we read this episode as a Jewish-Christian midrash, its lesson

The barren, windswept wilderness of Judea. *(Courtesy of* Biblical Archaeologist.*)*

was that the old children of God had proved faithless; Jesus, by his great trust in God, had qualified as the representative head of the new Israel, the true Son of God. Unquestionably the narrative has symbolic features that reflect the story of Israel's wilderness experience. Yet it is as improbable that anyone in the early Church would have had the imagination to create this narrative, as it is that the idea of Jesus' temptation originated in the Church. The Q account possibly preserves the substance of an internal conflict that Jesus faced before his active ministry began. Jesus might have told his disciples this story as it stands in Matthew's version. We cannot, of course, be sure of this.

John's preaching aroused the hopes of many in the advent of a messiah. It is natural to expect that Jesus considered the course of his life's work in terms of such popular expectations. In the story of Jesus' baptism the term *messiah* does not appear, yet as Jesus identified himself with his people, and joined with them in their ardent longing for the salvation of God, he may have felt himself called to a life work that, for its characterization and measurement, demanded certain aspects of current messianic hope. It is against the background of this complex of Jewish messianic expectation that one may search for significant clues to Jesus' thinking and the moral courage of his decisions in the wilderness.[24]

THE GALILEAN MINISTRY

"Now after John was arrested, Jesus came into Galilee, preaching the gospel of God and saying, 'The time is fulfilled, and the kingdom of God is at hand;[25] repent, and believe in the gospel.' " (Mark 1:14f.) Like John the Baptist, Jesus was moved to action by his conviction that the eschatological Day was fast approaching. Like John also, Jesus called upon his hearers to repent. But the emphasis of Jesus lay not upon the threatening "wrath to come." Instead he spoke of the imminent coming of the reign of God as good news and, in the actions of his ministry, *he became more than a herald:* "Jesus not only issued a call to repentance but with full authority he granted to men the salvation expected in the future."[26] We may note also that Jesus was no ascetic. There is no trace in the earliest strata of the gospel tradition of Jesus' baptism of disciples. Hence he did not linger in the wilderness or stand by the side of running streams attracting people to himself. Rather, he moved from place to place, speaking in the synagogues or in the open countryside.

The earliest Gospel makes it clear that two kinds of activity were typical of Jesus' itinerant ministry in Galilee—teaching and healing. We have seen Mark's particular interest in Jesus' power over demons, but he does not neglect to report that Jesus' teaching astonished the people. "He taught as one who had authority, and not as the scribes" (Mark 1:21f.).

THE CALL OF THE FIRST DISCIPLES

Shoftly after the ministry began, Jesus called disciples. Two pairs of brothers, fishermen by trade, were invited to follow Jesus and to help him in his work.[27] The call of another disciple, a tax collector named Levi, is singled out by Mark.[28] Strange as it may seem, the gospel traditions do not enable us to know positively the names of all of the disciples.[29] Some scholars have identified stages in the relations of Jesus with his disciples. First there was the call of

The Sea of Galilee to the northwest from the southeastern shore. *(Courtesy of Consulate General of Israel.)*

an indeterminate number, followed by the appointment of "the Twelve," then the commissioning of "apostles." Some suppose that Jesus' formal choice of twelve men was "an acted parable" proclaiming his intention "to create a new Israel."[30] It is probable that the synoptists recognized that the elders, representing the twelve tribes of Israel, provided a type of Jesus' selection of twelve men. It is possible that at the end of his ministry Jesus treated these disciples as the nucleus of the true Israel. That Jesus consciously restricted his disciples to twelve is not consonant with his call to others to "follow" him. Jesus sought to extend his popular following, yet never without fair warning that his disciples must be ready at all times to make costly sacrifices.[31]

THE MIGHTY WORKS OF JESUS

Two closely related questions must be considered. Is it possible to know Jesus' attitude toward his mighty works? Can the actual situations from the ministry be reconstructed from the miracle stories of the Gospels? In attempting to answer both questions earlier observations should be recalled. The *kerygma* of the earliest Church, supported by the claim that God had wrought "signs and wonders" through Jesus the Christ, ensured the preservation of miracle stories from the ministry. It would not be correct to describe all, or even most, of these stories as "wonder tales," created from apologetic motives unrelated to the Christian proclamation and moral teachings. Nevertheless, their forms in the Gospels do reflect stages of development, the special interests of the synoptic Evangelists, as well as the earlier influences exerted during the course of their oral transmission.[32]

The Q story of Jesus' temptation reports his decision not to use marvelous power either to help himself or for self-exhibition as a means of attracting attention or compelling belief. It should be noticed now that throughout the ministry Jesus did not extricate himself from dangers, nor was he willing to comply with demands that he produce signs in support of his authority. He refused to give such signs and spoke of people's desire for them as morally reprehensible.[33]

The fact remains, however, that Jesus did perform mighty works. His antagonists were unable to deny this. They could only impugn the source of his powers and his motives for exercising them. Mark 3:19b–27 is particularly instructive in this regard. The importance of this passage lies chiefly in its revelation of Jesus' reason for alleviating the suffering of a particular group of persons, the demon-possessed. It was God's will that "the strong man—Satan—be bound by a stronger power." Jesus' victory in the wilderness was to be extended into the Galilean ministry. Matthew and Luke incorporated into this Markan passage a detached saying that they found in the Q source:

> if it is by the finger [Matt.: Spirit] of God that I cast out demons, then the kingdom of God has come upon you. Luke 11:20 (cf. Matt. 12:28)

This saying provides a further insight into Jesus' attitude. In his mighty works the powers of the Age to Come were being manifested. It could therefore be said that the eschatological kingdom had come.[34] Noteworthy also is Jesus'

Aerial photograph of excavations at Capernaum, a major center of Jesus' ministry, showing the ruins of a third- or fourth-century synagogue, which was probably built on the site of an earlier one. The octagonal structure *(left)* is known as Peter's house, Mark 1:21, 29; 2:1, and pars.; also Mt. 8:5; Lk. 7:1 (Q). *(Courtesy of* Biblical Archaeologist.*)*

condemnation of Chorazin and Bethsaida, Galilean cities where, according to Matthew, "most of his mighty works had been done":

> "Woe to you . . . for if the mighty works done in you had been done in Tyre and Sidon, they would have repented long ago . . . it shall be more tolerable on the day of judgment for Tyre and Sidon than for you."[35]

Since "the time is fulfilled," Jesus' acts stand in a particular relation to the eschatological judgment. The mighty works of Jesus should lead to repentance and to belief in the good news. In the absence of this response, the final judgment of the Galilean villagers was being sealed.*

*It is instructive to contrast here the defensive attitude of the Qumran community in its battle with evil spirits. The Essenes found refuge in the Law, and then in the community in which its precepts were revered. Jesus had no "sheltering camp . . . nor was the Law for him a bulwark be-

At first sight it may seem that the above evidence is contradictory. On the one hand, Jesus refuses to give signs. On the other hand, he regards his mighty works as signs validating his proclamation and testifying to its fulfillment. But the apparent contradiction disappears when it is noted that Jesus believed that the merely curious, the seekers after signs, would never be able to understand the true significance of his acts. "Those who had eyes to see," had "been given the secret of the kingdom of God." Sooner or later those persons would recognize that Jesus' acts were signs.[36] That Jesus was acutely sensitive to subjective attitudes of persons toward him (or, better, to the actions of God as king exercising his power through him) is supported by the numerous notices that faith, or unbelief, affected his willingness though not his power to heal.[37]

This emphasis on faith in the miracle stories of the Synoptic Gospels distinguishes them from the wonder stories reported in popular Hellenistic literature, as well as in Jewish rabbinical sources. Jesus' word "your faith has saved you" is not found in the alleged non-Christian parallels. The pagan narratives exhibit the marvelous powers of their charismatic healers; the Jewish wonder stories celebrate the exceptional piety of certain rabbis who, because of their practice of Torah, are endowed with exceptional curative powers. It would seem that this emphasis on faith in the stories of the Gospels is a unique historical development. It is an attitude expressed by a Samaritan leper, a Roman centurion, and a Syro-Phoenician woman as well as by "a daughter of Abraham."[38] Apparently this faith, implicit or explicit, that Jesus commended was not specifically Israel's faith that God delivers or will deliver from their distresses his law-abiding people, nor a confession that Jesus is the Messiah, the Son of God. Perhaps one can conclude that the faith Jesus acknowledged was a trust that God, whose sovereign rule he proclaimed, was willing and able to bestow health and wholeness to needy human beings, a faith not confined to any person's or communities' ideology.*

In his healing ministry Jesus' attitudes and actions are not those of an emancipated Jew. The faith of the historical Jesus must not be separated from Israel's hope that God keeps faith with his promises to redeem his creation from bondage to evil powers, disease, and death. Jesus' healing ministry was testimony that the blessings of God's eschatological kingdom were not future possibilities only, a utopian, visionary dream: the God worshipped in Israel, but not exclusively Israel's God, was now fulfilling his purposes of salvation, willing and able to fulfil them in the present.

The accounts of Jesus' exorcisms of demons are apt to be particularly offensive to the modern reader. Belief in demon possession was almost universal in the first century, and many mental and physical maladies were so diagnosed. Doubtless Jesus' power over the affected persons was great, and his exorcisms created a strong impression upon the masses. Yet few persons today would hesitate to attribute the belief in demon possession to the tendency of persons in the Hellenistic Age to ascribe to supernatural agencies phenomena that were not understood. Perhaps some may argue that in our present state of knowledge the possibility of demon possession should not be dismissed; at the least one can admit that some mentally ill persons are victims of forces that seem to lie altogether beyond one's control. But most modern persons believe that the symptoms attributed to demon possession in the Gospels are to be otherwise explained.**

Did Jesus believe in demon possession? Some persons have held that he accomodated himself to popular beliefs in order to gain rapport with those he intended to help. Demon possession was a dreadful factor in the minds of many, which could not be dispelled if attacked as an illusion. It seems more plausible, however, to assume that Jesus really shared the views of his contemporaries; to affirm his genuine humanity is to acknowledge that he was a first-century Jew.

In summary, it can be said that for Jesus' disciples—now as then—his acts of healing were perceived as arresting signs, events partly disclosing deeper mysteries than the miracle stories display, viewed separately or together. But

hind which one could take refuge against the devil. He therefore went over to the attack." O. Betz, *What Do We Know About Jesus?*, p. 60. See CD 2:4–10, 3:24; 1QH 6:25ff.

* The character of this faith "is so startlingly unlike anything we could parallel in Judaism and the early church" that it must be characteristic of Jesus himself. (N. Perrin, *Rediscovering the Teaching of Jesus*, p. 139). Bornkamm notes that faith for Jesus has not yet acquired the meaning of the obedient acceptance of his messiahship. In this respect the miracle tradition of the Gospels retain a pre-Easter perspective (*Jesus of Nazareth*, p. 129ff.)

** Advances in psychosomatic medicine make it possible for modern readers to explain many of the miracles of the Gospels differently. Certain maladies once believed and the result of physical causes are now recognized to be functional disorders

AROUND THE SEA OF GALILEE

Who then is this, that even wind and sea obey him?
(Mark 4:41)

Home of Mary Magdalene;
"Magadan"

Capital of Herod Antipas "The Fox"

Jesus performs many miracles in
"his own city"; Matthew follows
Jesus; 12 Apostles instituted

Sermon on the Mount

Woe to you Chorazin
(Matthew 11:21)

...He came to them,
walking on the sea
(Mark 6:48)

Multiplication of
loaves and fishes

...Woe to you Bethsaida...
Matthew 11:21
City of Andrew and Peter

Drowning of the
Gadarene swine

Storm
on the sea

G A L I L E E

Magdala

Tiberias

Gennesaret

Capernaum

Chorazin

Bethsaida

Gergesa

Hippus

H I P P U S

G A D A R A

Sennabris

Emmatha

Gadara

Matt. 4:18, 5:1, 8:18, 23–24, 9:1, 13:1, 14:13–34, 15:29–39;
Mark 2:16–20, 2:13, 4:1, 35–41, 5:1–21, 6:32–53, 8:1–10, 22;
Luke 5:1–11, 8:22–39, 9:10–17;
John 6:1–25

for those persons rejecting the significance that Jesus assigned his mighty works, or for those who demand signs, no such mysteries are disclosed, no proofs are provided to overcome the subjective uncertainty of faith.

JESUS AND THE TORAH SCHOLARS

In his ministry of healing Jesus perceived that the powers of the coming kingdom of God were already attacking directly the sources of evil and human distress, bringing health and joy to persons. For Jesus this meant that the time was fulfilled for a willing acceptance of *the demands* as well as *the gifts* of God. With great urgency he laid upon the conscience of his hearers the necessity of immediate, unreserved obedience to the Will of God. Jesus' eschatological proclamation of the good news and summons to repentance provide the proper context for understanding his teaching.

Jesus' teaching is also to be understood within the context of a dialogue with other teachers concerning the interpretation of "the Law, the Prophets, and the Writings," for the common assumption was that these sacred scriptures, though not yet finally fixed as a "canon," contained the revelation of God's will. For Jesus, as for all teachers who engaged him in debate, the scriptures, correctly interpreted, provided "the legal charter of national life, the foundation of public worship, the unique source for individual piety, and a text-book for the schooling of young and old."[39] Judaism's most treasured possession, "the study and observance of Torah were thought [by Jesus' contemporaries] to constitute at all times, during the eschatological age also, the quintessence of religion. No counsel among the Sayings of the Fathers is urged more pressingly than meditation on the Torah, and in apocalyptic and Qumran thought it was a return to this study that was to herald the onset of the final age."[40]

It is clear from the Synoptic Gospels that Jesus viewed his eschatological proclamation of the coming kingdom as the fulfilment of the scriptures of Israel, and that, in his exposition of that righteousness required of those who are to enter this kingdom, he was drawn into debate with the Torah scholars of his day—"the scribes," and "the sages" and "rabbis," as they were coming to be called.*

On occasions Jesus taught in the synagogues of Galilee and gave special instruction to disciples after the manner of the rabbis. Like them also, Jesus expressed his teachings in aphorisms, proverbs, and parables, drawing his vivid metaphors from the same sources from which his contemporaries derived their teaching—the scriptures, nature, and the everyday experiences of Palestinian Jews. Jesus was perceived by some as a rabbi, a teacher of Torah, although others among his hearers looked askance at his lack of formal schooling and observed differences between him and the sages.

According to the Earliest Evangelist, those persons most seriously offended by Jesus' teaching were "the scribes" (2:6f.), or "the scribes of the Pharisees" (2:16), or, simply, "the Pharisees" (2:24; 3:6). Recall the reports of Josephus concerning the *Pharisaioi*, participants in the power struggles among the citizenry during the Hasmonean Era. "After the death of Salome Alexandra Josephus mentions the Pharisees only sporadically."[41] One must turn to rabbinic sources for knowledge of the Pharisees in the Roman Period. In some sense

resulting from psychological maladjustment. Some of the so-called "modern parallels" demonstrate that much that Jesus did was not "against nature." At the same time, the evidence of the dramatic progress of a science yet in its infancy enforces the wisdom of refusing to accept only those miracles of Jesus that today's scientists can accomplish. The Christian is not alone in his unwillingness to dogmatize concerning what was possible for Jesus, but Christians especially will not wish to press their conclusions upon others.

*The title "rabbi" (my master) was given to Torah scholars after Hillel (ca. 20 C.E.), according to some historians. Alternatively, the first descendants of Hillel were known as "Rabban" (our master); only after Yavneh were individual Torah scholars given the title "rabbi." Rivkin, *A Hidden Revolution*, pp. 257f.

*Rabbinic Judaism—that mode of Judaic religion created by the rabbis of the first six centuries (C.E.) and embodied in the laws and doctrines of the Talmud. J. Neusner, ed., *Understanding Rabbinic Judaism* (1974), p. 1. For identification of the two Talmuds, Babylonian and Palestinian, see p. 197.

**A classic statement depicting the Jewish sage in the role of "scribe" is written in Sir. 39:1ff. "He devotes himself to the study of the law of the Most High," he "seeks out the wisdom of all the ancients," he is "concerned with prophecies." In sum, he "reveals [divine] instruction in his teaching, and glories in the law of the Lord's covenant."

†Targum (pl. Targumim). Since the emphasis in these translations was on understanding rather than literal meaning, the Targumim were often paraphrases, embellishments of the texts that were, in fact, commentary.

‡Midrash, Midrashim (from the root, *darash*, "to search out" or "to look for"), is the Hebrew word for biblical exegesis or

(admittedly difficult to trace and assess) these Pharisees were major contributors to the early development of "rabbinic Judaism."*

AN EXCURSUS: RABBINIC LITERATURE

An understanding of rabbinic literature can be useful for reconstructing Palestinian Judaism before 132 C.E., and for understanding "the historical Jesus" (also Paul and Jewish Christianity).

A dramatic event took place in Jerusalem early in the fourth century B.C.E. Under the leadership of Ezra, "the priest and scribe," returnees from Babylonian Exile were gathered "into the square before the Water Gate" for a public reading from "the book of the law of Moses which the Lord had given to Israel." Since it was intended that this reading would inspire far-reaching reforms (which it did), Ezra and his fellow priests not only read "clearly" but "they gave the sense, so that the people understood the reading."[42] There are two noteworthy elements in this narrative. (1) In the persons of Ezra "the scribe" and his priest colleagues, are the prototypes of a professional class whose members devoted themselves to the study, interpretation, and application of the scriptures.** (2) This Ezra narrative provides a plausible explanation for the early development of a legal tradition. Following Ezra's reading of the Hebrew scriptures, a translation into Aramaic (the language of the people) was given so that the reading was understood. This Aramaic translation-interpretation developed into an exegetical tradition. It was written down much later, at which time it became a type of literature known as the *Targum*.†

By the time of Jesus the public recitation of scripture was a regular feature of synagogue worship. The Torah scroll was read, section by section, from Genesis through Deuteronomy, followed by an appropriate passage from the Prophets known as the *haftarah*.[43] The reading of both texts was accompanied by an Aramaic Targum, and probably followed by a sermon or homily.[44]

The activities and public image of the priest-scribes who functioned during the period of the Hellenistic kingdoms are shrouded in obscurity. During the reign of the Hasmoneans, "scribes" constituted a class of professional Torah scholars. Yet the status of the priest-scribes was not unrivalled. Influential sages emerged from all walks of life, functioned as Torah scholars alongside the priest-scribes, and seemed to have overshadowed the professional class in establishing legal prescriptions.

These ancient scholars, referred to in the rabbinic literature as "sages," have been likened "to the early prophets, Nathan, Gad, Ahijah, and Elijah—reprovers of kings and despots. Only their reproof did not emanate from prophecy and their influence was not due to charisma, but to their wisdom," and this wisdom consisted in a knowledge of the written and oral Torah.[45] Their expository method came to be known as *midrash*.‡ The midrashim consisted of commentary on the sacred text, intended to demonstrate its binding, legislative function in relation to all of life.

The development of midrash reflects the two types of material in the written Torah: (1) the rules of conduct—legal statutes, ordinances, and so on, and (2) the narrative. The midrash on the former, known as *halachah* or halachic midrash, sought to apply the original Mosaic laws to the constantly changing situations of life. Midrash on the narrative portions of the Torah, known as *haggadah*, or haggadic midrash, sought by means of parables, historical anecdotes, legends, and the like, to inspire and instruct the pious in the ways of God.*

While one can assume that the priest-scribes and other sages sought to base their teaching upon scripture, it is clear that their targumic and midrashic operations contributed to the expansion of "the oral law" or "the traditions of the fathers." Presumably, it was believed that they were merely unfolding the Torah itself, or applying ancient legislation, which, like the written Torah, had its origin in the Mosaic revelation.

One is not able to trace step by step the formation and transmission of the oral law in the late Second Temple Period; however, the *Mishnah* and the *Tosefta* are literary deposits of this "tradition of the fathers," and provide important clues concerning the methods and objectives of those scholars of the twofold law who flourished from around 70 to 220 C.E.**

The Mishnah edited by Rabbi Judah ha-Nasi ("the Prince," or "the Patriarch") around 220 C.E., was received as an authoritative collection of the oral law, arranged according to subject matter into six major divisions or "orders": "Seeds," "Set Feasts," "Women," "Damages," "Hallowed Things," and "Cleannesses."

These tracts were subdivided into sixty tractates. Rabbi Judah's Mishnah soon superceded all other attempts to record the halachoth of scholars of the twofold law, most of whom are designated as the *Tannaim*.†

The document written in the middle of the third century, known as the Tosefta, resembles the Mishnah of Rabbi Judah in its form and contents. Its halachoth are of quite diverse origins, and it contains more haggadoth than the Mishnah.

The Mishnah and Tosefta differ radically in their form from the Targumim and Midrashim. In the latter the teaching is aligned with the text of scripture and is its exposition. In the Mishnaic tradition, halachoth are ascribed to the sages (most are named, others are anonymous), and when scripture is cited its function is to provide a proof text.[46] One tractate in the Mishnah of Rabbi Judah is quite different from the rest, namely *Pirqe Aboth*, which is known as "the Sayings of the Fathers." It is a collection of sayings and anecdotes ascribed to notable Tannaim or their predecessors.

The collection and codification of oral law did not cease with Rabbi Judah's Mishnah, which was completed in the early years of the third century. Subsequent collections are represented by the Babylonian and Palestinian (or Jerusalem) *Talmuds*. The first redactions of the Palestinian Talmud date from the second half of the fourth century. The larger and more significant Babylonian Talmud was, for the most part, edited at the beginning of the fifth century.

The two Talmuds preserve the legal prescriptions of the *Amoraim*, those rabbis who taught in the years between Rabbi Judah's redaction of the Mishnah and the editing of the Talmuds.‡ The sayings of the Amoraim are referred to as *Gemara*, for they were purported to be "the completion" of Mishnaic and Tannaitic scholarship.

Other respositories of oral law are the Tannaitic Midrashim, described above

exposition. Literary works preserving this exegesis are known as Midrashim.

*In sum, *halachah* (pl. halachoth) is regulative material; *haggadah* (pl. haggadoth) is illustrative and hortatory, showing what the narratives of the Torah "tell" in addition to their literal sense. Bowker, *The Targums and Rabbinic Literature*, p. 40.

**Mishnah, from *shanah*, meaning "to repeat," hence a title given to recensions of oral law, fostering learning by repetition. Tosefta, "supplement." A document intending to supplement the Mishnah? "The actual relations between the two remains one of the most vexing problems of rabbinical scholarship." Bowker, *The Targums and Rabbinic Literature*, p. 61f.

†Tannaim (sing. Tanna), "reciters," "repeaters," a designation for the "generations" of Torah scholars who lived from ca. 70 to 220 C.E. Their teaching is preserved in the Mishnah and Tosefta, and the Tannaitic Midrashim. Also ascribed to the Tannaim are the Baraita (pl. Baraitoth), miscellaneous legal prescriptions scattered throughhout the Talmuds.

‡Amoraim (sing. Amora), "speakers" who sought to elucidate and clarify the text and meaning of the Mishnah, which (after scripture) became the object of their study. The word *Talmud* means "teaching, learning."

as commentaries on the written Torah. The oldest Midrashim are expositions of legal material in the Pentateuch. They are the Mekilta (on parts of Exodus), Sifra (Leviticus), Sifre Numeri, and Sifre Deuteronomium.

With an understanding of the rabbinic literature most relevant to a study of first-century Judaism, it is important now to hold in mind a methodological principle: rabbinic sources deriving from early in the third century and later are primarily testimonies to the views of the Tannaim and their successors, the Amoraim, even when such views are attributed to Torah scholars known to be their predecessors. Only with caution can one employ these sources as preserving the halachoth of legal authorities who lived before 70 C.E. The task, then, is a complex one: to discover the contributions of this rabbinic literature to a portrayal of "the historical Pharisees" described by Josephus and appearing before us in the pages of the New Testament.

Probably all or most of the sages who, according to the Mishnah, flourished in the first century before 70, were Pharisees or tended toward Pharisaism. Yet only two persons who are named in the Mishnah are designated in extra-Mishnaic writings as "Pharisees": Gamaliel[47] and Simeon b. Gamaliel.[48] The remaining Tannaitic sources reveal nothing concerning the sectarian affiliation of those pre-70 Torah scholars identified in the Mishnah. The quest of the historical Pharisees is further complicated by the fact that post-70 rabbis rarely identify their predecessors by sectarian designations corresponding to the *Pharisaioi* in the Greek sources (Josephus and the New Testament).

In the Semitic sources (rabbinic literature) references can be found to *perushim*, which, like *Pharisaioi*, can be transliterated loosely to "Pharisees." But not every appearance of *perushim* can be taken as a reference to the Pharisees of Josephus and the Gospels. When the *perushim* are sharply opposed by the *zedukim* in the Tannaitic sources, there would seem to be a clear reference to the Pharisees and Sadducees of the Greek sources; and when other passages report clashes between "the sages" (hakhamim) and the *zedukim*, apparently the legal prescriptions of these sages represent the views of Pharisees. In still other passages, however, *perushim* does not refer to members of a particular sect but to one or more deviant types.[49] Perhaps one may conclude that *perushim* ("separated ones") had both good and bad meanings. Doubtless some sages/Pharisees separated themselves from situations incurring ceremonial defilement in accordance with the twofold law. But the term "separated ones"— "seceders"—may have been used by critics of some extremists who, by insisting upon increasingly scrupulous degrees of holiness, were inflated with pride, withdrew from community affairs, and were perceived by their critics to be hypocrites.[50]

In rabbinic writings, as in the Gospels, "the scribes" and the sages/*perushim* are sometimes distinguished. Again we note that since the days of Ezra it is probable that "scribes" continued to function as a distinct professional class. Doubtless some of these scribes joined the sect of the Pharisees from time to time (which may account for the reference to "the scribes of the Pharisees" in Mark 2:16). The views of scribes are not distinguished from those of the Pharisees in the Gospels.

The name of Hillel is prominent in the rabbinic traditions concerning the pre-70 Pharisees. In fact most of these traditions concern Hillel, the group of his followers referred to as the House of Hillel, and their opponents within Pharisaism—Shammai and the House of Shammai. A major reason for Hillel's prominence is that by the close of the century his descendants and followers took over the leadership of Pharisaic Judaism from the followers of Shammai, who, in the lifetime of the two men, exerted the larger influence. At Yavneh (ca. 70–125 C.E.), and especially afterwards at Usha (ca. 140 C.E.), adherents of the House of Hillel edited the traditions relating to their founder.* Many of the reports concerning Hillel—his legislation, wise sayings, his Davidic origin, his rise to power—reflect less the historical person, Hillel, and more the interests of rabbis of the middle decades of the second century, those who had strong motives for developing traditions about the founder of their "House."[51] Although there are sharp differences of opinion concerning the use of the Hillel traditions for historical reconstruction, few would demur from the conjecture that Hillel was chiefly responsible for "changing the character of Pharisaism from a political party [which, we have seen it was in the Hasmonean Era] to a table-fellowship sect [in the time of Herod].[52]

At the present time scholars draw somewhat different pictures of pre-70 Pharisaic Judaism, corresponding to their assessments of historically reliable evidence in the rabbinic literature. By "concentrating on those sayings and stories that indubitably allude to Pharisees before 70 C.E.," one scholar concludes that their's was a cult-centered piety seeking "to replicate the cult in the home, and thus to effect the Temple's purity laws at the table of the ordinary Jew, and quite literally to turn Israel into 'a kingdom of priests and a holy nation.' "[53] This "late Pharisaism" corresponds to the Gospels' Pharisaic stories; both stress some of the same concerns: first, eating ordinary food in a state of ritual purity,[54] second, careful tithing and giving of agricultural offerings to the priests,[55] and obedience to biblical rules and taboos concerning raising and harvesting crops,[56] third, some special laws on keeping the Sabbath[57] and finally, a few rules on family affairs.[58]

The body of laws attributed to the Houses of Shammai and Hillel "apply in the main to the ritual cleanliness of food, and of people, dishes and implements involved in its preparation . . . laws regarding Sabbath and the festivals [also] involve in large measure the preparation and preservation of food." The impact of the dietary laws of the Pharisees "extended far beyond the table, however, for purity required one always to remain aware of the rules of table-fellowship," and "since the Pharisees claimed that the laws they kept were not 'sectarian,' but derived from the Torah of Moses at Sinai, they would have said they kept the rules and the regulations of the Creator of the world, and their laws constituted perpetual observance of his will."[59]

Other scholars describe the concerns of the rabbi's Pharisees as being broader than this nonpolitical concentration upon the sect's rules relating to table-fellowship and internal discipline. While recognizing that the ideal of the sages/Pharisees was "to facilitate the observance of the laws of purity in all their stringency," it is also claimed that leaders of the sect were actively involved in the governance of the temple and the nation, through their leadership in the Sanhedrin and in their schooling of the nation as the synagogue's esteemed Torah scholars.[60]

According to Matthew, Jesus in his teaching upheld the formal authority

*For a brief description of the activities and accomplishments of the rabbis at Yavneh under the leadership of the Pharisee, Yohanan ben Zakkai, and subsequently at Usha, under Simeon b. Gamaliel and Aqiba's followers of the House of Hillel, see J. Neusner, *From Politics to Piety*, pp. 97ff., and 123ff.

both of the written Torah (5:17) and of the oral "traditions of the fathers" (23:2f., 23). Nevertheless, it is reported that on occasions he revoked specific Mosaic commandments, and at other times invalidated prescriptions of the oral Law in commanding a more radical obedience to God, grounded upon his own teaching. (See pages 154–155.) Where obedience to the twofold Law conflicted with the demands of love—love of God and of neighbor—Jesus loosed his disciples from the law's binding authority. The twin love commandment summarily comprehended "the law and the prophets" (22:34–40). [61]

There would seem to be no reason to doubt that Matthew's basic interpretation of Jesus' attitude to the twofold Law reflects important aspects of the teaching of the historical Jesus, although we have noted a tendency in the First Gospel toward "a temporizing" of Jesus' counsels of perfection. A historian's assessment of Jesus' attitude to the Torah must, however, take into account other important evidence, that which is provided by stories in the Gospels reporting the controversies of Jesus with the Pharisees. The views of pre-70 sages/Pharisees and the self-understanding of scribes gleaned from the rabbinic literature may contribute to our understanding of Jesus' critics. In examining this Gospel material, most of which is in the form of the aphoristic narrative, our major question is this: when Jesus was accused of deviating from the Torah and the halachic midrashim of the scribes and Pharisees, how did he respond?

Ritual Purity/Defilement "Why do your disciples not live according to the traditions of the elders," complained some Pharisees (along with some of the scribes), "but eat with hands defiled?" (Mark 7:1–8, 14–23). The earliest Evangelist's note—that "all Jews" observed the purity laws concerning hand washing is doubtless an exaggeration, yet we have seen that such practices were important to the sages as an expression of an intention toward holiness comparable to the ritual of holiness in the Temple. The exact extent of these practices was a matter of dispute. Perhaps Mark described legal prescriptions too extreme for many Torah scholars, but they are by no means unlikely for some of the *hakhamim/perushim* depicted in rabbinical sources.*

* "For (the eating of food that is) unconsecrated or (Second) Tithe or Heave-offering, the hands need but be rinsed, and for Hallowed Things they need to be immersed; and in what concerns the Sin-offering water, if a man's hands are unclean his whole body is deemed unclean." *Mishnah:* Hagigah 2.5; Yadaim 1.1 ff.

Mark's penchant for inserting one traditional narrative into another may have resulted in the loss of the narrative frame for the halachic aphorism (7:15; see p. 117). Possibly the dialogue and interpretation that follow (17–23) were formulated in a Gentile Church as a reaction to conservative Jewish Christians adhering to traditional Jewish purity laws (Note 19b); however, inherited prejudices may have made people resistant to Jesus' radical views in this matter. Bultmann judges verse 15 to be a saying of Jesus, both in its form and content. [62]

According to Matthew 23:25f., Jesus criticized the Pharisees' purity rules as "full of anomalies": they "cleanse the outside of the cup and the plate," and not the inside. But his contention that "whatever goes into a man from outside cannot defile him" goes further than a rejection of traditional halachoth. Did Jesus call into question the written Torah's purity laws *in toto*? [63]

Contact with "Sinners" When the scribes of the Pharisees saw that Jesus was "eating with sinners and tax-collectors" they said to his disciples: "Why does he eat with tax-collectors and sinners?" (Mark 2:13–17 and pars). [64]

In the rabbinical literature the term *Am Ha-aretz* (pl. *Amme Ha-aretz*, "people of the land") identified Jews who were careless in their Torah observance and indifferent to the halakah of the sages. The sages seem to have taken an ambivalent attitude to the *Amme Ha-aretz* from whose social classes many of the sages were drawn. The sages thus are depicted as defending actions and customs of the *Amme Ha-aretz* in disputes with Sadducees. Yet the practical neglect by an *Am Ha-aretz* of the purity laws and the law of the tithe led the *perushim* to separate themselves from his or her company.* It is quite probable that the unrighteous *Amme Ha-aretz* of the rabbinic sources are the "sinners" of the Gospels, among whom are grouped especially odious characters, the corrupt agents of Rome—tax-collectors.

The Synoptic Gospels report that Jesus often befriended sinners. This free association was highly offensive to the Pharisees. Jesus and his disciples flouted the program of social ostracism necessitated by the ideal of a holy people. Jesus defended these attacks by saying: "Those who are well have no need of a physician, but those who are sick; I came not to call the righteous, but sinners." "The Son of man [or I] came to seek and to save that which was lost." These "lost sheep of the house of Israel" were his special care. God willed and rejoiced in their salvation. The danger therefore of eating untithed food in the homes of sinners, or of otherwise incurring ceremonial defilement through association, was no hindrance to his ministry among them.

Sabbath Observance   "One sabbath he was going through the grainfields; and as they made their way his disciples began to pluck ears of grain. And the Pharisees said to him, 'Look, why are they doing what is not lawful on the sabbath?' "

To preserve the sanctity of the sabbath, the sages/Pharisees constructed an elaborate fence around this commandment of the Torah.[65] Sabbath observance was a principal hallmark of piety in Palestinian Judaism.** The aphorism attributed to Jesus in Mark 2:27 is indeed remarkable. "For this to come from the lips of an ordinary rabbi is quite without parallel."[66] Coming from Jesus, what seems to have been his meaning? Not an abrogation of the commandment to keep the sabbath holy. The assumption underlying 2:27 is that Jesus and his disciples observe the sabbath; the issue is by what standard they keep it. According to Jesus, the fulfilment of human need overrode the many rules in the oral law concerning the sabbath. (And Jesus said [to those who criticized him for healing on the sabbath]: 'Is it lawful on the sabbath to do good or do harm, to save life or to kill?) (Mark 3:4). We report here a Mishnaic ruling declaring that "whenever there is doubt whether life is in danger, this overrides the sabbath." In the Gospel's pericopes, however, the grain pickers were in no dire need, nor were those persons healed on the sabbath.[67] It was enough for Jesus that God never proscribes acts of mercy. If it is permissible to pull an ox out of a well into which it has fallen or to lead a thirsty animal to water on the sabbath, then surely God wills on this day that humans who are suffering be given immediate relief.[68]

Divorce   The Torah provided that a husband could present his wife a certificate of divorce if he found in her "some unseemly thing" (RSV:indecency).[69] In

*"For *perushim* the clothes of an *Am Ha-aretz* count as suffering contact-uncleanness." (*Mishnah*: Hagigah 2.7). (He who is scrupulous) "must give tithe from what he eats and from what he sells and from what he buys (to sell again); and he must not be the guest of an *Am Ha-aretz*. (*Mishnah*: Demai 2.2) . . . he may not be the guest of an *Am Ha-aretz* nor may he receive him as a guest in his own raiment . . . (2.3).

**". . . the rules about the Sabbath Festal Offerings, and Sacrilege, are as mountains hanging by a hair, for (the teaching of) Scripture (thereon) is scanty and the rules many. . . ." (*Mishnah*: Hagigah 1.8).

"The main classes of work (forbidden on the Sabbath) are forty save one: sowing, ploughing, reaping, binding sheaves, threshing, winnowing, etc." (*Mishnah*: Shabbath 7.2)

"The Sabbath is delivered unto you, and you are not delivered to the Sabbath." (*Mekilta* Ex. 31: 14; R. Simeon b. Menasya, ca. 165–200 C.E.).

*"The House of Shammai say: A man may not divorce his wife unless he has found unchastity in her, for it is written, 'Because he hath found in her *indecency* in anything.' And the House of Hillel say: (He may divorce her even if she spoiled a dish for him, for it is written, 'Because he hath found in her indecency *in anything*. . . .'" (*Mishnah*: Gitten 9.10).

**An example from the *Babylonian Talmud*, Shab. 31a: "it happened that a certain non-Jew came before Shammai and said to him, 'make me a proselyte, on the condition that you teach me the whole Torah while I stand on one foot.' Thereupon he repulsed him with the builder's cubit which was in his hand. When he went before Hillel, he said to him, 'what is hateful to you do not do to your neighbor, that is the whole Torah, while the rest is the commentary thereof; go and learn it." (cf. Tobit 4:15.

†Philo summarized the piety of the Essenes as love toward God and one's neighbor (*Every Good Man is Free*, IX. 83f.) 1QS ii. 24, v. 25. This love of neighbor applied,

Jesus' day neither scribal sanction nor a wife's consent were necessary in divorce proceedings, but the question had arisen concerning how the Torah provision was to be interpreted.* According to Mark and the Q tradition Jesus refused to be drawn into this casuistic debate. Divorce, he taught, was contrary to the will of God whatever its cause.[70] In taking this position Jesus was rejecting the final authority of an explicit provision of the Torah. In doing so, however, Jesus appealed to the Torah, finding in its story of creation divine sanction for the teaching that marriage ought to be an indissoluble union. Jesus' intention therefore was not a repudiation of the Torah, but an interpretation of its basic intention.[71]

The Twofold Love Commandment   An important pericope in Mark 12 provides an essential focus with respect to Jesus' attitude to the Torah and the traditional halachoth of the Pharisees. The pericope, verses 28–34, does not reflect Mark's usual view of scribes; of the nineteen references to scribes in Mark only this man is portrayed in a favorable light.[72] The story was probably circulated in this form before Christians tended to disparage all scribes as Jesus' carping critics. Moreover, the scribe of Mark 12, who earnestly sought from Jesus a *kelal*, perceptively distinguished between the relative importance of the temple ritual and the paramount obligation to love God and neighbor.** The typical Torah scholar would certainly not have voiced this distinction in value among the commandments. For example, Rabbi (Judah) said: "be heedful of a light precept as of a weighty one, for thou knowest not the recompense or reward of each precept . . ." (*Mishnah*: Aboth 2.1) According to Luke, Jesus' answer to the scribe was "do this, and you will live" (10:28). Jesus thus is reported to have assigned a priority to the twin love commandments that is neither logical nor relative, but absolute. Without any supplement whatsoever this law is the complete guide to those who would enter the kingdom of God.†

The Question About Authority   One day as Jesus was teaching the people in the Temple and preaching the gospel, the chief priests and the scribes with the elders came up and said to him, "Tell us by what authority you do these things, or who it is that gave you this authority?"[73]

The reply of Jesus seems to be an evasion, although the clear inference to be drawn from his counterquestion is that his teaching was indeed "from God." As his end drew near, as at earlier times, Jesus refrained from defending his words and deeds by appealing to existing categories of authority. He did not put himself forward as a rabbi; yet he issued a new halachoth of binding authority.[74] He made no claim to be a prophet, although he was recognized as such, for he spoke and acted with an authority exceeding that of Israel's true prophets.[75] In his public utterance he did not explain his person in terms of any popular messianism; nevertheless "the higher righteousness" that he demanded of his disciples sometimes went beyond the prescriptions of the twofold Torah and required a personal obedience to his words for no other reason than this.[76]

In view of the way in which Jesus personalized obedience, it is not sufficient to say that he merely radicalized the Torah, subordinating all of its commandments to the demand to love God and neighbor.[77] "The conflict between Jesus and the Torah scholars arose out of the authority with which Jesus acted and taught—authority which he refused to explain or ground in any official position, but authority which equally he refused to renounce." The fact is that in the teaching of Jesus generally "there is an egoism that is inconsistent with good Jewish piety.[78] We have seen that this is manifested in some of the antitheses of Matthew's Sermon on the Mount, where Jesus opposed himself and his own authority to that of Moses. Possibly editorial interests have sharpened the contrast here, or, as some have held, weakened it. The contrast is already present, however, in Mark 10:21, where Jesus says to a man who has professed obedience to the whole law, "You are still short of one thing . . . come, follow *me.*" The law does not provide adequate direction for the people of God; its place must be taken by Jesus—and the fact that on ordinary occasions Jesus is willing enough to observe the law does not lessen the offense.[79]

however, only to members of the sect: one should "love all the children of light and hate all the children of darkness," 1QS i. 10 (cf. Mt. 5:43); see also 1QS x. 17–21.

TEACHING BY PARABLE

Jesus' teaching is revealed in his parables as well as in the conflict stories and controversial sayings of the Gospels. We cannot distinguish sharply between these materials as though they are different in type. If we use the term *parable* in its original and broadest sense, it can be said that Jesus seldom if ever taught except in parable. His poetic and imaginative mind conceived ideas in realistic images. His maxims and short pronouncements as well as his "parables" are pictorial and dramatic.[80] But the parables in narrative form, considered as a whole and apart from the similitudes and proverbial sayings of Jesus, provide material of special value for a recovery of Jesus' teaching.

The parables of the Gospels in their most typical form can be characterized as extended metaphors drawn from nature, common experience, or the Jewish scriptures and tradition, arresting the hearer with their vividness and strangeness and leaving the mind in sufficient doubt over their application to prod the hearer into active thought, and, hopefully, into right decisions.[81] Recent studies of the parables of the Gospels have demonstrated that various levels of meaning often can be distinguished. There is, first of all, a parable's original *Sitz im Leben,* the life-situation occasioning the parable as spoken by Jesus to specific groups—his disciples, opponents, or a crowd of listeners. It is probable that the meaning of many of Jesus' parables was not self-evident, that he appealed to the imagination of his hearers, thereby prompting self-examination and decision.[82] It follows from this supposition that at least some of the parables reflect the life-situations of the early oral witnesses who preserved them and applied them to their needs. Finally, one can locate the particular concerns and theological tendencies of the Evangelists and the communities they addressed by observing their selection and treatment of the parables of the Synoptic tradition (see p. 88).

It is clear that before Jesus' parables were given their canonical shape they were a highly treasured part of a living tradition, there being a sustained interest in applying Jesus' teaching to developing circumstances that daily challenged his followers. While this transformation of the parabolic tradition is a demonstrable fact, it can be said that recent studies have not diminished the grounds for confidence that the parables, taken as a whole, bear "the stamp of a highly individual mind." They are works of art whose author can rarely be in doubt.[83] In vivid and various images the parables of Jesus exhibit some of the essential elements in his teaching.

Several recurrent themes are prominent in the parables. Especially note-worthy is the motif of growth and the harvest.[84] The motif of the absent master is hardly less prominent.[85] Indeed, several parables utilizing these themes focus upon the idea of great expectations and emphasize the necessity of waiting patiently or alertly for their fulfillment. It is easy to say that the interest of the early churches in the consummation of the kingdom of God and in the return of the absent Lord explains the presence in the Gospels of such parables. Yet apart from some modifications in their application, these parables surely originated in the mind of Jesus and reveal his principal concerns.[86]

Another recurrent theme of the parables is the pathetic proclivities of persons to make excuses when it is time for decisive action, or, as a variation on this theme, tragic unpreparedness for the days of opportunity and a refusal to recognize, when caught unaware, the fault in having put other interests first.[87] Again, it is easy to show that parables such as these served practical ends in the early Church. But the presence of so many of them attests their origin in the teaching of Jesus. Apparently he was sensitive to the tendency in all human beings to excuse themselves and to evade their responsibility under God.

Like the stories of Jesus' mighty works, many parables of the Gospels reveal Jesus' conviction that the eschatological hope of Israel would soon be fulfilled, that the kingdom of God was at hand. Jesus' parables that have reference to the kingdom of God have been listed (see p. 175). In some instances the preface is secondary, which reads, "the kingdom of God is like . . ." Nevertheless, the study of these parables, apart from their editorial setting, often supports the view that the reality of the kingdom is their implied premise. The farmer waits with assurance for the harvest that is ripening, in spite of small beginnings and of the mysterious hiddenness of nature's powers;[88] servants await the master's return with mixed feelings of hope and fear—he is coming soon but will they be prepared?[89] The leaves of the fig tree are signs that the summer's end is close;[90] a cloud arises in the west, a shower is imminent, or a south wind rises warning that scorching heat approaches;[91] a treasure is found, but one must act at once to seize the opportunity;[92] a man is on the way to trial, he must be quick to clear himself;[93] a great banquet is prepared, invitations are being sent out, if the righteous who are bidden are refusing, then "sinners" must be seated at the board.[94] The people to whom Jesus spoke were in the position of the various characters of these parables. A crisis had arisen. The parables reveal Jesus' belief that the kingdom of God is at hand, for weal or for woe.[95]

A large number of parables reveal that Jesus kept in the forefront of his teaching God's mercy to "sinners."[96] The coming of the kingdom was "good news to the poor." Most of these parables of the Gospels were preserved as weapons against the synagogue or, perhaps, "Pharisees" in the Church. But it is probable also that they originated in controversy. We have seen that the scribes rejected Jesus because he gathered "sinners" around him and assured them of God's forgiveness, apart from obedience to the Torah. The parables reveal that Jesus sought to teach his critics that it is the "sinner" who can best realize the extent of God's goodness;[97] that the "righteous" have no reason for their indignation that the "good news" is being proclaimed to the poor;[98] that it is God's nature to seek the lost and to rejoice greatly when they are found, when they return.[99]

But there are other parables that are intended to stir Jesus' hearers to repentance. In view of the attitudes of many, the imminence of the kingdom is the imminence of catastrophe. The parables of the faithful and wise servant, of the talents (or pounds), and of the doorkeeper were probably addressed to the ranking scribes of Israel.[100] To them much had been entrusted, and the judgment of God was soon to be revealed. The parable of the mote and the beam was probably directed to the Pharisees, as well as the similitude about blind leaders of the blind who fall into the ditch with those whom they guide.[101] The parable of the fig tree appears to warn of the fate of Israel as a whole, whereas the parable of the wise and foolish builders is a warning of Jesus to his own disciples.[102] Apparently Jesus used the parable to warn various groups that the kingdom comes as judgment upon those who spurn the will and the word of God.

What is a person to do in view of the coming crisis? Jesus gave his answer in many parables. Adults are to become again like little children, that is to say they are to be little before God, to be trusting, and to find their security in his love.[103] The parables of the servants' wages and of the laborers in the vineyard emphasize Jesus' belief that obedience to all of the commandments does not put God in his debt, that all the rewards of God are, in the final analysis, the outcome not of human merit but of divine grace.[104] Accordingly, those who await the coming of the kingdom cannot pride themselves in their righteousness nor take security in it, but must be humble before God. Humility is certainly a predominant theme in Jesus' teaching, in his action, and in his attitude to God. In the age that is coming, God *is King*.

This repentance and self-abasement before God must be followed by recognition of the cost of "entering" or "receiving" the kingdom. The way of the penitent is not easy. The door is a narrow one that leads to life.[105] In vivid imagery Jesus warns his hearers not to act without counting the cost. The expense of a tower must be estimated by its builder; a king must muster his troops before a campaign, or there may be embarrassing shortages.[106] The plowman must set his eye on a mark ahead, lest, looking back, he should run a crooked furrow.[107]

What, according to Jesus, are the characteristic marks of those who await in penitence and faith the coming of the kingdom and who have made, or are ready to make, the necessary sacrifices? The twin parables of the hidden treasure and of the pearl speak of the unprecedented joy of those who have found the one thing of supreme value.[108] But above all else, Jesus expected persons to learn the spirit of forgiveness and forbearance toward one another, and to love both friend and foe. In the parables of the unmerciful servant and the prodigal son, Jesus teaches that the requirement of forgiveness is grounded in the limitless willingness of God to forgive, to show mercy to the undeserving.[109] In the parable of the good Samaritan, Jesus depicted neighborly love in action.[110] Besides the extended metaphors of Jesus' parables, concrete examples of neighbor love are given in brief word pictures: "If anyone strike you on the right cheek, turn to him the other also. . . . If anyone forces you to go one mile, go with him two miles. Give to him who begs from you. . . . Sell your possession and give alms . . ."[111] Such precepts are not reducible to statute laws, to a code morality. Rather they remain a continuous stimulus to the imagination, prodding the hearers of Jesus to consider what such forbearance and love require of them in concrete situations.[112]

Let us consider here Mark 4:10–20. A strong case has been made for attributing 4:11f. to Jesus if allowance is made for an Aramaic original, or, alternatively, if a common misunderstanding of Mark's Greek statement is rejected.

On the assumption that Jesus spoke Aramaic, several attempts have been made to restore the saying to its original meaning. It has been suggested that Jesus used the Aramaic word *mathla* (riddle, or dark saying), and the Aramaic particle *di* (which meant "who" as well as "so that"). Thus Jesus declared that whereas the Twelve possessed the secret of the kingdom of God, for those outside everything remained in riddles, who saw and heard but did not perceive.[113] Moreover it is further claimed that the citation in Mark 4:12 of Isaiah 6:9f. accords with an Aramaic paraphrase preserved in traditional Targumim: "in order that they [as it is written:] may see and yet not see, may hear and yet not understand, unless they turn and God will forgive them."[114]

Without resorting to conjectures concerning an Aramaic original, others have denied that Mark 4:10f. expresses a hard, predestinarian purpose. (This remains a false assumption of many interpreters.) Instead we may have here a generalizing statement of Jesus' observation concerning the aim and effect of his teaching in parables.[115] True learning is possible only when the learner is stimulated to think for himself:

> As soon as he was alone, those who were round him, together with the Twelve, used to ask him about the parables. And [on such occasions] he used to say: "to you the mystery of the kingdom of God has been given ["you" referring to those persons who respond positively to the parables and have come inside for elucidation]. But those who [stay] outside never get any further than the parables themselves, in order that [as the prophet said sarcastically] they may look without seeing, and hear without understanding, otherwise they might turn to God and be forgiven!

Mark 4:13–20, the explanation of the Parable of the Sower and the Seed, is considered by many scholars to be wholly a commentary of the early church, on the dubious assumption that Jesus never intended an allegorical treatment of any of the details of his parables. As we have seen, there is considerable evidence that Jesus' parables were adapted to situations in the early church. Mark 4:13–20 affords primary evidence supporting this thesis.[116] It is possible, however, that the Markan pericope is a reapplication of a semiallegorical explanation provided by Jesus himself.[117] To the extent that this is so, one can conclude that this parable and its explanation reflect Jesus' own reaction to the mixed results of his Galilean ministry, and that the parable was originally told to answer the question of failure and success encountered in his proclamation of the good news of God's coming kingdom.

Jesus' failure to appeal to certain persons is recognized, but this does not prevent his assurance of a final, overwhelming victory. Those who risk exclusion from God's kingdom are the hard of heart—the Pharisees, but even the Twelve—who give Satan the opportunity to contest the coming of the kingdom.[118] Other persons were responding by a withdrawal from Jesus because of the opposition to him. Some may be expected to defect when the final tribulations are experienced; while a present preoccupation with worldly interests may lead others to turn away from Jesus' challenge to heroic discipleship.[119] These groups are contrasted to those genuine disciples who must be willing to leave all for the sake of the kingdom. Jesus was confident that their reward would be truly great.[120]

RESPONSE IN GALILEE TO JESUS' TEACHING AND HEALING

Two incidents are located in the Gospels, near the close of Jesus' Galilean ministry, that appear to represent strategic turning points in the narrative: the mission of Jesus' disciples and Jesus' feeding of the multitude.[121]

It is probable that the principal reason for the disciples' mission was Jesus' eagerness to announce the imminence of the kingdom of God to as many people as possible while time remained. The power of God would be with the disciples to heal, and they were to call men to repentance and faith.[122] Embedded in the account of this mission is the ominous notice that Herod, receiving reports of the activities of Jesus and the disciples, spoke of having beheaded John the Baptist.[123] This traditional story is not untouched by early Christian apologetic. As its reads, it may do less than justice to the actual hostility toward Jesus of Herod Antipas and his partisans. The combined opposition of Herod and the *perushim* probably precipitated Jesus' decision to send forth the disciples.[124]

Jesus' action in feeding the multitude apparently resulted in a crisis in his relations with the Galileans. The question will naturally arise, What is the meaning of this story? It is puerile to suggest that during an afternoon picnic by the lakeside Jesus taught a lesson in sharing. Yet a literal multiplication of loaves and fish is difficult to reconcile with Jesus' refusal in the wilderness to turn stones into bread, and with his unwillingness in Galilee to give signs of his authority. It is probable that this meal was celebrated with a large company of Galilean followers in anticipation of the feast that Jesus believed would soon be enjoyed in the kingdom of God. Jesus frequently used the banquet image in parables and sayings, recalling prophetic and apocalyptic symbolism.[125] In another way, in deed as well as in word, Jesus expressed his conviction that the Age to Come was near.

Whatever uncertainty remains over the circumstances and original significance of this story, the immediate results of the feeding of the multitude are evident. Jesus promptly sent the disciples away by boat, persuaded the crowds to go home, and sought the seclusion of the hills. Why were such actions necessary? John's Gospel records a plausible explanation. The masses wished to make Jesus their king! After this, Jesus abandoned his work in Galilee.[126]

One might suppose that Jesus' popularity among the *amme ha-aretz* in Galilee would have warranted the continuation of the ministry there. Yet, as has been surmised, Mark 4:1ff. reveals Jesus' awareness that his message was not deep-rooted in the minds and wills of the masses. People came to be healed and to marvel at Jesus' teachings. But they had not repented nor believed his proclamation of the coming of the kingdom, nor surrendered themselves to the will of God.[127]

Why did Jesus abandon work in Galilee? Various answers have been given: the failure of the disciples' mission; the attempt of the multitude to draft Jesus as a leader according to popular expectations; Jesus' inner constraint to discover what his disciples thought of the ministry or to know the extent of their loyalty; his desire to escape arrest by Herod and a fate like that of the Baptist; his desire to concentrate upon the training of the Twelve. Surely one important factor was Jesus' conviction that Jerusalem and the nation's leaders must be confronted with his proclamation of the coming kingdom of God.

NOTES

1. Matt. 11:7ff.; Lk. 7:24ff.; 16:16 (Q); Acts 1:21; 10:36f.
2. Lk. 1:80; 3:2; Mt. 3:1. How John maintained life in the wilderness is something of a mystery. It was recalled that his diet had been limited to "locust and wild honey." Doubtless John's sympathizers believed that he had been sustained by divine providence, as had Elijah, his prototype; John's enemies attributed his survival to demon possession, Mt. 11:18; Lk. 7:33 (Q).
3. W. H. Brownlee in K. Stendahl, *The Scrolls and the New Testament* (1957), p. 35. See M. Burrows, *More Light on the Dead Sea Scrolls* (1958), pp. 56ff.
4. Jos. *B.J.* II. ii.1. K. Schubert lists evidence supporting the opinion that John's father held views similar to the Qumran sect: *The Dead Sea Community* (1959), pp. 126f.
5. Isa. 40:3 (Mk. 1:3 and pars.; 1QS viii. 13–16). It should be noted that others besides Essenes lived in the desert for religious convictions. See Josephus's description of such an ascetic named Banus, *Life*, 2:11.
6. Cf. Jn. 1:6–8, 15, 19ff.; 3:22ff.
7. Jos. *Antiq.* XVIII. v. 2.
8. For this apocalyptic image of judgment, cf. 2 Esd. 4:30ff.
9. See pp. 26f. C. H. H. Scobie, *John the Baptist* (1964), pp. 17–22, 110f. Cf. M. Enslin, "Once Again: John the Baptist," *RLife* (1958): 557ff.
10. C.T. Craig, *The Beginning of Christianity* (1943), p. 69; T. W. Manson, *Servant-Messiah* (1953), pp. 43ff. Cf. Scobie, *John the Baptist*, pp. 95–102.
11. As evidence that such a radical position can be attributed to John, cf. 1QM 1, ii; 1QH vi. 7f.; CD 2:14–3:20, Brownlee, in Stendahl, *Scrolls and the New Testament*, p. 37. The Qumran folk considered themselves the true Israel; outsiders belonged to the realm of Belial.
12. Cf. 1QS vi. 14ff., ii. 19, iii. 6; Jos. *War*, II. viii. 5 and 7.
13. Schubert, *Dead Sea Community*, pp. 80ff. H. H. Rowley, "Baptism of John and the Qumran Sect," in A.J.B. Higgins, *New Testament Essays* (1959), pp. 218ff. John had disciples who learned from him certain disciplines of the spiritual life, but he does not seem to have organized a sect. On the contrary, he directed his hearers to the coming One "mightier than I."
14. Dan. 7:10f.; 4 Ezra 13:10f.; 2 Thess. 2:8; Rev. 8:5ff.
15. C. H. Kraeling, *John the Baptist* (1951), pp. 117ff. See 1QpHab iii. 28ff. Cf. Scobie, *John the Baptist*, pp. 114–116.
16. Luke puts the baptism in a subordinate clause, probably viewing the fact as relatively

unimportant beside the experience of Jesus at the time. Second-century Christians offered more elaborate explanations (see M.R. James, *Apocryphal New Testament* (Oxford: Clarendon Press, 1924), pp. 6ff.). although Jesus was at no time reluctant to humble himself before God (Mt. 3:14f.), is probably secondary since it implies John's recognition of Jesus. Note 21, below.

17. Jn. 1:32–34. Scobie, *John the Baptist*, p. 147. See further, p. 439.

18. Jos. *Antiq.*, XVIII. v. c. For an account of the defeat of Herod's armies, see *Antiq.* XVIII. v.

19. Scobie, *John the Baptist*, pp. 178–186.

20. Mt. 11:2ff; Lk. 7:18ff. J. A. T. Robinson conjectures that John thought "the One who should come" was Elijah, *"Elijah, John, and Jesus: An Essay in Detection, NTS* 4 (1958), 263ff.

21. C. Kraeling, *John the Baptist*, pp. 137ff. M. Goguel's judgment that Jesus broke with John is without support, *The Life of Jesus* (1949), pp. 271ff. Cf. Robinson's view that Jesus accepted, then later rejected, John's Elijah *redivivus* teaching. Note 20.

22. Mt. 4:1ff; Lk. 4:1ff. Did Mt.'s order of the last two temptations stand in the Q source? D. Daube, *The New Testament and Rabbinic Judaism* (1956), pp. 406ff.

23. Bultmann, *History of the Synoptic Tradition*, pp. 253ff.

24. A. M. Hunter, *Work and Words of Jesus* (1950), pp. 38ff. F. Dostoevsky, *The Brothers Karamazov*, 5. J. Fitzmyer, *The Gospel According to Luke, AB*, Vol. 28, (1981, 1985), pp. 506ff. Cf. Marshall, *The Gospel of Luke* (1978), pp. 166ff.

25. Dodd's rendering "the kingdom of God has come" is to be rejected. See R. H. Fuller, *The Mission and Achievement of Jesus* (1954), pp. 20ff.; cf. N. Perrin, *The Kingdom of God in the Teaching of Jesus* (1963), pp. 64ff. O. Betz, *What Do We Know About Jesus?* (1968), pp. 34ff.

26. Pannenberg, *Jesus*, p. 217; Bornkamm, *Jesus*, pp. 82ff.

27. Mk. 1:16ff.; Mt. 4:18ff. The variant, Lk. 5:1ff., may be a transposed post-resurrection story, cf. Jn. 1:40ff.

28. Mk. 2:14; Mt. 9:9.

29. Mk. 3:16ff.; Mt. 10:2ff.; Lk. 6:14ff. (Acts 1:3); Jn. 1:40ff.

30. Hunter, *Work and Words*, pp. 60f.; Bornkamm, *Jesus*, pp. 144ff.

31. Mt. 8:19ff.; Lk. 9:57ff.; Mt. 10:34ff.; Lk. 12:51ff.; Mk. 10:21 and pars. Very probable is the view that the number of Jesus' disciples fluctuated from time to time.

32. A. Richardson, *The Miracle Stories of the Gospels* (1942), pp. 20ff.; R. H. Fuller, *Interpreting the Miracles* (1963), pp. 24ff. "Today . . . it is being increasingly recognized that the tradition of the miracle stories in the Gospels deserves much more serious attention than either the older liberal or the earlier form-critical scholarship gave it." N. Perrin, *Rediscovering the Teaching of Jesus* (1976), p. 132.

33. Mk. 8:12 and pars. The saying "no sign shall be given . . ." is doubly attested; see Mt. 12:38ff.; Lk. 11:29ff.

34. Kümmel, *Promise and Fulfillment* (1957), pp. 105ff.; Perrin, *Rediscovering Jesus*, pp. 63ff. Jesus' reply to John's question from prison implies the same: the Old Testament prophecies of the last days are being fulfilled in Jesus' marvelous acts. Mt. 11:2ff.; Lk. 7:18ff.

35. Mt. 11:20ff.; Lk. 10:13ff. (Q).

36. Mk. 4:10ff. and pars.; Mt. 13:16f.; Lk. 10:23f. (Q); Mk. 8:17ff.; Mt. 16:8ff.

37. Mk. 2:5 and pars; 5:34f. and pars.; Mk. 6:1–6 (Mt. 13:53ff.).

38. Lk. 7:11–19; Mt. 8:5–10; Lk. 7:1–10; Mk. 7:24–30 (Mt. 15:21–28; Lk. 13:16).

39. "By common though mysterious consent, and using criteria which largely elude us, the Palestinian religious authorities decided probably at about the end of the third century (B.C.E.) to arrest the growth of sacred writings . . . from then on the

nation's religious and moral guidance was entrusted not to writers but to interpreters." G. Vermes, "Bible and Midrash," in C.F. Evans and P. Acroyd, eds., *Cambridge History of the Bible*, Vol. 1 (1970), p. 199.

40. *Ibid.*, pp. 201f. Vermes cites Jub. 23:26 and 1QS VIII, 12–16. For the identification of "the Sayings of the Fathers" (Pirqe Aboth) see "Mishnah." While the "Torah" in the rabbinical writings and in Hellenistic Judaism designated particularly the five books of Moses, Torah included more: "the reprimands and promise of the prophecies [Dan. 9:10; Ezra 9:10], and the ethics of the Wisdom books" [Sir. 24:23; Bar. 4:I], also "the enactments serving as a 'fence' for the Torah . . ." E.E. Urbach, *The Sages* (1975), pp. 289ff.

41. E. Rivkin, *A Hidden Revolution* (1978), p. 33; also 49ff. Recall the thesis of J. Neusner, whose critical analysis of Josephus's descriptions of the Pharisees leads him to conclude that the Pharisees ceased to function as a political sect or party with the advent of Herod. *From Politics to Piety (1973)*, pp. 45ff.

42. Both the identification and dating of Ezra the priest are problematical. See S. Talmon, "Ezra and Nehemiah," *IDBS* (1962), pp. 317ff. The Ezra narrative, as reconstructed by Talmon, consists of Ezra 7:1–36; Neh. 7:72b–9:37; 13:1–3.

43. Mishnah: Megillah 4:1–5. For "Mishnah," see p. 197.

44. G. Vermes, *Scripture and Tradition in Judaism* (1973); J. W. Bowker, *The Targums and Rabbinic Literature* (1969). Cf. E. P. Sanders, *Paul and Palestinian Judaism* (1977), pp. 25–29. The dating of extant Targumic texts is extremely difficult. Most are quite late but some were composed in Palestine prior to 70 C.E., as Targum fragments were found in the Qumran caves, IV and XI. Schürer, *History of the Jewish People*, Vol. 1 (1973), pp. 96–98.

45. Urbach, *The Sages*, p. 571.

46. Rivkin, *A Hidden Revolution*, p. 128, 223–233. "The laws of the Mishnah and the Tosefta are *arranged*, for the most part, logically, whereas the laws of the Tannaitic Midrash are *derived*, for the most part, logically," from designated scriptures. p. 128.

47. Acts 5:34.

48. Jos. *Life* 191.

49. Rivkin, *Hidden Revolution*, pp. 129–138; J. W. Bowker, *Jesus and the Pharisees* (1973), pp. 4–8.

50. Perhaps this derogatory connotation is sufficient to explain why the Tannaim rarely refer to their predecessors as *perushim*/Pharisees. Also, the first-century sages wished "to live amidst the broad strata of the people . . . this was prompted to no small extent by the fact that they themselves came from all classes and strata." Urbach, *The Sages*, pp. 574f., 584, 588–593. Bowker, *Jesus and the Pharisees*, pp. 19–21.

51. Neusner, *From Politics to Piety*, pp. 13–44. Cf. Urbach, *The Sages*, pp. 576–593.

52. Cf. Rivkin, *A Hidden Revolution*, pp. 85–88.

53. J. Neusner, ed., *Understanding Rabbinic Judaism*, pp. 13f.

54. Cf. Mk. 7:1–5, 14:23; 2:15–17; Mt. 23:27f.

55. Mt. 23:23f.; Mk. 7:9–13.

56. Mk. 2:23–28.

57. Mk. 3:1–6.

58. Mk. 10:2–9.

59. Neusner, *From Politics to Piety*, pp. 82–90.

60. A comparison of two major treatises concerning the Pharisees, presented in popular, readily available sources, will acquaint the reader with the several reasons why "it is now virtually (perhaps) totally impossible to write an adequate history of the Pharisees" (Bowker). On the one hand, one has Neusner's research concerning the

rabbinic tradition about the Pharisees before 70, whose conclusions are presented in *From Politics to Piety*; on the other hand, Rivkin's definition of the Pharisees, and his account of their teaching and institutional innovations, are to be found in the *IDBS*, pp. 657–663, and in *A Hidden Revolution*.

See also Urbach, *The Sages*, pp. 571–593; Safrai, "Jewish Self-government," in *The Jewish People in the First Century* (1974), pp. 384–389; 396–400; G. Alon, "The Attitude of the Pharisees to Roman Rule and the House of Herod," in *Jews, Judaism and the Classical World* (1977), pp. 18–47.

61. Cf. Mk. 12:28–34; Lk. 10:25–28.

62. Bultmann, *Synoptic Tradition*, p. 147, 105.

63. For some persons, Mk.'s parenthetical note (7:19b) is an explicit answer to this question, in the affirmative (e.g., Perrin, *Rediscovering Jesus*, pp. 149f.). Others deny that Jesus was "an iconoclast" who intended "to cross out entire chapters of the book of Leviticus." The early church would never have had to wrestle with the problem of table-fellowship with Gentiles if Jesus had unequivocally repudiated the entire ritual system enjoined in the twofold law (e.g., Craig, *The Beginning of Christianity*, pp. 98f. See pp. 154ff.

64. See also the following: from Q—Mt. 11:16–19; Lk. 8:31–35; from "Special Matthew"—21:31; from "Special Luke"—7:36–50; 18:9–14; 19:1–10.

65. Exod. 20:8–11; Lev. 19:3; Deut. 5:12–15.

66. Bornkamm, *Jesus of Nazareth*, p. 17.

67. Mk. 3:1–6; Lk. 13:10–17; 14:1–6.

68. Mk. 2:28 and pars. probably evidence that the earlier aphoristic narrative received a Christological interpretation. Accordingly, Jesus' teaching, which was a radical criticism of sabbath casuistry, was oriented towards his person and exalted status as "Lord of the sabbath." A. J. Hultgren, "The Formation of the Sabbath Pericope," *JBL* 91 (1972): 38–43; F. W. Beare, "The Sabbath Was Made For Man," *JBL* 79 (1960): 130–136. Cf. R. Banks, *Jesus and the Law in the Synoptic Tradition* (1975), p. 131.

69. Deut. 24:1.

70. Mk. 10:2ff. and pars.; also Mt. 5:32 and Lk. 16:18 (Q). The exceptive clause of Mt. 5:32 and 19:9 represents a qualification that probably derived from the Jewish-Christian community of the First Gospel. Mk. and Lk., as well as Paul (1 Cor. 7:11) agree against Mt.

71. In seeking to apply this and other moral absolutes of the Gospels, it should be remembered that "Jesus was not legislating for life's failures, but proclaiming the perfect will of God in the light of the dawning of his reign." Craig, *Beginning of Christianity*, p. 95.

72. Cf. Mt. 22:35; Lk. 10:25.

73. Lk. 20:1f.; Mk. 11:27f.; Mt. 21:23f.

74. C. K. Barrett, *Jesus and the Gospel Tradition* (1967), p. 29. Note Mk. 1:21f. (Mt. 7:28f.; Lk. 4:31f.

75. "It is very tempting to call [Jesus] a prophet. But this will not do at all. No prophet could remove himself from the jurisdiction of Moses without thereby becoming a false prophet." E. Käsemann, "The Problem of the Historical Jesus," *Essays on New Testament Themes* (1964), p. 42.

76. Mt. 11:28–30 (cf. Mt. 23:1–4). See also Mt. 7:24–28 (cf. Mt. 28:16–20). Also Mk. 8:38; 13:31.

77. Jewish law was never oriented to "an authority" to be obeyed, not even Moses.

78. Barrett, *Jesus and the Gospel Tradition*, p. 63. Barrett cites the following statement from Joseph Klausner's *Jesus of Nazareth* (1925), pp. 408f.: "Jesus possesses a belief in his mission which verges on the extreme of self-veneration . . . So strong was

Jesus' belief in himself that he came to rely upon himself more than upon any of Israel's great ones, even Moses.''

79. Barrett, *Jesus and the Gospel Tradition*, p. 64. W.D. Davies, *The Setting of the Sermon on the Mount* (1964), pp. 43ff.

80. Mk. 2:17, 19ff.; Mt. 5:39ff. (Lk. 6:29f.) Mt. 6:2f., etc. The Hebrew term *mashal* referred to a proverb, riddle, similitude, or allegory, as well as to a (proper) ''parable.''

81. Adapted from C. H. Dodd's definition, *The Parables of the Kingdom* (1961), p. 16. See further p. 206.

82. Baudelaire's comment concerning Flaubert's *Madame Bovary* may be applied to Jesus' parables: ''A true work of art does not need to make moral pleas. The inner logic of the work suffices for all moral implications, and it is the reader's task to draw the right conclusions from its outcome.''

83. Dodd, *Parables of the Kingdom*, p. 11.

84. Mk. 4:26ff.; 4:1ff. and pars.; Mt. 13:24ff.; Mk. 4:30ff. and pars.; Lk. 12:13ff.; Mt. 20:1ff.; 21:28ff.; Mark 12:1ff., and pars.

85. Lk. 19:12ff.; Mk. 12:1; 13:34.; Mt. 24:45 and Lk. 12:42 (Q); Mt. 25:14f.

86. H. J. Cadbury, *Jesus: What Manner of Man* (1947), pp. 39ff.

87. Mt. 22:1ff.; Lk. 14:15ff. (Q); Mt. 8:21f.; Lk. 9:59ff. (Q); Mt. 24:43ff.; Lk. 12:35ff. (Q); Mt. 25:1ff.

88. See Note 84.

89. See Note 86.

90. Mk. 13:28f.

91. Mt. 16:2f.; Lk. 12:54f. (Q).

92. Mt. 13:44ff.

93. Lk. 12:58f.; Mt. 5:24f. (Q).

94. Mt. 22:1ff.; Lk. 14:15ff. (Q).

95. Dodd's defense of a ''realized eschatology'' of the parables falls short of conviction. See Kümmel, *Promise and Fulfilment*, pp. 127ff.; J. Jeremias, *Parables of Jesus* (1963), pp. 115ff., 230.

96. Lk. 7:36ff.; 15:1ff.; Mt. 21:28ff. Jeremias, *Parables of Jesus*, p. 124ff.; Perrin, *Rediscovering Jesus*, pp. 90ff.

97. Lk. 7:47.

98. Mt. 21:28ff.; Mt. 22:8f.; Lk. 14:21 (Q); Mk. 12:9.

99. Lk. 15:7, 10, 32.

100. Mt. 24:45ff.; Lk. 12:42ff. (Q); Mt. 25:14ff.; (Lk. 19:12ff.); Mk. 13:33ff. Jeremias, *Parables of Jesus*, pp. 53ff.

101. Mt. 7:3ff.; Lk. 6:41f. (Q); Mt. 15:12ff.; Lk. 6:39.

102. Lk. 13:6ff.; Mt. 7:24ff.; and Lk. 6:47ff. (Q).

103. Mk. 10:15 and pars.; Jeremias, *Parables of Jesus*, pp. 190f.

104. Lk. 17:7ff.; Mt. 20:1ff.

105. Mt. 7:13f.; Lk. 13:23f.

106. Lk. 14:28ff.

107. Lk. 9:61f.

108. Mt. 13:44ff. Perrin, *Rediscovering Jesus*, pp. 87ff.

109. Mt. 18:23ff.; Lk. 15:11ff. See also Mt. 6:12, 14f., and Lk. 11:4 (Q).

110. Lk. 10:25ff.

111. Mt. 5:39ff.; Lk. 6:29f.; Mk. 10:21 and pars.

112. C. H. Dodd, *Gospel and Law* (1951), pp. 73ff.

113. T. W. Manson, *The Teaching of Jesus* (1945), pp. 76ff. ''The quotation from Isaiah is not introduced by Jesus to explain the purpose of his teaching in parables, but to illustrate what is meant by 'those outside': it is in fact a definition of the sort

of character which prevents a man from becoming one of those to whom the secret of the kingdom of God is given."

114. Jeremias, *Parables of Jesus*, p. 17.
115. C. F. D. Moule, "Mark 4:1–20 Yet Once More," in *Neotestamentica Et Semitica*, E. E. Ellis and M. Wilcox, eds. (1969), pp. 95–113.
116. This is one of three parables in the Gospels that is accompanied by an explanation attributed to Jesus. The others are Mt. 13:36–43 and 49f.
117. It is a tenuous position to declare that since the parables of the Gospels were interpreted allegorically in the ancient and medieval churches, *any* allegorical feature is a mark of nonauthenticity.
118. Mk. 3:5, 6:52, 8:14–21, 31–33; Mt. 13:36–38; cf. Mt. 6:13: "from the evil one?"
119. Mk. 13:19f.; cf. Mt. 24:10–12. Mk. 10:17–31 and pars.; Lk. 21:34–36.
120. See R. E. Brown, "Parable and Allegory Reconsidered," in *New Testament Essays*, (1968), pp. 320–333, and literature cited.
121. Mk. 6:6ff., and pars.; Mk. 6:30ff., and pars. See also John 6:1ff.
122. For comment upon Schweitzer's reading of Matt. 13:23, see p. 177.
123. Mk. 6:14ff. and pars.
124. Mk. 3:6 and pars. Since the sequence of conflict stories in Mk. forms a topical complex, the reader should be warned against assuming too precipitous a break in the relations of Jesus and the Pharisees. Cf. Lk. 13:31ff. See Goguel, *Life of Jesus*, pp. 343ff.
125. Lk. 14:15ff.; Mt. 22:1ff. (Q); Mt. 25:1ff.; Lk. 6:21 (Mt. 5:6). Cf. Isa. 25:6ff.; G.F. Moore, *Judaism in the First Centuries of the Christian Era* (1927–1930), V. 2, pp. 363ff.; D. Daube, *New Testament and Rabbinic Judaism*, pp. 36ff. On the miracle itself, see V. Taylor, *The Gospel According to St. Mark* (1952), pp. 121f.
126. Mk. 6:45ff. (Mt. 14:22ff.) Jn. 6:15. Was Jesus at this time confronted by "a Maccabean host with no Judas Maccabeus, a leaderless mob a danger to themselves and everyone else?" T. W. Manson, *Servant-Messiah*, pp. 70f. C.H. Dodd, *The Founder of Christianity* (1971) pp. 140–142.
127. Jesus' rejection at Nazareth may have forewarned him of the offense that would be taken by other Galilean communities sooner or later, e.g., Bethsaida and Chorazin, Mk. 6:1ff. (Mt. 13:53ff.) Lk., employing an independent source, makes the incident at Nazareth a prelude to the ministry (Lk. 4:16ff.) It is doubtful that Jesus ever anticipated mass repentance and belief, or that the Synoptic traditions support those biographers of Jesus who depict a "Galilean Springtime."

THE itinerary of Jesus after his retirement from Galilee is variously reported in the Gospels. Mark narrated that he led his disciples "into the region of Tyre and Sidon." Assuming a brief excursion into this territory beyond Galilee, it is not surprising that few stories of encounters of Jesus with non-Jews have survived. There is no evidence that he sought to extend his ministry among these Gentiles.[1] In the vicinity of Caesarea Philippi, Peter confessed his faith that Jesus was the Messiah whom he had been expecting.[2]

A MOMENTOUS CONFESSION AND ANNOUNCEMENT

The historicity of the incident at Caesarea Philippi has been denied by some scholars. It seems improbable, they say, that the disciples' confession, "Jesus is the Messiah," occurred during the ministry. Moreover, it is argued that Jesus did not at this time foresee his death and resurrection. The passion predictions, so-called, reported in Mark 8:31, 9:31, and 10:32f., are prophecies after these events. The post-Easter faith was projected backward into Jesus' ministry, by Mark or by Christian witnesses before him.[3]

This critical judgment is not sufficient reason to conclude that Jesus' ministry was originally nonmessianic. The Gospels provide strong support for the position "that Jesus actually awakened Messianic expectations by his coming and by his ministry, and that he encountered the faith which believed him to be the promised Savior. The faith which is expressed by the two disciples at Emmaus: 'But we hoped that he was the one to redeem Israel.' (Luke 24:21) seems to express quite accurately the conviction of the followers of Jesus before his death. This, too, is the only explanation of the attitude of the Jewish authorities and of Pilate's verdict."[4] The question of Jesus' awareness of impending sufferings and death is discussed in the next section.

On the assumption that Mark's account of Peter's confession of Jesus' Messiahship contains an historical kernel, how is one to explain the report of Jesus' response?

Although the term *messiah* had no fixed meanings, as our review of the evidence has shown, popular Jewish messianism was closely associated with the political independence and the national sovereignty of the Jews. If Jesus had made public a claim to be a messiah, or if he had encouraged others to make the claims for him, false hopes would certainly have been aroused that he was launching a political, perhaps a military, campaign. This was far from Jesus' intention, as the narratives of the Temptation and the Galilean ministry reveal. Yet it was inevitable that within the circle of Jesus' serious hearers the question should have arisen: What is the relation of the herald of the kingdom to its coming? Mark has probably exaggerated the extent to which the recognition of Jesus as a messiah was kept secret, yet it is not probable that the secrecy motif is altogether a post-Easter interpretation. Mark does report that when Jesus approached Jerusalem a blind beggar, Bartimaeus, hailed him as "Son of David," and that Galilean pilgrims welcomed him to the city with shouts of victory for "the kingdom of our father David that is coming."[5] The result was that within a few days Jesus was executed as a messiah, or, from the viewpoint of the Romans, a revolutionist. One may with reason suspect that messianic speculation centered around Jesus during the Galilean ministry and that he sought to quiet a premature, misguided popular movement. When Peter confessed his belief, "You are the Messiah," Jesus recognized that the term *as Peter understood it* should not be applied to him.[6]

From the moment of Peter's confession, Jesus turned to explain to "the Twelve" his understanding of his destiny and of theirs. He demanded of the disciples a loyalty to himself, not only an acceptance of his proclamation. The mission and fate of the "Son of man" became the principal subject of this teaching.

THE SON OF MAN IN THE SYNOPTIC GOSPELS

The frequent appearance of the phrase *Son of man* holds a particular fascination for students of the history of Jesus. According to the Evangelists, Son of man became Jesus' self-characterization. The phrase is employed in no other context except one in which Jesus himself speaks; neither friend or foe address him as Son of man.* One scholar comments: "Of all the problems of New Testament scholarship those relating to the Son of man are perhaps the most intractable. Whether or not Jesus designated himself such and what he might have meant by it may never be finally settled in our present state of knowledge of the background of the term and its usage in the earliest community."[7]

Passages in the Gospels refer to a future coming of the Son of man; to his present prerogatives or fortunes; and to the imminent suffering, death, and resurrection of the Son of man. This threefold tradition is set forth as follows, according to the sources in which it is found.

A. THE FUTURE COMING OF THE SON OF MAN

Mark:

1. ". . . whoever is ashamed of me and of my words in this adulterous and sinful generation, of him will the Son of man also be ashamed, when

* The following statement sharply poses the importance of the historical problem: " 'Son of man' is the only title that can be traced back to Jesus himself with much credibility." If this is denied to him "we shall be obliged to recognize that . . . (a) we cannot approach Jesus' own understanding of the significance of his death, and (b) that the syn-

optic tradition contains no serious thinking on the subject at all." C. K. Barrett, *Jesus and the Gospel Tradition*, p. 41.

he comes in the glory of his Father with the holy angels." Mark 8:38 (Luke 9:26; cf. Matthew 16:27).

2. "And then they will see the Son of man coming in clouds with great power and glory. And then he will send out the angels, and gather his elect from the four winds, from the ends of the earth to the ends of heaven." Mark 13:26 (Matthew 24:30–31–Luke 21:27).

3. ". . . and you [members of the Sanhedrin] will see the Son of man sitting at the right hand of Power, and coming with the clouds of heaven." Mark 14:62 (Matthew 26:64; cf. Luke 22:69).

Q:

4. "And I tell you, everyone who acknowledges me before men, the Son of man [Matthew: "I"] also will acknowledge before the angels of God; but he who denies me before men will be denied before the angels of God." Matthew 10:32–33–Luke 12:8–9.

5. "But know this, that if the householder had known at what hour the thief was coming, he would have been awake and would not have left his house to be broken into. You also must be ready; for the Son of man is coming at an hour you do not expect." Matthew 24:43–44–Luke 12:39–40.

6. And he said to his disciples, "The days are coming when you will desire to see one of the days of the Son of man, and you will not see it. And they will say to you, 'Lo, there!' or 'Lo, here!' Do not go, do not follow them. For as the lightning flashes and lights up the sky from one side to the other, so will the Son of man be in his day . . . as it was in the days of Noah, so will it be in the days of the Son of Man . . . likewise as it was in the days of Lot . . . so will it be on the day when the Son of man is revealed." Luke 17:22–30; (cf. Matthew 24:26f, 37–41).

"Special Matthew":

7. "When they persecute you [the disciples] in one town, flee to the next; for truly, I say to you, you will not have gone through all the towns of Israel, before the Son of man comes." Matthew 10:23.

8. "The Son of man will send his angels, and they will gather out of his kingdom all causes of sin and all evildoers, and throw them into the furnace of fire . . . then the righteous will shine like the sun in the kingdom of their Father. . . ." Matthew 13:41–43.

9. Jesus said to them [the disciples], "Truly, I say to you, in the new world, when the Son of man shall sit on his glorious throne, you who have followed me will also sit on twelve thrones, judging the twelve tribes of Israel." Matthew 19:28 (cf. Luke 22:28, 30).

10. ". . . then will appear the sign of the Son of man in heaven, and then all the tribes of the earth shall mourn. . . ." Matthew 24:30a.[8]

11. "When the Son of man comes in his glory, and all the angels with him, then he will sit on his glorious throne. Before him will be gathered all the nations. . . ." Matthew 25:31ff.

"Special Luke":

12. ". . . when the Son of man comes, will he find faith on earth?" Luke 18:8.

13. ". . . watch at all times, praying that you may have strength to escape all these things, and to stand before the Son of man." Luke 21:36.[9]

B. THE PRESENT PREROGATIVES OR FORTUNES OF THE SON OF MAN
Mark:
14. ". . . the Son of man has authority on earth to forgive sins. . . ." Mark 2:10 (Matthew 9:6–Luke 5:24).
15. And he said to them [the Pharisees], "The Sabbath was made for man, not man for the Sabbath; so the Son of man is lord even of the Sabbath." Mark 2:27–28 (Matthew 12:8–Luke 6:5, both omitting verse 27).
Q:
16. "For John came neither eating nor drinking, and they say, 'He has a demon'; the Son of man came eating and drinking, and they say, 'Behold, a glutton and a drunkard, a friend of tax collectors and sinners. . . .' " Matthew 11:18–19–Luke 7:33–34.
17. . . . a man [Matthew: a scribe] said to him, "I will follow you wherever you go." And Jesus said to him, "Foxes have holes, and birds of the air have nests; but the Son of man has nowhere to lay his head." Matthew 8:19–20–Luke 9:57–58.[10]
18. "This generation is an evil generation; it seeks a sign, but no sign shall be given to it except the sign of Jonah. For as Jonah became a sign to the men of Nineveh, so will the Son of man be to this generation." Luke 11:29–30 (cf. variant Matthew 12:39–40).
"Special Luke":
19. And Jesus said to him [one of those who murmured against him] "Today salvation has come to this house, since he [Zaccheus, a tax collector] is also a son of Abraham. For the Son of man came to seek and to save that which was lost." Luke 19:9–10.

C. THE IMMINENT SUFFERINGS, DEATH, AND RESURRECTION
OF THE SON OF MAN
Mark:
20. And he [Jesus] began to teach them that the Son of man must suffer many things, and be rejected by the elders and the chief priests and scribes, and be killed, and after three days rise again [Matthew, Luke: "on the third day be raised"]. Mark 8:31 (Matthew 16:21–Luke 9:22).
21. And as they were coming down the mountain [of transfiguration], he charged them [Peter, James, and John] to tell no one what they had seen, until the Son of man should have risen [Matthew: "is raised"] from the dead. Mark 9:9 (Matthew 17:9).
22. . . . he was teaching his disciples, saying to them, "The Son of man will be delivered into the hands of men, and they will kill him . . . after three days he will rise [Matthew: "he will be raised on the third day"]." Mark 9:31 (Matthew 17:22–23; Luke 9:44 omits the prediction of the resurrection).
23. "Behold, we are going up to Jerusalem; and the Son of man will be delivered to the chief priests and the scribes, and they will condemn him to death, and deliver him to the Gentiles; and they will mock him, and

spit upon him, and scourge him, and kill him; and after three days he will rise." Mark 10:33–34 (note variants, Matthew 20:18–19–Luke 18:31–33).

24. ". . . the Son of man also came not to be served but to serve, and to give his life as a ransom for many." Mark 10:45 (Matthew 20:28; cf. Luke 22:27).

25. "For the Son of man goes, as it is written of him, but woe to that man by whom the Son of man is betrayed!" Mark 14:21 (Matthew 26:24–Luke 22:22).

26. ". . . the hour has come; the Son of man is betrayed into the hands of sinners." Mark 14:41 (Matthew 26:45; cf. Luke 22:48 below).

"Special Luke":

27. . . . Jesus said to him, "Judas, would you betray the Son of man with a kiss?" Luke 22:48.[11]

The expression "Son of man" is as unnatural in the Greek of the Gospels as it is in English. It is a literal translation from the Aramaic *bar ᵉnāsh(ā)*. In the native tongue of Jesus this was a familiar expression, referring either to "man" in the generic sense, a human being, or in the indefinite sense, "someone," "anyone."[12] It is disputed that *bar ᵉnāsh(ā)* was at this period a surrogate for the personal pronoun "I," but the speaker as a human being could in a reserved manner include himself or herself.

Now since the expression "son of man" is Aramaic in its origin, it is plausible that Jesus may have used *bar ᵉnāsh(ā)* as an idiosyncrasy of speech with reference to human beings, at times including himself.[13] "There are indeed sayings attributed to Jesus that are so astonishingly bold that their very boldness might seem to justify the avoidance of direct statement in the first person."[14]

Note the five sayings, 14–17, printed in group B above. Possibly, knowledge that Jesus on occasion referred to his human fortunes and aims as those of "man" led to an early Christian extension of the expression to other sayings of Jesus. It appears that the Evangelists made some editorial changes of this sort. A majority of the "Son of man" sayings in the Gospels have been transmitted in two forms, one version containing the expression, the parallel saying without it. One scholar counted fifty-one "Son of man" sayings in the four Gospels of which no fewer than thirty-seven have a variant: the term "Son of man" is absent from one text, and "I" (usually) stands in its place.[15]

It is reasonable to assume that a kernel of traditional, genuine "Son of man" sayings must have existed as a point of departure for the Gospels' widespread use of the "Son of man" *as Jesus' self-designation.*[16] There are few who would contend, however, that the origin of the entire tradition can be explained as an editorial expansion of Jesus' (sometime) avoidance of direct speech in the first person. It is far more likely that the sayings collected above in Group A represent that "kernel" of genuine "Son of man" sayings spoken by Jesus *in which "Son of man" was intended as a title.* Sayings in this group were preserved in all strata of the Gospel tradition, and ten of them "have been handed down, without competitors, only in the Son of man version and in which even the possibility of mistranslation is excluded."[17] It would seem that alongside its everyday use, *bar ᵉnāsh(ā)* came to refer to a particular, somewhat mysterious man—the Man, the agent of God's final judgment and salvation. Beyond doubt this august use of *bar ᵉnāsh(ā)* was derived, directly or indirectly, from an apocalyptic vision recorded in Daniel 7:1–14.

In Daniel's vision four beasts are successively arraigned before the throne of God and condemned (each, one is told, represents a kingdom oppressing the people of God). After this a fifth being appears, having not the form of a beast but of man:

> 13. Behold there came kebar ᵉnāsh (one in human likeness; RSV, "one like a son of man") in heavenly clouds and came to the Ancient of Days and was presented before him.
> 14. And to him was given dominion and glory and a kingdom, that all peoples, nations and languages shall serve him; his dominion is an everlasting kingdom, which shall never pass away.

According to Daniel 7:18, "the one in human likeness"—the Man—served as a corporate image symbolizing "the saints of the Most High, who receive the kingdom (of God) and possess it forever."

In a few later Jewish texts Daniel's apocalyptic Son of man is interpreted to refer to a messianic individual, a heavenly being who is to appear as the eschatological judge and redeemer of the world: the Sibylline Oracles 5:256 (70–100 C.E.), and 2 Esdras 13:2ff. (around 90 C.E.). Many scholars have abandoned the hypothesis that 1 Enoch 37–71, "the Similitudes of Enoch," are Jewish texts of the First Century B.C.E.

Opinions differ sharply concerning the origin of the titular use of *bar ᵉnāsh (ā)*. Some scholars deny that in Palestinian Judaism "Son of man" was current as a title, equivalent or alternative to "messiah," or indeed as a title at all.[18] But other scholars, drawing upon the Jewish texts noted above, are convinced that they provide "valuable evidence for the existence of belief in certain circles in the time of Jesus in the Son of man as a messianic heavenly judge and ruler, and deliverer of the righteous from their oppressors . . . It is this idea of the apocalyptic Son of man which Jesus adapted in his teaching."[19]

Although there remains uncertainty concerning the existence and influence of Jewish precedents for the Son of man sayings in Group A, this by no means rules out the possibility that these Gospel passages (directly or indirectly referring to Daniel 7) can be traced back to Jesus himself.

Among scholars who consider that at least some of the "Son of man" texts in group A are genuine sayings of Jesus are those who make a distinction between the "I" of the speaker (Jesus) and the Son of man who is to come (the latter being referred to in the third person).[20] According to this view, Jesus did not envision that he was to be this Son of Man.

The hypothesis that Jesus never spoke of himself as Son of man but only proclaimed the coming of another whom he so designated contains serious difficulties. When it is recalled that Jesus designated John the Baptist as the precursor of the coming age, and that in his own word and action he himself inaugurated the kingdom of God, one may well ask what place there would have been in Jesus' teaching for the coming of some other eschatological figure. Moreover, the judgment of the coming Son of man "so precisely corresponds to a person's response to the earthly Jesus that there must exist so close a connection between Jesus and 'the Man' that the question of identity is at least suggested."[21] The fact that this identity is veiled may mean that a distinction is made not between two persons, but between two periods of activity of the same person. It is plausible that by his use of the third person Jesus intended to express the mysterious relationship that exists between himself and the coming Son of man: he is not yet the glorified Son of man that he is destined to be or become.[22]

It should be noted that if the alternative reading is adopted, that is, that Jesus never spoke of himself as Son of man, it follows for some scholars that sayings in group A may consistently be adjudged post-Easter formulations giving rise to the full development of the tradition: the church's heavenly Lord was identified with the apocalyptic Son of man; predictions of his coming were put into the mouth of Jesus. Gradually, the title Son of man was pressed back to his resurrection, his passion, and his earthly life.[23]

There would seem to be a more plausible explanation for the growth of the Son of man tradition, which will be given later. For the present, a few comments are needed about the sayings in groups B and C. It is noteworthy that the "Son of man" sayings in group B, although fewer in number, are nevertheless attested in multiple sources. The Q saying, number 16, merits special attention. It is unlikely that one can account for this saying in its present form as an example of Jesus' use of the familiar colloquialism *bar ᵉnāsh* to avoid direct speech. Nor is the view more satisfactory that this saying originally lacked the expression 'Son of man,' that the presence here of this quasimessianic title is a post-Easter product. The sharp contrasting of Jesus and John does not correspond to the church's estimate of John as forerunner or, in some quarters, as a competitor of the Christ. Moreover, the criticism of Jesus that the saying reflects corresponds to what is known of the opposition to Jesus, hardly that experienced by the early Christians. There is "not the slightest reason for refusing to credit this saying to Jesus."[24]

The other sayings in group B, with the probable exception of Mark 2:28 (see p. 201) can best be explained as coming from Jesus. The affirmation that the Son of man has power on earth to forgive sins, Mark 2:10 and parallels, can hardly be taken to ascribe to men indiscriminately this divine prerogative. The Son of man's homelessness, number 17, cannot be said to characterize the fate of men generally. In these sayings the reference is without doubt to Jesus, the Man, and there is no substantial reason why Jesus himself should not have spoken them. It is indeed likely that the basis of the self-recognition of Jesus as the Son of man arises from "the depths of a religious spirit that, grasping that the true nature of all glory and service, especially redemptive service, is revealed in suffering and sacrifice, applied this conception to the fate of the Son of Man."[25]

Attention must be given now to the "Son of man" sayings cited above in group C. It is generally acknowledged that these passion-resurrection predictions, in their present forms, are summaries formulated after these events. In recognition of this close correspondence between prophecy and fulfilment, some scholars conclude that early Christians (who identified the risen Christ with the apocalyptic Son of man, and who were convinced that Jesus had not been surprised by his fate in Jerusalem) wrote into the tradition these "Son of man" sayings. To claim from them that Jesus foretold his suffering, death, and resurrection is considered by some scholars to be wholly without warrant.[26]

Unfortunately, the almost exclusive attention given to Mark 8:31, 9:31, and 10:33f., has fostered a neglect of the large amount of evidence provided by the Gospels that Jesus did expect and forecast a violent death for himself, as well as vindication beyond it. Of special significance are his announcements concerning his sufferings and their outcome that were *not* fulfilled. Such predictions surely would not have originated in post-Easter churches. And then one should note the curious phrase in the Markan summaries with reference to Jesus' resurrection, "after three days," independently edited by Matthew and Luke to read "on the third day." "After three days" does not seem to be based on the Easter narratives but is an imprecise Semitic expression with respect to time, and may report an indefinite forecast of Jesus: his resurrection would occur "soon," shortly after his death.[27]

If Jesus forecast his violent death, it is highly probable that he gave thought and voice to the meaning of that death and its consequences for himself and his disciples. Moreover, it follows that his views would be related to the same eschatological context in which he interpreted his ministry as a whole: his role as the Son of man.[28]

Because of this probable connection it is unwise to reject all of the "Son of man" sayings in Group C as only secondary formulations yielding no words of Jesus. For example, because of its brevity, indefiniteness, and terminology, Mark 9:31 does not read like a prophecy *ex eventu*. Something like Mark 8:31 also was probably spoken by Jesus; otherwise how is Peter's rash protest to be understood, a protest evoking Jesus' harsh rebuke, which could not have originated in the church? The frequent connection between the title "Son of man" and the verb "to hand over" also may betray Jesus' own speech preserved within the Markan tradition.

An attempt will now be made to gather together these various strands of the Son of man tradition. The evidence seems to support the view that the self-designation of Jesus as "Son of man" (the Man) is the source of this tradition in its threefold development. It is probable that Jesus, early in his ministry, perceived a fateful connection between his own person and activity (both present and future) and the realization of the vision recorded in Daniel 7. For Jesus, this vision represented the fulfillment of God's ultimate purpose, the execution of a final judgment and the establishment of a universal, everlasting kingdom.

There is no reason why Jesus should not have used *bar ᵉnāsh (ā)* as a self-designation, unless this would have been tantamount to saying, "I am Israel's Messiah." But on the basis of the evidence available, it cannot be said that this Danielic symbol had become a popular messianic title.[29] The public would have been able to read into Jesus' use of Son of man only that which they had already learned from his teaching and his actions. Moreover (and this is a more important consideration), by adopting an eschatological symbolism that was only loosely related to traditional messianic expectations, Jesus was able to provide the subject of his teaching such content and significance as he desired. At the same time, in relating his ministry to the coming of the Son of man, Jesus could proclaim that in his own words and deeds, God's purpose, set forth in

Daniel's triumphant vision, would be fulfilled in history and beyond it.[30]

Support for the conclusion that Jesus spoke of his present and future activities as inseparably related (both being complementary aspects of the Son of man's role), is found in Jesus' proclamation of the kingdom of God.

One can apply here the criterion of coherence or consistency. For Jesus, the kingdom had not come in its fullness, yet in his ministry—his proclamation, his mighty works, his supersession of the formal authority of the Law as it applied to the present age, his teaching by parable—Jesus declared that the coming rule of God was already being manifested in history. Likewise, Jesus' claim to authority, while grounded in his election and faithful witness to God's kingdom as Son of man, is not fully realized; nevertheless, because he is fulfilling the role of Son of man he will be vindicated and exalted as such by God, and stand as the chief witness in the last judgment.

It is at this place that one can see the appropriateness of the phrase "*Son of man*" as the subject of Jesus' prophecies concerning his suffering and death. It is precisely in this context in the Gospels that the third usage of the Danielic image is found: "The Son of man must suffer many things and be rejected . . ." As one writer has reminded us, "The Son of man [in Daniel] is not simply one who appears at the end of time to act as judge; rather it is because he is Son of man *now*—i.e., elect, obedient, faithful, *and therefore suffering* that he will be vindicated as Son of man in the future . . ."*

*Attempts to bring the Son of man tradition within the frame of a "consistent" or a "realized" eschatology have not been successful. The *kingdom has not yet come;* nevertheless, in the word and deeds of Jesus, God's final rule is even now being manifested. Even so, *Jesus is not yet the glorified Son of man;* nevertheless, he acts on earth as possessing in the present the authority he will exercise as Son of man when he comes.

There are no primary texts in the Gospels that link directly the kingdom and the Son of man. Yet these allegedly disparate sayings are juxtaposed in the same strata of the Gospel tradition, and what is said about the Son of man corresponds closely with what is said about the kingdom.[31]

Another form of the argument opposing the view that Jesus thought of his ministry as that of the Son of man is that the prophecies in the Gospels of the future coming are never brought into direct relation with the prophecies of Jesus' passion and resurrection as Son of man. It is true that sayings in group A refer to the exaltation or glorification of the Son of man, while sayings in group C refer only to his resurrection. This observation has led some to conclude that since exaltation appears to be the more primitive concept than the resurrection of Jesus, the authenticity of the group A sayings, as deriving from Jesus, is confirmed.[32]

There is, however, no a priori reason why Jesus should not have spoken of the vindication of the Son of man alternatively as resurrection and as exaltation. While some texts of the Gospels relate these alternative modes of speech very closely indeed, the relationship is not sufficiently coherent and unified to support their origin in the witness of post-Easter community.[33] The detachment and reserve in Jesus' speech concerning the future role of the Son of man, the lack of explicit teaching relating his present work to God's future vindication, are more adequately explained as resulting from Jesus' own readiness to accept his present mission and fate as the Son of man, and to give this the principal focus in his teaching: Suffering and death he must endure before the Son of man appears as a witness in the last judgment, when God's kingdom, which cannot be destroyed, will be established.

Several "Son of man" sayings may appear to contradict this almost exclusive focus of Jesus upon accomplishing his present mission. One may point especially to passages found in the "little apocalypse" of Mark 13 and its parallels. It must be recalled, however, that a great many scholars hold that this discourse is a composite document originating in the early Church. Many if not all of these sayings might be genuine utterances of Jesus. But the total effect of the discourse creates an impression inconsistent with Jesus' teaching elsewhere. Mark's own purposes, as well as the theological and practical interests of the early Church, have decisively affected the form and content of Mark 13.

Most of the sayings of Jesus referring to the future coming of the Son of man emphasize the unpredictability of this event. Even in Mark 13 there is a passage that stresses this fact. The following words provide a strange ending to a discourse ostensibly providing a "blueprint" of the End:

> Truly I say to you, this generation will not pass away before all these things take place . . . But of that day or that hour no one knows, not even the angels in heaven, nor the Son, but only the Father. Take heed, watch; for you do not know when the time will come. (Mark 13:30ff.; 9:1, 14:62)

Apparently Jesus' certainty of God's imminent vindication of his word and work was joined with a disinterestedness in calculating its calendar date.

THE SUFFERING SERVANT OF THE LORD

If Jesus believed himself to be the Son of man while reckoning with the likelihood of a violent death (as we have held), then he must have given thought not only to its meaning for him but *the effect of his death upon his disciples.* There is some evidence that Jesus (for a time at least) believed that his disciples might die with him; for example, Mark 8:34–37 and 10:35–40. But at other times Jesus spoke of suffering and dying in place of his followers and for their sakes. In the same context in which Mark reports Jesus' prediction that James and John should "drink his cup" and "be baptized with his baptism," Jesus declares that "the Son of man . . . came not to be served but to serve, and *to give his life as a ransom for many.*" And on the occasion of his last supper, Mark reports a similar word of Jesus: "this is my blood . . . which is poured out for many." (Mark 10:45 [Matthew 20:28], and Mark 14:24)

On the basis of these two passages (with glances at Mark 9:11–13 and Luke 22:35–38), an impressive number of scholars have concluded that Jesus came to speak of the atoning power of his death, perceiving that he was called to fulfil the role of the suffering *Ebed Yahweh* (the Servant of the Lord) portrayed in Isaiah 53.*

Some of the "righteous sufferer psalms" also may have contributed to Jesus' understanding of the redemptive significance of his suffering and death. In these scriptures one reads of the sufferings of the righteous that are patiently borne in obedience to God, and in these scriptures the faith is expressed that the suffering of these innocents, and their intercession for the guilty, have a vicarious value, that they serve as God's means of redeeming "the many."

It is not possible to prove that Jesus found in "the Servant Songs of Isaiah" a key to the meaning of his death. Some have argued that the earliest strata of the Gospel tradition provide no support for this assumption.[34] The title "Servant" is nowhere the subject of Jesus' pronouncements concerning his fortunes

* Some scholars who are doubtful that Jesus spoke of the Son of man (in a titular sense with reference to himself), have concluded that "the evidence, although not extensive, clearly points to Jesus having regarded his death as including the fulfilment of the pro-

phetic ideal of the Suffering Servant, and as possessing redemptive significance for all who united with him." A.J.B. Higgins, *Jesus and the Son of Man*, pp. 196f., 204–206; C. H. Dodd, *Founder of Christianity*, pp. 112–121; E.W. Saunders, *Jesus in the Gospels* (1967), pp. 240–243.

or mission,[35] yet it is probable that Isaiah's servant supplied the principal scriptural basis for the predicate: "The Son of man goes *as it is written of him*. . . ."[36]

The story called "the Transfiguration" presents special problems for historians. Some are content to treat Mark 9:2–8 and parallels as patently legendary. A few have designated the passage a postresurrection story read back into Jesus' ministry.[37] While few persons would claim to know what actually happened on this mountain, it is probable that at this time Peter, James, and John became convinced that Jesus was indeed their God-appointed teacher, even though the mystery of a suffering messiah was to remain for them a stumbling block. They knew that they must wait upon his words and follow him. Still it was with fear and trembling that they turned toward Jerusalem, and at the end of their journey their courage collapsed.

JUDEA AND BEYOND THE JORDAN

Passing through Galilee, escaping (so far as it was possible) the public eye, Jesus came into the region of Judea.[38] We have seen that many readers consider that Mark telescoped Jesus' ministry leading up to his final visit to Jerusalem. We cannot be sure that Mark possessed any record at all of Jesus' movements during this time. None of the narratives strung together by Mark's incidental notes of Jesus' forward progress is strictly relevant to the circumstances of the journey.[39] Luke mentions a frustrated attempt to enter "a village of the Samaritans." Jesus may have journeyed into the region of Samaria. Limited contacts with members of this hated group resulted in mutual appreciation, but the evidence hardly supports the notion of a ministry in Samaria.[40] There seems no reason to doubt that in leaving Galilee behind, Jesus deliberately "set his face" to go to Jerusalem.*

*According to the Fourth Gospel, Jesus came to Jerusalem during the Feast of Tabernacles (September–October). Although opposed by the chief priests and Pharisees, Jesus remained in Jerusalem or its environs until the Feast of Dedication two months later. After this, Jesus crossed the Jordan and, seeking greater privacy, took his disciples to Ephraim. Some scholars have accepted these references to Jesus' itinerary, noting certain passages in the Synoptic Gospels that hint that Jesus' "final" visit to Jerusalem was not his first but a return visit.

LAST DAYS IN JERUSALEM

The passion narratives of the Gospels are, as has been observed, full of detail, and in each the sequence of events is closely connected. The first impression is that historical reminiscences were retained here to a greater extent than was the case in earlier portions of Jesus' story. And this is doubtless true. It must be remembered, however, that the passion of Jesus was "preached" from the earliest days of the Church, and that apologetic and missionary motives surely influenced the narratives: the earliest witnesses were convinced that Jesus' death was by no means "accidental"; God's purpose was fulfilled in and through it, although those men who brought Jesus to his cross were fully responsible for their actions.

The high incidence of references to the fulfillment of "scripture" in the passion narratives inevitably raises questions that cannot be answered positively: To what extent was "proof from prophecy" added later as a result of Christian interpretation? Were scriptural passages "creative" of some of the detail in the story? Although scholars differ with respect to the historicity of its details, "nothing would be more wrong to deny that there is any historical truth in the story . . . simply because the church's faith was specially concerned with this

A skyline photograph of the old city of Jerusalem, viewed from the Mount of Olives, showing the temple area. A silver-capped dome of the mosque of El Aqsa is visible on the left. El Aqsa is a much venerated Muslim shrine facing the mosque of Omar (known as the Dome of the Rock). This gold-domed mosque was built in the eighteenth century, and, like its predecessors, was constructed on the site of Solomon's temple. When Jesus entered Jerusalem, it was the second temple, which was being remodeled according to Herod's plan, that he frequented.

piece of tradition, and has filled it in with the aid of passages from the Old Testament."[41]

All of the Gospels agree that Jesus' last visit to Jerusalem occurred a few days before the Passover.[42] At this time the city was teeming with pilgrims. They had come from every place to commemorate the redemption of Israel from bondage by the grace and power of God. From the time of his arrival in Jerusalem, Jesus' actions are best understood as acted parables. Like the Old Testament prophets, who sometimes dramatized their oracles concerning coming events, Jesus declared by actions more eloquent than words the meaning and outcome of his ministry. It is probable too that, like the prophets' "signs," Jesus' actions were more than vivid illustrations. The relation of Jesus' deeds to realities to come were as yet unseen, but Jesus acted in the faith that what he was doing was instrumental to their fulfillment.[43]

Consider, first, the story of *the triumphal entry into Jerusalem.*[44] One can ask the probable meaning of this demonstration for the crowd who participated in it, and then what meaning the incident might have had for Jesus. It is often asserted that the disciples and other Galilean pilgrims who accompanied Jesus to Jerusalem hailed him as Messiah. It must be noticed, however, that Mark 11:9 contains citations from a Hallel Psalm, which was regularly sung by pilgrims at a number of Jewish festivals. Even the unusual cry, "Blessed be the kingdom of our father David that is coming," does not hail Jesus as a messiah.[45] Perhaps the sight of the city alone, and the joy of their festival journey, led the multitudes to voice their intense eschatological hopes. At the same time, the spreading of garments and leafy branches before Jesus shows that special homage was being given to him.[46]

Against the background of this tense situation the action of Jesus is to be understood. Jesus could not control the outbreak of popular enthusiasm. He could not avoid personal involvement in this nationalist demonstration. But by acted parable he could associate himself with an Old Testament prophecy depicting a messiah without pomp, a king of peace. As at the time of Peter's confession, Jesus was unable to deny the homage paid him, but the disciples and the crowd could be shown the only kind of leadership he offered them. In retrospect this day of his "visitation" would be understood.

There is irony in this situation. Unknown to themselves, the crowds shout for the restoration of David's kingdom, confessing that in Jesus, as he goes to his death, the kingdom of God is coming. There was on Jesus' part no deliberate messianic claim. But the truth was soon to dawn upon those who had eyes to see—the truth concerning the messianic secret and the mystery of the kingdom of God.[47]

The second acted parable of Jesus is *the cleansing of the temple*.[48] Again it is not altogether clear what happened on this occasion. How was Jesus able to drive from the large Court of the Gentiles the money-changers and sellers of sacrifices and to prevent the area from being used as a thoroughfare? Jesus' action cannot have been intended as a reform measure only. Shortly afterwards he left the temple and the city, and traffic was resumed. But Jesus' action could have been understood as a messianic sign, and it probably was so intended. In Old Testament prophecies and in ancient Jewish traditions, the Messianic Age is associated with the renewal of the temple and with the expectation that in that day Gentiles will worship at Mount Zion.[49] The people generally may not have understood this messianic significance of the disturbance in the temple. Mark reports that it was Jesus' teaching there that astonished the multitudes.[50] But, for the chief priests, such popular demonstrations were the stuff from which messianic movements began. They might have been totally blind to the purposes of Jesus, but his action in the temple had challenged their authority and offered a serious threat to the peace. A tense situation was developing that required that they be cautious.

Some of the conflict stories that follow this incident in the temple may have been situated earlier in the Ministry of Jesus.[51] Nevertheless, it is likely that the stories concerning the challenge of Jesus' authority and his views on the traditional resurrection hope belong to the passion week.[52] The Sadducees put to Jesus their stock question designed to reduce to absurdity the belief of the Pharisees in a general resurrection. In his reply, Jesus dismissed as profitless all idle curiosity concerning the manner of the resurrection and turned to the ground for belief in it as a fact. In the Torah, which the Sadducees considered to be the

The Mosque of Omar, or Dome of the Rock, is richly decorated with colorful mosaics. Muslims believe that Allah transported Mohammed from Mecca to Jerusalem by night. Visitors are shown Mohammed's mark upon the sacred rock. *(Courtesy of Pictorial Archive.)*

sole authority, God is revealed as "the God of the living." Jesus taught that the faithful of all ages enjoy unbroken communion with Him.

The Last Supper of Jesus is the third of his acted parables in Jerusalem.[53] The interpretation of this event is partly determined by the answer given to the question: Was the Last Supper a Passover meal? The following table presents the sequence of events associated with this important Jewish feast, and approximate times (according to modern reckoning):

Nisan 14: The day of preparation.
  Noon Use of leaven and leavened foods prohibited.
  1:30 P.M. Slaughter of the daily evening sacrifice.
  2:30 P.M. The offering of this sacrifice. From this time until sunset everyone fasted. The Passover lambs were slain.

Nisan 15: The day of Passover, or the first day of Unleavened Bread.
  Around 6:30 P.M. Sunset, the end of Nisan 14: The beginning of Nisan 15; the Passover was celebrated.

Mark, followed by Matthew and Luke, report that Jesus' Last Supper was a proper Passover eaten in the early hours of Nisan 15. The Gospel of John, however, presents contradictory statements. It is reported that when Jesus was tried before Pilate, the Passover had not been eaten by the priests.[54] In view of these discrepant versions the reader must decide between the following alternatives: Either all that happened from the Last Supper to the burial of Jesus took place on the day of Passover, Nisan 15, which, in the year Jesus died, fell on a Thursday/Friday; or these final events occurred on the day of Preparation which, in that year, was Thursday/Friday, Nisan 14.[55]

It is sometimes argued that the Last Supper of Jesus with his disciples was their celebration of a proper Jewish Passover meal because the oldest Gospel traditions display its typical features. Jesus and his men formed a group of typical size, they reclined while eating, the traditional bread and red wine were given a ceremonial interpretation, the poor were remembered, songs of thanksgiving were sung, and afterwards a journey was taken within the limits of the city.[56]

But there are serious objections to the Synoptic accounts. Several questions seem to demand answers favoring the Johannine narrative. Would Jesus' disciples and the arresting party have carried arms on the evening of Passover? During the night, would the Sanhedrin have met, tried, and condemned Jesus? Allowing for the possibility that an extraordinary session of the Council was held, would the high priest have violated the oral law by tearing his robe in protests of blasphemy? Would Jesus have been executed on the Day of Passover? Would he have been taken down from the cross, prepared for burial, and entombed during the feast?

It cannot be denied that the super traditions are fragmentary and lack consistency. Which account is the most apt to be authentic: the "tradition" Paul had "received" (reported in the earliest literary source, I Cor. 11:23ff.), the Markan version (Mark 14:17ff.; Matthew 26:20ff.), or the tradition drawn from "Special Luke" (Luke 22:15ff.)?[57] The present writer believes that Mark's Gospel reports the oldest form of Jesus' words:

> Distributing bread to his disciples, Jesus said: "Take; this is my body." And when the cup was given to them, he said: "This is my blood [of the covenant] which is poured out for many.[58] Truly, I say to you, I shall not drink again of the fruit of the vine until that day when I drink it new in the kingdom of God."

Our interpretation of these words should depend upon the following facts. In his parables Jesus had spoken of the coming kingdom as a banquet or feast. He had employed this image in feeding the multitude, and possibly at other fellowship meals with his disciples. Jesus had spoken of giving his life as a ransom for "many." He had also spoken of his forthcoming suffering as his "cup." And now, Jesus distributes bread as representing himself on the eve of his death; he hands around the wine cup promising the disciples a share in the eschatological kingdom made possible by his death. No longer does Jesus expect them to die with him. But they were to have a share in the benefits of his death, in the consequences of his death. By eating and drinking, the disciples were given the privilege of experiencing in advance the "messianic banquet." To Jesus, they were the Israel of the Age to Come. They were being allowed to experience in the present those benefits soon to be realized when the kingdom of God came "in power."

This is a remarkable thing that Jesus did for his disciples. Before the night

Fresco of the Last Supper, painted in 1980 on the chancel wall, Holy Trinity Church, Glendale Springs, N.C., by the artist, Ben Long. Local mountain people served as models for the disciples of Jesus. *(Courtesy of the rector, J. Faulton Hodge.)*

was over, one of these men was to deny him. All were to forsake him. Since Jesus knew this, it can be said that his action at the Last Supper was his most impressive declaration that the gifts of God are given to the undeserving. Jesus came, as he said, "not to invite the righteous, but sinners."[59]

GETHSEMANE: THE ORDEAL OF GOD'S SON

When Jesus left "the upper room" with "the Twelve," he went toward the Mount of Olives, a usual trysting place at nightfall. In a garden called Gethsemane Jesus lingered. Separating himself from the disciples, he fell upon his knees in agony of spirit: "Abba (Father), all things are possible to Thee; remove this cup from me; nevertheless, not my will, but thine be done."[60] It is not surprising that this scene should be reported with slight variations in the Gospels, for the disciples were at some distance removed, and dozing. Yet it is

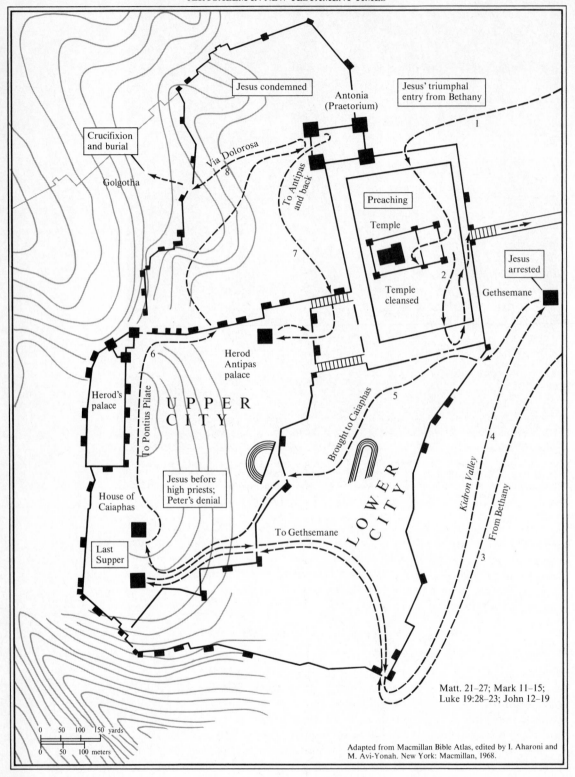

Jesus condemned

Antonia (Praetorium)

Jesus' triumphal entry from Bethany

1

Crucifixion and burial

Via Dolorosa

Golgotha

8

To Antipas and back

Preaching

Temple

7

2

Temple cleansed

Jesus arrested

Gethsemane

6

Herod Antipas palace

5

To Pontius Pilate

Herod's palace

U P P E R
C I T Y

Brought to Caiaphas

Kidron Valley

4

From Bethany

Jesus before high priests; Peter's denial

House of Caiaphas

L O W E R
C I T Y

3

Last Supper

To Gethsemane

Matt. 21–27; Mark 11–15;
Luke 19:28–23; John 12–19

0   50   100   150 yards
0   50   100 meters

Adapted from Macmillan Bible Atlas, edited by I. Aharoni and
M. Avi-Yonah. New York: Macmillan, 1968.

beyond question that on this night Jesus knew that his ordeal was imminent, that he recoiled from it, that he experienced a terrible anguish. It is equally certain that Jesus' serenity at the time of his arrest was not a stoical courage. Through communion with God as "Father," he had found the spiritual resources enabling him to accept violence and death.[61]

At this point a question can be raised that could have been dealt with at numerous points in the ministry. Whence arose the belief of early Christians— most explicitly set forth in the First and Fourth Gospels—that Jesus was (and is) "the Son of God"? Several answers have been given to this important historical question. That the title arose *ab extra* in Hellenistic Christianity, under the influence of the common notion that the great saviors of mankind were divine men or "sons of God," is now commonly denied. Later on such influences may have had an impact on the development of the Son of God Christology. But its origin must be otherwise explained. A popular view is that Son of God was first used in the post-Easter Palestinian church as a fitting title for Jesus the Messiah whose earthly career had ended and who was now adopted by God and enthroned in heaven.[62] Still other scholars have traced the term back to Jesus' self-disclosures. It is said that "the earliest use of the Son of God in relation to Jesus derives (a) from his activities as a miracle-worker and exorcist, and (b) from his own consciousness of an immediate and intimate contact with the heavenly Father."[63]*

For an understanding of Jesus' intensely personal consciousness of God as his Father, we are led to the Gethsemane setting. According to Mark, Jesus directs his earnest prayer to *Abba* (Father), (14:36). Two reasons suggest that Jesus was accustomed to employ this Aramaic mode of address elsewhere in his prayers. First, in the Gospels the Greek vocative form is sometimes rendered without a modifier; at other times, with a personal pronoun or an article.[64] This variation probably points to an underlying *Abba* which, in colloquial speech, expressed these various forms. Second, from Romans 8:15 and Galatians 4:6 we learn that the cry "Abba, the Father," uttered in the Spirit, was widespread in the early church. The preservation of the Aramaic term in Greek texts probably reflects a traditional reminiscence of the prayers of Jesus.[65]

Palestinian Jewish sources supply no parallel to this form of address to God.[66] Since *Abba* was a children's word in common usage, it may have seemed irreverent, "indeed unthinkable to the sensibilities of Jesus' contemporaries, to address God with this familiar word." In reporting the prayers of Jesus the Gospels show "that *Abba* expresses the heart of Jesus' relationship to God. He spoke to God as a child to its father: confidently and securely, and yet at the same time, reverently and obediently."[67]

If Jesus knew himself to be God's Son, a *yahid* "beloved" of God, it is clear that Jesus did not perceive this knowledge to be a privilege to be enjoyed but a gift to be shared. As the true Son of *Abba* he was called to reveal *Abba's* gifts and demands to his people. A Q tradition, Matthew 11:27 and Luke 10:22, affirms these two complementary realities: Jesus not only believed himself to be a recipient of this divine revelation but its mediator. It is often stated that this saying is a late product of Hellenistic Christianity. Yet other scholars have held that the saying reflects "a Semitic-speaking milieu."[68] Possibly this saying has a parabolic origin. While "the father"/"the son" were doubtless understood

*A first-century (B.C.E.) sage, Honi the Circle-drawer, after praying unsuccessfully for rain, "drew a circle and stood within it and said before God, "Lord of the universe, Thy children have turned to me, for that *I am as a son of the house before Thee.* In this mishnaic tradition a holy man's intimacy with God can be described fittingly as that of a son with his father. Vermes, *Jesus the Jew*, pp. 209f. Cf. Wis. 2:12–20 and Mt. 27:39–44, 54.

The Mount of Olives, east of the temple mount, rising from the Kedron Valley. The garden of Gethsemane lies to the left of the Basilica of the Agony (also known as the Church of All Nations). The traditional site of Gethsemane does contain some very venerable olive trees. For seven centuries the place of Jesus' betrayal and arrest has been guarded by Franciscan monks.

later as titles, originally the saying might have been a quite general observation concerning an ordinary but highly meaningful human experience in Galilean society: the unique, loving relation between a Jewish son apprenticed to his father.*

It is perhaps fruitless to speculate when Jesus might have spoken in this self-conscious way. That the saying, if genuine, was addressed to his disciples only, within the ministry, is supported by Mark 13:32, which is also spoken to the disciples.[69] Only 14:61 and its parallels are the exception,[70] which report the response of Jesus to the high priest's query: "Are you the Christ, the Son of the Blessed?" This important pericope will be considered later.

THE ARREST OF JESUS; BETRAYAL BY JUDAS; PETER'S DENIAL

In the garden of Gethsemane Jesus was arrested. The temple police, accompanied perhaps by deputies, were led to the spot by Judas Iscariot, "one of the Twelve."[71] In this way the authorities were able to avoid an open arrest of Jesus, a thing they had feared would result in a riot. Did Judas sell to the authorities his inside knowledge of Jesus' nocturnal meeting place? Albert Schweitzer has suggested that for a price Judas revealed the messianic secret, reporting to the priests Peter's confession and the incident of Jesus' anointment in Bethany as the Messiah. Conjectures over the possible motives for Judas' act, which can only be described as a betrayal, began in the first century and persist in the present.[72] Such curiosity is understandable, but since it is not possible to provide historical confirmation for any of these "explanations," there is little profit in raising the question of motive. Jesus himself could only say: "Woe to that man . . . It would have been better for that man if he had not been born."[73]

The story of Peter's denial is woven into the synoptic story of Jesus' trial.[74] Yet it is appropriate to consider it here. The Gospels variously report that Jesus had predicted Peter's denial.[75] Why should this be considered a prophecy after the event? Peter's brashness and self-confidence are broadly attested in the Gospels, and reports of Jesus' rebuke of his disciples' foolishness refer to his fore-knowledge of their behavior based on his understanding of their natures. The story of the denial is told with such vivid detail that some have suspected a legendary origin, or else the whole is attributed to a storyteller's art.[76] But is it credible that anything like this could have arisen in early Christian traditions? It is a sad fact that not even Peter, the man Jesus likened to a rock, remained loyal in the crisis. Jesus faced abuse and death without any human supports.

CONDEMNATION OF JESUS BY THE SANHEDRIN; TRIAL BY PILATE; THE SENTENCING OF JESUS

The Gospel narratives of the trial(s) of Jesus are not without difficulties, both historical and legal. The outline on page 234 offers a probable reconstruction of the course of events, but it is not possible to harmonize with complete satisfac-

* Perhaps the intention of the original saying may be conveyed in the following: "*My father has passed on to me his knowledge. Only a father knows his son, and only a son knows his father*" [a Semitic formulation meaning that only a father and a son really know each other]. "*And anyone* [who obtains this knowledge of the father is one] *to whom the son chooses to reveal him*" [since only the son is in a position to receive and mediate this personal knowledge]. Cf. Jeremias, *New Testament Theology*, pp. 56–61.

tion the various details of the Gospels. Christian, Jewish, and Roman sources agree, however, that Jesus was sentenced to die by crucifixion upon the order of the Roman governor, Pontius Pilate, on a serious political charge. He was accused of claiming to be a messiah, an anointed "king of the Jews."[77]

It is probable, as we shall see, that the charge that Jesus' aims and activities were seditious was utterly unfounded. Neither Jesus nor his disciples sought to provoke insurrection (although a few historians have argued that if the truth be told Jesus had active militant leanings; the evidence against this is impressive and persuasive).[78] It also is highly doubtful that during his public ministry Jesus ever openly claimed to be a messiah.[79] On the first day of the week following his crucifixion, however, Jesus' disciples became convinced that he had indeed been the Messiah. The resurrection of Jesus was viewed as God's vindication of Jesus' past and present messiahship.

There is a tragic irony in the circumstances of Jesus' death. He who in his public life did not claim to be a messiah was condemned for "saying that he himself [was] Christ a king."[80] Moreover, Jesus' executioners—not his sympathizers—were the first to take decisive public action based on their conviction that Jesus was a messiah (from their perspective, a messianic pretender, and thus a threat to the established order).[81]

A plausible outline of the judicial proceedings against Jesus is as follows:

1. Examination by the chief priests and their scribes.
   a. After his arrest Jesus is informally examined in the high priest's house.
   b. At dawn the Sanhedrin is convened; testimony against Jesus is sought: two issues are discussed—Jesus' saying about the Temple's destruction, and his alleged claim to be the Messiah. The silence of Jesus regarding the first, his (qualified?) acknowledgment concerning the second, lead to the verdict: blasphemy!
2. The Trial before Pilate.
   a. Jesus is accused of treasonable words and deeds, of the claim to be "a king." Pilate judges the prisoner to be politically harmless.
   b. Pilate offers to release Jesus pursuant to the governor's decision to release a prisoner (at Passover?), believing that Jesus is the people's favorite. Instead, the crowd cries for the release of Barabbas, an imprisoned insurrectionist.
   c. Confronted by importunate priests and a disturbing popular demonstration, Pilate condemns Jesus to death by crucifixion.

Several questions attract the interest of historians in reviewing the trial narratives of the Gospels: who was responsible for Jesus' crucifixion? By whose instigation and under whose authority did Jesus die? What motives led the persons involved to condemn him to death?

From time to time historians have adopted the extreme view that no Jewish authorities participated in the crucifixion of Jesus; all references to them in the Gospels reflect an apologetic falsification of history. This radical skepticism regarding the historical value of the Gospels is surely unwarranted, since the oldest Jewish, as well as Christian, sources acknowledge the involvement of Jewish authorities in Jesus' death.[82]

A second view tilts too far in the opposite direction, contending that Jewish authorities were the prime movers in Jesus' arrest, trial, and sentencing. Because the Romans alone could execute capital offenders or because the Jewish authorities wished to pass to the Romans the public responsibility for killing Jesus (or perhaps both), he was handed over to Pilate. In this view the Romans were little more than executioners.[83]

The initial impression may be that the Gospel's passion narratives support this position. But two types of evidence qualify this impression. First, as one moves from the earliest to the latest Gospel (and beyond, to the apocryphal gospels), a tendency is detected to lighten the responsibility of the Romans for the crucifixion of Jesus and to increase that of the Jews. Pilate's image is bettered; that of the Jewish authorities is blackened.[84] Is it not likely, one is asked, that "in the pre-Markan tradition the Jews appeared less and the Romans more responsible for the crucifixion and that this probably corresponded to the facts?"[85]

Second, the Third and Fourth Evangelists seem to agree independently on a version of Jewish involvement that does not include a trial, the calling of witnesses, a sentencing of Jesus to death.[86] Mark, followed by Matthew, records a night session of the Sanhedrin, at which a death sentence is declared, but describes also a second formal session of the Sanhedrin in the morning![87] The Markan tradition possibly reflects a fusion of two accounts of the same meeting.

The improbability of a formal nocturnal trial of Jesus by the Jewish Sanhedrin is increased when Mark's narrative is examined in the light of the criminal code set forth in the Mishnaic tractate, *Sanhedrin*. As many as twenty-seven infringments of rabbinic law have been counted. It should be noted, however, that these mishnaic procedures were promulgated a century after Jesus' death.* Since no agreement has been reached concerning the customs of the Sanhedrin in the early decades of the first century, or on whether the Sanhedrin at this time was governed by Sadducean or Pharisaic codes, a wholesale dismissal of Mark's trial scene is unwarranted.

A part of the confusion concerning the action of the Sanhedrin is attributable to the uncertainty regarding the competence of the Jewish court in cases of capital punishment. Despite John 18:31, which declares that the Jewish authorities could not execute a death sentence, some scholars maintain that the Jews did have the power of execution, even for political crimes. If that were so, then the very fact that Jesus was handed over to the Romans would be proof that Jesus was not sentenced to die by the Sanhedrin, for the Sanhedrin sentence could have been carried out without direct Roman involvement.[88] The Fourth Evangelist's report may be correct, however, at least as regards political crimes.[89] Perhaps we can conclude that the Sanhedrin was empowered to question a suspect, to obtain a deposition of witnesses, and then to decide whether there was sufficient provocation to send the prisoner to the Roman governor for trial.

All attempts to reconstruct details of the Sanhedrin hearing are sometimes dismissed as futile, the reason being that none of Jesus' disciples witnessed the proceedings; however, Mark's narrative is limited to two issues: allegations that Jesus had said "I will destroy the temple made with hands and in three days I will build another not made with hands" (14:58), and that he had himself confessed, "I am the Messiah" (14:61f.). According to Mark's crucifixion scene, these were the two issues that immediately became public knowledge (15:29–32).

It is hardly to be doubted that Jesus had spoken of the destruction and re-

* Examples of the infringement of rabbinic law in the Markan narrative are: the night session of the Sanhedrin; a trial on a feast day; the omission of the statutory second session; the discrepancy between the contention that Jesus was a blasphemer and the rule regarding the same, *M. Sanh.* 7: 5. Luke's independent source may have provided a more accurate sequence: the Council met "when day came," in the Council-chamber, and Jesus was not condemned formally for blasphemy. (Lk. 22: 66–71).

building of the Temple, the obscurity of the saying favors its genuineness. According to Mark 13:2 and parallels, Jesus spoke to his disciples of the temple's destruction, but he did not say that it would be destroyed by him.[90] Yet the witnesses against Jesus before the Sanhedrin were not able to reproduce, much less to understand Jesus' words concerning the Temple. They therefore failed to establish his guilt (hence Mark's statement that they were false witnesses).

After this failure to obtain unequivocal evidence, the high priest interrogated his prisoner. At first he was unsuccessful, but then, by asking a direct question, it was supposed that Jesus condemned himself.[91] The situation was further complicated by the fact that although Jesus gave an affirmative answer to the question, "Are you the Christ, the Son of the Blessed?" he goes on to speak of the elevation of the Son of man. "It is in harmony with Mark's total presentation of the messiahship of Jesus that Jesus should affirm it positively only at the moment when none of his hearers could possibly believe him, and even then abandon the theme of messiahship for the preferred title Son of man."[92]

These proceedings have seemed to some to be an incredible historical sequence, to which is added the puzzling claim of the high priest that Jesus had spoken blasphemy. If one follows the ruling of the Mishnah, this accusation is without foundation. Yet although Jesus was technically no blasphemer, he had (or so it seemed to his opponents) intruded upon God's special prerogatives.[93]

A first-century interpretation of 2 Samuel 7 provides an intriguing explanation for the proceedings of the Sanhedrin and, of greater significance, may contribute to an understanding of the responses of Jesus to the two issues before the court: the building of a new Temple, and the identity of Jesus as Messiah, God's Son. In a previous chapter our attention was drawn to a Qumran fragment in which Nathan's word to king David, 2 Samuel 7, is interpreted eschatologically.[94] One of David's descendants is to be established in his kingdom forever. God will be his father and he will be God's son. And he shall build God's temple not made with hands, the community of God's people in the Endtime.

Perhaps it can now be seen why the high priest, when the witnesses failed to agree concerning Jesus' temple saying, put the direct question concerning messiahship and forced Jesus' confession. Jesus' response was an acknowledgement that he was indeed God's Son, but that in place of a messiahship in terms of the Davidic ideal he had accepted the fate and the destiny of the Son of man.[95]

The procedures in Pilate's court can be determined with greater clarity than those supposed to have taken place before the Sanhedrin. Luke reports the prosecutor's charges: "We found this man perverting our nation, and forbidding us to give tribute to Caesar, and saying that he himself is Christ a king." (23:2). Mark 15:2 implies that Pilate had been told that Jesus was being acclaimed king.[96]

Some historians are ready to take at face value the notes in the Gospels that Pilate was never convinced that Jesus was guilty of any crime deserving death, that the responsibility for the execution of Jesus must be placed upon those Jewish officials who persisted in their accusations against him.[97] The aforementioned progressive betterment of Pilate's image in the Gospel traditions must be taken into account, however, in apportioning degrees of responsibility. (See p. 235.) Pilate's term as governor was accompanied by uprisings provoked by Jewish nationalists, and he had good reasons to be suspicious of someone who was being hailed as "king of the Jews."[98] It is understandable that Pilate might have decided to take precautions, and that he might have participated in the arrest and detention of Jesus before the Passover.[99]

It is important to observe that fears of the political implications of Jesus' teaching and activity may have contributed to the priest's determination to silence Jesus and to their cautious procedures in apprehending him. "Christian writers often assume that all of the Jewish leaders were aware that Jesus was not a potential revolutionary and so used the political charge as a smoke screen for their religious antipathy to Jesus. The situation was not so simple."[100] The Fourth Evangelist reports that on the basis of rumor concerning Jesus' activity, a special session of the Sanhedrin had been convened some time before Jesus' arrest, and the fear expressed that because of Jesus' popularity he might stir unrest among the masses ("and the Romans will come and destroy both our holy place and our nation.")[101]

Political motives apparently prompted Jewish as well as Roman authorities in arresting, interrogating, and trying Jesus. One must be cautioned, however, against discounting religious motives as real factors in explaining the pressure exerted upon Pilate by the Jewish delegation.

Throughout his ministry to his people Jesus avoided titles ready at hand that were descriptive of messiahship in one form or another because these titles were uncongenial to his purposes. Yet, as has been noted, it was unavoidable that at the final crisis of his ministry persons should have seen messianic significance in his actions. Now it is not self-evident that the identification of Jesus as the Messiah would have aroused such religious antagonism as would lead to his death; however, a messiah who (according to rumor) threatened the Temple, and who on occasion encouraged nonobservance of the Torah and the oral law, could well have provoked intense religious opposition.[102]

In the Torah two types of presumptuous spiritual leaders are condemned as capital offenders: prophets who are judged to be false (Deut. 13:5 and 18:20), and rebellious elders (Deut. 17:12).

Some historians have judged that the real religious charge against Jesus was that he stood condemned as a false prophet. Support for this hypothesis is found in the Synoptic passion narratives, which report Jewish mockery of Jesus (Mark 14:65 and parallels), and in one of the few references to Jesus in the Babylonian Talmud (43a), in which it is recorded that Jesus was executed for practicing sorcery and for enticing Israel to apostasy.[103]

Alternatively, it has been argued that Jesus' refusal to answer the high priest's questions or to accept the discipline and warning of constituted priestly authorities was contempt of court. As "a rebellious elder" Jesus thus condemned himself to death.[104]

All speculation aside, it is certain that to Pilate the disposition of his prisoner boiled down to a single issue (and Jesus' accusers saw to it that this single issue remained up front): was Jesus guilty of high treason against the Roman government, was he in fact a political rival to the Emperor and his deputy? Pilate's verdict was that Jesus was guilty. Whether or not he believed the truth of the

The Via Dolorosa. A passageway from the Lion's Gate, located at the northeast corner of the temple mount, threading through a part of the old city known as "the moslem quarter," to Golgotha—the way Jesus trod to his crucifixion. In this photograph persons walk under the Ecce Homo Arch, so named because of its traditional association with Pilate's presentation of Jesus, "Behold the man" (Jn. 19:5).

charge, it was the only charge that would justify the execution of Jesus—and justify Pilate, in his own eyes and in those of others. Over the priest's objection, Pilate ordered a *titulus* affixed to the cross of Jesus that read "The King of the Jews."

In accordance with Roman law, with reference to condemned slaves and rebel provincials, Jesus was subject to flogging before execution. Tied to a flagellation post, the victim was severely beaten with leather whips stiffened with metal rods.[105] Before leading Jesus out to be crucified, the Roman soldiers brutally mauled and mocked their prisoner.

THE CRUCIFIXION AND BURIAL OF JESUS

From the days of the Punic wars, the Romans had used crucifixion as a means of capital punishment. This was an extreme form of torture that could last for a day or longer. Mark writes that Jesus was crucified between two thieves (or political terrorists); that he refused opiates of any kind; and died within six hours. By a harmonization of the Gospel traditions, the Church speaks of "the seven last words from the Cross." Only one of these stands in the Markan passion narrative, the loud "cry of desolation" based upon Psalm 22:1. Either it was known from actual hearers that Jesus had shouted thus, or else in the absence of testimony it was assumed that this psalm, which so strangely prefigured events of the passion, was fulfilled up to the last moment.[106] In either case, a word from scripture on the lips of a righteous man at death is no cry of despair.

It would have been a violation of Jewish law to have left Jesus' lifeless body hanging on the cross overnight.[107] Its removal was all the more urgent since death had occurred within a few hours of the Sabbath. Joseph of Arimathea risked public scorn in order to be loyal to the traditions of piety. After securing Pilate's permission, Joseph hastily laid the dead stranger's body in a tomb and rolled a stone against its door.[108] "The curtain seemed to have fallen on unrelieved tragedy."[109]

THE RESURRECTION OF JESUS

The formation of the traditions concerning the resurrection of Jesus was discussed in Chapter 5, where it was noted that the earliest Christians seem not to have compiled a connected narrative of the events following the burial of Jesus. There is no narrative of the resurrection of Jesus as such in the New Testament, only of its accompanying phenomena: the empty tomb and the appearances of the risen Christ. "In the early community the resurrection was not narrated but proclaimed."[110]

Historians should begin their examination of the resurrection evidence with the experiences of the disciples. Unquestionably, the crux of the matter is here. Paul's "received tradition" stated that the risen Jesus had "appeared to Cephas [Peter], *then* to the Twelve." Yet if one proceeds from this point, puzzling discrepancies are soon encountered. What happened to Peter's story? Mark implies a first meeting with all of the disciples in Galilee, and Matthew reports the same. Luke and John report that it was in Jerusalem or in Judea that Jesus first appeared to the disciple band, although in "the appendix" of the Fourth Gospel a meeting in Galilee is reported.[111] "The tradition here was, for a longer time" than the passion narratives, "in a fluid state," the consequence being that "we have to reckon with gaps, but also with legendary additions."[112] It is perhaps too hasty to conclude, however, that such divergences as do exist render futile all efforts at historical reconstruction.

A popular harmonization has it that Jesus first appeared to "the Twelve" (Eleven) in Jerusalem, that they subsequently went to Galilee, where Jesus appeared to them again, and that finally the disciples returned to Jerusalem, where Jesus appeared to them once more before his ascension. It has been objected that the charge to the disciples to go to Galilee seems to exclude an immediate appearance in Jerusalem, and that it is unlikely that after an initial appearance of Jesus in Jerusalem (according to this hypothesis) and a commissioning of his disciples, some of them would have resumed their occupations as Galilean fishermen.[113]

More logical is the alternative view, which postulates first appearances of

Jesus to Peter and others of the Twelve in Galilee. Probably the Lucan and Johannine placements of appearances to the disciples on Easter Sunday were prompted by theological interests. Nothing in these appearances themselves rules against placing these happenings in Galilee. On the assumption that Jesus commissioned his disciples in Galilee, it is plausible that they returned to Jerusalem and, encouraged by the word of women who spoke of Jesus' appearance to them, began to proclaim boldly their "resurrection *kerygma*."[114]

Attention has been called to the fact that despite these differences in time and place one basic pattern is evidenced in the Gospel accounts of Jesus' appearances to the Twelve (certainly the primary testimony to his resurrection):

1. The situation presupposed: Jesus' followers are bereft of him.
2. The appearance of the risen Christ.
3. His greeting to his followers.
4. Their recognition of him.
5. Jesus' word of command or mission.[115]

The conclusion that can be drawn from this typical pattern is that "it makes little sense to construct a series of such appearances to the Twelve; each Gospel witness is reporting a slightly different version of an appearance that was constitutive of the Christian community."[116] The least we can say is that the "concise" appearance stories bear the marks of "a tradition shaped and rubbed down to essentials in the process of oral transmission."[117] The more circumstantial stories owe their origin and form to a variety of interests in the early churches.*

Two important distinctions should be kept in mind in considering evidence relating to the discovery of the empty tomb.[118] First, it is one thing to assert that the narratives of the finding of the vacant sepulcher were no part of the primitive "resurrection *kerygma*" (which they do not seem to have been). It is quite another thing to say that the empty tomb was not presupposed by the "resurrection *kerygma*," that the accounts of its discovery are late and largely apologetic. Second, a distinction within the various stories should probably be made between their basic narrative and later accretions resulting from Christian commentary (midrash).

Several considerations support the view that the earliest testimony to the resurrection presupposed that the body of Jesus was no longer in the place of its burial. The following question can be asked: If Jesus' appearances became the basis of the reports that he had been seen, what gave rise to the affirmation that he "was raised?" Even though one follows those who contend that the empty tomb was neither narrated nor proclaimed in the earliest *kerygma,* Jesus' resurrection from the grave is surely implied by the statement that God raised him, since the apocalyptic conception of resurrection is precisely resurrection from the grave.[119] Two points are taken from 1 Corinthians 15. (1) The apostle's reference to Christ's burial, and to his resurrection "on the third day" seems to be the earliest testimony that Jesus' tomb was found to be empty. The discovery itself probably gave rise to the precise note of time, included in Paul's formula, and in the Gospels of Matthew and Luke. (2) In 1 Corinthians 15:20 ff., Paul writes concerning the mystery of a believer's resurrection, likening it to Christ's. Again, resurrection, as in apocalyptic eschatology, is not depicted as a

*Some features can be recognized as secondary elaborations. (1) People felt a need to expand the accounts of Christophanies with sayings of the Risen One; (2) Christian communities developed an apologetic in reaction to the doubt and ridicule that the reports of the resurrection evoked; and, (3) the sheer delight in the story itself introduced accretions reflecting contemporary narrative style (haggadic midrashim?) Jeremias, *New Testament Theology,* pp. 300ff. E.g., Lk. 24:13–35; Jn. 21:1–14; (Jn. 20:11–17?)

noncorporeal victory over death but as a transformation of the body that at death is buried to an entirely new mode of existence.

Early arguments against the resurrection of Jesus, reflected indirectly in Matthew and John, and in second-century apologetics, never claim that the corpse of Jesus remained in the tomb. Moreover, the contention that the body of Jesus was stolen, or disposed of in a common burial ground, is patent slander; opponents seem to accept the fact that the body of Jesus could no longer be found.[120]

The careful reader will note the discrepancies in the stories of the women at the tomb. Mark says they found the stone rolled back, and that upon entering the tomb they met a young man there. Matthew reports that they saw an angel descend and roll away the stone. Luke says that they saw two men. In John's Gospel, Mary Magdalene discovered that the stone had been taken away. She reported to Peter and another disciple who found the tomb empty, except for the grave cloths. Mary herself subsequently looked into the tomb and saw two angels in white. The message to the women and their reactions are also variously reported. Did they or did they not find the disciples? And if they did, what message did they deliver? Did any of these women see the Lord? Is it possible to recover an original account on the basis of which one can explain the origin of the other stories, or must independent witnesses be weighed one against another?

A critical consensus has not been reached on these questions. All would agree that the events of Easter morning cannot be woven into a single narrative. For some scholars the very nature of these discrepancies "proves" the fact of the empty tomb. For others the same data point to late and possibly legendary origins. It can plausibly be contended that the various angelic manifestations and revelations "represent a dramatization of the import of the empty tomb." But behind these and other variations "there is a basic tradition that some women followers of Jesus came to his tomb on Easter morning and found it empty—a tradition that is older than any of the preserved accounts."[121] Whatever influences shaped these traditions, they arose as particular expressions of faith in Jesus's resurrection and not as providing evidence to establish its historicity.

In conclusion we can say that the origin of the resurrection faith was based on the appearances of the glorified Jesus. This belief, in turn, interpreted the fact of the empty tomb, otherwise ambiguous. Faith did not depend on the reality of the empty tomb—it was not an essential article of faith. But it was a sign of what had taken place: Christ had been raised, he had appeared to chosen witnesses, therefore, the tomb was empty. It would seem quite probable that the tradition also reflects the influence from the other direction, namely, that stories of the finding of the empty tomb contributed to the growth of narratives relating Jesus' postresurrection appearances. For example, the absence of Jesus' body from the tomb led to stress on the continuity between the man who was crucified and the man who was raised. According to Luke 24:39–43, Jesus offered his disciples material evidence that it was their recently beloved table companion who was appearing to them.

It may be a source of disappointment to some readers that the narratives in the New Testament do not provide cogent proofs for the resurrection. But,

The Triumphant Lamb. Early Christians associated Jesus' death with the slaying of the Passover Lamb (1 Cor. 4:7; 1 Pet. 1:18; cf. Jn. 1:29 and Rev. 5:6). The vicarious benefits of this sacrifice are celebrated in later eucharist liturgy, which was the inspiration for this iron altar panel of the fifteenth century. *(Courtesy of the Museum of Art, Duke University: Ernest Brummer Collection of Medieval and Renaissance Decorative Art.)*

when we think of it, this is not surprising. Suppose, for the sake of argument, that evidence for the empty tomb could be undeniably established; this would not prove that Jesus was still alive, still less that, as the consequence of his death, Jesus had been invested by God with "all authority in heaven and on earth."[122] Or suppose that the manner or mode of Jesus' appearing could be "explained," that one's curiosity could be satisfied concerning the so-called "subjective" or "objective" factors, or both, that *caused* faith in the resurrection; it would not thereby be established that in this event a new age began in history of the world, that God, by turning the defeat of his Anointed into triumph, gave to Jesus "the name which is above every name, that at the name of Jesus every knee should bow . . . every tongue confess that Jesus Christ is Lord, to the glory of God the Father."[123] Whatever the manner of his appearances, the Risen Christ was only seen *for what he is* through the eyes of faith.[124]

THE NATIVITY TRADITIONS

At first sight it may seem strange to direct attention to historical questions concerning Jesus's birth after a sketch of his public ministry. Is not this the very thing one has sought to avoid, a failure to adhere to the perspective of the Gospels? Paradoxically, this is not the case. It was only after the ministry of Jesus had resulted in belief in his resurrection that there was any interest in the circumstances of his origin. The central events in the New Testament's witness to Jesus are his death and resurrection. His birth is viewed in the light of the interpretation of these events, and not vice versa.

Other than the opening chapters of Matthew and Luke, there are no references in the New Testament to the virginal conception of Jesus.[125] Efforts have been made to discredit these passages by regarding them as scribal interpolations. But it cannot be said that the textual and literary evidence impugns their genuineness. The absence of all mention of the occasion of Jesus' birth in the Gospels of Mark and of John, in Paul's letters, and in other writings earlier than Matthew and Luke, is not prima facie evidence opposing these traditions. The most that these data prove is that in several important churches either nothing was known of unusual circumstances surrounding Jesus' birth, or, if the stories were current, they were not felt to contain any matter essential to the *kerygma* of the Church.

In Chapters 7 and 8 consideration was given to the interests that might have led the First and Third Evangelists to adapt as well as to report the traditions of Jesus' nativity.[126] At this point let us admit the likelihood that the stories in the Gospels are traditional, and not altogether the creations of the Evangelists, and raise the question: What is the historical evidence for the miracle?

It must be admitted that the nativity stories manifest irreconcilable differences in detail. There has been a freedom of development in this tradition that has no parallel in the Gospels. Both Matthew and Luke agree that Joseph was not the natural father of Jesus, but in almost all of the particulars they differ. Both report that Jesus was born in Bethlehem and reared in Nazareth, but there is no agreement as to the cause of the movements of Jesus' parents. Neither evangelist directly describes the event of Jesus' birth. The language of their narratives is poetical and influenced by Old Testament narratives and prophecies.

The nature of this evidence leads some to affirm that the birth narratives are an insecure basis for the belief in the virginal conception of Jesus.[127] Others take the opposite position. It is said that the discrepancies in the stories are those most likely to have occurred before the facts of the case became the object of scrutiny some thirty years or so afterward.[128] Moreover, the central claims are doubly attested since two independent stories agree in reporting them. It has been cogently argued that this agreement may have antedated Matthew and Luke in three respects: (1) the literary form of an angelic annunciation of birth was a well-known Old Testament literary pattern and provided a natural medium for Christians of Jewish descent for expressing their reflections on the birth of Jesus the Messiah; (2) the theological message in the annunciation, which placed side by side the Davidic descent of the Messiah and the begetting of God's son through the power of the Holy Spirit, was cast in the language of the early Christian creedal affirmations, expressing a Christological insight that was earlier associated with the resurrection and baptism of Jesus; (3) the annunciation involved the person of Mary, who was betrothed but still a virgin. The real historical problem is focused in the question: How is this third traditional element to be explained? Perhaps the catalyst for the idea of the virginal conception of Jesus was a combination of historical and nonhistorical factors.[129] Legends contain a kernel of fact; figurative speech and song are often deeply meaningful expressions of belief in astonishing events, concerning which very little of a factual nature can be recovered. It is not surprising that among many who confessed Jesus to be "the Son of God" there would have been little disposition to doubt that Jesus came from God in a way that was wholly unique. If, as seems likely, the nativity stories of the Gospels had their original setting in the worship of early Palestinian churches, many different influences might have converged to give them their distinctive traditional forms.[130]

For many readers a discreet veil of reverent agnosticism must ever surround historical questions concerning Jesus' birth. But the value of the nativity stories of the Gospels is not thereby depreciated. Be they fact or fiction or a combination of both, the faith they express is a faith that the whole of the New Testament proclaims: Jesus came from God; it is not possible to "explain" him as merely the product of Israelite piety. In his historical existence he was a new creation, accomplished by the power of God in and through Israel's history "when the time had fully come."[131]

NOTES

1. Mk. 7:24ff. Lk abandons Mk's account of journeys to the north. See the judicious comments of S. Johnson concerning Jesus' contacts with Gentiles, *Jesus in His Homeland* (1957), pp. 78ff., and J. Jeremias, *Jesus' Promise to the Nations* (1958).
2. Mk. 8:27ff. and pars.
3. See pp. 97, 102. R. Bultmann, *History of the Synoptic Tradition* (1963), pp. 257ff.; *Ibid. Theology of the New Testament* (1951, 1955) Vol. 1, pp. 26ff. Cf. G. Strecker, "The Passion and Resurrection Traditions in Mark's Gospel," *Int*, 20 (1968): 421ff., who locates pre-Markan traditional units, Mark 8:27–29, 31, 32–33.
4. G. Bornkamm, *Jesus of Nazareth* (1960), pp 169ff.; O. Betz, *What Do We Know About Jesus?* (1968), pp. 85ff; C. H. Barrett, *Jesus and the Gospel Tradition* (1967), pp. 23f.
5. Mk. 10:46ff.; 11:1ff. and pars.
6. Mk. 8:31 and pars. C. H. Dodd, *The Founder of Christianity* (1970), pp. 111f. The thesis that Jesus was in fact a revolutionist has been advanced from time to time since the inception of "the quest of the historical Jesus." In the interest of Christian apologetics, some have claimed, the Evangelists (and others who earlier transmitted the Gospel tradition) depoliticized Jesus' ministry. In their present forms nearly all of the pericopes in the Gospels portray Jesus as a peacemaker; however the Evangelists were not quite successful in suppressing evidence to the contrary. For an examination of this improbable thesis and of recent literature on the subject, see W. D. Davies, *The Gospel and the Land* (1974), pp. 336ff.
7. R. Morgan, "A Concluding Unscientific Postscript," in E. Bammel, ed., *The Trial of Jesus* (Naperville: Allenson, 1970) p. 144.
8. Probably an editorial addition (cf. Mk. 13:24ff.), similar to Mt. 16:28 (cf. Mk. 9:1).
9. Lk. 22:69 is probably an editorial modification of Mk. 14:62.
10. The recovery of this saying and its meaning is notoriously difficult. To which of the three contexts does it belong? Lk. 6:22 is probably not derived from Q. Cf. Tödt, *Son of Man in the Synoptic Tradition* (1965), pp. 123f. Mt. 13:37 is usually typed as secondary, Tödt, pp. 93, 135.

11. This passage may have belonged to Lk's special passion narrative (see pp. 130, 140), although it could be an editorial gloss (cf. Mk. 14:45f.). Lk. 17:25 and 24:7 appear to be editorial; however, on Lk. 17:25 cf. W. G. Kümmel, *Theology of the New Testament* (1973), pp. 89f.
12. G. Vermes. "The Use of bar nash/bar nasha in Jewish Aramaic," in M. Black, *An Aramaic Approach to the Gospels and Acts* (1967), pp. 310–328. Cf. J. Fitzmeyer, *A Wandering Aramean* (1979), pp. 143ff.
13. Cf. J. Jeremias, *New Testament Theology* (1971), p. 261.
14. Dodd, *Founder of Christianity*, p. 120.
15. Jeremias, *New Testament Theology*, pp. 262f. Cf. Mt. 5:11, Lk. 6:22; also Mk. 8:27; Mt. 16:13.
16. N. Dahl, *The Crucified Messiah and other Essays* (1974), p. 30. Italics mine.
17. Jeremias, *New Testament Theology*, p. 263, lists the following: Mk 13:26, 14:62; Mt. 24:27 (Lk. 17:24); Mt. 24:37 (Lk. 17:26); Mt. 10:23; 25:31; Lk. 17:22, 30, 18:8, and 21:36.
18. Dodd, *Founder of Christianity*, p. 119. G. Vermes, *Jesus the Jew* (1973): "In Galilean Aramaic . . . no trace survives of 'the titular use' of *bar nash(a)* . . . there is no case to be made for an eschatological or messianic officeholder generally known as 'the son of man' . . . none of the interpretive sources [of Dan 7:13] employ 'one like a son of man' as a title." pp. 168, 176f. J. A. Fitzmyer, *A Wandering Aramean*, pp. 153–155.
19. A. J. B. Higgins, *Jesus and the Son of Man* (1964), pp. 15, 197–200; Jeremias, *New Testament Theology*, pp. 268–272; W. G. Kümmel, *Theology*, pp. 77f.
20. Bultmann, *Theology of the New Testament*, Vol. 1, pp. 29–31; H. E. Tödt, *Son of Man*; Higgins, *Jesus and the Son of Man*, pp. 199f. The genuineness of these sayings is supported by the application of the criterion of dissimilarity to the extent that it is unreasonable (so it is said) that such sayings as Lk. 12:8 originated in some early Christian community. It is incredible that the Church should have created sayings that seem to distinguish between Jesus and the Son of man.
21. Kümmel, *Theology*, p. 80; Barrett, *Jesus and the Gospel Tradition*, pp. 32ff.
22. Jeremias, *New Testament Theology*, pp. 275ff.
23. See H. Conzelmann, *The Theology of St. Luke* (1960), pp. 136f.; *ib. Jesus* (1973), pp. 136f. The contributions of Christian "prophets" are sometimes offered to explain the origin of the tradition (e.g., Bornkamm, *Jesus of Nazareth*, pp. 230f.) This is hardly credible. Would prophets have confined the expression "son of man" to Jesus' speech? In some sense the Son of man tradition is attributable to Jesus.
24. Kümmel, *Theology*, p. 81. Cf. Eduard Schweizer's defense of the genuineness of this and other sayings in Group B, "The Son of Man," *JBL*, 79 (1960): 119–129.
25. W. Manson, *Jesus the Messiah* (1946), pp. 164f. Cf. Otto Betz's novel thesis (*What Do We Know About Jesus?*, p. 112). The words of Jesus concerning the present fortunes of the Man refer to "the man after God's own heart who does God's will"— the eschatological offspring of the house of David, who, like David before his coronation, is homeless, hungry, and misunderstood. Note Mk. 2:25–28; Mt. 8:19f., and Lk. 9:57f.
26. Probably this assimilation of prediction to fact preceded the composition of Mk. (Strecker, "The Passion and Resurrection Traditions," *Int.* (1968), pp. 421ff. It is demonstrable that Mt. and Lk. worked over the Markan summaries, e.g., Mt. 20:19 (Mk. 10:34); Mt. 26:1f. (Mk. 14:1); Lk. 18:31f. (cf. Mk. 10:33f.).
27. Jeremias, *New Testament Theology*, pp. 282–286; Barrett, *Jesus and the Gospel Tradition*, pp. 46–53, 77. (Kümmel also summarizes the evidence that Jesus reckoned on his own violent death, *Theology*, pp. 86f.)
28. Barrett, *Jesus and the Gospel Tradition*, pp. 35–45. "The title Son of man does more than any other to cement the unity of the gospel tradition." p. 67.

29. The Danielic Son of man is probably identified with the Davidic messiah in 1 Enoch 37–71. Since the Gospels do not echo the teaching of 1 Enoch, it is a dubious hypothesis that Jesus and his hearers were influenced by it. The Son of man passages in 1 Enoch are of doubtful origin.

30. While it may seem incredible that Jesus would have consciously chosen a self-designation that was vague and mysterious, Jesus knew the extent to which the Twelve shared the popular eschatologies and might well have wished to avoid clearly messianic titles. See Knox, *The Sources of the Synoptic Gospels* (1953), Vol. 2, pp. 143ff.

31. Barrett, *Jesus and the Gospel Tradition*, p. 31; Kümmel, *Theology*, pp. 83f.; cf. Tödt's critique of P. Vielhauer's thesis, *Son of man*, pp. 329–347.

32. Bultmann, *Theology of the New Testament*, Vol. I, pp. 29f.

33. Barrett, *Jesus and the Gospel Tradition*, pp. 81–86; Jeremias, *New Testament Theology*, pp. 285f.

34. Bornkamm, *Jesus of Nazareth*, pp. 226f.; M. Hooker, *Jesus and the Servant* (1959), p. 23; Barrett, *Jesus and the Gospel Tradition*, pp.39–41.

35. See, however, W. Manson, *Jesus the Messiah*, pp. 154ff.; W. Zimmerli and J. Jeremias, *The Servant of God* (1957), pp. 98ff.; J. L. Price "The Servant Motif in the Synoptic Gospels," *Int* 12 (1958): 28ff.

36. The rarity of "Servant texts" in the Gospels is explained by Jeremias as follows: "Only to his disciples did Jesus unveil the mystery that he viewed the fulfilment of Isaiah 53 as his God-appointed task, and to them alone did he interpret his death as a vicarious dying for the countless multitude." *New Testament Theology*, p. 104.

37. Bultmann, *History of the Synoptic Tradition*, pp. 259–261, 428f.; cf. Dodd's rejection of this opinion, in which he shows that a form-critical analysis of the transfiguration gives no support to an antedated postresurrection tradition (D. E. Nineham, *Studies in the Gospels* (1955), p. 25). See also R. H. Stein, "Is the Transfiguration (Mark 9:2–8) a Misplaced Resurrection-Account?" *JBL* 95 (1976): 79–96.

38. Mk. 9:30, 10:1.

39. Mk. 10:17, 32, 46; 11:1. V. Taylor, *Mark, IB*, V. 7, (1951), p. 132.

40. Lk. 9:51ff.; 10:30ff.; 13:22; 17:11ff. Cf. Mt. 10:5f.; 15:24; Jn. 4:4ff. S. Johnson, *Jesus in His Homeland* (1957), pp. 82ff.; Jeremias, *Jesus' Promise to the Nations*, pp. 19ff., 42f.

41. Bornkamm, *Jesus of Nazareth*, pp. 157f.

42. Mk. 11:9f., and pars; Jn. 12:12ff.

43. H. W. Robinson, "Essay on Prophetic Symbolism," in D. C. Simpson, ed., *Old Testament Essays* (1927), pp. 10ff. Cf. Isa. 20; Jer. 27f.; Acts 21:10ff.

44. Mk. 11:1ff. and pars.

45. "The Son of David" (Mt. 21:9) is doubtless an editorial gloss. Cf. Mt. 21:12. Schweitzer's view that some may have hailed Jesus as the Elijah who is to come deserves serious consideration.

46. Kümmel, *Promise and Fulfilment*, pp. 115f. Note 2 Kg. 9:13; 1 Macc. 13:51 (Jn. 12:13).

47. Kümmel, *Promise and Fulfilment*, pp. 117f.; Taylor, *The Gospel According to St. Mark* (1952), p. 452. This entrance of Jesus to Jerusalem "would be inconceivable without his powerful claim that the kingdom of God is dawning in his word, and that the final decision will turn upon himself." Bornkamm, *Jesus of Nazareth*, p. 158. Note the Fourth Evangelist's comment, Jn 12:16.

48. Mk. 11:15ff. and pars. (Cf. Jn. 2:13ff.) W. D. Davies, *The Gospel and the Land*, pp. 349, note 45, and 350–352, note 46.

49. Mk. 11:17 (Isa. 56:7); also Ezek. 43:6ff.; 44:5ff. Jeremias, *Jesus' Promise to the Nations*, pp. 57ff. Jesus' action may have been inspired by Mal. 3:1ff., as many

believe, but there is no purging of the priests. Perhaps Zech. 14:21b is the prophecy fulfilled.

50. Mk. 11:18. Cf. Lk. 19:47f.; Jn. 7:14f. Instead of acting to rid Jerusalem of Gentiles, Jesus provided for their worship at the Temple.
51. Mk. 12:28ff. Cf. Lk. 10:25ff. Taylor *The Gospel According to St. Mark*, pp. 101, 468.
52. Mk. 11:27ff.; 12:18ff. and pars.
53. Mk. 11:12ff. and pars.
54. Jn. 18:28. See also 19:14, 31, 42.
55. All harmonizing efforts seem to have failed. See J. Jeremias, *The Eucharistic Words of Jesus* (1955), pp. 5ff.
56. *Ibid.*, pp. 14ff.
57. For evidence favoring the longer text of Lk., and its independence, see Jeremias, *Eucharistic Words*, pp. 87ff.
58. Serious consideration must be given to the view that Paul preserved the oldest form— "this cup is the new covenant in my blood," since it is difficult to suppose that a Jew would have commanded the drinking of blood, and since the Markan phrase, "my blood of the covenant" is not possible in Aramaic. Kümmel, *Promise and Fulfilment*, pp. 120f.; Jeremias, *Eucharistic Words*, pp. 133f.
59. Mk. 2:17; Mt. 9:13. Also Lk. 19:1-10.
60. Mk. 14:26, 32ff., and pars. Cf. Jn. 12:27ff. and 18:11, which appear to be echoes of a precanonical Gethsemane tradition.
61. Lk. 22:42 and Jn. 12:28f. lay stress upon this fact implicit in the Markan narrative; however, it is possible that Jesus' cries in Gethsemane and from the cross imply that he hoped for God's intervention, that he was disappointed, yet remained determined to be faithful. Barrett, *Jesus and the Gospel Tradition*, pp. 46ff.
62. E.g., F. Hahn, *The Title of Jesus in Christology* (1969) pp. 284ff.; Bornkamm, *Jesus of Nazareth*, p. 226. Rom. 1:3f.
63. Vermes, *Jesus the Jew*, pp. 209–212.
64. Mt. 11:25f.; Lk. 10:21; 11:2; 22:42; 23:34, 46. "My Father": Mt. 26:39, 42. "The Father": Mk. 14:36; Mt. 11:26; Lk. 10:21.
65. Jeremias, *New Testament Theology*, pp. 61ff.
66. See Vermes, *Jesus the Jew*, pp. 210ff. The Talmudic anecdote concerning Hanan, grandson of Honi the Circle-drawer, is no exception. Although Hanan distinguishes between "the *abba* who has the power to give rain" (God) and "the *abba* who has not" (himself), he addresses God not as *abba* but in the typical rabbinic manner: "Lord of the universe."
67. Jeremias, *New Testament Theology*, pp. 65–68. Mt. 23:9.
68. *Ibid.*, p. 57.
69. Was "the handing down" of the Father's revelation an accompaniment of Jesus' baptism, as attested by the Synoptists, and the Q narrative of Jesus' earlier ordeal based on Jesus' self-disclosure to his disciples? Mk. 1:11; Mt. 3:17; 4:3, 6; Lk. 3:22; 4:3, 9. See p. 186. Since in Mk. 13:32 ignorance concerning the End time is attributed to "the Son," it is often said that the offense of this passage "seals its genuineness" (Taylor, *The Gospel According to St. Mark*, p. 522.).
70. Mk. 12:6 is probably a secondary feature of Jesus' parable spoken to "the chief priests and the scribes and the elders." Mt. 21:23, 33. Cf. Lk. 20:1, 9 ("the people," but see 20:19).
71. Mk. 14:43ff., and pars. Cf. Jn. 18:2ff.
72. Mk. 14:3ff. (Mt. 26:6ff.) Cf. Lk. 7:36ff.; Jn. 12:1ff.
73. Mk. 14:21; Mt. 26:24.
74. Mk. 14:66ff., and pars. Cf. Jn. 18:17, 25ff.

75. Mk. 14:26ff.; Mt. 26:30ff. Cf. Lk. 22:31ff.
76. Mk. 9:33ff. (Lk. 9:46f.); Luke 9:54f.; Mk. 10:35ff.; Mt. 20:20ff.; Mk. 14:37f.; Mt. 26:41.
77. See R. Brown's "Historical Reconstruction of the Arrest and Trial of Jesus," *The Gospel According to John* (1970), Vol. 26A, pp. 791ff.
78. See note 6, p. 244.
79. For a brief, judicious comment on the evidence, see Barratt, *Jesus and the Gospel Tradition*, pp. 20–24.
80. Luke 23:2.
81. N. Dahl, "The Crucified Messiah," in Dahl, *The Crucified Messiah* (1974), pp. 10–36. See also p. 236.
82. Brown, *The Gospel According to John*, pp. 793f.
83. P. Benoit, "The Trial of Jesus," in *Jesus and the Gospel*, Vol. 1, (1973). Brown, *The Gospel According to John*, p. 794.
84. Cf. Mk. 15:14f. Lk. 23:4, 13–16, 22 Mt. 27:19, 24f. and Jn. 18:38, 19:6. Brown, *The Gospel According to John*, pp. 294f.; Barrett, *Jesus and the Gospel Tradition*, pp. 53f.
85. Brown, *The Gospel According to John*, p. 54.
86. Lk. 22:66–70; Jn. 18:12–24, 28. See also Acts 13:27f.
87. Mk. 14:53–64; Mt. 26:57–66. Note also Mk. 10:33; Mt. 20: 18; 26:3f.
88. Brown, *The Gospel According to John*, p. 797.
89. E. Bammel,"The Historicity of the Sanhedrin Trial," in E. Bammel, ed., *The Trial of Jesus* (1970) ". . . the balance of probability favors the view that the Jews could at that time pass capital sentences, but were prevented from executing them." pp. 59–63. See also E. W. Saunders, *Jesus in the Gospels* (1967), pp. 277f.
90. Mk. 14:58; 15:29. Cf. Mt's variant: not "I will" but "I am able to destroy . . . ," 26:61. Cf. Jn. 2:19; Gospel of Thomas, 71; Acts 6:14.
91. Mk. 14:60–64 and pars.
92. Barrett, *Jesus and the Gospel Tradition*, p. 58 ". . . whether even so much can be judged historical is open to question."
93. *Mishnah: Sanh.* 7:5 "The blasphemer [Lev. 24:10ff] is not culpable unless he pronounces the Name itself." Cf. Mk. 2:7 and pars. E. W. Saunders conjectures that Jesus' reply to the high priest—I am (he)—was understood as a naming of the holy hidden name of God [I am I AM, Exod. 3:14] *Jesus in the Gospels*, pp. 280f. Jesus' religious offense is discussed on p. 237.
94. Recall the Third Evangelist's application of this testimonium to the birth of Jesus, Lk. 1:32f. above, p. 133. 2 Sam. 7 is reinterpreted, legitimating Israel's messianic hope in the following: Pss. 89:20–38; 132:11–18; I Chron. 22:8–10.
95. Betz, *What Do We Know About Jesus?* pp. 87ff.
96. Jn. 18:33ff.
97. E.g., Saunders, *Jesus in the Gospels*, p. 282; J. Blinzler, *The Trial of Jesus* (1959). P. Benoit, "The Trial of Jesus," pp. 140–142.
98. Brown, *The Gospel According to John*, p. 798. Jos. *Antiq.* XVII. x. 8; Mk. 15:7; Lk. 23:19.
99. Jn. 18:3, 12.
100. Brown, *The Gospel According to John*, p. 799; Barrett, *Jesus and the Gospel Tradition*, p. 57.
101. Jn. 11:47–53. Note also that Jesus is "questioned" by Annas the high priest "about his disciples and his teaching." Jn. 18:19f.
102. There were many would-be messiahs in the first century who were not condemned to death by the Sanhedrin, but it is important to note that these other "messiahs" were ardent nationalists whose success would have meant political independence

for the Sanhedrin, for Jerusalem, and for the Temple. Brown, *The Gospel According to John*, p. 801.

103. E.g., R. H. Fuller, *The Foundations of New Testament Christology* (1965), pp. 125–129.
104. Mk. 14:60f. (Mt. 26:62). Note the suggestion of evasiveness in Jesus' answer, Lk. 22:66–70; Mt. 26:63f.; Jn. 18:19–21. J. Bowker, *Jesus and the Pharisees* (1973), pp. 45–52.
105. Saunders, *Jesus in the Gospels*, cites Josephus, *B.J.* II. xiv. 9; V. xi. 1; VI. v. 3.
106. Mk. 15:34 (Mt. 27:46). Cf. Mk. 15:24 (Ps. 22:18); 15:29 (Ps. 22:7).
107. Deut. 21:22f.
108. Evidence concerning the anointment of the body of Jesus for burial is equivocal. Cf. Mk. 15:42–47; 16:3, also, Lk. 24:1–3 (23:54–56) with Mt. 28:1, and Jn. 19:39f.
109. A. M. Hunter, *The Work and Words of Jesus* (1950), p. 121.
110. 1 Thess. 1:10 and 1 Cor. 15:4b are summaries of "the resurrection kerygma." R. H. Fuller, *The Formation of the Resurrection Narratives* (1971), pp. 16f.
111. 1 Cor. 15:5; Mk. 16:7; Mt. 28:16–20; Jn. 21:15–23. Cf. Lk. 24:13–32, 36–53; and Jn. 20:19–29.
112. Bornkamm, *Jesus of Nazareth*, p. 182.
113. Brown, *The Gospel According to John*, pp. 971f.
114. *Ibid.*, p. 972. R. H. Fuller, *The Formation of the Resurrection Narratives* (1971), pp. 49, 171. Mary Magdalene's report to the disciples was not the origin of their Easter faith but it was welcomed by them as congruous with the faith that they had attained in Galilee.
115. See the important study of C. H. Dodd, "The Appearances of the Risen Christ," in Nineham, *Studies in the Gospels*, pp. 9–35, cited with approval by Brown, *The Gospel According to John*, pp. 972–975.
116. *Ibid.*, p. 973.
117. Dodd, "Appearances of the Risen Christ", p. 13.
118. Brown, *The Gospel According to John*, pp. 976ff.
119. Fuller, *Resurrection Narratives*, pp. 48ff., who cites Isa. 26:19; Dan. 12:2; 1 Enoch 92:3
120. Mt. 27:62–66, 28:11–15; Jn. 20:15f. Cf. the noncanonical Gospel of Peter 8:28ff., and the Acts of Pilate 13:1f.
121. Brown, *The Gospel According to John*, p. 977.
122. Mt. 28:18.
123. Phil. 2:9ff.
124. For a helpful discussion of "contemporary faith and proclamation," see Fuller, *Resurrection Narratives*, pp. 168ff. W. Marxsen et al., *The Significance of the Message of the Resurrection for Faith in Jesus Christ* (1968). Anderson, *Jesus* (1967), pp. 205ff.
125. R. E. Brown, *Birth of the Messiah*, pp. 518–521. Also, large parts of the pre-Gospel narratives employed by Mt. and Lk. contain no explicit reference to the virginal conception of Jesus. There is no clear reference to a virginal conception other than the angel's annunciation of Jesus' birth (Mt. 1:18–25 and Lk. 1:26–39.)
126. See pp. 133 and 148. "Both evangelists, having picked up elements of the tradition, have freely cast them in their own molds—[Mt.] in terms of dreams [Lk.] in an OT birth-announcement pattern." Fitzmyer, *The Gospel According to Luke*, p. 335.
127. E.g., P. Gardner-Smith, *The Christ of the Gospels* (Cambridge: W. Heffer & Sons, 1938), pp. 61ff.
128. J. K. S. Reid, "Virgin (Birth)," in A. Richardson, *Theological Wordbook* (1967),

pp. 275ff. The influence of doctrinal considerations is succinctly summarized by Brown, *Birth of the Messiah*, pp. 528–531.

129. Brown, *Birth of the Messiah*, pp. 521f. Fitzmyer, *The Gospel According to Luke*, pp. 336ff.

130. P. Minear, "The Interpreter and the Nativity Stories," *Tht* 7 (1950): 358ff. R. H. Fuller, "The Virgin Birth: Historical Fact or Kerygmatic Truth" (1956): 1–8.

131. Gal. 4:4. F. V. Filson, *A New Testament History* (1964), pp.86f.

PART II

EARLY EXPANSION OF CHRISTIANITY AND THE CAREER OF PAUL

The Environment of Gentile Christianity

O NE Christian missionary towers above all others in the first generation because of his strategic role in transplanting the gospel of the early Palestinian Church to the great cities of the Roman Empire. He is Saul of Tarsus, better known as Paul, "bond-slave of Jesus Christ," the "Apostle to the Gentiles." The life and thought of this premier apostle now concern us. But before we consider his great achievement we must view that larger area of the world into which we are drawn when we return to the reading of Acts, and follow this with a study of the letters of Paul. The gospel was successfully transplanted in the Roman world because, we may say, the soil was prepared and the atmosphere conditioned for its rapid growth.

The most lasting effect of the conquest of Alexander was the dissemination of the Greek language and culture and the consequent dissolution of many of the city-states and small kingdoms of Europe and western Asia. A common culture was vigorously fostered in the numerous cities built by Alexander and his successors. This culture was the legacy of the golden age of Greece; yet in the process of its extension it was enriched by many Oriental contributions.[1]

The resistance to Hellenization by the Maccabees in Judea was symptomatic of a broader Oriental reaction to all Greek influences in western Asia and Egypt.[2] Yet in spite of this reaction, the mighty tide was not turned. The influence of Hellas continued to permeate human life. With the triumph of Rome, political stability made possible the flowering of a culture commonly called *Hellenistic*, or *Hellenistic-Roman*.

The Roman genius for organization brought about the conditions for extending the Greek notion of the unity of all humankind. Yet with the unification of the world by Roman power, large masses of people were deprived of opportunities for participation in local government. Patriotism no longer furnished an organizing principle for their thought and energies. Instead, the search was begun for a meaningful existence in personal rather than in public affairs. The family, the trades, and the professions became more important, and social life found expression in small associations of persons who shared common occupations or aspirations. Thus, as has been frequently observed, the dominant spirit of the Hellenistic Age had two components: cosmopolitanism and individualism. At first sight these components may appear contradictory. Yet the arts and sciences, the philosophies and religions of the Hellenistic Age afford evidence that they were complementary and broadly characteristic of the spirit of the times.[3]

Of principal interest to readers of the New Testament are the religions and philosophies of the Hellenistic Age that flourished in the regions beyond Palestine where Christian missions were begun. In this chapter the following topics will be discussed briefly: the national cults and the "mysteries" of Greece; the religion of imperial Rome; the popular appeal of the Oriental mystery religions; the widespread belief in astrology and magic; the religious interpretations of life offered by two popular "schools" of Greek philosophy; and the religions of a more speculative and mystical type attested in "the Hermetica" and in "pre-Gnostic" writings. The chapter will conclude with a brief discussion of the Jews of the Diaspora ("Dispersion").

CULTS AND MYSTERY RELIGIONS

THE GREEK CITY-STATES

When the Greeks conquered the East they practiced on foreign soil some of the cults of their native city-states. With establishment of the Hellenistic cities, efforts were made to promote the worship of Zeus, Hermes, Apollo, Artemis, and other deities of the Greek pantheon. Homer remained a first reading book in the schools.[4] The results, however, were meager, for the foundation of the Hellenistic kingdoms marks the twilight of the gods of Olympus. Their fate was sealed with the break-up of the Greek city-states.[5] The failure of the Olympian gods to conquer the East also resulted from the fact that the Greeks honored the gods of the vanquished countries. The foreign gods were given the names of Greek deities upon the assumption that they were the same, that the change in their names was not a change in their natures. But this was often not the case; for example, the Artemis worshiped at Ephesus was not the chaste Greek goddess but a sensuous mother deity of the mountains.[6] Early in the second century B.C.E. an attempt was made in Greece to revive the worship of the Homeric deities. New epiphanies and new oracles were claimed, especially of Apollo at Delphi; some new festivals were added to the traditional calendar. But the pomp and circumstance of public worship failed to disguise the loss of a living faith. When honors were accorded the Greek gods in Asia and Africa, they were mere formalities.[7]

Following the death of Alexander, a sense of insecurity was felt everywhere. The belief arose that Chance (Tyche) ruled the destinies of persons. In some places, where the forms of national religion were without meaning, the Greeks personified Tyche and erected temples and statues in her honor. Tyche became the patron goddess of a number of Hellenistic cities, for example, Antioch in Syria. Criticism and unbelief "had wrenched the tiller from the hands of the gods, and men were driven hither and thither at sea without a rudder, at the mercy of the waves." Tyche was the last stage in the secularizing of classical Hellenic religion.[8]

Nevertheless, one form of ancient Greek religion survived the wave of skepticism and unbelief—the "mysteries." Indeed, the spirit of the times was con-

Mosaic from Cento Celle, Italy, depicting the head of Bacchus (Dionysus), ca. 200–250 C.E. *(Courtesy of the University of Pennsylvania Museum.)*

genial to their revival.* Among the Greek mystery religions that flourished in the Hellenistic Age were the Eleusinian, the Dionysiac, and the Orphic.

The Eleusinian mysteries centered on Demeter, goddess of the field; Kore (Persephone), her daughter, the spirit of vegetation; and Hades (Pluto), god of the dead. It was believed that Hades carried Kore to the underworld for eight months of the year. The initiates of this mystery apparently believed that just as nature is reborn in the spring, so by participation in the secret rites of Eleusis, people were reborn and secured a blissful immortality.[9] Dionysus was originally a Thracian fertility god who became known as the god of wine (Bacchus). His early worshipers roamed the countryside in states of sacred intoxication, tearing living animals to pieces and eating their raw flesh. Through these wild revelries the spirit of the god, incarnate in the potency of nature's life-forces, was possessed and immortality gained. Such savage practices were no longer encouraged by the devotees of the Dionysian mysteries in New Testament times. Instead, it was taught that the meaning of the Dionysian myths had been re-

*A *mysterion* was a sacred rite in which individuals participated by their own free choice. By means of it, initiates, called *mystai*, were brought into close relation to the deity honored. They were given a new nature, delivered from the cycle of reincarnation, and assured happiness after death. The "experience" of the *mystai* resulted either from an act done to them or by them, or from watching a sacred drama.

vealed to the ancients by Orpheus. The fate of Dionysus, child of Zeus, was that he was destroyed by the Titans, who, in turn, were destroyed by Zeus. Out of the ashes of the Titans humans were created, who possess both a divine and a destructively titanic nature. The soul, the divine element that derives from Dionysus, can be set free from its union with an inherently natural wildness only as it is liberated from the body. Orphism depicted the pleasures of the initiated and the horrible punishments of the wicked in the after life. Orphism showed the way, through strict diets and ritual purifications, to an eternal salvation.[10]

RELIGION IN IMPERIAL ROME

The religion of early Rome was in many respects parallel to the polytheistic cults of the Greek city-states. Jupiter, the great god of the sky and weather, was worshiped with Mars, who doubled as the god of war and agriculture, and also Quirinius, a minor war god. Juno, the fertility goddess of the moon, was another local deity. Because of its central location, Rome was influenced by gods of surrounding states at an early date. From Latin neighbors came Diana, Hercules, Castor, and Pollux; from Greece came Demeter, Dionysus, Kore, Apollo, and others. With the exception of Apollo, the Greek deities were given Roman or Etruscan names. When "the Romans established correspondence between their gods and those of the Greeks, they also appropriated the abundant myths that had been developed in Hellas; in this way the Roman gods, who protected the sanctity and inviolability of the traditional order, acquired a history."[11]

One feature of Roman religion that distinguished it from that of ancient Greece was its priesthood. The clergy were organized into a hierarchy of *collegia*, or boards. One priest, the *pontifex maximus*, outranked all of his colleagues. The principal function of the priest was to see that the numerous sacrifices and other traditional rites were scrupulously performed. All right-thinking Romans believed that such observances were necessary to maintain *pax deorum* (peace with the gods.)

No more than the cults of the Greek city-states was the religion of early Rome able to maintain itself as a living faith after the extension of the Roman power into the Mediterranean world. The cults of the Capitoline gods lived on in the form of local patriotism, to be revived only as a means of its support. But it became evident after the Punic wars that the new world needed a religion as all-embracing as the empire itself. In place of the old state religion, imperial Rome attempted to establish the cult of its emperors. The idea of deifying men, either living or dead, was not native to Italy. It was taken from the Greeks, who considered that a people's gratitude to heroes providing days of peace and social well-being was sufficient cause for paying them divine honors. Alexander and his successors had foreshadowed the emperor cult, but the first of the emporers, Augustus (27 B.C.E–14 C.E.), established the practice when he declared the apotheosis of Julius Caesar (*Divus Julius*) and dedicated a temple in his honor.[12]

During the reign of Caesar Augustus a deliberate effort was made to revive the old state cult and its *collegia* of priests. Although this "return to religion" had important political consequences, it did not succeed in breathing new life

Augustus (30 B.C.E.–14 C.E.) is represented in this sculpture as Pontifex Maximus, head of the Roman religion. Cast in this role, the emperor is pictured as the great restorer of Rome's moral and spiritual power. *(Courtesy Alinari/Art Resource.)*

into the old dry bones. Instead, the Romans of the new "republic" venerated their living "savior." Augustus refused to permit Romans to worship him directly. Nevertheless, his "genius" was venerated, and the poets sang the praises of the reigning god and the dawn of the Golden Age. In the eastern provinces, temples were built in honor of Augustus and Roma and sacrifices were offered to them. Herod the Great rebuilt Samaria, naming it Sebaste, the Greek equivalent of Augustus, and erected a temple in the emperor's honor. The worship of the dead emperor, and of the "genius" of the living emperor as divine, had an important bearing upon the organization and solidarity of the Empire. The emperor cult gave to the heterogeneous Roman army a feeling of pride in the unity and greatness of the empire. Associated with the cult of the military standards, representing the soldierly virtues, the veneration of the emperor was an important aspect of the legion's *disciplina Romana*.[13] It also became an important touchstone of political loyalty of subject peoples, especially in the eastern provinces.

Among the peoples of the empire only the Jews were exempt from the cult of the state and its emperor. Anyone refusing to take part in simple ceremonies acknowledging the divine source of the benefits of the *pax Romana* was suspected of revolutionary activity. It was inevitable that tension should develop between Christianity and imperial Rome as the Church became largely Gentile in membership and was recognized as a religious society distinct from Judaism. To the representatives of the state, the Christian proclamation "Jesus Christ is Lord," easily might be considered a treasonable statement. To Christian ears, the assumption by emperors of the titles "Son of God," "Savior," and "Lord" would appear blasphemous. Of the Roman emperors in New Testament times, Domitian was the most zealous in claiming divinity, but Gaius (Caligula) and Nero also sought divine honors during their reigns (see pp. 425f., 51f., and 124).

Like all religions constructed by politicians, the emperor cult had fundamental weaknesses. It lacked all genuine religious content. It afforded no satisfactory substitute for a personal religion or philosophy.[14] Before the time of the Augustan Restoration, mystery religions from Anatolia, Syria, and Egypt had been brought to Rome.

THE POPULAR APPEAL OF ORIENTAL MYSTERY RELIGIONS

Belief in divinely inspired prophetesses, called *sibyls*, originated in Greece, as did the idea that the state should collect, preserve, and consult these oracles upon whose fulfillment the fortunes of the state depended. Sibylline Books were introduced into Italy through Greek colonizers and provided the means of access to Rome for the earliest mysteries. Following a famine in the fifth century B.C.E., a Sibylline oracle was obeyed and a temple was built in Rome to Demeter, Dionysus, and Kore. In 205 B.C.E., after the long years of war with Hannibal, Rome was showered with volcanic stones on several occasions. Hannibal was no longer a serious menace, but Romans grew panicky and the Sibylline oracles were again consulted. It was learned that the enemy would not be defeated unless a Phrygian goddess was brought to Rome. Accordingly, a deputation went to Pessinus to procure the holy stone of Cybele, the *Mater Deum Magna* (great mother of the gods). Subsequently, a temple to the earth-mother was erected on the Palatine.*

*The cult's legend told of the love of the goddess for Attis. When the youth became unfaithful, Cybele drove him mad. He emasculated himself and died, becoming a god of the underworld. Like the

Having obeyed the divine command to receive the Great Mother, the Romans "took measures to keep her respectable and Roman."[15] Annual festivals continued, and during the reign of Claudius (41–54 C.E.) they were made more elaborate and given official sanction. Besides the public rites, the cult of Cybele-Attis probably had a number of sacraments. A blood-bath of initiation, called the *taurobolium*, is known from a number of inscriptions. In this ceremony the devotee descended into a pit covered with a grate. Onto the grate was led a bull or a ram, adorned with garlands of flowers. The beast was mortally stabbed by the priest and the devotee drenched with its blood. From the pit the initiate emerged, convinced that his or her sins had been washed away, and that the initiate was reborn forever, having acquired something of the nature and power of deity.[16]

Egypt's contribution to the Graeco-Roman mysteries was the cult of the god Osiris; his consort, Isis; and their son, Horus (or Anubis?). Accounts of the Osiris myth make it clear that the Egyptians worshiped a dying and rising god who offered people the hope of a happy immortality. Under the dynasty of the Ptolemies, the mysteries of Osiris assumed a less markedly national character. The Greeks at Alexandria called their god Sarapis and gave him the attributes of Zeus and other Greek deities. They hoped to unite in common worship the two races inhabiting the Ptolemaic kingdom.[17]

When the worship of Sarapis-Isis first reached beyond Alexandria, it was confined to private associations, but later the cult was officially established in

Greek Eleusinian mystery, this Anatolian cult was related to the annual death and resurrection of vegetation.

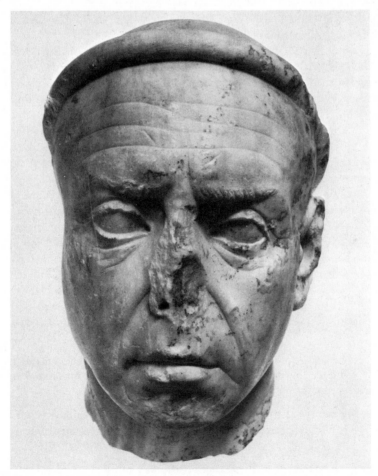

Sculpture of a priest of Isis, first century B.C.E. Found in the agora excavations, Athens. *(Courtesy of the American School of Classical Studies, Athens.)*

such prominent Greek cities as Athens, Thessalonica, and Delos. It is thought that the mystery became established at Rome during the time of Sulla (80 B.C.E.). There it continued to win followers in spite of the repeated attempts on the part of the government to suppress it. Chapels to the Egyptian gods were torn down four times in the decade 58–48 B.C.E. but the cult was not to be denied. At last the mad emperor, Caligula, put up a temple to Isis in the Campus Martius (ca. 38 C.E.). From this time the Egyptian mystery enjoyed the favor of the emperors.

The action of Caligula calls attention to the fact that Isis was often worshiped apart from the other Egyptian deities. While Sarapis was never invoked without Isis, she was often invoked alone. Indeed, of all the pagan deities of the Graeco-Roman world, Isis was probably the greatest. She became identified with every goddess; yet the Lady of the Myriad Names was more than a composite deity. She had little in common with Diana, the virgin huntress, as cold as her own moon; still less with Aphrodite, or with Athena, a man's goddess. Isis was a friend of women and the greatest of them all; she was a wife and mother who had suffered and who understood. It was no small part of the success of the Sarapis-Isis cult that for the first time in the pagan world one-half of the race had a friend in the court of heaven.[18]

There were many features that added to the popularity of this Egyptian mystery. The twice-daily sacrifices, the penitential practices, the continual round of duties performed by the black-stoled priests in the service of Isis impressed upon observers the reality of ever-present deities, ready and willing to enter into commerce with persons in need. Public ceremonies were regularly scheduled, and at such times the image of Isis was displayed. The November festival was the passion and resurrection of Osiris. In the spring, the festival of the launching of the symbolic ship of the goddess was held, at which time a gorgeous procession made its way from the temple to the seashore.

We can know what the cult of Isis meant to individuals because of the second-century romance by Apuleius, *Metamorphoses* (which is known, since Augustine, as *The Golden Ass*).[19] It is the story of a young nobleman named Lucius, who is led into careless dabbling in magic. As a result he is changed into the shape of an ass. After he has undergone many fantastic adventures, Isis appears to him in a dream, reveals her many divine names and powers, and speaks of her festival on the morrow. Lucius is told to approach the procession and take a rose from the priest's hand and eat it. Thus he will be rid of his animal nature. Isis claims his devotion and promises.

> Your life will be happy, nay glorious under my protection . . . And if by acts of diligent obedience, faithful devotion, and steadfast self-discipline you deserve well of my godhead, you shall know that I and I alone have the power to prolong your life beyond the bounds appointed by your fate.[20]

Lucius obeys the command of Isis, and later becomes initiated into her mysteries. He is not permitted to divulge the cultic secrets but his hints are revealing:

> I visited the bounds of death; I tread Proserpina's threshold; I passed through all the elements and returned. It was midnight, but I saw the sun radiant with bright light. I came into the very presence of the gods below and the gods above and I adored them face to face. . . .[21]

On the morning after these nocturnal revelations, Lucas was exhibited to a congregation of people in the dress of a sun god. Later on, Lucius passed through the other initiations and became a minor priest of Isis at Rome.

Brief notice should be taken of the cult of Mithra, a religion that spread with amazing rapidity throughout the Roman army and became, during the third century, a strong competitor of Christianity. According to the cult legend, the god Mithra had been born from a rock. After various exploits he caught and tamed a huge bull created by the Persian high god, Ahura-Mazda. Later Mithra slew this bull and from it there sprang the plants and animals useful to humans.[22] In early representations, Mithra is associated with the sun god, feasting with him and riding in his chariot. Indeed, by the time Mithra reached Rome in the first century B.C.E. he had become a solar deity. In later inscriptions he is invoked as *deus Sol invictus Mithras* (the unconquerable sun-god Mithra). His birthday was celebrated when the sun, passing the winter solstice, began its movements toward its summer position, a date fixed at December 25.[23] Among his worshipers Mithra was exalted as a righteous and holy god, a lover of truth and a hater of deceit, the guardian of contracts and the inviolability of oaths.

The shrine of the Mithra cult, of which there are many ancient remains, consisted of a pillared vestibule that led to an underground grotto. On the back wall facing the entrance was a bas-relief of Mithra the bull-slayer. It is probable that these chapels were not used for public worship but for initiations into the sacred mysteries. Only men were allowed to be devotees of Mithra. These passed through seven ascending stages of initiation, probably corresponding to the popular belief that the soul passed through seven planetary spheres on its way to the abode of the blest. The object of the initiatory rites was the progressive attainment of moral purity.[24] The initiate was promised eternal life in the general resurrection at the end of history, and an escape from the great conflagration that would finally consume all demonic powers and evil-doers.

THE WIDESPREAD BELIEF IN ASTROLOGY AND MAGIC

We have already noted that when the small "worlds" of the Greek and Roman city-states were shattered by the political changes of the Hellenistic Age, the fear arose that human life was a plaything of blind Tyche or Fortuna (Lat. fortune). Many people turned to astrology in the hope of understanding the universe and of finding security in it. Astrology is based on a belief that the stars influence life on the earth and determine the fate of every human being. The popular astrology of New Testament times was the adaptation by Greek science of ancient Babylonian observations and calculations concerning the movements of the heavenly bodies.

The logical implication of astrology is atheism, since belief that the cosmos is a giant, clocklike mechanism eliminates the possibility of interference by the gods. This conclusion was drawn by a few persons, notably by the avid student of astrology Emperor Tiberius, who reigned during Jesus' ministry. Belief in blind, merciless fate drove persons into the arms of priests of the mystery cults. The stars and other planetary "powers" were gods or demons *(daimones)* who could be appeased by sacrifices and prayers or mastered by magical means. Some of the mystery religions readily embraced the beliefs of astology and offered freedom from the tyranny of the *stoicheia* (elemental spirits of the universe). Thus Mithra, a solar deity, guided the souls of humans through the planetary spheres; Attis was called "the shepherd of the bright stars"; and men such as Lucius became convinced that Isis was the mistress over fate, able to prolong life beyond its appointed bounds.

Superstition and magic are weeds that grow in the same soil as religion. In Rome's golden age, Augustus sought to curb the traffic in sorcery and magical materials, as had the Athenians in the classical period of Greece, but with less success. The popular demand for love potions, conjurations, "the evil eye," amulets, statuettes of gods, and so on, netted fabulous profits for businessmen. Prevalent also was belief in oracles and in dreams and omens.[25]

THE POPULAR "SCHOOLS" OF HELLENISTIC PHILOSOPHY

Two philosophies that arose at the beginning of the Hellenistic Age were dominant in the period of Christian origins, Epicureanism and Stoicism. Both of these schools appealed to the educated who had lost faith in the traditional gods and were seeking some rational understanding of nature and the world as an alternative to skepticism.

While Alexander's generals were fighting over political control of the world, a philosopher named Epicurus (342–270 B.C.E.) taught at Athens. His understanding of the physical world was based upon the theories of Democritus. Nothing exists except atoms moving downward in empty space. The human being is thus a chance compound of atoms, which at death dissipate "like smoke." It is somewhat surprising that Epicurus believed in the existence of the gods. Yet he held that persons could contemplate their blissful existence with a religious emotion devoid of fear and selfishness, for the gods have neither the power nor the interest to hurt or help human beings. They dwell in the empty spaces between the stream of atoms, far removed from the world. They know no trouble and give none to anyone else. In his ethical teaching, Epicurus affirmed that pleasure is the fulfillment of life. The good person has the capacity to enjoy pleasure and is untroubled by pain or fear. It is important to recognize that "enjoyment" did not imply uninhibited pleasure; on the contrary, it connoted "the condition of human well-being which is achieved when one gains true wisdom and, therefore, is able in every situation to find the right thing to do."[26]

The philosopher's mission was to deliver human beings from their dread of life and of death. Since Epicurus believed that the popular forms of religion encouraged fear of the gods and of what comes after death, he became the foe of the traditional cults. The great poem of Lucretius, *De Rerum Natura*, composed early in the first century B.C.E., provides the fullest exposition of the teachings of Epicurus and also reveals the ecstasy of a man delivered from dread of life's mysteries.[27] Yet the influence of Epicurus was not extensive. Stoicism offered a more satisfactory solution to the theoretical and practical problems of

The agora of Athens was, by New Testament times, encircled by "stoa," or porches, such as the one depicted above, the Stoa of Attalos, which stood at the east side of the market place. (This second-century B.C.E. edifice was restored during the years 1953–1956.) The north side of the agora *(below)* was closed by "the Painted Stoa," which is unexcavated but is known to have been built during the fifth century B.C.E. and later became the birthplace of Stoic philosophy. *(Photos courtesy of the American School of Classical Studies, Athens.)*

persons in the Graeco-Roman world. It therefore became "the noblest and most influential religion for intellectuals." Through its street preachers, Stoicism also became a popular religious philosophy.[28]

The founder of Stoicism was Zeno (336–263 B.C.E.), a contemporary in Athens of Epicurus. He taught in the "painted porch" *(stoa)* from which his philosophy derived its name. Two of Zeno's pupils, Cleanthes and Chrysippus, elaborated his system. A brilliant representative of Stoicism in the second century B.C.E. was Posidonius, the teacher of Cicero. During this century the religious mysticism latent in Stoic philosophy was developed under the influence of the contemporary revival of Platonism. Also, the traditional polytheistic myths were allegorized to accommodate them to Stoic doctrines. After Posidonius, the ethics of Stoicism were emphasized by Seneca and Epictetus and the Stoic emperor, Marcus Aurelius.[29]

The Stoics taught that ultimate reality is a rational *pneuma* (breath or spirit). The universe is perpetually passing to and from alternative states: God in his proper being, the *Logos* (Pure Reason) or the Divine Fire; and the world in its plurality of *spermatikoi Logoi* (seminal rational forms), into which the one Logos is distributed as sparks of the Divine Fire. "The whole of reality," wrote Chrysippus, "forms a unity because a breath permeates it throughout, and by it the universe is held together and stays together and forms an organic unity."[30]

As a consequence of this world view, the Stoics believed that everything that happens to humans is in accordance with necessity, or "the providence which pervades the universe." This belief brought to the Stoics no terrors; they held in religious awe the universal law of Nature:

> Lead me, O Zeus, and thou, O fate,
> To the goal which you have ordained for me.
> I will follow without shrinking. Were I a miscreant,
> And would not follow, I should have to nonetheless.[31]

Since persons possess a spark of the divine, to live according to reason is "to live according to Nature" and to find true happiness. To attain this virtue requires constant self-examination and self-restraint. The "wise person" seeks to be wholly dependent upon Nature and completely independent of externals, as Epictetus wrote:

> I am free, I am a friend of God to render him willing obedience. Of all else, I may set store by nothing—neither by my own body, nor possession, nor office, nor good report, nor, in a word, anything else.[32]

The Stoic ideal was *apatheia* (freedom from all emotion). Reason must be the autocrat over the passions. An unfortunate person should be helped, the evil should be punished, without empathy.* Stoic doctrine was compatible with belief in the multiplicity of gods. The supreme god, the Divine Fire (habitually referred to by the traditional name, Zeus) was one; yet other reasonable beings besides humans existed. The Stoics followed the Platonists in designating such beings "demons." These inhabited the ether and were invisible. Stoics did not accept the popular mythologies in the literal sense but, according to Posidonius, even the obscenities in these myths could be explained as figurative expressions of truths taught plainly in Stoicism. Since the Stoics believed that a human

*This ideal of self-sufficiency could lead to an individualistic and negative ethic. Happiness could be conceived as the withdrawal into oneself. But Stoicism did not ordinarily lead to

being was by nature akin to God, the ceremonies of cultic religion had no significance. Prayer was the communion of the mind with God; whoever imitates God—that is, who lives according to Nature—has adequately worshiped him.[33] On the question of the survival of the soul, the Stoics were not fully agreed. Some denied personal immortality; others held that some souls survived the periodic world conflagrations wherein humans and demons were reabsorbed into the Divine Fire. According to Stoic theory, Zeus alone was imperishable.

At the time of Christian origins, the Stoic platform extended from the classroom into the marketplace. Stoic preachers, like the early Christian missionaries, visited the teeming cities of the empire taking their message to all classes of people. The "soapbox" speeches of the Stoics gave rise to a new type of literature called the *diatribe* (conversation-discourse).[34]

social indifference. Humans are destined by nature for society and given duties to fulfill. "The Logos which commands us what to do and what not to do is common. If this is so, then there is likewise a law in common. If this is so, we are fellow-citizens, and if this is so we are members of the same community . . . a single state." Marcus Aurelius, *Meditations*, IV. 4.

MYSTICAL RELIGIONS OF THE GRAECO-ROMAN WORLD

In its broadest sense, *mysticism* defines a tendency in all religions. But as ordinarily used by historians, mysticism describes the religion of persons who believe that they have experienced a direct knowledge of and communion with the divine. In this *unio mystica* the spirit of humans is joined with the divine spirit and set free from the limitations of mortality. Such an experience may be brief or prolonged, but in any case it transcends all ordinary conditions of human consciousness. The sensations of the mystic may result from the contemplation of some natural phenomena, but ordinarily they are thought to arise from supernatural revelation or illumination.

The mystical type of religion discussed in this section is sometimes classed among the "mysteries," but it can be distinguished from the latter by its lack of dependence upon cultic rites. The only kind of initiation that these mystics recognized was the purely spiritual initiation into the truth about God, the cosmos, and human nature revealed to the elect. From the human side, this truth could be gained only through the discipline of meditation.

There were intellectuals of the empire who found no lasting satisfaction in the popular philosophies and eventually turned to mystical or to occult beliefs. The god of the Stoic, "being immanent in everything, satisfied to some extent the mystical seeking of unity with the All . . . but the mystic demanded not only unity with God but also that he should be exalted. . . ."[35] God must be more than Reason or Spirit immanent in the world; he must be their transcendent Cause. It was under the pressure of this need that in the second century B.C.E. persons were attracted to the mystical (or Pythagorean) element in Plato's philosophy. Plato's mysticism was fused with Stoicism, as in the teaching of the Stoic Posidonius, or else Platonism was maintained as a system tinged with Stoic ideas.[36] In New Testament times the mystical longings of many persons burst the bounds of rational thought and found personal satisfaction not in speculative thought but in an experience of divine illumination.

This is evidenced by the popularity of "the Hermetica," an extensive body of writings that has survived from the second and third centuries C.E. Some tractates belonging to this literature are dated in the first century. Thus it is possible that Hermetic teaching was known in New Testament times. The Hermetica are monuments to the cross-fertilization of Greek and Oriental thought, which was characteristic of the Near East in the Hellenistic-Roman period. The Hermetic tractates are in the form of dialogues containing the communications of the god Hermes "Trismegistus" (thrice-greatest) to his sons, Tat and Asklepius.[37] The writers of the Hermetica probably did not form a "school," and their books were not the sacred canon of a "church." At the same time, small associations of mystics may have cultivated this Hermetic lore.

The doctrines of the Hermetica cannot be reduced to a consistent pattern of thought. Nevertheless, a Platonic-Stoic world view and a common religious spirit are manifest in them all. The Hermetists believed in one God, maker and father of the universe, and that knowledge of God provided the only way of human salvation. God demands from people no cultic ceremonies. "The service of God is one thing alone, to refrain from evil."[38] This ethical demand concentrated upon personal purification and detachment from material things. The mind was set upon God and his eternity.[39] To possess this knowledge was to be a complete person and to partake of immortality:

> "O earth-born men," cries the prophet in the first Hermetic tractate, "why have you given yourselves over to death, when you have the right to partake of immortality? Repent, you who have made error your fellow-traveler and ignorance your consort. Depart from that light which is darkness! Leave corruption and partake of immortality!"[40]

According to the Hermetica, knowledge of the invisible and visible world and of human nature has saving power. But this knowledge is not considered the product of rational observation or speculation. The writers believed that they were transmitting revelation and that the practical object of all knowledge is a vision of God. God wills to be known, and to know him is life eternal.

In the thirteenth tractate, the Hermetists' doctrine of regeneration is set forth.

While waiting upon God, Hermes directs the process by which Tat passes through the experience of rebirth. Tat is required to discipline his mind and will, to renounce "the irrational torments of matter" inherent in his material body, so that the essential man in him can be liberated. Then follows a period of silence when Hermes and Tat wait upon "powers of God" to possess Tat's nature and to expel the "torments." After the declaration by Hermes that Tat has been regenerated, Tat is assured that he has "become a god and a child of One." After singing the hymn of rebirth, Hermes warns Tat not to divulge the mystery, and declares: "Now you know with your mind both yourself and our Father."[41]

THE RISE OF GNOSTICISM

The terms *gnostic* and *gnosticism* are used by modern writers in a bewildering variety of ways. Etymologically, the terms are derived from *gnosis*, the Greek word for "knowledge." Through long usage among historians, "Gnostic" became a label for a large and somewhat amorphous group of speculative theological systems of the second century C.E., described by Justin Martyr and Irenaeus, and later by Hippolytus and others, in their refutations of heresies. Some scholars insist that the use of the terms should be limited to these Christian heresiologies.[42] But there are others who have brought forward evidence to support the hypothesis that Gnosticism developed as a movement or way of thinking independent of Christianity, paralleling and probably antedating the latter's origin. This proto-Gnosticism, so-called, found expression in a great variety of writings ranging from serious philosophical discourse to wild speculative teachings based on astrological and magical lore. Yet within a rich profusion of forms one is able to trace a cluster of motifs, which has affinities with second-century, classical Gnosticism, and the term *gnostic* may be appropriately used in a broader sense.[43]

The origin of Gnostic motifs is a subject of vigorous debate. But it is widely held that a Gnostic movement absorbed features from Judaism before its interaction with Christianity. Conversely, the writings of several Jewish apologists and sectarian groups reflect Gnosticising tendencies. Perhaps it is a sound assumption to explain the rise of Gnosticism as a syncretistic phenomenon, like so many popular religions and philosophies of the Hellenistic Age, a fusion of Greek and Oriental thought.[44]

After contact with Christianity, Gnosticism gathered momentum, and there arose "that rank growth of Christian, or semi-Christian and quasi-Christian systems" that are derided, and in some measure described, by the second-century Christian apologists.[45] It is a plausible but controversial theory that in the early period of Christianity's development Gnostic teachings were tolerated and that a mutual interpenetration of thought ensued; but that during the post-apostolic age resistance and rejection set in. In this book the earliest manifestation of Gnostic ways of thought—pagan, Jewish, Christian—will be termed *pre-Gnostic* to distinguish these ideas or motifs from the Gnostic systems of theology attributed to teachers within or on the fringe of the Christian Church in the second century and later.[46]

Reconstructions of pre-Gnosticism inevitably contain speculative features. Sources earlier than Christian writings are meager in the extreme, and the problem of methodology is an acute one. Some scholars believe it is possible to work backward from late sources, some of which date from the fifth or sixth centuries C.E. They have been provided a wealth of new and earlier material in the Nag-Hammadi discoveries, which preserve approximately a thousand pages of original Gnostic writing containing ideas similar to those attacked by Irenaeus and others, and numerous variations thereof.[47] By abstracting from the known sources of developed Gnostic systems some common and interrelated themes, these scholars have attempted to recover modes of thought important to several New Testament writers or at least to various persons and groups with whom New Testament writers interacted.

The constructive method described above is not inhibited by chronology and "has the advantage of presenting what early Gnostics may well have thought."[48] Nevertheless such synthetic abstractions should not be mistaken for the recovery of pre-Christian "sources." The problem for the interpreter is "to avoid reading back into first-century terminology the associations and connotations which that terminology does have in the second century," and at the same time to recognize, already in the first century, "the emergence in embryonic form

(Above) The Nag Hammadi codices, containing fifty-two tractates composed in Greek and preserved in these Coptic texts. Discovered in 1946 and now conserved in the Coptic Museum in Cairo, Egypt, these codices are believed to have belonged to the library of heretical Christian monks who were expelled from their solitary monastic settlements by those established in this region by St. Pachomius, because of their Gnostic views. *(Below)* Jabal at Tārif, site of the discovery by two Arab brothers of the Nag Hammidi codices, buried in a sealed stone jar in fallen rock at the foot of the cliff on the southern side of the mountain. *(Courtesy of the Institute for Antiquity and Christianity, Claremont, Calif.)*

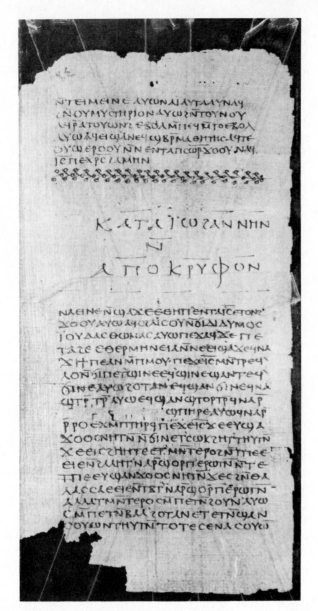

The opening page of the Gospel of Thomas, Nag Hammadi Codex II, p. 32, a tractate containing 114 sayings attributed to Jesus, some previously unknown, others reflecting a familarity with parables and aphorisms of Jesus contained in the Synoptic Gospels. *(Courtesy of the Institute for Antiquity and Christianity, Claremont, Calif.)*

of incipient Gnostic systems which only come to full development later."[49] Because of the dangers of this method, other scholars "refuse to admit that later developments can explain what earlier writers had in mind."[50]

The following tentative description attempts to set forth some of the motifs present in pre-Gnosticism. (It must not be supposed that this basic pattern was

everywhere explicit, or indeed found in any one document in this simple form.)
The principal characteristic of the pre-Gnostic world view is its radical dualism
between the visible and invisible worlds. Ultimate reality—God, the Good, the
Unknown Father—is supramundane and absolutely alien to anything human.
Indeed, knowledge of this invisible reality cannot be attained by the human
mind unaided; it derives from supernatural revelation. Even so, knowledge thus
given can only be expressed in negative terms. Over against God are other
orders of being, a spin-off of the divine nature, represented perhaps as the
creation of lower powers, who are termed demons, elemental spirits, and the
like. At any rate, the imperfect world of human beings is dominated by these
lesser powers; their home is the innermost dungeon of the domain governed
by these world rulers. Around and above this world is a system of spheres or
aeons—the *pleroma* (fullness)—which is the abode of the invisible spirits.

By their birth humans belong to the lowest order of beings. Yet the innate
feeling that a person is a prisoner in this world and under a fateful, destructive
tyranny, indicates a primordial relation to the invisible world. In the human
body, or in the bodies of the elect, a divine spark, which is immortal, is lodged.
The liberation of this spark or spirit is possible through *gnosis*, that "knowledge" of the divine mysteries reserved for the initiated. The goal of Gnostic
teaching is therefore the release of the inner life, in order that a person may
participate in the life of the invisible, eternal world—the realm to which he or
she belongs, from which he or she has fallen—and thus realize his or her true
destiny. *Knowledge is power.* This is the faith of the Gnostic teacher. "He who
knows what he is and whence he is can find his way home. He who knows the
nature of the governing world and its governing powers can overcome these
powers."[51]

Another way to describe the characteristics of pre-Gnosticism is to consider
its social history, reflected in the peculiar "stance" taken by the authors of
typical texts, such as their feeling of "an estrangement from the mass of humanity, an affinity to an ideal order that completely transcends life as we know
it, and a life-style radically other than common practice. This life-style involved
giving up all the goods that people usually desire, and longing for ultimate
liberation." Pre-Gnosticism, and later, Gnosticism, was not an aggressively revolutionary movement, but "a withdrawal from involvement in the contamination that destroys clarity of vision."[52]*

One of the most controversial aspects of research concerning ideas intrinsically pre-Gnostic is the postulation of a redeemer myth. In numerous classical
Gnostic systems it was taught that a redeemer descended to earth to impart
knowledge about the unknown God and the divine spark in human beings.
Having brought to humans redemption by this *gnosis*, he ascended to the realms
above. The question is: Did this myth of the Gnostic redeemer originate in
Eastern antiquity and, in the course of time, influence Jewish, Christian, and
pagan thinkers of the first and second centuries; or was the Gnostic redeemer
myth a culmination of a long process of development that derived its principal
content from Adamic speculation in Judaism or from Christian messianism or
both? In several ancient myths there appear ideas of a Heavenly or Primal Man
imprisoned in the material world and who, upon his release and ascension, left
behind something of his nature to be recovered. But it is a broad leap of the

* This "gnostic
stance" reflected a
common yearning for
deliverance from the
dominion of evil, or
for inner transcend-
ance—a yearning that
was pervasive in Hel-
lenistic-Roman times
and that emerged in
Jewish apocalyptic-
ism, Neoplatonism,
the mystery reli-
gions, and the like.
This pervasive world
view "was held to-
gether by a very de-

imagination to assume that such pre-Christian ideas conveyed the full implications of the alleged Gnostic redeemer myth which, according to some, influenced the Christology of the writers of New Testament books, e.g., Ephesians and the Fourth Gospel (see also pp. 386, 436).

The objectives of pre-Gnostic teachers were not unlike those of the Hermetists and the priests of the mysteries. They sought to provide the initiate a means of escape from bondage to matter, fate, and the demons, and to enable him or her to attain immortality. Yet pre-Gnosticism, like Hermetism, can be distinguished from the mysteries by the absence of public ceremonies and the cultus.[53]

It should be noted that the practical effects of *gnosis* upon human conduct produced two opposites: The enlightened could express their liberation of the spirit from the tomb of the body by adopting ascetic practices—dieting, sexual abstinence, and so on. Or the Gnostic doctrine of a radical freedom of the human spirit from matter could lend encouragement to moral license.

JUDAISM OF THE DIASPORA

At the time of the birth of Jesus "it was not easy to find a place [in the whole world] where they [the Jews] had not penetrated, and which was not dominated by them."[54] The Jews of the Diaspora actively participated in the commercial and social life of the cities and villages of the Graeco-Roman world, and sometimes enjoyed full citizenship rights. At the same time, they zealously maintained their national identity and religion and, where possible, some type of civic organization of their own. In Alexandria, for example, where the Jews were settled in unusually large numbers, theirs was a semi-autonomous community. In more sparsely settled areas, the synagogues served as centers of Jewish religious and political life.[55]

Like a magnetic pole, the temple in Jerusalem held the Jews of the Diaspora together. Thousands visited Jerusalem annually for the feast of the Passover, and every Jew of twenty years or older acknowledged his duty to support the temple with the yearly half-shekel tax. But more important for the preservation and propagation of Judaism abroad was the allegiance given to the commandments of the Torah. The Diaspora Jew was often ignorant of the burgeoning oral or unwritten Law formulated by the scribes of Palestine. Greek-speaking Jews could study the Septuagint, but language as well as geography rendered the teaching of the Mishnah (Hebrew) and the Gemarah (Aramaic) inaccessible to many. To the best of their ability Hellenistic Jews adhered to the precepts of the Law of Moses, but generally speaking the standards of piety among Palestinian Jews were higher.[56] At the same time there is some evidence that, under the influence of the text of the Septuagint, a tendency existed toward separation of Torah from the vital context of the covenant, and its "petrifaction" into "legalistic formulae."[57]

The sarcastic comments of such Roman writers as Horace and Juvenal indicate that the Jews impressed their Gentile neighbors by their observance of circumcision, Sabbath rest, and the avoidance of swine meat. Obedience to the ceremonial prescriptions of the Torah, together with monotheism, imageless

cided stance, which is where the unity amid the wide diversity is to be sought." Robinson, *Nag Hammadi Library*, p. 9f.

worship, and ethical conduct were indeed the essential characteristics of Hellenistic Judaism. This distinctive way of life made the Jews the object of both admiration and scorn among the Gentiles. By their belief that they were the chosen people of the one living and true God, by their ridicule of all forms of Gentile worship and idolatry, the Jews provoked some pagans to keen resentment.[58] Yet, as we have observed, there was much in Judaism that attracted high-minded Gentiles. The synagogues of the Diaspora were sensitive to this opportunity and actively sought converts. "Propaganda and the mission to the Gentiles appear in the Septuagint as a specific task incumbent on Jewish piety." As a result, proselytes and "God-fearers" were a conspicious element in the synagogues of the Diaspora.[59]

It has been said that Gentiles "were attracted to Judaism first as a philosophy and later as one of the Oriental mystery cults offering eternal life."[60] Judaism is called a "philosophy" by several Roman writers, a conception fostered by Jewish apologists. Josephus, as we have seen, identified the major Jewish parties and sects as the "four philosophies." Philo of Alexandria taught that the religion of Moses was the highest philosophy. He attempted to demonstrate the correspondence between the teaching of the Old Testament and the Stoicized Platonism of his time through an allegorization of the scriptures. In this he may be likened to Posidonius, who sought to show that Stoic doctrines could be found in the myths and cults of the popular religions.*

* The Wisdom of Solomon, the Letter of Aristeas, and 4 Maccabees are Hellenistic Jewish writings tinged with Platonic and Stoic doctrines. 4 Maccabees defines "wisdom" as did the Stoics: "the knowledge of things human and divine, and their causes." Wisdom-Torah is represented as the source of moral and spiritual education of humanity.

The traffic was by no means one way. Evidence of the direct influence of Hellenistic Judaism upon pagan philosophers and religious writers is not plentiful. Nevertheless, the fascination of the Westerner for things Oriental, the aforementioned apologetic writings of the Jews, the dissemination of the Hebrew scriptures in Greek, were not without their effects beyond the limits of the synagogues.[61] Some of the tractates of the Hermetica and pre-Gnostic texts reflect ways in which the Old Testament and ancient Jewish teachings contributed to the amalgam of Greek and Oriental thought.[62] It can be argued that Jewish ideas were little understood by these Gnosticizing writers. But to some extent Greek and Jewish thinkers employed common speech and discourse. This fact holds obvious implications for the Gentile mission of the Christian Church.

It is easy to see how some Gentiles could have mistaken Judaism for an Oriental mystery religion. Proselyte baptism might have suggested the lustrations and baths of initiation into the mysteries. Jewish fasts and other penitential acts could have been (wrongly) related to the deprivation of the flesh advocated by the popular cults.

Judaism could better satisfy the religious aspirations of men in the Hellenistic Age than could the mystery religions. Judaism taught the unity of God and of the world, and satisfied the longings of individuals for a purification from the passions of the flesh and for eternal happiness. At the same time, the ceremonial and dietary laws and the practice of circumcision gave Judaism a national character that remained a deterrent to its missionary enterprise.[63]

NOTES

1. R. H. Pfeiffer, *History of New Testament Times* (1976), p. 99.
2. *Ibid.*, p. 97. V. Tcherikover, *Hellenistic Civilization and the Jews* (1959), pp. 11f.

3. Pfeiffer, *New Testament Times*, pp. 98ff.

4. M. P. Nilsson, *Greek Piety* (1968). For a brief description of the cults of the Greek city-states, see S. V. McCasland, "The Greco-Roman World," *IB*, vol. 7 (1951), pp. 88ff. E. Lohse, *The New Testament Environment* (1976), pp. 222f.

5. The agnosticism of the fifth-century philosophers had been a strong corrosive influence. See Pfeiffer, *New Testament Times*, pp. 128ff.; Nilsson, *Greek Piety*, pp. 70ff.

6. Acts 19:23ff. At Lystra, Barnabas and Paul were worshipped as Zeus and Hermes, but to the townspeople they were not epiphanies of the Olympian gods but of local deities bearing their names, Acts 14:11ff.

7. W. W. Tarn and G. T. Griffith. *Hellenistic Civilization* (1952), pp. 337f.; Pfeiffer, *New Testament Times*, p. 130.

8. M. Nilsson, *Greek Piety*, pp. 85f.

9. See an inscription honoring priests of Eleusinian mysteries, F. C. Grant, *Hellenistic Religion* (1953), pp. 15f. The cult spread from Eleusis to Athens and from there to the world. Initiation was opened to all. Cicero commented on its spread: "the most distant nations were initiated into the sacred and august Eleusinia," *On the Nature of the Gods* 1. 42.

10. On the Orphic and Pythagorean influences upon the Bacchic mysteries and the initiation of young children, see M. Nilsson, *The Dionysiac Mysteries of the Hellenistic and Roman Age* (1957). F. W. Beare, "Greek Religion and Philosophy," *IDB*, 2 (1962), 492d. For Orphic texts, see Grant, *Hellenistic Religion*, pp. 105f.

11. Lohse, *New Testament Environment*, p. 224.

12. H. J. Rose, *Religion in Greece and Rome* (1959), pp. 197ff.; D. Winslow, "Religion and the Early Roman Empire," in S. Benko and J. J. O'Rourke, eds., *The Catacombs and the Colosseum* (1971), pp. 246–248. Lohse, *New Testament Environment*, pp. 216–221.

13. Nilsson, *Greek Piety*, pp. 277f.; C. D. Morrison, *The Powers That Be* (1960), pp. 83ff., 131ff.

14. It was even deficient as a social force, see Nilsson, *Greek Piety*, p. 178. D. Winslow, "Religion and the Early Roman Empire," pp. 247f.

15. Rose, *Religion in Greece and Rome*, pp. 273f.

16. The taurobolium (bull's blood-bath) was also used for the consecration of priests. See a description of the rite in Barrett, *New Testament Background*, pp. 96f.

17. For a summary of the Osiris myth reported in Plutarch's *Iside et Osiride* 12–20, see Pfeiffer, *New Testament Times*, pp. 141ff.

18. "Isis was a phenomenon which had not appeared in the Mediterranian world in historical times, but having once appeared has never since quitted it; she was the woman's goddess," Tarn and Griffith, *Hellenistic Civilization*, p. 359.

19. Apuleius, *Metamorphoses* XI. 8ff.

20. *Ibid.* Quoted from A. D. Nock, *Conversion* (1933), p. 139. For excerpts from *Metamorphoses* describing the initiation of Lucius, see Barrett, *New Testament Background*, pp. 97–100, Grant, *Hellenistic Religion*, pp. 136ff.

21. Nock, *Conversion*, p. 145. A. J. Festugière, *Personal Religion Among the Greeks* (1954), pp. 68ff.

22. Cumont, *Oriental Religions*, pp. 142ff.; for "A Mithras Liturgy," see Barrett, *New Testament Background*, pp. 102–104. J. R. Hinnells, ed., *Mithraic Studies: Proceedings of the First International Congress of Mithraic Studies*, Vols. I and II (1975).

23. See Cullmann, "Origin of Christmas," in O. Cullmann, *The Early Church* (1956), pp. 21ff.

24. The emperor Julian (261–287 C.E.) wrote of "the commandments which Mithra taught his followers," but no record of the moral code of Mithraism has been preserved. It probably contained the soldierly virtues.

25. For a selection of "Magical and Religious Papyri," see Barrett, *New Testament*

Background, pp. 29–36; F. C. Grant, *Ancient Roman Religion* (1957), pp. 238ff. Morrison, *The Powers That Be*, pp. 75ff.

26. Lohse, *New Testament Environment*, pp. 243f.
27. Passages from Lucretius and Epicurus cited in Barrett, *New Testament Background*, pp. 72–75.
28. Pfeiffer, *New Testament Times*, pp. 140ff.; E. Bevan, *Later Greek Religion* (1950), pp. 1f., 102ff.; Lohse, *New Testament Environment*, pp. 244ff.
29. Seneca (4–65 C.E.), Epictetus (60–110), Marcus Aurelius (121–180). The writings of Zeno's earliest pupils have perished except for a few fragments quoted by other writers, Barrett, *New Testament Background*, pp. 61ff.
30. Quoted in R. Bultmann, *Primitive Christianity in its Contemporary Setting* (1956), p. 135.
31. *Ibid.*, p. 139, attributed to Cleanthes.
32. *Discourses* IV. 3. 9ff. For other excerpts from the *Discourses* see Barrett, *New Testament Background*, pp. 66ff.
33. IX. 40. Theoretically the Stoic god is hardly personal, yet in practice Stoics often felt toward the all-encompassing Logos as toward a Person, a Father to be obeyed, to whom gratitude and praise could be offered. Bevan, *Later Greek Religion*, pp. 106ff.
34. Pfeiffer cites an excellent example from Horace, *Satires* II. 3. Imitations of the diatribe, which echo Stoic themes, are found in Hellenistic-Jewish writings, e.g., Wis. and 4 Macc. Pfeiffer, *New Testament Times*, p. 143.
35. Nilsson, *Greek Piety*, pp. 126f.
36. The amalgam of Platonic and Stoic ideas produced an *organon* for many writers of the Graeco-Roman world who attempted a rational justification for religion. Bevan, *Later Greek Religion*, pp. xxvi f. See Festugière, *Personal Religion among the Greeks*, pp. 123ff., for a description of this world view so congenial to the mystics' temperament.
37. The Hermetists, while writing in Greek, claimed to be translating ancient books of the Egyptians. Hermes is the Greek equivalent of the Egyptian god, Thoth, the inventor of writing, the first master of wisdom. The epithet "thrice-greatest" is an Egyptian formula often applied to the gods.
38. *Corpus Hermeticum*, X. 15.
39. C. H. Dodd, *The Interpretation of the Fourth Gospel* (1953), pp. 13f.
40. Corpus Hermeticum, I. 28.
41. Dodd, *Fourth Gospel*, pp. 44ff. Tractate 13 is one of the later Hermetic writings, and the possibility of Christian influence cannot be denied. Nevertheless, the substance of its teaching can be documented from other tractates, which reveal no Christian influence.
42. R. P. Casey, "Gnosis, Gnosticism and the New Testament," in W. D. Davies and D. Daube, *The Background of the New Testament and Its Eschatology* (1956), pp. 42ff.; J. Munck, "The New Testament and Gnosticism," in W. Klassen and G. F. Snyder, eds., *Current Issues in New Testament Interpretation* (1962), pp. 224ff.
43. H. Jonas, *The Gnostic Religion* (1958); Bultmann, *Primitive Christianity*, pp. 162ff.; R. M. Grant, "Gnosticism," *IDB* 2 (1962), p. 404; E. Pagels, "Gnosticism," *IDBS*, 364ff.; Lohse, *New Testament Environment*, pp. 253ff.
44. Lohse, *New Testament Environment*, pp. 254f.
45. Dodd, *Fourth Gospel*, p. 101; W. C. van Unnik, *Newly Discovered Gnostic Writings* (1960), pp. 28ff.
46. For a distinction commonly drawn between the terms *pre-Gnostic* and *proto-Gnostic*, see R. McL Wilson, *Gnosis and the New Testament* (1968), pp. 16ff.
47. J. M. Robinson, ed., *The Nag Hammadi Library in English* (1977).

48. R. M. Grant, "Gnosticism," p. 404.
49. Wilson, *Gnosis and the New Testament*, p. 23.
50. As reported by R. M. Grant, "Gnosticism," p. 404.
51. Dodd, *Fourth Gospel*, p. 113. For "an appropriate presentation of the basic structure of gnosticism" see Lohse, *New Testament Environment*, pp. 255–262. This and other syntheses of the motifs of gnostic thought are derived in large part from the influential book by H. Jonas, *Gnostic Religion*.
52. Robinson, *Nag Hammadi Library*, p. 1.
53. The Hermetica are often referred to as "gnostic writings" because of the basic similarities of beliefs and attitudes. Among the Nag Hammadi texts preserved by Christian gnostics is a previously unknown Hermetic tract (second century C.E.?) entitled by modern editors, Discourse on the Eighth and Ninth [spheres surrounding the earth], VI. 6, Robinson, *Nag Hammadi Library*, pp. 292–297. Lohse, *New Testament Environment*, pp. 262–268.
54. Strabo, quoted by Josephus, *B.J.* VII. 3. See also Philo, *Against Flaccus*, 7. For a history of Jewish settlements in foreign lands, see Tcherikover, *Hellenistic Civilization*, pp. 272–291; M. Stern, "The Jewish Diaspora," in S. Safrai and M. Stern, eds., *The Jewish People in the First Century* V. 1 (1974), pp. 117ff.
55. Where permissible, separate law courts may have been maintained, e.g., Sardis (ca. 50 B.C.E.), Jos. *Antiq.* XIV. iii. 17. The autonomy of the Jewish community was, however, not political but religious and social only. For a description of the internal organization of these communities, see Tcherikover, *Hellenistic Civilization*, pp. 301–332; S. Appelbaum, in Safrai and Stern, *The Jewish People*, pp. 472–490.
56. R. A. Kraft, "Judaism on the World Scene," in Benko and O'Rourke, *Catacombs and Colosseum*, pp. 84f.
57. H. J. Schoeps, *Paul* (1961), pp. 29f. It is a common but erroneous impression, acknowledged by Schoeps, that distinction should be made between Palestinian and Hellenistic Judaism. See W. D. Davies, *Paul and Rabbinic Judaism* (1948), pp. 6ff. M. Stern, "Relations Between the Diaspora and the Land of Israel," in Safrai and Stern, *The Jewish People*, pp. 186–199. Cf. Tcherikover, *Hellenistic Civilization*, pp. 344ff.
58. *Ibid.*, pp. 364–377. Pfeiffer, *New Testament Times*, p. 184.
59. Jos. *B.J.* VII. iii. 3; *Against Apion* 2. 39.
60. Pfeiffer, *New Testament Times*, pp. 192f.
61. Cf. Cicero, *De Officiis* 1. 43; Seneca, *Epis.* 89; Bultmann, *Primitive Christianity*, pp. 94ff.
62. See the Gnostic texts, *The Apocalypse of Adam* (Vol. 5), and *The Paraphrase of Shem* (VII, 1), Robinson, *The Nag Hammadi Library*, pp. 256ff., and 309ff.
63. Pfeiffer, *New Testament Times*, pp. 193f.

Chapter 13

The Acts Narrative of Paul's Missions

LETTERS of the apostle Paul form the centerpiece of the New Testament. Of its twenty-seven books, thirteen bear his name. It is probable that not all of these come from Paul himself. Some were written later by others to preserve the Apostle's legacy. Yet the letters of the New Testament authored by him put one "in direct contact with Paul and his message, furnish an extremely vivid picture of the Apostle's activity and struggles, his experiences and ideas, and at the same time afford us unique glimpses into the history of primitive Christianity."[1]

Alongside the Pauline Corpus, the New Testament provides a second important source, The Acts of the Apostles. More than half of its narrative focuses on Paul's career, and a popular view is that Acts is *the* source for knowledge of Paul's (public) life, providing an indispensable supplement to the letters that reveal essential aspects of Paul's person and theology. Accordingly many efforts have been made to dovetail into the Acts' narrative the letters of Paul and an exposition of their contents. Aside from the fact that the chronology of Paul's letters is uncertain, such synchronizations are often more confusing than clarifying. The dramatic progress of the Acts' narrative and its impact upon the reader are greatly diminished by the interpolation of Paul's letters. If Acts is read in bits and snatches, as the background for a study of Paul's letters, the distinctive literary and theological features of Acts are apt to be lost. One tends to "corrrect" its narrative by allusions to events in Paul's letters, or to "fault" Luke's theology as aberrant Paulinism. The reverse also may happen: the synchronization of Acts and Paul's letters may become a task of such interest and complexity that too little thought is given to the special contribution of each letter. Minor details in Paul's letters may be attended to in the search for clues to the solution of historical problems presented in Acts.[2]

In whatever way or ways one seeks to relate Acts to Paul's letters, it should never be forgotten that Acts 13–28 are the concluding part of Luke-Acts and contribute to the overriding purpose or purposes of a document that addresses issues of its own period. By the time Luke-Acts was composed (some 30–40 years after Paul's letters) "the conditions and events, the controversies and conflicting views of the earlier period . . . had given way to new questions, new views, new tasks."[3]

In this chapter it will be assumed that Acts 13–28 should be read as a literary unit. Only when it is important to acknowledge discrepancies or concurrences

Mosaic portrait of Paul from the Baptistry of the Arians in Ravenna, Italy, ca. 493–526 C.E. *(Courtesy of Michael Glazier, Inc. and* Biblical Archeologist.*)*

between events reported in Acts and by Paul will reference be made to the letters. Likewise, in the chapters on Paul's letters (which follow in this book), Acts will not be referred to directly, unless items in its narrative clarify one's understanding of the Apostle's situations prompting his letter writing.

THE COMPOSITION OF ACTS 13–28

The introductory verses of chapter 13 make it quite clear that the story Luke tells is still *the story of what the risen Lord accomplished, through his chosen witnesses and by means of the Holy Spirit*.[4] Christians at Antioch were "worshipping the Lord" when they were directed by the Holy Spirit to proclaim the gospel, just as were the earliest Christians in Jerusalem. "In Jerusalem and in all Judea and Samaria" the apostles had borne their witness; now other disciples received power to proclaim the gospel "to the ends of the earth." The world mission of the Church has its origin in the divine will and prospers under the Holy Spirit's direction.[5]

Although the essential unity of Luke-Acts should not be overlooked, Acts 13 introduces a new series of events. We are told of the first extensive missionary journey undertaken by Paul, a mission which resulted in the opening of "a door of faith to the Gentiles."[6] It is also a church-sponsored mission. Barnabas and Paul were not "free-lancing" missionaries, like Philip and the other "scattered brethren," but representatives of the congregation at Antioch. A single church stood behind the work of Barnabas and Paul and sent them forth with fasting, prayer, and the laying on of hands.

The author of Acts presents the story of Paul's missions in the form of a travel narrative. In addition to describing the chief centers of missionary activity, Luke notes the ports of embarkation (13:4, 13, and so on), landing points (13:5, 13, and so on), and other places to show the direction of the itinerary (14:24 and so on). One influential scholar has argued that this form of the narrative was determined by Luke's "travel diary." For reports of earlier times, in his absence he relied on oral or written traditions, for example, in narrating the "first missionary journey"; yet he cast the whole into the form of his itinerary source, inserting numerous anecdotes and speeches. This compositional pattern was followed in the remainder of the Acts narrative, although the pattern is broken with Paul's arrest in Jerusalem. An alternative theory is that Luke composed the itinerary narrative using another's firsthand account, composed by one of Paul's travel companions, which he edited and, by inserting "we," emphasized the eyewitness character of his source. The occasional disappearance of "we" may simply be the result of Luke's desire at such places to exalt Paul.[7]

Before picking up the thread of Luke's narrative, notice should be taken of prior references to Saul (Paul), a consideration of which was deferred in our earlier studies of Acts (Chapters 1 through 12).

THE ACTS STORY OF PAUL'S CONVERSION AND EARLY EXPERIENCES

"And Saul was consenting to his [Stephen's] death." Thus Luke introduces the man of Tarsus.[8] We are also told that Saul (Paul) zealously took part in the persecution that Stephen's martyrdom touched off in Jerusalem. "Entering house after house," Paul dragged both men and women "to prison." So bent was he upon extending the persecution of Christians beyond Jerusalem that he gained letters from the high priest and journeyed to Damascus.

What actually took place on the Damascus road is a mystery that becomes no less one by appealing to so-called parallels in the phenomenology of religious mysticism or to psychologists' data concerning visions and auditions. Luke's story in Acts 9:3–9, recounted in 22:6–11 and again in 26:12–18, reveals the extraordinary importance that the author assigned to this event. Some light may be shed upon its significance by reconsidering what Luke reports of Paul's experiences before it.

From Luke we learn that Saul was a native of Tarsus, a prominent city of Cilicia, and that by birthright he was a Roman citizen.* Far more important to Saul than his privileged civic and social status was his Jewish heritage. Luke's

*Presumably Paul's father or grandfather

The stoning of Stephen. A tapestry based on a design by the artist Raphael.

description of his hero's birth and early education (Acts 22:3) represents Paul as declaring: "I am a Jew born at Tarsus in Cilicia, but my parental home, where I received my upbringing, was in this city [Jerusalem] where also, under Gamaliel, I received strict training as a Pharisee, so that I was a zealot for God's cause."[9] Luke also locates Paul's spiritual home in one or more of the Greek-speaking synogogues in Jerusalem (note Acts 6:9), where the highly offensive preaching of Stephen, the "Hellenist," led to an outbreak of violence. There Paul became a zealous persecutor of the "sect" represented by Stephen, a fact amply supported by the testimony of Paul's letters. Luke's record provides a circumstantial narrative in agreement with the Apostle's statements that his militancy against those belonging to "the Way" was the measure of his zeal for the Torah and the traditions of the fathers.[10]

A close observer of Luke's thrice-narrated account of Paul's conversion on the Damascus road may recall specific features of ancient biblical stories. We noted earlier that Luke's narratives of the births of John the Baptist and of Jesus reflect Septuagintal models. One scholar has called attention to near parallels in Acts 9, 22, and 26 to the Old Testament narrative form, "the apparition-dia-

had rendered some outstanding service to Rome. The citizen's legal advantages included recourse to a fair and public trial if accused of any crime, exemption from certain degrading forms of physical punishment, and protection against summary execution (Acts 6:37; 22:26). The few Roman citizens of Tarsus constituted a social elite. A. N. Sherwin-White, *The Roman Citizenship* (1973).

logue," which appears in the scriptures in a long and a shorter form. The divine commission is also a feature of the shorter form.[11]

In addition to Luke's use of these traditional forms, one may recognize the influence of the biblical narratives of the calling or commissioning of Israel's prophets.[12] Perhaps Luke was also following literary convention in introducing variations into his parallel accounts, for example, the intensification of the light image and its effects.[13]

If one allows for the presence of these compositional forms and techniques, it follows that the three reports in Acts of Paul's conversion (or, better, his calling) are not to be read as verbal transcripts of what really happened on the Damascus road. Yet it would be a serious error to judge that these narratives are only fictional or legendary. Luke's retrospective view of the significance of Paul's call to mission derives from his own theological perspective. Paul was not (technically) an "apostle" (see p. 68), yet the care with which Luke has composed his narrative places Paul within the company of Christ's incomparable witnesses. It was certainly no part of Luke's purpose to put Paul down, so to speak. By the literary technique of repetition, and of others we have noted, Luke stresses the extraordinary significance of Paul's call. He also illustrates his main theme: the irresistible power of the risen Christ. No less than Paul is Luke concerned to derive the Gentile mission from the divine will—God moved the Gentile mission along by intervening at every crucial stage. Luke, no less than Paul, was concerned with showing that God's promises to the prophets of Israel—that the nation would be the instrument of salvation to the Gentiles—found fulfilment in the missions of Paul (and others).[14]

At first sight it may seem that Luke did not connect the Damascus road revelation and Paul's call to become an apostle to the Gentiles, as Paul clearly did. Only as a consequence of a revelation to Ananias did Paul receive his commission, which later was confirmed by a visionary experience in Jerusalem (Acts 22:12–21). Yet in Luke's third account of Paul's conversion the vision of the risen Jesus is accompanied by the call to mission: Paul is sent to the Gentiles (Acts 26:15–18). It is probable that the full meaning of his calling was not perceived by Paul all at once, but that Luke no less than Paul believed that it was all implicit in the Damascus road "revelation."*

Perhaps it is not possible to trace Paul's activity immediately after his Damascus road experience. Luke knows nothing of a mission to Arabia,[15] but he (rightly) supposes that the Apostle began at once to preach the gospel of Jesus, first in Damascus and not "many days" afterwards, in Jerusalem. Paul was soon forced to flee Judea to save his life. From Caesarea he returned to the city of his birth. Sometime thereafter Barnabas went to the region of Syria and Cilicia, found Paul, and brought him to the Christian congregation at Antioch-on-the-Orontes. Luke's interest in this important Syrian city and the development of its Christian community and missions may afford indirect support for the tradition that he was an Antiochene by birth.[16]

*The term "call" is to be preferred to "conversion," since the latter term is misleading. Paul was not rescued from an immoral life (as penitent sinner); nor (in his view) from one religion, Judaism, to another, Christianity, but from one kind of devotion, from one way of honoring God—that of obedience to Torah—to another kind of devotion, to another way of honoring the same God—that of obedience to Christ as Lord.

H. Mission to Cyprus and Galatia ("the first missionary journey") 13:1–14:28
　　1. The commissioning of Barnabas and Paul, 13:1–4
　　2. Mission on the isle of Cyprus, 13:5–12
　　3. The mainland mission begins, 13:13–14a

"The street called Straight . . ." (Acts 9:11). In a house located on this ancient street in Damascus, Saul (Paul) awaited Ananias, who restored the stricken man's sight and spoke of Paul's missions to the Gentiles. *(Courtesy of the* Biblical Archaeologist.*)*

The choice of Cyprus as the launching point of the mission from Antioch may have been derived from the wish of Barnabas to return to his homeland. But Luke's interest does not dwell upon the advantage that previous contacts might have afforded. One episode is singled out for attention. The very first Roman official whom Paul encountered was favorably disposed toward hearing "the word of God." In spite of the opposition of "a Jewish false prophet," the proconsul of Cyprus, Sergius Paulus, believed. Similar reactions to Paul's preaching are reported over and over again.[17] The Apostle's troubles did not originate from the custodians of the Roman peace or from the Gentile population, but from the Jews. Paul and his companions regularly went first to the synagogue, not merely out of convenience, but because they were convinced that "it was necessary" that the word of God should be spoken first to the Jews.[18] The people of God must not have any grounds for complaint or for excusing themselves.[19] Following the violent opposition of "unbelieving Jews" to those who offered them divine forgiveness, Paul and his party turned to the Gentiles.[20]

It is doubtful that Acts 13:16–41 represents a free composition. We have seen that the resemblance of this speech to those of Peter has led many scholars to consider that it too is a summary of the original gospel of the Church. At the same time, the Pisidian Antioch sermon is peculiarly appropriate to the occasion and contains a few distinctive Pauline features. Luke had more than oral and written versions of typical early sermons to guide him. He had heard Paul preach to Jews and Greeks in the synagogues of the Diaspora.[21]

The reactions of persons at Iconium and Lystra to the first Christian missionaries are consistent with the reputation of the peoples of this region. The Phrygians were highly emotional folk, easily excited to mob action and to mass movements. When Paul and his associates left the city of Antioch for the outlying districts, they showed great courage. They were almost lynched in Iconium, and at Lystra a very different but equally dangerous enthusiasm was manifested. According to an old legend, Zeus and Hermes had once visited the earth in disguise. None of the Phrygians had given them hospitality, with the exception of an old man and his wife. As a result the entire population was destroyed, but the two peasants were transformed into great trees when they died. The people of Lystra must have thought that history was being repeated, that Barnabas and Paul were the gods incognito. The ancient mistake would not be made over again.[22]

In appealing to the people of Lystra to abandon their idolatrous beliefs and practices, Paul argued from nature to nature's God. To the Jew, God's goodness was revealed in His patience in withholding His judgments upon evil men in history. But among pagans, who did not consider that history was ordered by a divine providence, the power and mysteries of nature awakened religious awe.

Paul argued that the beneficent aspects of nature disclosed the claims of a Creator upon His creation.

Note the contrast between the attitudes of the volatile crowds in verses 18 and 19. From offering sacrifices to throwing stones certainly shows a radical change of heart on the part of the crowd. But the most remarkable feature of this story is the courage of Paul. Nearly dead from the pummeling, he spent the night in the city, and after a brief visit to Derbe, came back to Lystra to "strengthen the souls of the disciples."

In Acts 13 and 14 we read of church-sponsored missionaries, moved by the Holy Spirit in a high moment of worship, going forth with the full support of their people. Wherever possible, the gospel is proclaimed by them against the background of the story of salvation revealed in the Old Testament.[23] At other times advantage is taken of some local custom, belief, or situation, and converts are offered salvation but not security.[24] Guidance is given new disciples in organizing themselves, but such steps are taken in the atmosphere of worship, turning the confidence of young churches away from human founders to the Lord. From first to last, Luke represents the Christian mission as the work of "a living God."*

> I. The Jerusalem Conference on the "Gentile Question," 15:1–35
>   1. Judean Christians pressure Antiochenes to require circumcision, 15:1
>   2. Conference in Jerusalem convened 15:6
>   3. Peter's speech, 15:7–11
>   4. Summary: the report of Paul and Barnabas, 15:12
>   5. The speech of James, 15:13–21
>   6. The Apostolic Decree adopted, 15:22–31
>   7. Antioch given instruction, 15:32–35

The narrative of Acts 15 has attracted an extraordinary interest, chiefly because of the importance of the events it reports, but also because Paul's account of an apostolic council or conference, which he details in his Letter to the Galatians, contains statements that are difficult if not impossible to reconcile with Luke's narrative. These discrepancies have placed serious obstacles to historical reconstruction, not the least for establishing the chronology of the life and letters of Paul. But first let us attend to Luke's version. What significance does Luke assign to the episode reported in chapter 15, what is its relation to the scheme of Acts?

Up to this point in Luke's narrative all roads have led to Jerusalem. "Wherever Christianity is implanted, the town or region concerned is in one way or another subordinated to the capital of Judea," and to the apostles, the eyewitnesses of Jesus' ministry and of his resurrection.[25] Chapter 15, which stands at the exact midpoint of Luke's narrative, marks several deliberate shifts. Peter and the other original "apostles" make their last appearance here. Henceforth they are replaced by James, the brother of Jesus, and by "the elders."[26] But the most important change is the shift from the Antiochene missions of Barnabas and Saul to the independent mission of Paul and his co-workers.[27] The stage is set for a decisive forward movement of the Gentile mission by the council convened in Jerusalem and by the decision to endorse Paul's gospel and to reject the position of the "Judaists," or "Judaizers," who were demanding

*It is sometimes said that Luke's account of the so-called "first missionary journey" was intended to epitomize the whole Pauline mission, or that Acts 13:13–52 served to summarize Paul's preaching and experiences in Syria and Cilicia and possibly in adjoining areas, during the "fourteen years" (Gal. 2:1) after Paul's first visit to Jerusalem following the Damascus road event (in lieu of reliable sources). Acts 13–14 is plausibly based on pre-Lukan material from Antioch.

PAUL'S VISITS TO JERUSALEM
(reported in Galatians 1–2, Acts 9:26ff.)

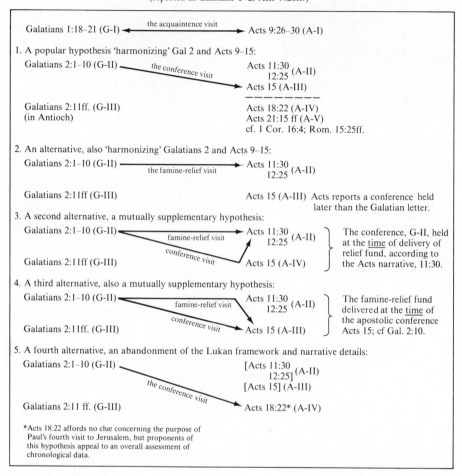

Galatians 1:18–21 (G-I) ◄——— the acquaintence visit ———► Acts 9:26–30 (A-I)

1. A popular hypothesis 'harmonizing' Gal 2 and Acts 9–15:

Galatians 2:1–10 (G-II) ——— the conference visit ——► Acts 11:30
12:25 (A-II)
► Acts 15 (A-III)

Galatians 2:11ff. (G-III)   Acts 18:22 (A-IV)
(in Antioch)   Acts 21:15 ff (A-V)
                                 cf. 1 Cor. 16:4; Rom. 15:25ff.

2. An alternative, also 'harmonizing' Galatians 2 and Acts 9–15:

Galatians 2:1–10 (G-II) ——— the famine-relief visit ——► Acts 11:30
12:25 (A-II)

Galatians 2:11ff (G-III)   Acts 15 (A-III) Acts reports a conference held
                                 later than the Galatian letter.

3. A second alternative, a mutually supplementary hypothesis:

Galatians 2:1–10 (G-II) ◄—— famine-relief visit ——► Acts 11:30
12:25 (A-II)   ⎫ The conference, G-II, held
Galatians 2:11ff (G-III) —— conference visit ——► Acts 15 (A-IV)   ⎬ at the <u>time</u> of delivery of
                                                                   relief fund, according to
                                                                 ⎭ the Acts narrative, 11:30.

4. A third alternative, also a mutually supplementary hypothesis:

Galatians 2:1–10 (G-II) ◄—— famine-relief visit ——► Acts 11:30
12:25 (A-II)   ⎫ The famine-relief fund
Galatians 2:11ff. (G-III) —— conference visit ——► Acts 15 (A-III)   ⎬ delivered at the <u>time</u> of
                                                                     the apostolic conference
                                                                   ⎭ Acts 15; cf Gal. 2:10.

5. A fourth alternative, an abandonment of the Lukan framework and narrative details:

Galatians 2:1–10 (G-II)   [Acts 11:30
12:25] (A-II)
[Acts 15] (A-III)
Galatians 2:11 ff. (G-III) —— the conference visit ——► Acts 18:22* (A-IV)

*Acts 18:22 affords no clue concerning the purpose of
Paul's fourth visit to Jerusalem, but proponents of
this hypothesis appeal to an overall assessment of
chronological data.

that all male converts receive circumcision as a prerequisite to "salvation." According to Luke, the conversion of Cornelius (confirmed by a "second Pentecost") was a sufficient precedent for the council's decision. Having won the major battle with the Judaists, Paul and the Antiochenes endorsed the decree introduced by James as a means of facilitating fellowship between Jewish and Gentile Christians.

Brief notice must now be taken of the historical problems resulting from the alleged discrepancies in the two more-or-less parallel accounts, Acts 9–15 and Galatians 1–2. Synchronization of the sources can begin with the independent reports of Paul's first visit to Jerusalem following his conversion Acts 9:26–30; Galatians 1:18–21; the so-called "acquaintance visit." Beyond this point the sources differ as to the number and purpose of Paul's visits to Jerusalem. Luke reports four additional visits—11:27–30; 15:1ff.; 18:22; and 21:15ff. In his Galatian letter Paul "swears" (1:20) that at the time of his second visit to Jerusalem "fourteen years," later he laid before the apostles the gospel that he preached among the Gentiles (2:1ff.) and received their endorsement.

Numerous hypotheses have been advanced to relate the data provided by the two sources. Few persons have wished to contest the principle that Paul's report is to be favored where there is evidence of conflicting testimony, but while some have concluded that the two sources are irreconcilable and that Luke is in error, others are persuaded that in important ways the accounts of Paul and of Luke are mutually supplementary (although a recovery of the actual course of events is an acute problem for any two-source hypothesis).[28]

One "solution" (A) preserves the framework of Luke and much of the data in the two sources by distinguishing between a "conference visit," described by Paul in Galatians 2:1–10 (which it is supposed occurred during "the famine-relief visit," Acts 11:27–30), and "the apostolic assembly visit" reported only in Acts 15. The absence of any reference in Galatians to the Jerusalem "assembly" is explained by the conjecture that the mission and letter to the Galatians predated the assembly. The expansion of the Gentile churches (Acts 13–14) and the agitation caused by the presence at Antioch of certain "men from James," gave rise to the controversy reported in Galatians 2:11ff and led to the convening of the assembly and the Antiochenes' acceptance of "the apostolic decree" (Acts 15).[29]

This attractive "solution" is not without its difficulties. The identification of Acts 11 and Galatians 2 (A-II = G-II, see the first and "second alternatives"), severely compresses the seventeen-year span from Paul's conversion (which could hardly have been earlier than 33 C.E.) to the famine-relief visit (ca. 43–45?; note Galatians 1:18; 2:1). Of course, Acts 11 makes no reference to a conference of Paul and Barnabas with James, Cephas, and John reported in Galatians 2:1ff., and Galatians 2:10 scarcely alludes to the relief mission of Acts 11.

This "solution" (2) introduces the anomaly of a double apostolic conference, first Galatians 2:1–10, and later Acts 15. It also proposes an earlier date for the Letter to the Galatians than most would assign. A further difficulty arises for the defenders of this "solution" who date the apostolic assembly ca. 48 or 49 C.E. The result is that an insufficient interval of time is allowed for Paul's activities from the beginning of his "second missionary journey" (Acts 15:36ff.) to his mission in Corinth and his arraignment before Gallio (Acts 18:1–18).[30]

Perhaps the most popular "solution" is the equation of Galatians 2:1–10 and Acts 15, "solution" (1) which retains some data gleaned from Acts but less than solutions (2) and (3). Advocates of this hypothesis usually assume at the outset that Paul was right in designating "the conference visit" his second, and that Luke was in error in associating Paul with the famine-relief delegation.[31]

Turning to the two accounts of the meeting with the apostles, it would seem at first sight that Acts 15:2f. is not compatible with Galatians 2:2 (1). Yet Paul's interest may have been to score the point that "it was not the word of a community but a divine command which caused him to undertake the difficult journey to Jerusalem."[32] While the meeting Luke describes is not a private conference, doubtless Paul understood that the real business was to reach agreement with James, Cephas, and John.

The most serious discrepancy is the adoption of "the apostolic decree" (Acts 15:19–21). Paul's declaration in Galatians 2:6 that "those who were of repute added nothing to me," excludes the possibility that the "decree" derives from this conference. It probably was drafted later in Jerusalem, without Paul's collaboration and was a compromise prompted by the dispute in Antioch and intended to ensure that fellowship between Jewish and Gentile Christians be maintained.[33]

"Solutions" (1) and (4) involve difficulties with respect to relative dating. If Paul arrived in Corinth early in 50 C.E., the apostolic assembly must have been sufficiently early to accomodate the land and sea journeys detailed in Acts 15:36 to 18:18 (ca. 46 or 47 C.E.). Also, working backward from 50 C.E., there is insufficient room for the seventeen years separating Paul's conversion and the conference.[34]

One other "solution" (5) can be noted, which in effect rejects the Lucan framework of five visits and relates the two visits of Paul to Jerusalem reported in Galatians to evidence gleaned from other letters of Paul; from the writings of Josephus and Roman historians; inscriptions, and so forth (including incidental notes from Acts). The actual setting for the apostolic conference, according to "solution" (5) is "the strangely compressed account of the trip 'up' to Jerusalem in Acts 18:22."[35] By dating the conference according to this scheme, the itinerary of Paul from Jerusalem to Corinth is accomodated, and also the full seventeen years from Paul's conversion to the conference. Moreover, the curious popular opinion of early, "silent years" (and of late, "too-crowded years") is somewhat alleviated.*

* Paul's conversion (Gal. 1:15) 34 C.E.; 3-year interval (Gal. 1:18) 34–37; Escape from Damascus (2 Cor. 11:32f.) late 37; First Jerusalem visit (Gal. 1:18f.) late 37; 14-year period—Cilicia, Cyprus, etc. (Gal. 1:21; 2:1) 37–51; Paul's arrival in Corinth (1 Cor. 1:1ff., 16:1ff.) Early 50; Departure from Corinth, Late 51; Apostolic conference (Gal. 2:1–10) late 51; Conroversy with Peter in Antioch (Gal. 2:11ff.) 51–52.

Although this "experimental" hypothesis has a number of attractive features, it is doubtful that its hypercritical treatment of Acts 9–15 will commend it to most readers of the New Testament. Some form of the "solution G-II = A-III," (1) or (4), which acknowledges the limitation of Luke's sources, seems more satisfactory, but none are without difficulties.

In reading Acts or Galatians it is important to keep the following in mind. There is no doubt about the final outcome of the debate in the early Church concerning the terms of admission for Gentiles. Nor is there any serious difference of opinion concerning the significance of this historic decision for the future of Christianity; both Paul and Luke, in different ways, let us see this.

What was this so-called "Gentile Question?" Some of the Jewish Christians of Jerusalem insisted that Gentile converts to Christianity should be circumcised. These Judaists, or Judaizers, held that until God's commandment is fulfilled, no assurance of salvation ought to be given to any male received into the Church.[36] Christian baptism was not a substitute for circumcision, any more than was Jewish baptism of Gentile proselytes in the synagogues. Circumcision was *the* sign of membership in the covenant community and the condition of God's convenanted mercies.

The fact that some of the first Christians championed this position is significant. But it was not a view by only a handful of Jewish Christians in Jerusalem. Paul's letters, especially the Letter to the Galatians, reveal that there were advocates of circumcision in Christian churches of the Diaspora.[37]

There was another aspect of the Gentile Question. The Judaizers also insisted upon the continuing authority of the food laws of the books of Moses. They probably did not teach that Gentile converts were bound to observe all of these dietary regulations in order to be saved. But Paul was surely right in concluding that so long as distinctions were drawn between "clean" foods and "unclean" foods, Gentiles were being compelled "to live like Jews."[38] Christian communities would become hopelessly segregated, and the vision of a community in which Jew and Greek would be brothers in Christ would be an empty dream. Also, by refusing to eat with Gentiles, Jewish Christians were guilty of insincerity; they were denying by their actions their pretensions to equality and unity in the Church.[39]

Without Paul's version of the great debate in Galatians 1 and 2, the reader of Acts 15 might fail to see that there is any connection at all between the stated purpose of the Jerusalem Conference and the final "decree." Yet it is clear from Galatians that the two issues of circumcision and the observance of Jewish food laws were closely related. Both involved the fundamental question: Upon what does salvation rest according to the Christian gospel?[40] Is salvation ultimately the reward for a righteousness achieved in obedience to Law? Or does full assurance of salvation depend upon the glad response of faith to the proclamation of God's saving action in Christ?

Paul saw much more clearly than did anyone else this fundamental issue. If the position of the Judaizers had been adopted, believers in Jesus as the Christ would have been confined to a sect *within* Judaism. The practical effect of their demands would have been to force Gentiles to become Jews in the course of becoming Christians. The new mission to the Gentiles, begun by the Antioch congregation and spreading so rapidly, would have been set back. But more important than the practical handicap imposed upon subsequent missions to the Gentiles was the threat to the gospel itself. Paul was convinced that if a works-righteousness was accommodated to the Christian message of salvation, the cross of Christ would no longer effect its saving power. If salvation was to be won by obedience to the Law "then Christ died to no purpose."[41]

> J. Mission to Macedonia and Achaia ("The second missionary journey") 15:36–18:18
> 1. An altercation over John Mark, 15:36–40
> 2. Summary: Paul revisits churches; is joined by Timothy at Lystra, 15:41–16:5
> 3. Paul is guided to Macedonia, 16:6–10 (Note introduction of "travel diary.")
> 4. At Philippi: Lydia's conversion; a slave girl is healed; Paul and Silas are beaten and jailed; the deliverance and public apology, 16:11–40
> 5. At Thessalonica and Beroea: a summary of the missions, 17:1–15
> 6. Paul at Athens; awaits Silas and Timothy, 17:16–21
> 7. Paul's speech in the Areopagus, 17:22–34
> 8. At Corinth: Paul lives, works with Aquila and Priscilla; preaches in the home of a "God-fearer"; is arraigned before Gallio, 18:1–18

When Paul set sail from Troas for Macedonia he carried the gospel of Jesus Christ from one continent to another.[42] Of course the map of Paul's world was not the same as that of today's. The Romans referred to the Mediterranean as *Mare Nostrum* (our sea), and the crossing of the Aegean was from one province of the Roman Empire to another. Nevertheless, the modern reader can realize the dramatic significance of Paul's penetrations westward into regions destined to become a part of modern Europe.

Paul and Barnabas parted company at the outset of the "second missionary journey." Paul argued that John Mark should be left behind this time.[43] How could such a relatively small matter lead to "sharp contention" between friends of long standing? In his Galatian letter Paul wrote that Barnabas as well as Peter had been rebuked for shrinking from table fellowship with Gentiles. Perhaps the dispute over Mark ruffled feelings that were already severely strained.[44]

On this mission Paul journeyed overland to the Galatian cities. Silas (Roman name, Silvanus) was his companion, and another helper, Timothy, joined them at Lystra. In order to avoid needless antagonisms Paul circumcised Timothy "because of the Jews." It was no sacrifice of principle to circumcise a half-Jew, and it was expedient to do so since Timothy would be visiting Jewish synagogues with Paul.[45]

The brief notices of Paul's northward and northwesterly trip toward Troas have led to a variety of speculations.[46] Luke was interested only in stressing that the mission to Macedonia represented an urgent, divine call. Some plans had to be given up in order to follow the leadership of the Holy Spirit.

A woman was Paul's first convert on the soil of Europe. Lydia was one of the highminded women of the Gentile society who had been attracted to Judaism. In Philippi the Jews met outside the city gate, by the river where the ceremonial washings could take place. It cannot be said for certain whether a synagogue was located there. But to this accustomed place of worship came Paul on the Sabbath and "spoke to the women who had come together." It is clear from Luke's identification of Lydia and from the nature of her gracious invitation to the Christian missionaries that she was a wealthy merchant. While it is true that Christianity held an attraction for the depressed classes of Roman society, persons from the top of the social scale also became converts.

In view of Paul's cordial relations with the Philippians one might wish that more details relating to the Apostle's establishment of this church had been reported (see p. 361f.). But the author wishes only to show how Paul's stay at Philippi ended.[47] The story of the healing of the mad slave girl is told with consummate artistry. People of the ancient world were curiously fascinated by insane persons. It was supposed that the gods had deprived such folk of their sanity in order to make them their spokesmen.

The mob's attack upon Paul and Silas was violent and disorderly. The missionaries may have thought it pointless to protest brutal treatment. Legal proceedings might result in long delays and restrictions upon their freedom of movement. Only when the situation became desperate did Paul appeal to Caesar.

The author's comment upon the bearing of Paul and Silas in the inner prison is indeed moving. No wonder "the prisoners were listening to them."[48] Freakish earthquakes were common enough in this region, we are told, and when we put out of mind modern penal establishments and consider the typical wooden-beam dungeons of the period, there is no reason to deny that there is a kernel of fact in this dramatic story. At any rate, it is not the miraculous aspect of the story that interests Luke, but the effect of the courage and the responsible action of his prisoners upon the Philippian jailer. Filled with a shuddering fear, and knowing that his life was no longer worth anything, the jailer was ready to commit suicide. Whatever, the jailer meant by his "Save me!" the apostles took him at his word. They offered him a salvation not from punishment for a supposed dereliction of duty, but for life eternal.

Let no reader suppose that Paul's wounded pride led him to demand a police escort out of the city.[49] For the sake of the gospel, the Philippian Christians (and Theophilus?) it was important that the missionaries be vindicated of charges that they had breached Roman law.

The winning of converts in Thessalonica brought further opposition from the Jews, who stirred up the mobs against the apostles, depicting them as aliens and insurrectionists.[50] In the uproar that followed, the city authorities intervened and the apostles were urged to move on to another place.

At Beroea, the apostles were more favorably received. Luke notes (with a probable appeal to Theophilus) that confirmation of the gospel is to be sought by "examining the scriptures." Some Jews at Beroea gave an intelligent response to this argument from the Old Testament. They recognized that the gospel provided a key to the unity of the Bible and its message: the crucified Christ fulfils the Old Testament drama of salvation; and the cross itself is to be understood in the light of God's mighty acts in that history that led up to it.[51] Ironically, at Beroea Paul was subjected to persecutions like those he had given others; Jews from Thessalonica came to persecute the Christians, following the same course that Paul had determined to follow as a zealous Pharisee in his journey to Damascus. In the face of his antagonists, Paul must have seen his former self. The critical situation that developed at Beroea led to a temporary separation of Paul, Silas, and Timothy. Paul, we are told, was carried to Athens.[52]

Our imagination is quickened by the thought of Paul in the Athenian *agora* (marketplace) with its architectural gems and its monuments to the heroes and the gods. Just so, Luke's imagination must have been stirred. The Areopagus speech provides primary evidence of important aspects of Luke's theology. Neither in its style nor in its content does this sermon correspond to the gospel Paul proclaims in his letters. Is it possible that Paul would have claimed common ground between himself and the popular beliefs of his listeners? For example, where in his letters does Paul hold to the Stoic thesis that men are by nature akin to God?[53]

It is too much to claim that Paul's mission to Athens is derived from an eyewitness account, and that this speech is a verbatim report. Yet some scholars claim that the difficulties in the way of accepting the substantial historicity of Luke's narrative at this point have been exaggerated.[54]

Luke mentions three types of response to Paul's preaching at Athens. in the first place, we are told that "some mocked."[55] The Epicurean and Stoic philosophers would probably be among this number. They contemptuously dismissed his ideas as a throwing together of scraps of learning picked up hither and yon.[56] When Paul proclaimed "Jesus and the resurrection," some supposed that he spoke of *foreign* divinities."[57] Finally, we notice that "some men joined him [Paul] and believed": an aristocrat named Dionysius, a woman named Damaris, and "others with them."[58]

Since there is no reference to a Christian church at Athens in New Testa-

A view of Athens toward the northeast. On the right, the Areopagus (Mars' Hill) and the Acropolis; at the center lay the agora. The distant side of the marketplace was closed by the Stoa of Attalos (see p. 264). *(Courtesy of the American School of Classical Studies, Athens.)*

ment times, it would seem that whatever the results of Paul's visit there, they were ephemeral. The intellectual atmosphere in Athens encouraged the novelty of ideas, talk, not personal commitment.

While waiting at Corinth for the arrival of Silas and Timothy from Macedonia, "Paul was occupied with preaching."[59] Luke's portrayal corresponds with the impression one gains from reading Paul's letters. Tireless and unwilling to wait for one situation to become stabilized before starting other ventures, Paul seldom missed opportunities to proclaim the good news of Jesus Christ. Perhaps, as Paul wrote to the Corinthians later, he was spurred on to activity by his belief that "the appointed time has grown very short," that the "form of this world is passing away."[60] But it is more likely that the essential sanction for Paul's perseverance was the fact that he was constantly under the control of Christ's love for all men.[61]

A sidelight upon Paul's personality is afforded in the reference to his move from the synagogue to the house of Titius Justus next door. Perhaps Luke wished to show that although Paul reacted in a conventional way to the Jews who "opposed and reviled him," he did not abandon his kinsmen by race. The Jews and the God-fearers who frequented the synagogues had to be given every opportunity to hear and heed the gospel. It must have been galling to the Jews that "Crispus, the ruler of the synagogue, believed in the Lord." Continuing to preach within the shadow of the synagogue, Paul must have faced daily the scowling countenances of his enemies. Luke reports that the Lord was revealed to Paul in order that his fears of bodily harm might be allayed.[62]

Gallio, the proconsul of Achaia, saw through the tissue of trumped-up charges brought against Paul. He was not going to be imposed upon, nor was he willing to begin his rule in the region with a religious squabble. The incident is entirely credible: the roughing-up of Sosthenes by onlookers who are encouraged by Gallio's snub; Gallio's indifference to—perhaps amusement over—the commotion that followed. Gallio's judgment was not to be swayed by mob scenes.[63]

As usual, Luke brought his narrative of Paul's activities in one city to a close with a public notice and a general disturbance. But this time the reason for Paul's departure is not given. Did Paul leave Corinth on his own initiative to visit Jerusalem at the Passover season?

> K. Mission of Paul to Asia: The Ephesian Ministry ("the third missionary journey") 18:19–20:38
> 1. Brief visits to Ephesus, Jerusalem, Syrian Antioch, 18:19–22
> 2. Summary: Paul visits Galatian and Phrygian disciples, 18:23
> 3. Apollos at Ephesus, 18:24–28
> 4. Paul's preaching accompanied by "a new Pentecost," 19:1–7
> 5. Summary: the more than two-year Ephesian ministry, 19:8–12
> 6. Paul and the Jewish exorcists, 19:13–16
> 7. Summary: public book burnings, 19:17–20
> 8. The Roman journey projected, 19:21f.
> 9. The riot in the theater, 19:23–41
> 10. Brief visits to Macedonian and Achaian churches, 20:1–6 ("the travel diary" resumed, 20:5ff.)
> 11. Paul in Troas; a near-tragic accident, 20:7–12
> 12. Plans in the light of Pentecost, 20:13–16
> 13. Paul's farewell speech to the Ephesian elders, 20:17–38

When Paul received the call to become an apostle of Jesus Christ he did not consider that he ceased being a Jew. The gospel was not antithetic to the religion of Israel but a development and final expression of its revealed truths. Luke correctly reported that although Paul vigorously championed the freedom of the Gentiles concerning the requirements of the Law, he still honored many of them. No longer did his salvation, nor that of any man, depend on obedience to its letter, but the Law contained divinely sanctioned religious customs as well as moral commandments. "At Cenchreae," Paul "cut his hair, for he had a vow."[64]

With Acts 18:23 the story of Paul's "third missionary journey" begins. One wishes that Luke had reported beforehand the nature of Paul's receptions at Jerusalem and Antioch. Were relations with the leaders of these churches further strained at this time?[65] Luke seems impatient to get Paul back to the mission field, to tell of his experiences at Ephesus, the principal city of the Roman

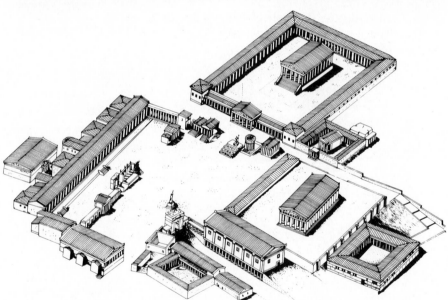

Above, ruins of the ancient city of Corinth viewed from the east, with Acrocorinth rising to the southwest. *Below,* an artist's reconstruction of the agora, 50 C.E., based on a plan drawn up by C. K. Williams, director of the Corinth excavations. The south stoa (far left) housed the city council chamber, headquarters for the Isthmian games, shops, etc.; the central terrace, running somewhat parallel to this stoa, contained the bema (tribunal) and other shops. According to Acts, Paul stood on the pavement before Gallio, the proconsul, who gave Paul's accusers a brief scolding from the bema (18:12–17). *(Photos courtesy of the American School of Classical Studies, Athens, and J. Murphy-O'Connor.)*

province of Asia. But before he does this, he introduces Apollos, a brilliant Alexandrian who knew something about Christianity, but whose experiences had been limited. "He knew only the baptism of John," we are told.[66] This expression is cryptic. Perhaps Apollos knew a tradition that declared John and Jesus were heralds of the coming kingdom of God, preachers of repentance. Like them, Apollos preached with eloquence and power concerning the coming judgment, and the heroic ethic required of those who were to share in the new age. But one thing Apollos lacked. He did not know that the Christ had come, that the new age had dawned, and that persons who were baptized "in the name of Jesus," as Christ and as Lord, were experiencing the very thing that had been promised—the power of the Holy Spirit.[67]

Paul labored in Ephesus for two or three years, preaching daily in "the hall of Tyrannus." As we have noted earlier, Luke seemed especially interested that Paul's ministry was marked with the same evidence of divine favor as had marked Peter's ministry in Jerusalem. Special notice is taken of the fact that "a number of those who practiced magic arts brought their books together and burned them in the sight of all."[68] According to several Latin and Greek authors, Ephesus was known the world over for its magic books, the "Ephesian Letters." It was thought that they would ensure safe journeys, success in love and business, and so forth. The public "book burning" in Ephesus doubtless created quite a stir.*

Before narrating the threatening demonstration in the theater, Luke noted Paul's plan upon leaving Ephesus. A determination to revisit Jerusalem has top priority. Eventually he "must also see Rome"; but first, Palestine.[69] "After the uproar ceased," Paul departed for Macedonia and Achaia. From Luke's brief notices it might be surmised that Paul's purpose was to give further encouragement to his young churches, but from letters written at this time it is learned that the Apostle's real purpose was to bring to completion a project dear to his heart, the collection of monies to alleviate "the poor" in the Jerusalem church.[70] From Paul's Letter to the Romans (probably written during the "three months" spent in Greece),[71] it is learned that the collection was completed and Paul, accompanied by representatives of the contributing churches, was ready to deliver to the saints in Jerusalem "what has been raised."[72]

It is strange that at this point, and subsequently in his narrative of the visit to Jerusalem of Paul and his Gentile delegation, Luke makes only an unclear reference to this collection (24:17). Possibly Luke knew nothing of this project and of its relation to Paul's purpose in undertaking this hazardous journey, but it is probable that Luke "intentionally suppressed any obvious mention" of the collection. Luke may well have feared that Theophilus would regard this transport of substantial sums of money as an illegal operation, ground for official suspicion of Christian missions. Perhaps in view of Rome's special concession to the Jews, allowing for the transport of the temple tax,[73] Luke "tersely portrayed the collection in Acts 24:17 as the delivery of religious contributions recognized as legally permitted."[74]

A plot against his life prevented Paul from realizing his hope of arriving in Jerusalem for the Passover. He determined if possible to make it for the day of Pentecost.[75] From Miletus (about thirty miles from Ephesus) Paul sent for the elders of the Ephesian church. Paul's words with his friends are, from one point

* Scant information is given about Paul's relatively lengthy ministry in Ephesus, although what Luke reports is of great value (Cadbury, *The Book of Acts in History*, pp. 41ff.) It is often assumed from notices in the Corinthian letters that Paul was imprisoned at least once in Ephesus (1 Cor. 15:30–32; 2 Cor. 1:8–11), and that during this imprisonment he wrote Philippians, Philemon, and (if by Paul) Colossians. Galatians is also dated during the Ephesian ministry, and Romans at its close.

Ephesus. *(Above)* Ruins of the Roman theater, site of the riot instigated by Demetrius in protest against the results of Paul's mission in the city (Acts 19:23ff.). *(Opposite page)* The half-mile road that in ancient times led to the harbor, long since filled with silt. *(Courtesy of Elizabeth Harris.)*

of view, a sad farewell.[76] From another, they are an eloquent apology for his life.[77]

    L. Paul's Last Visit to Jerusalem, 21:1–23:32
        1. The voyage to Palestine; Paul is forewarned, 21:1–7
        2. Paul among the prophets at Caesarea, 21:8–14
        3. James and the elders receive Paul, and give advice, 21:15–26
        4. Paul is dragged from the Temple and mobbed, 21:27–30

In spite of his fears in coming to Jerusalem, Paul did not resign himself to them. He made every effort to disarm the opposition. His friends in Jerusalem were faced with a delicate situation. Rumors had spread that Paul encouraged the Jews to forsake their Law and traditions upon becoming Christians. Paul had to in some way demonstrate his true attitude if he hoped to dispel the ugly rumors concerning him. Four men, we are told, were in the process of observing the Nazarite vow.[78] The time approached for the purchase of the animals and other items to be sacrificed. Perhaps Paul would agree to pay the expenses of the four men.[79]

Paul must have followed the suggestion of James and the elders with considerable reluctance.[80] Such an action could be interpreted as hypocrisy. It is probable that Paul knew that a compromise was necessary, which could be agreed upon without sacrificing his principles. In this case the outcome of Paul's action was disastrous. Asian Jews were responsible for bringing a slanderous charge against Paul.

Whether Paul's antagonists really believed that he had carried into the temple his Gentile companion from Ephesus, Trophimus, or whether the whole thing was trumped-up, we cannot say. It was, of course, a very serious charge, involving a death penalty, and the reaction of the pious Jewish pilgrims, massed in Jerusalem for the festival, was instantaneous.[81] Maltreatment by outraged mobs was nothing new to Paul; however, the anger of the incensed Jews in Jerusalem was a murderous anger. If the Roman tribune (commanding about 1,000 soldiers) had not intervened, Paul would certainly have been lynched.

The tribune suspected that Paul was a notorious criminal, the Egyptian revolutionary who, some time earlier, had marched on Jerusalem with a large force.[82] Paul's Greek speech led the tribune to realize his mistake, and Paul was able to gain his consent to address the mob.

A touch of personal admiration is revealed in the author's comment: "Paul, standing on the steps, motioned with his hands to the people; and when *there was a great hush*, he spoke to them in the Hebrew language. . . ."[83] Tradition has it that Paul was not an impressive man in his physique and appearance.[84]

It is hard to believe that Paul could have spoken formally and at such length to this restive mob. Has Luke introduced proof of Paul's innocence by means of a conventional literary device, the speech? Paul's words are altogether appropriate to the occasion, and even mobs have been known to become quiet when someone yells, "Let the scoundrel have a chance to speak!" Paul stressed his strict loyalty to the Law by identifying himself with the people to whom he spoke. He once stood where they were standing, persecuting men like himself with a zeal no less than their own. It was true that a change had taken place, but Paul argued that he had not abandoned his old faith. He had rather found its fulfillment. The Christ of promise had revealed himself to Paul as being none other than Jesus of Nazareth, risen from the dead. To what conclusion was Paul's defense tending? The question is not answered in Acts, for, with the mention of the word "Gentiles," the smoldering fury of the crowd was fanned into flame.

The view is taken above that Paul acted with prudence in Jerusalem. Some aspects of the story of the "trial" might seem to deny this claim. His defense was not begun in the usual formal manner; he railed out against the court official, "the high priest Ananias."[85] Perhaps he added insult to injury by excusing himself, saying, "I did not know, brethren, that *he* [that a man with his reputation] was the high priest."

There is a kind of reckless abandon in Paul's bearing before the Sanhedrin, sharply contrasted with the regal dignity of Jesus before the same body. "When he [Jesus] was reviled, he reviled not in return; when he suffered, he did not threaten; but he trusted to him who judges justly."[86] It is not surprising that few if any men, even the great Apostle, measure up to Jesus' example. But again let it be said: Paul could not believe that his work was done. Jesus went to Jerusalem expecting his death. Paul was determined to "see Rome."

Perhaps it is from this point of view that one must interpret Paul's words, "Brethren, I am a Pharisee, a son of Pharisees; with respect to the hope of the resurrection of the dead I am on trial."[87] It was a tactic designed to divide the court and to divert the body from the main question before it. The second part of Paul's claim raises a more serious question. He was not on trial concerning the hope of the resurrection. Perhaps Paul decided to throw "an apple of discord" among his judges, to remind them of the enmity existing between themselves, drawing attention away from their common enmity toward him.[88] It is possible that, like Stephen, Paul saw the futility of answering the specific charge brought against him, and that he took the opportunity to call attention to the centrality of the resurrection hope in the Christian gospel.

Sometime during the following night, Luke reported that Paul had had another vision. The Apostle became convinced that "the Lord stood by him," that he would indeed be given opportunity to "bear witness also at Rome."[89] But there is a threatening sequel in the story. Paul's enemies sought by devious means to circumvent "justice." Forty men, in a solemn confederation, planned to kill Paul, but a relative heard of the ambush and tipped him off.

Claudius Lysias recognized his duty and did it. A letter was dispatched to the governor Felix, and asylum provided for Paul at the seat of the Roman government in Palestine, Caesarea. According to the records, Antonius Felix was procurator in Judea from 52 to 59 C.E.[90]

M. Paul in Custody at Caesarea, 23:33–26:32
1. Paul arraigned before Felix; his accusers arrive; Paul defends himself, 23:33–24:21
2. Paul's trial delayed; on several occasions Felix interrogates Paul, 24:22–27
3. Festus suceeds Felix; Paul is charged again; appeals to Caesar, 25:1–12
4. Paul defends himself before king Herod Agrippa, 25:13–26:32

There is every reason to suppose that Felix found himself in a difficult corner. How could he gain from Paul's enemies the true facts of the case? The whole incident had begun in a mob scene; its instigators were unknown. Since they were "Asian Jews" they had probably returned to their homes. The only crime of which Paul was accused that was punishable by death was the charge that he had desecrated the temple. But it would be almost impossible to establish his guilt. If Paul had been "a nobody" Felix could have settled the tiresome affair as he pleased. But Paul was a Roman citizen, and Felix was a "freedman" (according to Tacitus).[91] Hence it was necessary for Felix to proceed with caution. Some degree of freedom was doubtless allowed Paul.[92]

The arrival of the new governor, the procurator Festus, provided another opportunity for Paul's enemies to convict him. A special favor was requested of Festus by the group from Jerusalem: let Paul be returned to the scene of his "crime" for trial. Were the forty men still holding themselves to their vow? Festus, however, was no fool. Let the accusers come to Caesarea, he replied. When he returned, a hearing was set, and Paul was again given an opportunity to defend himself.*

*According to Luke, Paul's apologies stressed the relationship between the Old Testament and the Christian gospel. He argued that the hopes of Judaism found fulfillment in Christ and, that Paul as a Christian Jew, far from forsaking the scriptures, had faithfully honored them. Even in his preaching to the Gentiles he had sought to fulfill the divine mission of the people of Israel. Luke may have been prompted to give so much space to Paul's hearings before governors and other officials since he knew that Theophilus (and readers of his station) would have a particular interest in the attitudes that officialdom had taken toward Paul.

In the months of waiting Paul had not been preparing legal briefs, but the issues had become crystal clear. "Neither against the Law of the Jews, nor against the temple . . . have I offended at all," Paul declared.[93] Since the only matter worthy of investigation was the charge of sedition, there was no warrant for transporting Paul to Jerusalem, and Paul certainly did not desire it. But perhaps Festus was guided by considerations other than logic. Since Felix had been recalled for his inability to govern the Jews, Festus may have been inclined to accede to the Sanhedrin's request. What chance did Paul have in Jerusalem of seeing "justice" done? The situation was indeed desperate. He was therefore forced to seize upon his last defense. He appealed directly to Caesar. A step had now been taken from which there was no turning back.[94]

N. Paul Conducted to Rome by a Centurion: Experiences at Sea Logged by Diarist, 27:1–28:16
    1. Adverse winds make for slow progress, 27:1–8
    2. Paul warns of hazards ahead; other's advice followed, 27:9–13
    3. The violent storm; Paul assuages fears, 27:14–38
    4. All personnel escape onto the island of Malta; Paul not hurt as a viper strikes; islanders are healed, 27:39–28:10
    5. Last leg of the voyage, 28:11–14

Luke's story of Paul's ship foundering in a storm, pounded to pieces upon the shoals, its passengers in the water narrowly escaping with their lives, has fascinating elements of surprise. It is no wonder that readers of Paul's voyage to Rome become absorbed in the nautical or heroic aspects of the story. But the narrative's theological significance ought not to be overlooked. Luke would not have gone to such lengths merely to tell an exciting episode.

By this time, the reader of Acts may have noticed that its ending closely parallels the conclusion of Luke's Gospel. Some have referred to Acts 21:1 as the beginning of "a passion narrative." Like his Lord, Paul went to Jerusalem to be rejected by the Jews, to suffer indignities at their hands, to be examined by the high priest, to be given a hearing before the Roman procurator and the regnant Herod. The storm and shipwreck appear as the nadir of Paul's fortunes.

Yet the hope of reaching Rome was realized after all. The reader is meant to realize that, from first to last, "the acts of the apostles" were wrought by God, in the fulfillment of his saving purpose for mankind in and through Christ and his Church.

Only when such considerations as the above are taken into account is there value in tracing the sea journey of Paul in some detail. Even then the commentator is bound to acknowledge that his own notes can hardly "improve" the narrative. Luke's abilities as a storyteller and historian are demonstrated impressively in the concluding section of Acts.

O. Paul in Rome; for Two Years Under House Arrest, 28:15–31
  1. Paul appeals to Jewish leaders, 28:15–22
  2. Paul's sermon results in a schism; Isaiah's prophecy recalled, 28:23–28(29)
  3. Summary: the two-year ministry in Rome, 28:30f.

When, at long last, Paul arrived in Rome it was "to the Jew first" that he proclaimed the good news of Jesus Christ. One might suppose that after a quarter-century Paul would have abandoned all hope of laboring profitably among the Jews and turned his full attention to the Gentiles. But three days after arriving in Rome, he "called together the local leaders of the Jews."[95] The motive for his persistence is clear: "It is because of the hope of Israel that I am bound with this chain." Israel's hoped-for Messiah had come. This was the theme of Paul's preaching until the end.

No unfavorable report concerning Paul had come to the Jews in Rome, yet it is obvious that they were primed for him. They desired to hear Paul, but they made it plain that they knew that "this sect" (Christianity) was spoken against everywhere. Unable to go to the synagogue, Paul encouraged the Jews to come to his lodgings. There "from morning to evening" he attempted to "convince them about Jesus, both from the law of Moses and from the prophets." Once again there was a mixed reception. The passage that Paul cited from Isaiah was a popular "testimony" in the early Church to account for the resistance of the Jews to the preaching of the Messiah.[96]

It was beyond the scope of the writer's purpose to deal with the fate of Paul after "the two years" he resided in Rome.[97] To Paul these months were a time of opportunity. While waiting to appear before Caesar or for his prosecutors to bring their charge to Rome, he kept right on doing what he had always done. Within the limits imposed upon him, he earned his keep, preached, and taught.[98]

The story of Paul's missions from Jerusalem to Rome ends on a note of victory. In the language of the writer of Acts, "quite openly and unhindered" is one word: *akolutos*. It expressed the faith of Luke, as well as of Paul: nothing could stop the advance of the Christian mission in the world.

THE PURPOSE OF LUKE-ACTS

Thus far no effort has been made to synthesize the interests and objectives of the author of Luke-Acts in order to reach conclusions concerning the purpose or purposes of this massive work. No collation of the theological tendencies revealed in Luke's two volumes has been undertaken. Now that the reading of Luke-Acts is completed consideration can be given to the writer's distinctive aims and beliefs. The more explicit features of Luke-Acts will be recalled, and several problems briefly noted.

In the Gospel part of Luke's narrative Jesus is portrayed as God's anointed one whose coming was foretold by all the prophets from Moses onward. From his birth to his resurrection-ascension, proofs from prophecy interlard the story of Jesus, supporting the Evangelist's proclamation that the salvation of God promised to Israel was truly manifested in his person and ministry. Especially noteworthy is the Gospel's conclusion when the disciples are taught, by the risen Jesus himself, that what had happened to him conformed to what was written in the scriptures about the Messiah.[99]

In Acts, Luke told how the appointed witnesses to Jesus' resurrection-ascension proclaimed this salvation promised to Israel, and proofs from prophecy continue to connect the ancient history of Israel and the story of the apostles' missions, those of Stephen and the Hellenists, and those of Paul. As in the Gospel, so in Acts, Luke undertook to write a sequel to the biblical narrative and, as we have seen, his thoughts were much influenced by the Greek version of the scriptures. Once again, in Acts as in the Gospel, "the sufferings of Christ" are explained as the fulfillment of the scriptures.[100]

A corollary of Luke's theme that, in both the preaching of Christ and in the apostolic *kerygma*, God's promise of salvation to Israel is fulfilled, is the theme of reversal or, as one writer described it, "the turning of tables." This theme, like the other, is anticipated in the nativity story and receives development in the Gospel: the whole ministry of Jesus is designated as "the year of the Lord's favour" (NEB) in which the poor and the captives are released from their plights while the rich and the powerful are humbled; the kingdom of God is given to "the little flock" who share in the "trials" of Jesus, in contrast to Israel's leaders who reject him.[101]

The theme of reversal is also prominent in Acts. Not only are the successes of the apostles made possible by divine intervention,[102] but the adversities of the witnesses to Jesus are turned into miraculous deliverances and result in a further promotion of the gospel.[103]

Another prominent theme in Luke-Acts (again illustrative of the writer's interest in the fulfillment of the scriptures) is that the salvation *of Gentiles* is a necessary consequence of the eschatological action of God's Annointed One, an accompaniment of Israel's renewal and glorification. Isaiah 49:6 is applied to Jesus in the infancy gospel and to Paul in the Acts.[104] "The conclusion of the whole narrative is that the salvation promised to and realized in Israel has been sent to the Gentiles."[105]

It is important to recognize that this scenario—Israel first and after that the Gentiles—is not to be understood as an unsuccessful proclamation to Jews, which thereby compelled the proclamation to Gentiles so that Gentiles form a substitute for the lost people of God. For Luke, "Israel" does not refer to a church made up of Jews and Gentiles, but to the repentant portion of empirical Israel, the Jews who have accepted the gospel.[106] Luke not only stresses the fact that after the resurrection of Jesus salvation was first preached to the Jews but that large numbers did believe.[107] The promises of God to the fathers have thus been fulfilled: Gentiles have been joined to the reconstituted Israel, those from among the sons of Abraham believing in Jesus and receiving forgiveness of sins through his name.

Now it is unlikely that persons with little knowledge of or interest in Judaism would have understood this approach to Christianity or this interpretation of its origin. At least Luke must have been assured that his readers were inclined toward belief in the God worshiped by the Jews and toward a reverence for the scriptures of Israel.

This evidence possibly leads to the conclusion that Luke-Acts was written for those Gentiles who were known to the Jews as "devout" or "God-fearers." Numerous Gentiles were attracted to the monotheistic faith and moral ideals of Judaism. Although they had not become proselytes, they attended the synagogues, "gave alms liberally" to the Jews, and "prayed constantly" to the God of Israel.[108] According to Acts, these God-fearers heard Christians proclaim the gospel in Jewish synagogues. Many had become converts; others had held back.[109] But for the God-fearers among them there were reasons for resistance to the gospel. Did conversion to Christianity mean that a person could no longer worship the God revealed in Israel's scriptures? Had not a large majority of the Jewish nation rejected as blasphemous the claims concerning Jesus? *Was the gospel a corruption or a fulfillment of Israel's hope?*

For Gentiles who had gratefully received from the synagogue the Septuagint, it was a serious matter that the Christian gospel had been rejected by untold numbers within the Jewish nation and that, with the passage of time, the offense had not been overcome. Luke's selection and treatment in Acts of the "fulfilled-among-us" events makes it probable that Theophilus, and the circle of the "devout" he represented belonged to this group. Luke would have his God-fearing readers "know the truth": the rejection of the gospel by many Jews and its acceptance by Gentiles, far from giving cause for offense, was indeed the fulfillment of the scriptures. By the power of His Holy Spirit, God had spoken through the scriptures concerning these "last days," in which the Messiah had been revealed and vindicated, and his disciples inspired to bear faithful witness to his mission. Members of the ancient people of God who had resisted the gospel resisted the Holy Spirit and thereby forfeited their privileges and their inheritance.[110] To accept Jesus as the Messiah and "to continue in the apostles' teaching and fellowship" is truly to revere the scriptures and to inherit the promises made to God's covenant people. It is consistent with this understanding of Luke's purpose that he "does not claim that the church has replaced Israel as the people of God, nor does he call Gentile believers "Abraham's children . . . Luke wants to make it clear beyond doubt that in the course of events due respect has been paid to the priority of Israel . . . The main point would be that the continuity with [Israel's] history has in no way been broken, either by the emerging of Gentile Churches, or by the exclusion of disobedient Jews."[111]

It is probable that another dimension of the purpose of Luke-Acts is revealed in its reports that the earliest Christians were forced to defend themselves before the established order. Several arrests and trial scenes are reported.[112] Luke makes it clear, however, that the Jewish authorities who held their powers under Roman rule were unable to convict the apostles as political offenders. When official action was taken against them, they were vindicated by heavenly visions, or they were released from prison by divine intervention. The judicial death of Herod who "laid violent hands" upon some in the Church is reported, and the conversion of a notorious persecutor. Luke seems sensitive to a political dimension of the religious problem facing persons like Theophilus. He is intent upon resolving misgivings they may have, based on derogatory reports of subversive acts and teachings of Jesus and his followers.

There is some evidence from New Testament books written at the time of the composition of Luke-Acts that the church existed in uneasy tension with Rome. Judaism was an officially recognized religion, but the Christian communities, largely composed of Gentiles, could not take for granted that this toleration would be extended to them. Some scholars have held that the principal purpose of Luke-Acts was the defense of this privilege: Christians are true Jews and thus deserve toleration. The extent to which Luke's narrative was consciously shaped as a "political apology" remains questionable. Yet from his reading of Luke-Acts Theophilus learned that Christians are not only legitimately attached to Israel, but also that Jesus and his followers were innocent of politically subversive activities.[113]

The above evidence supports the conclusion that Luke's primary purpose was to show that in Jesus, the risen and reigning Messiah, God's promises to Israel were being fulfilled: final salvation is granted the repentant "sons of the prophets and of the convenant," and is also proclaimed to Gentiles who call upon the name of the Lord Jesus. In addition a "secondary, but not unimportant aim"— a defense of Christians against the charge of enmity towards Rome—may have influenced Luke's selection and treatment of the gospel and apostolic traditions.*

*In the reading of Luke's Gospel, notice was taken of the Third Evangelist's editing of several Markan and Q passages reporting Jesus' teaching concerning the future. The claim is often made that a principal stimulus for the writing of Luke-Acts was the non-occurrence or delay of Christ's (second) coming. No agreement has been reached, however, concerning the nature of the theological problem facing Luke or his proffered solution.

THE IDENTITY OF THE *AUCTOR AD THEOPHILUM*

The author of the Third Gospel and the Acts was probably "Luke, the beloved physician," a sometime travel companion of the Apostle Paul.[114] He may have joined Paul and Silas on "the second missionary journey" so-called, and later traveled with the Apostle from Troas to Jerusalem, and still later, from Caesarea to Rome, for in narrating these itineraries the author includes himself, employing the first person plural.[115] The traditional (probably correct) explanation for the appearances of the personal pronoun "we" in the travel account is that Luke simply wanted to indicate that he was there, and so Theophilus must have understood these notations.[116]

It is sometimes said that the unanimous ancient church tradition concerning authorship could have been deduced from New Testament references in the absence of any external support. But this is hardly the sole basis for the tradition. If it had not been known that a Gospel and the Acts were authored by Luke (hardly a prominent person in the apostolic age), there is no apparent reason why tradition should have associated these writings with him.[117]

The most serious obstacle to acceptance of this tradition of authorship is the presence of discrepancies (some of which have been noted) between the events of Paul's career, and a description of his preaching reported in Acts, and Paul's own statements in his letters. It is often asserted that the "Paulinism" of Acts is substantively different from Paul's theology and renders untenable the idea that a companion of the Apostle could have written Luke-Acts.[118]

Some of the undeniable differences may be the result of Luke's limited acquaintance with Paul. For example, if Luke was not personally involved in Paul's critical struggle with Judaizers, if he had never read Paul's Letter to the Galatians, if he was writing some thirty years after the events and was in possession of insufficient sources, one can account for such differences as do exist. Moreover, it is not unreasonable to suppose that after Luke became a coworker with Paul he might fail to assimilate some aspects of Paul's theology.[119]

Questions of this sort involve a consideration of Luke's heritage and background. For some while the present writer has held that Luke was a Gentile, as ancient church tradition portrays him.[120] Yet Luke's profound knowledge of the scriptures suggest that before his conversion he had embraced Judaism, not as a proselyte but as a God-fearer. We have noted above that it is possible that Luke-Acts was especially directed to God-fearers such as Theophilus represented. We now follow the suggestion of some scholars that formerly Luke himself may have been a God-fearer. The attention that Luke gives to the conversion of Cornelius and to the faith of an unnamed centurion in the Gospel may point inward.[121] Cornelius was known to have been "a devout man who feared God . . . gave alms liberally to 'the people' and prayed constantly to God; the Gospel's centurion is described by Jewish elders as a man who 'loves our nation' and who 'built our synagogue.'"[122] If Luke was formerly a God-fearer, this would explain his knowledge of the scriptures and his interest in "proofs-from-prophecies," his belief in the priority of Israel, his respect for the Law, but also his joy in proclaiming that Gentiles are fully incorporated into the eschatological people of God without the requirement of circumcision.

While it is true that many concede "that the question of authorship is almost incapable of solution,"[123] it would seem that "most of the arguments brought forth in modern times to substantiate the distance of Luke from Paul do not militate against the traditional identification of the author of the Third Gospel and Acts with Luke, the Syrian from Antioch, who had been a sometime collaborator of the Apostle Paul."[124]

NOTES

1. G. Bornkamm, *Paul* (1971), p. xiv.
2. That studies conceived along these lines have often been unsatisfactory should not lead one to conclude that all efforts to fuse the data of Paul's letters and the Acts are without value. An example of a stunning achievment is F. F. Bruce's *Paul: Apostle of the Heart Set Free* (1977).
3. Bornkamm, *Paul*, pp. xv., xiiiff. Beyond question, Paul's letters are authoritative as sources, for his life as well as his thought, providing the primary data. Concerning the supplementary value of Acts the issue throughout is not whether Luke was historian *or* theologian, but whether in addressing contemporary issues Luke the theologian has taken "his bearings on what was for him the authoritative primal age of faith" (Hengel), i.e., whether his narrative of past history effectually served his theological aim(s) without loss of its primary factual ingredients.

4. Acts 1:8.
5. Acts 13: 2,4.
6. Acts 14:27
7. See M. Dibelius, *Studies in the Acts of the Apostles* (1956), pp. 5f., W. L. Knox, *The Acts of the Apostles*, pp. 57f. Cf. E. Haenchen, " 'We' in Acts and the Itinerary," 1, (1965): 65ff. See also p. 302.
8. Acts 8:1. At this point the following passages in Acts should be reread: 8:1–3; 9:1–30; 11:19–30; 12:25.
9. See also Acts 26:4f.; Phil. 3:4f.; Rom. 11:1. Against this Lucan tradition it is sometimes argued that during his formative years Paul lived at Tarsus where he was influenced by Hellenistic-Jewish ideas; that his linkage with Gamaliel (I), the son or grandson of Hillel, is mere legend. According to M. Hengel, however, "only in the period after the Bar Kochba rebellion do we hear of the founding of Pharisaic schools outside the Holy Land." It is evident that Paul received formal training as a Pharisee, *Acts and the History of Earliest Christianity* (1980), p. 82. W. C. van Unnik, *Tarsus or Jerusalem: the City of Paul's Youth* (1962) Cf. Bornkamm, *Paul*, pp. 3–12.
10. 1 Cor. 15:9; Gal. 1:13f.; Phil. 3:6. J. Knox's doubt that Jerusalem was the place of Paul's education for the rabbinate *and* of his activity as a persecutor of Christians is unjustified (*Chapters in a Life of Paul* (1954), pp. 34ff.). Paul's statements in Gal. 1:13f. are not specific, but Gal. 1:22 does not imply that Acts 8:3; 22:4; and 26:9–11 are erroneous. F. F. Bruce, *Paul*, pp. 69f.; A. J. Hultgren, "Paul's Pre-Christian Persecutions of the Church: Their Purpose, Locale and Nature, *JBL* 95 (1976): 97ff.
11. Cf. Acts 9:10f., and Gen. 22:1f.; also, 1 Sam. 3:4ff. (LXX).
12. Jer. 1:4f.; Ezek. 2:1ff.; Isa. 6:1ff.; Acts 22:10; 26:16–18. Note that Paul's understanding of his call also reflects the narrative of the call of a prophet to address the nations, cf. Gal. 1:15f., Jer. 1:4f. (Isa. 49:1–6).
13. Acts 9:3f.; 22:6f.; 26:13f. Paul also compared the "revelation" given to him as a light shining out of darkness, 2 Cor. 4:5f. (Col. 1:12–14).
14. Acts 9:10; also 8:26ff.; 9:31; 10:1–11:26; 15:6–9. "Luke constantly drives home the idea that *Christ himself* brought about this change in front"—from its mission to the Jews to its mission to Gentiles. Haenchen, *Acts*, p. 328. Cf. Gal. 1:15f.; "seized by Christ," Phil. 3:12; 1 Cor. 9:16f. J. Dupont, *The Salvation of the Gentiles* (1979), pp. 11–33.
15. Cf. Gal. 1:17.
16. For this tradition and for the importance of Antioch, see Bruce, *Paul*, pp. 130ff. Both canonical sources are wanting in their accounts of Paul's activity from the time of his call to his ministry in Antioch. Both Paul and Luke were interested in Paul's relations to Jerusalem but for different reasons: Paul in reducing to a minimum his connections, Luke in tying Paul as closely to the mother church as possible.
17. Many passages ahead confirm that Luke wanted to emphasize this development, "but we could also look back to the story of Cornelius: the first Gentile convert was actually a Roman officer." Haenchen, *Acts*, pp. 403f.
18. Acts 13:46; cf. Rom 1:16; 9:1–5; 10:1.
19. Acts 13:40, 46, 51. Cf. Rom 10:18–21.
20. Acts 18:5ff.; 19:8f., etc.
21. The assumption here is that the author of the itinerary, 16:10ff., is also the author of Luke-Acts, W. L. Knox, *Acts*, pp. 94ff.
22. Ovid, *Metamorphoses* 8. 626ff. The identification of Barnabas with Zeus may indicate his more impressive physical appearance. The apocryphal "Acts of Paul" contains the story of Thecla, an Iconium convert. This legendary account may possibly

preserve a description of Paul's personal appearance: "a man of small stature, with his eyebrows meeting and a rather large nose, somewhat bald-headed, bandy-legged, strongly built, of gracious presence; for sometimes he looked like a man and sometimes he had the face of an angel." (Cited from *IB*, 9 (1952), 185).

23. Significant is the fact that "it is not in the Book of Acts but in the final chapter of his Gospel that Luke gives us his clearest definition of the systematic use of proof from Scripture among the early Christians." Luke 24:13–32, 44–48. J. Dupont, *Salvation of the Gentiles*, pp. 129ff.
24. Acts 14:22f.
25. Acts 8:14–25; 9:31–35; 11:27–30. Haenchen, *Acts*, p. 461.
26. Note the introduction of James (12:17) and of the elders (11:30), and their leadership positions (15:13–21 and 15:2, 22), which they retain at the time of Paul's last visit to Jerusalem (21:17ff.).
27. Acts 13:2; 14:12–14; 15:2, 12, 22. Cf. Acts 15:36–41, 40; 16:1ff.
28. Standard treatments of the chronology of Paul's life and letters are C. B. Caird, "Chronology of the New Testament," *IBD* 1 (1952), 599–607; J. C. Hurd, Jr., *IDBS*, (1976), 167; G. Ogg, *The Chronology of the Life of Paul* (1968); R. Jewett, *A Chronology of Paul's Life* (1979).
29. See, e.g., Bruce, *Paul*, pp. 148–159, 173–187. For comment on the defense of representatives of this "solution" see Jewett, *Chronology of Paul's Life*, pp. 69ff., 90–93; and the bibliography, note 36, p. 144.
30. The proconsulship of Gallio is dated 51–52 C.E., "an externally ascertainable date" which is an important benchmark for chronologists, Jewett, *Chronology of Paul's Life*, pp. 38–40. See also p. 331, note 28.
31. E.g., Hengel, *Acts*, pp. 111f.
32. *Ibid.*, p. 114.
33. *Ibid.*, p. 117. "One may perhaps infer from Acts 21:25 that Luke knew that Paul himself had not recognized the 'apostolic decree': there James presents it as something new and apparently unknown to him."
34. For advocates of this "solution," see Jewett, *Chronology of Paul's Life*, pp. 64–69, 89–93, and note 17, pp. 141–143.
35. Knox's statement of this "solution" is most widely known. For other exponents of it see Jewett, *Chronology of Paul's Life*, who seeks to refine and elaborate this hypothesis, pp. 78–85, 95–104, and note 77, pp. 147f. How does the personal involvement of Barnabas fit into this picture?
36. Gen. 17:9ff.;
37. Gal. 5:2; 6:12f.; Phil. 3:2f.
38. Gal. 2:14
39. Gal. 2:11ff.
40. Gal. 5:2–6; cf. Col. 2:3–17, 20–23; 1 Cor. 8:8; 10:23–26.
41. Gal. 2:21.
42. Acts 16:11.
43. Acts 15:36ff. Recall Acts 13:5, 13.
44. However sharp the rift at Antioch, Paul continued to recognize Barnabas as a valued colleague, see 1 Cor. 9:6. Mark seems to have redeemed himself in Paul's sight, Col. 4:10; Philem. 24; 1 Tim. 4:11.
45. Acts 16:3. See Bruce, *Paul*, pp. 214–216. Cf. Haenchen, *Acts* pp. 480–482.
46. Haenchen, *Acts*, pp. 489–491.
47. Recalling Luke's account of "the first missionary journey" (Acts 13–14), one may notice a common sequence of events: the founding of a church, Sabbath preaching in the synagogue, followed by persecution. This is not to suggest that the narrative

is merely contrived but it does reflect a limitation of the author's interest. Fortunately the Apostle's letters "fill in the gaps in the Lucan description." Haenchen, *Acts*, pp. 510f.

48. Acts 16:25ff.

49. Acts 16:37.

50. 1 Thess. 2:14, 17 and 3:2f., imply that Paul was persecuted by Gentile anti-Christians, but he may have judged that the real instigators were his countrymen, as he recalls the persecutions in Judea.

51. Acts 17:11.

52. Acts 17:14ff.

53. See "Paul on the Areopagus," in Dibelius, *Studies in the Acts*, pp. 26ff. One should not overlook the important fact that Paul's letters were written to Christians; in this speech Paul addresses pagans.

54. B. Gärtner, *The Areopagus Speech and Natural Revelation* (1955); Bruce, *Paul*, 243–247. Cf. Flender, *St. Luke* (1967), pp. 66ff.

55. Acts 17:32.

56. Acts 17:18.

57. *Anastasis* (Greek "resurrection") may have been mistaken for the name of a goddess.

58. Acts 17:34. Cf. 1 Cor. 16:15. Paul's only indirect reference to the unproductivity of his preaching in Athens. See also 1 Cor. 2:1–5.

59. Acts 18:5.

60. 1 Cor. 7:29, 31.

61. 1 Cor. 9:16ff.; 2 Cor. 5:14f.

62. Acts 18:6ff.

63. Did Luke intend to commend Gallio's attitude to his Roman readers, to recognize that Christianity "is an inner-Jewish affair which Rome would do well not to meddle?" Haenchen, *Acts*, p. 541. For the importance of Gallio's proconsulship in fixing Pauline chronology see note 30.

64. This notice, along with other evidence in Acts that presents Paul as an observer of Jewish Law (e.g. 16:3; 21:20–24), indeed as one who remained "a Pharisee" to the end of his life (23:6–9), appears incredible to some scholars, a denial of that self-understanding of the Apostle revealed in his letters. See, e.g., discussions of the issue in L. Keck and J. L. Martyn, eds., *Studies in Luke-Acts* (1980), pp. 37ff. (Vielhauer), and pp. 194ff. (Bornkamm). Cf. Bruce, *Paul*, pp. 255, 346–348, and note 1 Cor. 9:20; Rom. 3:9; 9:3; 11:1ff.

65. Admittedly Luke intended to report a fourth visit to Jerusalem (18:22), but was a visit actually made at this time? Haenchen, *Acts*, p. 544, note 5; also 547f.: "that the apostolic conference took place at this time is a mistaken hypothesis." See also p. 286.

66. Acts 18:24f.

67. Perhaps Luke's conviction is again shown, vis., that it was intrinsically impossible that a missionary should work in independence of "the apostles" (Paul and his co-workers being considered an extension of their influence).

68. Acts 19:19; cf. 5:12ff.

69. Acts 19:21f.

70. 1 Cor. 16; 2 Cor. 8:1–9:14. Note also Gal. 2:10.

71. Acts 20:3.

72. Rom. 15:25–29.

73. Jos. *Antiq.* XIV. x. 9–26; XVI. ii. 3, vi. 2–7; XIX. v. 2f., vi. 3; XX. 1. 2; *B.J.* VI. vi. 2.

74. K. F. Nickle, *The Collection* (1966), pp. 148–151; Bruce, *Paul*, pp. 296f., See also,

J. Jervell, *Luke and the People of God* (1972), pp. 42ff.; cf. Haenchen, *Acts*, pp. 612–614.

75. Acts 20:3, 6, 16.
76. Since Luke did not intend to tell the story of Paul's death, it may be said that in this emotional speech he presses "the crown of martyrdom" upon Paul's head. Dibelius, *Studies in the Acts*, pp. 157f.
77. The only speech in Acts that is addressed to Christians. It is not surprising that "it presents in a far greater degree than any of the other Pauline speeches, features of affinity with the letters of Paul." Bruce, *Paul*, p. 342. Cf. Haenchen, *Acts*, p. 596, who considers it unlike Paul (and like Luke) to extol the speaker in this manner.
78. Acts 21:20ff.
79. Num. 6:1ff.; Jos. *Antiq.* XIX. vi. 1.
80. The various reactions of modern historians to this episode underscore the difficulty and delicacy of Paul's dilemma: see G.H.C. Macgregor, "The Acts of The Apostles," *IB*, 9, 283f.; J. Munck's account based on textual emendation (*Paul and the Salvation of Mankind* (1959), p. 238ff.); and Bornkamm, in Keck and Martyn, *Luke-Acts*, pp. 204f.
81. Jos., *B.J.* V. ii. 1f.
82. *Ibid.*, II. xiii. 3f.
83. Acts 21:40.
84. See note 22. Cf. 2 Cor. 10:10.
85. Acts 23:3.
86. 1 Pet. 2:22.
87. Acts 23:6ff.
88. C. S. C. Williams, *A Commentary on The Acts of the Apostles* (1964), p. 248. Jos. *Life.* 139ff.
89. Acts 23:11.
90. See p. 53. Bruce succinctly summarizes Roman and Jewish sources concerning Felix, pp. 354f.
91. Tacitus, *Annals* XII. 54; *Histories* V. 9.
92. Some scholars assign two or more of Paul's "prison" or "captivity letters" to his years of Roman custody in Caesarea. Perhaps a larger number favor a Caesarean provenance for Colossians and Philemon, but some are convinced that the Letter to the Philippians was dispatched at this time. See Kümmel, *INT²*, pp. 324ff.
93. Acts 25:8.
94. The accounts of Rome's protection of Paul and of the several hearings before the procurators and king Herod have been said to contain many historical improbabilities. See Haenchen, *Acts*, pp. 635–694. Cf., however, Bruce, *Commentary on the Book of Acts* (1956), pp. 351–367.
95. Acts 27:17.
96. Cf. Matt. 13:14f.; John 12:40; also Mark 4:12 (Luke 8:10).
97. For a summary of various accounts of this omission, see Macgregor, "Acts of the Apostles," pp. 349ff.
98. Ancient church traditions report that Paul wrote four of his letters during this period of imprisonment in Rome: to the Philippians, to the Colossians, to Philemon, and to the Ephesians. See pp. 352, 361, 368.
99. Luke 24:26f., 44–47. Cf. 9:18–45; 18:31–34.
100. Acts 2:23; 3:17f.; 8:26–35; 13:26–29; 26:22f.
101. N. Dahl, "The Purpose of Luke-Acts," in *Jesus in the Memory of the Early Church* (1976), p. 91. Lk. 1:51–53; 4:16–21; 6:17ff.; 12:32; 22:28–30. Note the citation of Ps. 118:22, Lk. 21:17, and Acts 4:11.
102. Acts 2:4, 47; 3:13–15; 4:31; 5:32; 9:31.

103. E.g., Acts 12:1–17; 16:16–34.
104. Lk. 2:32; 13:47.
105. Dahl, "The Purpose of Luke-Acts," p. 91. Acts 28:23–28; also 13:46; 18:6.
106. Jervell, "The Divided People of God," in *Luke and the People of God* (1972), p. 53.
107. E.g., Acts 2:41, 47; 4:4; 5:14; 6:7; 8:4–8; 9:31; 14:1; 28:24.
108. Acts 10:2; 13:43. Note also Lk. 7:1–10.
109. Acts 13:16, 26; 14:1ff; 17:1, 4; 18:4.
110. Acts 3:17–26; 7:51.
111. Dahl, "The Story of Abraham in Luke-Acts," in *Jesus in the Memory of the Early Church*, pp. 82f. (also in Keck and Martyn, *Luke-Acts*, pp. 151f.). See also, E. Franklin, *Christ the Lord: A Study in the Purpose and Theology of Luke-Acts* (1975), pp. 77ff.; A. C. Winn, "Elusive Mystery: The Purpose of Acts," *Int* 13 (1959): 151ff.
112. Altogether there are ten trials narrated in Acts, as well as several official investigations of political charges against the followers of Jesus.
113. H. Conzelmann, *Theology of St. Luke* (1960), pp. 137ff.; Kümmel, *INT*[2], pp. 140f., 162f. (Lk. 23:2, 13:16, 22, 47; Acts 17:6f.; 25:1–8; also 23:26–30). Cf. Franklin, *Christ the Lord*, pp. 134ff.
114. Col. 4:14; cf. Philem. 24.
115. Acts 16:10–17; 20:5–15; 21:1–18; 27:1–28:16.
116. M. Hengel, *Acts*, p. 66; J. Fitzmyer, *Luke*, pp. 36f.
117. A point scored by J. M. Creed (*The Gospel According to St. Luke* [1942], pp. xiiif.), and cited with approval by Fitzmyer, *Luke* p. 41.
118. P. Vielhauer, "On the 'Paulinism' of Acts," in Keck and Martyn, *Luke-Acts*, pp. 33–49; Kümmel, *INT*[2], pp. 176–185.
119. J. Fitzmyer, *Luke*, pp. 47–51; Hengel, *Acts*, pp. 66f.
120. Some hold that Luke was a Jewish Christian, e.g., E. E. Ellis, *The Gospel of Luke*, pp. 51–53.
121. Franklin, *Christ the Lord*, pp. 178f. Dahl calls attention to Luke's interest in and appeal to God-fearing Gentiles, "The Purpose of Luke-Acts," pp. 96f.
122. Acts 10:1–11:18; 15:7–11; Luke 7:1–10.
123. C. H. Talbert, "An Introduction to Acts," *Review and Expositor* (1974): 446f. See a valuable analysis of various points of view by A. J. Mattill, Jr., "The Value of Acts as a Source for the Study of Paul," in Talbert, ed., *Perspectives on Luke-Acts* (1978), pp. 76–98.
124. J. Fitzmyer, *Luke*, p. 51. Fitzmyer argues that the internal evidence supports the ancient tradition that Luke was an Antiochene, pp. 42–47. F. F. Bruce, "Is the Paul of Acts the Real Paul?", *BJRL* 58 (1976): 282–305.

<table>
<tr><td>

Paul's Letters to Thessalonica and Corinth

</td><td>

Chapter

14

</td></tr>
</table>

T HE Apostle Paul was a prolific letter writer. His ambition to preach the gospel where Christ had not been named kept him on the move,[1] but by means of letters, often hand delivered by co-workers, he was able to keep in close touch with the churches he established. Evidently Paul expected his letters to be read at congregational meetings, thus to serve as apostolic directives in lieu of personal visits.[2]

Since the Apostle's letters in the New Testament canon (the Pauline Corpus, so-called) were written within a relatively short period, within a decade or a little more, one might not expect to trace in them a progressive sophistication of Paul's theology, or to find evidence of substantive change or development. Nevertheless, Paul was acutely sensitive to new, ever-evolving problems, and in his responses Paul brooded over a wide range of theological and ethical issues that he sought to address with "the mind of Christ," or, as he averred, "taught by the Spirit."[3] Paul's letters are an *ad hoc* disposition of special problems as these were brought to his attention. In every case his letters served as substitutes for or preparatory steps toward direct pastoral action. Because of the non-literary nature of Paul's letters, the term *epistle,* which is commonly applied to them, can be misleading.[4]

The letters of Paul bear formal resemblance to the common types written during the period. Yet they are "like rare and attractive wild plants growing in the conventional and well-kept garden of contemporary Greek writers,"[5] The Apostle's passionate concern led him to subordinate the well-turned phrase and the orderly application of his metaphors to forthrightness in speech. Apparently he visualized his readers and their reactions as he dictated his letters, and his words were charged with feeling.

It is this quality of passionate concern that draws the modern reader of Paul's letters into a vigorous dialogue. Behind the specific local conditions that confronted Paul and led him to write lie ever-present human concerns.

THE LETTERS TO THE THESSALONIANS

The Authenticity of the Letters and Their Relationship

Students of Paul declare that 1 Thessalonians is conspicuously characteristic of him in language and personal qualities. But two major difficulties are said to stand in the way of accepting Paul's authorship of 2 Thessalonians. First in importance is the matter of similarity and difference in language and style. Portions of 2 Thessalonians resemble so closely 1 Thessalonians that some interpreters suspect that Paul's ideas have been paraphrased by another person. Why, it is asked, should Paul have written almost identical letters to the same church within a short interval of time? Besides this verbal similarity, one must reckon with a difference in the tone of the letters reflected in their styles. The mood of 1 Thessalonians is warm, affectionate, personal; that of 2 Thessalonians, cool, formal, official, and, some would add, "grim and vengeful."[6]

A second major objection relates to the alleged difference in the eschatology of the two letters. The writer of 1 Thessalonians expects an imminent coming of the Lord Jesus without signs.[7] In 2 Thessalonians it is declared that certain signs will precede the coming of Christ, and that an indeterminate time may elapse before the End comes.[8] By itself this objection to a single authorship is not serious. The notion that the End is near and that premonitory signs are to be expected are not mutually exclusive ideas in Jewish or Christian apocalypses. Nevertheless, some have concluded that since the language and style suggest that 2 Thessalonians is a pseudonymous writing, the different emphases in the eschatology of the two letters is also evidence of different authorship.[9]

While certainty is not possible, most scholars affirm Paul's authorship of both letters and conclude that these difficulties have been exaggerated. The situations and purposes of both letters are credible on the assumption that the Apostle wrote them in their canonical order.*

*Two major proposals have been made to meet objections to Pauline authorship. Perhaps Paul addressed 1 Thess. to Gentile Christians; 2 Thess. to Jewish Christians, chiefly to clarify points in the longer letter. A second view reverses the canonical letters, and alleges that in 1 Thess. the sufferings of the church are treated as belonging to the past, whereas in 2 Thess. they are at their height.

INTERPRETING 1 THESSALONIANS

A. Address and Greeting, 1:1
B. Thanksgiving, 1:2–3:13
  1. The Apostle's gratitude for the Thessalonians' endurance and progress 1:1–10
  2. Paul's defense of his mission, 2:1–16
  3. Paul comments on developments since his recent mission, 2:17–3:10
  4. Paul's prayer for his converts' perfection in holiness, 3:11–13

The reader gains a vivid impression that in the first part of this letter Paul's assurances are mingled with anxiety. He is grateful and relieved that the Thessalonian Christians have stood firm under very trying circumstances, but he is anxious lest impugners of his character and motives destroy his work and the confidence that the church has placed in him. From the moment he left, Paul wished to return to Thessalonica. Timothy's report (and perhaps a letter from the church) had increased his longing.

Luke provides an account of Paul's departure from Thessalonica.[10] He reports that Jews in the city had stirred up the crowd against the missionaries, and a Christian named Jason and some others in the church had been brought before the city authorities, rightly identified by Luke as politarchs. In the absence of the missionaries there was a judgment against them, probably condemnation by default. In his letter, Paul acknowledged that determined opponents sought to thwart the Christian mission in Macedonia. He wrote: "you suffered the same things from *your own countrymen* as you did from the Jews."[11] Would the new converts stand firm? Timothy was sent from Athens to encourage the church.

When Timothy rejoined Paul at Corinth, Paul learned that the enemies of the church had been attacking the Apostle's behavior during the Thessalonian mission and making capital of his failure to return. Paul's defenses may disclose the character of these attacks. Probably his enemies were depicting him as just another egotistical purveyor of a popular religion or philosophy, a "fly-by-night" street-preacher claiming to possess superhuman powers, and not averse to greedily exploiting his credulous followers.[12] Apparently Paul believed that by explaining the methods and motives that prompted his missions, he could counteract these malign misconceptions.

Among the several reasons given for earnestly desiring a face-to-face meeting with his recent converts is Paul's hope that he "may supply what is lacking" in their response to the gospel.[13] These deficiencies are discussed in the remainder of the letter.

> C. Some Deficiencies in the Church, 4:1–5:22
>   1. The apostle's admonitions, 4:1–12
>   a. General encouragement, 4:1f.
>   b. Sexual purity, 4:3–8
>   c. Concerning love of the brethren, 4:9–12

Twice in this passage Paul uses terms that translate "more and more."[14] The Apostle sensed that his young converts had begun well; what they needed was encouragement, lest they resume former habits in their relations with others. They would be especially susceptible to relapses in sexual behavior. There is some obscurity in Paul's admonition, but his intention seems to be to urge husbands to restrict their sexual activity to their own wives, and not to look upon them merely as a means to satisfy lust or only to produce children. "Sanctification" is a religious ideal, but for Paul it was to be expressed in all human acts, not only in those commonly considered religious.

> C. 2. Instruction concerning the Parousia of Christ, 4:13–5:22
>   a. The dead have not forfeited their salvation, 4:13–18
>   b. The Day of the Lord, an indeterminate date, 5:1–3
>   c. Conduct befitting "sons of the Day," 5:4–21
> D. Final Prayer and Farewell, 5:23–28

It is often commented that in the Thessalonian letters there is a notable absence of the great theological themes considered by all to be essentially Pauline: justification by faith, the new life in Christ, to name two prominent doctrines. Apparently the most pressing need of the Thessalonian Christians at this stage of their development was practical encouragement; less urgent was the need for doctrinal clarity, with one exception. Paul's converts were seriously deficient in their understanding of the Christian's hope.

A common view is that the question troubling persons in this church was whether the situation of those who were dying would be any different from the living at the time of Christ's coming. It is probable, however, that their distress was grounded in a fear that the dead have forfeited their salvation, that only those alive at the coming of Christ would be saved. If the problem is thus defined, Paul's purpose was "not to assuage normal grief caused by death, but to deal with despair." The need then was for instruction.[15]

Notice Paul's development of this instruction. First he cited a common creed of the church: "we believe that Jesus died and rose again" (even so, through Jesus God will bring with him those who have "fallen asleep"). Paul then appealed to a "word of the Lord (Jesus)" (4:15); again, he employed a metaphor used by Jesus to affirm the unpredictability of the coming of the Day of the Lord—"like a thief in the night" (5:2).[16] Paul concluded this instruction with a statement of faith: as a consequence of the death and resurrection of Jesus, the Day of the Lord is anticipated as present reality ("Behold! Now is the day of salvation").[17]

In the Thessalonian letters Paul affirmed the Christian hope for the future centering on "the coming of our Lord Jesus Christ with all his saints."[18] The Greek term Paul used, translated "coming," is *parousia*, probably chosen because of its associations in a Gentile cultural setting with a ceremonial visit of an emperor or other dignitary to a village or city. By appealing to this familiar event perhaps Paul sought to aid his readers in grasping the significance of that dramatic sequence of events associated with the End in a literature alien to most Gentiles, Jewish, and Jewish Christian apocalypses.*

*The root of the noun, *parousia*, means to arrive or to be present. Already in the classical period the Greek term was applied to the arrival of a king or god. In Hellenistic times it acquired a technical sense in connection with a state visit to a community of the emperor or some other high official. The imagery Paul uses with reference to the *parousia* of the Lord Jesus is borrowed from this secular ceremony as well as from Jewish Christian apolcalyptic sources. F. W. Beare, *IDB*, 4 (1962) 624ff.

The task of rendering credible to Gentiles the eschatology of the early Christian *kerygma* was exceedingly difficult. The Greek mind resisted the idea of a resurrection of the body, although the belief was common that the souls of men were subject to reincarnations, being essentially immortal. Moreover, the Greeks thought of history as an ever-recurring circle, not as a forward-moving line of time directed toward a day of judgment and a general resurrection.[19] Doubtless Paul's eschatological proclamation baffled many of his Gentile hearers. But there is no evidence that on this account Paul resorted to speculative reasoning or to an allegorizing of Jewish apocalyptic symbols in describing the Christian hope. His contagious assurance that death brings no separation of the believer from his Lord, and that an eternal fellowship with Christ is promised, must have brought comfort to mourners where knowledge failed. We have seen that in the Hellenistic Age confidence was placed in the illumination of the mysteries of life and death through revelation when rational thought was unable to penetrate the darkness.

The moral delinquencies of the Thessalonian Christians probably were related to their failure to grasp the full significance of the Christian hope. The Greek view of the human personality was dualistic. Where religion permeated philosophy, the belief was sustained that the spirit or mind of persons was by nature divine or, if properly enlightened, destined to share the life of eternity. But the "flesh" had no decisive influence upon "spirit"; bodily impulses and actions were merely instinctive or morally indifferent. Only the disposition of a person's mind or spirit affected his or her eternal destiny.

Paul inherited from Judaism a belief in the profound unity of a human being's nature as wholly related to God. Moreover, as a Christian apostle, Paul envisaged a new stature of personhood in Jesus Christ. He experienced the indwelling of the Holy Spirit and proclaimed the hope of the resurrection of the body.

Accordingly, the Apostle's ideal was the life of total consecration, "unblamable in holiness" before God. Christians were called to be "saints," that is to say, persons who acknowledged that they were chosen by God and thus consecrated unto Him. Paul repeatedly commends the Thessalonians for their "love of the brethren." Nevertheless, he reminded the "loafers" in the church that they lacked love unless they aspired to live quietly, minded their own affairs, worked with their hands, and were dependent upon no one. To the rest Paul wrote that love is always patient, even with loafers.[20]

Apparently the proclamation of the imminence of the Day of the Lord had led some Christians at Thessalonica to become overly excited. Their hope had reached such a feverish state as to be morally enervating. They had abandoned their work and become wards of the community. Paul reminded his converts that a proper understanding of the Parousia hope would not lead to a fanatical otherworldliness, but to a tranquillity of mind, to such industry as would leave no time for meddling in others' affairs, and to an honorable independence that would command the respect of outsiders.

The patterns of ethical instruction in 1 Thessalonians are found in several non-Pauline letters of the New Testament and in other early Christian literature. This teaching is parallel in its forms to ethical instruction in Hellenistic writings generally. It is therefore probable that the Thessalonian letters contain typical expositions of "the Christian Way" in the Hellenistic churches.[21]

INTERPRETING 2 THESSALONIANS

A. Address and Greeting, 1:1f.
B. Thanksgiving, 1:3–12
   1. Commendation of his converts' faith, love, and endurance under persecution, 1:3f.
   2. Encouragement for the afflicted; warnings for the afflictors, 1:4–12
C. Further instruction concerning the Parousia and (last) judgment, 2:1–12
D. Statements and prayers expressing confidence in the Lord, and in the salvation of his elect, 2:13–3:5
E. Further admonitions concerning the idle, 3:6–15
F. Final prayer and farewell, 3:16f.

Within a few weeks after dispatching his first letter, Paul learned that the problems at Thessalonica were more serious than he had supposed. This church was not only ignorant of the Christian hope concerning the dead and the dying, and needed encouragement in view of the coming Day of the Lord; there was a fundamental misunderstanding of this aspect of the Christian *kerygma*. Paul could not wait to visit the church, for some persons were misrepresenting his views and thereby causing great excitement. Moreover, the enemies of the church had stepped up their persecutions, and loafers in the church were creating a serious problem. A short letter was therefore written to recall his teaching while in their midst and to beg the Thessalonians to adhere to "the traditions" that had been passed on to them orally or by letter.[22]

As we shall see, it was not a total misrepresentation to declare, as some were doing, that Paul proclaimed a "realized eschatology."[23] Yet it is certain that at the time of the Thessalonian correspondence Paul shared the perspective of the early Church: the hope of Israel had not been completely fulfilled; salvation through Christ was a present reality and also a future hope.

It is futile to seek a full exposition of Paul's eschatology in 2 Thessalonians since in this letter he did not recall his teaching but asked his readers to do so. His immediate purpose was to quiet the fanatical excitement in the church, not to detail a blueprint of the close of the age. As a result, certain of Paul's statements in this section defy understanding. The "rebellion" referred to the commonplace apocalyptic belief that religious apostasy precedes the coming of the Day of the Lord.[24] But what is the meaning of Paul's reference to "the mystery of lawlessness already at work"? And who is this "man of lawlessness," claiming divinity and enthroning himself in the temple? A further problem is the identification of the force or person "restraining" this lawlessness.[25]

Some have held that "the man of lawlessness" refers to an emperor or agent of Rome, and that by the mystery of lawlessness Paul meant the power regnant in the imperial administration. But it is consistent with other statements by Paul that Rome should be considered the restrainer not the cause of lawlessness.[26] Accordingly, others interpret Paul as referring to Judaism as "the mystery," and some leader—perhaps a wicked high priest—as "the man of lawlessness." Another suggestion can be traced, like the above alternatives, to ancient Christian sources. Paul, it is claimed, was the restrainer of the mystery of lawlessness, and that which restrained (or delayed) the revelation of the man of lawlessness was the Christian gospel, which must be proclaimed to the Gentiles before the End comes.[27]

It is probable that Paul had in mind definite historical situations and persons, but we cannot be certain of this. The Apostle's vision included more than the observable events of history. His thought is mystical and soars to cosmic dimensions. The revelation of the man of lawlessness, with "pretended signs and wonders," is described as "the activity of Satan." With the coming of the Day of the Lord the lawless one is to be slain as the result of a cosmic conflict. Paul's imagery contains some of the characteristic stage properties of Jewish and Christian apocalypses.*

While the two Thessalonian letters are not the greatest of Paul's writings, they are certainly distinctive and of undoubted value. They reveal in marvelous ways the personal and pastoral qualities of Paul, and also the strength and weakness of a small Christian community, but a few weeks old, struggling to understand the gospel of Jesus Christ and to maintain itself against overwhelming odds.

*Perhaps Paul's mental state at this particular time contributed to this apocalyptic scenario. Not only was Paul experiencing alienation in synagogue after synagogue, but many Jerusalem Christians were opposing Paul's version of the gospel. Such threatening factors may have generated this vision of the End, a "resolution" of the apparent contradiction between Paul's confidence in the Christian's hope and his experience of alienation and isolation.

THE CORINTHIAN CORRESPONDENCE
PRELIMINARY QUESTIONS

The narrative of Acts enables us to identify the period of the Apostle's contacts with the Corinthian Christians; Paul's letters shed remarkable light upon his relations with them.

Paul's mission to Corinth began in the winter of 49–50 C.E. and ended in the summer of 52.[28] After this, the Apostle returned to Judea and Syria. We are left to guess how long it was before the "third missionary journey" began, but it is probable that the visitation of the churches in the regions of Galatia and Phrygia was started in the early spring of 53.[29] The eventual destination of this trip was Ephesus, and Paul labored there for the better part of three years, 53–56.[30] Upon leaving Ephesus, he visited the churches in Macedonia and Achaia. Luke implies that this time Paul stayed at Corinth for three months before going through Macedonia en route to Jerusalem. This, his last visit to the Corinthians, probably occurred late in 56.

For the story of Paul's relations with the church at Corinth during the last two or three years of this period we turn to 1 and 2 Corinthians.

1 Corinthians was not Paul's first letter to the church at Corinth. In it (5:9) he referred to another written earlier and to a misunderstanding that it had caused. The full text of this "previous letter" ("Letter A") is lost, but numerous scholars have held that a fragment of it is embedded in the canonical writing, 2 Corinthians. The six verses that follow 2 Corinthians 6:13 interrupt the train of thought, while 2 Corinthians 7:2ff. can be joined smoothly to 6:13. Moreover, it is thought by some that the teaching of this "erratic block" answers to Paul's description of his previous letter and is of such a nature as to necessitate clarification.

"Letter A," from Paul to the Corinthians, was followed by a letter from the church to the the Apostle, requesting his guidance on a number of controversial issues.[31] Paul acknowledged the receipt of this letter: "and now for the matters you wrote about (NEB) . . ."[32] Before Paul found time to address the Corinthian's questions he received a disturbing report, delivered in person by some of "Cloe's people."[33] In writing 1 Corinthians ("Letter B"), this oral communication from Corinth demanded the Apostle's prior attention.

INTERPRETING THE CANONICAL LETTER CALLED "1 CORINTHIANS"

A. Introduction, 1:1–9
    1. The address, 1:1–3
    2. The thanksgiving, 1:4–9
B. Admonitions Based on Reports Concerning Quarreling and Factions, 1:10–4:21
    1. The acknowledgment of partisan alignments, 1:10–12
    2. The primacy of Christ crucified, 1:13–17
    3. "The wisdom of men" and "the foolishness of God." 1:18–31
    4. Paul's initial visit recalled, 2:1–5
    5. God's "wisdom" revealed and taught by the Spirit, 2:6–16
    6. Who are "the spiritual (persons)"? and who are "the apostles"? 3:1–15
    7. Those who are Christ's are God's temple, and possess all things, 3:16–23
    8. Summary: the apostles' example; plans for an early visit, 4:1–21

The organization of Paul's letter follows spontaneously along the lines suggested by the impending crisis in the leadership of the Corinthian church and by the expressed need for instruction in particular matters. One looks in vain for an orderly exposition of the Apostle's gospel. It would be false, however to describe the content of the letter as "practical" rather than "theological"; Paul's admonitions are at every point related to some aspect of the Apostle's *kerygma*.[34]

One cause of the divisions at Corinth arose from a misguided loyalty attached to various leaders. Apollos, who had been instructed by Paul's converts at Ephesus, had conducted a mission at Corinth in Paul's absence. Some Christians there had championed the leadership of Apollos and had compared his preaching with that of Paul, to the latter's disadvantage. Others had championed Peter. It is not possible to know whether or not Peter preached at Corinth; Paul himself may have told them about his special relation to Christ. Some deny that the words "I belong to Christ" referred to a fourth party at Corinth, but others believe its existence is implied from Paul's remarks in 2 Corinthians 10:7. The "Christ party" probably identified those persons professing direct visions of Christ, an unbounded freedom resulting from their faith and baptism in his name, and repudiating all human leaders.[35] *

*Some scholars have attempted to show that these particular groups are presupposed throughout the Corinthian letters. Thus, it is said, "the weak" referred to in 1 Cor. 8 belonged to the "Cephas party"; those who denied a future resurrection of the dead (1 Cor. 15:12) belonged to the "Christ party"; and so on. There are large elements of conjecture in such connections, and it is perhaps futile to base interpretations of particular passages upon a partisan alignment. Other divisions seem to have been caused by the social stratification of its membership; still others by the presence in the community of Gentiles and Jews representing various backgrounds.

With fine tact, Paul pointed to the error of his own champions. He had not spent his time in Corinth making Paulinists. He was indeed "the father" of the Corinthian church, but even the few persons he had baptized stood in no special relation to him.[36] Those who were initiated into the mystery religions might hold in reverence their priests or mystagogues, but it was not so, according to Paul's understanding, in Christianity. All Christian apostles were subordinate to Christ. They were not rivals but "fellow-workmen for Good," and no one should attempt to pass judgment upon the relative values of their work.

The words of Paul in 1:17ff. were probably not directed solely against those who "belonged to Apollos." These partisans may have been chiefly responsible for criticizing Paul's lack of "wisdom," but there was a pervasive tendency to depreciate Paul's preaching, and he addressed his notes on "the foolishness of the *kerygma*" to the entire congregation.[37] No brief comment can exhaust the meaning of this remarkable passage. The Apostle affirmed that the powerful effect of the gospel does not depend on anyone's special comprehension or literary adornment of it; its salvific effect does not derive from any preacher's personal dynamism or eloquence of speech. The *kerygma* accosts every person as an effective witness to God's deed, accomplished in and through the passion, crucifixion, and resurrection of Jesus the Christ. Lest the Corinthians conceive of the gospel as similar in kind to some popular Greek philosophy, integrating human knowledge into a sophisticated credible system or else to some esoteric cult, another oriental "mystery" accomplishing salvation through initiation, Paul made two vital points. First, admittedly the Christian *kerygma* is offensive to some, absurd to others. To Jews, the idea of a crucified messiah is an offense. They seek and expect a victorious messiah who will overthrow the oppression of God's people, whose coming will be heralded by miraculous signs. To Greeks, it was foolishness to make of a crucified felon either a teacher of "wisdom," or a strong hero—a divine man! Yet Paul reminded the Corinthians that "the word of the cross" was doing something "for those who are called" that all the wisdom and power of humans could never accomplish. Second, Paul asked his readers to consider their former lives, the occasion of his coming to them and their reception of the gospel. Nothing in these human circumstances could justify boasting, the exaltation of oneself over other selves. The Christian *kerygma* is a "mystery" revealed by "the Spirit which is from God" for the salvation of all, not reserved for the few who consider themselves "the spiritual ones" or "the mature."

It is a popular view that in the Corinthian letters Paul fought against "a Gnostic perversion of the Christian message which attributes to 'the spiritual,' as those liberated from 'the flesh,' a perfect redemptive state and an unconditional moral freedom."[38] Some have gone so far as to conclude that since Paul himself distinguishes between those who are "mature" and those who are "babes in Christ," between human natures that are "spiritual" and others that are merely "natural," one can infer that the Apostle's theology was affected by Gnostic tenets.[39] It is a controversial question whether the presuppositions and positions of Paul's opponents can be properly described as "Gnostic" or "pre-Gnostic," but it is highly improbable that Paul, wittingly or unwittingly, countenanced such ideas. "The mystery" of which Paul spoke, "the wisdom" that the Apostle imparted, was not something added to "the word of the cross"; it is in Christ crucified and risen that the wisdom of God is embodied. Paul did not have a simple gospel for "babes" and a different wisdom-gospel for "the mature"; the distinction was in the degrees of comprehension on the part of those receiving the *kerygma*.[40]

It is noteworthy that Paul called upon the Corinthians to stand with Apollos and himself under "the word of the cross," under the same norms of judgment: the gracious calling of God and the Parousia of Christ.[41]

C. Admonitions Based on Reports Concerning Sexual Immorality, and Legal Disputes Among Members, 5:1–6:20
1. Paul judges the case of incest, 5:1–8
2. The church vis-à-vis the world: internal discipline versus the judgment of "outsiders," 5:9–6:11
3. Summary: "the body is not meant for immorality," 6:12–20

The Apostle next commented on a case of incest, perhaps reported to him by Chloe's household. It was not only the sin that shocked Paul but the condoning attitude of the church at Corinth. Paul's decision implied more than the separation of the offender from the Christian community, although this would surely be the practical result of the church's action. To be excluded from the church was tantamount to being cut off from the sphere of Christ's influence and thrust back into Satan's dominion with dreadful, but not necessarily final, destructive consequences.[42]

There were many factors in the Corinthian environment that encouraged extramarital relations. Not only were there numerous brothels in the city to accommodate sailors, but the worship of Aphrodite, the goddess of love, led to intercourse with her "sacred" prostitutes. Since the Christian community could not isolate itself from Corinthian society and its influence, Paul insisted that it must maintain internal standards of purity and of discipline. It must judge the evil of its own members; God would judge those without.[43]

Paul's attack upon the sexual immoralities and debauchery at Corinth reveals a principal cause for the seriousness of the situation. Some Christians were not merely excusing extramarital relations as a common human weakness, but defending them. It was being said that physical actions such as eating and drinking, involving the appetites of the body, which perishes, would not affect the spirit of people. Paul countered this dualistic conception of the human personality by proclaiming the sanctity of the body.[44] The new life of the Christian had been purchased at great cost; the entire body of the believer was the temple of the Holy Spirit.

> D. Paul's Replies to the Corinthian's Letter, and Related Matters, 7:1–16:12
> 1. Paul discusses the ascetics' advocacy of abstinence from sex, 7:1–40
>   a. A Christian's understanding of marriage, 7:1–7
>   b. Advice to the unmarried and widows, 7:8f.
>   c. Counsel concerning separation and divorce, 7:10–16
>   d. The *status quo* is Paul's "rule," 7:17–24
>   e. "The eschatological reservation" concerning marriage, 7:25–35
>   f. A quandary for those who are bethrothed, 7:36–38
>   g. A widow's choice, 7:39f.

Paul's answer to certain questions raised in the letter from the Corinthians concerning marriage and celibacy reveal that there were persons in the church who took the opposite position from those who considered the sex act nonmoral or amoral. Ascetics were claiming that sex was inherently sinful. "Spiritual persons" avoid marriage or, if married, depreciate coitus. Perhaps the slogan of this ascetic group was, "it is well for a man not to touch a woman."[45]

Paul deals with this situation by first insisting that husbands and wives must not deny one another their conjugal rights, unless it be by mutual consent, and then only for a season lest Satan take advantage of their continence. Paul also asserted the positive value of marriage by referring to Jesus' commandment forbidding divorce. Moreover, he declared that Christian partners in marriages with pagans should not take the initiative in seeking separation; indeed the shared life might lead to the conversion of their mates. At the same time, Paul assured the Corinthian ascetics that celibacy was to be preferred to marriage, provided one has one's "own special gift from God"—an important qualification. Indeed, one gains the impression that Paul tolerated marriage because he disapproved so strongly of extramarital sexual relations.[46]

In defending his principle of maintaining the status quo, and his preference for the unmarried state, Paul declared his principal reason for doing so: Christians are called to give single-minded devotion to the Lord. Since the time is short, all impediments and conflicts of interest subject to choice must be forestalled. The unmarried are better able to do this. The Apostle's eschatology does not focus only upon the temporal imminence of the End, however, for already "the form of this world is passing away," being replaced by "the new creation in Christ."[47] Not only will all human relationships be governed by different standards in the (near) future but "from now on" by one's allegiance to Christ as Lord.[48]

Apparently Paul was convinced that the ideal of asceticism was impractical for all Christians, and not binding upon those who unwisely aim to live the celibate's life.*

*Perhaps one can summarize Paul's views on the subject as follows: celibacy is preferable provided one has the special gift and is able to avoid

> D. 2. Paul discusses the question concerning "food offered to idols":
>   a. The effects of "knowledge" and love, 8:1–3
>   b. The application of both to the issue at hand, 8:4–9
>   c. Admonitions to those who "possess knowledge," 8:10–13

The public rites of pagan religions, as well of Judaism, included animal sacrifices. Parts of the slain animals would be consumed by the altar fires, but the left-overs might be disposed of as gifts to priests, or sold in the marketplaces. Some worshipers used their portions for private banquets, and sent out invitations, as illustrated in this papyrus: "Antonius, son of Ptolemaeus, invites you to dine with him at the table of our lord Sarapis."[49] Could Christians accept such invitations from pagan neighbors?

Christians of Jewish background had obvious scruples against such a thing. The issue was complicated by the common belief that spirit powers, both good and evil, possessed persons through the eating of food.[50]

Paul considered the problem from various angles. First, he agreed in principle with those at Corinth who denied the existence of the pagan gods. Theoretically, the question about what to do about things "offered to idols" was morally indifferent. But there were weaker brothers and sisters in the church, recent converts from paganism, who ate food "as really offered to an idol." Out of consideration for these persons Paul advised those possessing "knowledge" (8:10) to impose a voluntary limitation upon the exercise of their freedom. To encourage persons to act against their conscience, even though they think these scruples absurd, is an evil that love avoids. Whatever privileges "knowledge" brings, the violation of the commandment to love is not one of these. It is clear that whereas Paul shared the conviction of the advocates of Christian liberty, he did not share their spirit.[51]

D. 2. *d*. The Apostle's privilege and example: self-renunciation of his "rights," 9:1–23
  e. Persons having "knowledge" must accept discipline and resist temptation: an example from scripture, 9:24–10:22
  f. Summary: The meaning of "the table of the Lord" as applied to the question; conscientious opinions and neighbor-love, 10:23–11:1

In appealing to his own example, Paul revealed his sensitivity to criticism and self-consciously expressed a principle that determined the special form of his defense of the Christian gospel and ethic: "I have become all things to all men, that I might by all means win some." By thus adapting his counsel to the situation Paul left himself open to misunderstanding.[52] But, according to his own testimony, the Apostle deliberately adopted this flexible approach. It was for him a calculated risk. No interpreter of Paul can ignore this autobiographical clue, both to the working of the Apostle's mind and to his missionary strategy.[53]

Paul's allusion to the Exodus experience of the Israelites and his curious haggadah concerning the "Rock which followed them" in their wilderness wanderings, may detract the modern reader from the course of the Apostle's argument. At this place he reminds the Corinthians, who prided themselves that their conscience was enlightened and who believed that they were secure from infection by demons, that pride invites a fall. Furthermore, Paul argues that a person who sits at "the table of the Lord" cannot feast at the table of a pagan god, even though the so-called god is only an idol. Once more Paul's faith that the believer is a member of Christ's body is introduced, and the connection of

sexual immoralities; less desirable is marriage, yet for most Christians their sexuality prompts this life-style and if adultery and lust are curbed, marriage "is no sin"; least desirable is the state of those who need to marry because of their sexuality but who attempt to live as an ascetic, or those who after marriage refrain from sex. Cf. Barrett, *1 Corinthians* p. 161.

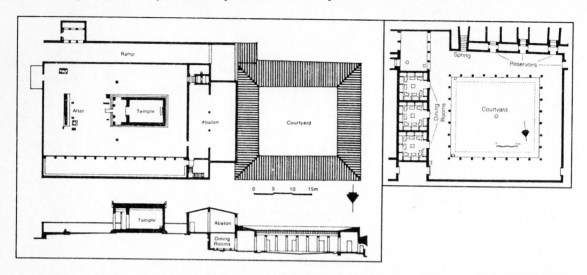

(Above) The Asclepion at Corinth. The temple of Asclepius, the god of healing, was rebuilt by Roman colonists in 44 B.C.E. Paul had to deal with the dispute concerning a Christian's presence at the cult meals honoring pagan deities (1 Cor. 8–10). *(Courtesy of J. Murphy-O'Connor.) (Below)* Ruins of the temple of Octavia, looking toward Acrocorinth. *(Courtesy of the* Biblical Archeologist.*).*

this idea with the bread of the Eucharist may point to the source of its inspiration.

Paul concluded this discussion of idol meats and idolatry with practical advice about what to do when a Christian is invited to a pagan home. He reminded his readers of their responsibility to avoid wherever possible giving offense to anyone, and appealed to his own conduct as the imitation of Christ.*

> D. 3. Paul discusses the "head covering" women are to wear in leading public worship, 11:2–16
> 4. Paul's warning concerning the scandalous behavior at the Lord's Supper; the rite's traditional meaning, 11:17–34

Beginning with 11:2, and continuing to 14:40, Paul treats a series of problems relating to the conduct of the Corinthians in their public assemblies. Perhaps "chaotic" is the one word that describes these noisy meetings.

It is not clear from Paul's introduction of the next topic whether women in Corinth, who were leading in public worship, were wearing a "head covering" because of Paul's instruction or because of a local, established custom.[54] In either case Paul commends this tradition and opposes some antilegalists in the church who were urging its abandonment.

In the defense of his position Paul uses a word meaning both (physical) "head" and "source" (origin). His elliptical argument is based on the Genesis stories of the creation of man and woman, on social conventions concerning hair styles, and the directions nature affords. Two very different readings of the drift of Paul's thesis are given. A common interpretation is that the Apostle understood the head covering (lit. "authority") worn by women participating in Christian worship to be a visible sign to all assembled—angels as well as human beings—that women are subordinate to men.[55] An opposing interpretation is that the head covering is a sign of woman's authority, enabling her to do that which was commonly denied her within the old creation, namely, to participate in Christian worship as man's equal.[56]

In defense of the first reading it is said that Paul's Jewish predisposition, based in part upon a traditional understanding of Genesis, which he cites, and in part upon synagogue practice, inhibited the Christian apostle from following to its logical conclusion the faith he enunciated in Galatians 3:26–28. Did Paul also fear that the antilegalist's enthusiastic flaunting of social conventions might provoke derogatory comment concerning women in the church?

By pointing to 11:12f., defenders of the second interpretation have shown that Paul's partially realized eschatology has a bearing on his equivocal position. The old creation, with its established order (while not wholly superseded), is giving place to the new creation: "in Christ's fellowship woman is as essential to man as man is to woman . . . and [God] is the source of all." (NEB)

In this matter, as in others, Paul's social conservatism drew support from his belief in the imminence of the End. It is probable that Paul's concluding arguments (11:13–16) appeared to his first readers as they may to us, as rationalizations in defense of a custom, logically inconsistent but nonetheless strongly held.[57]

The Apostle's words concerning the behavior of the Corinthians at their

*Are Paul's admonitions contradictory, as some readers suppose, or does Paul develop two complementary arguments? In 1 Cor. 8:1–13 and 10:23–33, Paul declares that eating idol meats is in some situations of no moral consequence (agreeing in principle with those possessing "knowledge"); in 1 Cor. 10:1–22, Paul condemns participation in temple ceremonies paying homage to pagan gods as an act of idolatry!

community meal (11:17ff.) has attracted unusual interest because of his reference to the liturgical tradition establishing the celebration of "The Lord's Supper." At this place, however, Paul is less concerned with the form of the sacramental service than he is with the spirit of its participants. Before the Lord's
Supper a common meal was held but not shared. The richer members, concerned only with the satisfaction of their hunger and thirst, went ahead with
their own meals, leaving little if any food for late-comers (the poorer, working-
class members?) when they arrived. In their greed and selfish indifference to
other's needs, some Corinthian Christians were bringing upon themselves the
Lord's judgment, not his blessing.

For Paul the sacrament was the locus of Christ's self-manifestation. By their
lack of reverence these celebrants did not "render his gift ineffective nor turn
the presence of Christ into absence." As a means of grace and a call to obedience, the Lord's Supper is a source of great blessing, but as a self-manifestation
of Christ *as Lord* the sacrament is also a means of judgment. Therefore those
who partake of it must "examine" and "judge" themselves lest they incur the
Lord's condemnation. "Wherever the Savior is scorned, the Judge of the world
nevertheless remains and manifests himself."[58] Paul's reference to "discerning
the body" has been understood either as an indication of Christ's presence in
the bread and wine or to the church as Christ's body. Both meanings can be
implied.

> D. 5. Paul discusses the significance of various "spiritual gifts," 12:1–14:39
>   a. A mark of authenticity; "to each . . . for the common good," 12:1–11
>   b. The body of Christ and its many members, 12:12–31a
>   c. The "more excellent way": the nature of love; its permanence; its su-
>   periority, 12:31b–13:13
>   d. Prophecy and speaking in tongues, 14:1–25
>   e. Summary: order in the church, 14:26–40

The assembly of Christians at Corinth for worship led to other disorderli-
ness. Members were vying with one another, speaking in tongues and prophesying. Paul did not question the reality or validity of these spiritual gifts.[59] But
it is clear that he considered them relatively unimportant, especially when they
were disruptive of community, led to private incommunicable teaching, and
invited criticism from outsiders. This section has attracted an extraordinary interest because in the course of his discussion Paul developed his famous metaphor of the Church's unity as the body of Christ having many interdependent
members and composed his lyric description of enduring love.

The survival of the church at Corinth was threatened because some members—the prophets and the "spiritual"—considered themselves all-important
and the rest nonessential. Paul declared that what is valued highest by God and
in the church may seem foolish to the world, which commonly honors spectacular gifts in its leaders (cf. 1:26ff.). Mystical overtones have been detected in
Paul's figure of the Church as Christ's body, but the emphasis here is upon the
interdependence of the fellow members of Christ's visible body, the Corinthian
congregation. God's gifts to this church were intended to serve the needs of the
entire community rather than bring honor to isolated individuals.

Since love is not one of the "gifts" in chapter 12, and prophecy as "a higher gift" (12:31a) is discussed in chapter 14, some scholars have conjectured that the famous hymn extolling love is an interpolation, perhaps written by Paul for another occasion. The location of the passage in 1 Corinthians is not inappropriate, however; in chapter 12 Paul stresses that the church is a community of persons whose fellow-feeling leads them to care for and fully share with each other, and at the beginning of the hymn on love the phenomena of speaking in tongues and prophesying remain in the foreground. Also, after his incomparable description of love's enduring qualities, Paul places in proper perspective the more ephemeral gifts of prophecy, tongues, and knowledge. The Corinthians had a too exclusive, too acquisitive, interest in these spectacular gifts; above all else they should aim to excel in love.

D. 6. Paul discusses the Christian hope of resurrection, 15:1–58
    a. The received tradition; its significance, 15:1–11
    b. The risen Christ "the first fruits," "then at his Parousia those who belong to Christ," 15:12–23
    c. Christ's mediatorial role completed at the End, 15:24–28
    d. Some consequences "if the dead are not raised," 15:29–34
    e. The "mystery" of the resurrection body; "the work of the Lord" is profitable labor, 15:35–58
  7. Paul discusses "the Contribution for the Saints," and describes his contingent plans, 16:1–12
E. The Conclusion, 16:13–24
  1. Final admonitions, 16:13–24
  2. Greetings, 16:19f.
  3. Inscribed salutation, with an imprecation; the advent prayer, 16:21f.
  4. Benediction, 16:23f.

The teaching of Paul in 1 Corinthians concludes with a reminder of the essentials of the Christian *kerygma*, and with an exposition of the Christian hope of the resurrection of the body. Our attention has been repeatedly drawn to the opening statements of this classical passage. In it Paul declared that the validity of the entire structure of the *kerygma* rested upon a mighty act of God: Jesus had been raised from the dead. This event gave assurance that the eschatological victory of Christ had begun and that his reign must continue "until he has put all his enemies under his feet" and destroyed death.[60]

It is doubtful that any at Corinth denied this proclamation of the risen Lord, although aspects of the apocalyptic end-drama were puzzling. Some in the church, probably Greek in background, may not have been able to conceive of any *bodily* form of life after death. This incredulity might have led them to deny the resurrection of the dead.[61] The world view of popular religions and philosophies, as we have observed, envisioned the disembodied spirit passing through the planetary spheres, finally sloughing off every part of the temporal flesh-and-blood existence, even self-consciousness and reason. Paul acknowledged the element of truth in this Greek (or Gnosticizing?) tradition: "Flesh and blood cannot inherit the Kingdom of God." But he went on to proclaim "a mystery": those who hope in Christ will not merely experience a passage from death to an eternal incorruptible state, but a change from a "physical body" to a "spiritual body." Paul associated this change with the coming of Christ.

Alternatively, the deniers of a future resurrection of the dead at Corinth may have been those "spiritual" Christians who understood, one-sidedly, Paul's preaching that believers in Christ have been raised with him.[62] If such were the situation, Paul would have wished to make clear that the new life in Christ, in which the power of his resurrection is being experienced, is nevertheless a life lived in hope of a final resurrection.[63]

The burden of Paul's teaching in the important passage concerning the nature of the resurrected body is that there is both a radical difference and a real continuity between the human body that dies and the "body" that is raised. While Paul attempts to provide analogies from nature to support his position, he affirms that the paradoxical hope of receiving a "spiritual body" derives its reality and meaning from Christ's own resurrection. Paul's use of the term translated *immortality* is not to be confused with the commonplace belief in man's survival as a disembodied spirit. His expression "put on immortality" resembles superficially the language of the mystery religions, but Paul's teaching opposes the contemporary "gospels" of rebirth and deification.

INTERPRETING CANONICAL 2 CORINTHIANS: FRAGMENTS OF SEVERAL LETTERS

Reconstructions of the course of events between the writing of 1 Corinthians and later letters and the situations alluded to must rely on speculation. But certain points seem clear. Timothy's return from Corinth (1 Cor. 16:10f.) must have brought news of no improvement in the church. Soon afterward, Paul went directly to Corinth by sea. This journey, referred to in 2 Corinthians 2:1, is commonly called "the painful visit." It seems to have been a complete fiasco. One member of the Corinthian church rebelled against Paul's authority, and the congregation as a whole acted defiantly.

Upon Paul's return to Ephesus he wrote again to the Corinthians "in anguish of heart and many tears."[64] This "tearful," or "severe" letter, as it is sometimes called (Letter C), probably was dispatched by Titus and contained an ultimatum from the Apostle. Certainly he demanded punishment of the offender.[65] While awaiting the return of his fellow-worker, Paul suffered deep anxieties. Had he dealt too harshly with the Corinthians? It is probable that this "severe letter" was not preserved; however, according to many scholars, 2 Corinthians 10–13 contains a significant part of this letter that so deeply grieved its recipients.*

When Paul left Ephesus and came to Troas he found the situation opportune for the preaching of the gospel, but his "mind could not rest." Hoping to find Titus, who would bring him news of Corinth, Paul "went on to Macedonia." If the reader turns from these notes (from 2 Cor. 2:12f.) to 7:5, it will be evident that Paul's narrative is resumed after a lengthy excursus. Have fragments of one or more letters been interpolated into the text of Paul's letter? Some scholars conjecture that 2 Corinthians 2:14–7:4 (excepting 6:14–7:1) was originally part of a letter written by Paul as a self-defense upon hearing of the presence in Corinth of "apostles" who were opposing him.[66] Since Paul's outburst of praise (2:14ff.) is understandable in its canonical context, there would seem to be "no inescapable necessity" to regard this passage as "a secondary insertion."[67]

*It has been often claimed that after writing 2 Cor. 1–9 Paul could not have written the angry, sarcastic words that follow. Therefore 2 Cor. 10–13 must be a part of another letter, the tearful, severe letter written after Paul's "painful visit" to Corinth.

The most serious objection to this view is that the defiance dealt with in the se-

When Titus joined Paul, the Apostle learned that the Corinthians had been moved to grief and repentance by his severe letter. The offender had been punished by the congregation, although the specific action had occasioned some disagreement.[68]

Paul experienced great relief from his depression. As soon as possible he began a letter to the Corinthians, 2 Corinthians 1:1ff., "the thankful letter," so-called (Letter D). He wrote in a reminiscent mood. The contrast of his states of mind when writing the "severe letter" and when receiving the report from Titus gave expression to a predominantly confident mood. At the same time, there is a defensive undercurrent of anxiety that resonates throughout; an ambivalence of feeling (such as one may sense in reading the early statements in 1 Thessalonians). In acknowledging his gratitude and basic confidence in the establishment of a new plateau in his relations with the Corinthians, Paul makes frequent digressions to avoid misunderstandings, or, defensively, to clarify the import of his ministry as it relates to them.[69]

vere letter (2 Cor. 2:3f. and 7:8f.) is not treated in 2 Cor. 10–13. Also, in 12:14, 13:1, 10 Paul writes of his purpose of an early visit; when Paul wrote the severe letter he had decided against an early visit, disdaining another confrontation.

PAUL'S "THANKFUL LETTER" TO THE CORINTHIANS

A. Introduction, 1:1–11
1. The address, 1:1f.
2. The thanksgiving: gratitude for God's consolation; for his deliverance from earth, 1:3–11
B. Paul's defense of his integrity: a change of plans explained; the severe letter sent in lieu of another painful visit, 1:12:4
C. The offender's punishment sufficient; Paul's relief with the coming of Titus, 2:5–17

The "thanksgiving" of this letter celebrates God's mercy and unfailing comfort made known to Paul as a sharer in the sufferings of Christ. Elsewhere Paul describes the vital union between the believer and his Lord, which faith establishes, as a crucifixion with Christ.[70] This cannot mean that the sufferings of an apostle of Christ afford a complementary redemptive value, that alone the cross of Jesus is lacking efficacy.[71] Yet in Paul's mind, the life of the Church, as Christ's body, is inseparably related to the eschatological events of Christ's death and resurrection: as founder of the Corinthian church, Paul is called to bear a special "affliction" on its behalf; as fellow-members of Christ's body, the Corinthians are themselves sharers of the same sufferings. Paradoxically, in the midst of these afflictions both share abundantly divine comfort. One finds in these words a profound theological context for the whole of 2 Corinthians.[72]

Vigorously defending himself, Paul declares that his dealings with the Corinthians had always been forthright and consistent. He was under compulsion to specify his legitimate claims since they were being disputed, to commend his actions that were made to appear vicious. Paul twice takes an oath supporting the truth of his statements.

While Paul's rehearsal of recent events here and later in the letter is an appeal to let bygones be bygones—the Apostle devoutly wished to put the dreadful crisis behind him—the possibility that the church at Corinth would fail to meet "the test" cannot be completely dispelled.

As he launches a sustained defense of the source and nature of his ministry Paul is haunted by thoughts of those who impugn his motives and question his credentials.[73]

Paul's comments on the ministries of the old and new covenants emphasize the lasting splendor of the new age manifested in Christ as contrasted with the ephemeral, fading splendor of the revelation to Moses, whose authority is now superseded in the present age by the apostles and their ministry. Some interpreters consider that Paul is disputing here the visiting teachers alluded to in 2:17; 3:1, who, in their Judaizing zeal, were seeking to impose upon the Corinthians obedience to the Mosaic Law. But the thrust of the Apostle's words about the two dispensations (literally; "ministries") is not that the gospel abrogates the demands of the "written code," e.g., circumcision and food laws. He seems intent only in declaring that the transient glory of the old covenant has been surpassed by the glory of Christ proclaimed in the Apostle's *kerygma*. This passage, then, affords no substantial evidence for equating the activities of Paul's Jewish Christian opponents in Corinth with those of the Judaizers in Galatia.

The undercurrent of defensiveness, never far beneath the surface of Paul's statements of confidence, a confidence bolstered by Titus' assurance, erupts in the following section.[74] The invisible world-rulers of this age reinforce the resistance of men to God's revelation in Christ, and his apostles contend with the same demonic forces seeking to frustrate their ministries. Yet in the face of such formidable and crushing opposition, Paul writes that he does not "lose heart." In the consummation of the age now inaugurated, the "god of this world" and all other antithetical powers will be subjugated by God, who will raise from the dead those persons belonging to the Lord Jesus. Just as Paul does not consider the benefits of his suffering and consolation apart from his Corinthian converts (1:6f.), he is not minded to think of his own salvation apart from theirs.

Paul's description of the Christian's hope of inheriting "a house not made with hands, eternal in the heavens" has led some scholars to distinguish the eschatology expressed here from that set forth in 1 Corinthians and the Thessalonian letters.[75] The language contrasting the visible world with the perfect and enduring, invisible world and his distinctions between the outward and inner person do appear Greek. Nevertheless, Paul's rabbinical traditions and his apocalyptic eschatology remain in the background for correctly interpreting this passage. The prospect of the full exposure of everyone's life "before the judgment seat of Christ" was an essential element in Paul's eschatology. He believed that no person is saved by his or her "works"—such an assurance was grounded solely in a faithful response to God's grace offered in Christ—yet what a person "has done in the body," his or her "work" must be, and certainly will be, submitted to Christ's judgment.[76]

> D. 6. The controlling love of Christ, the one for all, 5:11–15
>   7. The new creation in Christ, 5:16f.
>   8. The ministry of reconciliation, 5:18–21
>   9. The paradoxes of the Apostle's experiences, 6:1–10

It is helpful in understanding the conclusion of Paul's apology concerning his ministry as an apostle, under the imagery of "reconciliation," to read without a pause 5:11–6:10. The grand themes developed in this passage catch our attention as, no doubt, they held Paul's. Note, however, should be taken of Paul's defensiveness (5:12f. and 5:3f., 8). The Apostle is unable to free his mind of his detractors and their calumnies.

As at the creation, so in the time of Christ, all is the work of God, wrote Paul. The "new creation" is viewed by Paul against the background of the creature's revolt. God is declared to be the Reconciler—not the one to be reconciled—even though He is the one perennially opposed by all humankind. The gospel of the death of Christ revealed to Paul the gravity of the rebel's situation: banishment from God's presence, subjection to God's wrath, as well as the wonder of God's reconciling grace.[77] Theologians find in Paul's statements *loci classicus* for discovering his doctrine of the atonement: What did Paul mean in saying: "he [Christ] died for all," or again, "for our sake he [God] made him [Christ] to be sin who knew no sin, so that in him we might become the righteousness of God"? A comparison with Paul's Letter to the Romans, especially 5:1ff., shows that the interpersonal imagery of enmity and reconciliation runs parallel in Paul's thought to his juridicial imagery of guilt and justification or vindication. In his application of both images Paul teaches his distinctive soteriology. In the Corinthian passage, however, the emphasis is not upon the meaning of God's action per se, but upon the agency of the Apostle as "ambassador" for Christ. Paul offers the Corinthians no "theory" of the atonement. Rather he proclaims that the way of reconciliation has been provided for overcoming their estrangement.

Paul puts his battle-scarred life on the line, so to speak, to reinforce his written appeals. Abused at Corinth and elsewhere, the Apostle's participation in the afflictions of Christ are his substantial credentials. "Working together, with him [i.e., Christ] we entreat you. . . ."[78]

> E. An Apostrophe: Paul's Special Appeal for Purity of Life, 6:14–7:4
>   1. For large-heartedness, 6:11–13
>   2. For consistency in faith and practice, 6:14–7:1
>   3. For mutual confidence, 7:2–4

As noted above, the poor connection of 6:14–7:1 in the context of this letter demands some explanation; however, it is doubtful that a satisfactory explanation can be found.[79] It cannot be denied that Paul's impassioned apostrophe, beginning at 6:11 and resumed at 7:2, is clumsily interrupted and that new subject matter is abruptly introduced. Yet Paul's letters contain numerous digressions and seemingly irrelevant asides, and 2 Corinthians, written during a greatly disturbed period, may contain more of the same. Already with 6:3 the emotional quality of Paul's entreaties disrupts the logical development of his ideas, and in recalling the dreadful vicissitudes and dramatic paradoxes of his life as an apostle, Paul may have been driven to abandon indirect discourse and resort to forthright exhortation. Perhaps it is too much, where such trauma of feeling is in evidence, to expect precise logical connections in Paul's correspondence. Possibly a loose connection may be found in free association with the following idea: openheartedness, i.e., uninhibited receptivity of persons with whom one has had differences, must not be mistaken for a careless tolerance. In Corinth such openheartedness had led repeatedly to indiscriminate accommodation of Christian attitudes, beliefs, and behavior to those of "unbelievers."

> F. Paul Recalls the Crisis Prior to the Report of Titus, 7:5–16
> 1. Paul's state before receiving encouraging news, 7:5–7
> 2. The severe letter in retrospect, 7:8–13a
> 3. Paul's comfort in the joy of Titus, 7:13b–16

The Apostle's long apology having ended in a flood tide of feeling, he returned to his reminiscence of the most recent crisis in his relations with the Corinthian congregation (7:5ff.), the details of which we have already considered. Apparently this crisis had frustrated Paul's earlier plans for a collection of money from the Corinthians for the relief of impoverished Christians in Jerusalem (1 Cor. 16:1ff.). Since Titus and two associates, who were to be the bearers of Paul's letter, were also being sent to assist the Corinthians in raising these relief funds, Paul writes to facilitate their work. The abrupt transition from 2 Corinthians 7:16 to 8:1 is not sufficient to support the hypothesis of some scholars that two different letters have been put together by a later editor of the Corinthian correspondence. Also, the contents of 9:1–15 seem to be a continuation from 8:24, presupposing the same situation in Corinth with respect to the collection, rather than part of a different letter.[80]

Notice the variety of motives to which Paul appealed in seeking to promote a generous offering for the poor in Jerusalem. Because he sought to remove all suspicion that these funds were being misappropriated, and because he spoke of desiring further proof of the Corinthian love, we may suspect that he was still uncertain of the church's attitude towards him.

> G. Paul Warns Against the Pseudoapostles; Identifies "the Signs of a True Apostle," 10:1–13:10
> 1. Paul's weapons of warfare, 10:1–6
> 2. Paul's words and deeds consistent, 10:7–11
> 3. Paul's sphere of authority includes Corinth, 10:12–18
> 4. Paul warns against beguiling preachers, 11:1–6
> 5. Paul sarcastically contrasts his relations to the church with those imposed by the "deceitful workmen," 11:7–21a
> 6. Paul boasts of his weaknesses; affirms his love, 11:21b–12:21
> 7. Paul threatens not to spare the Corinthians, 13:1–10
> H. Conclusion, 13:11–14
> 1. Final admonitions, 13:11f.

2. Greetings, 13:13
3. Benediction, 13:14

After giving his counsel concerning the offering, Paul's thoughts naturally turned to his chief purpose in writing the letter, the preparation of the church for a third visit from the Apostle. If the unity of 2 Corinthians is assumed, we must ask why thoughts of this visit should have led Paul to conclude the letter as he did.

Trivial reasons have been given for his allegedly abrupt change of mood at 10:1, such as a sleepless night or an attack of indigestion. It is certainly wise to depend on clues provided by the letter itself rather than resort to mere fancies. Perhaps 2 Corinthians was written piecemeal, and several days passed before Titus and the other emissaries to Corinth took leave of Paul. Meanwhile bad news was received. Other Jewish Christian apostles had come to Corinth, who were now claiming personal loyalty, superior knowledge, and demanding the church's support. By their preaching and other actions they seemed to be stirring up dying embers of resistance to Paul. Receiving such news as this, at the point of sending his thankful letter and his delegation to collect the Jerusalem offering, Paul was provoked to anger. The situation could become more critical than ever before. The Apostle was bound to assert his authority in no uncertain terms.[81]

An unending debate has centered upon the identity and purpose of Paul's aggressive opponents to whom harsh reference is made in 2 Corinthians 10–13. Are "the superlative apostles" the same persons as "the false apostles," or do the terms refer to different groups? Probably the latter alternative is supported by the references to them: "the superlative apostles" (to whom Paul is "not in the least inferior") are the Jerusalem apostles, James and the Twelve.[82] "The false apostles," "the deceitful workmen" (whom Paul derogates as "servants of Satan"), are the trouble-makers in Corinth.

What now can be inferred concerning the objectives of those persons who were preying upon Paul's converts? The intruders were Jewish Christians.[83] May they be identified as Judaists or Judaizers? Some scholars say yes. Claiming to be true apostles of Christ or authorized representatives of the original apostles and "servants of righteousness," they strongly opposed Paul's teaching that Gentile converts were wholly free from the requirements of the Mosaic Law. Some have claimed that Paul's reference to "letters of recommendation" in 2 Corinthians 3:1 shows that these Judaizers came as official representatives from Judea. They had brought to Corinth letters of introduction from James and the church of Jerusalem. The notice taken of Peter and "the brothers of the Lord" in 1 Corinthians 9:4ff. has been judged by some as evidence that a Judaizing element connected with Jerusalem was active in Corinth before the later arrival of these visiting brethren. In any event, sometime before the correspondence preserved in 2 Corinthians, Judaising opposition to Paul at Corinth was intensified.[84]

A principal objection to this Judaizer theory is that circumcision and the food laws are not alluded to in the Corinthians letters. According to Galatians and Romans, these were the issues in Paul's struggles against the Judaizers. It is possible, however that some Jewish Christians adopted other stratagems in opposing Paul. Since in his self-defense Paul insisted that he was as good a Jew as any of his opponents, it is said that they must have insisted not only on their Jewishness but upon the incompatability of Paul's gospel with Judaism.[85] Perhaps a principal stratagem of Paul's Jewish Christian opponents is disclosed in their insistence that Hellenistic criteria be applied in determining who possessed and who did not possess apostolic authority.[86] In this respect their receptivity to extra-Palestinian cultural influences is shown.

The major alternative to the theory that Paul's opposition came from Judaizers is the opinion that his latest rivals were Jewish Christians whose understanding of the gospel was pre-Gnostic. Early in the Corinthian correspondence Paul contended with persons claiming to possess "knowledge" and "spiritual gifts" that distinguished them from others who still "walked according to the flesh." According to this theory "the false apostles" of 2 Corinthians 10–13 (and some would include "the superlative apostles") were anonymous visitors who aggravated this incipient Gnosticism, preached "a different gospel," and downgraded the authority of Paul as one who "acted in a worldly fashion."[87]

The existence in Corinth of a pre-Gnostic Jewish Christianity can only be a speculative hypothesis.[88] The most that can be concluded with assurance is that Paul's most threatening opposition came from Jewish Christians who, in the Apostle's opinion, preached "another Jesus." Paul does not say wherein their "gospel" differed from the early Christian *kerygma* that he preached. Indeed, Paul made no attempt to refute the claims of his rivals. He could produce more impressive credentials of the sort they prized. But the signs of a true apostle are manifested in other ways—not in one's commissioning by the right ecclesiastical authorities, not in the power of an apostle's personality, not in one's extraordinary spiritual experience, not in the emoluments of the office, but only as one's life and preaching proclaim the crucified Jesus. In the weakness of Christ, and of his servants, the power of God and the wisdom of God are mediated.[89]

NOTES

1. Rom. 15:20.
2. Col. 4:16; 2 Cor. 1:23–2:9.
3. 1 Cor. 2:13, 16; 7:40.
4. A. Deissman, *St. Paul* (1912), pp. 9–13.
5. H. Lietzmann, *The Beginnings of Christianity* (1949), p. 114. C. K. Barrett presents specimens of letter writing in the Hellenistic Age, preserved in papyrus fragments, *The New Testament Background* (1957), pp. 27ff.
6. F. W. Beare, *St. Paul and His Letters* (1962), p. 42; McNeile-Williams, *Introduction to the New Testament*, p. 128f.
7. 1 Thess. 5:1ff.
8. 2 Thess. 2:1ff.
9. Kümmel (INT²) contests the arguments against the unity and authenticity of Paul's Second Letter to the Thessalonians, pp. 264–269. See also E. Best, *Commentary on The First and Second Epistles to the Thessalonians* (1972), pp. 45–58.
10. Acts 17:5ff. The Thessalonian mission was probably longer than three weeks. Cf. 1 Thess. 2:7ff.; 2 Thess. 3:7ff.; Phil. 4:15.

11. 1 Thess. 2:14. The vehemence of the indictment of "the Jews" that follows this notice of the sufferings of the Thessalonian Christians, verses 15f., is without parallel in Paul's letters. Some exegetes argue that this bitter complaint and malediction is unsuited to the context and is probably an interpolation.

12. G. Bornkamm, *Paul* (1971), pp. 63–65.

13. 1 Thess. 3:10.

14. 1 Thess. 4:1, 10; see also 3:12; 5:11.

15. L. Keck, "The First Letter of Paul to the Thessalonians," in *Interpreter's Bible One-Volume Commentary* (1971), p. 871; Best, *First and Second Epistles*, pp. 180–184.

16. Mt. 24:43f.; Lk. 12:39f. Acts 1:7; 2 Pet. 3:10.

17. 2 Cor. 5:17–6:2; Rom. 6:4–13.

18. 1 Thess. 3:13; also, 1 Thess. 2:19; 4:15; 5:23; 2 Thess. 2:1, 8. With the exception of 1 Cor. 15:23, Paul uses other terms with reference to the final coming of Christ. Later New Testament writers employ the term *parousia*: Mt. 24:3, 27, 37, 39; Jas. 5:7f; 1 Jn. 2:28; 2 Pet. 1:16; 3:4-12.

19. O. Cullmann, *Christ and Time* (1950), pp. 51ff.

20. 1 Thess. 5:14.

21. C. H. Dodd, *Gospel and Law* (1951), pp. 12ff.; D. G. Bradley, "The Typos as a Form in Pauline Paraenesis," *JBL* 72 (1953): 238ff.

22. 2 Thess. 2:15; 3:11. That another letter on similar subjects would be needed so shortly after the first is sufficient explanation for their close resemblance and sufficient cause for the sharpness of the Apostle's words in the second letter. Best, *First and Second Epistles*, p. 59.

23. 2 Thess. 2:2.

24. 2 Thess. 2:5f. Cf. 2 Esdras 5:1ff; Jub. 23:14ff; Mt. 24:10ff.

25. Both neuter (2:6) and masculine (2:7b) forms are used.

26. Cf. Rom. 13:1ff, see also p. 356.

27. Cf. Mk. 13:10; Acts 1:6–8; 3:19–21.

28. This absolute dating is based on the concurrence of Acts 18:11–16 and a Delphi inscription noting Gallio's proconsulship in Achaia.

29. R. Jewett, *A Chronology of Paul's Life* (1979), pp. 38–40. Acts 18:18, 22f.

30. Acts 19:1, 8–10.

31. Probably brought by Stephanus and two colleagues, 1 Cor. 16:15–18. N. Dahl conjectures that the three were partisans of the Apostle, 1 Cor. 1:12: "The Church at Corinth," in *Studies in Paul* (1977), pp. 40ff.

32. 1 Cor. 7:1; 8:1; 12:1; 16:1. Also 15:1.

33. 1 Cor. 1:11f. The letter to Paul may have aggravated the "quarreling" reported by members of Chloe's household. Were some contending "why not write Apollos instead?" Perhaps others were protesting, "why not write Cephas (Peter)?" Were still others, those claiming to "belong to Christ," insisting that they were wise enough to do without an apostle's counsel? Dahl, "The Church at Corinth," pp. 40ff.

34. Some scholars have argued that 1 Cor. is a secondary assemblage of several letters, but the arguments for partitioning the canonical text into two or more letters are not convincing. Kümmel, *INT²*, pp. 276–278. C. K. Barrett, *A Commentary on The First Epistle to the Corinthians* (1968), pp. 12–15.

35. C. T. Craig, "I Corinthians," *IB*, 10, (1954) 21f.; cf. J. Munck, *Paul and the Salvation of Mankind* (1959), pp. 142f.

36. 1 Cor. 1:13–17; 4:14f.

37. 1 Cor. 1:2, 26; 2:1–5.

38. Kümmel, *INT²*, pp. 274f.

39. W. Schmithals, *Gnosticism in Corinth* (1971), pp. 151–155. Cf. H. Conzelmann, *1*

Corinthians (1975), pp. 15, 56ff.; Kümmel, *INT²*, pp. 274ff.; R. Funk, *Language, Hermeneutic, and the Word of God* (1966), pp. 275–305.

40. W. Baird, "Among the Mature," *Int* 13 (1959): 425ff.; F. F. Bruce, *I and II Corinthians* (1971), p. 38.

41. R. Funk, *Language, Hermeneutics and the Word of God*, pp. 298–300. 1 Cor. 4:6f., 14–17; also 1:10.

42. Cf. Paul's comments concerning his threat to the whole congregation in his "severe letter," 2 Cor. 10:2; 13:7. Note also Rom. 9:3; Gal. 4:8. J. Munck, *Paul and the Salvation*, pp. 189ff. Cf. Barrett, *1 Corinthians*, pp. 125ff.

43. The thought of judgment leads to a digression in which Paul condemns Christians for legal actions against each other in pagan courts, 1 Cor. 6:1–8.

44. A common view is that for Paul the anthropological term *body* referred to the whole person, the self. The distinction is between "I am a body," and "I have a body."

45. Paul seems to agree in principle with the ascetics, since in 1 Cor. 6:12 he accepts the antilegalist principle, but serious qualifications follow in both instances. H. Chadwick, "All Things to All Men," *NTS* 1 (1955): 263ff.

46. Note the grudging formula, 1 Cor. 7:9b; but see p. 311.

47. 1 Cor. 7:31; 2 Cor. 5:16f.

48. G. Bornkamm, *Paul*, pp. 209f.; C. H. Dodd, *Gospel and Law*, pp. 28ff. In defending a maintenance of the *status quo* (which has been wrongly said to disclose Stoic influence) Paul refers to those who were slaves when they were called. His counsel is obscured by a text that has been taken to have opposite meanings (1 Cor. 7:21). See pp. 369f.

49. Cited by W. Barclay, *Letters to the Corinthians* (1957), p. 80

50. Lake quotes a comment of Porphyry, preserved by Eusebius: "most of all [evil spirits] delight in blood and impure meats, and enjoy these by entering into those who use them." *Earlier Epistles of St. Paul*, p. 195.

51. Since Paul does not invoke "the apostolic decree" in this letter (*contra.* Acts 15:28f., 16:4), support may be given to the view that he was not party to its provisions. See pp. 285f.

52. 1 Cor. 9:19–23. Note 2 Cor. 1:13ff.; Gal. 5:11.

53. Chadwick, "All Things to All Men," pp. 261ff. In his article, "The Missionary Stance of Paul in 1 Corinthians and in Acts" (Keck and Martyn, *Studies in Luke-Acts* (1980), pp. 194ff.), Bornkamm's interpretation of 1 Cor. 9:19ff. is sound, but the contrast between Paul's statement of his strategies and Paul's actions in Acts is too sharply drawn.

54. 1 Cor. 11:2. J. C. Hurd, *The Origin of 1 Corinthians* (1965), pp. 182ff.; cf. Conzelmann, *1 Corinthians*, p. 191.

55. E.g., J. Héring, *The First Epistle of St. Paul to the Corinthians* (1962), pp. 102–110. Héring, however, senses the tension in the Apostle's argument between the demands of "the natural order" (11:8f.), and "the Christian order" (11:11).

56. M. D. Hooker, "Authority on her head; an examination of 1 Cor. 11:10," *NTS*, 10 (1963): 410–416; R. Scroggs, "Paul and the Eschatological Woman," *JAAR* 40 (1972): 283–303; also *JAAR* 42 (1974): 532–537. One wonders what sense Paul's Gentile readers made of his comment: "because of the angels" (11:10). Jewish Christians might have understood that Paul referred to a common tradition that angels were guardians of the Law (B. Reicke, "The Law and This World According to Paul"; *JBL* 70 (1951): 261f.), a view that was extended by the priests at Qumran to apply to the offense given to the angels by infraction of the communities' purity rules in their assemblies. 1QSa ii. 3–11; 1QM vii, 4–6. J. Fitzmyer, "A Feature of Qumran Angelology and the Angels of 1 Cor. 11:10," *NTS* 4 (1957): 49ff.

57. Note Barrett's comment on the half-concealed motives prompting Paul's intransi-

gence on this issue, *1 Corinthians*, pp. 255–258; cf. Conzelmann, *I Corinthians*, p. 191.

58. E. Käsemann, "The Pauline Doctrine of the Lord's Supper," in *Essays on New Testament Themes* (1963), pp. 119–127.

59. 1 Cor. 14:5, 18, 39; cf. 1 Thess. 5:19; (Rom. 8:26f. ?).

60. For an analysis of various contemporary readings of Paul's intention, see H. W. Boers, "Apocalyptic Eschatology in 1 Corinthians 15," *Int* 21 (1967): 50ff.

61. 1 Cor. 15:12, 35. Cf. Justin Martyr, *Dial. with Trypho* 80.

62. Rom 6:5ff.; 2 Cor. 5:15; Gal. 2:19f.

63. 1 Cor. 4:8; 6:14f. See Barrett, *1 Corinthians*, pp. 347f.; Hurd, *Origin of I Corinthians*, pp. 282ff. Hurd believes that Paul's earlier eschatology (which he abandoned) contributed to the misunderstanding that he sought to overcome in 1 Cor. 15.

64. 2 Cor. 2:4f; 7:8f.

65. Munck surmises that Paul, nearing despair, threatened to deliver the church over to Satan if the offender was not disciplined, *Paul and Salvation*, 190ff.

66. G. Bornkamm, *Paul*, p. 245; D. Georgi, "Second Letter to the Corinthians, *IDBS* (1976) 185.

67. Kümmel, *INT²*, p. 291; Barrett, *2 Corinthians*, pp. 97, 23–25.

68. 2 Cor. 2:6ff.; 7:6–16.

69. Comment concerning the problems posed by 2 Cor. 8 and 9 will be deferred in order now to give consideration to the contents of 2 Cor. 1–7. See p. 328.

70. Rom. 6:6; Gal. 2:20.

71. Cf. 1 Cor. 1:2. Barrett, *2 Corinthians*, pp. 61f. See Col.: 24.

72. See J. L. Price, "Aspects of Paul's Theology and Their Bearing on Literary Problems of 2 Corinthians," in J. Geerlings, ed., *Studies and Documents* (1967), Vol. 39, pp. 95ff.

73. 2 Cor. 2:17–3:6.

74. 2 Cor. 4:1ff.

75. 2 Cor. 4:16–5:9. Cf. 1 Cor. 15:42ff.; 1 Thess. 4:14ff.; 2 Thess. 2:1ff. See Barrett, *2 Corinthians*, pp. 145–159; Bruce, *Paul*, pp. 300–313.

76. Cf. 1 Cor. 3:10–15; 4:1–5.

77. Rom. 1:18ff.; 5:12ff., see also pp. 386f.

78. 2 Cor. 6:1–10.

79. J. Fitzmyer identifies 2 Cor. 6:14–7:1 as a non-Pauline interpolation ("Qumran and the interpolated paragraph in 2 Cor. 6:14–7:1," in *Essays on the Semitic Background of the New Testament* [1971], pp. 205–217); H. D. Betz: an interpolation opposing Paul's teaching ("2 Cor. 6:14–7:1: An Anti-Pauline Fragment," *JBL* 92 [1973]: 88–108). Cf. Barrett, *2 Corinthians*, pp. 193ff., 23–25. Perhaps the tendency of some outspoken Corinthians to distance themselves from Paul was related to their readiness to resume their pagan ways.

80. An influential partition hypothesis is that originally 9:1–15 followed 7:16 and that 8:1–24 is an earlier letter (whose conclusion has been cut off), possibly sent by Titus "to speed up the collection for Jerusalem." This was before the return of Timothy (1 Cor. 4:17–21; 16:10), who brought the bad news that occasioned Paul's painful visit"; also before the writing of canonical 1 Cor. J. Weiss, *The History of Primitive Christianity* (1937), Vol. 1, pp. 353–357. Alternatively, 8:1-24 was written by Paul as an appendix to "the thankful letter" (2 Cor. 1:1–2:13, 7:5–16), and 9:1–15 was written later, before the visit Paul anticipates (2 Cor. 9:5, 11). G. Bornkamm, *Paul*, pp. 245f.

81. It is possible that 2 Cor. 10–13 was not originally a part "the thankful letter," but was written shortly afterwards when Paul received distressing news on the eve of

his departure for Corinth that his opposition was now intensified with the arrival of Jewish Christians from Jerusalem. Barrett, *2 Corinthians*, pp. 243–245. The assumption is that two letters, written with only a brief interval between, were put together in the correct chronological order to form canonical 2 Cor.

82. Cf. the temperate irony employed by Paul with reference "to those who were apostles before [him]," Gal. 1:17; 2:2, 6, 9.

83. 2 Cor. 11:22.

84. Barrett, *2 Corinthians*, pp. 28ff.

85. 2 Cor. 11:16–23.

86. Barrett surmises that Paul's opponents sought to establish in Corinth "a new, non-Pauline apostolate, emanating from Jerusalem, fundamentally Jewish, or Judaizing, but ready (as Paul was not) to adapt itself to criteria of apostleship proposed, or exacted, by the mainly Gentile church of Corinth." *2 Corinthians*, p. 40.

87. 2 Cor. 10:2.

88. Kümmel, *INT*², pp. 284–286.

89. 2 Cor. 11:23–12:10; also 2 Cor. 4:7–11; 6:4–10; I Cor. 1:18–25.

The Galatian and Roman Letters

Chapter
15

P AUL'S Letter to the Galatians was probably written while the controversies still raged at Corinth;[1] the Letter to the Romans within a few months. Thus we possess two other writings that shed light upon the concerns of the Apostle at this time. Yet the principal justification for grouping Galatians and Romans is not the temporal proximity of their composition. Both documents reflect Paul's vigorous response and defense in answer to a particular devastating attack upon the legitimacy of his work. In order to preserve "the truth of the gospel"[2] among his own converts in Galatia the Apostle developed his historic doctrine, "justification by faith," which many consider the heart of Paul's gospel. In writing to the Christian community at Rome, the fruit of the labor of others, Paul expounds the same doctrine hoping to extend its influence, and to counter opposition on a broader front.

THE LETTER TO THE GALATIANS

Galatians was written in hot indignation. From beginning to end Paul vigorously defended his right to speak as an apostle commissioned by the Lord Jesus Christ, his independence of all human authority, and the total adequacy of his gospel and its moral dynamic for all people. As one reads the letter—if possible without interruption, which is its best introduction—several interrelated questions arise. Who were these Galatians? What was their geographical and ethnic identity? Can a place be found in the New Testament records for the establishment of churches by this name? Can we know the particular circumstances that led Paul to write this letter?

Answers to these questions must be drawn from Galatians and a few unclear references in Acts, but there is no consensus concerning them. With a few notable exceptions, scholars are fairly certain that the situation which prompted this impassioned letter can be identified. But there is no agreement over the destination of the Galatian letter or the social milieu of its recipients. Fortunately it is not necessary to solve these critical problems fully in order to appreciate the essential meaning of this book, either in the early or the modern Church.

HISTORICAL QUESTIONS

Who were the "foolish Galatians"?[3] In the third and fourth centuries B.C.E. hordes of Celtic people invaded the Italian and Greek peninsulas. Eventually they were contained in the interior of Anatolia, where they built settlements. Chief among these were Pessinus, Ancyra, and Tavium. The Greek called these barbarians *Keltai* or *Galatae*, the Romans, *galli*. During the Roman conquests this territory was annexed and gradually extended. In 25 B.C.E. Galatia became an imperial Roman province. Its area included districts adjacent to the old kingdom of Galatia—Lycaonia and Pisidia—and parts of Phrygia and Cappadocia. We thus can see that in Paul's day the term *Galatians* was ambiguous.

From the ancient times to the present, many have believed that Paul addressed his letter to the people who lived in inner Anatolia who were Galatians by racial heritage or assimilation. In Acts 16:6 it is reported that Paul and his fellow missionaries "went through the region of Phrygia and Galatia." Again, on his next journey, Paul "went from place to place through the region of Galatia and Phrygia, strengthening all the disciples."[4] On the basis of these notes in Acts the assumption has been that Paul preached the gospel to the Galatian people during his "second missionary journey," having been frustrated in his attempt to proceed to Asia.[5] Churches were established at Pessinus and other settlements along the western border of the old kingdom of Galatia, perhaps at the chief city, Ancyra. An interval of three years may have elapsed before Paul's second visit to this region during the "third missionary journey." Several statements in the Galatian letter suggest that by this time disturbing symptoms of trouble had begun to appear.[6] Sometime later, when Paul was either at Ephesus or in the region of Macedonia, news was received that prompted the Letter to the Galatians.[7]

Since the late eighteenth century this account of the origin of Galatians has come under attack sporadically. But at the turn of the present century Sir William Ramsay, English archeologist and historian of the region of Asia Minor, persuaded numerous New Testament scholars that Paul's Galatian letter was written to the churches founded on his "first missionary journey"—Antioch, Iconium, Lystra, and Derbe.[8] This position became known as "the South Galatian theory"; the older view was called "the North Galatian theory." Some scholars refer to these opposing theories as "the province hypothesis" and "the territory hypothesis."

In defense of the South Galatian, or province, theory it is argued that Paul's allusions to geographical or political areas must not be made to conform to Luke's usage. The Apostle almost always names the Roman province in which his churches were located.[9] "Galatia" was the only inclusive term that could have been used to identify churches at Antioch, Iconium, Lystra, and Derbe. While it is not necessary to the South Galatian theory to show that Paul founded no churches in North Galatia, it has been observed that, contrary to his usual custom, the author of Acts mentions no cities in the travel notes of 16:6ff. and 18:23. In the latter passage it is said that Paul strengthened all "the disciples," not the churches.[10]

Other things are said to point to South Galatia as the designation of Paul's letter. In Galatians 2:9 and 13 Barnabas is mentioned as though he were known to the readers. According to Acts, Barnabas was with Paul on his mission in South Galatia but the two had parted company at the beginning of the next journey when, it is supposed, churches were established in North Galatia. Some claim that churches in the more populous cities of South Galatia would have been subjected to the propagandizing activity of Paul's opponents from other places more than would those of the relatively inaccessible region of North Galatia.

A question related to the geographical location of the Galatian churches, but more important, is that of the ethnic character and social status of these converts. Perhaps the majority of scholars have held that the Galatians were Gentiles.[11] But a case can be made for the view that in Galatia, as elsewhere, Paul's congregations were composed of proselytes and god-fearers drawn from Judaism as well as Greeks. The susceptibility of the Galatians to the pressures of anti-Pauline Judaizers is more understandable if one assumes that Hellenistic Jewish Christians were being addressed in Paul's apology along with the Gentile majority in the Galatian churches.[12]

In view of the highly sophisticated and refined literary manner in which Paul addresses the Galatians it would seem that they were an urban, relatively prosperous, civilized group.[13] This may seem to support the South Galatian destination, yet it is possible that the Celts living in the old Galatian territory had been assimilated into a Hellenized, Romanized society, and were no longer the rough and ungovernable barbarians of an earlier time.

INTERPRETING GALATIANS

A. Introduction, 1:1–10
   1. A prescript containing a declaration of Paul's authority and independence as an apostle; an ascription of praise, 1:1–5
   2. Concerning the apostasy of the Galatians; a double curse, 1:6–9
   3. A defensive apostrophe, 1:10
B. Paul and Jerusalem: A Personal Apology (Mostly Narrative), 1:11–2:14
   1. Paul's gospel based on "a revelation of Jesus Christ," 1:11f.
   2. Paul's early life opposed to the gospel and the church, 1:13F.
   3. Paul's conversion isolated him from Jerusalem, 1:15–17
   4. The fifteen-day "acquaintance visit" with Peter and James, 1:18–20
   5. After a lapse of fourteen years, the conference visit, 2:1–10
   6. Paul's altercation with Peter and Barnabas in Antioch, 2:11–14

In his salutation Paul wrote an unequivocal declaration of his apostleship and independence, suggesting at once that his detractors were attempting to subordinate him to others and derive his authority from them. The emphatic denial "not from men" should not be understood as meaning that he had derived nothing from those "who were apostles before" him. Paul made it clear that there was but "one gospel" from the beginning, and that the apostles were in full accord concerning its essentials.[14]

Dispensing with the customary "thanksgiving," Paul came directly to the point of his letter. He expressed dismay that the Galatian churches were "so quickly turning to a different gospel." The statement is not a decisive clue to the date or destination of the letter.[15] Paul's astonishment may spring from the fact that some of his churches had so readily succumbed to the teaching of Judaizers when this was the very danger against which he had warned them. During a second visit Paul had pronounced a curse on any man who claimed that a message other than the one the Galatians had received was the gospel.

The question interjected at this point (1:10) reveals Paul's acute sensitivity to the charge that he was a publicity seeker. But without further delay, Paul reviewed his relations with the Jerusalem church. The Apostle's reference to his conversion attracts our attention. But the curious who wish to know "what really happened" are disappointed. Paul only said: it was "a revelation of Jesus Christ," and that his life as a Jew—as his first readers knew—had not disposed him toward Christianity. Like the great prophets of Israel, Paul spoke of his calling as antedating his birth—and, also echoing the oracles of the prophets, declared that when God's call came to him the purpose of his life had been revealed.[16]

Paul had not gone directly to Jerusalem after his conversion. It is not likely that he felt compelled to detail his itineraries. Even in the specific references—"after three years . . . after fourteen years"—he does not say from what points he reckons these intervals of time. Paul wished to emphasize that there had been no need for him to consult the original apostles. He was not their emissary. Nevertheless they knew what he was doing and did not oppose him. When he did revisit Jerusalem "after fourteen years" it was only "by revelation" that he was impelled to go up.

We face again the question: Does Paul in Galatians 2 report the same meeting described in Acts 15? In the latter source, Paul went up to Jerusalem as a commissioner of the church at Antioch. Galatians stresses Paul's independence, contradicting perhaps a delegate status. Yet in spite of this and other differences in detail, the circumstances of Galatians 2 and Acts 15 are so closely parallel that both would seem to be describing the Jerusalem Conference (see p. 285). The perplexity arises from Paul's statement that the authorities had "added nothing" to him at this time. The author of Acts was probably in error in connecting the decree of 15:19ff. with this Jerusalem Conference.*

Paul's narrative ends with his report of a distressing sequel to the Jerusalem Conference.[17] A few historians would place this incident at Antioch before the Conference, arguing that Peter and Barnabas would not have acted in this way after the decision reached in Jerusalem.[18] Others do not see how Paul could have ignored the decree so quickly and dared rebuke Peter and Barnabas for their vacillation. But the episode is intelligible as an aftermath of the Conference, especially if 15:19ff. was no part of its proceedings. The Conference had dealt with the crucial issue of circumcision and the Gentiles. But what of Jewish Christians and the law? Were they released from its demands, especially the food laws, which distinguished Jews of the Diaspora and helped to prevent their absorption by paganism? The two issues were logically related, as Paul contended. But they probably arose separately. Luke may have failed to recognize this in retrospect.

However one deals with the historical problem, one can see that Paul appealed to the Antioch incident to prove his independence. And to clarify "the truth of the gospel" he proclaimed: that "a man is not justified (or made righteous) by works of the law, but through faith in Jesus Christ. . . ." Paul re-

* Gal. 2:3 presents an important textual problem. Should one read "to those [demanding that the Greek, Titus, be circumcised] we did not yield by submission for a moment?" Or, with some witnesses, declare that "for a moment" Paul did yield to this demand? Some scholars refer to 1 Cor. 9:19–23 and Acts 16:3, and conclude that Paul agreed to the circumcision of Titus. But Paul's point is that to have yielded in this instance would have meant that "the truth of the gospel" would have been compromised.

ferred to the Antioch incident to lead his readers into the heart of the gospel's message for all, Gentiles as well as Jews. Having vindicated the divine origin of his apostleship and the legitimacy of his gospel, he turned to teach the truth of his universal gospel and to oppose its perversion by the Judaizers.

C. The Gospel of Justification by Faith Proclaimed in Opposition to Judaizers (A Vigorous Polemic), 2:15–4:31
   1. Paul affirms an essential agreement with Jewish Christians, 2:15f.
   2. Paul denies (false) inferences drawn from this teaching, 2:17f.
   3. Paul's self-apology summarized in four statements, 2:19f.
   4. Paul refutes his opponents' serious charge, 2:21
   5. The evidence of experience, 3:1–5
   6. The argument from the Abraham tradition, 3:6–14
   7. An argument from legal practice, applied to Abraham, 3:15–18
   8. A digression on the purpose of Torah, 3:19–25
   9. An appeal to Christian beliefs and hopes, 3:26–4:11
   10. An appeal to friendship, 4:12–20
   11. An allegorical argument: an interpretation of the Abraham tradition, 4:21–30
   12. Summary of Paul's argument, 4:31

Paul's argument in Galatians revolves around two poles: (1) an appeal to the experience of his converts and for consistency in their belief and practice, and (2) an appeal to scripture purposed to show that God's promise to Abraham and to his posterity was to those who believe instead of to those who are observers of the Law of Moses.[19]

The first appeal to experience, launched in a series of questions, is linked to the preceding self-apology (2:15–21). The Galatians' experience of salvation did not conform to human expectations, for it was not the consequence of human achievement or merit. This was consistent with the experience of Paul and that of others. Paul's call to apostleship, which his opponents represented as lacking legitimacy, occurred nevertheless, clearly the result of God's grace. The gospel Paul preached should, according to ordinary expectations, never have been recognized as valid. Yet it had been approved by the authorities in Jerusalem. Jewish Christians (one might reasonably assume) should never have agreed to table-fellowship with Gentiles, but it was done in Antioch following Peter's leadership. Consistent with these unexpected events is the present reality of salvation in and through Jesus, the crucified Messiah. According to Jewish theology this never could have happened. But as a consequence of God's resurrection of Jesus, it was in fact happening. The Galatians who were being "delivered from the present evil age,"[20] were participants in "a new creation,"[21] and salvation was being offered to all who "have believed in Christ Jesus, in order to be justified by [the] faith of [or "in"] Christ."[22]

It is significant that Paul appealed first of all to the experience of his converts. It is also significant that he took his case to the scriptures. Apparently the Judaizers had been defending their position by appealing to Genesis 17. God's promises to Abraham and to his offspring applied to Jews and to circumcised Gentiles only. Paul took his stand upon Genesis 15:6 and employed this test as the basis of a long and sustained argument, which recalls other aspects of the Genesis story concerning Abraham as well as oracles from the Prophets. Paul was as eager as were his opponents to link the Christian gospel with God's former revelation recorded in the scriptures. He was certain that the good news that God justifies persons having faith is implicit in the whole history of salvation.[23]

Paul's use of scripture may appear to some readers as not only obtuse but perverse, especially when he claims that God's promise made to Abraham's "offspring" referred to one, not to many.[24] Surely Paul knew a collective noun when he saw one. But underlying these rabbinical subtleties are convictions that combine to form a profound theology of history. The ideal of a holy people—the true offspring of Abraham—envisioned by the prophets of Israel under various images, was not fully realized until the coming of the Messiah. But when "the time had fully come," Jesus in his own person fulfilled this ideal, and through the gift of the Spirit, an ever-widening inclusive fellowship was being formed. The Church of Jesus Christ is the new Israel of God, the eschatological community, inheriting the promises of God unto the fathers. Paul quotes the Old Testament "to show that already in Israel (not only in the church) are found justification by faith, the promise as basis and scope of the law, and the covenant with the free children of God."[25]

Paul's valuation of the Mosaic Law in Galatians seems to be almost wholly negative. Some interpreters have concluded that this is indeed so. All persons who "rely on the works of the law" to merit God's blessing are under its curse.[26] It is declared that God's gift of the law, "four hundred and thirty years" after the promise to Abraham, certainly did not set aside the promise.[27] The law was provided to expose the sinfulness of God's people and to keep them dependent upon his gracious promise. Nevertheless, Paul writes that the law was not given directly to God, or it would have had the power "to make alive."[28] Instead, the law had been given by angels and by the hand of an intermediary, Moses.[29] The law was a temporary and provision means of discipline to bring persons to Christ. Accordingly, believers in him are free from the tutelage of law; to seek salvation out of the law is to seek bondage.[30]

Although some interpreters of Galatians 3 view Paul's statements as primarily intended to depreciate the Mosaic Law, the thrust of Paul's argument is rather against those who misuse it by seeking to impose certain of its commandments or prohibitions upon Gentiles. The practical effect of this was to exclude some persons from the covenant promises of God. Against the Judaizers, Paul fought for a community of God's people—his true "sons" and daughters, "heirs according to promise"—in which none are excluded. In Galatians 3:26–4:7 Paul's intention is stated quite explicitly. (For an understanding of Paul's evaluation of the law per se, one must also turn to certain of the Apostle's statements in his Letter to the Romans. See p. 353.)

If careful attention is given to Paul's use of another term, beginning with his important assertion in 2:16, further insight into the Apostle's specific concerns can be grasped. This term is *faith*, associated with Christ, whose name is written in the genitive case. In the RSV the Greek phrase is translated "faith *in* Christ," but it can equally well read "the faith of Christ," as other scholars have contended.[31] One writer argues persuasively that Paul's thought, throughout this section of the Galatian letter—which is concerned with the relation between the Christian and the Mosaic Law—is influenced by his own and his reader's knowledge of transactions prescribed by Roman law for the transmission of inheritances.[32] According to ordinary legal procedures, a testator assigned to a sole heir his legacy. In the testament, or covenant, provision was made for a *fidei commissum*, a trust, which, when accepted by the sole heir, gave him the right to designate beneficiaries who would share this legacy and who would thus themselves become heirs of the testator. Moreover, a Roman could, by his testament, adopt aliens or strangers so that in every sense they became sons and heirs. He could also provide testamentary "tutors" for them, as for his minor children designated beneficiaries, until the death of the sole heir, at which time the inheritance would be shared.

Paul's argument does seem to draw upon these analogies provided by Roman legal practices. He writes of Abraham and of his rightful descendants; of Christ as the sole offspring through whom God's blessing of Abraham comes to the Gentiles; of those who are heirs, yet subject to a tutelage until Christ accepts and fulfills the testamentary *fidei commissum* (summarily, the faith of Christ), whereby he makes them sons and heirs of the testator, i.e., God. Paul's primary use of the term *faith* is therefore analogous to the *fidei commissum* on which the testament or covenant is based and through which it is effectuated. This is the faith that Paul attributes to Christ, i.e., the faithful execution of his trust. But, it should be noted, "faith" is used by Paul in other contexts—as in the case of Abraham in the past and Christians in the present—to signify that trustfulness befitting those who have been chosen beneficiaries, who are "heirs according to promise."

At 4:8 Paul appeals directly to his converts from paganism. He asked if they wished to become enslaved again "to the weak and beggarly elemental spirits." Paul presupposed belief in invisible demons or world rulers, a commonplace, as we have seen, of the Graeco-Roman world. Were the Judaizers in Galatia pandering to popular Gentile superstitionn, claiming that adherence to Jewish dietary laws and the ritual calendar delivered persons from the baneful influences of the spirit world? Tendencies toward syncretism were certainly present in Galatia. Was there an incipient Gnosticism in the Galatian Judaizers' doctrine? Some find evidence supporting an affirmative reply; others deny its sufficiency.[33]

An allegory based on the Genesis story of Abraham's sons follows an impassioned, personal appeal, and provides a transition to Paul's moral exhortation. The controversial mood is sustained. The allegory introduces the theme of freedom and slavery by sharply contrasting two mutually exclusive ways of salvation. The responsible use of this freedom informs the admonitions of Paul that follow, which are concerned with those who are not under law but who are led by the Spirit.

D. Exhortations: "For Freedom Christ Has Set Us Free," 5:1–6:10
    1. A solemn warning concerning alternatives; circumcision—perfect obedience versus a faithful response to the Spirit's prompting—"the hope of righteousness"; an angry aside, 5:1–12
    2. The hallmark of freedom: neighbor-love, an antidote to selfish contention, 5:13–15

3. The dualism of "flesh" and "spirit"; their respective "fruit," 5:16–24
4. Important ethical maxims; summary of Paul's exhortation, 5:25–6:10

It is probable that one reason the Galatian Christians were wavering in their belief in the viability of Paul's version of the gospel was that their initial sense of freedom was being dampened by problems with the "flesh." Paul's opponents were capitalizing on this low morale and were claiming as safeguards the Torah and circumcision.[34] Paul countered by declaring that the freedom of believers is not a state of deprivation and impotence. Christ has enabled his followers to live in freedom; by means of the Spirit he enables them to shake off all forms of slavery. "If the Galatians' 'freedom in Christ' is to be preserved, it can be done only by the same means by which their freedom was created: the work of Christ and the Spirit. Those who were liberated by the Spirit can protect their freedom only by 'walking by the Spirit,' by 'being led by the spirit,' and by 'following the Spirit.' "[35]

Paul's argument in this hortatory section is a further attack upon the central problem in Galatia. One need not suppose what he has turned from the Judaizers to inveigh against another group. When first attacking the Judaizers Paul asked them: "Having begun in the Spirit are you now ending in the flesh?" Moreover, Paul's reference to those "who are spiritual" has no derogatory implication, and at the close of the letter Paul is still opposing those "who would compel" the Galatians to be circumcised and who thereby exalted "the flesh."

E. The Letter's Conclusion, 6:11–18
1. Authentication by Paul's own hand, 6:11
2. Recapitulation of charges against his opponents, 6:12f.*
3. Paul's position restated, 6:14f.
4. A blessing upon "the Israel of God," 6:16
5. A personal appeal, 6:17
6. Final benediction, 6:18

*The point of Paul's stinging attack upon his opponents in the "epistolary postscript" is not altogether clear (Gal. 6:12f.) Why would Judaizers fear persecution, and by whom? Probably the anti-Paulinists were fearful of expulsion from the synagogue (which they wished to avoid, believing Christianity to be a sectarian movement within Judaism?). By insisting upon the circumcision of Gentile converts, Judaizers sought to avert the charge that their proselytes were not being subjected to the Torah.

The letter ends on a very personal note. We can reflect upon it in relation to the other personal appeals that break through Paul's argument toward the end of the doctrinal section.[36] The reader may have noticed that in these passages Paul's state of mind and manner of speaking are reminiscent of 2 Corinthians. In both letters the Apostle's estrangement from his churches led him to anguished expressions of emotion, to bitter irony, and to scornful reproach of his enemies. He contrasted sharply the reception that these churches had given him with their present attitudes, to their shame. He was much occupied with the mystery that spiritual strength is made perfect in weakness. In both letters Paul was forced to self-assertion. When we consider these things, along with the similarities between Galatians and Romans, which shall be shown presently, it is reasonable to conclude that Galatians was written during the Corinthian crisis. Henceforth Paul asked to be spared the anxiety caused by the backsliding Galatians, the physical effects that his sufferings and persecution had had upon him. If he must boast, he would boast of the things that showed his weakness. He would point to "the branding marks of Jesus" that were upon his body, for he is Christ's slave.[37] Christ may do with him as he wills. Throughout the

Letter to the Galatians, Paul exalted Christ and claimed a subservience to him alone.

THE LETTER TO THE ROMANS

THE SETTING OF ROMANS IN PAUL'S CAREER

The Letter to the Romans is, by common agreement, the most considered and systematic statement of Paul's gospel. Its great—many would say incomparably great—influence upon the history of the Christian Church is a matter of record. Because of this it is sometimes thought that Romans manifests a timeless quality. Yet the book is a genuine letter and not a theological treatise. Its exposition of the gospel reflects the controversies, pastoral problems, and spiritual experiences of its author.[38] A knowledge of the setting of Romans in Paul's career contributes much to its understanding.

Before reading Romans through one should examine its introduction (1:1–15) and the personal notes at the end (15:14ff) to observe the letter's testimony to its origin. For some while Paul's eyes had been turned toward Rome. He longed to preach there and to follow this visit with a mission in Spain. (One may notice Paul's confession that he preferred the work of a pioneer evangelist to that of a pastor who must build on the work of others. Indeed Paul would rather that others build on the foundations that he himself had laid, so that he might be free to press on to other places.)[39] Before Paul could visit Rome, however, he had an obligation to discharge. He must deliver the contribution for the Christian poor in Jerusalem.*

The content of Romans 16 presents some puzzling data. Could Paul, a stranger to Rome, have known more than twenty-six persons in its church? When Paul wrote 1 Corinthians from Ephesus, he sent greetings from "Prisca and Aquila together with the church in their house." Perhaps this point was not noticed, but examine 1 Corinthians 16:19 and Romans 16:5. Is it conceivable that within such a brief period this couple had returned to Rome, and that their house had become a gathering place of Christians? Another surprise is that "the dissensions and difficulties" referred to in Romans 16:17f. are not alluded to in chapters 1–15. Paul's warning against the creators of dissension sounds like the authoritative directive of a pastor to his people, hardly one written by a missionary to a church he had neither founded nor visited.[40] For these and other reasons many persons believe that Romans 16 was not a part of the letter written to the Romans. Rather it is an extant fragment of what was probably a brief letter of commendation for Phoebe, and of greetings to friends, written from Corinth or Cenchreae to the church at Ephesus.[41]

The question of the integrity of Romans having been raised, brief notice must be taken of the curious textual variations in its last three chapters. The doxology (16:25–27) appears at several different places in copies of the letter, while others omit it altogether. In the oldest Greek manuscript of Paul's letters, the third-century codex, Papyrus 46, the doxology follows 15:33. In other valuable manuscripts it stands after 16:23, or else after verse 24. Second-century Christian writers reported that copies of the letter in Rome and in African

*This prospective journey to Jerusalem cannot be the one noted in Acts 18:22, for at that time the ministry of Ephesus lay before Paul. It must be the journey narrated in Acts 20, the object of which was delivery of the collection gathered among his Gentile churches.

churches contained only chapters 1–14.[42] The conclusion is that this doxology was not written by Paul but by some editor. Perhaps it was composed as a suitable ending for a short form of the letter.*

*Beyond this conclusion, opinions can be grouped into two major alternatives: Paul wrote the short letter (Rom. 1–14) intending it for his churches in the East (later editing a copy to be sent to Rome, with a "covering letter"); or Paul originally wrote one of the longer versions. It is a plausible view that Paul wrote chapters 1–15 to the Romans and that a copy (with its postscript, chapter 16) was sent to Ephesus. T. W. Manson's hypothesis, summarized with approval by J. Munck (*Paul and Salvation of Mankind,* pp. 197ff), and G. Bornkamm (*Paul,* pp. 88–96).

Although some uncertainty remains concerning the exact content of Paul's letter and whether or not he wrote it only for the Roman Christian community, the immediate purpose in sending this letter to Rome is clear. By means of it Paul announced his coming, explained the delay, and sought to gain the understanding of this important church, and perhaps its assistance, before visiting Rome en route to Spain. Can one say more concerning the purpose of the Letter to the Romans? Some scholars have felt that the broad lines of Paul's theological argument suggest "other, deeper grounds."[43] We press, then, beyond the relatively simple query "Why did Paul send this letter to the Romans?" to the more difficult question "Why did he write it in the way he did?"

The letter's testimony to Paul's lack of direct relationship to the church at Rome makes it very unlikely that its subject matter stands in apposite relation to specific controversial issues within the Roman congregation. A few scholars have adopted the opposing hypothesis, namely, that Paul was informed of specific problems in the Roman church and addressed these in his letter.[44] Still others have detected a self-conscious defensiveness and believe that Paul at this time was moved to write an impassioned apology for his life and mission.[45] Many scholars have concluded that Paul composed this letter for the purpose of clarifying his principal convictions—for the benefit of the Romans and others—convictions that had been hammered out in the fires of controversy, convictions that needed to be drawn together in a constructive relation to one or more major truths of the gospel. Perhaps Paul realized that his opportunities for doing such a thing might be severely limited in the future.[46]

The history of this letter's interpretation shows that many generations of readers, especially since the Protestant Reformation, have tended to fix their attention upon its teaching concerning justification by faith *interpreted in the context of an individual's experience.* The significance of justification by faith for Christian theology has been very great indeed. Yet the result of this concentration of reader interest has been that segments of Romans have become somewhat tangential to its "main theme" containing, it is said, irrelevant or at least unnecessary excursuses.[47] This letter has long suffered from interpreters who, for one good reason or another, have limited their interest in its teaching too narrowly, and then assumed that Paul's interest was likewise limited. Perhaps the Apostle's statement that the Christian gospel reveals "the righteousness of God" affords the surest clue to his overarching purpose in writing to the Romans.

INTERPRETING ROMANS

A. Introduction, 1:1–15
  1. The superscription containing a credal statement, 1:1–7
  2. The thanksgiving (including Paul's wish to visit Rome) 1:8–15
B. The Gospel According to Paul, 1:16–11:36
  1. The gospel reveals God's righteousness, 1:16–18
  2. The righteousness of God manifested in judgment: the Gentiles who refuse

the (general) knowledge of God are without excuse, 1:19–23; idolatry and the resultant depravity of human beings, 1:24–32

3. The righteousness of God manifested in judgment: the self-esteemed "innocent critics," 2:1–11; the impartiality of divine retribution, 2:12–16
4. The righteousness of God manifested in judgment: Jews, their privileges and practices contrasted, 2:17–24; circumcision and the mark of "a real Jew," 2:25–29; some Jewish objections countered; 3:1–8
5. Provisional summary of Paul's position, 3:9–20

Christianity was for Paul a dynamic religion. Its gospel was "the power of God working toward salvation." The realities signified by the terms—*salvation, to be saved*—held a more prominent place in Paul's thought than a statistical summary of their use in his letters may suggest.[48] In biblical and ancient Jewish traditions salvation had become increasingly an eschatological idea. And thus it is in Paul's teaching. It remained a future hope. But true to the perspective of the Christian *kerygma*, Paul proclaimed that God's future was being anticipated in the present.[49] The gospel had proved to be the power of God put forth to bring salvation to all.

Paul's synonym for salvation was "the righteousness of God." It is this that the gospel reveals. The modern reader may assume that Paul was affirming his belief that God is a just being, that righteousness is one of his attributes. This common sense inference is not to be rejected, yet it is important to know that in ancient Judaism the phrase connoted an active as well as a passive meaning. And the more the Jews looked toward "the end of the days" for the vindication of God, and of "the righteous" whom he approved, the more this active meaning of the term *righteousness* became associated with eschatology.

Several passages in the prophets and Psalms of the Old Testament illustrate this theology of hope, that God will reveal his salvation, his righteousness:

> *I [Yahweh] will bring near my righteousness [deliverance, RSV]*
> *it is not far off,*
> *and my salvation*
> *will not tarry;*
> *I will put salvation in Zion,*
> *for Israel my glory.* Isa. 46:13; cf. 51:5ff.; 56:1, 62:1.

> *O sing to the Lord a new song,*
> *for he has done marvellous things!*
> *His right hand and his holy arm*
> *have gotten him salvation [victory, RSV].*
> *The Lord has made known* his salvation [*victory*],
> *his righteousness has he openly shown*
> *[he has revealed his vindication, RSV]*
> *in the sight of the nations.* Ps. 98:1f.

Within the eschatology of ancient Judaism, this thought of the revelation of the righteousness of God was associated with a day of judgment. When the coming manifestation of righteousness was celebrated, therefore, it was with assurance that God would bless "the righteous":

> *O let the evil of the wicked come to an end,*
> *but establish thou the righteous,*

> *Thou who triest the minds and hearts,*
> *Thou righteous God.*   Ps. 7:9

Or again, in Ps. 31:1 the writer's plea, "in thy righteousness deliver me!" is accompanied by his faith that "the Lord preserves the faithful, but abundantly requites him who acts hautily." Israel's faith was that Yahweh, as righteous Judge, would restore the right of those who are deprived of it. Thus the revelation of God's righteousness would be the assertion of his power to accomplish this, Ps. 17.[50]

As we have seen, this belief in the imminence of divine judgment was especially prominent in Jewish apocalyptic writings. In them the faith of the Old Testament writers that the righteous would be vindicated by God in the coming judgment becomes intensely nationalistic.[51] But even more significant a development is the belief, persistently asserted, that God in judging persons must surely vindicate himself. In several apocalypses the revelation of the righteousness of God principally focuses upon the establishment of God's right, as sovereign ruler of all nations, a vindication of the trust of his faithful people in his right action and righteous judgments toward all persons in their history.

The writers of 2 Baruch and 4 Ezra raised the question of the righteousness of God in the face of historical events that seemed to impugn it, and sought to defend his "righteous judgments." When Ezra is condemned for judging God, he is called upon both to give thanks for his place among the elect, and not to doubt God's justice. In the Psalms of Solomon we read:

> [And yet] I will justify Thee, O God, in uprightness of heart,
> For in Thy judgments is Thy righteousness (displayed), O God . . .
> God is a righteous judge,
>   And he is no respecter of persons.

This writer likewise defends the righteousness of God's judgment. God's judgment, which falls on every nation, is just, but also that judgment which comes upon his own people: "behold, now, O God, Thou hast shown us Thy judgment in Thy righteousness." In these contexts the righteousness of God is virtually synonymous with his faithfulness, his constancy.[52]

Against this background of Jewish eschatology Paul's proclamation in Romans 1:17 and 18 is to be understood: "For in it [the gospel] the righteousness of God is being revealed . . . for the wrath of God is being revealed from heaven against all ungodliness and wickedness of men . . ." In these statements Paul certainly claimed that the eschatological day of salvation and of judgment was no longer a future event only. Do historical considerations enable us to say more? What specific meanings are present in Paul's declaration that now "the righteousness of God has been manifested" (3:21)? Does Paul refer primarily to that righteousness that through Christ is given to persons by God, and is now accounted valid before Him? Or does Paul chiefly proclaim how the righteousness that is God's is being manifested; how God's dominion as Savior and Judge is being revealed to all persons in and through Jesus Christ? The alternatives have been often debated.[53] The present writer believes that the second expresses the central motif in Paul's proclamation of the gospel. Paul does not *begin* with the question of how sinful persons can be made or accounted "righteous" but rather how the right of God over his creation is being and will yet be realized in a manner consistent with his promises and covenant. For Paul, the Christian *kerygma* vindicated the judgments of God, past and present, and proclaimed his coming victory! All persons, therefore, who accept God's judgments (proclaimed in the gospel as righteous judgments), and who acknowledge his claim upon them for believing obedience, receive their vindication, and are given a share in his present and future victory.

The meaning of the crucial word *faith* is deepened in the course of the argument in Romans. But one should note that in the superscription Paul announced that his mission was "to win believing obedience . . . among all the Gentiles."[54] In his confessional statement, (1:3f) emphasis is placed on the fact that *all*—not only the Jew to whom the gospel was first proclaimed, but also the non-Jew—are able to render this obedience that God requires. The power of God for salvation is available now to everyone on equal terms: "to everyone who has faith."

Paul's appeal to the prophecy of Habbakuk 2:4 makes it plain that God's revelation in Jesus Christ had radically revised his understanding, both of the means whereby a person may hope to obtain righteousness, and of the nature of saving faith. The oracle of the prophet—"the righteous shall live by faith"— was understood by rabbinical Judaism "as a comprehensive fulfillment of the commandments in meritorious faithfulness."[55] One Jewish sect in New Testament times understood the prophet's oracle to have an eschatological as well as a hortatory meaning. At first glance it may seem that the writer of the Qumran Habbakuk Scroll approaches the thought of Paul. For this writer, Habbukuk referred to "all those of the house of Judah *who live according to the Torah*, whom God will rescue from the place of judgment because of their labor and their faith in the teacher of righteousness."

Paul's teaching sharply contrasts with this. The righteousness of God was being manifested *apart from law*,[56] and those who are experiencing salvation "in the place of judgment" are not "the righteous" but sinners from among Jews and Gentiles. The writer of the Qumran commmentary did teach that those who hope in God's vindication must have faith—faith in a person, "the teacher of righteousness." But obedience to the Torah and the laborious discipline of the sect gave meaning to this saving "faith" in the righteous Teacher. For Paul, reliance upon "the works of the law" was a flat denial of "faith in Jesus Christ."[57]

Once again, interpreters of Paul are presented with an ambiguous use of the genitive case. Should we read "faith in Jesus Christ" or "the faith of Jesus Christ," and accordingly what was Paul's primary reference when he used the single term *faith*? Perhaps one's answer should be deferred until the passage 3:21ff. is examined (see p. 341).

Paul's exposition of the gospel begins, however, with Romans 1:18, not with 3:21. Paul did not write that "the wrath of God" was revealed *before* the gospel was proclaimed or received or that it will be revealed only on *the last day*. "The wrath of God *is being revealed*," he wrote, here and now. The eschatological moment had come and, in accord with current Jewish eschatology, Paul believed that the wrath of God belonged to the same disclosure as His righteousness. God is now revealing his righteousness, Paul affirmed, by no longer withholding his wrath. God stood against persons in their sin and was ready to save them. It is doubtful that Paul would have agreed with some of his modern interpreters who say that "the gospel proclaims not God's wrath, but his righteousness . . ." Romans 1:18ff. may be correctly entitled: "The Gospel as God's Condemnation of Man."[58]

It is a testimony to Paul's Hellenistic-Jewish background as well as to his allegiance to Christ as Lord that he indicted Gentile society for its idolatry and saw in this the root of sexual perversions and other social vices.[59] The refusal to acknowledge God as God, to honor God, was essentially an idolization of self. As a result, human beings dishonor their own bodies. Worshiping beasts, humans become like them. Paul also believed that God permitted this evil to bring its tragic consequences, for idolatry and vice could not be attributed to ignorance but to the defiance of His will.

Students of Paul's thought have quite naturally been attracted to the way in which Paul sought to establish the fact that all persons are accountable to God for their behavior and stand under His judgment. Did Paul believe that all humans know the claim of the divine Creator by the mere fact of their existence, that humans have an innate consciousness of God's moral order? Does one find in Romans evidence for Paul's belief in a "natural" knowledge or "general" revelation of God? Perhaps the majority of Paul's readers have said yes. As a Hellenistic Jew, Paul had come under the influence of Stoic beliefs in natural law and in the universal phenomenon of moral consciousness or "conscience." Perhaps these beliefs (without some of the inferences drawn from them by the Stoics) had come to Paul through the Jewish "wisdom theology" of the period, which taught that the Torah had been both the plan and the instrument in God's creation of the world.[60] The creation was conceived as a manifestation of God's Wisdom—Torah. Therefore some Gentiles could (and all others ought to) "do by nature what the law requires," since the Law was written on their hearts. "By their wickedness they suppress the truth" and bring upon themselves God's just judgment.

But this interpretation of Paul's argument is by no means self-evident to others. Paul wrote to Gentiles who had been confronted by the gospel. He declared that in the gospel there is revealed something that they did not already know, the objective fact that God had been declaring himself unto his creatures, that his will had been impinging upon human wills since the creation of the world. Now they could and must know, through the truth revealed in Christ, that as God's creatures they are accountable to him.[61]

Neither way of explaining Paul's argument here is fully adequate. Although this indictment of Gentiles is grounded formally upon Paul's belief in anyone's natural knowledge of God and capacity to make moral judgments based upon the human situation, *the starting point for Paul is the revelation of the truth revealed in Christ and His cross.* That the gospel is Paul's norm of judgment throughout Romans 1–2 is evidenced when "the edge of the argument is turned, as it is at 2:16: God's judgment now, as at the last day, is a judgment through Christ."[62] Paul argued that only from the perspective of the gospel is the depth and seriousness of human evil fully exposed, and only its revelation of God's righteousness provides a basis for meeting the objections of anyone who questions the rightness of God's judgments, who protests his justice. One thing seems certain, Paul was not advancing rational proofs for the existence of God in Romans 1–2. The prevalence in the Graeco-Roman world of idolatry, not of atheism, is the human tragedy Paul deplores.

The Apostle evidently assumed that while some of his readers would join him in his condemnation of common social vices, they would fail to see that his indictment applied to themselves.[63] But, said Paul, pious Jews (as well as Gentile moralists?) who pass judgment upon others, "are doing the very same thing"—glorying in themselves and not in God's grace toward sinners. Paul's words at this point concerning the coming "day of wrath" disclose once again his eschatological perspective. The judgment, like the salvation of God, is future, even though—or one might say because—it is being revealed in the present. The impartiality of God's judgment consists in the fact that all persons are judged according to the light that has been given them. The Jew is not excused because he or she has the Law, nor the Gentile who disavows all knowledge of the truths that it teaches.

Paul knew that this position would not go unchallenged. He was bound to make clear his understanding of the teaching of scripture: God the creator is a righteous judge; he is no respecter of persons. When viewed from the perspective of the gospel, Israel's election and special privileges were fully consonant with this teaching. But at this place in the letter Paul only denied the common distortions of his position in this regard.[64] His immediate concern was to clinch the point: "there is no distinction . . ." between Jews and Gentiles, *insofar as their culpability is concerned*, ". . . since all have sinned and come short of the glory of God . . ."*

> B. 6. The righteousness of God manifested in the faithfulness of Christ: the justification of believing sinners, 3:21–4:25 (justification defined, 3:21–26; three inferences, 3:27f; the relation of Law to the covenant of promise, 3:31–4:25)

Paul's deep pessimism concerning the possibilities of any human being apart from Christ is not to be attributed to his Jewish apocalypticism but to his belief that the gospel revealed the only means whereby right relations can be established between God and his estranged creatures; justification can be achieved only by God's "grace as a gift through . . . Jesus Christ."[65]

The crucial term *justification* needs further clarification. What the verb *to justify* meant for Paul depended on its reference. With reference to God, it meant "to accept as righteous" His action or his judgments. With reference to humans, *to justify* may mean "to make or declare righteous," or "to secure the vindication of someone." In the present context Paul did not claim that from the moment persons are declared righteous they become, as we should say, virtuous or moral. He did not say that sinners are treated by God as if they are righteous (when in fact they are not). For Paul, God's justification of persons—his act of making righteous—denoted a change in a person's relation to God (and consequently to other human beings), not a change in a person's moral qualities. The believer is told that in the acknowledgment of sin and of God's righteous judgment upon it, a person is vindicated by God, his or her sins are not held against him or her. In the language of the law court that Paul employed, the gospel proclaims the sinner's acquittal.

*In this summary statement we may be provided an important clue to Paul's conception of the nature of sin. So far he had said that anyone's sin consisted in a willful refusal to acknowledge God, in the false assumption that life is one's own and not a gift of the Creator. This is the essential sin, and from this disorientation all material sins arise. Paul had inherited these conceptions from Judaism. But as a Christian, Paul believed that the Creator had revealed "the light of the knowledge of the glory of God in the face of Christ." Thus, when Paul declared that all persons "fall short of the glory of God," he may have been saying that none reflect the glory of Christ's manhood, a nature faithfully submitted to the will of God, in obedience and in trust. (2 Cor. 4:6; also 3:17f.; 1 Cor. 11:1; Col. 1:25ff.).

This justifying act of God is further described as "the redemption" and also as "an expiation by his (Christ's) blood to be received by faith." These two biblical terms—*redemption, expiation*—further emphasized the gratuitious nature of God's act, and point to the historic deed whereby this deliverance is accomplished. Both terms had special associations with Israel's deliverance from Egyptian bondage by God's grace and power. *Expiation* may refer to the act of the priest on the day of atonement, the sprinkling of the lid or cover of the ark of the covenant with blood of the sacrificial animal. Symbolically this act was reminiscent of the great events revealing to Israel the divine mercy. It was a present and continuing means of receiving God's mercy and forgiveness. Paul's use of the image proclaimed that the cross of Christ was the place where God revealed his mercy. The shedding of the blood of Christ was the divine means whereby atonement was made for human sin.[66]

The question is raised here whether any individual's "faith" is the principal reference when Paul writes of the instrument whereby God's justification of persons is accomplished. According to the RSV, Paul wrote that the gospel manifested "the righteousness of God *through faith in Jesus Christ* for all who believe" (3:22). As noted above, throughout this passage (3:21ff.) Paul's emphasis is upon what God has accomplished through Christ, especially through his death. It is probable, then, that it is the faithfulness of Christ that is first of all being proclaimed, "the faith of Christ"—the fulfillment of his trust.[67] In this context "faith" therefore as any human being's response fundamentally consisted in an acknowledgment that God's judgment through Christ, upon anyone's sin, is indeed just. No longer is any person able to claim that his or her own acts are the basis upon which God will declare one "righteous" (3:20); the gospel calls upon persons to believe in the efficacy of Christ's faith, in his "act of righteousness" (5:18), if they themselves are to be declared righteous by God.[68] The gospel demonstrates that *God is righteous and that he declares righteous whoever has faith in Jesus* (3:26).

The justification *of God* was probably still uppermost in Paul's mind when he asked his reader to consider three questions, all of which related God's justifying act in Christ to His former revelations to Israel.[69] God's deliverance of persons "on the ground of their faith" in Christ's faith removed all cause for pride in one's own moral achievements, all causes for interpreting God's favors as His favoritism, and, rather than destroying the authority of the Torah, established it.

Realizing that this final claim was far from self-evident, Paul introduced the case of Abraham, which, as we learned from the Galatian controversy, had been thrown into his face as a witness against the truth of his gospel. But Paul had found that Abraham's story strengthened rather than weakened his position. Since much of the argument in this section of Romans parallels Galatians, no exposition of it will be undertaken here. Again Paul seems to draw upon Roman testamentary law in defining concretely the nature of that faith appropriate to all who receive and inherit God's promises and who are accounted righteous in His sight.

B. 7. The righteousness of God manifested in his salvation of all humankind: the character of the new life in Christ, 5:1–8:39 (justification and salvation,

5:1–11; Adam and Christ—the corporate effects of sin and their remedy, 5:12–21; death to Sin and the Law—three analogies, 6:1–7:6; life under the Law—a perception of faith, 7:7–25; new life in the Spirit, and the assurance of ultimate salvation, 8:1–39)

This section is introduced by a recapitulation and an *a fortiori* argument: *If God has through Christ's death delivered us from the guilt and threatening consequences of sin and restored us to right relationship with himself, how much greater* is the assurance that "we shall be saved by his (risen) life."[70]

Paul's exposition of the life "in Christ" (or "in the Spirit") follows the pattern of answering questions that are either implied or stated.[71] (The accompanying structural outline identifies a major theme developed in Romans 5–8, that of freedom from a hopeless bondage through the action of Christ, with the consequence that one now belongs forever to Him as Lord and inherits final salvation.)

In the Adam–Christ typology (5:12–21), Paul pursued further the question: how can *one* man's "act of righteousness" make it possible for any person to "rejoice in the hope of sharing the glory of God"? The discussion assumed the current Jewish belief that all human beings became subject to sin and death as

Romans 5–8, The Nature of the New Life "in Christ"
(or "in the Spirit"), Present and Future

Delivered from "wrath", for life eternal—saved by one man's obedience	a. The provisional nature of a Christian's existence in the present—a life of faith, grounded upon the grace and love of God, sustained and completed in hope, 5:1–11; b. The present, powerful effects of the grace of God abounding for all, anticipating the final conquest of Sin and death: the contrasting, corporate (and potentially universal) effects of Adam's disobedience/Christ's obedience, 5:12–21;
Freed from bondage to Sin to become servants of God	c. Because of Christ's death and resurrection, the (baptized) believer is set free from bondage to Sin; one is therefore obligated to live under grace, surrendering oneself to God in the service of his will, 6:1–14; d. Two contrasting states of servitude, emphasizing the outcome of each, entailing for the present a release from bondage to the Law ["the performance principle"], 6:15–7:6; [you once were…but now you are]
Freed from the dominion of Law to be under the dominion of Christ	e. The objective situation (as distinct from a subjective awareness) of the person prior to, and apart from, faith in Christ—as faith perceives this situation (7:5), Paul rejects the equation law = Sin (7:7–11), also the supposition that the Law causes death. Sin is the cause of death, but Sin worked (works) death in persons through that which is good, i.e., the Law of God (7:12–25);
Freed from death's power—destined to obtain "the glorious liberty of the Sons of God."	f. "The new life of the Spirit" (7:6), and the assurance of ultimate salvation, i.e., deliverance from death through God's love manifested in Christ, 8:1–39.

the result of Adam's fall.[72] Sin existed in the world when the first man set himself against God, and its effects were continued and compounded "because all men sinned. . . ."[73] In the "Augustinian theology" of the Church, Paul is held responsible for the doctrine of sin as a hereditary disease. It is difficult to defend or deny this from the passage before us, for Paul limited himself to the thought of Adam as "a type" of unredeemed humanity and also of Christ. The fact that Paul said both things simultaneously makes it difficult to follow him. The differences brought to expression in the Adam–Christ analogy are stressed particularly, for Paul does not view Christ as simply a better Adam who balances the effect of Adamic sin.[74]

Throughout the passage Paul is concerned chiefly with the corporate reality of sin, not with its origin. Since the life of the individual in society is corrupted by sin and death, salvation must consist in overcoming that "corporate wrongness which underlies individual transgression." This "social salvation" was now possible "in Christ"; through faith in him, believers are lifted into a new order of life in which goodness is more powerful than evil, in its corporate as well as its individual manifestations.[75] The background of Paul's confidence is his conviction that in the life, death, and resurrection of Jesus Christ the Age to Come had dawned. Christ's coming had made possible a radically new order of life: "if anyone is in Christ *there is a new creation.*"[76] Paul's Adam–Christ typology may have been influenced by current Jewish speculation about Adam as the first man, but elements in this speculation had been "demythologized" by the appearance in history of the Man of Heaven, Jesus of Nazareth, "the Son of man."[77]

"Where sin increased, grace abounded all the more." In writing this, Paul was reminded of a common objection to his doctrine that persons are justified by God's grace: then "why not do evil that good may come?" This question was raised earlier and brushed aside with disgust. But now Paul faced it seriously.[78] The question was rooted in a serious misunderstanding both of the nature of saving faith and of the new life "in Christ." In his or her baptism the Christian renounced his or her past and its ways, as certainly as Christ's death had brought to an end one phase of his work. The believer's new life was a life risen with Christ.

This passage has attracted an unusual amount of interest and discussion for it sets forth Paul's view concerning baptism as well as his conception of the "mystical" life *in Christ.* Some scholars have detected the influence of the mystery religions upon Paul's conception of an initiation by sacramental death and resurrection. It is indeed probable that Paul's language was shaped by a reaction to ideas of the pagan cults. But his teaching concerning the effect of Christ's death and resurrection originated in Jewish beliefs concerning the atoning value of the sufferings of the righteous—or of a representative "Righteous One"— which had found concrete fulfillment in the crucifixion and resurrection of Jesus the Christ.[79]

Moreover, baptism "in the name of Christ" derived its meaning for the early Church and for Paul from Christian eschatology. This is seen in the fact that the new life participated in the continuing realities of sin and death as well as in a victory that had overcome the dominion of both. At times Paul may seem to speak of the new life as did the initiates of the mystery cults; Christians are "dead to sin" and "alive to God in Christ Jesus"; they have crucified "the flesh." But the realism of the Christian *kerygma* is not lost sight of. Paul must exhort Christians against allowing sin to "reign" in their "mortal bodies." It was because the power of God for salvation had been anticipated in the believer's experience, not yet fully realized, that this paradoxical manner of speaking could not be avoided. For Paul the life in faith is never a self-assured possession. Yet when the Apostle speaks of "what the believer essentially is . . . he is always thinking of what he will be. The sureness of that future . . . enables him to refer to it as though it were an actual present fact."[80] But Paul was bound to acknowledge the reality of sin in himself and in every believer.

With Romans 7:7, Paul's thought progresses by means of another question: "What then shall we say, that the law is sin?" Earlier Paul had flatly stated that "through the law comes knowledge of sin."[81] He now supports this, saying that given human nature, the effect of the law actually becomes an enticement to wrongdoing.

Paul's use of personal pronouns at this place has given rise to an unsettled controversy. Is he remembering his old life under the Torah or is he speaking throughout or at some particular place of his present Christian experience? Those who defend the latter viewpoint stress Paul's use of present tenses, and notice that this passage falls within Paul's description of the new life in Christ.[82] But defenders of the alternative viewpoint argue that Paul could not have considered the life of peace and freedom in Christ to be beset by such torment.[83] Perhaps it is best to hold in abeyance one's decision in this matter until Paul's question has been considered: Is the law sin?

Paul answered negatively by pointing to the positive value of the law. Since human beings rebel against external restraints, even the knowledge of God's commandments, which are "holy and just and good," sets up an intolerable tension between the will and the deed. Paul's poignant description of this split between intention and action needs no commentary. But the depth of the tragedy so described can be perceived when we remember what Paul has written elsewhere in Romans. His position can be summarized. The ineradicable problem of legalistic morality is that persons tend to employ law for their own glory. Instead of being humbled by the commandments of God, they use them as the criteria for establishing their own righteousness.[84] Sin thus finds opportunity in the commandment, which promises life, and destroys life. Salvation lies not in reforming old laws or in discovering better ones, but in the obedience of faith, which is the submission to God's righteousness, established through the faithfulness of Christ.

If in Romans 7 Paul wrote of his life under the law, he was not recalling his former attitudes, but the tragedy of a situation that became visible to him "only after he had attained the viewpoint of faith." Whatever frustrations the old Paul may have experienced, he had not realized the desperateness of his life under the law "until the message of grace hit its mark in him."[85] But is it not possible that Paul also described the life of the Christian as well, beginning perhaps with 7:14, the situation of a person who is dead to sin and yet alive to it? The Christian is being saved, but he or she is "saved in hope."[86]

It is this thought that underlies the poetic prose of Romans 8, for it was in the positive meaning of the Christian hope that Paul had found the way out of the subjective uncertainties of faith. There is a pathos in the recognition that these statements of assurance and certainty were written by Paul just before his fateful journey to Jerusalem. But in these words Paul exposed his innermost convictions. As C. H. Dodd has commented: "There is no arguing with such a certainty. Either you simply don't believe it or you recognize it as the word of God."[87]

> B. 8. The righteousness of God manifested in his saving purpose in history, 9:1–11:36:
>   a. Paul's persisting concern for his unbelieving "kinsmen by race," 9:1–5
>   b. A future for the people of Israel, 9:6–11:36: (the unbelief of many Jews not a failure of God's purpose, 6:6–13; God's election, although appearing arbitrary, not unjust, 9:14–29; God's election not arbitrary, 9:30–10:21; Israel's rejection not total, 11:1–6; those who have stumbled are serving God's purpose, 11:7–24; eventually "all Israel will be saved," 11:25–32; in praise of God's wisdom, 11:33–36).

This section of the letter is a unit of thought that to some readers may seem an irrelevance. It is suggested that one can pass directly from 8:39 to 12:1 without being conscious of any omission. Interpreters who understand Romans as the gospel of salvation whereby individuals are delivered from sin and guilt, made righteous and engrafted into Christ by means of the spirit and faith, have the greatest difficulty finding a place for chapters 9–11 in this letter. But we have held that Paul was chiefly concerned in Romans in demonstrating that the gospel establishes the righteousness of God, his rightful dominion over the world—a revelation purposed to benefit "the Jew first" as well as "the Greek" (1:16f.). Early in the letter Paul recognized that an objection could be raised, "that God is unjust" if, as Paul affirmed, he inflicts wrath "upon the Jews," upon the very people "entrusted with his oracles," attempting to live by His law and deriving their hope from it (3:5, 2). Paul abruptly repulsed this objection and went on to assert that every mouth protesting that God is unrighteous is, in fact, being silenced, for the gospel renders the whole world accountable to God (3:19f.). Only if God proves himself a just God and a Savior, only if God can "prevail when he is judged" (3:4), is there hope for humans that they will be delivered from the wrongs they commit and suffer.

But how was Paul able to maintain God's righteousness in the face of his belief that Gentiles, who did not aspire to "righteousness," i.e., who did not acknowledge God's rightful dominion over His creatures, were being assured in the gospel of God's blessing; while many in Israel, laying claim to God's dominion by acknowledging his law, were being condemned? What credibility could Paul hope to gain in claiming that God had revealed his righteousness in the gospel, which on the one hand, was being presented as something "promised beforehand through his prophets in the holy scriptures"[88] and yet, on the other hand, took away any special privilege for Israel and—as experience had shown—resulted in the exclusion of so many of God's chosen people?

The reader will find the suggested outline of Paul's defensive argument helpful. Viewing the chapters 9–11 as a whole, we can conclude that Paul saw two principles revealed in the history of salvation: selection and representation. God had chosen Israel to be his people and purposed through them to accomplish his salvation. But with the passage of time there had been an increasingly smaller number within Israel who truly represented this people of God in history. Then, with the coming of Christ, and with the formation of the "remnant chosen by grace" from among Jews and Gentiles, there had come into existence a community of persons who responded to God's word with the faith of Abraham, and who therefore represented the true people of God. Because of these eschatological developments and because of his belief in the triumphant power and love of God over all evil, Paul dared hope that when "the full number of the Gentiles come in" then "all Israel will be saved." Yet Paul was overcome with awe when he considered this "mystery," and prognostication gave place to praise.*

C. The Obedience of Faith: Conduct Within the Church, and Regarding Others, 12:1–15:13:
   1. The basis of Christian morality, 12:1f.; love among fellow members of "the one body in Christ," 12:3–13; love of enemies, 12:14–21
   2. The relation of Christians to "governing authorities," 13:1–7
   3. The debt of love, 13:8–10; the eschatological sanction, 13:11–14
   4. The relations of "the weak" and "the strong" in the church, 14:1–15–6
   5. In the church's unity God is glorified, 15:7–13:
D. Conclusion, 15:14–16:24:
   1. Paul's work and future plans, 15:14–32
   2. A benediction, 15:33
   3. A commendation of Phoebe; greetings; an appeal and warning; a grace, 16:1–24

We have noted that opinions differ concerning the subject matter of the concluding chapters of Romans. Many scholars hold that Paul's exhortations were not prompted by the Apostle's knowledge of specific problems in this church, but reflect situations that had arisen in his own churches and the strategies he employed in dealing with them.[89] Still others believe that Paul was not without friends in Rome, who had informed him of conditions in the church, and that Paul addressed several local issues.[90] In either case, some of the teaching in this part of the letter may have been drawn directly from Paul's reflection upon "the mercies of God" revealed in the gospel, and the teaching of Jesus that he had received as a part of the Church's "tradition." Paul derived the essentially Christian moral attitudes from the gospel and showed how these might be applied to conduct both within and outside the Church.

How is the person who accepts as righteous the sentence of God upon sinfulness, who believes that God has accounted righteous the one who has faith in the faithfulness of Christ—how is one to respond? Like the Old Testament prophets, Paul proclaimed that the only response acceptable to God is the offer of the self in obedience to God. Conformity to the divine will, not to socially acceptable patterns of behavior, is "the spiritual worship" of all who are in Christ.[91]

In the paragraph that follows (Romans 12:3ff.), Paul's words recall those of an earlier letter addressed to the church from which he was now writing, Corinth.[92] The Christian's independence of moral judgment led neither to an irresponsible individualism nor to arrogance. A person who is a fellow member of

*Interpretations differ over the meaning of Paul's conclusion: "all Israel will be saved." *All* Israel probably does not refer to everyone but to potential believers among "the others," as distinguished from those who are presently the believing remnant (11:23, cf. 11:5). Some scholars note that in expounding this "mystery" Paul does not claim that all Israel will come to believe in Jesus as the Christ. Rather, it is said Paul refers to the exclusive activity of God toward Israel at the End. See W. D. Davies, "Paul and the People of Israel," *NTS* 24 (1977): 4–39.

the body of Christ must act accordingly. As in 1 Corinthians, Paul acknowledged that love is the most excellent of all gifts, that many of the attitudes that
are characteristically Christian are the expression of love that is genuine, for
fellow-believers and for the enemy.

It is difficult to understand Paul's counsel concerning the subjection of Christians to "the governing authorities."[93] Had the Apostle's own experiences conditioned him? Paul had traveled with comparative safety on land and sea, and
sometimes he had escaped a lynching because of Roman law and order. Yet he
also had seen the arbitrary and ruthless character of some governors, and he
did not commend submission to the state for reasons of expediency, but "for
the sake of conscience." Moreover, he appealed to the love commandment. Love
required that men make every effort to "live peaceably with all men," and
"vengeance" must be left to God.[94] But love also required more of the Christian, not less, than was required of patriotic, law-abiding citizens.[95] Paul had
encountered civic irresponsibility in those who prided themselves in their freedom in Christ.

The disclosure of Paul's eschatological sanction affords perhaps the principal
clue to his counsel in this matter. But to some extent the interpreter must read
between the lines. Did Paul associate the nearness of the end with the onslaught
of demonic powers, and did he consider "the governing authorities" a restraining power, or their agents?[96] In any event, the Church must take advantage of
limited opportunities to proclaim the gospel.

To the Galatians Paul had written that the Christian's special responsibility
was toward "those who are of the household of faith."[97] So to the Romans,
Paul's last exhortations appeal to the maintenance of love within the Church
when conscientious differences of opinion arise. His advice to "the weak" and
"the strong" in the Corinthian church should be remembered, but rather than
pointing out to the Romans his own practice of avoiding giving offense to "the
weak," Paul appealed to the example of Christ.[98]

The last words in the letter have to do with his own plans. But before disclosing these, Paul tactfully wrote:

> I myself am satisfied about you, my brethren . . . But on some points I have
> written to you boldly by way of reminder. . . ."[99]

In sum total these "points" give us one of the greatest letters ever written.
In each generation Romans has served, "by way of reminder," to recall the
Church to its reason for being—the proclamation of "the gospel of God."

NOTES

1. Ca. 54 or 55, from Ephesus or Macedonia, Kümmel, *INT*[2], pp. 303f.; "the years
   between 50–55 . . . a reasonable guess," H. D. Betz, *A Commentary on Paul's
   Letter to the Churches in Galatia* (1979), pp. 11f.
2. Gal. 2:5, 14.
3. Gal. 3:1.
4. Acts 18:23.
5. Acts 16:6; cf. Gal. 4:13f.

6. Gal. 4:13, 16, 20; 5:21 (1:9?)
7. A classic statement in English of this territory hypothesis is given in J. B. Lightfoot, *St. Paul's Epistle to the Galatians* (1905), pp. 1ff. Kümmel, *INT*[2], pp. 296f.; Betz, *Churches in Galatia*, pp. 3–5.
8. W. M. Ramsay, *St. Paul the Traveller and Roman Citizen* (1920), and *A Historical Commentary on St. Paul's Epistle to the Galatians* (1900); E. D. Burton, *A Critical and Exegetical Commentary on the Epistle to the Galatians* (1920), pp. xxvff.; G. S. Duncan, *Epistle of Paul to the Galatians* (1934), pp xviiiff.
9. Cf. Kümmel, *INT*[2], pp. 296–298. E.g., 1 Cor. 19:19; 2 Cor. 1:1; 8:1. Note, however, Gal. 1:21, which refers to Syria in the narrower sense.
10. Cf. Acts 14:23; 15:14; 16:5.
11. See H. D. Betz, who contends that the Galatians were Gentiles, "whether originally Greeks, Celts or a mixture of diverse character is impossible to determine." *Churches in Galatia*, p. 4. The following passages are cited: Gal. 4:8; 5:2f.; 6:12f.
12. See important reviews of Betz's weighty commentary by W. D. Davies, P. Meyer, and D. Aune, *RSR*, Vol. 7 (1981): 310–328.
13. Betz, *Churches in Galatia*, pp. 2f.
14. Gal. 1:7, 23f.; 2:0, 16.; 1 Cor. 11:23; 15:1ff. J. T. Sanders, "Paul's Autobiographical Statements in Galatians 1–2," *JBL* 85 (1966): 335ff.
15. Betz, *Churches in Galatia*, pp. 47f.; cf. Duncan, *Epistle of Paul to the Galatians*, pp. 19f.
16. Cf. Gal. 1:15 and Jer. 1:4f; Isa. 49:1ff. Does Acts 18:9 echo Jer. 1:8?
17. Gal. 2:11–14.
18. E.g., Duncan, *Epistle of Paul to the Galatians*, p. 40.
19. See the valuable exposition of the theological argument of the Galatian letter in Betz, *Churches in Galatia*, pp. 14–33.
20. Gal. 1:3f.
21. Gal. 6:15; 2 Cor. 5:17.
22. Gal 2:16. This phrase presents a grammatical ambiguity. See the discussion on p. 341.
23. The excision of Gal. 3:6–9 from Marcion's text is not surprising.
24. Gal 3:16. Cf. Gen. 22:17f. (LXX). D. Daube, "The Interpretation of the Generic Singular in Galatians 3:16," *JQR* 35 (1944): 227ff.
25. M. Barth, "The Kerygma of Galatians," 21 (1967): 138. Paul's theology of history is more explicitly developed in Rom. 9–11. See pp. 354ff.
26. Gal. 3:10.
27. Gal. 3:17f.
28. Gal. 3:19a, 22.
29. Gal. 3:19b–21. Cf. Acts 7:38, 58; Heb. 2:2; Deut. 33:2 (LXX); Bk. Jub. 1; Jos. *Antiq.* XV. v. 3.
30. Gal. 3:24; 4:2.
31. E.g., Gal. 2:15; 3:22. Cf. [the] faith in [or, "of"] the Son of God, Gal. 2:20.
32. G. M. Taylor, "The Function of 'Pistis Christou' in Galatians," *JBL* 85 (1966): 58ff.; also G. Howard, "On the Faith of Christ," *HTR* 60 (1967): 459ff. See also p. 341.
33. See Kümmel, *INT*[2], pp. 298–301; Betz, *Churches in Galatia*, pp. 5–9.
34. In the absence of Law how can one deal with transgressions? Gal. 6:1.
35. Betz, *Churches in Galatia*, pp. 32, 272–274.
36. Gal. 4:12–20. Also 5:7–12.
37. Gal. 6:17; cf. 2 Cor. 11:23ff.
38. ". . . So far as we know . . . [Paul] always took up his pen under the pressures of

the urgencies of his mission. There is nothing in him of the academic theologian. The letter from Corinth to Rome is no exception." F. J. Leehardt, *The Epistle to the Romans* (1961), p. 14.

39. How else can one explain Rom. 15:23a?

40. For a concise account of the obscure origin of the Roman church, see Kümmel, *INT*[2], pp. 307–309.

41. J. Knox, "The Epistle to the Romans," *IB* (1954) pp. 365ff.; T. W. Manson, "St. Paul's Letter to the Romans—And Others" *BJRL*, 31 (1948) pp. 224ff.

42. Kümmel, *INT*[2], pp. 314ff.

43. *Ibid.*, 312.

44. See K. Donfried, ed., *The Romans Debate* (1977) especially pp. 120–151.

45. E.g., A. Nygren, *Commentary on Romans* (1949), pp. 3f.

46. See Note 42.

47. E.g., Rom. 5:12–21; 9–11, and so forth.

48. See the still valuable exposition of Paul's theology under the concept of salvation, C. A. A. Scott, *Christianity According to St. Paul* (1927).

49. E.g., Rom. 5:9f.; 8:24; 10:9; 1 Cor. 1:18, 21.

50. E. R. Achtemier, "Righteousness in the O.T.," *IDB* 4 (1962): 82ff.; R. Bultmann, *Theology of the New Testament* (1951, 1955), Vol. 1, pp. 270ff.

51. D. S. Russell, *The Method and Message of Jewish Apocalyptic* (1964) p. 301.

52. 2 Esd. 2:15ff.; 7:17ff.; 8:37ff.; 2 Bar. 78:5; 1 En. 108:13; Ps. Sol. 2:16–18; 8:7f., 21–24; 9:2f. Parallel ideas are found in the Qumran texts, e.g., 1QH ii, 24; 1QS, i, 26, xi, 14.

53. M. T. Brauch, "Perspectives on 'God's righteousness' in recent German discussion," in E. P. Sanders, *Paul and Palestinian Judaism* (1977), pp. 523ff.; S. K. Williams, "The 'Righteousness of God' in Romans," *JBL* 99 (1980): 241ff. Arguments seeking to establish a single meaning for the term "righteousness of God" are probably in error, but it is always pertinent to ask which meaning is called for by the context.

54. C. K. Barrett's translation, *A Commentary on the Epistle to the Romans* (1957), p. 21.

55. G. Schrenck in *Theological Dictionary* 22 (1964): 187.

56. Rom. 3:21a, 28.

57. Rom. 3:20; Gal. 5:2ff. Cf. 1QS, xi, 12f. S. Johnson, "Paul and the Manual of Discipline," *JBL* 48 (1955): 160ff.

58. K. Barth, *A Shorter Commentary on Romans* (1959), pp. 24ff.; C. K. Barrett: "the revelation of wrath . . . is a clear signal of the revealing of God's righteousness." *Commentary on Romans*, p. 34.

59. Wis. 14:12. Paul's statements throughout 1:18–32 are paralleled at many points with this book.

60. W. D. Davies, *Paul* (1948), pp. 115ff., 165ff.

61. K. Barth, *Shorter Commentary on Romans*, pp. 26ff. Cf. C. H. Dodd, "Natural Law in the New Testament," *New Testament Studies* (1953): 129ff.

62. W. Manson, "Notes on the Argument of Romans 1–8," in A. J. B. Higgins, ed., *New Testament Essays* (1959), pp. 154ff.

63. Rom. 2:1–16.

64. Rom. 3:1–8. 3:1–6 anticipates 9:1–11:36, and 3:7f. anticipates 6:1–7:6.

65. Note Paul's tautology: "grace as a gift." "Free for nothing," that is, from the side of the recipient.

66. C. K. Barrett, *Commentary on Romans*, pp. 77ff. Probably Rom. 3:21–31 is constructed around a pre-Pauline formula, but there is disagreement concerning its limits. See J. Reumann, "The Gospel of the Righteousness of God," *Int.* 20 (1966):

432ff. For a careful discussion of the meaning of Paul's terms, "expiation," "redemption" (or "redemptive liberation"), and "justification," see J. Fitzmyer, *Pauline Theology* (1967), pp. 44–53 (also *JBC*).

67. For the probable correctness of this interpretation, see Williams, "The 'Righteousness of God' in Romans," pp. 272–276; also J. L. Price, "God's Righteousness Shall Prevail," *Int.* 28 (1974): 259ff.

68. Rom 4:1, 9, 18f.; 8:3f. That righteous persons accept as righteous the sentence of God is found in Jewish apocalypses, e.g., 2 Esd. 10:16, a position "in accord with the favorite usage of the rabbis." G. Schrenck, *Theological Dictionary* 2, 212f.

69. Rom. 3:27ff.

70. Paul's development of the imagery of reconciliation (of enmity-estangement giving place to reconciliation-peace) in Rom. 5–8 closely parallels his use of other salvific images in 3:21ff., justification, redemption, expiation. 2 Cor. 5:17–19.

71. Rom. 6:1, 15; 7:1, 7, 13. On the difficulty of finding a logical thread running through Rom. 5–8, see Knox, "Epistle to the Romans," pp. 450, 469ff.

72. Cf. 2 Esdras 3:21f.; 4:30.

73. Rom. 5:12.

74. Cf. 1 Cor. 15:22. A valuable discussion of this section is given by E. Brunner, *The Letter to the Romans* (1959), pp. 44ff.

75. C. H. Dodd, *The Epistle of Paul to the Romans* (1932), p. 82.

76. 2 Cor. 4:6; 5:17; Gal. 2:20; 5:14f.; also, 1 Cor. 15:20ff.

77. Davies, *Paul*, pp. 37ff.; E. Best, *One Body in Christ* (1955), pp. 34ff.

78. Rom. 6:1ff.; note 3:8.

79. R. Bultmann, *Theology of the New Testament*, Vol. 1, pp. 311f., 140ff. Cf. G. Wagner, *Pauline Baptism and the Pagan Mysteries* (1967); R. C. Tannehill, *Dying and Rising with Christ* (1967); Barrett, *Commentary on Romans*, pp. 121–123.

80. Knox, "Epistle to the Romans," pp. 480f.; Barrett, *Commentary on Romans*, pp. 128–130. A better explanation of this Pauline paradox may be that it reflects the Apostle's distinction between the believer's *participation* in the effects of Christ's death/resurrection, and the believer's *possession* of one's inheritance: the first is present; the second, future.

81. Rom. 3:20.

82. Knox, "Epistle to the Romans," pp. 498ff.; Nygren, *Commentary on Romans*, pp. 287f., 296.

83. Dodd, *Epistle to the Romans*, pp. 104ff; F. Leenhardt, *Epistle to the Romans*, pp. 182ff.

84. Rom. 9:31f.

85. R. Bultmann, *Theology of the New Testament*, Vol. 1, p. 266. Cf. Phil. 3:4ff.; Gal. 1:13f.; C. L. Mitton, "Romans 7 Reconsidered," *Exp T* 65 (1953–54): 78ff., 99ff., 132ff.

86. Rom. 5:3ff.; 8:22ff.

87. Dodd, *Epistle to the Romans*, p. 146.

88. Rom. 1:2; 3:21b.

89. E.g., Nygren, *Commentary on Romans*, pp. 3–5; Dodd, *Epistle to the Romans*, p. xxviii.

90. E.g., W. Marxsen, *Introduction to the New Testament* (1968), pp. 92ff; P. Minear, *The Obedience of Faith* (1971).

91. E. Käsemann, *New Testament Questions of Today* (1960), pp. 188ff.

92. Rom. 12:4ff.; 1 Cor. 12:12ff.

93. The question concerning Paul's specific reference to "the governing authorities" (or "powers") has been vigorously and profitably discussed, raising the larger issue of Paul's views concerning the invisible spirits or demons ("principalities and powers,"

his usual terminology) and their relation to God and the redemptive work of Christ. See C. D. Morrison, *The Powers That Be* (1960), pp. 11ff.

94. Rom. 12:17ff.

95. Rom. 13:8ff. Käsemann disputes the common views that Paul's teaching concerning subjection to civil magistrates should be "directly associated" either with his love ethic or with the "eschatological conclusion" in 13:11ff. (*New Testament Questions*, p. 199). But if, as he affirms, the whole section "stands under the sign of 12:1f.," the eschatological situation of the Christian is an underlying assumption.

96. Cf. 2 Thess. 2:3ff.; 1 Cor. 2:5ff.; 5:1ff. (see pp. 314f.); 1 Thess. 4:9ff.

97. Gal. 6:10; 1 Thess. 4:9ff.

98. Cf. Rom 14:1–15:6 and 1 Cor. 8. See pp. 320. It is important to recognize that Paul's principles are applicable to a restricted range of problems: Dodd, *Epistle to the Romans*, pp. 219f.

99. Rom. 14:14f.

<table>
<tr><td>

Letters from Prison

</td><td>

Chapter
16

</td></tr>
</table>

PAUL, an ambassador and now "a prisoner (also) for Christ Jesus." When these words were written, the Apostle's contact with Philemon and the church in his house was restricted to letter-writing and messages sent by a friend.[1] Three other letters of the New Testament were written, ostensibly by Paul, under similar circumstances: Ephesians, Philippians, and Colossians.[2] Ordinarily, readers of the so-called "Prison (or Captivity) Epistles" have pictured the Apostle imprisoned, under house arrest in Rome, awaiting the outcome of his appeal to Caesar. These writings—especially Ephesians and Philippians—have been considered his testaments, written at the end of his spiritual pilgrimage, his last witness to the Church before martyrdom.[3]

In recent times confidence in this picture has been shaken. The opinion often voiced today is that Paul did not write the Letter to the Ephesians. Also suspect in some quarters is the Letter to the Colossians. But Colossians, along with Philemon and Philippians, is probably a genuine letter of Paul. Some persons believe that one or all of the letters from prison may have been written at Ephesus, while a few favor Caesarea. Questions concerning the genuineness and occasion of the Prison Epistles are subjects for lively debate and cannot be lightly dismissed. If Ephesians or Colossians, or both, are denied Paul, then some features of the familiar outlines of Paul's theology and its development must be sacrificed. Decisions concerning dates have important implications. If Ephesus is preferred to Rome as the place of writing, then descriptions of the development in Paul's thought between the earlier and later letters (which are based on the traditional chronology) will have to be rejected.[4]

THE LETTER TO THE PHILIPPIANS

The Letter to the Philippians stands apart from the other three in the group. Colossians, Philemon, and—if written by Paul—Ephesians were sent by the same messenger. A perusal of their contents may suggest that all three were written within a few weeks. But Philippians was dispatched by another messenger under different circumstances.

THE CHURCH AT PHILIPPI

The writer of the travel diary of Acts reports Paul's establishment of a Christian community at Philippi.[5] Historians of the Church have recognized this mission as Paul's first in the West. Perhaps one can detect in the Apostle's comment a consciousness of its special importance. He associated it with "the beginning of the gospel." This is an extraordinary phrase when one thinks of Paul's previous work, to say nothing of the earlier witness of other apostles.*

Luke passes over the development of the mission at Philippi and reports a series of incidents that brought it abruptly to a close.[6] Paul wrote to the Thessalonians shortly after this that he had "suffered and been shamefully treated at Philippi."[7] And so, we may believe, were Paul's converts after he left them. But the church maintained its life and did not forget "the partnership in the gospel" that its members shared with Paul. Nor did they forget him. Twice they sent supplies to support Paul's work, and they remembered him when he was at nearby Corinth.[8] In this connection, Paul's tribute to the generosity of the churches of Macedonia should be recalled.[9]

Perhaps as many as five years elapsed before Paul was able to revisit the Philippians. After his ministry in Ephesus, and in the midst of the Corinthian crisis, he undoubtedly went to Philippi. Perhaps he wrote the letter called 2 Corinthians there.[10] Beyond this, our knowledge of the church must be gleaned from allusions in the Letter to the Philippians.

*When Caesar Augustus rebuilt Philippi he gave it the rank of "a colony"—a military outpost of Rome with special privileges for its inhabitants. As the first station on the Via Egnatia, the main highway leading from the east toward Rome, Philippi stood at an important crossroads. F. W. Beare, *A Commentary on the Epistle to the Philippians* (1959), pp. 7ff.; F. F. Bruce, *Paul* (1977), pp. 218–222.

THE PLACE AND DATE OF THE LETTER

The traditional belief that Paul wrote Philippians from Rome draws principal support from its references to "the whole praetorian guard" and to "those of Caesar's household," and also to second-century Church tradition.[11] In recent times inscriptions and papyri have been discovered that prevent us from taking for granted the Roman provenence of Philippians. It seems that "the praetorium" was the government quarter in many important provincial cities, and that the expression "those of Caesar's household" referred to Rome's civil servants wherever situated.

Since scholars had already noticed several difficulties in the tradition that Philippians originated in Rome, the discovery of these inscriptions led to a thorough investigation of possible alternatives. It was recalled that in addition to his imprisonment at Philippi, the Apostle had been confined for two years at Caesarea.[12] Allusions in Paul's Corinthian correspondence also intimated one or more imprisonments during his ministry at Ephesus.[13]

A principal difficulty calling into question the traditional view is that Rome and Philippi were separated by a distance of nearly eight hundred miles, and Paul's letter implies that he had been in close communication with the Philippians for some while. Four trips between Paul's prison and the Macedonian city are suggested: the message of Paul's situation was sent and received at Philippi; Epaphroditus had come from the church to Paul; word was sent to Philippi that their messenger had been mortally ill; word had come back to Paul's prison revealing their anxiety. To these journeys should be added the prospective ones: Epaphroditus was being sent with Paul's letter; Timothy was to go to Philippi when Paul's situation was clarified, and then Paul hoped to visit Philippi himself. According to some estimates, a one-way trip from Rome to Philippi would take over seven weeks; approximately ten months would have been needed for the journeys that had already taken place when Paul wrote Philippians. Once "the Ephesian hypothesis" is entertained, these difficulties are obviated. Ten to twelve days for travel between Ephesus and Philippi would suffice.

Other evidence has been claimed to support "the Ephesian hypothesis." Paul assured the Philippians that he would come to them if and when his release was obtained.[14] In Acts it is reported that upon leaving Ephesus Paul went into Macedonia.[15] Some scholars have argued that 1:30 and 4:15f. imply that Paul had not been to Philippi since founding the church there. If Paul were writing from Rome this would not have been true. Moreover, when writing to the Romans Paul declared his intention to evangelize Spain. The Philippian letter gives no hint of this plan.

When Paul wrote Philippians he was contending with strong Jewish opposition.[16] According to Acts, this was Paul's situation at Ephesus.[17] But the same source reports that leaders of the synagogues in Rome had received Paul cautiously. It does not report that they persecuted him.[18] The letter reveals also that the Apostle was contending with strife among Christians.[19] Paul's speech to the Ephesian elders in Acts manifests his sensitivity to this problem at Ephesus.[20] (If Romans 16 was addressed to the Ephesians, we have evidence that Paul's fears materialized.[21]) Reference to Acts also discloses that Timothy was with Paul at Ephesus; no notice is taken of his presence in Rome.[22]*

The Ephesian origin of Philippians is not improbable,[23] but the theory is open to some serious objections. It cannot be established that Paul was imprisoned at Ephesus. Indeed the supposition that he was confined shortly after the work in Asia began may be nothing more than a conjecture framed to support the Ephesian origin of "the Prison Epistles." But granting the possibility that Paul was jailed in Ephesus, do the fragments of indirect evidence support a theory of an imprisonment of not less than three months' duration under conditions permitting Paul to receive and dispatch messengers and letters? The only reference in the New Testament to a prolonged imprisonment allowing for such activities is the house arrest at Rome.[24]

The matter of distance is a formidable objection to the older view (and also to the Caesarean theory), but possibly too much is made of this point. Being a Roman colony, Philippi was in close communication with the capital and was connected with it by a good road affording overland travel in all seasons. Moreover, the number of journeys between Rome and Philippi, and the estimated time necessary for them, may have been exaggerated.[25]

The absence of any notice of the mission to Spain in a letter from Rome is surely not an insuperable difficulty. Four or five years in prison was a sufficient setback to alter the Apostle's plans. He commented in the letter that he had learned to adjust to altered circumstance.[26]

From the teaching of Philippians very little, if anything, can be inferred about its place and date of writing. Its similarities to Paul's early letters are not sufficiently close to prove that it belongs to the period of the Ephesian mission.

When all the arguments have been read, one faces the inescapable conclusion that no open-and-shut case is possible. The vital question becomes, In which of the settings do the mood and situation of the Apostle seem to fit? The uncertainty of the answer should inhibit interpretations of Philippians based upon an imprisonment in one place or the other.**

*Other difficulties in the tradition of Roman origin and seeming to favor Ephesus are the gifts of the Philippians and their acknowledgment. In the letter Paul said that the Philippians lacked opportunity to help him over a period of time, and later revived their concern for him (4:10). According to Acts, Paul visited Philippi twice after receiving the gifts at Corinth. Eight to ten years may have passed before his imprisonment in Rome. But if Philippians was written from Ephesus, then the time interval is reduced to no more than three years, during which period Paul had been in Judea and Syria.

**Some scholars have hypothesized that Philippians is a composite of several letters. F. W. Beare identifies three: 4:10–

20, a letter of thanks (perhaps complete except for its salutation) acknowledging the gift brought to Paul by Epaphroditus; sections 1:1–3:1; 4:2–9 and 21–23 are a letter carried by Epaphroditus on his return to Philippi; and 3:2–4:1 is a fragment of a letter to the Philippians, of uncertain date, in which Paul warns against Jewish propaganda and shameful self-indulgence.

INTERPRETING PHILIPPIANS

The purpose of Philippians is so interwoven with the development of its thought that it can be examined in the course of an exposition of the letter. No neatly logical sequence of ideas can be traced in Philippians. "Paul writes out of a full heart, putting down his ideas as they come to him, and personal notices, outbursts of tenderness and thanksgiving, warnings, profound reflections are all mingled together."[27] Nevertheless, several divisions of the letter are discernible.

    A. Introduction, 1:1–11
        1. The prescript, 1:1f.
        2. A thanksgiving containing Paul's expressions of affection, 1:3–8
        3. Prayer for the increase of the Philippians, 1:9–11
    B. The Apostle Reports His Situation, 1:12–26
        1. The by-products of his imprisonment in the local church, 1:12–18
        2. Paul's only desire for deliverance is to serve the Church, 1:19–26

There was no need to lay emphasis upon his apostleship in the prescript to this letter. Paul's authority was not disputed at Philippi. He simply identified himself with Timothy as "slaves of Christ." The special deference shown to "bishops and deacons" (RSV) is noteworthy. But theories of Church polity in the Apostle's communities rest insecurely upon this address.[28] Paul's words could mean "overseers and assistants." He may have remembered those persons who administered the church's funds so liberally placed at his disposal.

The thanksgiving in Philippians is far more than a gesture of conventional piety. It bespeaks a deep affection freely given and received.[29] Paul's prayer for his friends held in mind "the day of Christ." The hope of the believers was being fulfilled, but it was not yet completed.[30]

It is tempting to read between Paul's lines depicting his own situation (1:12ff.). Is the main thought here that the gospel is being proclaimed at Rome, even though the publicity is of another sort than Paul had expected? Uncertainty must remain. But can we account for Paul's vagueness? Perhaps he did not wish to be unduly alarming, but rather wished to emphasize the positive results of an imprisonment that might eventuate in his own death. Paul simply did not know what the outcome would be. At times he thought his deliverance likely and hopefully planned for the future;[31] at other times his death seemed imminent and he faced this prospect realistically. Paul was, as he wrote, "hard pressed between the two."[32]

Why should Paul's imprisonment have given some persons of good will boldness, while others sought by their preaching "to afflict" him? Paul's confidence had inspired the former to be more courageous. But one must speak less confidently concerning the preachers whose motives were mixed. The question involves Paul's situation. In any case, Paul did not psychoanalyze his detractors. He did not charge them with false teaching. What did it matter: "Christ is proclaimed; and in that I rejoice."[33]

Like Job, Paul was confident of his ultimate vindication.[34] Whether "salvation" was to be release from prison, or from life by death, Paul's thought was influenced directly by his eschatology. His only point in living now was the need of the churches; he yearned "to depart and be with Christ." There was some satisfaction that the choice was not his own. Paul's own anxiety was that Christ be honored, whether through a continuation of his ministry or through his martyrdom.[35]

  C. Exhortations to Unity, 1:27–2:18
    1. An appeal for unity and confidence while suffering for the sake of Christ, 1:27–30
    2. An appeal for unity remembering Christ's divine condescension, 2:1–5
    3. A hymn to Christ—humiliation in death; exaltation as "Lord," 2:6–11
    4. An appeal for sobriety and joyful obedience unto the End, 2:12–18

The exhortations in Philippians emphasize the need for unity in the Church. Paul sensed first of all the disruptive power of fear and a natural impulse to shrink from suffering pain (1:27ff.). But he also recognized that selfishness and self-conceit insidiously destroyed the unity of a church, doing violence to love that is Christlike. It was usual for Paul to ground his ethical teaching in some aspect of the Christian *kerygma*. But this time he incorporated a poetic version of the story of salvation. Various attempts have been made to show that the structure of the passage resembles a hymn:

> *Though he was in the form of God,*
> *(He) did not count equality with God*
> *A thing to be grasped,*
>
> *But emptied himself,*
> *Taking the form of a servant,*
> *Being born in the likeness of men.*
>
> *And being found in human form*
> *He humbled himself*
> *And became obedient unto death*
> *(Even death on a cross).*
>
> *Therefore God has highly exalted him*
> *And bestowed on him the name*
> *Which is above every name*
>
> *That at the name of Jesus*
> *Every knee should bow,*
> *In heaven and on earth and under the earth,*
>
> *And every tongue confess*
> *That Jesus Christ is Lord*
> *To the glory of God the Father.*

This "hymn" provides the sanction supporting Paul's exhortation to unity. A continuing Christological discussion has been provoked by this passage.[36] It probably prompted the Philippians to worship, not to debate and speculate. Yet questions concerning the hymn's origin and meaning relate to the important subject of the development of Christology in the early Church.[37]

Paul's exhortations often call to mind Old Testament scenes. The closing part of this section may have been influenced by Paul's recollection of Moses' charges to the children of God, and of temptations that beset Israel in their day of salvation.[38] There is an apparent paradox in the thought that persons must work out their own salvation, for God is at work in them to will his good pleasure. Yet this was a succinct statement of Paul's belief in a divine providence that entails the calling to a serious life. The Christian calling is founded upon the grace of God, which, when apprehended, requires not less but more of one.[39]

    D. Plans Concerning Paul and His Fellow-workers, 2:19–30
        1. Timothy to come soon; his worth is extolled, 2:19–23
        2. Paul to follow shortly—God willing, 2:24
        3. Epaphroditus, now recovered, to come at once; his service and courage are commended, 2:25–30

When Paul noted future plans, it looks as though he intended to bring his letter to a close. But postscripts are sometimes incorporated in the body of Paul's letters.[40] The prospective visits to Philippi were discussed above. It is interesting at this point to contrast Paul's lavish commendation of Timothy with the slur upon the rest.[41] Would Paul have spoken so uncharitably of Christian leaders at Rome (or at Ephesus), especially after the magnanimity shown in the introduction of the letter? Perhaps he had asked several others to undertake the mission he was now entrusting to Timothy. Paul expected much of others while expecting the "impossible" of himself.

Paul's commendation of Epaphroditus may reveal the specific purpose of the letter. Did Paul fear that the church would think their emissary had been derelict in his duty? Was he writing to ensuure Epaphroditus a cordial homecoming?[42] But why, one may ask, was Paul "less anxious" with Epaphroditus in Philippi than with him? The question may provide a clue to the abrupt transition at 3:1 and further unravel the purpose of Philippians. Several developments required the presence in Philippi of one of Paul's trusted fellow-workers who knew the community and its leaders.

    E. A Fresh Start in the Act of Saying Farewell (Warnings, mingled with an apology for his life), 3:1–4:1
        1. An emotional warning against Jewish propaganda, 3:1–4
        2. Paul renounces his former Judaism; an avowal of undying devotion to Christ, 3:5–16
        3. Two contrasting mind-sets: earthly and heavenly, 3:17–4:1

Paul was angry when he lashed out against Jewish propaganda. Of course he did not have in mind all of his kinsmen by race. His choice of words reveals his contempt for the fanatics who, in their zeal for proselytizing, had preyed upon Paul's converts like scavenger dogs. When circumcision was made an end in itself, was it of greater religious value than other mutilations of the flesh?[43] Paul's spiritualization of the Jewish rite is reminiscent of his words in Romans.[44] In contrast to those men who could pride themselves that the covenant sign was upon their flesh, Paul wrote of others whose only glory is Christ Jesus.

The contrast is wrought out in a passage that was a personal confession. If any man had grounds for "confidence in the flesh," Paul surely had. But his past, his "blameless" righteousness under the Law, had been renounced as amounting to nothing. The gospel had revealed "the righteousness of God," in the first instance, "through the faith of Christ," but received by Paul as "the righteousness from God [given men by God] that depends on faith." Paul affirmed once again what he had written in Romans: this gospel undercuts every reason for human pride.

Paul's strong denial of his own perfection may sound to some readers like histrionic mock humility.[45] But other letters of Paul reveal his conviction that the mark of Christian maturity is a frank recognition of one's own weaknesses and imperfections, and that it is developed through a vigilance that opposes self-conceit.[46] The Apostle's reference to the figure of his never-ending race led directly to another sharp warning. Paul always found persons who distorted his gospel of freedom from Law. Some claimed that Christians are free from sin; others found in his emphasis on freedom a sanction for self-indulgence or moral indifference. In Philippians as in Galatians, Paul balanced a warning against legalism with a warning against license. A graphic description is given of the materially minded person.[47]

But by way of contrast, a marvelous picture is drawn of a believer's orientation. The Christian's "commonwealth is in heaven." His or her mind cannot be fixed upon "earthly things." Perhaps Paul was thinking of the pride of the Philippians, living in an outpost of Rome, anticipating a visitation of Caesar their savior.[48]

    F. Conclusion, 4:2–23
       1. Admonitions concerning unity, forbearance, joy, and constancy in prayer; a plea for excellence, 4:2–9
       2. Personal notes: Paul acknowleges the church's concern; their gifts are "a sacrifice . . . pleasing to God," 4:10–20
       3. Final greeting; a benediction, 4:21–23

One marvels at Paul's tactful approach to two quarrelsome women. He had spoken of his love for everyone in the church. He had dealt with their need for unity in Christ. And now, while rebuking the troublemakers, he commended them and asked someone—their "true yoke-fellow"—to help them.

The next two paragraphs appear to be a fresh attempt to bring the letter to a close. They are the words of a man reluctant to say good-bye for fear it may be his last. Paul cannot close without remembering especially the kindnesses of this church, but his words reflect a mood of resignation. His need is for peace and inner strength, not for gifts of money and more helpers. And Paul believed that God would supply these needs. It was not the serenity of the Stoics, nor their schooling in indifference to outward circumstance, that Paul had learned. He had discovered the secret of true contentment. Even when bound with chains, Paul was a man "in Christ."

THE LETTER TO PHILEMON

The remaining letters from prison will be considered in this order: Philemon, Colossians, Ephesians. It is easy to justify placing Colossians in the middle. Colossians is closely linked to Philemon in that both letters were carried by the same bearer and contain identical personal references.[49] But Colossians is also closely related to Ephesians, which will be discussed in Chapter 17. Again there is a common bearer. There is also a striking parallelism in language, style, and leading ideas that sets these two books apart from the rest in the collection (see p. 370).

Colossians, then, stands in the key middle position. But there is value in studying these books from left to right. A decision relating to the origin of Philemon obviously affects one's judgment concerning the more substantial writing, Colossians, and, some would claim, by a chain of inferences, the Letter to the Ephesians. One can speak with greater assurance about the origin of Philemon than the others. Some words of John Knox bear this out:

> No reputable scholar doubts its authenticity [Philemon]. The little letter bears in itself every mark of genuineness. Its vocabulary and style are those of Romans, Corinthians, Galatians, and Philippians; and the personality of its author is unmistakable. Besides all this, the letter brings us a dramatic moment in the life of Paul which no later writer would have had either the skill or the motive to invent.[50]

THE PLACE AND TIME OF PHILEMON

Where was Paul when he said good-bye to a slave named Onesimus and handed him over to Tychicus with this brief letter to Philemon? The traditional answer has been, "At Rome." But we have seen that this judgment may have depended on references in Philippians and also in Colossians, which do not bear the weight put upon them. Many scholars champion the Ephesian origin of the letter.[51]

Several passages have been thought to support the new theory. Observe, first of all, that Philemon lived at Colossae, a town in the Roman province of Asia, about one hundred miles inland from Ephesus.[52] When Onesimus escaped, where would he most likely have run? To Ephesus, say the proponents of this theory, to the metropolis of his province rather than to faraway Rome. Morever, if Paul was at Ephesus, then his request to Philemon that a guestroom be prepared is a reasonable one. But if Paul was in Rome (planning a mission in Spain?) what would have been the point of such a request? Finally, two of Paul's friends, sending greetings to Philemon, were with him at Ephesus, while others had connections with this city, or the province of Asia. Only one of them, Luke, is known to have been with Paul at Rome.

The above arguments are not without merit, but they fall short of a demonstration.[53] Surely a fugitive slave carrying stolen money might put as much distance as possible between himself and his master, especially since his apprehension would result in a severe flogging. Where could one get lost in a crowd better than in Rome? Paul's request for lodgings does not necessarily imply an early visit to Colossae. He may have intended to say no more than "keep the latch key out, I'll be along some day."[54] And finally, with respect to the group of friends, both Timothy and Aristarchus (who were with Paul at Ephesus) accompanied Paul on his journey to Jerusalem, which resulted in the Roman imprisonment. Even if Timothy was not on shipboard with Paul, he may have arrived at Rome a few weeks or months later. We should not expect such a detail to be recorded at the conclusion of Acts.[55]

The Letter to Philemon provides no compelling reasons for adopting the Ephesian hypothesis. Some passages in the letter are better suited to an imprisonment at Rome. Paul had known Onesimus long enough to become attached to him as a "father," and as Paul wrote he needed him for a longer service during his "imprisonment for the gospel."[56] The provenience of Philemon must remain *sub judice*, at least until its companion letter is examined.[57]

INTERPRETING THE LETTER TO PHILEMON

A. Introduction, 1–3
   1. The prescript, 1f.
   2. A grace, 3
B. Thanksgiving, 4–7
   1. Gratitude for Philemon's witness, 4–6
   2. Philemon's benefactions have brought Paul "much joy and comfort,"7
C. The Request Concerning Onesimus, 8–20
   1. Paul rejects his right to command: prefers an appeal "for love's sake," 8f.
   2. The usefulness of Onesimus, 10f.
   3. Paul suppresses a reluctance to part with Onesimus, 12–14
   4. Providence turns evil into good, 15f.
   5. Charges, receipts, indebtedness, 17–20
D. The Conclusion, 21–25
   1. Paul's confidence that Philemon will do more than he asks, 21
   2. Plans for a visit, 22
   3. Greeting from Paul's friends, 23f.
   4. Benediction, 25

After a reading of this brief letter, one may conclude that its purpose is self-evident. Yet its very brevity leaves many questions in our minds. The raising of some questions is a mere pastime. But others lead to the purpose of the letter. It is well to keep three of these questions before us. What does Paul ask of Philemon? Upon what does he base his appeal? With what results?

Paul's approach was extremely tactful. He warmly acknowledged Philemon's reputation for faith and love of the brethren. He was, as Paul wrote, a refreshing person.[58] Paul's prayer was that Philemon's benefactions might result in bringing the two men into closer union with Christ.[59]

Paul had every reason to be tactful. He was asking Philemon to pardon a legally very serious offender. He was also asking to be excused the presumption of detaining Onesimus. Strictly speaking, Paul was at risk of defrauding his friend.[60] It was necessary to avoid every appearance of dictating to Philemon, lest his purpose in writing be defeated.

Paul was not self-conscious about his authority as an apostle. Our reading of his letters has surely confirmed this. Yet Paul chose to appeal to Philemon "for love's sake." What did he want Philemon to do? Was Paul asking for Onesimus? Was he requesting Philemon to send him back his "child"?[61] Some of Paul's expressions suggest this.[62] But can we be sure? The Apostle knew that Philemon could and might retain Onesimus.

Does Paul ask for the slave's freedom? Not explicitly.[63] The important thing to notice is that Onesimus was sent home for the service of the gospel. Whether he remained with Philemon or was returned to Paul, whether he remained in bonds or was set free, Paul asked that Philemon treat Onesimus as "a beloved brother." Philemon was to acknowledge the fact that a new relation existed between master and slave, not merely within the church, but with respect to law and social custom. Onesimus is "more than a slave," he is Philemon's brother—both as a man and as a Christian.[64]

Paul asked a lot of Philemon. Could he acknowledge this difference, in fact as well as in principle? Onesimus was now a man "in Christ." Could Philemon receive him as though Paul himself were coming to his home?

Paul seemed confident that he would—that Philemon would do even more than he asked—for Philemon owed Paul his Christian existence.[65] The reader may notice Paul's play on the word "Onesimus" (used or profitable) and observe his use of commercial formulae, the scribbling of his I.O.U. Could Paul count on Philemon's sense of humor? Or was he being careful to respect the rights, the liberty of Philemon?

The concluding words of the letter reminded his readers that the appeal was being made from prison. Like Onesimus, Paul and his associates did not know what the future held. But it mattered not. Like the slave, these men had found their freedom "in Christ Jesus."

THE LETTER TO THE COLOSSIANS

The apparent close connection between Philemon and Colossians suggests that Paul wrote both letters. Yet some persons have had grave doubts. They consider that the type of error being promoted in Colossae hardly existed in Paul's lifetime; that the letter presents—in a distinctive style and manner—a view of Christ and the Church not developed in other letters of the Pauline collection (excepting Ephesians); and that its peculiar literary relation to Ephesians and earlier letters by the Apostle casts suspicion upon Pauline authorship. Accordingly, several alternative theories have been advanced, each claiming that Colossians is a pseudonymous writing. Some scholars hold that the writer of Colossians had access to several of Paul's letters and drew upon these to combat error at the Colossian church. Others conjecture that an authentic letter of Paul to the Colossians has been adapted by another person in order to apply the authority of Paul's teachings to a new situation in the church.

How is one to decide? The issue depends mainly on the answer to two questions. First, do the verbal parallels or similarities between Colossians and earlier letters by Paul suggest that Paul wrote Colossians, or that someone composed it who had access to one or more of his letters? Second, is it probable that the type of error implied by Colossians appeared during Paul's lifetime and that Paul dealt with it (if it did arise) by developing the theological conceptions contained in this letter? Neither question can be answered simply; it cannot be denied that the origin of Colossians is a complex problem. For many persons, the scales teeter uncertainly. But for the majority they tip in favor of Pauline authorship.[66]

The Church at Colossae

The ancient Phrygian settlement at Colossae had by Paul's time declined to the status of a small town.[67] It was situated on the Lycus River, a tributary of the Meander. Within a radius of twelve miles were the twin cities of Laodicea and Hierapolis, overshadowing Colossae in their significance. During most of the centuries of Roman rule, the district belonged to the province of Asia.

Colossae was probably destroyed by a regional earthquake in 61 C.E. Unlike nearby Iaodicea, Colossae was not restored.[68] (This supposition militates against attributing Colossians to a Paulinist writing in the last decades of the first century, as some propose.)

Apparently the founder of the churches in the Lycus valley was Epaphras (1:7). He may have owed his conversion to Paul. In any event, he became a "beloved fellow-servant," whom Paul counted among his associates. As Epaphras was a Gentile, one naturally concludes that his converts also were. Inferences from the Letter to the Colossians bear this out, but the district was not exclusively Greek. Numerous Jews resided in the Lycus valley, and some of the churches' leaders may have been drawn from Gentile proselytes to Judaism or from the "God-fearers."

Paul had never visited Colossae.[69] Epaphras had come to see him in prison, bringing news and affectionate greetings from the Lycus Valley churches. As a result of conversations with Epaphras, two letters were written by Paul: the canonical Letter to the Colossians and a lost writing, the Letter to the Laodiceans (4:16).

If Paul wrote Colossians, then the traditional view of its Roman origin has high merit. To argue that Colossians was written at Ephesus involves more than the questionable assumptions noted in the study of Philemon. One must adopt an almost incredible hypothesis, that the conceptions of Christ developed in Colossians were of passing significance, of apologetic value only, for Paul. They do not appear in Romans, which sets forth a summary of the Apostle's gospel up to the time of its writing. Contrary to the opinion of some, denial of the Pauline authorship of Ephesians is not sufficient to discredit Colossians. The relation between these writings is not circumstantially the same as between Philemon and Colossians.[70]

Interpreting Colossians

A. Introduction, 1:1–4
  1. The prescript, 1:1f.
  2. The thanksgiving, emphasizing Paul's satisfaction in hearing of the progress of the Colossians, 1:3–8
  3. A prayer for the increase of the church ends with an affirmation of the eschatological victory, 1:9–14
B. Christ, the Mystery of God, 1:15–2:5
  1. The Son and his relation to God (1:15a); the universe (15b–17); the Church (18)
  2. The Son as reconciler of all things (1:19f.); of the Colossians who were formerly pagan (21–23)
  3. Paul's office is to make known the mystery, through sufferings for the sake

of the church (1:24); through preaching Christ among the Gentiles (25–27); through the nurture of Christians (28f.)

4. Paul's concern for the churches of the Lycus Valley (2:1–5); that they gain a full understanding of God's mystery—of Christ (1–3); resist "beguiling speech"; be established in the received faith (4f.)

C. A Human Condition Contrasted with the Tradition According to Christ, 2:6–3:4 (Admonitions)

1. The fullness of Christ, and of life in him, 2:6–10
2. Buried and raised with Christ, 2:11–13a
3. Christ's triumph in death, 2:13b–15
4. The shadow of ritual; the substance that is Christ, 2:16f.
5. Growth results from holding fast to Christ, not from asceticism and angel-worship, 2:18
6. Ascetic taboos are a futile submission to vanquished spirits, 2:20–23
7. Submit your minds to Christ who is your life, 3:1–4

In "the thanksgiving" Paul reported to the Colossians that the gospel, "the word of the truth," was everywhere "bearing fruit and growing," as it was among themselves. Already one detects the apologetic purpose of the letter. The propagandists were pressing upon the Christians their so-called true version of the gospel, proclaimed by Epaphras in its simplicty, a version alleged to possess universal appeal and able to produce superior results. In his prayer for the church Paul desired that his readers recognize that this so-called "fulness of knowledge" or "spiritual wisdom" was not needed. God the Father had delivered them from "the dominion of darkness" and transferred them to "the kingdom of his beloved Son," in which they had their "redemption."

The assurance that closes the first section proclaimed Christ "the beloved Son" of God the Father. Associated with this is a remarkable confessional statement concerning the significance of the Christian redeemer (1:15–20). Some scholars have suspected a later interpolation, arguing that the passage is unparalleled in Paul's writings. Alternatively, other scholars, noting the liturgical form and mythical content of the passage, conjecture that Paul, or an early churchman, took over a pre-Gnostic myth concerning the Heavenly Man who is also man's Redeemer, and composed a Christian hymn to Christ.[71]

Leaving open the questions of the source of these ideas, or an earlier form, we may say that there is no valid reason for assigning this passage to a later period. It is admirably suited to the purpose of Colossians and the development of its teaching. Either the author of Colossians composed the passage, or he adapted an earlier baptismal (?) hymn, to combat the specific danger facing the Lycus valley Christians. He reminded the church that its Lord is mightier than all cosmic powers and holds sway over them all.

For a knowledge of the teaching being opposed by Paul we are dependent on inferences from Colossians. But our study of "the Gentile environment of Christianity" should enable us to understand better the nature of the danger confronting this church in the hinterland of Asia. After a first reading of Colossians, the following brief analysis of the "philosophy" and discipline being urged upon the Colossian Christians may be helpful and may lead to a greater appreciation of its marvelous apology.

THE ERRONEOUS TEACHING AT COLOSSAE

The propagandists at Colossae described their teaching as "a philosophy" and also as a "tradition," claiming that it was a sophisticated system of thought sanctioned by antiquity (2:8). A central position was given to invisible spirit-beings, twice referred to in Colossians as the *stoicheia* (the "elemental spirits of the universe") (2:8, 20). These cosmic powers were also called "principalities and authorities." It was taught that together they constituted the *pleroma* (the "fulness," or full complement) of divine powers through whom God ruled the world. These powers were the means whereby divine revelation was given; they controlled the ways of access whereby mortals (or at least some) ascended to their eternal destiny.

Essentially the propaganda at Colossae bears the characteristics of pre-Gnostic thought. But we can go further and identify the system as a Jewish type of Gnosticism. The propagandists judged piety by a legalism that reflects, at some remove, the Torah of Judaism. For them "questions of food and drink" were of great importance, as well as particular observances, "a festival or a new moon or a sabbath" (2:16). They also imposed ascetic practices that went beyond the requirements of the Law and the scribal traditions of Palestine. Perhaps a manual of discipline is implied in the reference to their commandments, "do not handle, do not taste, do not touch. . . ." We also learn that they sought to promote "rigor of devotion and self-abasement and severity to the body. . . ." (2:20–23).

The relation of these legalistic and ascetic practices to the "philosophy" of the propagandists may be found in the belief that the Law was given by the angels. If so, they might have taught that the keeping of the Law was a form of self-abasement and veneration required by the angels (2:18). The Colossian Christians were being offered a religion of "knowledge" that enabled them "to disarm the principalities and powers" of the invisible world, and also "to put off the old nature" and attain "fulness of life."

Had the erroneous teaching absorbed some of the aspects of the mystery cults that flourished in the region of Phrygia? An a priori probability may find support in Paul's reference to one propagandist who "took his stand on visions" (literally, "entered into what he had seen"). Some inscriptions from Asia Minor indicate that this expression was used in a technical sense by the mystery religions, describing the act following initiation whereby one entered the place of vision (the forbidden sanctuary?) to receive a revelation from the god (2:18). Perhaps Epaphras had reported that one of the propagandists at Colossae boasted of an initiation into the higher mysteries. Paul's frequent use of his term "mystery" in this letter further suggests that the syncretistic error at Colossae derived some of its aspects from the mystery cults.[72]

Paul would not have been content merely to denounce the propagandists at Colossae. He had been ready to contend with the Judaizers in the Galatian churches on their own terms. And so, we may believe, Paul proclaimed Christ as the One who alone embraced in himself all the functions that were being falsely ascribed to "the elemental spirits of the universe." Christ bestowed upon his Church all the benefits of redemption being sought through the merely "human" traditions and profitless ascetic disciplines of the propagandists. Christ was the pre-eminent mediator between God and humans—as One exalted above all "the authorities" (by whatsoever name they were called), since they were a part of the created order and derived their being from him. Moreover, as "the first-born from the dead," Paul proclaimed Christ the revealer and mediator in the new creation, especially with respect to the Church, the eschatological community—his body, of which he was the Head. Indeed, Paul affirmed that "all the fulness of God"—the full complement of divine powers—dwelt in Christ alone. The conclusion followed: the *stoicheia* possessed no power superior to nor in any way qualifying the power of the Christian redeemer.[*]

* Special interest has been shown in the writer's description of Christ "as the head of the body, the Church." Paul's use of the metaphor in 1 Corinthians and Romans differs from this, leading some scholars to deny Pauline authorship of Colossians. However, it is quite conceivable that the erroneous teaching in the church prompted Paul to extend his metaphor.

Paul described the gospel as "the mystery hidden for ages . . . but now made manifest"; and, again, he described it as the "mystery which is Christ in you, the hope of glory."[73] As in the pagan mystery cults, the term *mysterion* represented for Paul something given through revelation. But the Christian "mystery" referred neither to an initiatory rite, nor to disclosed secrets that were to be withheld from the uninitiated. Rather, the mystery was to be proclaimed to everyone. Its benefits were not restricted to the few persons who through cultic rites, ascetic discipline, mystical contemplation, or other means qualified themselves to receive the mystery. It was the Father who qualified believers in Christ "to share in the inheritance of the saints in light."[74] Therein was established a relation to one in whom are found "all the treasures of wisdom and knowledge" necessary to their salvation and to spiritual maturity.[75]

D. The True Discipline of Men Who Declare the Mystery of Christ, 3:5–4:6 (exhortations):
  1. The reformation of life, 3:5–17
  2. Household duties, 3:18–4:1; wives and husbands (18f.); children and parents (20–21); slaves and masters (3:22–4:1)
  3. A call to prayer, 4:2–4
  4. Behavior toward outsiders, 4:5f.
E. Conclusion, 4:7–18:
  1. Commendations of Tychicus and Onesimus, 4:7–9
  2. Greetings from Paul's associates, 4:10–14
  3. Personal greeting and final requests, 4:15–18a
  4. Benediction, 4:18b

The heart of the *kerygma* proclaimed the death and resurrection of Jesus Christ, events that freed persons forever from the ancient dread (3:6, 3). No longer need they anxiously strive to secure their salvation through meticulous performance of "legal demands," to "disarm the principalities and powers" so-called. Such "human precepts and doctrines have the appearance of wisdom," Paul admonished his readers, "but they are of no value in checking the indulgence of the flesh."[76]

In this declaration Paul indicated the moral impotence of the propagandist's philosophy and practices, and introduced a series of moral exhortations that were intrinsic to his gospel.[77] The form of this teaching was probably not original. A list of traits to be discarded like a filthy garment, others to be "put on," may have been compiled by the propagandists at Colossae. Similar lists were drawn up by contemporary Jewish rabbis and pagan moralists.[78] But in introducing the distinctive moral sanctions of the gospel, Paul charged these conventional ideas with new meaning and directed his readers to the source of power that enabled men to live by them.

The second table, the "household duties," is unique among Paul's letters. It has been compared with similar ones compiled by Jewish and pagan teachers, and by other early Christian writers.[79] The Christian tables are distinguished by their emphasis on the reciprocal nature of household rights as well as duties. This applied to wives, children, and slaves, not just to their (according to custom) social superiors. But the distinctive Pauline teaching, which transformed the conventional patterns of domestic morallity, was that the Christian recognized that other persons are "in Christ."[80]

NOTES

1. Philem. 9 b; also verses 1, 10, 12, and 23.
2. Eph. 3:1; 4:1; 6:20; Phil. 1:7, 13f.; Col. 4:18.
3. Some persons would extend this traditional picture by adding later letters, 1 and 2 Tim. and Titus. These writings, however, contain developments that are difficult if not impossible to accomodate Paul's release and a second imprisonment and subsequent martyrdom in Rome. See pp. 388f.
4. C. H. Dodd, *New Testament Studies*, pp. 67ff.; J. Fitzmyer, *Pauline Theology* (1967), pp. 4f. Cf. G. Bornkamm, *Paul* (1971), pp. 79f.
5. Acts 16:9ff.
6. Acts 16:16–40.
7. 1 Thess. 2:2.
8. Phil. 4:15f.; 2 Cor. 11:8f.
9. 2 Cor. 8:1ff.
10. 2 Cor. 2:4, 12f.; 7:5f. Cf. Acts 20:3, 5.
11. Phil. 1:12f.; 4:22. The Marcionite prologue to the letter dating from the second century reads: ". . . The Apostle praises them [the Philippians], writing to them from Rome, from prison, by Epaphroditus."
12. Acts 24:22ff., 27.
13. 2 Cor. 1:8ff.; 11:23ff.; 1 Cor. 15:32.
14. Phil. 2:23 (1:26).
15. Acts 20:1f.
16. Phil. 1:28f.; 3:2f.
17. Acts 19:8f.; 20:19.
18. Acts 28:17ff.
19. Phil. 1:15ff.
20. Acts. 20:29f.
21. Rom. 16:17ff. Note: "Andronicus and Junius . . . my fellow prisoners" (Rom. 16:7).
22. Acts 19:22. Cf. Acts 27:1ff. Phil. 1:1; 2:19ff.
23. The alternative theory that Philippians was written from Caesarea is not as probable, although Kümmel and some other scholars incline toward it. The difficulty of distance; Paul's relative safety at Caesarea (Acts 24:26); and the unlikelihood that Paul thought of an early visit to Philippi at this time militate against this hypothesis. F. F. Bruce, *Paul* (1977), pp. 359f.
24. F. W. Beare, *A Commentary on the Epistle to the Philippians* (1959), pp. 22f.
25. G. B. Caird writes: "Perhaps Epaphroditus fell ill on the way to Rome, and nearly

died because he insisted on joining Paul in Rome, 2:30. Word of his illness reached the Philippians before he reached Rome, 2:26, and a report of their anxieties reached Paul before E. had fully recovered. Did Paul wait to thank his friends until he had good news to report concerning E., indeed, until he was well enough to travel?" *Paul's Letters from Prison* (1976), pp. 99f.

26. Phil. 4:11.
27. E. F. Scott, "Philippians," IB 11 (1955):12.
28. *Ibid.*, p. 16; Beare, *Epistle to the Philippians*, pp. 49f.
29. One can detect in Phil. 1:8 Paul's eagerness to include everybody in his affectionate embrace, those whom he must reprove and those whom he commends. There are few references in the letter to individuals. He names a certain Clement and two women who followed in the footsteps of Lydia who have "labored side by side with [Paul] in the gospel."
30. Phil. 1:6, 10; 2:12f., 16; 3:12–14, 17–21.
31. Phil. 1:19, 22, 24–26; 2:24.
32. Phil. 1:22; 2:17. Cf. 4:6 and 11.
33. Phil. 1:8. Beare looks to Rome for the explanation (*Epistle to the Philippians*, pp. 59f.).
34. Phil. 1:19, possibly an echo of Job 13:16 (LXX).
35. Phil. 1:20.
36. For a discussion of the origin and structure of the passage see Beare, *Epistle to the Philippians*, pp. 74f.; E. Käsemann, "A Critical Analysis of Philippians 2:5–11," JthCh 5 (1968): 45ff. Cf. C. H. Talbert. "The Problem of Pre-existence in Philippians 2:6–11," *JBL* 86: 141ff. Kümmel noted: "the separating out of the Pauline additions from the traditional text on the basis of formal criteria is extremely uncertain . . . even if Paul did incorporate an older hymn . . . he has by this means expressed his own proclamation of Christ . . ." *INT*[2], pp. 114f.
37. E.g., H. Anderson, *Jesus and Christian Origins*, pp. 267ff., and 278f. R. P. Martin, *Carmen Christi* (1967).
38. Cf. Deut. 31:25ff., and Phil. 2:15f.; Beare, *Epistle to the Philippians*, pp. 88f.
39. Phil. 2:12f. Cf. Rom. 8:26ff.; 1 Cor. 15:9f.; Gal. 2:19ff.
40. 1 Thess. 4:1–12. Cf. 2 Cor. 13:11ff. Kümmel, *INT*[2], p. 333.
41. Phil. 2:20f.
42. Phil. 2:29f.
43. Paul's terms for circumcision and mutilation are a cruel pun. His attack is vicious but no more so than the legal purists who in ancient Jewish writings condemn the indifferent or apostate as "dogs." Paradoxically, by their emphasis on good works as salvific, they are "evil doers," according to Paul.
44. Cf. Phil. 3:3 and Rom. 2:28f.
45. Phil. 3:12ff.
46. Note Phil. 2:3; Rom. 12:3, 16; 1 Cor. 1:28f.
47. Phil. 3:19.
48. Note Phil. 1:27 (literally, "behave as citizens worthy of the gospel").
49. Cf. Col. 1:1, 7; 4:7ff., and Philem. 1:1f., 110, 23f.
50. Knox, "Epistle to Philemon," *IB*, 11, (555):555.
51. E.g., G. S. Duncan, *St. Paul's Ephesian Ministry* (1929); *id.*, "The Epistles of the Imprisonment in Recent Discussion," *ExpT* 46 (1934): 296; E. Lohse, *Colossians and Philemon* (1971), p. 188.
52. See p. 371 and a map of the region.
53. C. H. Dodd's defense of the Roman origin of Philemon is assesed by F. F. Bruce, *Paul* (1977), pp. 396–399. See Dodd, *New Testament Studies*, p. 95.
54. Beare, *IB*, 11: 137; "the developing situation in the province of Asia, as Paul learned

it from Epaphras and other visitors, may well have seemed to him to call urgently for his presence there as soon as he regained his freedom (if indeed he did regain it)." Bruce, *Paul*, p. 398.

55. Dodd, *New Testament Studies*, pp. 92f.

56. Philem. 10, 13.

57. For a statement and criticism of an original, highly speculative reconstruction of the circumstances prompting the letter and also explaining its preservation, proposed by E. J. Goodspeed (*New Solutions of New Testament Problems* [1927]) and expanded by John Knox (*Philemon Among the Letters of Paul* [1959]), see Bruce, *Paul*, pp. 401–406; also C. F. D. Moule, *The Epistles of Paul the Apostle to the Colossians and Philemon* (1957), pp. 14–18.

58. Philem. 7b, 20b.

59. A paraphrase. The meaning of verse 6 is obscure. Moule, *Colossians and Philemon*, pp. 142–144.

60. For a discussion of Roman laws relating to the case of Onesimus, see P. R. Coleman-Norton, "The Apostle Paul and the Roman Law of Slavery," in P. R. Coleman-Norton et al., eds., *Studies in Roman Economic and Social History* (1951), pp. 175–177. Lohse, *Colossians and Philemon*, pp. 196f.

61. Philem. 10. Onesimus while with Paul was converted. Note Paul's use of the metaphor of begetting (1 Cor. 4:14–17; Gal 4:19).

62. Without explicitly saying so Paul asked Philemon "not only to pardon his slave Onesimus and give him a Christian welcome, but to send him back so that he can go on helping Paul as he had already begun to do." Bruce, *Paul*, p. 406; Knox, "Epistle to Philemon," pp. 566f.

63. Philem. 16: "no longer a slave. . . ." need not imply Philemon's manumission of his fugitive slave. Cf. Gal. 3:27. "In 1 Cor. 7:21 Paul simply referred to the possibility that a Christian in slavery might become a freedman; he said nothing about the 'how' and 'why' of the manumission," S. S. Bartchy, *Mallon Chrésai: First-Century Slavery and 1 Corinthians 7:21* (1973), p. 175.

64. Philem. 16b. This would seem to be the meaning of the phrase "in the flesh and in the Lord." Moule, *Colossians and Philemon*, p. 148.

65. While it is unlikely that Paul had conducted a mission in Colossae, where Philemon lived and his house-church was located (see p. 368), Philemon had met Paul at Ephesus or elsewhere for he was converted by the Apostle. Lohse, *Colossians and Philemon*, p. 192, note 9. Cf. B. Reicke, "The Historical Setting of Colossians," *RevExp.* 70 (1973): 432f. Bruce. *Paul*, p. 406, note 37.

66. Modern criticism of Colossians is summarized concisely by F. W. Beare, *Colossians* (1955), pp. 143ff. Kümmel, *INT*[2], pp. 340–346. E. P. Sanders examines passages in Colossians that appear to be verbatim or serial quotations from indisputable Pauline letters or conflations thereof and concludes that Paul did not write Colossians as we have it. "Literary Dependence in Colossians," *JBL*, 85 (1966): 28ff. Lohse, *Colossians and Philemon*, pp. 177ff.

67. Strabo *Geography* XII. 8. 13. Colossae seems to have lost all importance when Pliny collected materials for his history of the region (ca. 75 C.E.).

68. See B. Reicke, "The Historical Setting of Colossians," *RevExp* 70 (1973): 429–432.

69. See, however, Note 66.

70. Moule, *Colossians and Philemon*, pp. 13ff.; Bruce, *Paul*, pp. 408–412. Cf. F. W. Beare's cautious statements, pp. 143ff. Caesarea still has its champions, e.g., B. Riecke, "Historical Setting of Colossians," pp. 435f.

71. Col. 1:15–20 is commonly held to form "a hymnic section which has been appropriated from the tradition." This surmise is supported by observations concerning literary form and theological content. Although scholars differ concerning the extent

of editorial modification, it is probable that the words "of the church" were inserted to give the term *body* (in the original a reference to "the cosmos"?) a Pauline interpretation. Also the words "through the blood of his cross" were added to point (with typical Pauline emphasis) to the crucifixion as the place where reconciliation was accomplished. Lohse, *Colossians and Philemon*, pp. 41ff. E. Schweizer, "Christ in the Letter to the Colossians," *RevExp.* 70 (1973): 455–459. Cf. Moule, *Colossians and Philemon*, pp. 58ff.

72. Scholars differ over the influence of Judaism, perhaps a local variety of Judaism practiced in the synagoguues of the Lycus valley, upon the false teachers. According to Bruce, "their teaching seems to have been Jewish" (*Paul*, pp. 413ff.). E. Schweizer detects Pythagorean teaching ("Letter to the Colossians," pp. 452f.). Lohse stresses the diversity of elements that "can be termed Gnostic, or if a more cautious designation is desired, pre-Gnostic." Perhaps all would agree that the Colossian false teaching represents a kind of syncretism of Christianity and non-Christian, late Hellenistic piety of a speculative bent. *Colossians and Philemon*, pp. 127–131.

73. Col. 1:25ff.

74. Col. 1:12; cf. 2:18.

75. Col. 2:2, 1:9ff.; 2:10, 19. Paul's use of the term *mystery* as a reference to God's eschatological act of salvation is in agreement with 1 Cor. 2:7, 10. Kümmel, *INT*[2], p. 344.

76. Col. 2:23. The reference to circumcision (3:11; cf. 2:11, 4:11) suggests that the propagandists were urging it, not in order to contain Christianity within Judaism, as did the Judaizers in Jerusalem and Galatia, but as one of "the severities of the body" (2:23) that promoted a higher degree of piety. See Lohse, *Colossians and Philemon*, pp. 101ff.

77. Col. 3:5ff.

78. Moule, *Colossians and Philemon*, pp. 126ff.

79. For examples of the latter see 1 Pet. 2:13ff.; Titus 2:1ff.; also Did. 4:9ff.; 1 Clem. 21:6ff.

80. This practical interest in domestic relations has been contrasted with Paul's admonitions in 1 Cor. 7. Is this evidence of another's teaching or that the Apostle's eschatological perspective had changed?

PART III

CONFLICT AND CONSOLIDATION IN THE POSTAPOSTOLIC AGE

<table>
<tr><td>

Writings from the Pauline Circle

</td><td>

Chapter
17

</td></tr>
</table>

T HE four or five decades following 65 C.E. are commonly called "the post-apostolic age," or the "precatholic period." The first description acknowledges the passing of "those who were from the beginning eyewitnesses and ministers of the word."[1] By 70 C.E. the chief apostles were dead, and the influence of the survivors was attenuated by the geographical spread of the gospel and the predominantly Gentile character of the churches. The term *precatholic* acknowledges an equally significant fact about this period. It was only well into the second century of the Common Era that those forms of doctrine and organization prerequisite to the establishment of a "catholic" (universal) Church were achieved.[2]

We have examined the proclamation and pattern of teaching "declared at first by the Lord," and attested "by those who heard him."[3] We have followed Paul's vigorous advocacy of Christianity among the Gentiles, and read his main writings. The question now becomes: What are the lines connecting this nascent Christianity and the ancient catholic Church of the second century?

The difficulty and perennial challenge of this question is partly due to the lack of a narrative sequel to the Acts of the Apostles. It might seem that adequate compensation for this lack is found in the more than a dozen New Testament writings commonly assigned to this time. Yet critical scholars have not reached settled conclusions concerning the origins of the majority of these books. Consequently, all efforts to relate them to each other and to other Christian writings of the same general period are inevitably conjectural and tentative. Some pieces of the "picture puzzle" are missing. Without these, the existing parts do not form a wholly intelligible pattern.

Beyond question there were many Christians at this time who were actively writing.[4] Yet their letters and tracts were intended to meet local or regional needs. Later generations were not interested in preserving these writings that did survive from the earlier period. Some of them were stigmatized as heretical; others were inadequate for the current needs of the Church.[5]

Shall we abandon our study of the New Testament books as units, and from the various writings quarry material for constructing a history of Christianity in the postapostolic age? Some authors of books on the New Testament have followed this method. Passages have been selected from the New Testament and from contemporary documents that illustrate the principal interests and problems of second- and third-generation Christians. This material is then presented according to such various topics as the relation of the Christian movement to society and the state, the development of forms of organization, types of apology, and so forth. From these authors much can be learned about the next half-century. But in the chapters that follow, the remaining canonical books will be studied as units. As in the previous sections, interest will center upon the special problems relating to the origin and interpretation of each.

Although some have supposed that the Apostle Paul was forgotten for a period, it is unlikely that this was ever the case in important areas of the Church. Second- and third-generation Christians drew inspiration from the story of his life, and his letters were copied and quoted as possessing unusual authority.[6]

In addition to Acts, several books of the New Testament witness to the influence of Paul after his martyrdom. Four of these will be studied in this chapter—Ephesians, 1 and 2 Timothy, and Titus.

LETTER TO THE EPHESIANS

Ephesians is a theological tract having the formal appearance of a letter. It has been described as "the crown of Paulinism," for its writer reduced some of the principal ideas of the Apostle to a system dominated by a single theme. According to ancient Church tradition, as we have noted, Paul wrote Ephesians from his Roman prison shortly after he wrote Colossians. But many modern critics agree that Ephesians is a later work written by a Paulinist. In any event, the choice lies between Paul and someone well acquainted with his thought.

A completely satisfactory solution of the origin of Ephesians has not been reached. Indeed, arguments for and against Pauline authorship are so evenly matched that protagonists tend to overstate their cases and persuade others to the opposite opinion. Only a brief discussion of this perplexing critical problem is necessary.[7]

THE PROBLEM OF AUTHORSHIP

There are fundamental differences in the style and language of Ephesians and those of the unquestionably genuine letters of Paul. The great sixteenth-century classicist Erasmus commented on the literary peculiarities of Ephesians. Those who read Paul's letters in Greek are most sensitive to this, but the English reader can notice the differences in style between, let us say, the Corinthian letters and Ephesians. In the latter the sentences are long and involved, containing many participles, relative pronouns, and synonyms joined together. Paul's style has been likened to a cascade. It is quick, light, allusive. The style of Ephesians is more like a glacier—slow-moving, massive, majestic. Some have sought to account for this by noting the noncontroversial and meditative mood of Ephesians, as well as the devotional nature of its theme. Others have conjectured that Paul relied on a trusted helper to compose the final draft of the letter. All agree that the criterion of style must be employed with caution.

The unusual vocabulary of Ephesians is another linguistic element of the problem. More than ninety words that are not found elsewhere in Paul's letters appear, and this novel vocabulary is akin to Christian writings after Paul. Common Pauline words are put together in unusual ways, and others are used with different shades of meaning.[8] Some persons consider that the subject matter of Ephesians is sufficient to explain these facts. But when it is observed that identical words, e.g., *mystery* and *fullness,* are used differently in Colossians and Ephesians—two letters composed at nearly the same time if both were written by Paul—there is reason to question the adequacy of such explanations.[9] Moreover, in no other letter does "Paul" depend so extensively upon reproducing ideas previously expressed in writing. Much weight is given to this evidence of literary dependence by those who view Ephesians as a pseudonymous work.[10] Some worthy disciple of Paul, it is claimed, created a mosaic of "tiny elements of tradition," and the result is a carefully worked-out theme. Of course, it can be shown that in his major letters Paul relied on tradition—hymnic fragments, primitive confessions, and the like. Yet the Apostle did not employ these pieces of tradition to help express his ideas, but to buttress them, just as he did with scriptural proof.[11]

Several theological aspects of Ephesians are important to the question of origin. In 1 Corinthians, Paul wrote that "no other foundation can any one lay than that which is laid, which is Jesus Christ." In Ephesians "the apostles and prophets" are called the foundation of the Church.[12] In the main letters of Paul, God is the reconciler of men, working through Christ. In Ephesians Christ is the reconciler, and the death of Christ, so central to Paul's gospel, is subordinated to his exaltation.[13] Peculiar to the Pauline letters is the declaration in Ephesians that Christ "descended into the lower parts of the earth."[14] There is no suggestion of the coming of the Lord, whether soon or late.[15] For the author of Ephesians the object of Christ's ministry had been to break down "the dividing wall of hostility" between Jew and Gentile.[16] As ardently as Paul longed for harmony between both ethnic groups in the churches, he did not speak of this as the primary object of Christ's mission.* Some say that Paul developed in Ephesians some of the deeper implications of his earlier teachings. Others consider that this "unprecedented development," in certain instances, amounts to contradiction, providing a chief objection to apostolic authorship.[17]

Any solution of the problem of authorship contains large elements of subjective feeling. Either Ephesians is an original, noncontroversial writing composed, in whole or in large part, by Paul shortly after Colossians (with a greater than usual reliance upon an amanuensis?); or it is the writing of a follower of Paul, whose mind was steeped in the language and thought of Colossians and of other letters of the Apostle, but who was also a theologian in his own right. The cumulative weight of the internal evidence seems to support the latter alternative. The question is still in debate. Perhaps it will never be answered with certainty.[18]

THE DESTINATION OF THE LETTER

Two facts lead the majority of scholars to say that Ephesians was not written for the church at Ephesus, at least not exclusively for this Asian church. Several of the best manuscripts omit the address "at Ephesus," as the editors of the RSV acknowledge.[19] Moreover, the absence of greetings and other personal no-

* Since there is every reason to believe that a Paulinist should have employed some of Paul's primary ideas, more weight must be given to lesser ideas that also reflect a changed perspective. An example would be the conception of Paul's mission recorded in Ephesians 3:4–13. The passage states that Paul was entrusted with a particular revelation, namely, that the Gentiles should be "fellow heirs, members of the same body [with Jews], and partakers of the promise in Christ Jesus through

the gospel." According to Paul his fundamental revelation was that the principle of obedience to the Torah as a means of salvation was now set aside. The corollary of this proclamation was the admission of Gentiles into the Church. In Ephesians the means and the end are reversed.

tices is conspicuous. These facts defy explanation if the letter was addressed directly to a church in which Paul had labored for from two to three years. Some statements in Ephesians imply that its readers knew Paul only by reputation, and that the writer had hearsay knowledge of his readers' Christian witness.[20]

There are two principal explanations for these facts. A popular view is that Ephesians was composed as a circular letter to be carried from place to place by a single courier (Tychicus?). Perhaps the author left a blank space in the letter's prescript, expecting the reader to supply the appropriate address: "at Laodicea," "at Hierapolis," and so on.[21] The alternative to the circular-letter theory is that a second-century scribe supplied the words, "at Ephesus," bringing the letter into conformity with its traditional title and the prescripts of other Pauline letters. The original address was therefore "to the saints who are also faithful in Christ Jesus." This mode of address would be strange from Paul's pen; from a writer in the postapostolic age, appropriate.[22] Nothing is certain about the destination of this letter except that it was not written for one church, at any rate not for the Ephesians alone.

A date for the writing of Ephesians around 90 C.E. is consistent with the allusions to it in the writings of the Apostolic Fathers and with the supposed influence of Acts. Yet if 1 Peter reflects the influence of Ephesians, as many believe, Ephesians might be dated a decade earlier. The closeness of the author to Paul's situation supports a date not long after the Apostle's death.

INTERPRETING EPHESIANS

A. Introduction, 1:1–2:10
   1. The prescript, 1:1f.
   2. A doxology, proclaiming the purpose of God to unite all things in Christ, and the benefits of believers, 1:3–14
   3. A prayer for the reader's enlightenment, passing into praise of the greatness of God's power, 1:15–2:10
B. An Exposition of the Unity of All Believers in Christ, 2:11–23
   1. The former hopeless state of the Gentiles, 2:11f.
   2. The reconciliation of Jew and Gentile "in one body through the cross," 2:13–18
   3. The household of God, 2:19–23
C. The Mystery of Christ Made Known to Paul, 3:1–13
   1. The revelation mediated through the "holy apostles and prophets": the Gentiles are fellow heirs of the promise, 3:1–6
   2. The plan: the Church is to make known to the invisible powers "the manifold wisdom of God," 3:7–13
D. Paul's Prayer is Resumed; a Doxology, 3:14–21
   1. Prayer for the readers fulfillment, 3:14–19
   2. In praise of the divine power and glory, 3:20–21

The first three chapters of Ephesians are a meditation in praise of God, beginning and ending in prayer. The letter's introduction has been likened to the flight of an eagle "rising and wheeling round, as though for awhile uncertain what direction in his boundless freedom he shall take." Just so the thought of the writer of Ephesians "ranges this way and that in the realm of the spirit, marking out no clear course, but merely exulting in the attributes and purposes of God."[23] The conviction that gives a unity to the whole is that there is a predestined purpose working in history, and beyond it, toward some marvelous, all-embracing goal. Christ has revealed the mystery of the divine will. Through Christ and his Church, God is accomplishing an ultimate unity, the reintegration of every conflicting, disintegrative force in the universe. Does the writer envision that in the end the judgment of wrath will be set aside?[24]

In the thought of the writer, God "the Father" is the absolute prototype of all authority. God's sovereignty was not for him an abstract concept, but a personal relation: "the Father of our Lord Jesus Christ."[25] This apprehension of God as "the Father" is the ground for the writer's belief in the primordial and predestined unity of creation. Yet his emphasis is not placed upon some speculative, ideal unity, but upon the revelation of God's will toward unity, and of his power to achieve it in historical events: the resurrection of Christ, and the union of formerly hostile segments of humanity in a visible community.

Since Ephesians declares that the Church is the primary stage in the accomplishment of the unification of the universe, the letter's teaching concerning the nature and role of the Church merits special consideration. Let us notice, first of all, the author's mystical conception of the Church as the necessary complement of Christ. As the head of the Church, Christ is its "fullness"; but the Church as his body brings to completion the purposes conceived by Christ.[26] It is in accord with this belief that the writer prays that the Church's membership may be "filled with all the fullness of God," and that the perfected life of the Church may express the totality of God's purpose revealed in Christ.[27] This purpose is to be fulfilled when all things are united in Christ, and to that end all things are tributary to him who is the head of the Church.

This mystical conception of the relation of Christ to his Church is set forth also in the hortatory section of Ephesians.[28] The writer's ideal of Christian marriage was that husbands and wives should conceive of their relations to each other in the light of the archetypal union existing between Christ and his bride, the Church.

The transcendental significance of the Church is most clearly taught in the idea that "through the church the manifold wisdom of God" is being made known to "the principalities and powers in the heavenly places."*

Nevertheless, the mystical and transcendental significance of the Church was not the principal interest of the writer of Ephesians. He was concerned chiefly to proclaim the importance of the Church as the *historical* agency purposed by God to reconcile person to person and to lift the human spirit into communion with the divine.[29] Now that Jews and Gentiles had been made one, there was no limit to the power of Christ the Reconciler. Through him all men could find a basis for unity; through him they might "have access in one Spirit to the Father." A new human type had been created by God in Christ that was not determined by national, cultural, or racial factors. This new person was not "Jew" or "Gentile," but "Christian."

*It is difficult to understand how the formation of the Church could have some unprecedented effect upon the world rulers. But the writer believed that the unity of Jew and Gentile in one body gave prescience of the ultimate unity of "all things," heretofore unknown to human beings or to the world of spirits. (See the essay and bibliographical notes on Gnosticism and Ephesians in M. Barth, *Ephesians*, pp. 12–18. "The development of Christology and ecclesiology [in Ephesians] . . . can only be understood against the background of a christianized mythological gnosis." Kümmel, *INT²*, p. 365. See note 36.

E. Exhortations to Unity, 4:1–6:9
   1. A call to consecration, 4:1–6
   2. God's various gifts intended for the unity and maturity of the saints, 4:7–16
   3. Their former lives contrasted with their new natures, 4:17–24
   4. A description of Christian behavior as the opposite of pagan immoralities, 4:25–5:20: specific commands (4:25–5:2); light opposes darkness (5:3–14); a summary (5:15–20)
   5. Mutual subordination in the household of God, 5:21–6:9: the relation of husbands and wives is that of Christ and his Church (5:21–33); children and parents (6:1–4); slaves and masters (6:5–9)
F. Christian Warfare, 6:10–18
   1. Be strong in the Lord, 6:10
   2. Put on the whole armor of God, 6:11–17
   3. Pray at all times, 6:18a
G. Conclusion, 6:18b–24
   1. Appeal for supplications for the saints, and for the writer, 6:18b–20
   2. Commendation of Tychicus, 6:21f.
   3. Benediction, 6:23f.

Moral exhortation is found early in the letter, when the Paulinist's predestinarian theme is given somewhat curious expression: "created in Christ Jesus for good works, which God prepared beforehand that we should walk in them."[30] Once again, the readers are urged to conform the pattern of their lives to the holy purpose that the Church was intended to serve. They should be eager to maintain within their fellowship that unity which God willed for his Creation. Christ had provided the Church with the essential gifts for the attainment of this end (4:1ff.).

For the writer and his readers the time of "the holy apostles and prophets" appears to have ended.[31] The Christian faith is now being transmitted by evangelists, pastors, and teachers.[32] The interest of Ephesians in these charismatic ministries of the church and the absence of any reference to "bishops," in contrast with the Pastoral Letters, suggests a "pre-Catholic" origin for Ephesians, yet a setting in which there was a keen yearning for ecclesiastical unity.[33] The author, however, does not attack errorists directly; rather, in keeping with the approaches of the writers of the Pastorals and the Fourth Gospel, he opposes them "with the fascinating phenomenon of the *una sancta apostolica*."[34] Prominent attention is given to Christian baptism in Ephesians, which is to be expected in a Pauline writing, but what explanation is there for silence concerning the Lord's Supper?

The midrash in Ephesians 4:8ff. is connected with the thought of Paul in Colossians 2:15, but the pre-Gnostic view that the rulers of the heavenly spheres are by nature evil is not found in the Paulines. The writer of Ephesians took a further step in the direction of the developed Gnostic systems when he wrote that the Reconciler descended through the heavenly places, and ascended through the same spheres, leading "the host of captives."[35] Yet the purpose of "the gnosis of redemption" in Ephesians was not the enlightenment or apotheosis of individuals. Christ's gifts were provided for the achievement of the corporate unity of his Church, "for the building up of the body of Christ . . . in love."[36]

After sharply contrasting pagan and Christian morality, the writer solemnly warned his readers against relapsing into their "former manner of life." His references to "the unfruitful works of darkness" done "in secret," and to the deceivers, suggest that the temptation toward impurity and other forms of self-indulgence came from within the Church and not only from pagan society.[37]

The ethical section of Ephesians concludes with a brief table of household duties modeled upon the conventional pattern of moral teaching in the Hellenistic Age but especially upon Colossians. Particular stress was placed upon the mutual subordination of husbands and wives because the writer saw in marriage a profound symbol of the nature of the Church.*

The familiar passage depicting the Christian warrior in full armor has been described as a sublimation of the apocalyptic image of the final conflict. The evil day is no longer the apocalyptic "tribulation," but the present time; Christ is no longer conceived as the One who shall destroy evil with the fiery breath of his mouth.[38] But the Christian life is depicted (as in the whole of the New Testament) as an unremitting warfare against evil, for which struggle all the resources of the gospel are needed.

THE AIM OF THE WRITER OF EPHESIANS

Is it possible to describe more specifically the circumstances leading to the composition of Ephesians? A principal element in Edgar Goodspeed's thesis has many advocates: the chief purpose of Ephesians was to serve as a prefatory statement, a general introduction to Paul's gospel, on the occasion of a major collection of Paul's letters. The present writer believes that a specific historical situation in the church rather than a literary intention provides a more plausible circumstance for the writing of Ephesians. Its author was probably faced with an attitude among Gentile Christians that Paul had anticipated but that developed into a crisis only in the postapostolic age.[39] The writer knew of Gentile Christians who were disparaging the Jewish past of the Church. This past was represented by Jewish Christians, the remnant of the Israel of God in and through whom the Christian Church held continuity with the people of the old covenant and the eternal promises of God. The author of Ephesians, doubtless a Jewish Christian himself,[40] met this situation by emphasizing that the Church's Lord had reconciled, in one body, Jew and Gentile. This fact gave prescience of a final integration of "all things" in Christ and hope for the emergence of a truly universal Church.[41]

THE PASTORAL LETTERS

Three letters of the New Testament are called "the Pastorals"—1 and 2 Timothy, and Titus. The original contents of these writings explain the derivation of this description. They were composed by a "pastor," that is, by one who had the concerns of a shepherd or caretaker.[42]

The primary problem facing the interpreter is whether or not Paul was the pastor. From the late second century until modern times, the assumption was that Paul's appeal to Caesar resulted in his acquittal. After his release he resumed missionary work in the East and wrote 1 Timothy and Titus. He was

*Three relations are treated as analogous in this passage: husband–wife, Christ–Church, person–body. The realistic, coordinate union between Christ and the Church is affirmed. The exclusiveness of the physical-spiritual union of husband and wife provides a significant symbol of the unity existing between members of Christ's body and of the subjection of the Church to Christ as Lord.

arrested again and brought back to Rome. During this second imprisonment, and shortly before martyrdom, Paul wrote 2 Timothy. A critical examination of the letters demonstrates that this tradition cannot any longer be maintained with confidence. A full statement of the case is not necessary to feel the cumulative weight of the evidence against Pauline authorship.

THE PROBLEM OF THE PASTORALS

It is the internal evidence that is decisive. The vocabulary and style of the Pastorals reflect a marked difference from the indisputably genuine letters of Paul and point to a postapostolic provenience. More than a third of the words in the Pastorals are non-Pauline, and many Pauline terms are used differently. There are also at least 170 words in the Pastorals that are not found elsewhere in the New Testament.[43] The significance of this linguistic data can be seen best when the doctrinal connotations of the vocabulary are studied.*

*The Pastorals are missing from Marcion's collection of the Paulines and also from the earliest codex, Papyrus 46. This evidence can be interpreted in several ways. It is almost certain that there are allusions to the Pastorals in the writings of the Apostolic Fathers that establish their origin before Marcion's time. It is quite possible, however, that Marcion's New Testament did not contain these letters. Since the ending of the papyrus codex is lost, nothing can be established by its omission of the Pastorals.

A consideration of the personal and historical allusions in the Pastorals reveals other aspects of the problem. The following passages should be noted: 1 Timothy 1:3; Titus 1:5 and 3:12; and 2 Timothy 1:8, 15ff., and 4:9ff. Although these passages have suggested to some persons that these letters were written during Paul's imprisonments at Ephesus or at Caesarea, they demand the tradition of the Apostle's release and second Roman imprisonment if written by Paul.[44] Yet this assumption is not free of difficulties. Is it conceivable that Paul should have urged Timothy to remain at Ephesus and carefully instructed him concerning his mission there, and then commanded him to come to him at Rome? Again, Timothy is said to have witnessed Paul's sufferings at Antioch, Iconium, and Lystra, all of which occurred before Timothy became Paul's associate.[45]

The theological outlook of the pastor is an important element in the problem. Beyond question, some of Paul's distinctive teaching is set forth in the Pastorals, and the Apostle's gospel is the norm of "sound doctrine." But, as E. F. Scott has written, this manifest desire of the writer to think like Paul makes more significant his failure to understand several of Paul's key doctrines. "He does not know what Paul meant by the Law; he confuses Pauline faith with loyalty to a Church tradition; he forgets the central value which Paul attached to the Cross; he has nothing to say of the conflict between the flesh and Spirit; his thought is quite untouched by the Pauline mysticism."[46]

The Pastor's portrayal of the Christian's life as a life of "piety" is often contrasted with Paul's delineation of the moral qualities of the life "in Christ." "The assertion that the Pastorals contain a moralized version of Paulinism is not without foundation." For Paul, "righteousness," as it pertained to the individual, denoted his new status or relation vis-à-vis God; "righteousness" in the Pastorals refers to a person's uprightness, his or her moral respectability, we might say. Is it possible that Paul should have laid stress upon the value of "good works," which sometimes appear in the Pastorals as ends in themselves?[47] Modern writers have referred to the "bourgeois" morality of the Pastorals. Words rarely used by Paul illustrate the appropriateness of this description, at least as a tendency: "sobriety," "a godly life," a "good conscience," are set forth as identifying marks of the Christian. It appears that in settling down in the world, churches Christianized some of the secular virtues.[48]

Another element in the problem is the Church situation reflected in the Pastorals. The leaders of the earliest churches, "the apostles, prophets, teachers," have been succeeded by the bishop and elders or by the elder-bishops—the point is debatable—and by the deacons. Moreover, the positions of "Timothy" and "Titus," and the prerogatives given them through their ordination by elders, suggest that they were bishops even though the title is not used.

A survey of the contents of the letters reveals the extent to which the pastor was preoccupied with attacking false teachings. But the only way he could cope with the situation was to contradict, denounce, and ridicule. Unlike Paul, who in Colossians offered a creative interpretation of the gospel to refute the distortions of pre-Gnostic speculations and asceticism, the pastor resorted only to name-calling, and appealed to "the truth," "the good teaching," and the like. His conservative mentality is shown in his concern that the deposit of faith be guarded.[49] All in all, he represents a very different spirit from that revealed in the nine Paulines. Furthermore, whether or not Ephesians was written by Paul, it is in every respect worthy of the Apostle. The same cannot be said of the Pastorals. Yet like the writer of Ephesians, the pastor commended Paul to his churches as the great exemplar of Christianity, and in this he rendered a service of inestimable value.

The conclusion seems to be irresistible: 1 and 2 Timothy and Titus were written by a Paulinist who is known to us only through his letters. It is a safe surmise that he was a convert from Hellenistic Judaism and that, by the time of his writings, he held a position of eminence in the Pauline churches of Asia Minor. There is no difficulty in the view that the Pastor chose to write under the pseudonym of "Paul." He was "fighting the good fight" in the Apostle's name. The only difficulty in the theory of pseudonymity concerns the Pauline personalia. Notice has been taken of the view that the Pastor built up his letters from fragments of the Apostle's personal correspondence with colleagues. This is an attractive but fanciful hypothesis.[50] The problem concerning the personalia is literary and historical, not moral. No agreement over the identification or origin of "precious fragments" has been reached, and perhaps never will be. What "rings true" to one reader seems obvious "fiction" to another. The significance of the matter can easily be exaggerated. In any event, the teaching of the letters is not directly Paul's but that of a Paulinist.

The dates of the three letters and the order of their composition are determined chiefly by decisions concerning the so-called parallels in the writings of the Apostolic Fathers, and by the identification of the schismatic teaching that the pastor opposed. The type of Church organization also has been used as a clue, some persons placing the Pastorals before, others after, the Letters of Ignatius (ca. 110 C.E.). A choice lies between dating them within a decade on either side of 100 or later in the second century.[51] The order of reading suggested here is: 1 Timothy → Titus → 2 Timothy.

INTERPRETING 1 TIMOTHY

A. Introduction, 1:1–17
1. The prescript, 1:1
2. The purpose of Timothy's ministry at Ephesus, 1:3–11
3. Thanksgiving for the grace of Christ toward Paul; the Apostle's witness; a doxology, 1:12–17

Several features of this letter's prescript imply non-Pauline authorship. The formal greeting would be odd if addressed by Paul to his intimate disciple. But as the introduction to a charge from a bishop to younger subordinates, the address is thoroughly appropriate. The words *God our Savior* are not paralleled in the main Paulines and reflect the language of the postapostolic Church.[52]

The letter's first paragraph clearly reveals the pastor's purpose. The Pauline gospel was being perverted by persons occupying themselves with "myths and endless genealogies," and claiming to be "teachers of the law." That this mythical speculation was of Jewish origin is explicitly stated in the Letter to Titus.[53] Some consider that the reference was to second-century Gnostic teaching concerning the emanations that proceed from God. But it is more probable that the pastor scorned pre-Gnostic Jewish speculations involving a mystical or allegorical interpretation of narrative portions of the Torah.[54] It is difficult to imagine Paul writing that the Law was not given for "the just" but only for "the ungodly and profane." Yet the pastor's insistence reveals that a new type of ascetic legalism had arisen. He was confident that if Paul were living he would vigorously oppose it.

In the references to Paul that follow, one sees why the pastor wrote in his name (1:12ff.). For him, Paul was the foremost exponent of the Christian tradition. The saying in verse 15 is not an expression of Paul's, yet the Apostle surely would have approved his follower's impression of his witness.

Before proceeding to the particulars of his "charge," the pastor stated the credentials of the ideal type of Church leader for the second generation (1:18–20). The apostles and prophets had selected promising men who had been ordained by the elders. The contrasting apostate leaders served as a warning to the faithless and erring.

Recall that Paul expressed equivocal views concerning the participation of

Sculptures of a young woman and a young man, first century C.E. *(Photographs by Agora Excavations, courtesy of the American School of Classical Studies, Athens.)*

women in public worship. Although the Apostle commanded that in praying and prophesying women should cover their heads, it is doubtful that in principle he intended to restrict their freedom.[55] The pastor's views are beyond doubt. Women must not be permitted to speak. This was not commanded for reasons of expediency but in recognition of an inviolable order of creation. Women are by nature transgressors, easily deceived, by temperament (especially the younger ones) too garrulous.[56] In selecting widows for orders the pastor enjoins the application of strict standards.[57]

The pastor took for granted that Timothy knew the status and function of the bishop, the leaders, and the deacons. His concern was that those selected be known for their moral stability, for their adherence to conventional standards of morality.[58] Also, they must have no conscientious doubts concerning "the faith."[59] In the midst of this counsel relating to church officers, the pastor gave his reasons for his concern. They may be summarized as follows: The Church must be ordered in its corporate life, not because this is an end in itself, but because it is "the pillar and bulwark of the truth" (3:14f.). The Church's purpose for being is to confess the mystery of Christ's Lordship over heaven and earth. (This is emphasized by the inclusion of a liturgical fragment.[60]) But the Church exists also as a defense and a security against destructive doctrine.

The Pastor did not for long refrain from attacking the false teachers. We are now informed that they advocated a rigorous asceticism. Paul counseled tolerance of "the weak" who held ascetic views concerning marriage and matters of diet. The pastor allowed no such toleration. Even "Timothy" was not free to associate spiritual discipline with "the training table," not free to be a "teetotaler."[61] The pre-Gnostic notion that the "fleshly" appetites invariably were evil put the issue of asceticism for religious motives in a new context. If Paul had lived in these "later times," when the imminence of the End was no longer expected, would he have affirmed, without qualification, the positive value of life in this Age?[62] The pastor thought so, provided Christians remained chaste, temperate, and void of greed, especially in money matters, and fulfilled their station in life and its duties.

The concluding appeal provides the most direct justification for describing as pre-Gnostic the teaching opposed by the pastor (6:20f.). His antagonists laid claim to a *gnosis*. Some scholars have detected a reference in this passage to a lost book called "the Antitheses," which was written by Marcion and dealt with the "contradictions" between the Law and the gospel. But this is a slim basis for dating 1 Timothy around 150 C.E. or later. Throughout the letters the author displays a temperamental distaste for argument. One of the things that distressed him most was that the schismatics had "a morbid craving for controversy."[63]

INTERPRETING THE LETTER TO TITUS

A. Introduction, 1:1–4
  1. The superscription containing a statement concerning Paul's credentials, 1:1–4a
  2. A grace, 1:4b
B. The Purpose and Conduct of Titus's Ministry in Crete, 1:5–2:15
  1. A recollection of the Apostle's instructions, with special reference to elders and the bishop, 1:5–9
  2. The activities and reputation of the Cretan false teachers, 1:10–16
  3. Regulations concerning the conduct of the minister and the congregation, 2:1–10
  4. The training and behavior of persons who have seen manifested "the grace of God," 2:11–14
  5. Summary concerning the general functions and status of Titus, 2:15
C. Christian Conduct in a Pagan Society, 3:1–8a
  1. The Christian witness in the community, 3:1–2
  2. Contrast between the Christians' former paganism and their present standing and future hope, 3:3–8a
D. Conclusion, 3:8b–15
  1. Good deeds attest sound doctrine; the lives of false teachers are "unprofitable and futile," 3:8b–9
  2. A rule concerning the treatment of factious men, 3:10–11
  3. Personal services requested, 3:12–13

4. The importance of "good deeds" stressed again, 3:14
5. Greetings and a grace, 3:15

The shortest of the Pastorals has the longest prescript. Its formal, liturgical character is incongruous in a personal letter. It reveals the pastor's conception of his own ministry. He was entrusted with the apostolic *kerygma*. His right to command was given by the Supreme Commander. From the beginning the special emphasis of this letter is upon the inseparability of knowledge of the truth and true piety.

The author makes no effort to relate his addressee to the Titus of Paul's letters. It is profitless to seek a historical setting for the Cretan mission.[64] The ministry of "Titus" is a type of the successor to the apostles; their missions were to be extended and the Church was to be provided a qualified ministry.*

The instructions to Titus concerning various groups within the Church resemble closely those given in 1 Timothy.[65] The rulings echo Paul's counsel, conditioned by the conventional moralism of the age, and introduce the distinctively Christian sanction for complete fidelity. The epithet "our great God and Savior Jesus Christ" drew the notice of early scribes of the letter, and it has continued to provoke theological discussion. The Pastor's ordinary practice was to write "God the Savior," and to refer separately to Christ.[66] Have we here an expression framed, in the worship of the Church, as a reaction to the liturgies of the emperor cult and mystery religions?

Like Paul, the pastor wrote concerning the moral responsibilities of Christians in a pagan society. Like Paul, he called his readers to a deepened appreciation of "the grace of God" and of the character of their new life and eternal hope by reminding them of their former situation apart from faith in the gospel.[67] But the idea that by God's grace persons are "trained to renounce" godless ways is not found in Paul. "In Paul grace is not educative but liberating": by it persons are set free from "worldly passions."[68] Also, unlike Paul, the pastor conceived of salvation as a past event, although still a matter of hope; and baptism as "the washing of regeneration." This entire passage is instructive, as evidence of early Paulinism giving place to the theology of the later catholic church.[69]

Titus ends on a note that dominates the Letter of James: true faith is known by its works, not its words. The times demanded this emphasis.

*The pastor's contempt for "Cretans" and his refusal to counsel patience in dealing with them may be compared with Paul's failure to castigate all Corinthians as sensuous merely because of their popular reputation. The writer's source of the generalization concerning Cretans was a popular tag attributed to Epimenides (ca. 500 B.C.E. but the origin is uncertain of the proverb, "to the pure all things are pure . . ." (cf. Lk. 11:41; Rom. 14:20).

INTERPRETING 2 TIMOTHY

A. Introduction, 1:1–18
   1. The prescript, 1:1f.
   2. A thanksgiving recalling Timothy's heritage, Paul's testimony and suffering; and containing an encouragement to Timothy, 1:3–14
   3. Some experiences of Paul in Asia, 1:15–18
B. The Charge to Timothy, 2:1–4:5
   1. Various analogies depicting the calling of the Church leader, 2:1–7
   2. Paul's gospel and personal witness recalled, 2:8–13
   3. Things to do and things to avoid, with special reference to promoters of controversy, 2:14–3:9
   4. Another reminder of Paul's life and persecutions, 3:10–13

5. Another reminder of Timothy's heritage, especially his long acquaintance with the scripture, 3:14–17
6. A summary of the charge emphasizing steadfastness, 4:1–5
C. Paul's Farewell, 4:6–22
   1. The reward of faithfulness: "the crown of righteousness," 4:6–8
   2. Paul's situation; personal requests; a statement of confidence ending in a doxology, 4:9–18
   3. Greetings and an urgent request, 4:19–21
   4. Benediction, 4:22

At its beginning 2 Timothy more closely corresponds in form to Paul's letters than do 1 Timothy and Titus. Yet the pastor's vocabulary reveals striking differences.[70] Moreover, the bases upon which the addressee was given encouragement suggest that "Timothy" typified the leadership of a later generation (the third?). He is summoned to be loyal to a faith that was not new in his time. It was an established "pattern of sound words," espoused by his family, by the great Apostle Paul, and tested by much suffering. As Timothy had been properly ordained, he could expect the powerful guidance of the Holy Spirit.

Loyalty to the gospel of the martyred Apostle is the keynote of 2 Timothy. Various teachings of the Apostle are utilized by the pastor, but in his summary of the effect of "the appearing of our Savior Christ Jesus," there is reflected the language generally used by the Hellenistic church in its worship.*

*2 Timothy, like 1 Timothy and Titus, was probably written by a representative of churches (in which Paul's influence and authority were recognized), who employed the pseudonym of the Apostle when writing to a recognized disciple, in order to instruct the community in sound doctrine, correct church polity, and to set forth an ideal of individual piety, to the end that false teaching and disillusionment respecting the Christian's hope might be resisted and overcome.

The warnings in 2 Timothy concerning the rebellion "in the last days" superficially resemble passage in 2 Thessalonians and those in other Christian writings concerning the tribulation preceding the End.[71] But the apocalyptic ideas have been significantly transformed. According to the pastor, the "rebellion" had already begun. The future tense of apocalyptic prediction—the literary device of pseudonymity to describe post-Pauline conditions—was not consistently retained. Nor was the exposure of corruption thought to be coincident with the coming of Christ as judge. Rather it was the triumph of orthodoxy over "counterfeit faith." Even when the pastor warned that "evil men and imposters would go on from bad to worse," there was no reference to signs of the End. The antidote to this distressing prospect was that the faithful, under the leadership of "Timothys" who follow the example of the Apostle, continue in what they "have learned and have firmly believed." Furnished with inspired scripture, church leaders are equipped to fight against false teaching (3:14–16).

The need for steadfastness did recall the advent hope of the church. But the pastor's charge pointed backward to the ordination liturgy rather than forward to the Parousia.

Readers will not agree concerning the letter's farewell. Some will judge that Paul certainly wrote it. Others will consider that this is most unlikely, that these words are the pastor's loving tribute to his hero. In either case this celebrated passage expressed the contagion of Paul's robust hope. Following the example of Paul who "kept the faith," Timothy is challenged to "fulfil" his "ministry."

Many readers are attracted to the view that the pastor tacked onto his writing a "precious fragment" of a letter written by Paul on the eve of his martyrdom. There is no completely satisfactory explanation for the origin of this passage, but the preoccupation of "Paul" with his own discomforts, and with the deceitfulness of men, does not conclude the letter. The last word is the witness of hope and praise.

NOTES

1. Luke 1:2. Some historians prefer the term "subapostolic."
2. For the earliest use of the term *catholic,* see Ignatius, *Smyr.* 8:2. The term "early-catholic" is employed by some modern scholars who detect catholic tendencies (variously defined) in some of the latest writings of the New Testament.
3. Heb. 2:3f.
4. H. J. Cadbury, "The New Testament and Early Christian Literature," *IB* 7 (1952): 32ff.
5. M. H. Shepherd, Jr., "The Post-Apostolic Age," *IB* 7 (1952): 215.
6. Note the accolades of the late first-century writer of 1 Clem. 5:22ff. It must be said that there was also hostile resistance to Paul and to his continued influence, e.g., Jewish-Christian writers reflect an opposition to Paul that did not abate with the Apostle's martyrdom. See Hennecke and Schneemelcher, *New Testament Apocrypha* (1965), Vol. 2, pp. 71f., 103ff.
7. F. W. Beare, "The Epistle to the Ephesians," *IB* 10 (1955): 597ff.; E. J. Goodspeed, *The Meaning of Ephesians* (1933); C. L. Mitton, *The Epistle to the Ephesians* (1951). Cf. M. Barth, *Ephesians* (1974), pp. 36–59; and Kümmel, *INT*², pp. 357–366.
8. Note the examples given in the following studies and the different conclusions drawn: Beare, "Epistle to the Ephesians," pp. 598ff., and M. Barth, *Ephesians,* pp. 4–6.
9. Cf. Eph. 3:3ff. and Col. 1:26f (1 Cor. 2:1); also Eph. 1:9; 5:32. Kümmel, *INT*², pp. 358–360.
10. E.g., Mitton, *Epistle to the Ephesians,* pp. 86ff. Cf. F. F. Bruce, *Paul* (1977), pp. 425–427.
11. E. Kasemann, "Ephesians and Acts," in L. Keck and J. L. Martyn, eds., *Studies in Luke-Acts* (1966), pp. 288f.
12. Cf. 1 Cor. 3:11 and Eph. 2:20.
13. Cf. 2 Cor. 5:18ff., Rom. 5:10f., and Eph. 2:16. Also Col. 1:20, 2:13f.
14. Eph. 4:9f. Cf. 1 Cor. 15:4f; Rom. 10:6f.
15. The consummation of the Church's hope "in the coming ages" [sic] is the perfecting of the unity of all things, including "the faith."
16. Eph. 2:13ff.
17. For a judicious assessment of the "doctrinal considerations," which frankly acknowledges that the evidence can be used for or against Pauline authorship, see M. Barth, *Ephesians,* pp. 31–36.
18. *Ibid.,* pp. 37–39. N. Dahl, "Ephesians," *IDBS* (1976), 268f.; H. J. Cadbury, "The Dilemma of Ephesians," *NTS* 5 (1958–1959): 91ff.
19. Eph. 1:1b. Kümmel, *INT*², pp. 352–356.
20. Note Eph. 1:15 and 3:2. "If Paul himself wrote this epistle, then it could hardly have been addressed to Ephesus. Or if it was really written for the Ephesians, then Paul was most likely not its author." M. Barth, *Ephesians,* pp. 10f.
21. J. A. Robinson, *St. Paul's Epistle to the Ephesians* (1909), pp. 11f. Cf. F. L. Cross, ed., *Studies in Ephesians* (1956), pp. 14ff., also, pp. 21ff.
22. M. Barth accounts for the impersonality of Paul's address by supposing that Ephesians was directed to only one group in the Ephesian congregation. The mutual acquaintance of the Apostle and recently baptized Gentiles would be based on indirect information only. *Ephesians,* pp. 11, 58, 328.
23. Robinson, *St. Paul's Epistle* p. 19.

24. Eph. 2:3; 5:6. G. Johnston, *Ephesians, IDB,* 2 (1955): 113. Cf. Rom. 2:3ff., 5:9.
25. Eph. 1:3, 17. Also 2:18; 3:14f.; 4:6; 5:20; 6:23.
26. Eph 2:22f. M. Barth, *Ephesians,* pp. 158f., 200–210.
27. Eph. 3:19. Cf. Col. 1:18f.; 2:9.
28. Eph 5:2ff. See p. 387.
29. The writer of Ephesians is definitely interested in "the redemptive-historical an-chorage of the church." F. W. Beare, *"Epistle to the Ephesians,"* p. 607. Käsemann, "Ephesians and Acts," p. 291.
30. Eph. 2:10; also 1:4, 12. "Good works" (plural) is a phrase ordinarily avoided by Paul.
31. Eph. 3:5.
32. Eph. 4:11f.
33. Eph. 4:3–7, 11–16. Also 2:14–16.
34. E. Käsemann, "Ephesians and Acts," p. 292.
35. In Colossians the invisible powers are harmless provided they are not worshiped; in Ephesians they are "the spiritual hosts of wickedness." Eph. 6:11f.; also 2:1f.
36. J. Murphy-O'Connor has sought to show that the writer of Ephesians was influ-enced by pre-Gnostic Jewish thought and modes of expression, closely resembling Qumran texts. *Paul and Qumran,* (1968), pp. 115ff.; 159ff. Cf. M. Barth, *Ephe-sians,* pp. 18–21.
37. Eph. 5:3ff. Cf. 1 John 1:6, 3:20f.
38. Eph. 6:13ff.; 4:15.
39. Cf. Rom. 11:17ff., and Paul's repeated emphasis: "the Jew first but also the Greek."
40. Eph. 2:3, 11, 17. Beare, "Epistle to the Ephesians," p. 607.
41. See Kümmel, *INT*[2], p. 364, who cites with approval the thesis of H. Chadwick. Käsemann's interpretation is similar, but H. Conzelmann argues that this contro-versy was acute when Paul wrote Rom. 9–11, and that the writer of Ephesians views the situation theoretically and from a distance. Cf. M. Barth, *Ephesians,* pp. 56–59, for a trenchant criticism of the Goodspeed hypothesis.
42. The term *Pastorals* is at least as old as the eighteenth century and although its appropriateness has been questioned, especially as descriptive of 2 Tim., no better common designation has been suggested. P. N. Harrison, *The Problem of the Pas-toral Epistles* (1921), pp. 13ff.
43. *Ibid.* Harrison's study of the vocabulary is the most complete. His evidence is sum-marized and evaluated by F. D. Gealy, "I and II Timothy, Titus," *IB* 11 (1955): 360ff.; Kümmel, *INT*[2], pp. 372f. Cf. D. Guthrie, *The Pastoral Epistles* (1957), pp. 212ff.; J. N. D. Kelly, *A Commentary on The Pastoral Epistles* (1963), pp. 21ff.
44. G. Duncan, *St. Paul's Ephesian Ministry* (1929) pp. 184ff.; P. N. Harrison, "The Pastoral Epistles and Duncan's Ephesian Theory," *NTS* 2 (1956), and Duncan's reply, *NTS* 3 (1957). Cf. Barrett, *The Pastoral Epistles* (1963), pp. 7ff. For difficulties inherent in the tradition of Paul's release, resumption of missions in the East, and a second Roman imprisonment, see *INT*[2], pp. 375f., M. Dibelius and H. Conzel-mann, *A Commentary on the Pastorals* (1972), p. 3.
45. 2 Tim. 3:10f. If the personalia in the Pastorals are historical, it is more probable that the Pastor incorporated fragments of Paul's correspondence concerning events covered by Acts. "The fragment hypothesis" will receive further notice below.
46. E. F. Scott, *The Pastoral Epistles* (1937); B. S. Easton, *The Pastoral Epistles* (1947), pp. 22ff. Cf. Guthrie, *Pastoral Epistles,* pp. 38ff.
47. C. K. Barrett, *Pastoral Epistles,* pp. 25f.
48. 1 Tim. 2:10; Tit. 2:14. Cf. 1 Tim. 1:5.
49. E.g., 1 Tim. 1:19; 3:9; 4:1; 2 Tim. 3:8; 4:7; Tit. 1:13. The self-understanding of the pastor and others of his generation became "objectified in a particular image of

the apostle and a specific understanding of doctrine." The reader of the Pastorals is faced with the question: "How and in what sense the *kerygma* of the apostles, during the course of transmission, becomes doctrinal authority?" Dibelius and Conzelmann, *The Pastoral Epistles*, p. 1.

50. Barrett, *Pastoral Epistles*, pp. 17ff. J. A. T. Robinson offers a reconstruction from Acts of the historical framework of Paul's missions described in the Pastorals without positing a period of activity after the house arrest described in Acts 28, *Redating the New Testament* (1976) pp. 67–85.

51. "The most likely assumption is the very beginning of the second century." Kümmel, *INT*[2] pp. 386f. No agreement has been reached concerning the order of composition. Cf. Easton, *Pastoral Epistles*, pp. 17ff. Defenders of Pauline authorship usually date 1 Tim. and Tit. before the winter of 64; 2 Timothy within the year.

52. Gealy, "I and II Timothy, Titus," pp. 377f.

53. Tit. 1:14; 3:9. Note also Tit. 1:10. Dibelius and Conzelmann, *Pastoral Epistles*, pp. 16f.

54. R. M. Wilson, *Gnosis and the New Testament* (1968), pp. 41ff.

55. 1 Cor. 11:2–16. It is probable that 14:33b–36 is an interpolation. Paul's essential principle is stated in Gal. 3:26–28.

56. 2 Tim. 3:6; 1 Tim. 5:11ff.

57. 1 Tim. 3:11; 5:9ff.

58. Note this prior concern: 1 Tim. 3:3ff.; 8:12f.; 5:9f.; Tit. 1:7f.

59. 1 Tim. 3:6, 9. Cf. Tit. 1:9; 2 Tim. 2:24.

60. This confession reflects other postapostolic writings. Cf. Jn. 1;14; 3:13f.; 6:62f.; 16:28; 1 Pet. 3:18; Heb. 1:14ff. The first two lines present a theme similar to the confession Paul incorporated in Rom. 1:3f. The proclamation of the cosmic rule of Christ approximates Phil. 2:9ff., although it may represent a later development. E. Schweizer, *Lordship and Discipleship* (1960), pp. 64ff.

61. 1 Tim. 5:3.

62. Cf. the advice of the pastor concerning young widows with that given by Paul, 1 Tim. 5:14; 1 Cor. 7:8f., 39f.

63. 1 Tim. 6:3ff.

64. Gealy, "I and II Timothy, Titus," *IB*, 11, p. 525; Dibelius and Conzelmann, *Pastoral Epistles*, pp. 152ff. Cf. Guthrie, *Pastoral Epistles*, pp. 183f.; Robinson, *Redating the New Testament*, pp. 71–85.

65. Because of this the question is raised: What was the need and occasion for two letters so much alike? Perhaps the admonitions in 1 Timothy were directed to a leader of congregations already organized while Titus was written to an organizer of churches. Dibelius and Conzelmann, *Pastoral Epistles*, pp. 153f.

66. Cf. Tit. 1:3f.; 2:10; 4:4, 6; 1 Tim. 1:1; 2:3; 4:10; 2 Tim. 1:6f. Also Jude 5; Lk. 1:47.

67. Cf. 1 Cor. 6:11.; Col. 1:21ff. (Eph. 2:11ff.)

68. Barrett, *Pastoral Epistles*, p. 137. Cf. Tit. 2:11ff.; Rom. 6:15ff.

69. Tit. 3:4–7. Note the implicit trinitarian teaching.

70. Gealy, "I and II Timothy, Titus," pp. 460ff.

71. 2 Tim. 3:1ff. Cf. 2 Thess. 2:1ff.; Mk. 13; Acts 2:17ff.

Chapter 18

Five "Open Letters"
to Christians

S EVEN letters of the New Testament have been known as "General (or Catholic) Epistles" since the early fourth century: James, 1 and 2 Peter, 1, 2, and 3 John, and Jude. This description applies to writings intended for groups of Christians in various places. The "open letter" serves as a modern equivalant for the ancient "Catholic Epistle."

Four of the General Letters are the subjects of this chapter. The three letters of John will be considered in Chapter 20, along with the Gospel of John. To the remaining four will be added the Letter to the Hebrews, a writing that is grouped with the Pauline corpus. The writing, however, does not profess to be by Paul, and it is certain (as any conclusion drawn from the internal evidence can be) that Paul did not write it. Hebrews has sometimes been called "a general letter" so there is reason to include it here. In many respects, however, Hebrews is a unique document.

THE FIRST LETTER OF PETER

The First Letter of Peter is addressed to Christians residing in five of the provinces of Asia Minor who were being disturbed by the ill-will, slander, and abuse being heaped upon them by non-Christian opponents. The purpose of its writer was to recall to his readers the resources of the gospel, inherent in their baptism, and to rally their courage and hope. The result was that the whole Church received a beautiful and very appealing book as a priceless legacy. It is easy to see why 1 Peter is a favorite among Christians today. As one commentator observes, "this gallant and high-hearted exhortation breathes a spirit of undaunted courage and exhibits as noble a type of piety as can be found in any writing of the New Testament outside the gospels."[1]

THE DESTINATION OF THE LETTER; THE SITUATION
OF ITS RECIPIENTS

Reference has been made to the successive migrations into Anatolia (Asia Minor) of Celtic folk in pre-Christian times who settled in the territory of Galatia (see p. 336). To the indigenous population in this and neighboring areas had also been added a significant Jewish element. As a result, this vast plateau was settled by a "mixture of races, cultures, and religions" overlaid with "a firm Hellenistic veneer,"[2] The writer of 1 Peter addresses his letter to the widely scattered Christian communities in this region, many of whose members seem to have been recent converts (1:12; 2:2), saluting them as "exiles [sojourners] of the Dispersion" (1:1; 2:11). While it is likely that the writer was a Jewish Christian, it seems that references to his readers imply that they were converts from paganism (1:18; 2:10; 4:34.)[3]

Clearly the most significant aspect of the situation of these Anatolian Christians is that they were suffering (unjustly) "various trials," referred to collectively as "the fiery ordeal" (1:16; 2:19; 4:12).*

Scholars views have differed widely concerning the question of what occasioned this suffering and its nature. The significance of the question is enhanced by its association with the issues of the date and authorship of 1 Peter. Many interpreters have concluded that the writer's references to suffering, especially in 4:14ff., imply that Christians were being arraigned before imperial or at least official courts, and that the mere fact that one was identified as a Christian was a capital offense.[4] Alternatively, others have concluded that the hostility, harassment, and social ostracism alluded to in the letter was of a local, unofficial sort.[5]

To the present writer this second view is a more likely explanation of the disturbing situation addressed in 1 Peter. There is no mention in the letter of a demand that sacrifices be offered to the emperor, which was a serious problem confronting some Christians during the reigns of Domitian and Trajan. "Indeed it is scarcely credible that under either Trajan or Domitian the writer could have linked 'reverence for God' and 'honour to the emperor' in the positive and unqualified manner of 2:17."[6] There would therefore seem to be no indications concerning the date or authorship of 1 Peter in these passages referring to the "various trials" being suffered by its recipients.[7]

*The distinction is sometimes made between the ill treatment alluded to in 1:3–4:11 (as being merely potential) and in 4:12ff (as an actual harsh reality). This alleged contrast has suggested that canonical 1 Peter is a joining of two letters: (A)1:3–4:11; (B) 4:12–5:11. The present writer is persuaded that the canonical letter is a unity and that its references to suffering presuppose the same circumstances.

1 PETER AND OTHER CANONICAL AND NONCANONICAL WRITINGS: LITERARY AND THEOLOGICAL AFFINITIES

Modern studies of 1 Peter have stressed the resemblance of much of its teaching to that of the Apostle Paul. Several passages are said to reflect the writer's dependence upon letters of Paul, especially Romans and (if by the Apostle) Ephesians.[8] The theology of 1 Peter "has been described as Pauline to a degree unexampled in the rest of the NT," but "parallels with 1 Peter have also been discovered in both James and Hebrews."[9] Outside the New Testament, yet still within the First Century, "1 Peter stands in a close relation with 1 Clement" (ca. 95).

Correspondences between 1 Peter and 1 Clement are best explained as either Clement's familiarity with the canonical letter, or as dependence of both writers upon common Christian traditions. The same explanation is to be preferred with reference to the so-called canonical "parallels." Instead of resorting to theories of literary dependence, one can judge that Paul, and the authors of 1 Peter, James, and Hebrews, drew upon shared traditions, upon relatively fixed patterns of liturgical, hortatory, and catechetical material.[10]

Bust of the Roman emperor Trajan, 98–117 C.E. *(Courtesy of the Trustees of the British Museum.)*

AUTHORSHIP, DATE, AND PLACE OF ORIGIN

In the prescript to 1 Peter the author identifies himself as "an apostle of Jesus Christ," and, later in the letter, as an "elder and a witness of the sufferings of Christ" (5:1). That the document was originally anonymous (but later attributed to Peter by the addition of 1:1 and 5:12–14) is pure speculation. An impressive case can certainly be made for Petrine authorship, whether directly or "through Silvanus."[11] There are, however, many readers who have found incredible the attribution of the letter to the disciple of Jesus.*

It is the letter's testimony to its origin that has called into question the ancient Church tradition. Aside from the perceived circumstances referred to as "the fiery ordeal" (which for some is conclusive evidence), there are three major objections to Petrine authorship. First of all it is said that there are few of any direct references in 1 Peter to the words and deeds of Jesus, and an absence of personal testimony, which one might expect in a letter from an intimate disciple of Jesus.

This objection is not without foundation. In 5:5f. the writer expresses the thought of Luke 14:11, but it is formulated not in Jesus' words but in those of Proverbs 3:34. Also at first sight it is surprising that Christ's suffering is described in terms of Isaiah 53 rather than an eyewitness' memory. Allusions to

* Among the Apostolic Fathers, there is no unequivocal testimony to the origin of 1 Peter. In his writing "Against Heresies" (ca. 180 C.E.) Irenaeus introduced a quotation from 1 Peter with the words, "Peter says in his epistle, 'whom though you see him not' . . ." (IV. 9. 2, cf. 1

Jesus' words have, however, been detected in the letter. One writer contends that these are specially connected with narrative contexts in the Gospels where Peter is an active participant.[12] Perhaps the most that one can say is that the perceived textual affinities between 1 Peter and the canonical Gospels demonstrate a common tradition but do not authenticate such material as Peter's own testimony or redaction.[13]

A second objection to Petrine authorship is the letter's "Paulinism" (noted above). This objection seems to rest insecurely upon the largely abandoned theory that the theology of 1 Peter has been directly influenced by several of Paul's epistles.[14]

A third objection is that the writer's educated use of Greek and his citations from the LXX make improbable Petrine authorship. This objection is often met by noting that the writer himself states that he has written "by Silvanus, a faithful brother as I regard him. . . ." It is commonly believed that this Silvanus (Silas) was a sometime companion of Paul (1 Thessalonians), and that this identification may account for Pauline conceptions in 1 Peter, the linguistic competence of the writer, and his use of the Greek Old Testament.

The letter is addressed from "Babylon." Some have taken the term to apply generally to the Church in exile, recalling the letter's initial reference to Christians as "exiles of dispersion." But the author represented the authority and conveyed the greetings of a particular church. It is far more likely that "Babylon" stands for Rome than for the ancient city of Mesopotamia or the Roman frontier post on the Nile. The Christian use of Babylon as a code word for Rome is attested by the book of Revelation.[15]

Some readers will conclude that on balance the evidence suggests that whoever wrote the letter it "comes from Peter's lifetime and that he is in the fullest sense 'behind' it."[16] Yet the possibility remains that 1 Peter is a pseudonymous writing composed not long after the apostle's death (within the period, say, of 72–90 C.E.?), a product of Petrine tradition preserved by "a Petrine circle" in the church at Rome. Over the whole debate one senses the shadow of a great unknown: the missions and teaching of the Apostle Peter. The problem of Paul's relation to the Pastorals is less acute, since we know much from Paul's letters about the Apostle's thought, the regions in which he was active, and so forth. We have no such direct information concerning Peter.[17]

Pet. 1:8). Eusebius reported that polycarp used 1 Peter (*H.E.* IV. 14). He also recorded that Papias knew Peter's "former epistle" (*H.E.* III. 29.17).

INTERPRETING 1 PETER

A. The Prescript, 1:1f.
B. Thanksgiving, 1:3–12
   1. For the imperishable inheritance of those receiving baptism, 1:3–5
   2. For the assurance of salvation that makes possible joy in the midst of suffering, 1:6–12
C. The Call to a Holy Life as Befits God's People, 1:13–2:10
   1. Ransomed by the blood of Christ, the newly born are called to "sincere love of the brethren," 1:13–25
   2. Privileges and responsibilities of the elect people of God, 2:1–10

The hypothesis that 1 Peter is, in its essential form and content, really a baptismal liturgy although outwardly a letter, has had long-lasting influence.

In its most elaborate statement this hypothesis declares that the letter's thanksgiving is a prayer-psalm introducing an actual baptismal service (1:3–4:11). Instructions are given the candidates (1:3–21), after which the rite is administered. Thereafter the tense changes: "having purified your souls . . ." marks the continuation of the liturgy, which includes exhortations (1:22–25; 2:11–3:12) and hymns (2:1–10, 21–24), a revelation shared by a charismatic bystander (3:13–4:7a), and a closing prayer (4:7b–11). 4:12–5:11 stands as an exhortation addressed to the entire congregation in which the newly baptized with the rest are challenged to face their "fiery ordeal" with joy and fortitude, making it an occasion for glorifying God.

This reconstruction is a tour de force but some versions of the hypothesis have commendable features.[18] Instead of saying that 1 Peter is a baptismal liturgy in the form of a letter, "it seems better to regard 1 Peter as a real letter into which a baptismal exhortation had been incorporated, or at least materials that often were used in such an exhortation."[19]

Some historians, observing that the initiates into the "mysteries" of Isis, Cybele, and Mithras were depicted as persons "reborn," derive the writer's conception of supernatural begetting from this source (1:23; 2:2). Probably more direct is the influence of the metaphor applied in Judaism to proselytes, and by Jesus to the inheritors of the kingdom of God (Mark 10:15 and pars.; also John 3:3).

The exultant thanksgiving of 1 Peter arises from the conviction that the inheritance of believers is indestructible, grounded upon the resurrection of Jesus (1:3, 21; 3:21). Their salvation is so certain that the "various trials" (which must be suffered for a brief time) become the occasion not for alarm or depression of spirit, but for rejoicing (1:6, 8; 4:12f.)

From 1:13–25 the readers ("children of obedience") are exhorted to holiness and love and are reminded of the great cost of ransoming them from their former "futile ways." By a curious (to us) mixing of metaphors (2:2–10), the summons to holiness is reinforced.[20] The newly elect people of the Holy One must be themselves holy in all their conduct.[21]

    D. Practical Admonitions, 2:11–3:12
        1. Relations with defamatory Gentiles, 2:11f.
        2. Subjection to governing authorities, 2:13–17
        3. Domestic relations, 2:18–3:12
    E. Instruction Concerning the Endurance of Ill-treatment, 3:13–4:19
        1. Revilers of good deeds may be put to shame, 3:13–17
        2. As a consequence of Christ's death and resurrection "the unrighteous" are brought to God through baptism, 3:18–4:6
        3. The eschatological sanction, 4:7–11
        4. Sharing Christ's suffering "as a Christian"—expecting the revelation of his glory, 4:12–19
    F. Protocol in the Brotherhood, 5:1–11
        1. Instruction to "the elders," 5:1–4
        2. To younger people, 5:5
        3. Encouragement to humility and watchfulness, 5:6–11
    G. Conclusion: Commendation of Silvanus and Greetings, 5:12–14

To assist his readers in maintaining good conduct among non-Christians, the writer of 1 Peter describes some practical moral imperatives (2:11–3:12). Although they are "aliens" with respect to the mores of their communities, the Anatolian Christians are to be no less concerned to "do right" than the most moral folk (Stoics, Jews?); indeed they should exemplify in their daily lives the ideals of one's heavenly citizenship, however brief one's earthly "sojourn." [22]

1 Peter 2:13–17 will remind the attentive reader of Romans 13:1ff. There are, however, differences that argue against literary dependence. It would seem that Christians adapted conventional moral codes to regulate their corporate societies and included among the classification of duties the obligation of civil obedience. [23] The ethic of submission—of slaves to masters, of wives to husbands (2:18–3:7)—reflects the social conservatism of the writer, which many modern readers will find abhorrent. One should note, by way of compensation, that a slave's acceptance of patently unjust treatment makes him a partner (as it were) with his Lord in his passion. And although the writer assumes that husbands have authority over their wives, it is required that they show them proper deference. [24]

Many students of 1 Peter are in agreement that 3:18–22 contains traditional liturgical or catechetical material. But efforts to understand the writer's adaptation of these formulae (3:19–21?) have provoked a variety of interpretations. It is probable that "the spirits in prison" are the fallen angels, and that the writer's contention is that Christ (in his ascension) proclaimed that the power of these disobedient spirits had been overcome. As a result of their baptism (more potent than the rite of circumcision), Christians enjoy the lasting consequence of Christ's victory over all evil powers, seen and unseen. [25]

Clues for interpreting the remainder of 1 Peter were noted above in the introduction to this letter. The limits of space forbid extending comment. It may be noted that the writer's final appeals to his readers to trust and glorify God are joined with exhortations to humility, self-control, and watchfulness. This two-fold concern is summarily stated in the concluding declaration: "this is the true grace of God; stand fast in it."

THE LETTER TO THE HEBREWS

"My word of exhortation"—this is the phrase employed by the author of Hebrews to describe his writing (13:22), the product (we may say) of his pastoral preaching. The "Letter" to the Hebrews is a misnomer. It does not begin as one, and the epistolary ending may only give the author's sermon the semblance of a letter. The literary form of the document has been variously identified as a Christian tract modelled upon an early form of Greek admonitory speeches, or as a Christian's exegesis patterned after Hellenistic-Jewish midrashic discourse. However one describes its form, the writing was clearly designed by its author to establish his practical exhortations concerning Christian behavior upon "mature" Christological doctrine, or, conversely, to affirm that the Christian's "confession" must evidence one's acceptance of its moral imperatives. [26]

The first writer known to refer to Paul as the author of Hebrews noticed its differences from letters certainly attributed to the Apostle. Clement of Alexandria (ca. 150–215) surmised that Luke had translated into Greek a letter written by Paul in Hebrew. Origen (ca. 180–250) speculated that someone who knew Paul must have written down his thoughts at a later time. According to Eusebius, Origen knew of traditions from an earlier period ascribing Hebrews to Clement of Rome, others to Luke. But Origen's own, oft-quoted judgment concerning the authorship of Hebrews was, "Who wrote it, God knows."

It is very probable that the Eastern churches, with the exception of Alexandria, accepted Hebrews as a letter of Paul. But in the West doubts persisted because of the author's apparent denial of the efficacy of a second repentance (6:4–8; 10:26–31). Western churches were troubled by some members who wished to exclude all persons who had apostasized in times of persecution. The earliest direct evidence from Rome assigning the authorship of Hebrews to Paul and according the book canonical status dates from the middle of the fourth century.

Evidence for the date of the writing of Hebrews is no earlier than Clement of Rome (96 C.E.), and efforts to designate some well-known author other than Paul belonging to the Apostolic Age—Barnabas, Apollos, Luke—are not likely to succeed, for several statements in the text itself suggest that both the author and recipients of Hebrews belonged to the postapostolic era (2:3 and 13:7). In spite of these and other indicators, however, it is sometimes argued that the writer of Hebrews implies that the temple is still standing, suggesting a date for the document before 70 C.E. "The trouble with this argument is that the author is expounding scripture. He is speaking of what the priests do in the Book of Leviticus, not of what was going on in the temple. The (earthly) sanctuary he refers to is the tent in the wilderness, not the temple at Jerusalem."[27]

There is today little difference of opinion concerning the destination of Hebrews. Its concluding note points to Rome: "those who come from Italy send you greetings" (13:24). Other passages support its Roman destination. For example, the notice taken of the endurance of the church's former members who were "publicly exposed to abuse and affliction;" and another, which speaks of the eminence of its former leaders.[28]

INTERPRETING THE LETTER TO THE HEBREWS

A. Introduction, a Statement of the Speaker's Central Thesis, 1:1–4:16
   1. The Son of God, final revealer of the divine purpose in creation and redemption, has performed the high priestly act of making purification for sins, 1:1–3
   2. The uniqueness of the Son's mission, 1:4–14
   3. Exhortation: neglect not the superior revelation, 2:1–4
   4. The Son's temporary, essential subordination in suffering and death, 2:5–18
   5. Exhortations: to follow the examples of Jesus' faithfulness, contrasted with the responses of Moses and the rebellious generation of the Exodus, 3:1–4:13
   6. Statement of the central thesis with an accompanying exhortation, 4:14–16

The earliest Christians proclaimed that the risen Jesus was seated at the right hand of God having completed his historic saving work. This imagery of Christ's heavenly session was derived from Psalm 110:1.[29] The writer of Hebrews takes this traditional "confession" and develops the Christology of his sermon by offering an extended treatment of the Psalm, noting that in verse 4 the enthroned Lord is designated "a priest forever after the order of Melchizedek." (This midrash on Psalm 110 constitutes the major part of the author's grand theme, 5:1 to 10:39; it is anticipated in three earlier references to Christ as "high priest," 2:17; 3:1; 4:14.)

Before explaining why one can speak of Jesus as solitary high priest "after the order of Melchizedek," the author of Hebrews declares that the enthroned Lord of Psalm 110:1 is the "Son of God," citing Psalm 2:7.[30] Two truths about Jesus' person and work are affirmed by this "name"—the Son of God: God's appointment of him as "the heir of all things," the anointed one—the Messiah, and his own complete submission and obedience to the will of his Father.[31]

For the author, the Son's temporary humiliation in his passion and death was essential to the fulfillment of his priesthood and antecedent to his exaltation: "he had to be made like his brethren in every respect, so that he might become a merciful and faithful high priest in the service of God, to make expiation for the sins of the people."[32]

As further preparation for an exposition of Christ's priestly office, the author reinforces the moral seriousness of his appeal. A comparison is drawn between the reader's position and Israel's sojourn in the wilderness.[33] Like the people of the Exodus, the followers of Jesus lived between the times: the former between Egyptian bondage and freedom in the land of Canaan; the latter between the first and second comings of Christ. For each interim there was provided a priesthood and sacrificial cultus to enable God's wandering folk to enter his eternal rest. But within each interim there was the danger of forfeiting the inheritance. "Take care, brethren (the author warns), lest there be in any of you an evil, unbelieving heart, leading you to fall away from the living God."[34]

B. Preliminary Development of the Author's Central Thesis, 5:1–6:20
   1. The nature of the Son's role as "priest forever after the order of Melchizedek"; his qualifications, 5:1–10
   2. Exhortation: a rebuke for the reader's lack of development; no second repentance possible; assurances, 5:11–6:20

By applying to Jesus the early testimonium, Psalm 110, the author was able to offer scriptural warrant for a priestly order distinct from the Levitical. Although Jesus was descended from the tribe of Judah, he possessed proper, indeed unique, qualifications to become a high priest. Note the various ways in which the author argues for the superiority of the priesthood of Christ to that which Moses instituted, appealing once again to the psalm-words (2:7 and 110:4).

One of the most serious problems facing the modern reader of Hebrews concerns its rigorous teaching concerning repentance. It is noteworthy that the author limits his denial of a second repentance to those who are guilty of apostasy, and that he disallows it, not after, but before apostasy had occurred. This preacher is given to uttering dire warnings.[35]

C. Extended Treatment of the Central Thesis: Christ the High Priest and Mediator of the New Covenant, 7:1–10:18
   1. Melchizedek, the type of the perfect high priest, 7:1–3
   2. This priesthood superior to the Levitical, 7:1–28
   3. Christ's ministry in the "heavenly sanctuary" effectively mediates the new
      covenant of promise, 8:1–10:18; the reader's need for endurance, 10:19–
      39

The strange story in Genesis of the encounter between Abraham and Melchizedek was obviously of great importance to our author.[36] Unlike the Levitical
priests, who were legitimated by their genealogy, Melchizedek had neither predecessor nor successor. Yet his supremacy was acknowledged by Abraham, who
paid his tithes and received from him a blessing. Psalm 110, which was composed after the books of Moses, demonstrates that the Levitical is not the only
priesthood. Moreover, since the established priestly system is connected with
the Mosaic law, both fail and fall together. Several inadequacies of the holders
of the Levitical priesthood are indicated: they are not appointed with an oath;
their tenure ends with their death; their ritual is necessarily repetitive.[37] But
Christ performed his priestly service perfectly, once-for-all, and therefore its
effects last forever. Moreover, the Levitical priests ministered in the tent in the
wilderness; Christ performed his priestly service in heaven, in the true sanctuary of which the wilderness tent was "a copy and shadow."[38] Finally, the
earthly ritual was ineffectual because it could only atone for breaches in the
ceremonial law; "but when Christ appeared as a high priest of the good things
that have come . . . he entered once for all into the Holy Place, taking not the
blood of goats and calves but his own blood, thus securing an eternal redemption."[39] The introduction of Psalm 40:6–8 recalls that Christ's sacrifice had
ethical meaning, for it was his volantary obedience to the will of God.[40]
Once again our author concludes his Christological teaching with an exhortation (perhaps to reinforce his initial exhortation, 5:11–6:20).[41] To the whole
he then appends his major hortatory section (11:1–12:29).

D. Extended Exposition of the Moral Demands upon Those Who Have Faith, 11:1–
   12:29
   1. Perseverance of faith (hope), the correlative of God's promise, in salvation
      history, 11:1–12:2
   2. The divine discipline of sons, 12:3–13
   3. Urgent appeal in view of apocalyptic fulfillment, 12:14–29
   4. An appendix, with an epistolary ending, 13:1–25

This eloquent section has attracted different interests on the part of its readers. Notice can be taken here of certain influences that have shaped the author's
theology. The role of the heroes of faith highlights his indebtedness to Hellenistic-Jewish literature, reflected throughout his sermon.[42] His concept of faith
very likely reveals his postapostolic situation. He celebrates faith as insight into
an invisible reality that supports a persistence in hope, rather than (with Paul),
as that means whereby one accepts the grace of God apart from human works.
Great importance is given to the role of corporate worship. The Christian
assembly is likened to the gathering of Israel at Sinai.[43] Not only is the old

covenant, with its (ceremonial) law, rendered obsolete, but in their liturgy the people of the new covenant participate in the worship ascribed to God and Jesus in the heavenly (eschatological) Jerusalem.

The "appendix" was probably added by the author, including the epistolary ending by which he converted his sermon material into a document intended for its Roman recipients, possibly directed especially to a group of potentially able "drifters" within a larger Christian community.[44]

THE CULTURAL ENVIRONMENT OF THE AUTHOR AND HIS READERS: JEWISH-CHRISTIAN APOCALYPTICISM OR HELLENISTIC IDEALISM?

Some interpreters of Hebrews have concluded that this writing presents a radical modification of the *kerygma* of the early Church. Instead of the "horizontal eschatology" with its familiar perspective on the present and future, the writer assumes two coexisting worlds and, in his "vertical eschatology" contrasts the material and heavenly spheres. Like Philo and the author of the Wisdom of Solomon, the writer of Hebrews reveals his indebtedness to Hellenistic imagery. Heaven is conceived to be the sanctuary of a temple-structured universe; the sea and earth, its outer courts (9:24; 10:19–20; 6:19–20?). Christ has entered into this invisible heaven to open the new and living way for all believers to enter. Further evidence of Hellenistic influence is that the author employed Greek allegorical methods in his exegesis of scripture.[45]

Alternatively, other scholars argue that the writer's imagery of the heavenly sanctuary reflects the influence of Jewish apocalypticism. The Old Testament notion that the wilderness tabernacle was constructed according to a divine pattern (Exod. 25:9; 1 Chron. 28:19), had become, in apocalytic thought, a belief in the existence of a temple in heaven, a model for the earthly sanctuary (Wis. 9:8; Ethiopic Enoch 14; Test. of Levi 5:1; Rev. 11:19). It is said that this apocalyptic heavenly sanctuary imagery is found in Hebrews 8:1–5; 9:11–14, 23. Believing that "Christ had offered for all time a single sacrifice for sins," and entered the heavenly sanctuary inaugurating the end time, our author developed an original statement of the traditional futurist eschatology, containing the typical Christian paradox that the future has already been anticipated. See Hebrews 10:19–25.[46] With respect to the author's exegetical methods, a close examination reveals that the alleged resemblance to Greek methods of allegorizing is more apparent than real.[47]

One scholar has argued that both types of the heavenly temple imagery and both types of eschatology—the horizontal and vertical—are found in this writer's homily. The realized eschatology expressed in the Hellenistic mode (the writer's perspective) is used "to shore up the apocalyptic hope of his hearers, in the face of persecution and flagging perseverance."[48]

THE LETTER OF JAMES

Apart from its prescript, "the letter" of James does not read like one. Its author appears to be a Christian leader, yet the address of the book is completely impersonal; the circumstances of the writing are not explicitly set forth;

there is no epistolary ending. If there is a unity in James, it is found in the writer's practical purpose.

It has often been noted that there is lacking any apparent connection between the various admonitions in James. One can, however, identify three homilies or treatises: 2:1–13; 2:14–26; and 3:1–12. Before and after these homilies, abbreviated admonitions are grouped according to catch phrases; still others, self-contained, are scattered throughout the letter, for example 3:18; 4:17; and 5:12.

Several features of this book have suggested an early, Palestinian origin. Its "Jewish tone" has given currency to a theory that its ideas were originally written down by a Jew named "Jacob." Some Christian editor interpolated a few references to Jesus Christ and produced the canonical book. This theory can be maintained only by drastically underestimating the contributions of the "Christian editor." The doctrinal presuppositions of the writer are scarcely disclosed, but one finds in James references that certainly imply ascription to the Christian *kerygma,* not to Judaism.[49]

Many studies of James refer to the "primitive simplicity" of its Jewish Christianity. The author's religion is said to be a religion of the Law, purified by the influence of Jesus' teachings but unaffected by the theology set forth in the letters of Paul and other later books. For some modern critics this evidence confirms the Church's tradition that the book was written by James, the Lord's brother, or at least supports a theory of mediate authorship.[50]

There are features of James that render implausible these accounts of its origin. The author's moral exhortations are presented in typical Hellenistic forms. The book is written in prose, in the second person used by writers of popular moral tracts, and its illustrations and style often resemble the Stoic-Cynic diatribe. The author was able "to write easily and fluently in Greek," and to employ various rhetorical devices utilized in Hellenistic literature.[51] He was familiar with the terminology and content of Stoic ethics. There are echoes in James of the Septuagint and of Jewish wisdom books of Hellenistic Judaism. Such signs of "the Greek shape"of James indicate that its author's background was Diaspora Judaism, but this is not undisputed.[52] The same literary features, however, make incredible the theory that the canonical book is a translation from Aramaic or from the colloquial Greek of Palestine.

Reminiscences in James of Jesus' teaching are sometimes said to support a Palestinian provenience and the tradition concerning its authorship. It can be argued that a brother of Jesus, writing before 62 C.E. (the date of James' martyrdom), would not have failed to witness to his death and resurrection or to other events from the ministry. But an alternative defense of the primitive Palestinian origin of this teaching is that only some of this tradition may have been derived from the Apostle James.*

The sum total of the internal evidence supports the view that James is a pseudonymous writing. Jerome reported that this belief was "not uncommon" in the ancient church, and 2 Peter and the Pastorals provide New Testament parallels, although the choice of James as the patron may be explained somewhat differently from (let us say) the pastor's use of Paul's name and authority. The "innocent labeling" of James in no way intends a literary imitation or disguise. Nowhere in the text does the author seek to shore up the authority of his words by reference to the teaching or experience of the Apostle or other

*The modern reticence concerning James may have been felt in the ancient Church. The judgment of Eusebius in the fourth century still holds true: "Certainly not many of the ancients have mentioned it." No

person; only 1:1 constitutes a mark of pseudonymity. "In the mind of the author, to whom the actual struggles over the Law in the first generation were foreign, James the "Just," who was zealous for the Law, seemed an appropriate literary patron for such a document."[53]

INTERPRETING JAMES

A. The Prescript, 1:1
B. Introduction: The Trials of Life, and the Perfecting of Religion, 1:2–27
   1. Only the tested faith is perfect and complete, 1:2–4
   2. Only those who pray with faith for wisdom will receive it, 1:5–8
   3. Only the lowly and steadfast, among the poor or rich, will receive "the crown of life," 1:9–12
   4. Only one's own desire tempts toward evil; every "good endowment" is from "the Father of Lights," 1:13–18
   5. Only moderation in speech and meekness promote "the word of truth," 1:19–21
   6. Only those who persevere "in doing the word" shall be blessed, 1:22–25
   7. Only those who bridle their tongues escape self-deception and vanity, 1:26
   8. The marks of "religion that is pure and undefiled," 1:27

writer before Origen is known to have attributed the book to James, "the Lord's brother." A century later, Eusebius placed James among the "disputed books." Martin Luther questioned the theological value of James and referred to it as "a rather straw-like epistle," though he conceded that it contained "many good sayings." S. Laws, *Commentary on James*, pp. 1f., Kümmel *INT*[2], pp. 405–407.

Moffatt's paraphrase brings out the wordplay that introduced the writer's exhortations: "Greeting. *Greet* is as pure joy. . . ." Like the Stoics, James taught that the trials of life are not evils to be avoided; rather they are character-building experiences to be accepted joyfully. The author was more directly influenced by the common Christian teachings than by Stoicism, but he found elements of the latter congenial.[54] The letter's references to "trials" and "sufferings" are too slight to show their external causes. "Trials" also refer to inner constraints, to "temptations."[55]

The connection of the next exhortation can be found in the author's recognition that the capacity of Christians to endure trials is proportionate to their dependence upon divine wisdom. Yet, again, a single word may provide the only link: lacking . . . lack.

From the beginning of the book the author reveals his "pet peeve": the double-minded person, that is, the Christian whose profession of piety is insincere. A doubter's prayers have no results at all; the prayer of the truly righteous person has powerful effects.[56] In the thought of James, "wisdom" and "righteousness" are inseparable, as in the Wisdom Literature of Judaism.[57]

Another animus of James is introduced: his contempt for selfish, rich Christians, especially the social snobs among them. But James does not dwell upon this subject. He was anxious to assure his readers that God rewards those who endure trials, and that the trials cannot be interpreted as God's attempt to break down faith.

The thought of God's "gifts" may have suggested to James the "perfect gift" of the new creation. The writer's references to "the word of truth," and to God's people as "a kind of first fruits," derive ultimately from the scriptures. But his further description of "the word" discloses his Christian presuppositions. The word implanted in the reader's heart is the gospel that is powerful unto salvation.[58]

The rebuke of the quick-tempered and thoughtless in speech becomes more direct later in the letter.[59] Its connection here with the writer's doctrine of regeneration reflects again his basic concern that Christians be morally sound: the implanted word needs clean soil in which to grow. This idea is given further application in the admonition against only hearing the word and not doing it.

James defined the marks of true religion as public charity and personal purity. Thoroughly Jewish is this close association of the idea of "defilement" with belief that self-knowledge depends upon the study and practice of "the perfect law." But it is evident that the writer's ideal of "unstained" religion was ethical rather than ceremonial. Nothing is said in James concerning the necessity of pious acts such as fasting, public prayers, and the like. These are not the "works" to which he refers. The admonition that Christians should avoid the contamination of the world is repeated later in the letter, but in neither place does the author say how this is to be accomplished.[60]

    C. A Homily on Partiality, 2:1–13
       1. Partiality toward the rich is contrary to the gospel's "royal law," 2:1–9
       2. Whoever is guilty according to one law is guilty of all, 2:10–13
    D. A Homily on Faith and Works, 2:14–26
       1. Faith by itself, if it has no works, is dead, 2:14–17
       2. A diatribe: a braggart is bested, 2:18–19
       3. Faith and works are inseparable: the cases of Abraham and Rahab, 2:20–26

Martin Dibelius has argued persuasively that the "stylized" examples James gives to support his admonitions "cannot be used as a historical source for actual situations within the Christian communities."[61] The objection can be raised, however, that James' illustrations "would only serve to reinforce his general admonitions if they bore some relation to the actual experience of those who read them."[62]

The passages concerning the rich raise a serious objection to an early, Jerusalem origin of the book. It is true that the writer's tendency to equate the pious and the poor reflects the perspective of Palestinian Judaism. But it is highly doubtful that there were rich members in the Jerusalem church in sufficient number to call forth the reproofs of James. One may recall the pastor's charge to Timothy with reference to the "haughty" members of the postapostolic Church who were "rich in this world."[63]

To the writer of James, partiality toward rich people was especially obnoxious in public assemblies devoted to the worship of "the Lord of glory." He reflected the teaching of Jesus and the whole Church when he recognized in such discrimination a serious breach of "the royal law." In the Christian fellowship all men were "neighbors" regardless of the social and economic distinctions of society. But James was not content to say that rich and poor should be treated alike. He had special words of condemnation for the rich. He accused them of exploiting the poor, of being insensitive to the needy. Because of their attachments to wealth they suffered the illusion that they were secure to make whatever plans they might wish. It is refreshing to find in the New Testament an echo of the voices of the great prophets of Israel. Yet James did not glorify poverty as such. The "lowly brother," not merely the poor Christian, may boast in God's exaltation.

A perennial problem for interpreters of James is a clarification of the author's views concerning faith and works and their relation to the teaching of the apostle Paul. The evidence of literary dependence is inconclusive, yet the statements of James in 2:14–26 "are inconceivable unless Paul had previously set forth the slogan 'faith, not works.' "[64] It seems highly probable that James was attacking views that did not directly derive from Paul but represented a perversion of Paul's doctrine of justification by faith and not by works of the Law. Such misrepresentations arose during Paul's lifetime and, according to 2 Peter, continued to arise in postapostolic times.[65]

The wrong impression that James opposed Paul may result from a failure to recognize the different connotations of their words. The same terms could be used differently by the two authors because their situations were different. By "works" Paul meant acts of obedience to the moral and ritual requirements of the Torah. James clearly implied that the essential "works" are acts of disinterested love for one's neighbor in need. By "faith," pure and simple, James meant an intellectual assent to certain doctrines, such as the belief that God is one.[66] Such "faith" could be either sincere or feigned. For Paul, "faith" was a personal response to God revealed in Christ, establishing a relation in which genuine obedience became possible for the first time. What James derided as a feigned faith, or "dead faith," Paul would have said was not Christian faith at all.

Faith was essential to both, and to both love of one's neighbor was the necessary consequence and proof of faith.[67] Doubtless, Paul would have preferred to speak of Christian acts of compassion as the "fruits" of the Spirit, but he would have had no substantive quarrel with James.

Even though all this is conceded, it cannot be said that James' position represents an adequate restatement of Paul's great doctrine. The Apostle, as we have seen, placed the reality of justification at the very moment a person responded in faith to the *kerygma*. The believer in Christ anticipated in the present time God's final judgment and salvation. James does not seem to have grasped the full measure of God's gift in Christ. He could speak of the Christian's hope of "righteousness" as the harvest of the good life.[68] Nevertheless, one wonders if it was any part of James' purpose either to qualify or to defend Paul's doctrine. The practical tone of the entire letter reveals his primary concern: the exposure of the moral sterility of Christians whose faith is mere talk. James's grasp of the theological significance of the gospel may have been deficient, but his stern insistence upon the obedience of faith provided a wholesome antidote to all evangelicalism that would save its own soul while it lets a brother suffer the want of life's elemental needs.

The third homily of James expresses his lively concern for the uses and abuses of speech (3:1–12). Following this are admonitions that, for the most part, develop further some subjects earlier expressed. The following outline without commentary may serve to delineate these developments.

    E. A Homily on the Tongue, 3:1–12
       1. Teachers are especially exposed to sins of speech, 3:1–2
       2. The power and destructiveness of the untamable tongue, 3:3–12
    F. Sayings Attacking Jealousy and Selfish Ambition, 3:13–18; 4:1–12
       1. Heavenly wisdom is peace-loving; contentious wisdom, demonic, 3:13–18
       2. A sermonic series of admonitions, 4:1–12

       G. Sayings Against Arrogant Merchants and Self-indulgent Rich People, 4:13–17; 5:1–6
         1. Humans propose; God disposes, 4:13–17
         2. The destruction of riches; the guilt of rich people, 5:1–6
       H. Sayings Commending Patience, Honesty in Speech, and Prayer, 5:7–11
         1. Patient waiting for the Parousia, 5:7–11
         2. Swearing is prohibited, 5:12
         3. Christian reactions to pain and pleasure, 5:13–15
         4. The role of elders in healing; confession; intercessory prayer, 5:16–18
         5. The reward of the reclaimer of an erring member, 5:19–20

THE LETTER OF JUDE

The "general letter" of Jude can more appropriately be called a tract. The brevity of Jude is not the chief cause of uncertainty concerning its origin and value. The author suppressed a desire to write about the Church's "common salvation" and in so doing veiled his particular understanding of the gospel from later readers. He wrote, as he says, to attack certain "ungodly persons." Apparently he felt no need to refute their teaching; he only vituperates against them.[69]

The prescript identifies the author as Jude [Judas], "the brother of James," and therefore of Jesus. But it is most unlikely that this Jude wrote the tract, or that the association of the book with "founder's kin" resulted in its preservation. According to some scholars, the words "the brother of James" were added by a later scribe. Others suggest that the tract first circulated under the name of "Judas [son] of James," who was one of "the Twelve."[70] The majority of critics hold that Jude is patently a pseudonymous writing, and that probably it was recognized as one from the beginning.

Two facts support the postapostolic origin of Jude: the author's references to "the predictions of the apostles" and to the imperative need that the lives of Christians be established on "the most holy faith," and the affinities of Jude with the Pastoral Letters and, possibly, with 1 John. In the first place it seems evident that neither the author nor his readers belonged to the first generation of Christians. The second fact, that there is close affinity with other writings of the postapostolic period, is established less securely since it is difficult to determine the nature of the false teaching opposed by Jude.

The use of Jude by the writer of 2 Peter supports a date for the writing of Jude before 150 C.E.*

*If there are echoes of Jude in the Didache or Polycarp then its composition may be as early as 100. The locality of the author or his first readers is mere guesswork. The historical importance of this letter, as of 2 Peter, lies in the evidence it affords that radical differences in

INTERPRETING JUDE

  A. Introduction, 1–4
     1. The prescript, 1–2
     2. The exigency prompting the letter: an insinuation into the church of "ungodly persons," 3–4
  B. The False Teachers: Their Character Described, Their Doom Foretold, 5–16
     1. Examples from scripture of the punishment of rebels; dire warnings, 5–7
     2. The errorists portrayed and denounced, 8–13
     3. Apocalyptic writings proclaim judgment, 14–16

C. The "Most Holy Faith," the Sure Foundation, 17–23
  1. The apostles foretold the coming of "scoffers," 17–19
  2. The Christian's defense, 20–21
  3. Some are to receive mercy, 22–23
D. A Doxology, 24–25

theology and ethics forced the churches "to establish the 'apostolic' norms of canon, tradition and of an authoritative interpretation" of the faith.

The writer's appeal that his readers "contend for the faith" shows that he was convinced that there was such a thing as a common Christian tradition. Certain "ungodly persons," however, were perverting this gospel "into licentiousness." Either because of their actions, or in addition to them, they were denying the Church's "only Master and Lord Jesus Christ." It is doubtful that these errorists can be shown to have advocated Gnostic views, but Jude provides further evidence of "lawlessness" in the postapostolic Church, and Gnostic views can be detected in some oblique references in the letter.[71]

As a proof of the gravity of the errorists' situation, Jude recalled the testimony of the scriptures concerning God's severe judgment upon rebels (verses 5–7). Jude's reference to the presumptuous angels and their imprisonment "in the nether gloom" until judgment day, echoes 1 Enoch and possibly the Book of Jubilees.[72] The references to the errorists' licentiousness may indicate generally their susceptibility to idolatrous pagan practices. The defilement of "the flesh" (verses 8, 23) is associated with their rejection of constituted authorities.

We have seen that several books in the New Testament refer to a popular belief that the Law of God had been mediated by angels.[73] Jude implied that faithful angels also sought to ensure that men honor it. But the errorists were rejecting all authority and reviling "the glorious ones." Like "irrational animals" their knowledge was limited to the things of sense. Jude's reference to the selfish carousings of the errorists at the Church's love-feasts reminds us of Paul's rebuke of certain Christians at Corinth for similar actions.[74]

The thought of the impending doom of the errorists led Jude to recall the picture of the final judgment in 1 Enoch.[75] The writer's effective use of scripture and his original application of its vivid imagery deserve notice. But the reader is not impressed by Jude's "name-calling."

Perhaps there are two values preserved in this little book. The inspirational phrases of its noble doxology somewhat redeem the vitriolic quality of the writer's polemics. And the insistence of the writer that the Church's security against error rests upon the grace of God and the *kerygma* it has received is the more impressive when we realize that persons of the temper of Jude contended for it. There was "a faith which was once for all delivered to the saints," as we have seen—not a fully articulated system of doctrine, but faith in Jesus as the one by whom human salvation was inaugurated and was to be consummated. That the "most holy faith" survived such pettiness and licentiousness within the Church as well as attacks from without is cause for wonder.

THE SECOND LETTER OF PETER

Scarcely an independent scholar maintains that Jesus' disciple from Galilee composed the letter called 2 Peter. This writer's art has not hidden the conventional marks of a pseudonymous writing of the second-century Church. Ancient Church tradition contains no evidence of the existence of this letter before Justin Martyr (ca. 155 C.E.), and it is not certain that Justin refers to 2 Peter. Its admission into the New Testament as a canonical writing was certainly later. Notable exceptions were still being taken to its authenticity in the lifetime of Jerome.[76]

The writer claims the name and authority of "Simon Peter." He refers to the Apostle's presence on "the holy mountain" of Jesus' transfiguration, and to Jesus' prediction concerning his death. But his knowledge of Peter and of these things was derived from the Church's traditions.[77] His reference to "our beloved brother Paul" is also a device of pseudonymity. When 2 Peter was written, collections of Paul's letters were being used and probably accorded canonical authority.[78]

The secondary character of 2 Peter is revealed most clearly in the passages that seem to have been lifted by its author from Jude. Besides padding his source, he has changed Jude's present tenses into future and removed the reference to Enoch, which are other marks of a pseudonymous writing.[79] Since there were being circulated at the time at least two writings attributed to Peter—an apocalypse and a gospel—there is no difficulty in accounting for the origin and survival of a pseudonymous letter.[80] The writer of 2 Peter should not be charged with lacking integrity. He sought to discredit views that he sincerely believed were opposed to the apostles' proclamation. As defender of the faith, i.e., the Church's doctrinal tradition, against error, the author stands in the shadow of the Prince of the Apostles.

A date for 2 Peter sometime within the period 125 to 150 C.E. commands the widest assent among scholars. Any date up to the third century is possible, but an early second-century dating is more probable.

INTERPRETING 2 PETER

A. Introduction, 1:1–21
  1. The prescript, 1:1–2
  2. The Christian's privileges: an enabling power; a call; the promises, 1:3–4
  3. The Christian's responsibilities to confirm the call and election, 1:5–11
B. The False Teachers: Their Character Described; Their Doom Foretold, 2:1–22
  1. The antecedents of the false teachers, and the consequences of their "destructive heresies," 2:1–3
  2. Examples from scripture of the punishment of rebels, 2:4–10a
  3. The errorists denounced, 2:10b–22

It is probable that the early reference to the "knowledge of God" was more than a liturgical formula for the writer of 2 Peter.[81] Had *gnosis* become a technical religious term in our writer's circle? As we shall see, it is possible that *Gnostic* may be the label we should apply in describing the writer's principal adversaries. According to the teaching of 2 Peter, a personal acknowledgement of the truth revealed in "Jesus our Lord," not mystical or mythical speculation, makes for sound and steady growth in all things pertaining "to life and godliness." Only by such means are men enabled to "become partakers of the divine nature."

An intimation of our writer's concern to affirm (against the false teachers) the certainty of Christ's return in glory is evidenced in 1:16ff. Jesus' transfiguration, witnessed by "Peter," is viewed as a proleptic event guaranteeing that the advent hope cannot be dismissed as a "cleverly devised myth." Prophecy also confirms the reality of Christ's final coming, (19–21).

Apparently the writer of 2 Peter was impressed with Jude's description of the false teachers plaguing the church, considered it a classic and, in a general way, descriptive of his adversaries, (2:1ff.). His reference to the errorist's promise of "freedom" (2:18ff.) suggests that they were representatives of a Gnostic libertinism.

C. The Defense of "the Promise of His Coming," 3:1–13
1. Prophecy and the apostolic witness are recalled, 3:1–2
2. The scoffers' taunt and their claim, 3:3–4
3. Things have not, and will not, "remain the same": the flood a type of the coming judgment, 3:5–7
4. The Day of the Lord: reasons for patience and repentance, 3:8–10
5. Summary: the Lord's promise and its implications for the Church, 3:11–13
D. Conclusion, 3:14–18
1. The exhortation of Peter is supported by Paul "in all his letters," but the latter's difficult doctrines are being distorted, 3:14–16
2. A final warning and admonition, 3:17–18a
3. A doxology, 3:18b

How can one describe the position of the "scoffers" who were saying, "Where is the promise of [Christ's] Parousia?" Their chief concern seems to have been not with delay but with denial. It is likely that they were Gnostics who were rejecting the traditional eschatology of the early church, with its prospect of a Last Judgment. In its place they had adopted a spiritualized eschatology that equated their esoteric enlightenment with a resurrection with Christ. Our writer accuses them of "deliberately ignoring" the fact that their licentious behavior will incur the divine wrath with the coming of "the day of judgment and [its] destruction of the ungodly."

The writer vigorously attacked the errorists' skepticism. He denied that all things "have continued as they were from the beginning of creation," and he reasserted and re-emphasized the apocalyptic message of the early Church. The biblical account of the flood in the days of Noah proclaimed the truths that the universe was subject to the rule and the judgments of God and that the ungodly perish.[82] Our writer's restatement of the traditional hope of the Church contains two distinctive aspects. Instead of emphasizing the suddenness and unpredictability of the Lord's last day, he called to mind the scriptural teaching that God's time scheme differed from clock-time. He also stressed the catastrophic nature of the End. Alone among the New Testament writers, the author of 2 Peter employed an apocalyptic symbol reminiscent of the Stoic doctrine of world conflagration.

That the writer in this restatement remained true to the hope embedded in the primitive Christian eschatology has been denied. It is claimed that the early expectation of God's triumph through Christ is replaced by a proclamation of the apotheosis of the pious, destined to become partakers "of the divine nature," rewarded for righteousness and escaping the destruction of the wicked. The writer's thought, it is said, "marks the relapse of Christianity into Hellenistic dualism": this version of the Christian *kerygma* offered persons a way of escape from the corrupt world and safe transit to the eternal realm.[83]

Although it must be conceded that the writer's teaching contains Hellenistic elements, this reading of the eschatology of 2 Peter, as nearly indistinguishable from Gnosticism, seems to be one-sided. The writer's hope reflects—at some remove it is true—the same tension between the "now" and the "not yet" present in the early *kerygma*, and his moral imperatives, as in Paul's letters, are based upon the indicatives of the gospel.[84]

Some readers will doubtless conclude that the theology and manner of defense adopted by the writer of 2 Peter leave much to be desired, and may find his apocalyptic literalness unappealing. Yet his moral admonitions, which were prompted by a steadfast hope and maintained in the face of widespread skepticism, eventually won for this book a place among the Christian scriptures.

NOTES

1. J. W. C. Wand, *The General Epistles of St. Peter and St. Jude* (1934), p. 1. J. H. Elliot cites others who extol 1 Peter, "The Rehabilitation of an Exegetical Step-child: 1 Peter in Recent Research," *JBL* 95 (1976): 243f.
2. J. N. D. Kelly, *A Commentary on the Epistles of Peter and Jude* (1969), p. 4.
3. Perhaps one ought to include Gentile "God-fearers" among the addressees who would find the writer's frequent appeal to the scriptures impressive, as well as his insistence that Gentile believers in Jesus Christ are truly "God's own people," 2:9f. W. Van Unnik, *1 Peter, IDB* 3 (1962) 764f.
4. Some scholars presupposing persecution of Christians (a) during Trajan's reign (98–117), ca. 110, are F. W. Beare, *The First Epistle of Peter* (1970), pp. 29–34; J. Knox, "Pliny and 1 Peter," *JBL* 72 (1953): 187–189; (b) during Domitian's reign (81–96), ca. 90–95, Kümmel, *INT*[2], p. 424f,; E. Goodspeed, *INT* (1937), pp. 283f.; (c) during Nero's reign (54–68), 64, or early 65, J. A. T. Robinson, *Redating the New Testament* (1976), pp. 151–160: B. Reicke, *The Epistles of James, Peter and Jude* (1964), pp. 71f. Cf. W. van Unnik (*IDB*, 3 (1952) 762): "no state persecution in any period is reflected in the letter."
5. Kelly, *Epistles of Peter and Jude*, pp. 5–11; E. Best, *I Peter* (1971), pp. 39–42; Elliott, "Rehabilitation of an Exegetical Stepchild," pp. 251–253.
6. Robinson, *Redating the New Testament*, p. 72.
7. A date in the sixties and Petrine authorship are compatible with the view that the letter alludes to spontaneous and sporadic expressions of hostility and abusive conduct on the part of pagans toward Christians; however, a setting of the epistle in either Domitian's or Trajan's time requires a postapostolic dating and pseudonymous authorship.
8. See Kelly, *Epistles of Peter and Jude*, p. 11.
9. *Ibid.*, pp. 11f. M. Dibelius and H. Greeven, *A Commentary on the Epistle of James* (1976), pp. 30f. For a note concerning 1 Pet. and the synoptic gospel tradition, see pp. 400f.
10. For evidence of liturgical influence, see p. 402. That 1 Peter presupposes Pauline theology is taken by some scholars to exclude Petrine authorship (F. W. Beare, *First*

Epistle of Peter, pp. 54ff.; Kümmel, *INT*[2], p. 423). An appeal to literary affinities and the use of tradition, however, neither excludes nor establishes authorship by the apostle. Elliott, "Rehabilitation of an Exegetical Stepchild," p. 248.

11. From among a sizable number of English scholars who attribute 1 Pet. to the apostle and date it before 70, see the arguments advanced by Robinson, *Redating the New Testament*, pp. 150–169. The reserve shown in Kelly's comments (*Epistles of Peter and Jude*, pp. 30–33) is perhaps more typical of English scholarship.

12. R. H. Grundry, " 'Verba Christi' in 1 Peter," *NTS* 13 (1966–1967): 336–350. Cf. E. Best, "1 Peter and the Gospel Tradition," *NTS* 16 (1969–1970): 95–113.

13. Elliott, "Rehabilitation of an Exegetical Stepchild," pp. 247f.

14. Kelly, *Epistles of Peter and Jude* p. 30; F. L. Cross, *1 Peter: a Paschal Liturgy* (1954), pp. 43f.

15. Rev. 14:8; 17:5; 18:2; 2 Esd. 3:28, 31; 2 Bar. 11:1; 67:7; Or. *Sibyll.* 5:143, 159: writings composed after 70 C.E. with the possible exception of Revelation. See p. 426. Perhaps 1 Peter is the earliest literary reference extant.

16. Robinson, *Redating the New Testament* p. 169.

17. Kelly, *Epistles of Peter and Jude*, p. 32. See R. E. Brown, K. Donfried, and J. Reumann, eds., *Peter in the New Testament* (1973). Cf. E. G. Selwyn (*The First Epistle of St. Peter* [1947], pp. 33–36) who traces theological affinities between 1 Pet. and the Apostle's preaching according to the Acts.

18. See F. W. Beare's statement of the baptismal-liturgy-transcript theory advanced by H. Preisker and subsequent modifications by others, *First Epistle of Peter*, pp. 220ff. Also Cross, *I Peter*; B. Reicke, *James, Peter and Jude*, pp. 74f. Cf. C. F. D. Moule, "The Nature and Purpose of 1 Peter," *NTS* 3 (1956): 1–11; Kelly, *Epistles of Peter and Jude*, pp. 15–20.

19. J. Fitzmyer, "The First Epistle of Peter," *JBC* 58 (1968): 363.

20. In addition to baptism, this passage may contain a Eucharistic reference, 2:3, 5b.

21. Note also 1:15f.

22. Phil. 3:20; Heb. 13:14; Col. 3:1–17.

23. Tit. 3:1; 1 Tim. 2:2.

24. Kelly, *Epistles of Peter and Jude*, pp. 107–134.

25. 1 Pet. 4:5ff. has been taken to confirm the alternative view that 3:19 refers to Christ's descent into the realm of the dead; however 4:6 refers to preaching done by others (earlier Christians) to persons physically dead (at the time of the writer) but who belong to him who is Lord of the living and the dead. 1 Thess. 4:13–18; Heb. 9:27. W. J. Dalton, *Christ's Proclamation to the Spirits* (1965).

26. Even into sections chiefly advancing the writer's Christology, urgent admonitions are inserted. E.g., 2:1–4; 3:7–15; 6:1–8.

27. R. H. Fuller, "The Letter to the Hebrews, James, Jude, Revelation, 1 and 2 Peter," in G. Krodel, ed., *Proclamation Commentaries* (1977), pp. 3–4.

28. Heb. 10:32–34; 2:3–4; 5:12. The first allusion to Hebrews is in 1 Clem., written at Rome. It is unlikely that this exhortation was written for either Jewish Christians or Gentile Christians, but to Christians as Christians who were suffering a lethargy of hope. See Kümmel, *INT*[2], pp. 398–401.

29. Acts 2:34–36; 1 Cor. 15:25; Col. 3:1; Eph. 1:20.

30. Heb. 1:5; also 5:5–9.

31. Heb. 1:1–2, 5, 8–9; 5:7–9; 10:5–7.

32. Heb. 2:10, 14–18. See also 4:14–15; 5:8.

33. Heb. 3:6–4:13.

34. Heb. 3:12–19.

35. With 6:46 read 10:26–31 and 12:16–17, 25–29. Note also 2:3; 4:11–13; 12:28–29.

36. Gen. 14:17–20; Heb. 7:1–19.

37. Heb. 7:20–28.
38. Heb. 8:1–5; 9:24.
39. Heb. 9:11–14.
40. Heb. 10:11–14; 9:14.
41. Heb. 10:19–39.
42. Sir. 44.
43. Heb. 12:18–29. See 10:24–25; also 3:13–14.
44. Heb. 2:1; 5:12; 6:9–12; 13:24.
45. J. Moffatt, *A Critical and Exegetical Commentary on the Epistle to the Hebrews* (1924), pp. xxxiff.; Kümmel *INT*[2], pp. 395f.; J. W. Thompson, " 'That Which Cannot Be Shaken,' Some Metaphysical Assumptions in Heb. 12:27," *JBL* 94 (1975): 580–587.
46. C. K. Barrett, "The Eschatology of the Epistle to the Hebrews," in W. D. Davies and D. Daube, eds., *The Background of the New Testament and Its Eschatology* (1956), pp. 363ff. Fuller, "Letter to the Hebrews," pp. 25–27.
47. Barrett, "Eschatology of Hebrews," p. 389.
48. G. McRae, "Heavenly Temple and Eschatology in the Letter to the Hebrews," *Semeia* 12 (1978): 179ff. McRae also notes that the author's peculiar understanding of faith ("insight into the heavenly world") functions as a homiletic support for the perseverance of the reader's (apocalyptic) hope: "hope is the goal and faith is the means towards its full realization" (p. 192).
49. Besides 1:1 and 2:1, see 1:18, 21; 2:7; 5:8, 12. Noteworthy also are the echoes of sayings attributed to Jesus, e.g., 1:5, 17, 22; 4:12.
50. R. V. G. Tasker, *The General Epistle of James* (1956); R. Heard, *INT*, pp. 164–166; Robinson, *Redating the New Testament*, pp. 130–139. Cf. S. Laws, *A Commentary on the Epistle of James* (1980), pp. 38–42; Reicke, *The Epistles of James, Peter and Jude*, (1964), pp. 3–6; Dibelius and Greeven, *Epistle of James* (1976), pp. 17–21; Kümmel, *INT*[2], pp. 411–414.
51. *Ibid.*, pp. 413f.; Dibelius and Greeven, *Epistle of James*, pp. 34–38.
52. Kümmel, *INT*[2], pp. 413f. Cf. R. M. Grant, *Historical Introduction to the New Testament*, p. 222.
53. Dibelius and Greeven, *Epistle of James*, pp. 18–21.
54. Cf. 1 Pet. 1:6f., 4:12f.; Rom. 5:3f. Seneca *Epis.* XXIII; *De Prov.* 4.
55. Jas. 1:12f., 5:10, 13.
56. Jas. 1:6f.; 5:16b. Cf. Mk. 11:23 and pars.
57. The influence of Jewish Wisdom books is evident throughout. For "the crown of life," cf. Wisd. 5:15f. 2 Tim. 4:8, 1 Pet. 5:4; Rev. 12:3. For the idea that God does not tempt persons, cf. Sir. 15:11f. 1 Cor. 10:13.
58. Jas. 1:21. Cf. Rom. 10:8f.; 1 Pet. 1:23; 2:1f.
59. Jas. 1:26. Note that a third homily has as its subject the uses and abuses of speech, 3:1–12. See also, 1:22–24 and 2:12. "Speech to God, prayer, is another of his interests." Laws, *Commentary on James*, p. 27. See 1:5–7; 4:2–4; 5:13–18.
60. Jas. 1:27; 4:4ff.
61. Dibelius and Greeven, *Epistle of James*, pp. 128–130.
62. Laws, *Commentary on James*, pp. 6–10, 97–101.
63. 1 Tim. 6:10, 17ff.
64. Dibelius and Greeven, *Epistle of James*, p. 179. See the entire essay, "Faith and Works in Paul and James," pp. 174–180. Kümmel, *INT*[2], pp. 414–416.
65. Rom. 6:1ff.; Gal. 5:1ff.; 2 Pet. 3:14f.
66. Jas. 2:19.
67. Cf. Jas. 2:8 and Gal. 5:6.
68. Jas. 3:17f.

69. Jude 3f.

70. Lk. 6:16; Jn. 14:22. For B. H. Streeter's view that the author was Jude, the third bishop of Jerusalem (ca. 125 C.E.), see *The Primitive Church* (1929), pp. 178ff. Robinson's placement of Jude in the late apostolic age (ca. 60–62) depends on an acceptance of the perceived parallels with the Pastoral Letters, which he dates 55–58 C.E.

71. Verses 8, 12, 16, 19. J. C. Beker, "Peter, Second Letter of," *IDB*, 2, pp. 1010f.; Kümmel, *INT²*, p. 426; Grant, *Introduction to the New Testament*, pp. 227f.

72. 1 En. 10:41ff.; Jub. 5:6 (Gen. 6:1ff.).

73. Gal. 3:19–20; Acts 7:38.

74. Jude 12; 1 Cor. 11:17ff. Did the errorists who joined other movements nevertheless come to the Christian "love feasts" in order to disrupt them and to lead some astray?

75. 1 En. 1:9; 60:8.

76. Kümmel, *INT²*, pp. 433f.

77. 2 Pet. 1:14 (cf. Jn. 21:18f.) Also 2 Pet. 1:16–18 (cf. Mk. 9:2–10 and pars.)

78. 2 Pet. 3:15f.

79. Cf. 2 Pet. 2:1–8; 3:1f., and Jude 4–19. The arguments against Jude's use of 2 Pet. (Luther's view) are persuasive. Cf. Reicke's view, *James, Peter, and Jude*, p. 189f.

80. M. R. James, *The Apocryphal New Testament* (1924), pp. 505ff. Also "the Preaching of Peter," 16ff., and "The Acts of Peter," 300ff., therein, 2 Peter is an early Christian adaptation of a Jewish literary genre known as the farewell speech or "testament." In the XII P. the dying patriarchs speak of things to come, and exhort the succeeding generation to pious acts. See also the Jewish book, Tob. 14:3–11.

81. 2 Pet. 1:3; see also 1:8; 2:20f.; 3:18.

82. C. H. Talbert argues persuasively that in its "testament" form, this letter aims to foretell the emergence of error after the death of Peter and to appeal to apostolic authority as a defense against some Christian Gnostics who were denying the church's conviction of a Parousia-judgment. "II Peter and the Delay of the Parousia," *VC* 20 (1966): 137–145.

83. Käsemann, "An Apologia for Primitive Christian Eschatology," in *Essays on New Testament Themes* (1964), pp. 169–195.

84. Beker, "Peter, Second Letter of," p. 769; Grant, *Introduction to the New Testament*, pp. 229–231; Reicke, *James, Peter and Jude*, pp. 174–183.

Chapter 19

The Apocalypse from the Johannine Circle

FIVE New Testament books are ascribed by tradition to John the son of Zebedee, one of Jesus' original disciples. Irenaeus, bishop of Gaul, voiced this belief in his church at the close of the second century with respect to the Gospel, Revelation, and the first two letters of John.[1] To Irenaeus also we trace the information that "John, the disciple of the Lord," bore faithful witness to the apostolic tradition in the church at Ephesus "until the time of Trajan."[2]

Questions relating to the origin of the Johannine writings are complicated by the fact that the internal evidence is not direct. Only the Revelation gives its writer's name, and that simply as John. The Gospel and 1 John are anonymous writings. The lesser letters, 2 and 3 John, were composed by a writer or writers identified simply as "the Elder."

The view taken in this chapter and the next is that whatever conclusions can be reached concerning the authorship of the Johannine books, the tradition that associates all five with a church or churches in Asia is probably correct. Their literary, historical, and theological affinities are striking, in spite of their differences. They are all associated with the testimony of the Apostle John. Thus they may be called, "writings from the Johannine circle."

THE REVELATION TO JOHN

The book of Revelation is one of the least read and the most misunderstood writings of the New Testament. Many Christians do not know what to make of it; a few make of it entirely too much. The book is commonly called "Revelations." This is an accurate description if it applies to the many visions of its author, but the title is singular, not plural. Unlike many writings of its type, Revelation is not a pseudonymous book. It contains a new message given to a contemporary seer under the authority of his own, not another's name. And it begins with a series of short letters. But otherwise Revelation is a typical *apocalypse.*[3] This fact should prevent the serious reader from being misled by some interpretations that have been imposed upon it.

That some modern Christians should have doubts about the authority of Revelation is not surprising. By the end of the second century its authority was generally acknowledged, but the voice of the Church was not unanimous.[4] The book's popularity with many raised the doubts of a few. It was as eagerly received by millenarians of the second as of the twentieth century, lusting for the pleasures of "reigning on the earth a thousand years" with Christ.[5] Some leaders of the ancient Church rejected this doctrine when interpreted literally. According to Tertullian, Marcion was repelled by its "Jewish" character and therefore denied to Revelation an apostolic authority. His followers are still among us. The Church of the West rose to the defense of the book. But not all misgivings were allayed by official declarations. The great Jerome expressed his personal doubt about its canonical standing, and, later, Protestant reformers did the same.

Christians at Alexandria in the third century found no great difficulty with the teaching of Revelation. This ease probably was the result of the tendency within this church to interpret scripture allegorically. Origen, a forthright foe of millenarianism, rejected a literal interpretation and exercised his ingenuity to recover the spiritual (allegorical) meaning of Revelation. The book still suffers from Origenesque interpretations. Dionysius, bishop of Alexandria (247–264 C.E.) was the first scholar to argue that Revelation could not have been written by the same hand as the Fourth Gospel. Its style, grammar, and ideas were not those of the Fourth Evangelist. Since the bishop accepted the apostolic authorship of the Gospel, he was bound to deny it to Revelation. Eusebius, who reported the bishop's views, found them convincing. He suggested that Revelation was written by a certain John, "the elder" of Ephesus, of whom Papias had written. The historian adopted an indecisive position; Revelation could be accepted or rejected as scripture "as may seem proper."[6] The attitude of Eusebius has been the practical position of many in the Church since his time.

THE WITNESS OF THE APOCALYPSE TO ITS ORIGIN

Four times the author of Revelation called himself "John." He wished to be known to his readers as God's "servant," and their "brother," sharing "in Jesus the tribulation and the kingdom and the patient endurance." It is doubtful that John's words claim an official position; it was enough that he had heard and seen "the revelation of Jesus Christ." Nevertheless, it is clear that he considered himself a Christian "prophet," and his message, "words of the prophecy,"[7]

In the light of the internal evidence, modern scholars do not hesitate to reject the equivocal witness of the second century concerning the apostolic authorship of Revelation. But this judgment rests upon broader consideration than the writer's references to himself. The general thought, vocabulary, and style of Revelation set it apart from the Fourth Gospel. One scholar summarizes the case in the following words:

> In the Revelation God's love is mentioned once, his fatherhood not at all, and the material imagery of the Revelation is in sharp contrast to the mysticism of the gospel. Many of the specially characteristic words of the gospel are absent from the Revelation, *e.g*, truth, or used in a different sense, *e.g.*, light, only with a physical meaning; different Greek words are employed in the two books for "the Lamb." The style of Revelation is barbarous, and only consistent with a very imperfect knowledge of Greek grammar.[8]

Obviously these negative judgments carry greater weight with those who hold that John the Apostle wrote the Fourth Gospel or that his typical witness is reported therein. Otherwise, some conjecture that the disciple's Galilean background could account for the form and content of Revelation. Yet the absence of any trace of the writer's association with Jesus in his ministry and his reference to "the twelve apostles of the Lamb," to mention but two considerations, make this surmise extremely improbable.[9] There were many persons named John in the early Church. An inspired writer such as this one might easily have been mistaken for the Lord's disciple with the same name, at a time when the sanction of apostolic authority was sought and Revelation was a controversial document. For those seeking a designation for the author more suggestive than "St. John the Divine," "John the Seer" may serve.

How far the contents of Revelation reflect John's ecstatic experiences on Patmos cannot be said. But at least three external influences upon the form of his message have been detected: the Old Testament, contemporary Jewish apocalypses, and the worship of the Christian Church. These three factors deserve brief comment.

Revelation contains over five hundred allusions to the Old Testament. The writer has reminted much of the imagery of scripture in presenting his visionary experiences.[10] But even more important may have been the influence of several Jewish apocalypses that were currently in circulation. Many scholars claim that the writer borrowed extensively from these. One "school" contends that the bulk of Revelation reproduces one or more of these Jewish tracts. But not many have been persuaded that the "seer" is only an "editor." The Christian aspect of Revelation cannot be reduced to a prologue, epilogue, and a few interpolations.

In recent times attention has been given to the impress of Christian liturgy upon the Seer's mental processes. One writer has said, "It is as if the author, cut off from the Church's worship on the Lord's day, meditates upon its offering of praise and thanksgiving which is counterpart of the heavenly liturgy."[11] The prayers and other liturgical materials in Revelation have been used as sources for reconstructing the worship in the postapostolic Church.[12]

References in the Apocalypse that provide clues to its occasion and date of composition will be noted in the survey of its content (see pp. 428f.).

INTERPRETING THE REVELATION TO JOHN

No book of the New Testament makes such demands upon its reader; no book so much requires a critical introduction as Revelation. At the same time, it is quite impossible to learn the message of Revelation from secondary sources. One must view with his or her own eyes this vast, fantastic panorama, even though one needs a guide map.

Unfortunately the reader does not find general consent as to the plan of the book.[13] On the one hand, some interpreters assume that its visions follow a consecutive, temporal series. If the text of the book does not display consistency, one must suppose either its dislocation or the hand of an editor, or both. Only by critical restoration can the progress of the Seer's thought be recovered.[14] On the other hand, many interpreters—perhaps the majority—believe that the Seer adopted some scheme of recapitulation. His visions are often parallel, repeating in various imagery the three conventional stages of the apocalyptic drama: the period of catastrophies in heaven and on earth; the coming of Christ to destroy the powers of evil; the final judgment with its eternal rewards and penalties. A third group of interpreters say that the book defies structural analysis, believing that the author was not interested in these matters. As in some modern impressionistic paintings, the viewer must not expect logical patterns but must seek to appreciate the kaleidoscopic nature of Revelation's many-splendored vision.

A. Prologue, 1:1–20
    1. A solemn superscription including a beatitude, 1:1–5a
    2. In praise of the risen Christ, 1:5b–6
    3. A solemn declaration: behold, he is coming, 1:7–8
    4. The revelation to John, 1:9–11
    5. The initial vision, 1:12–20
B. Letters to the Seven Churches, 2:1–3:22
    1. Ephesus, 2:1–7
    2. Smyrna, 2:8–11
    3. Pergamum, 2:12–17
    4. Thyatira, 2:18–29
    5. Sardis, 3:1–6
    6. Philadelphia, 3:7–13
    7. Laodicea, 3:14–22
C. A Vision of Heaven, 4:1–5:14
    1. The throne of the eternal God surrounded by his worshipers, 4:1–11
    2. The vision of Christ the conqueror—who is given the scroll with the seven seals, and worshiped with God, 5:1–14
D. The Effect on Earth of the Opening of the Seven Seals, 6:1–8:1
    1. The four seals and the four horsemen, 6:1–8
    2. The fifth seal and the cry of the martyred saints, 6:9–11
    3. The sixth seal: some brighter phases of the eschatological drama are anticipated, 6:12–7:17; the day of wrath and its universal terrors (6:12–17) contrasted with the "sealing" of the saints and their rapture (7:1–17)
    4. The seventh seal: silence in heaven, 8:1

As John meditated on the Lords's day upon the worship of the church from which he was separated, the significance of the critical times in which he lived dawned upon him. The ordeal of the present was the beginning of the End, "the woes of the Messiah." He addressed his book to Christians assembled for worship, for a blessing is pronounced upon the presiding reader, the listening congregation, and upon all who heed its message. Antiphonal choruses join in praise of the eternal God and of Christ, crucified and risen (1–3).

With this transcendent setting of the stage, the reader's curiosity may lead him or her to the panorama of visions that follow. But several striking facts about the letters should not be overlooked (B). The letters are addressed to the guardian angels of the churches of Asia. In keeping with this apocalyptic convention, the writer's messages are couched in symbolical language. His judgments were severe, for the practices of the seven churches (the Church at large?) were contrasted with his own ideals. In the visions of John, the Church is victorious. His condemnations fall upon pagan society, for over against it stands the Church of God.[15] The letters contain more than deprecations, however, for eternal rewards are promised to the martyrs.[16]

The writer's vision of heaven (C) is a *sursum corda*. The persecuted Church must look up to the awesome majesty of God the Creator. Just as Paul wrote, Christians set their minds "on the things that are above where Christ is. . . ."[17] Without this vision, faith cannot endure. Two features of John's symbolism may attract the reader, his "celestial mathematics," and his bizarre mythological beasts. Biblical and ancient Jewish tradition provide the safest contexts for interpreting this symbolism. For example, the Lamb with horns is derived from the horned ram of several Jewish apocalypses.[18] But behind the figure of "the Lamb that was slain," whose blood ransoms men for God, is surely the event of the crucifixion as understood in the light of Isaiah 53. The early Christian use of the Passover lamb as a type of the cross of Christ further enriched this imagery.[19]

A description of the woes preceding the End was a familiar apocalyptic feature, as we have seen. John developed this pattern in a distinctive way. Just as the reader is led to expect the opening of the final "seal," a new sequence of woes is initiated; before the last angel's trumpet sounds, another dreadful series begins. In the outline the proposal is made that at such places the writer has anticipated the brighter side of the judgments of God to hearten his readers.[20]

> E. A Vision of the Seven Trumpeting Angels Who Stand Before God, 8:2–11:19
> 1. The ministry of the angels at the altar of heaven, 8:2–6
> 2. At the sound of the trumpets of four angels, the earth is partially destroyed, 8:7–13
> 3. At the sound of the fifth angel's trumpet, demonic locusts are unleashed (the first of three woes), 9:1–12
> 4. At the sound of the sixth angel's trumpet, the second woe (again, brighter phases of the eschatological drama are anticipated), 9:13–11:14: four militant angels and their cavalry are released, bringing to the earth three plagues (9:13–19); the unrepentant survivors (9:20–21); the cosmic angel appears (10:1–7); the seer eats the scroll from the angel's hand (10:8–11); the measuring of a part of the temple and the two mighty witnesses (11:1–6); the death and resurrection of the witnesses and their final bliss, the terror of their foes (11:7–14)
> 5. At the sound of the seventh angel's trumpet, the announcement of the end brings joy in heaven and cosmic repercussions (the third woe), 11:15–19

As the writer of the Apocalypse introduces his lurid scenes of judgment, cosmic convulsions, and deadly plagues, the reader may be baffled by the array of symbols. Scholars of the Apocalypse acknowledge that clues are often lacking for determining the writer's meaning. Much of John's symbolism is, however, decipherable. It is important to read a version of the Book of Revelation that is annotated, e.g., *The Oxford Annotated Bibles:* one annotating the Revised Standard Version; the other, the New English Bible.

The obscurity of John's symbolism troubles us less than his morbid, pitiless preoccupation with scenes of punishment. Our moral consciousness, not our reason, is repelled. When we read that the opening of the seals by Christ brings war, civil dissension, famine, and other disasters; the prayer of the martyrs for blood revenge; and the dreadful series of woes, repeated thrice, we may ask: To what extent is Revelation "a Christian book"? Many have pondered this question. With regard to the wrath of God and the fearful prospect of judgment, the writer does not depart from the teaching of the New Testament generally.[21] When we read these disaster scenes we should not overlook the fact that Revelation was written to encourage persecuted Christians living in disastrous times, not to frighten pagans into repentance. Furthermore, the petition of the martyrs is more than an impatient cry for public justice; it is "a heartfelt self-identification with the purpose of God, imperfectly expressed, no doubt, but in essence identical with the prayer 'Thy kingdom come.' "[22]

Nevertheless, while these and other things can be said, the fact remains that John's vindictiveness is reminiscent more of Qumran's spirit than of Jesus'. But Christians have the Sermon on the Mount to purge Revelation of its dross. Some persons value Revelation as though it contained the whole gospel; others see no gospel in it. But there is another point of view, that which acknowledges Revelation to be an essential part of the gospel but by no means the whole of it.[23]

F. Seven Visions Concerning the Dragon and His Emissaries, and the Messiah and His Church, 12:1–15:4
1. First vision: the heavenly mother and the dragon; the birth of the heavenly child; the dragon is thwarted, 12:1–17
2. Second vision: the rise of the beast from the sea invested with the dragon's power; his blasphemy and his reprobate worshipers, 13:1–10
3. Third vision: the delegated power of the second beast "from the earth"; his persecutions, 13:11–18
4. Fourth vision: the conquering Lamb and the "redeemed from the earth," 14:1–5
5. Fifth vision: the angel with the "eternal gospel," followed by two angels of woe; a beatitude for the martyrs, 14:6–13
6. Sixth vision: "one like a son of man," and the angels of wrath, 14:14–20
7. Seventh vision: after the final judgment, the triumphant songs of Moses and the Lamb, 15:1–4

Our attention may now be directed to the seven visions concerning the dragon and his agents. In these scenes we see the conflict between Christianity and the dread forces of evil in a historical setting. Some of these scenes can be called "flashbacks." The birth of the heavenly child and the murderous attack of the dragon may have intended a transparent disguise of the birth of Jesus to Mary, and Herod's threat to his life (F.1). In the Apocalypse, events on earth have their counterparts in heaven. But it is more probable that the "woman clothed with the sun" is a symbol throughout of the Church.[24] Like Paul and the writer of Hebrews, John recognized the continuity between Israel and the Church. From the womb of Israel the Christ was born. In either case, the deliverance of this child from death surely symbolized the resurrection and heavenly exaltation of Christ. The war fought in heaven and also on earth represented John's adaptation of the teaching found in Paul's letters and elsewhere. The triumph of Christ resulted in the fall of the demonic powers but not their final conquest.[25]

The visions of the beasts are companion pieces (F.2–3). The blasphemous monster from the sea probably suggested the Emperor Domitian (81–96 C.E.), or the representative of his imperial power in Asia. The second beast symbolized the imperial priesthood or, more inclusively, the local government that vigorously fostered the emperor cult in Asia. Some commentators have detected an evil parody in these pictures. The dragon and the two beasts war in concert against God's Lamb and the divine Spirit incarnate in the Church. In John's day men worshiped the god of power incarnate in the Roman emperor and the State, rejecting the true trinity. The vision that pictures the conquering Lamb as the one who accepted suffering, instead of inflicting it upon men, provides welcome relief from the woeful scenes of judgment (F.4); likewise, the vision of the universal proclamation of "an eternal gospel," and the coming of "one like unto a son of man" (F.5–7). But in these brighter scenes all darkness is not dispelled, nor do the songs of the saved drown the woeful dirges. John believed, in company with other writers of the New Testament, that judgment attends the heralding of the good news for those who will not receive it.[26]

G. Visions Concerning the Seven Bowls Full of the Wrath of God, 15:5–16:21
  1. The opening of the temple of heaven, 15:5–16:1
  2. First bowl: the plague of sores upon the worshipers of the beast, 16:2
  3. Second bowl: plague of the sea turned to blood, 16:3
  4. Third bowl: plague of the rivers and springs, 16:4–7
  5. Fourth bowl: plague of fierce heat, 16:8–9
  6. Fifth bowl: plague of darkness upon the kingdom of the beast, 16:10–11
  7. Sixth bowl: plague of drought prepares for "the kings from the east" and for Armageddon, 16:12–16
  8. Seventh bowl: plague of cosmic upheaval, 16:17–21
H. Visions of the Judgment Upon Babylon, 17:1–19:10
  1. The great harlot is depicted, 17:1–6
  2. The scene is interpreted, 17:7–18
  3. Vision of the angel announcing Babylon's fall, 18:1–3
  4. A dirge and taunt song over Babylon, 18:4–20
  5. Vision of the millstone, and the violent overthrow of Babylon, 18:21–24
  6. The mighty voice of the heavenly multitude exults in the divine deliverance and worships God, 19:1–8

John's gruesome tapestry of the judgment is further embroidered by the visions of the seven bowls outpoured, leading up to the fall of "Babylon" as a symbol for Rome's tyrannical power structure. These scenes are richly interwoven with Old Testament symbolism and language (G.1–6). In the explanation of the vision of "the great harlot [the goddess Roma?]," the beast from "the bottomless pit" is recalled and his destined fate announced (H.2). The revelation to John of this "mystery" is not altogether clear to his modern reader, for there is a confluence of references, literary and historical, and the symbolism is complex.[27] By such means, however, John assured his readers that, in the clash of powers in history, the Lamb was destined to conquer. "Another angel" then appeared to chant a dirge announcing Babylon's doom (H.3–4). Zeal for the vindication of God's righteousness led John to echo the taunt songs of the Old Testament prophets. Other New Testament writings do not allow the Christian to believe that God exacts double punishment for sin. It is possible though not probable that one New Testament book was written to correct the effect of these impassioned songs of hatred against Rome.[28]

The seven visions that follow proclaim a temporary check upon Satan's power to deceive men, an interregnum of the Messiah, a world conflict and the consigning of Satan to a place of eternal torment, judgment day, and the beginning of the eternal reign of God and the elect.

Some of these scenes appear to be a gathering up of earlier ideas, in anticipation of the last "last things."[29] The Gog and Magog theme, which is derived from Ezekiel, recalls Armageddon (I.5).[30] The beasts are again disposed of; not finally, but their doom is announced. The thousand-year reign of Christ on earth is interposed. With John's development of the simpler patterns of doomsday one should compare several first-century Jewish apocalypses, which also depict a temporary messianic kingdom as the prelude to the Age to come.[31] While John's interest centered chiefly upon the ultimate, not this penultimate, kingdom, one cannot conclude that John was unwillingly a captive to traditional beliefs. The millennium was deliberately introduced to encourage a martyr church. The repeated attempts that have been made to literalize this fleeting vision and to fit it into the calendar time of the future have led to nothing but confusion and vexation.[32]

The imagery of John's vision of the last judgment (I.6) stresses his belief that

Bust of Domitian. Roman senatorial, Greek, and Christian writers of antiquity damned Domitian as a tyrant because of alleged attacks upon the aristocracy, Hellenism, and the Church. Modern scholars have difficulty assessing his accomplishments and failings objectively. Domitian's policies were generally intelligent and favorable to the middle class until he lost control in the final years of his reign. During this time the cult of Domitian was augmented in the province of Asia. *(Courtesy Alinari/Art Resource.)*

nothing—absolutely nothing—in the created order escapes the divine scrutiny; nothing remains beyond the reach of God's power. Death and Hades release their captives at God's command, and the final frustrations to the fulfillment of the purpose of the Almighty are removed. Whatever uncertainty may have lingered in the mind of Paul, John was no believer in universal salvation.

John's picture of the fate of the damned has been contrasted unfavorably with the mythologies of the End described by prophets of other religions. Yet his vision of the holy city is without parallel for the sublimity of its themes (J.1–5). Exploiting the rich and complex symbolism of the Old Testament to describe the new Jerusalem, he ends by stressing the Christian's attainment of the ultimate blessedness: God's "servants shall worship him; they shall see his face. . . ."[33] The power of these visions to move the human spirit is enshrined in the world's great art. Prosaic commentary runs the risk of botching the effect of this vivid canvas. John's "new Jerusalem" is not conceivable; it is only imaginable.

What can now be said about the occasion of the Apocalypse? In its completed form the Revelation to John can be dated in the closing years of the Emperor Domitian's reign, ca. 94 or 95 C.E. The internal evidence is consistent with ancient church tradition and Latin sources.[34] Neither support the view that Domitian ordered the deaths of Christians as a general policy, but the promotion of the cult of the living emperor in the province of Asia probably provoked a crisis, which, according to John, threatened widespread persecutions of Christians in the region; arraignments before Roman judges; and the likelihood of martyrdoms. John writes to give encouragement and hope to those who may share with him "in Jesus the tribulation and the kingdom and the patient endurance."[35]

NOTES

1. The Muratorian canon; Clement of Alexandria, *Strom.* III. 5, 45 (Eusebius *H.E.* VI. 14. 7); Origen (Eusebius *H.E.* VI. 25. 9f.). Irenaeus quotes from 1 and 2 John as though they were a single letter, *Adv. Haer.* III. 15. 5–8.

2. Eusebius (*H.E.* III. 23) cites the apology of Irenaeus (*Adv. Haer.* I. 9. 3; II. 22. 5; V. 33. 3.) Trajan, 98–117 C.E.

3. J. Kallas contends that the author has a nonapocalyptic eschatology and explanation of suffering, "The Apocalypse—An Apocalyptic Book?" *JBL* 86 (1967): 69–80.

4. R. H. Charles, *A Critical and Exegetical Commentary on the Revelation of St. John* (1920) V. 1, pp. cff.; A. S. McNeile and C. S. C. Williams, *Study of the New Testament* (1953), p. 263.

5. See Rev. 20:1–10. A widely influential, second-century heretical group, the Montanists, espoused millenarianism (belief in a visible reign of Christ for 1,000 years before the last judgment).

6. Eusebius *H.E.* III. 39. 6; also III. 24. 18 and III. 25. 4. For the tradition concerning John's exile on the island of Patmos, see Rev. 1:9; *H.E.* III. 18 and 20.

7. Rev. 1:3; 22:7–10.

8. Heard, *Introduction to the New Testament* (1950), p. 239. The comparative studies of R. H. Charles established beyond reasonable doubt a different authorship, *Revelation of St. John*, Vol. 1, pp. xxxixff.

9. Rev. 21:4. McNeile and Williams, *Study of the New Testament*, pp. 264f.

10. R. H. Preston and A. T. Hanson, *The Revelation of St. John the Divine* (1949), pp. 34ff.

11. R. H. Fuller and G. E. Wright, *The Book of the Acts of God* (1960), pp. 376f.

12. L. Mowry, "Revelation 4–5 and Early Liturgical Usage," *JBL* 71 (1952): 75ff.

13. For an assessment of several proposed outlines, see McNeile and Williams, *Study of the New Testament*, pp. 254ff.; J. W. Bowman, "Revelation, Book of," *IDB*, 4, 64ff.

14. E.g., Charles, *Revelation of St. John*, Vol. 1, pp. xxvff.

15. E. F. Scott, *The Book of Revelation* (1941), p. 61.

16. Rev. 2:7, 11b, 17b, 26–28; 3:5, 10–12, 20–21.

17. Col. 3:1–3; 2 Cor. 4:16–18.

18. Rev. 6:16; 17:14. Cf. En. lxxxixff.; Test XII Pat., xix. 8.

19. 1 Cor. 5:7; Jn. 19:31ff.

20. C. B. Caird, *A Commentary on the Revelation of St. John the Divine* (1966), pp. 82ff. 2 Thess. 1:5ff., 2:9ff.

21. Caird, *Revelation of St. John*, pp. 292ff.; W. Klassen, "Vengeance in the Apocalypse of John," *CBQ* 28 (1966): 300ff.; cf. Kallas, "The Apocalypse," pp. 74ff.

22. Fuller and Wright, *Book of the Acts of God*, p. 337; Preston and Hanson, *St. John the Divine*, pp. 29ff.
23. Kümmel, *INT²*, pp. 472–474.
24. Caird, *Revelation of St. John*, p. 149; cf. M. Rist, "The Book of Revelation," *IB*, 12, (1955) pp. 363, 452ff.
25. Rev. 12:7ff.; Col. 2:15 (Gal. 4:3ff.?); Luke 10:17; John 12:31f.
26. Rom. 10:15ff.; Heb. 2:2ff.; Jn. 3:17ff.
27. E.g., note the difficulty facing the interpreter in identifying the apparently straight-forward reference to the seven kings: Rev. 17:10f.; Caird, *Revelation of St. John*, pp. 217ff.
28. See Edgar Goodspeed, *Introduction to the New Testament* (1937), pp. 265ff., 283f. The book referred to is 1 Pet.
29. Some scholars find it necessary to resort to a displacement theory to understand Rev. 20–22. See Preston and Hanson, *St. John the Divine*, pp. 129ff.
30. Ezek. 29:17ff. Cf. Rev. 6:16.
31. 2 Esd. 7:27ff.; 2 En. 33:2. See Rist, "The Book of Revelation," Vol. 12, pp. 518ff.
32. For judicious comment on the interpretation of this problematical passage, see Caird, *Revelation of St. John*, pp. 248–252.
33. Rev. 22:4.
34. Irenaeus, *Adv. Haer.* V. 30. 3; 1 Clem. 5:2ff.; also Dio Cassius lxvii, 13; Suetonius, Dom. 13; Martial V. 8.
35. Rev. 1:9.

The Gospel and Letters of John

Chapter 20

ANCIENT Church tradition concerning the origin of the Gospel of John is at first sight bewildering. At the close of the second century there was agreement on a wide front that the Gospel had been written by the intimate disciple of Jesus, John the son of Zebedee.[1] But before ca. 180 C.E. there is no information concerning the Gospel's author as well as an absence of verbatim citations in the writings of the Apostolic Fathers (where one would expect to find them, if the work was published with the authority of apostolic authorship).[2] Ignatius, in writing to Christians at Ephesus, did not mention John's connection with them, although he emphasized their close relation to Paul. There is no reference to John in Polycarp's Letter to the Philippians, although, writing from Asia, he refers to Paul. (Indeed, Paul is the apostolic authority for Polycarp.) Justin Martyr, who possibly knew the Gospel, did not make use of it or comment on its origin, although he ascribed the book of Revelation to the Apostle John.[3]

Some Christians in the early second century rejected the apostolic authority of the Gospel. Irenaeus noted that certain persons disapproved its teaching concerning the Holy Spirit.[4] Epiphanius referred to a group, perhaps the same persons, ascribing the Gospel and Revelation to Cerinthus, a Gnostic teacher. Epiphanius called them the *Alogi* (anti-Word, or irrational, men).[5] The fact that the authority of the Fourth Gospel could be openly challenged by Christians at this time throws some suspicion upon the direct value of the Johannine tradition cited by Irenaeus and others.

Before examining the witness of the Gospel to its origin, notice must be taken of the oft cited account received by the Church concerning the circumstances leading to its writing. Eusebius quotes Clement of Alexandria as having said:

> last of all, John, perceiving that the external facts had been made plain in the gospels being urged by friends, and inspired by the Spirit, composed a spiritual gospel.[6]

Modern criticism seems to have established at least two aspects of this "precritical judgment," that John is the latest and the most theologically developed of the Gospels.

THE WITNESS OF THE GOSPEL TO ITS ORIGIN

The reader of John may conclude that its author was an eyewitness to Jesus' ministry. Since the Gospel is anonymous, inquiries have focused upon the identity of disciples who are mentioned. Most important of these is the man described as "the disciple whom Jesus loved." (13:23; 19:26f; 20:2; 21:20 and 24). The phrase suggests one of Jesus' intimate followers. According to the synoptic tradition, these would have been Peter, and Zebedee's sons, James and John. Since James was killed by Herod Agrippa I, and Peter is distinguished in the narrative from "the disciple whom Jesus loved," John alone remains. The sons of Zebedee are never named in the Gospel. May one conclude that the "beloved disciple" was John? Is he also "the other disciple" closely associated with Peter in the Gospel?[7]

Some interpreters, following this reasoning, have observed other evidence that suggests that the author must have been a Palestinian Jew. He knew the geography and customs of the region and the religious beliefs and ordinances of its people. Besides, it is said, there is an Aramaic quality about the Greek of the Gospel.[8]

These considerations were used by conservative scholars at the turn of the present century to support the traditional ascription of the Gospel of John to Jesus' disciple. More recently, some have claimed that archeological discoveries provide a broader confirmation for the Palestinian provenience of its traditions; its words and ideas have a close affinity with those of the Qumran scrolls.[9]

Other aspects of the Gospel are not favorable to the traditional account of John's origin. Chief among these is the striking difference between the portraits of Jesus in John and in the Synoptic Gospels. At first sight, the four Gospels have much in common. Jesus' ministry opens with the testimony of John the Baptist. Some disciples are called. There is a popular ministry in Galilee, during which time Jesus performed many cures. He fed five thousand by the lake, and at night came to his disciples on the water. Jesus' popularity declined, but Peter confessed him to be the Holy One of God. There is then a transposition of the ministry from Galilee to Judea. The passion and resurrection narratives in all the Gospels have much the same pattern. It is not surprising that John should supplement the synoptic tradition at various points.

There are, however, remarkable differences. In John, Jesus is publicly proclaimed the Messiah at the outset of his ministry. There are no baptism or temptation narratives in John; no proclamations of the near advent of the kingdom of God. There are no demon exorcisms. This is strange, since Mark reported that the ministry in Galilee was characterized by preaching in the synagogues and "casting out demons."[10] The early dating of the cleansing of the temple is surprising. In Mark this incident aroused the fury of the Sadducees and led to Jesus' crucifixion. But in John the provocative event is the raising of Lazarus, a story that is missing from the Synoptic Gospels.[11] Jesus' frequent visits to Jerusalem may be contrasted with the Synoptists' account of a single fateful journey.

Divergences are also found when the teaching of Jesus in John is compared with the threefold synoptic tradition. There are no parables in the Fourth Gospel, and the themes and the style of Jesus' discourses are unlike those of the other Gospels. These differences can be exaggerated, but there is a notable absence in John of Jesus' aphorisms, teaching presented in short, pictorial words so familiar to the reader of the Synoptic Gospels. Instead, in the discourses attributed to Jesus, the diction resembles that of the writer of 1 John.

Some scholars minimize these difficulties by emphasizing the fragmentary character of the Synoptic Gospels and the special purposes that informed the Evangelists' selections of traditional materials. They have preferred John's plan of a longer ministry and have found an emphasis upon the public teaching of Jesus in the synoptic sources, and upon Jesus' private instruction of the Twelve in the great discourses of John.[12] It should be noticed that the Fourth Evangelist seems to exclude this popular means of harmonizing.[13] Most modern critics agree that comparative studies of the Gospels make it very improbable that the Fourth Gospel, at least in its present form, should be regarded as the writing of Zebedee's son. But a decision concerning John's relation to the Fourth Gospel must depend upon additional considerations. In the next section we shall ask whether or not it is possible to reconstruct several stages in the composition of John's Gospel.

Indirect evidence in the Gospel, which sometimes has been used to buttress the tradition of John's authorship, probably points to a final composition at some remove from eyewitness testimony. Such familiarity as the author shows with Palestinian conditions could easily have been derived from his sources. The Fourth Evangelist presents Jesus as having a detached attitude to "the Jews" and "their Law."[14] The so-called eyewitness scenes are problematical. Sometimes they reflect the more circumstantial narratives of a developed tradition, while others seem relatively undeveloped. At some places the narrative can be attributed to the writer's dramatic skill: were eyewitnesses present when Jesus talked with the Samaritan woman or conversed with Pilate?[15]

QUESTIONS CONCERNING THE SOURCES AND COMPOSITION OF JOHN'S GOSPEL

Many scholars have held that the Fourth Evangelist's dependence upon one or more of the Synoptic Gospels renders improbable the apostolic authorship of John. The question of literary dependence does have this and other important implications and has been carefully examined.[16] Comparative studies in the modern period led first to a majority opinion that John knew one or more of the other Gospels. In recent decades this hypothesis has been challenged repeatedly.[17] John, some have said, had access to an independent tradition; others conclude that he drew independently upon traditions similar to those used by the Synoptics, at least by Mark and Luke.

It does not seem that John's many differences from the Synoptics can be explained satisfactorily by a theory of either deliberate change or misunderstanding, or both. Some scholars appeal to the few narrative sequences and striking "verbal reminiscences" that are found in the same order in John, as sufficient evidence supporting the hypothesis that John had read Mark or Luke or both.[18] In view of the extensive differences, however, neither these narrative sequences nor the linguistic parallels establish literary dependence. In any case, it is commonly acknowledged that the Fourth Evangelist did not draw upon any

Gospel as a source in the way that Matthew (let us say) seems to have used Mark. Cross-influence from the Synoptics upon manuscripts of John's Gospel may explain the "verbal reminiscences" better than surmising that John quoted from one or more of them, somewhat eclectically, perhaps from memory only.[19]

If the origin and special content of John cannot be explained satisfactorily by reference to other canonical Gospels, is it possible to identify otherwise unknown literary sources? Following through on numerous suggestions of earlier scholars, Rudolf Bultmann put forward in his commentary (1941) the view that the Fourth Gospel was based on several major sources: a revelation-discourse source; a miracle stories source (the *semeia* or "sign" source); and passion and resurrection sources.[20] Bultmann also hypothesized that the Gospel's present form is the result of apparently accidental displacement, and reflects a subsequent "restoration" through a process that he calls "ecclesiastical redaction." Bultmann's detailed analysis, in which every sentence or part of a sentence of the Gospel is ascribed to one of the Evangelist's sources or to the Evangelist himself or to redaction, "has not gained general acceptance," but his reconstruction "embraces critical elements which are widely regarded as well-established results of Johannine research." For example, the existence of a collection of miracle stories upon which the Evangelist drew ("a sign-source," note, 2:11; 4:54; 20:30?); as well as a passion tradition or source; a recognition of the secondary character of Chapter 21; and the reversal of the order of chapters 5 and 6. Although written sources "appear less likely for the discourses," it is possible that they reflect traditional patterns" (note 1 John). Moreover, chapters 15–16 "follow awkwardly after 14:31 ("rise, let us go hence"), and may represent traditional materials added rather late in the process of composition."[21]

Bultmann's theory of accidental dislocation, like those of other scholars, is surely not fantastic. Loose sheets of a book (unfinished?) could conceivably have become misplaced, and an editor-disciple may not have restored them to their proper order. But one must view with skepticism the proposed rearrangements. Some of Bultmann's alterations "improve" connections, others create new difficulties. All rearrangements must depend upon some doubtful assumptions: that the critic is able to restore the "original" while the hypothetical disciple-editor was not; that the Evangelist's narrative-discourse sequences were written in a logical, orderly way, and that his purpose required that he adhere to precise chronological and geographical connections. With good reason many interpreters have preferred to read the Gospel in its present order.[22]

Bultmann's assumption that the Evangelist was a consistent as well as an original and independent thinker led him to identify four major types of "ecclesiastical redaction": (1) ideas relating to a sacramental appropriation of the saving work of Christ;[23] (2) passages proclaiming a futurist eschatology in terms of Jewish-Christian apocalypticism;[24] (3) verses harmonizing John's Gospel with the Synoptics;[25] and (4) statements laying claim to apostolic and eyewitness authority.[26]

In developing this redaction theory Bultmann assumed a heavy burden of proof. Having followed his analysis of most of the theologically suspect passages, the present writer concludes that Bultmann's contentions fall short of being convincing. John's sacramental interest is far too pervasive to be eliminated by the excision of the passages Bultmann denied to him. The problem of the juxtaposition of a realized and a futurist eschatology in the Gospel may be solved in other, more probable ways than by Bultmann's resolution in removing the tension.

A more tenable alternative to Bultmann's theory is this, that the Evangelist was himself the principal "ecclesiastical editor" who, perhaps over a period of time, reworked the Johannine traditions. However uncertain our knowledge of the provenience of the sources used and obscure the circumstances surrounding the composition of this Gospel, it seems clear that its author assimilated congenial materials, adapting them to his special purposes. The excision from the text of the several passages, which may be attributed, with some confidence, to redaction by other hands (e.g., chapter 21), affects but slightly the task of interpreting the Gospel's teaching.[27]

EXPLORING THE CULTURAL BACKGROUND OF JOHN'S GOSPEL IN SEARCH OF PURPOSE

For an understanding of the evangelist's purpose, the importance of his own statement cannot be overemphasized.[28] Nevertheless, these words provide a starting point for, not the conclusion of, discussion. Was the Gospel written to confirm and instruct Christians or to convert unbelievers? Because of the prominence given the farewell discourses in this Gospel, which contain the prayers of Jesus for the community of his followers (chapters 13–17), one can conclude that its principal purpose was to assure believers that through the incarnation of the Son of God they have obtained eternal life, and will ever be supported by divine love (17:3, 34–26).[29]

It is unlikely that the Gospel's primary aim was missionary because of its persistent polemic against the sons of darkness. Yet it is plausible that the content of the Gospel was shaped by the extension beyond Jesus' ministry of the Johannine communities' dialogue with "the Jews" (those survivors of Pharisaic Judaism after 70 C.E.) who, in this Gospel, represent those who are "of the world," that is, persons who are in opposition to Jesus and his "own," and who refuse to come to him as the light.[30]

Johannine scholars have tended in recent times to stress the Jewishness of the Fourth Gospel's background.[31] This is reflected not only in its citation of (or implicit reference to) the Old Testament, but in the rabbinic modes of scriptural exegesis; in the way Jesus is compared with the leading figures of Jewish history, especially Moses (1:17; 5:45–47; 6:30–34; cf. 8:31ff.); and in the Evangelist's familiarity with Jewish customs and traditions. The Qumran scrolls provide important external evidence of the Jewishness of the Fourth Gospel. For some features of the Gospel, it is said, "the Qumran literature offers a closer parallel than any other contemporary or earlier non-Christian literature, either in Judaism or in the Hellenistic world."[32]

The question of the background of the Gospel is complicated by the fact that Hellenism and Judaism do not identify mutually exclusive cultures in a period when Oriental and Western ideas and modes of thought had met and intermingled. Some interpreters are convinced, after a wide canvass of non-Christian writings, that John's Gospel manifests affinities with a variety of literatures. Interesting parallels to passages in John have been found not only in the rabbinical and sectarian Judaism of Palestine, but in Philo's writings and other Hellenistic-Jewish books, especially in the Wisdom literature. Moreover, John's thought has been judged akin to a type of religious thought found in the Hermetic tractates, as well as to the Stoicized Platonism of popular philosophy. Thus it is claimed that the vocabulary and thought forms of John's Gospel were familiar to Jews and non-Jews of various cultural backgrounds, who shared a common universe of discourse.[33]

Others have rejected this broad, general view and claimed that it is possible to define with greater specificity and clarity the contours of John's immediate environment. As early as 1925, Bultmann's studies of the Fourth Gospel had led him to Ignatius and to the Odes of Solomon—evidences of early Syrian Christianity—and also to certain ancient texts preserved by a Mandean sect that had survived to the modern era. These resources seemed to provide the most direct access into the Gnostic, mythological world of ideas presupposed by John. Bultmann conjectured that a pre-Christian Gnostic movement had originated in Persia, spread westward, and influenced Jewish and pagan groups in Syria and Judea. Perhaps John himself was an ex-Gnostic. At least according to Bultmann, one of his major sources, the "revelation discourses," was Gnostic and was "Christianized" by the Evangelist.

This effort to characterize the Evangelist's thought as an interaction with Oriental Gnosticism and to reconstruct its background from a curious miscellany of texts, some dating from a much later time, seemed farfetched to many scholars. But the amazing discoveries in the 1940s at Qumran and Nag Hammadi led to a closer examination of the alleged Gnostic background of the Fourth Gospel. While Qumran provided evidence for (what some have called) a pre-Christian, Gnosticizing Judaism, Nag Hammadi revealed an early Christianity with Gnostic tendencies, reflecting both Jewish and non-Jewish ideas and motifs.

The outstanding problem concerns the conclusions to be drawn from the alleged "Gnostic terminology" of the Fourth Gospel. Should one conclude that John's thought world was broadly representative of the syncretistic culture of his period, and that his language was later borrowed by Gnostics and invested by them with specifically Gnostic connotations (Gnostic *use* of a document does not make the document itself "Gnostic")? Or, alternatively, should one conclude that John consciously attacked pre-Gnostic tendencies in the churches of his time, using the language employed by these errorists to repudiate the points of view expressed therein? "That there exists a relation of some kind between the Fourth Gospel and non-Christian Gnosticism is scarcely open to question; exactly what this relation is, is one of the most disputed problems in current New Testament scholarship."[34]

The picture is a confusing one, but several important gains may be noted. No longer can John's Gospel be considered "an acute Hellenization" of the *kerygma* of the early Church, far removed geographically and culturally from the Palestinian world of Jesus and his first interpreters. Apparently the Fourth Evangelist was sensitive to important currents of thought, widely influential in his age, but also those in ancient Palestinian Judaism and in early Jewish Christianity. One must be wary, then of the supposition of a late, extra-Palestinian provenience for Johannine tradition. Finally, it should be stressed that the more thorough the comparisons between John's Gospel and the relevant literatures, the more impressive is the evidence for the originality of the Evangelist's theology, for its specifically Christian content.[35]

DATE AND PLACE OF WRITING

Until recent times the consensus had been that the Gospel in its present form was published ca. 100 C.E. In the nineteenth century some argued that John appeared in the later half of the second century. The discovery of papyrus fragments containing parts of the text of the Gospel excludes this possibility.[36] If one could be certain whether or not Ignatius knew the Gospel (ca. 110 C.E.); if the date of Heracleon's commentary could be fixed; or, if the relation between the Gospel and 1 John were established, definite clues would be provided. In the present state of knowledge, however, we are faced with a string of uncertainties.

The place of the Gospel's origin is likewise uncertain. Three cities have been suggested: Ephesus, Antioch of Syria, and Alexandria. Although the claims of Alexandria have been somewhat strengthened by the recent discoveries at Nag Hammadi, Ephesus remains the most likely place.[37] Until further evidence comes

A page from a facsimile of a fourth-century Greek manuscript, Codex Sinaiticus, containing the beginning of the Gospel of John. This important codex, with its four-columned pages (15 × 13½ inches), contains the whole of the New Testament, two writings of Apostolic Fathers, and much of the Old Testament. *(Courtesy of the Trustees of the British Library.)*

to light, we must content ourselves with the realization that "it is more important to understand the theological task achieved by the Fourth Evangelist than to know his name and to know the materials with which he worked and the way he used them, than to know the date and place at which he wrote."[38]

INTERPRETING THE FOURTH GOSPEL

A. Introduction, 1:1–51
    1. The prologue, 1:1–18
    2. The testimonies of John the Baptist, and of the disciples, 1:19–51

A:1. "When all things began the *Logos* already was . . ." (NEB). This Greek term is found in numerous Hellentic-Jewish and pagan writings of the period. Logos ("word") referred to the mind's unspoken thought and also to the expression of thought in speech. With God, or the divine, as predicate, the Logos could refer to the disclosure of ultimate reality. Stoics employed the term to express their conviction that the divine Logos (immanent Reason) pervaded the universe, and that human beings possessed a seed or spark of the universal Logos to direct their lives according to reason. The Logos is a term frequently used by Philo in an undisciplined way, in the interest of furthering his aim to wed Jewish and Greek thought.[39] For Philo "the logos of God" identified the ideal world, and also the archetypic human, of which the phenomenal world and empirical human are copies. The Logos also identified an intermediary principle (the high priest allegorically interpreted) linking the two realms; however, "neither the personality nor the pre-existence of the *logos* was clear in Philo," and the *logos* did not impart (eternal) life.[40]

To a Greek-speaking convert from Judaism and to others versed in the Septuagint, the first statements in the Prologue doubtless recalled the Genesis story of creation and the historic missions of the Hebrew prophets. "By the word of the Lord the heavens were made, and all their host . . ." The logos of God, once spoken to and by the prophets had "a quasi substantial existence of its own."[41] But the most impressive background for understanding the thought of the Prologue is its affinity with Jewish Wisdom speculation. "Wisdom" (*Sophia*, LXX), like the Logos, was present with God before creation, and was an active agent in creation.[42] Wisdom, like the Logos, came into the world to impart life, "to make her dwelling place among the children of men," but found "no dwelling place."[43] Yet as the Word set up his "tabernacle" among humankind, so Wisdom established her "tabernacle" in Jacob.[44] According to Sirach (24:23ff.), Wisdom became identified in Jewish thought with Torah.[45] This idealization of the Law that arose in pre-Christian times was developed in late rabbinical tradition: Torah pre-existed creation and served as a pattern for the creation of the world.[46]

Now it is clear that in the Prologue personification is carried further than Wisdom/Torah was carried in Judaism, but belief in the incarnation of the Logos and the proclamation of "the Word" (*kerygma*) by the believing community led to this remarkable advance.[47]

"And the Logos *became flesh* . . ." With this declaration the man named Jesus was received by the Johannine community as being himself the eternal

Word, not merely another spokesman of it: "we have beheld his glory . . . No one has ever seen God; it is God the only Son, ever at the Father's side, who has revealed Him."[48] The Prologue to the Fourth Gospel thus provides an essential interpretive frame before *Jesus* is introduced.*

A:2. The story of Jesus' ministry begins with the witness of John the Baptist proclaimed on three days, days that have a programmatic rather than a chronological significance. This narrative sequence develops the initial statement concerning the Baptist in the prologue.[49] In the remainder of chapter 1 a typical literary design of the Evangelist is presented: realities that were manifested on later occasions from the ministry are proclaimed as having been revealed throughout Jesus' history. The Evangelist has the Baptist proclaim the saving benefit of Christ's cross; on the occasions of the call of the first disciples, they summarize the whole meaning of their discipleship. A synopsis is given of the gradual increase in the disciples understanding that took place during the ministry of Jesus, but chiefly *after* his resurrection and the coming of the Spirit. Perhaps this synopsis was intended to make explicit that the Christology of the Johannine community was founded on the apostles' testimony (1:41, 45, 49).[50]

The proleptic perspective also provides a basis for the juridical development of John's Gospel. In the Synoptics, Jesus' trials take place on the eve of his death; (in the Acts, those of his disciples, following their witness to his resurrection). Throughout John's account of the ministry persons seek to bring Jesus to trial; they pass judgment upon any person or anything purporting to witness to the truth. There are, of course, climactic "trial scenes" in the Gospel. For example, Jesus adduces a series of witnesses to the truth of his revelation, and Pilate judges Jesus.[51] There is irony in both situations: his antagonists, not Jesus, are being tried. But the point now stressed is the presence of legal terminology throughout John. It has been observed that "the Gospel opens with a trial and John the Baptist under interrogation."[52]

*A common view is that for the introduction to his Gospel the Fourth Evangelist adapted a hymn that he had composed at an earlier time (Schnackenburg), or one composed by another member of the Johannine community (Brown). After exploiting the usefulness of the term *Logos*, the Evangelist may have abandoned it, wishing to interpret Jesus by appealing to the traditions of his ministry rather than in terms of Hellenistic Word/Wisdom/Torah speculation.

B. The Book of the Signs, 2:1–12:50
   1. First episode—the new beginning, 2:1–4:42: the sign at Cana (2:1–11); the cleansing of the temple (2:12–25); first discourse—the conversation with Nicodemus (3:1–21); an appendix (3:22–36); second discourse—Jesus' conversations with the woman of Samaria, and the disciples (4:1–45)

Following the suggestion of several interpreters, chapters 2 through 12 are designated the "Book of the Signs" (B).[53] The word *sign* is used seventeen times by the evangelist to designate actions of Jesus, some of them miraculous, others nonmiraculous.[54] There are repeated references also to "the works" of Jesus.[55] His actions seem to be regarded as parables, directing attention to some significance beyond the happenings as such, a significance that only faith can properly understand. It is probable that this use of the terms *signs*, and *works*, is derived from the Old Testament. Like the "signs" performed by the prophets, Jesus' actions were more than illustrations of ideas; they anticipated events that were to take place. Jesus' signs are therefore not to be interpreted independently. They all point to a forthcoming event—the cross, which was Jesus' glorification, and the revelation of the Father's glory.

The first episode contains two narratives. The first is explicitly called a sign, but the second is implicitly one. Considered separately, as events from the ministry, these stories bristle with problems. The story of the water changed to wine is a celebrated stumbling stone. Would Jesus have acted in this way? The story of the cleansing of the temple raises other historical problems. It is as difficult to believe that Jesus would have prejudiced the authorities against himself at the beginning of the ministry as that he cleansed the temple twice. But the Evangelist's special interests often render profitless and distracting a concentration upon such matters. If the grouping of stories epitomized some central and abiding truth about the ministry, it mattered not to John that they were uprooted from their setting in life. If by altering the detail of some traditional story its implicit meaning was rendered clearer, can one properly speak of John's version as "fictional," as "a falsification of history"? One passage in the Fourth Gospel reveals how the mind of the Evangelist worked in selecting and reporting incidents from the ministry: the received traditions had been illumined by the testimony of the apostolic Church and the interpreting spirit of God.[57] None of the evangelists was interested in reporting bare facts concerning Jesus, but John's interest in the significance of Jesus' acts was more intense and sustained than that of the others. At every point he sought to grasp the Spirit-filled meaning of the facts relating to Christ so that his readers might have "life in his name."

A general observation can be made concerning John's predominant interest in the miracle tradition of the gospel. Each "sign," as the first makes quite explicit, manifests the glory of Jesus. One scholar has rightly observed that John's concern is "everywhere apparent that Christ himself may not be overshadowed by anything . . . Jesus alone is the true divine gift to which all other gifts can and should only point . . . Johannine criticism of miracles begins and ends where Jesus himself is sought, or forgotten, *for the sake of his gifts.*"[58]

Assuming that John's Christian readers may have had diverse origins, what possible range of meanings would the "signs" at Cana and in the temple signify? In the Dionysiac "mystery" it was claimed that the god Dionysus transformed water to wine.[59] Certain Hellenistic authors had "spiritualized" this pagan mythology. Wine signified divine inspiration, a *living* water bestowing life and truth.[60] Perhaps John's story proclaimed that only Jesus could truly give this benefaction. Humanity's quest for a life-giving draught, for a blissful immortality, could not be satisfied through mythical ritual or mystical ecstasy but only by believing in Jesus, the crucified and risen Son of God. A reader of Jewish background could hardly fail to see in the water that was transformed by Christ a symbol of the religion of ceremony and law.[61] By contrast, the wine provided by the Son of god symbolized the religion of the Spirit, the glad fulfillment of eschatological expectations. Christians familiar with the teachings of Jesus set forth in several similes preserved in the synoptic tradition, would also see the story as an acted parable: The gospel is the new wine, which "the friends of the bridegroom" receive with incomparable joy.[62]

The work begun in Galilee was completed in Jerusalem. Like Luke, John seems to have epitomized the rejection of Jesus by bringing forward an incident from the ministry. The story of the cleansing of the temple complements the sign at Cana: Christ not only perfected Judaism by transforming the old into something new, his coming resulted in judgment upon the old. The glory of God appeared in the temple to pass judgment upon its cultus and to render it obsolete. "He came to his own home, and his own people received him not."[63]

The first episode is further developed by means of two discourses. Throughout the Book of the Signs the Evangelist interprets traditional stories and sayings of Jesus by means of discourses. The dialogue of chapter 3, which passes into a monologue, emphasizes the necessity of regeneration. In chapter 4, narrative and discourse affirm that the new life, which belief in Christ produces, is a continuing experience since it is eternal.

In the hope of Israel and the early Church, the transformation of human nature was associated with "the new heavens and the new earth." The early Christians were of the belief that persons could enter now into the experience of that eschatological life, through faith in Christ and through the power of the Holy Spirit. The Age to Come had supervened upon the present age. The apocalyptic imagery was more or less adequate to express this paradoxical idea. In the Fourth Gospel both present and future aspects are retained, but it is clear from Chapter 3 onward where the Evangelist has placed the emphasis. "The hour is coming and *now is*."[64] Belief in Jesus Christ as the Son of God in the present was inseparably connected with the final transformation of human nature. The hope, which was even now being realized, anticipated an ultimate fulfillment. Conversely, a rejection of Christ brought one's present life under God's final judgment.

In offering his interpretation of the *kerygma*, John employed concepts familiar to Christians drawn from backgrounds other than Palestinian Judaism, although he may have assumed this origin for most of his readers. The term *the kingdom of God* was not the most familiar expression of Israel's hope, and the idea that a person must "be born again [or from above]" in order to have "eternal life" was a popular conception. The problem of Nicodemus was common to all whose thought was influenced by Hellenistic dualisms: "How can this be?" How can any person, a prisoner of the lower world ("that which is born of flesh is flesh"), enter the world of light and life ("that which is born of spirit is spirit")?[65] We have observed that many religions and philosophies of the Graeco-Roman world (not all of which can be considered Gnostic) sought to overcome, or at least to bridge, this radical dualism and to give to persons assurance of their eternal life. Like many persons, John believed that human beings were the children of God, potentially the inheritors of eternal life, and that eternal life must be received as a gift of God. Only through some revealer of God did a person receive the power to become a child of God. But contrary to popular belief, John affirmed that a person could not fan to flame the sparks of divinity within through participation in some "mystery" or through mystical self-transcendence. "Unless one is born of water and the Spirit he cannot enter the kingdom of God."[66]

The phrase just cited probably referred to Christian baptism, the sacrament of belief in "the name of Christ." The "appendix" to this discourse supports this assumption.[67] The Christian sacraments are not explicitly described in the Fourth Gospel; Jesus does not institute them. But baptism is presupposed in chapter 3, as is the Eucharist in chapters 6 and 15, and the sacraments possibly appear as subordinate themes elsewhere. Various reasons have been given for John's failure to deal explicitly with the sacraments of the Church.[68] In any case, he was less interested in the Church's acts of worship than in the Person and the deed giving them meaning. The acts themselves did not mediate "heavenly things"; only the one who had "descended from heaven" could do this.[69]

It is not possible within the limits of this chapter to comment upon the entire sequence of episodes in the Book of the Signs, or to do justice to the progress of the Evangelist's thought throughout. Only two other episodes will be considered, the second and the sixth.

> B. 2. Second episode—the life-giving word, 4:46–5:47: the second sign at Cana (4:46–54); the healing at Bethzatha Pool (5:1–9); discourse on Christ's power to give life and to judge (5:10–47)
>
> 3. Third episode—the bread of life, 6:1–71: the feeding of the five thousand (6:1–15); Jesus comes to the disciples on the sea (6:16–21); conversation concerning the true bread (6:22–59); appendix (6:60–71)
>
> 4. Fourth episode—light and life, 7:1–8:59: introduction (7:1–10); conversations during the feast of tabernacles (7:11–8:59)
>
> 5. Fifth episode—judgment by light, 9:1–10:42: the healing of the man born blind (9:1–7); a trial scene (9:8–34); a dialogue passing into the discourse on the shepherd and the flock (9:35–10:21); appendix (10:22–42)
>
> 6. Sixth episode—the victory of life over death, 11:1–54: the raising of Lazarus from the dead (11:1–44); appendix (11:45–54)
>
> 7. Seventh episode—life through death, the meaning of the cross, 11:55–12:50: the anointment at Bethany (11:55–12:11); the triumphal entry (12:12–19); the approach of the Greeks (12:20–26); judgment by the word (12:27–50)*

*With chapter 5 the Evangelist "transfers Jesus' words and signs to the public domain." The revelatory discourses become disputes with unbelief. The most impressive of the signs—the healing of the man born blind, and the raising of Lazarus—are the culmination of Jesus' revelation to the world: Jesus is hailed as the light and the life, the fundamental concepts announced in the Prologue. (Schnackenburg, *The Gospel According to John*, Vol. 2, pp. 1–3; see also Culpepper's attention to plot development, *Anatomy of the Fourth Gospel*, pp. 86–94).

The discourse that follows Jesus' healing of the official's son and the sick man at Bethzatha Pool turns upon the basic question of Jesus' authority (B:2.). His violations of the Sabbath are not the matter discussed, but the real issue underlying such actions. In them, it was said, Jesus made himself "equal with God."[70]

The Evangelist affirmed that the continuity and unity of action between the Father and the Son resulted from the latter's humble submission to the Father's will. Jesus exercised no independence of judgment; he was at all times subservient to the one "who sent him."[71] Yet because of this complete dependence, the Father committed to the Son divine prerogatives: the authority to bestow life and to judge. As one who exercised these divine powers, Jesus deserves the highest honors that persons could bestow upon him. Thus to refuse to honor the Son is to dishonor the Father.

The discourse deals also with the witnesses to Jesus' authority.[72] The Son did not bear witness to himself. The father bore witness to the Son in ways that He Himself had appointed: John the Baptist had been sent to bear witness to Jesus; the works done by Jesus in the Father's name bore him witness; the scriptures, rightly understood, testified to his authority.

In the conclusion of this discourse the blindness of unbelief is attributed to estrangement from God.[73] The way of faith was denied those who did not have the word *(logos)* within, or "the love of God within," or who did not seek His glory. As the scriptures testified, Israel was called to be "the son of God," to live the life of obedient trust in God as Father. This life Jesus lived. Therefore, John proclaimed, he was "the Son of God."

It can be concluded that the Evangelist asserted his faith in the equality of the Father and the Son in the strongest possible way. Yet he insisted that Jesus exercised divine functions *because* there had been in him a deliberate purpose to subordinate his will to God.[74] This subordination was so complete and perfect that there existed between the Father and the Son, throughout the latter's ministry, a unity of purpose and action. For men to see Jesus thus was to see the Father.[75] Other men may be called "the children of God"; there has been only one Son.[76]

No discourse is appended to the narrative in the sixth episode of the Book of the Signs (B:6). Instead, every feature of the story is weighted with meaning. Whatever the form of the tradition underlying it, the entire episode was rewritten by the evangelist to epitomize the theological significance of the ministry. The true meaning passed beyond the miracle itself and arose out of the event toward which it pointed—the death and resurrection of Jesus.[77] But the miracle was related also to an event that, for the reader, remained an outstanding promise: "He who believes in me, though he die, yet shall he live."[78] It is noteworthy that in the appendix to this episode the Jewish Council assembled to lay plans for putting Jesus to death. Here, as elsewhere, John taught that the sacrifice of Jesus' life made possible a resurrection.

The proclamation that Jesus is the giver of life moves along two planes in the Lazarus episode. The miracle anticipated the final resurrection of the dead from their graves. The story was thus a sign of that resurrection through which believers pass from physical existence into life that is eternal. But the narrative also laid stress upon the faith that Jesus possessed the power to make alive *before* the last day. Several commentators have noticed the correspondence between the word of Christ in John 5:28 and his action in the raising of Lazarus:

Those who are in the tombs . . .   He found Lazarus in the tomb (11:17, 38)
will hear his voice . . .   he cried with a loud voice (11:43)
and come out (5:28)   the dead man came out . . . (11:44)

One writer has concluded that the evangelist "has taken an event associated with the 'last day,' and transplanted it into the historic ministry of Jesus, thus making it a 'sign' of the life-giving which that ministry (when consummated) brought into effect."[79] To the Evangelist was it no less a miracle that believers in Jesus Christ "*have passed* from death to life" than that the body of a dead man should have been revivified? If, upon the testimony of the Gospel and the Church, the possibility of this new birth seemed fanciful, would people become convinced "if someone should rise from the dead"?[80]

John's Book of the Passion-Resurrection does not begin with the betrayal and arrest of Jesus, but with "farewell discourses." Chapter 12 marks the end of the public ministry and the beginning of the Passion. Instead of appending discourses to single incidents, as in the preceding section, the Evangelist interpreted the whole story beforehand. He therefore allowed the moving drama of the last week of Jesus' life to make maximum impact upon his readers.[81] Yet in composing this testament of Jesus, the Evangelist was prompted by historical as well as theological considerations. According to the earlier Gospels, Jesus devoted himself to death on the evening before his trials and crucifixion.

    C. The Book of the Passion–Resurrection, 13:1–20:31
        1. The farewell discourses, 13:1–17:26: washing the disciples' feet; the be-
           trayal foretold (13:1–30); dialogue on Christ's departure and return (13:31–
           14:31); discourse on Christ and his Church (15:1–16:33); the prayer of
           Christ (17:1–26)
        2. The passion narrative, 18:1–19:42: the arrest (18:1–11); trial before the
           high priest, Peter's denial (18:12–27); the examination before Pilate (18:28–
           19:16); the crucifixion (19:17–30); the burial (19:31–42)
        3. The resurrection narrative, 20:1–31: the finding of the empty tomb (20:1–
           10); the appearance of Jesus to Mary (20:11–18); the appearance to the
           disciples without Thomas (20:19–25); the appearance to the disciples with
           Thomas (20:26–29); the purpose of the Gospel (20:30f.)
    D. Conclusion, 21:1–25
        1. The appearance beside the Sea of Tiberius, (21:1–23)
        2. A testimonial, (21:24f.)]

    In the dialogue with Nicodemus it was proclaimed that the love of God prompted the gift of Christ to the world. It is noteworthy that after John described the manner in which this gift was given and received, he returned to the theme of divine condescension. The love of the Son for the Father led him to "lay down his life"; the Father loved the Son because of his willing and perfect obedience. It is now proclaimed that the object of this mutual love of the Father and the Son was the revelation of the divine love.[82] The farewell discourses range over many subjects, but there is one dominant note throughout, which is concisely stated in the words: "As the Father has loved me, so have I loved you; abide in my love."[83]

    In becoming the objects of divine love, the disciples of Jesus were bound together into a community with a mission to the world. They were governed by a new commandment. By this shall people know the disciples of Jesus, that they "love one another." The distinguishing mark of the new life into which persons were brought by virtue of Christ's death and resurrection was a love for the world that continued in the disciples, after the example of their "Teacher and Lord."[84]

    It is probable that John 13:31 to 14:31 forms a unity. The dialogue throughout is concerned with the "going" and "coming" of Jesus, his departure from the disciples and his return. According to some scholars, the Evangelist employed the traditional hope of Christ's (second) coming as the point of departure for a radical reinterpretation of the Gospel. John taught that Christ's death on the cross *was* his ascent to the Father (corresponding to the image of the heavenly session at God's right hand), and his return to his disciples after death (closely associated, if not identified, with the coming of the Holy Spirit) *was* the second advent.[85] Yet it is more probable that the difference between the eschatology of the Synoptic Gospels and of the Fourth Gospel is to be explained as a difference of emphasis, not of substance. Jesus not only promised his disciples that he would go to prepare a place for them, but also that he would come again to receive them unto himself. This is not the same as his abiding presence.[86]

    The conclusion of chapter 14 reads like a conclusion to "the farewell discourses." For this reason some interpreters have considered that these verses have been displaced. Others note the parallelism between sections 13:31 to 14:31 and chapters 15 to 17 and conjecture that alternate versions of the same discourse have been juxtaposed at some stage in the Gospel's composition. But 14:31 may possibly emphasize Jesus' acceptance of his destiny. He went forth to meet the adversary, not because he could not do otherwise, but because his love for the Father and for his own people led him to "do as the Father commanded." There is no movement to another place, but perhaps a change in temporal perspective is suggested.[87] The next discourse concerns Christ and his Church more than the previous one. The theological situation is focused more clearly beyond the cross, although the setting is still the eve of the crucifixion.

The passages in chapters 14 to 16 that tell of the coming of the *Paraclete* merit close attention. It is difficult to translate this Greek term in the contexts in which John used it.[88] The *Paraclete* will be a *witness* in Jesus' defense, and a *spokesman* for him, continuing Jesus' "suit" with the world. The basic passive form *paraclētos* means "one who is called alongside to help."[89] The *Paraclete* is also to be a *consoler* of the disciples in Jesus' absence. Moreover, he is to be their teacher and guide.

Different interpretations have been given of the relation of the *Paraclete* to Jesus, on the one hand, and to the Holy Spirit on the other. In 14:26, Jesus speaks of sending "another *Paraclete*." The close parallelism between the work of Jesus and the work of the *Paraclete,* and their corresponding relations to the disciples and the world, suggests that for John, Jesus continues his presence and ministry as the *Paraclete* in those who love him and keep his commandments. But as a spiritual presence, invisible to the world, witnessing against it in and through the disciples' witness, the *Paraclete* is "the Spirit of Truth" or "Holy Spirit."[90] In the teaching of the Evangelist, Jesus' promised coming is therefore partially fulfilled in the sending of the Spirit/*Paraclete*. By such means, Jesus "abides" with his own who are in the world, while yet present with the Father. The presence of Jesus with his disciples is not a substitute for or in opposition to the final coming of Jesus. But, as has been shown, a greater emphasis is placed upon the former in the Fourth Gospel.

The prayer of Christ in chapter 17 stands as more than a summary of the teaching of the Gospel, more than a discourse on the mission of the Church obedient to its Lord. This prayer represents the movement of Christ toward God, an equivalent of the narrative of the ascension in Luke-Acts. In the Gospel, it is the most impressive statement that the death of Jesus became the means whereby God's glory was manifested.

The prayer discloses five divisions. In the first, Jesus prayed that the hour that had come (the hour of his death) might be the means of God's glorification; of bringing eternal life unto his own; of reuniting the Son with the Father. The delegated work had been accomplished.[91] In the second division, the ministry of Jesus and its results (as set forth in John) are briefly summarized.[92] In the third division, Christ prayed for his disciples. He foresaw their situation in the Church after his departure and interceded in their behalf.[93] In the fourth division, Christ's prayer expressed his concern for all those persons who were to believe in him through the apostles' testimony. He prayed for their unity as a means of bringing to the world faith, and an experience of the love of God.[94] And last, Christ prayed for a final union of believers with himself in the presence of the divine glory.[95]

Much interest has rightly centered upon Christ's prayer for the Church. The following ideas are expressed: It is the glory of the Church that it should express in its fellowship a token of that love which unites the Father and the Son; not until the Church becomes "perfectly one" can the world know God's purpose of love in sending the Son. The triumph of the Church's mission in the world goes hand in hand with the perfecting of the unity of the Church.[96]

The kingship of Christ is a central aspect of the story of the passion in the Fourth Gospel.[97] Jesus went to his cross just as a king ascends to his throne. There is a characteristic irony in the emphasis of this Gospel that Jesus was "the King of Israel," since "the Jews" would have none of him. Yet the scene in Pilate's court makes it evident that Jesus' kingship could not be interpreted along national or merely this-worldly lines. His sovereignty lay in his witness to the truth. The allegiance that he claimed was that of obedience to truth.[98]

The evangelist emphasized that the death of Christ was a voluntary act. When the soldiers came, he gave himself up; when death approached, the initiative again was taken by Jesus.[99] He defended himself when falsely accused. But it is probable also that the Evangelist, like Luke, wished to stress Jesus' innocence.[100] One notices that in the action taken against Jesus, the Romans were involved from the beginning. Perhaps John sought in this way to emphasize that the whole "world" was aligned against him.

The word of Jesus from the cross, "I thirst," is reported as the fulfillment of scripture. One of several passages from "the Righteous Sufferer Psalms" have been suggested, but perhaps like other witnesses in the New Testament, the Fourth Evangelist perceived that the whole of the scriptures testified to a suffering Messiah.[101] The cry of Jesus may be understood as his thirst to drink to its last bitter drop "the cup which the father has given [him]." John knows no cry of derelicton from the cross, as reported by Mark: Jesus, always having the Father with him, was never alone.[102]

One interpreter of the Gospel, who rightly stresses its theme of the glory of Jesus, comments that one is tempted to regard John's story of the Passion "as being a mere postscript which had to be included because John could not ignore this tradition, nor could he fit it organically into his work."[103] On the contrary, the present writer agrees with another, who writes "that the Passion narrative and Resurrection come last in John because they are the climax of his thought, as they are the climax of the ministry of Jesus. The death of Jesus was the hour of glorification, when all the signs of his life were sealed by death, the ultimately real sign. It was the natural culmination of [Jesus'] work. The meaning of the cross and resurrection set forth *spiritually* in chapters 14–17 has validity only because Jesus did *actually* die and rise again."[104]

One of the most striking features of John's Easter Story is his report that Christ's ascension and gift of the Holy Spirit were the immediate sequel to the cross. Once again we see the Evangelist's lack of interest in temporal connections. His concern was that events not be separated that derive their meaning from Jesus' acts of self-oblation. It should be noticed also that the shepherd who lay down his life for the sheep was not long separated from his flock. Christ did not leave desolate his own.[105] From the day of his victory he gave to them, as he promised, the Holy Spirit that he might abide with them forever.[106]

Notice how pervasively there is woven into the narratives of the appearances of the risen Christ the motif of "seeing and believing." There is no depreciation of the eyewitness testimony, as the emphasis upon the "many signs" makes clear. It was no less important for John that Jesus really died and was raised from the dead as that the "word became flesh." Accordingly, the Evangelist emphasized the testimony of Peter, "the disciple whom Jesus loved," Mary Magdalene, the other disciples, and Thomas. Yet in the stories of Mary and Thomas, John claimed that the privilege of sight was not all-important. There was, after all, a relative value to the postresurrection "appearances," for those who witnessed them as for those who did not and cannot. Evidence of the risen Christ must be received and appropriated by faith, not simply observed.

Unquestionably the Evangelist believed that the first witnesses stood in a unique, unrepeatable position. It was of crucial importance that their words be true. Nevertheless, through their faith the successors of the apostles were united with the eyewitnesses: "We have beheld his glory. . . . Blessed are those who have not seen and yet believe."[107]

There were no days of anxious waiting for the disciples, no long separation from their Lord. But Mary was not permitted to cling to her departed "Master," to cling to the Jesus of the past. Thomas was invited to lay hold of the risen Christ. It was no longer the Word become "flesh" before whom Thomas bowed in adoration. It was the Son, existing in unity with the Father, now "with God," or simply, God.

THE THREE LETTERS OF JOHN

It is highly probable that 1, 2, and 3 John have a common authorship and presuppose similar circumstances.[108] While some scholars are of the opinion that the author of the letters, at least of 1 John, was the Fourth Evangelist, "the Elder" is more likely to have been another member of the Johannine community who wrote his letters after the traditions preserved in the Gospel of John had become the established norm of the community's beliefs, ca. 100–110 C.E.[109]

From 1 and 2 John one learns that a major schism had recently taken place, which had resulted in the secession of some Johannine Christians.[110] It seems quite plausible that the schism was the consequence of opposing interpretations of the Gospel, its doctrinal and ethical norms. The author of the letters contends for his own interpretations and those of his adherents and writes to warn against the erroneous teaching and moral indifference of the secessionists.

Although one can place the three letters after the major schism within the Johannine community, one cannot be certain of the situation of each in the subsequent course of events. Because the contents of 1 and 2 John are mutually illuminating, they should be read together. But first a few notes concerning 3 John.

AN OUTLINE OF THE THIRD LETTER OF JOHN

A. Introduction, 1–4
   1. Prescript and greeting, 1–2
   2. Expression of joy upon hearing the good report concerning Gaius, 3–4
B. Commendations, 5–8
   1. Of Gaius, for his "service to the brethren," 5–6
   2. Of the deserving brethren, 7–8
C. The Insubordination of Diotrephes, 9–12
   1. The offenses of Diotrephes are described, 9–10
   2. Counsel to imitate the good; a test of a godly man, 11–12
D. Conclusion, 13–15
   1. Reasons for brevity, 13–14
   2. Greetings, 15

The epistolary author identifies himself here and in the prescript of 2 John as "the Elder." In view of the positions he assumes and the probable meaning of this designation in Christian sources of the period, "the Elder" *(presbyteros)* identified one of that dwindling number of second-generation leaders who were disciples of the disciples of Jesus. In his own estimation, and that of his adherents, "the Elder" was a principal intermediary for the tradition about Jesus that came down from the Beloved Disciple of the Fourth Gospel.[111]

The occasion for this brief letter is the Elder's wish to thank Gaius (otherwise unknown) for the hospitality he has shown—and, hopefully, will continue to show—to the "brothers," missionaries from the main Johannine community who in the course of their travels sometimes sought lodging in outlying house-churches. The Elder also wishes Gaius to know of the rebuffs that he and his emissaries have received from a certain Diotrephes who has attained a position of preeminence in another house-church over which he presides. Not only is Diotrephes attacking the Elder's person, but "he refuses himself to welcome the brethren, and also stops those who want to welcome them and puts them out of the church."

The Elder does not directly accuse Diotrephes of erroneous teachings. He attributed his insubordination to personal ambition. Perhaps Diotrephes is to be regarded as a forerunner of the presiding bishop whose office is recognized in the letters of Ignatius, or as "the kind of upstart whose ambition made the emergence of the Ignatian bishop inevitable."[112] But can one surmise that the cause for the altercation ran deeper? Both the extreme measures taken by Diotrephes and the tenor of the Elder's rebuke suggest that something more than personal rivalry led to the rift. Did sharp doctrinal differences exist between the two concerning the gospel?[113] Perhaps 2 John can provide clues for an answer.

AN OUTLINE OF THE SECOND LETTER OF JOHN

A. Introduction, 1–3
   1. Prescript, 1
   2. Addressee; greeting, 2f.
B. A Summons to Follow the Truth, 4–6
   1. An expression of joy that some are following the truth, 4

        2. An appeal for loyal compliance, 5–6
    C. The Deceivers and Instruction Concerning Them, 7–11
        1. The deceiver's Christology, 7
        2. Warning against defection, 8
        3. The essential "teaching of Christ," 9
        4. No hospitality for the deceivers, 10–11
    D. Conclusion, 12–13
        1. Reasons for brevity, 12
        2. Greeting, 13

The letter before us was written by "the Elder" (very likely the same person who wrote 3 John) to a house-church warning its members against the dangerous influence of persons who had recently seceded from the main Johannine community, thereby revealing their radical departure from "the teaching of Christ." Apparently the church addressed as "the Elect (Lady) and her children" was an offshoot of the church of the Elder and of his adherents.[114] The Elder's love for the recipients of his letter is grounded in a common confession of the truth that Jesus is the Christ, the Son of God (A:2). He acknowledges that some of the children of the Elect Lady are "walking in truth" (living according to the love commandment of Jesus), but that the attitude of the secessionists poses a serious threat. Their error is that "the way one lives is of little salvific importance and that one need not show love for one's former Johannine 'brothers'."[115]

With verse 7 the Elder warns that the secessionists were spreading a serious doctrinal error: they "do not confess Jesus Christ coming in the flesh" (C:1). A similar charge is made in 1 John 4:2, where the context is more illuminating. Suffice it here to note that the Elder's adversaries were assigning a relatively slight significance to Jesus' earthly ministry, his passion and death. The letter implies that the trouble-makers had not yet reached the letter's recipients, but they had "gone out into the world" to proclaim their 'progressive' views."[116] These missionaries must not be given hospitality should they come (C:4), for they are the embodiment of the Antichrist (a Johannine figure expressing the apocalyptic diabolical opposition to Christ).[117] Grounded in the teaching of Christ, bound together in mutual love, the true children of God possess both the Father and the Son, and if they exercise due care will not lose their reward (in the Day of Christ?).

INTERPRETING 1 JOHN

The vocabulary, style, and the theological and practical concerns of the three Johannine epistles favor their ascription to a single author. The fact that the self-designation, "the Elder," is missing from 1 John may be explained by noting the absence of a prescript (and other features of a letter). Moreover, the writing was probably intended for members of the author's own community, rendering a formal introduction inappropriate. Since 1 John cannot aptly be described as a letter, to what literary genre does it belong? One interesting theory is that the writing is patterned upon the Gospel of John. Brown hypothesizes that "the peculiar format of 1 John may have been influenced by the author's attempt to refute the secessionists by commenting on the Gospel of John to which they also appealed as a justification for their views." His exposition of the Johannine gospel traditions would be directed to those persons in the community "still in communion with him, in order to strengthen them and to prevent them from being confused by the plausible presentation of the Gospel of John proclaimed by the adversaries."[118]

The reader of 1 John may wonder if the author was guided by any plan in its composition. The metaphor of the spiral has been suggested.[119] In the course of developing a theme the author sometimes brings one back to the starting point; almost, but not quite, for there is a slight shift that provides a transition to a fresh theme or to an old theme taken up again from a slightly different angle. Scholars have posited two, three, or seven main divisions of 1 John.[120] The suggested outline that follows calls attention to two major tests of "the truth"—the one, doctrinal, the other, ethical—that are the foci of the author's concerns.[121]

A. Prologue, 1:1–4
   1. Testimony to the gospel, 1:1–2
   2. A statement of purpose, 1:3–4
B. Fellowship with God: The Test of Behavior, 1:5–2:17
   1. Those who walk in the light (having fellowship with God who is light) live according to the truth and are cleansed from all sin, 1:5–7
   2. Those who are free from sin are those who confess sin, relying on him who is the expiation for sins, 1:8–2:2
   3. Only those who keep God's commandments know him, 2:3–5
   4. Only those who walk as Christ walked and who love their "brothers," abide in the light, 2:6–11
   5. The conquest of the Evil One and of the world, 2:12–17
C. Fellowship with God: The Confessional Test, 2:18–27
   1. The appearance of "many antichrists" signifies the arrrival of "the last hour," 2:18
   2. The secession of Johannine Christians, 2:19–21
   3. Their denial that *Jesus* is the Christ is tantamount to a denial of the Father, 2:22–25
   4. The assurances of those who have been anointed and who know the truth, 2:26f.

As in the Gospel of John, so in 1 John, a prologue establishes a conceptual frame for the writer's defense of the gospel. The epistolary author's use of the first person plural reveals his claim to testify to a tradition grounded in the sensory experiences of disciples who encountered Jesus historically (A:1, 2). Therefore those who have withdrawn from the Johannine community are not only rejecting the Elder's testimony but the witness of those to whom Jesus had revealed himself "from the beginning" of his ministry. Conversely, those who accept this gospel as imparting eternal life have communion with the Father and the Son, as well as with one another.

The writer's testimony to the "gospel" of God as light (B:1) may have been intended to correct the secessionist's claim that since light has come into the world (John 1:4f., 9) God is known by those who come to the light (John 3:19f.). For our author the entire ministry of the earthly Jesus manifested the light of life, revealing the Father (John 1:18, 8:12; 12:35, 46). This light continues to shine in the belief and behavior of the true followers of Jesus.

Three boasts of the Elder's adversaries are next sharply rejected (B:2, 3). While appealing to his own "children" ("if *we* say that . . ."), he is opposing secessionist's errors in claiming a special knowledge and love of God that frees them from sin and guilt. Their indifference concerning morality, coupled with a hatred of their "brothers," invalidated the secessionist's claim to know God, to abide in him, and to live in his light.

The Elder's urging that his adherents have no love for the world (B:5) seems to echo John 17:15f. Ironically the secessionists were repudiating this Johannine testimony: in "going out to the world" they revealed that they "belonged" to it,[122] and in turning their backs on Jesus' "own" they disobeyed his command to "love one another."[123]

In 1 John 2:19 the writer directly refers to the major schism in the Johannine community that occasioned his letters (C:2). In describing the action of the secessionists he insists that they are alone to blame and that their willful defection marked the arrival of the End. This imminent event makes all the more urgent the determination of a true Christological confession.

What light is now shed upon the nature of the controversy that had resulted in the secession (C:3)? Doubtless all members of the Johannine community confessed that "Jesus is the Christ, the Son of God" (John 20:30f.). The issue seems to have turned on the meaning of the subject "Jesus." For the Elder and his adherents the confession that *Jesus* was the Christ implied that his humanity and the way he lived ("walked") were essential for understanding his salvific work. For the secessionists, Christ, the Son of God, was the divine, pre-existent *Logos* whose coming into the world enlightened humankind; the career and death of Jesus were a nonessential aftermath, possessing relatively little import. To the Elder, the secessionist's failure to appreciate the importance of Jesus' exemplary life was a principal cause of their moral indifference. But more disastrous was their failure to appreciate the significance of Jesus' death on the cross (his blood).[124] Not through the incarnation alone, but through the crucifixion, one becomes a child of God.[125]

In the light of the above one can better understand the confessional test stated in 2 John 7 and later in this letter:

> Everyone who confesses Jesus Christ *come in the flesh* reflects the Spirit which belongs to God, while everyone who negates the importance of *Jesus* reflects a Spirit which does not belong to God. (1 John 4:2f.)[126]

In the present context (C:4) the Elder reassures his readers that since they were anointed by the Spirit when they first confessed Jesus, the same Spirit should keep them faithful to the true Christology in the face of the great apostasy and deceit of their former "brothers."

The remainder of the text of 1 John is a further development and application of the two tests thus far enunciated: the ethical and the Christological. There is much repetition as the Elder drives home his vigorous polemic against the secessionists, and seeks to reinforce the loyalty of his adherents during a crisis which, he believes, is "the last hour." The present reader is encouraged to follow to its conclusion the spiralling discourse of the author. It is hoped that the outline that follows can be an aid to that end. In conclusion there will be a brief discussion of the question: Does the description in 1 and 2 John of the secessionist views correspond to any "heresy" known to exist during the time and in the region in which the Johannine community flourished? Considerable interest focuses upon this subject in attempts to reconstruct the development of Christian theology and polity coincident with and shortly after the latest New Testament witnesses.

    D. A Reapplication of the Two Tests and Their Corollaries, 2:28–3:24
        1. The behavior of the children of God in view of Christ's [second] coming, 2:28–3:3
        2. The children of God, and of the devil; the tests of doing justly or doing iniquity, 3:4–10
        3. Abiding in death or in eternal life; the tests of hatred and love, 3:11–18
        4. A test of confidence before God, 3:19–22
        5. Summary: the two basic tests restated; the assurance of the Spirit, 3:23f.
    E. Testing the Spirits, of Truth and of Deceit, 4:1–6
        1. The Spirit of God prompts the confession of Jesus Christ come in the flesh, 4:1f.
        2. False prophets manifest the spirit of the Antichrist, 4:3 (1)
        3. The test revealing those who belong to the world, or to God, 4:4–6
    F. The Interrelation of the Tests of Behavior and Confession; the Assurances of the Children of God, 4:7–5:13
        1. The command to love is based on the revelation of love, 4:7–12
        2. The assurance of the Spirit is voiced in the confession that *Jesus* is the Son of God, 4:13–16
        3. Assurance concerning the Day of judgment: love casts out fear, 4:17f.
        4. Summary: the test for faith's reality—love of the brothers, 4:19–5:4a
        5. Faith's conquest of the world: the belief that Jesus is the Son of God who came in water and in blood; the witness of the Spirit is the testimony of God, 5:4b–12
    G. Conclusion, 5:13–21
        1. Statement of purpose, 5:13
        2. Reassurances concerning petition and intercession, 5:14–17
        3. Some Christian certainties, 5:18–20
        4. A postscript, 5:21

In conclusion, brief note will be taken of the opinions of scholars that the secessionists of 1 and 2 John were probably the "docetic" opponents of Ignatius or followers of Cerinthus or of other, better known second-century Gnostics.

Ignatius of Antioch was almost a contemporary of the Johannine writers. In letters to the Trallians and the Smyrnaeans, Ignatius contends that Jesus was truly born of a virgin, baptized by John, truly made to suffer, and was truly present after the resurrection.[127] This insistence was directed against some persons who said that Jesus only *seemed* to experience such things for, Ignatius wrote, "they do not confess that Christ was clothed in the flesh," and "they do not believe in the blood of Christ."[128] These opponents of Ignatius are called *docetists,* a term derived from the Greek verb "to seem." Their disdain for the humanity of Jesus was accompanied with a disregard of the need in the churches.[129]

It is claimed by some scholars that we "can be sure that the [secessionist's] denial that Jesus has come in the flesh was a form of the Docetic heresy, which is so strongly denounced in the letters of Ignatius."[130] The Elder's exposé of the secessionist's Christology does not attribute to them, however, a denial of the reality of the incarnation nor imply "that Christ had adopted only the outward appearance of human form."[131] Rather he criticized their failure to appreciate the essential salvific values of "the flesh" of Jesus and his bloody death. The identification of the adversaries of the Elder and of Ignatius seems unjustified, yet it is plausible that the secessionists moved in the direction of a docetic Christology.

Among the early Gnostics there was one, Cerinthus, who is reported to have been active in Asia Minor at the close of the first century. Some scholars claim that the teachings of Cerinthus (which are somewhat obscure) show "certain points of similarity with that which is attacked in 1 John." According to Irenaeus, Cerinthus taught that Jesus was merely human "and that after his baptism there descended into him from the Supreme Power Christ in the form of a dove, and that he proclaimed the unknown Father and performed miracles, but that finally Christ withdrew again from Jesus, so that it was Jesus who suffered and rose again, while Christ remained impassible, being pure spirit."[132] Cerinthus "denied that the human Jesus could in any real way be identified with the divine Christ."

Again, identification is unlikely, yet "one may surmise at least that 1 John 5:6 was attacking a Christological dualism which posited only a partial union between the divine and the human in Jesus Christ—a dualism less developed than that attributed to Cerinthus."[133]

Former advocates of a late dating for 1 and 2 John sought to relate the secessionist's teaching to better known, late second-century Gnostics, for example, to the followers of Basilides. Evidence for an earlier dating of the Johannine letters has not persuaded some scholars that the Elder's adversaries were not Gnostics: "an aberrant Christianity, which teaches salvation by esoteric knowledge, excites an enthusiasm devoid of moral concern, and nourishes a spirituality contemptuous of all things material, can be identified unmistakably as an early form of the movement which came to be known as Gnosis or Gnosticism."[134] Research on the Nag Hammadi documents has kept the question open. Perhaps some of the tenets of the secessionists would have been congenial to those who later composed these Gnostic texts; indeed, some of the converts of the Johannine adversaries may have eventually become Gnostics.[135]

In the Elder's time the "progressive" teachings of his adversaries seemed to be gaining an advantage, but his day was to come. By providing an anti-Gnostic interpretation of the Gospel of John he contributed to its canonization, helping to overcome the view of some that this Gospel supported a Gnostic version of the Christian faith.

NOTES

1. The Muratorian canon (Rome); Theophilus of Antioch; Polycrates of Ephesus (ca. 190 C.E.); Irenaeus, bishop of Lyon (178 to ca. 202), the "preeminent witness to the tradition of Asia Minor"; slightly later, Clement of Alexandria.
2. Copies of the Gospel were in existence at the beginning of the second century; C. H. Roberts, *An Unpublished Fragment of the Fourth Gospel in the John Rylands Library* (1935). P52, or Rylands Papyrus 457.

3. For a critical review of the texts disclosing the Early Tradition, see E. Haenchen, *A Commentary on the Gospel of John* (1984), Vol. 1, pp. 6–19; R. Schnackenburg, *The Gospel According to John* (1980), Vol. 1, pp. 77–86. Cf. Kümmel, *INT*², pp. 239–246.

4. Irenaeus *Adv. Haer.* III. II. 9.

5. "In the beginning was the *Logos*," John 1:1. Epiphanius *Panarion haer.* LI. 2f.

6. Eusebius *H.E.* VI. 17.7

7. 20:2–10; 1:37–40, 18:15f.; 19:35. For recent attempts to situate John the Apostle in the tradition history of the Fourth Gospel, see Schnackenburg, *Gospel According to John*, pp. 383–387; also R. E. Brown, *The Gospel According to John*, 3(1982), *AB*, V. 29, pp. xcii–xcviii, who, in a more recent study, changes his mind, *The Community of the Beloved Disciple* (1979), pp. 31ff. Cf. Kümmel, *INT*², pp. 234–239.

8. For discussions concerning the language of the Fourth Gospel, see Haenchen, *Commentary on John*, Vol. 1, pp. 55–66; Schnackenburg, *Gospel According to John*, Vol. 1, pp. 105–111.

9. W. F. Albright, "Discoveries in Palestine and the Gospel of John," in W. D. Davies and D. Daube, The *Background of the New Testament and its Eschatology* (1956), pp. 153ff.; Brown, *Gospel According to John, AB*, V. 29, pp. lxiiff.

10. Mk. 1:39.

11. Jn 11:1ff., verses 45–48; also 12:9–11, 17–19.

12. E.g., B. F. Westcott, *The Gospel According to John* (1903), pp. clvi–clxxff.

13. Jn. 18:19–21.

14. Jn. 8:17; 10:34.

15. Jn. 4:1–42; 18:23–38.

16. W. F. Howard, *The Fourth Gospel in Recent Criticism and Interpretation* (1955), pp. 128ff. See the extensive bibliography, and brief comment in Haenchen, *Commentary on John*, Vol. 1, pp. 67–70, 74ff.

17. P. N. Gardner-Smith, *St. John and the Synoptics* (1938); C. H. Dodd, *Historical Tradition in the Fourth Gospel* (1963); Brown, *Gospel According to John, AB* V. 29 pp. xliv–xlvii; Scknackenburg, *Gospel According to John*, Vol. 1, pp. 26–43.

18. E.g., C. K. Barrett, *The Gospel According to St. John* (1978), pp. 15–18, 42–54.

19. Brown, *Gospel According to John*, AB V. 29, p. xlvii.

20. For this brief description of Bultmann's proposals, I am indebted to D. Moody Smith's summary, "John, Gospel of," *IDBS*, 1976, pp. 482f.; for his full treatment, see *The Composition and Order of the Fourth Gospel: Bultmann's Literary Theory* (1965); Brown, *Gospel According to John*, pp. xxix–xxxii.; Haenchen, *Commentary on John*, Vol. 1, pp. 48–51, 80, 90.

21. Smith, "John, Gospel of," p. 483.

22. Haenchen states the principle as follows: "we must first of all attempt to interpret the text just as it stands, with all its difficulties, and reserve conjectured modifications for cases of extreme necessity, where several indications converge. . . . *Commentary on John*, Vol. I, p. 80; Barrett, *Gospel According to St. John*, pp. 21–26; C. H. Dodd, *Interpretation of the Fourth Gospel* (1953), pp. 289f.

23. E.g., Jn. 6:51c–58; 3:5 (water and . . .); 19:34b–35. "Ecclesiastical redaction" implies that revision was necessary to make the Gospel conformable to the communities' doctrine. Identification of such passages depends primarily on ideological rather than stylistic or contextual analyses.

24. E.g., Jn. 5:28f.; 6:39, 40, 44, 54; 12:48.

25. Jn. 12:3–4 (cf. Mk. 14:31; Jn. 21:5–11; Lk. 5:4–9).

26. E.g., Jn. 19:35; ch. 21:15ff.

27. Major Johannine scholars have in recent years sought to explain the substantial unity of the Fourth Gospel while acknowledging the several factors that render untenable the tradition of single authorship and suggest stages in the Gospel's com-

position. Brown, *Gospel According to John,* pp. xxxivff.; Barrett, *Gospel According to St. John,* p. 133; Schnackenburg, *Gospel According to John,* Vol. 1, pp. 68–74, 100–104; Haenchen, *Commentary on John,* Vol. 1, p. 90.

28. Jn. 20:30f.

29. Note also the commendation of Jesus at the close of the Gospel, of those who have not seen him and yet believe (20:29).

30. John's polemic against "the Jews" is not anti-Semitic: the attack is not upon a race or a people, but a condemnation of persons who refuse to believe that Jesus is the Christ, the Son of God. Brown, *Gospel According to John AB,* V. 29, pp. lxx–lxxv. Often "the Jews" refer to the religious authorities hostile to Jesus (9:22; 11:8; 18:3, 12), but depending on the contexts, "the Jews" can refer to a national or religious identity (4:22; 18:33, 35); the feasts and customs of a people so designated (2:6, 13; 7:2; 11:55); or simply to the residents of Judea (11:17–19, 36; 11:55).

31. D. M. Smith, "John, Gospel of," *IBDS,* pp. 484f.; Brown, *Gospel According to John,* pp. lixff. Cf. Schnackenburg, *Gospel According to John,* Vol. 1, p. 135: "Recent research has no doubt shifted the balance much more towards Palestinian and Hellenistic Judaism, but it would be an exaggeration to deny all contacts in the language, debate and mentality with the syncretist religions of paganism which were so much influenced by the East."

32. Brown, *Gospel According to John, AB,* V 29, pp. lxii–lxiv.

33. C. H. Dodd, The *Interpretation of the Fourth Gospel* (1953), Part 1: Background; Barrett, *Gospel According to St. John,* pp. 27–41; W. F. Howard, "Gospel According to St. John," pp. 452ff. For alleged Stoic parallels, see R. H. Strachan, *The Fourth Gospel,* (1941), pp. 42ff. Note Brown's reservations concerning Hellenistic influences apart from those derived from Diaspora Judaism. (*Gospel According to John AB,* V. 29, pp. lviff.)

34. Barrett, "The Theological Vocabulary of the Fourth Gospel and the 'Gospel of Truth'," in W. Klassen and G. F. Snyder, eds., *Current Issues in New Testament Interpretation* (1962), p. 210.

35. One great value of Bultmann's commentary is that while he interprets the Gospel against the background of Gnosticism, he shows that "at every crucial point the Gospel is in tension with the Gnostic point of view, indeed repudiates it." S. C. Neill, *Interpretation of the New Testament* (1964), p. 310.

36. See note 2, p. 453.

37. Brown, *Gospel According to John AB,* Vol. 29, pp. ciiif. Barrett, *Gospel According to St. John,* pp. 128–131; Schnackenburg, *Gospel According to John,* Vol. 1, pp. 149–152.

38. Barrett, *Gospel According to St. John,* p. 127. In the early decades of the twentieth century a stalemate was reached concerning the usual questions of origin. Johannine research was directed to a reconstruction of the background of thought that the Fourth Evangelist presupposed in his readers (e.g., C. H. Dodd, *Interpretation of Fourth Gospel*). A lack of consensus in this history of religions research has directed some scholars to an analysis of the narrative elements of the Fourth Gospel as it stands, such as the narrator's point of view, the Gospel's plot, characterizations, implicit commentary, etc. An important ground-breaking work is R. Alan Culpepper's *Anatomy of the Fourth Gospel: A Study in Literary Design* (1983).

39. For the affinities of Johannine and Philonic thought and a theory of dependence, see C. H. Dodd, *Interpretation of Fourth Gospel.*

40. Brown, *Gospel According to John AB,* V. 29, p. 520.

41. *Ibid.,* p. 521. Ps. 33:6; Is. 55:10f.; Ps. 147:15ff.

42. Prov. 8:22f.; Sir. 24:3.

43. Enoch 42:2; Sir. 15:7; Bar. 3:12.

44. Sir. 24:8ff.

45. Also Bar. 4:1.
46. P. Aboth 3.15.
47. In the New Testament the Word/Wisdom of God sometimes refers to the gospel (e.g., Lk. 8:11; Acts 8:29; Rev. 1:9; 1 Thess. 2:13; 1 Jn. 1:1), or to Christ himself (e.g., 1 Cor. 1:23; Gal. 3:1).
48. Brown's translation, *Gospel According to John AB*, Vol. 29, pp. 17f.
49. Jn. 1:6–8, 15. For the probable historical values of the Fourth Evangelist's Baptist traditions, see Dodd, *Historical Tradition in the Fourth Gospel* (1963), pp. 248ff. Cf. Haenchen. *Commentary on John*, Vol. 1., pp. 147–149, 159f.
50. For the Evangelist's use of prolepses and analepses (referring to events that took place later or earlier than the points at which they are reported in the narrative), see Culpepper, *Anatomy of the Fourth Gospel*, pp. 56ff. The two-part introduction of John's Gospel "is so rich in allusions to previous and coming events" that "a great deal of the story content" is communicated.
51. Jn. 5:31ff.; 18:28ff.
52. Brown, *Gospel According to John AB*, Vol. 29, p. 45; N. Dahl, "The Johannine Church and History," in Klassen and Snyder, *Current Issues*, pp. 125f.
53. Dodd, *Interpretation of Fourth Gospel*, pp. 497ff.; Brown, *Gospel According to John AB*, Vol. 29, pp. cxxxviiif. The present writer has adopted Dodd's outline.
54. Jn. 2:11; 3:3; 6:14, etc.
55. Note the equation, signs = works, in 6:20.
56. Barrett, *Gospel According to St. John*, pp. 75–78. Perhaps it matters less that an actual event is reported just as it occurred than that the "sign" reveals some truth concerning the cross of Christ. Note the reference to the "hour" of Jesus (2:4b), which is the moment when he lays down his life, the hour and time of his deepest humiliation and final glorification. 7:1ff., 30; 8:20; 12:23–33; 17:1; also 10:17f.
57. Jn. 16:13f.
58. E. Käsemann, *The Testament of Jesus* (1968), pp. 19f. Italics mine. "The significance of the wine is that it is Jesus' gift . . . given at the end, and it is so precious and copious that it is the eschatological gift of the Messiah." Schnackenburg, *Gospel According to John*, Vol. 1, pp. 337f. Joel 3:18; Jer. 31:5; En. 10:19; also Gen. 49:9–12. Haenchen, *Commentary on John*, Vol. 1, pp. 175–179.
59. "The Dionysus Legend" is cited by Schnackenburg, *Gospel According to John*, Vol. 1, p. 340.
60. Barrett, *Gospel According to St. John*, pp. 188f. For "theological motifs in the narrative," see, Brown, *Gospel According to John AB*, Vol. 29, pp. 103ff.
61. Jn. 2:6; 4:12f. Dodd, *Interpretation of Fourth Gospel*, pp. 311f.
62. E.g., Mk. 2:19ff and par.
63. Jn. 1:11. In this Gospel Jesus' "country" is "the land of Judea." Cf. Jn. 4:43–45 (3:22) and Mk. 6:1ff. For this reason, perhaps, the temple scene rather than the rejection at Nazareth symbolized the failure of Jesus' own (people) to receive him. Cf. Lk's prolepses, 4:16ff.
64. Jn. 4:23; 5:25, etc.
65. Jn. 3:6.
66. Jn. 3:5; 1:12f.
67. Jn. 3:22–36. Dodd, *Interpretation of Fourth Gospel*, pp. 309ff.; Brown, *Gospel According to John*, Vol. 29, pp. 141ff. Cf. Schnackenburg's literary criticism of Jn. 3, *Gospel According to John*, Vol. 1., pp. 360–363.
68. Brown, *Gospel According to John, AB*, Vol. 29, pp. cxiff.
69. Jn. 3:13f., 27, 31; 4:24; 6:32f., 50f., 63.
70. Jn. 5:16–18.
71. The authority of Jesus, like that of Israel's prophets, was a delegated authority. See

the discussion of important similarities and differences between Jesus and the prophets, Dodd, *Interpretation of Fourth Gospel,* pp. 255ff.

72. Jn. 5:31–37.
73. Jn. 5:37b–47; 10:22–28.
74. Note that the clearest statement of Jesus' independent action (10:17f.) is followed by the assertion: "this charge I have received from my Father."
75. Jn. 14:8–11; 10:30–33.
76. Cf. Paul who wrote that believers are sons by adoption, are servants who become sons only through grace. Rom. 8:14–17, 23; Gal. 4:5.
77. Jn. 11:4, 25. The remark of Thomas, verse 16, probably refers to Jesus' death also.
78. Jn. 11:25f.
79. Dodd, *Interpretation of Fourth Gospel,* p. 366. For a discussion of literary analysis and historical problems, see, Schnackenburg, *Gospel According to John,* Vol. 2, pp. 316–346.
80. Lk. 16:31.
81. Dodd, *Interpretation of Fourth Gospel,* pp. 289–291.
82. Jn. 13:1; 3:16f., 10:17; 16:27f.; 17:23ff.
83. Jn. 15:9.
84. Jn. 13:13ff.; 14:21; 15:12, 17. Cf. Mk. 10:43ff.
85. Dodd, *Interpretation of Fourth Gospel,* p. 395. See Schnackenburg, *Gospel According to John,* Vol. 2, "Eschatology in the Fourth Gospel," pp. 426–437; Brown, *Gospel According to John AB,* Vol. 29, pp. cxv–cxxi.
86. John 14:3; 17:24.
87. Dodd, *Interpretation of Fourth Gospel,* pp. 406f. Cf. Brown, *Gospel According to John AB,* Vol. 29A, pp. 581–604; also, Schnackenburg, who conjectures that chs. 15–16 were added as "a re-reading of the original farewell discourse, 14:1–31, with the existence of the community in the world especially in mind." Chapter 17 reflects the same situation and its placement in the text is attributed to the Johannine "school of disciples." *Gospel According to John,* Vol. 3, pp. 89–93.
88. Jn. 14:16f., 25; 15:26; 16:7–11, 13–15. It seems likely that the Evangelist received the term (already being used for the Holy Spirit) and made theological statements about the Paraclete that were in accord with the Johannine teaching about the Spirit. Schnackenburg, *Gospel According to John,* Vol. 3, p. 140.
89. See the valuable article on the Paraclete in Brown, *Gospel According to John AB,* Vol. 1, 29A, Appendix V, pp. 1135–1144.
90. Jn. 14:17; (16:13); 14:26.
91. Jn. 17:1–5.
92. Jn. 17:6–8.
93. Jn. 17:9–19.
94. Jn. 17:20–23.
95. Jn. 17:24ff.
96. Opinions have differed widely concerning the conception of the Church in the Fourth Gospel—its nature and mission. Cf. Brown, *Gospel According to John AB,* Vol. 29, pp. cvff., and Käsemann, *Testament of Jesus,* pp. 27ff. Also, Schnackenburg, *Gospel According to John,* Vol. 3, pp. 203–217.
97. Note Jn. 1:49; 12:13; 15:1ff.; 18:33, 39, 14f., 19ff.
98. Jn. 18:33ff.
99. Jn. 18:4–9; 19:17 (cf. Mk. 15:21). Jn. 19:28–30 (10:17f.)
100. Jn. 18:19–24, 33–38, 19:1ff.
101. Pss. 69:21, 22:14f. Note 1 Cor. 15:3; Lk. 24:25–27; Acts 13:29.
102. Jn. 18:11; 16:32f.
103. Käsemann, *Testament of Jesus,* p. 7.

104. Davies, *Invitation*, p. 482.
105. Jn. 14:18; 10:12ff.
106. Jn. 20:19–22; 14:16.
107. Jn. 1:14–18; 20:29.
108. Brown, *The Epistles of John* (1982), *AB*, Vol. 30, pp. 14–19, 30–32, 100–103.
109. *Ibid.*, pp. 19–30. Cf. Kümmel, *INT²*, pp. 442–445.
110. 1 Jn. 2:18f.; 2 Jn. 7–9.
111. Brown, *Epistles of John*, pp. 647–651.
112. C. B. Caird, "John, Letters of," *IDB*, 2, (1962) p. 950.
113. Brown proposes an interesting theory taking into account the complications caused by the activities of the secessionist missionaries. The strategy of Diotrephes was to refuse hospitality to *all* would-be missionaries. In effect Diotrephes becomes the teacher in the house-church over which he has primacy, and he moves away from "the pure Johannine tradition of the sole Paraclete-teacher so dear to the Presbyter." 1 John 2:26f. *Epistles of John*, p. 738.
114. For Hellenistic parallels to this mode of address, see C. H. Dodd, *The Johannine Epistles* (1946), pp. 144f.
115. Brown, *Epistles of John*, p. 684.
116. 2 Jn. 9.
117. "The term 'Antichrist,' peculiar to the Johannine Epistles in the New Testament, represents a convergence of various background factors in Judaism." For a discussion of these, see Brown, *Epistles of John*, pp. 333–337.
118. *Ibid.*, p. 90.
119. Dodd, *Johannine Epistles*, pp. xxif.
120. See charts 5 and 6 in Brown, *Epistles of John*, Appendix 1, pp. 764f.
121. McNeile, *Introduction to the New Testament*, pp. 300–302; Kümmel, *INT²*, pp. 435–437.
122. 1 Jn. 4:5f.
123. 1 Jn. 3:23; 4:7, 20f.
124. Familiarity with R. E. Brown's superb commentary on the Epistles will recognize the present writer's heavy indebtedness to this Johannine scholar's analysis of the Christological stance of the secessionists, and of the interrelatedness of the doctrinal and ethical issues in the controversy.
125. 1 Jn. 5:5–12. See also Jn. 1:29–31; 19:31–37.
126. Italics mine.
128. Ignatius *Trall.* 9–10; *Smyrn.* 1–3, 4:2; 5:2; 6:1.
129. Ignatius *Smyrn.* 6:2.
130. G. B. Caird, "John, Letters of," p. 947.
131. *Ibid.* Cf. Brown, *Epistles of John*, pp. 57–59.
132. Irenaeus *Adv. Her.* I. 26. 1, cited by Caird, "John, Letters of," p. 947.
133. Brown, *Epistles of John*, p. 67. Kümmel, *INT²*, pp. 441f.
134. Caird, "John, Letters of," p. 947. "Although the Gnostic false teaching cannot be determined with historical exactitude, it is nonetheless significant that here . . . enthusiastic Gnosticism has christological implications, so that here we have to do with a developed form of Gnosticism." Kümmel, *INT²*, p. 442.
135. Brown, *Epistles of John*, pp. 64f.

Abbreviations Used in Notes

AB	*Anchor Bible Commentary*
Bib	*Biblica*
BA	*Biblical Archaeologist*
BJRL	*Bulletin of the John Rylands University Library, Manchester*
BR	*Biblical Research*
CBQ	*Catholic Biblical Quarterly*
ExpT	*Expository Times*
Herm	*Hermeneia Commentary*
HNTC	*Harper's NT Commentary* (published in Great Britain as *Black's NT Commentary*)
HTR	*Harvard Theological Review*
IB	*Interpreter's Bible*
ICC	*International Critical Commentary*
IDB	*Interpreter's Dictionary of the Bible*
IDBS	*Interpreter's Dictionary of the Bible*, Supplementary Volume
Int	*Interpretation*
JAAR	*Journal of the American Academy of Religion*
JBC	*Jerome Bible Commentary* (one volume)
JBL	*Journal of Biblical Literature*
JHistSt	*Journal of Historical Studies*
JQR	*Jewish Quarterly Review*
JRel	*Journal of Religion*
JThCh	*Journal of Theology and Church*
MNTC	*Moffatt NT Commentary*
NCB	*New Century Bible Commentary*
NC1B	*New Clarendon Bible Commentary*
NIGkC	*New International Greek Commentary*
NTS	*NT Studies*
NovT	*Novum Testamentum*
Perkins	*Perkins School of Theology Journal*
PNTC	*Pelican NT Commentary*
PRS	*Perspectives in Religious Studies*
PC	*Proclamation Commentary*
RLife	*Religion in Life*
RSR	*Religious Studies Review*
RevExp	*Review and Expositor*
ScotJTh	*Scottish Journal of Theology*
ThT	*Theology Today*
TNTC	*Tyndale NT Commentary*
VC	*Vigilae Christianae*

Bibliography

The bibliography is presented by chapter, beginning with the third. Listed are the works cited in the text and endnotes, alphabetically according to author. (Occasionally references appearing in an earlier chapter are not repeated; for example, comprehensive introductions.) The purpose of the bibliography is to identify significant publications—not all, but some—that discuss matters treated in the text. A few noteworthy writings not referenced in this book have been added.

Chapter 3: Reconstructing the World of Jesus and His First Followers

ALON, GEDALIA. "The Attitude of the Pharisees to Roman Rule and the House of Herod." In *Jews, Judaism and the Classical World: Studies in Jewish History in the Times of the Second Temple and Talmud*. Translated by I. Abrahams. Jerusalem: Magnes Press, 1977.

AVI-YONAH, MICHAEL. *The Jews of Palestine: A Political History from the Bar Kokhba War to the Arab Conquest*. Oxford: B. Blackwell, 1976.

BARRETT, CHARLES KINGSLEY, ed. *The New Testament Background: Selected Documents*. New York: The Macmillan Co., 1957.

BRUCE, FREDERICK FYVIE. *New Testament History*. Garden City, NY: Doubleday, 1971.

CROSS, FRANK MOORE. *The Ancient Library of Qumran and Modern Biblical Studies*. Rev. ed. Garden City, NY: Doubleday, 1961.

————. "Early History of the Qumran Community." In *New Directions in Biblical Archeology*. Edited by D. N. Freedman and J. C. Greenfield. Garden City, NY: Doubleday, 1969.

GOLDSTEIN, JONATHAN A. I Maccabees: A New Translation with Introduction and Commentary. *Anchor Bible Commentary*, 41. Garden City, NY: Doubleday, 1976.

GOWAN, DONALD E. *Bridge Between the Testaments: A Reappraisal of Judaism from the Exile to the Birth of Christianity*. 2nd ed. Pittsburgh: Pickwick Press, 1980.

HENGEL, MARTIN. *Acts and the History of Earliest Christianity*. Translated by John Bowden. Philadelphia: Fortress Press, 1980.

JEREMIAS, JOACHIM. *Jerusalem in the Time of Jesus: An Investigation into the Economic and Social Conditions During the New Testament Period*. Translated by F. H. Cave and C. H. Cave. Philadelphia: Fortress Press, 1969.

KEE, HOWARD CLARK, compiler. *The Origins of Christianity: Sources and Documents*. Englewood Cliffs, NJ: Prentice-Hall, 1973.

GOWAN, DONALD E. *Bridge Between the Testaments; A Reappraisal of Judaism from the Exile to the Birth of Christianity*. 2nd ed. Pittsburgh: Pickwick Press, 1980.

LOHSE, EDUARD. *The New Testament Environment*. Trans. J. E. Steely. Nashville: Abingdon Press, 1976.

MURPHY-O'CONNOR, JEROME. "The Essenes in Palestine." *Biblical Archaeologist* 40 (1977): 100–124.

NEUSNER, JACOB. *From Politics to Piety: The Emergence of Pharisaic Judaism.* Englewood Cliffs, NJ: Prentice-Hall, 1973.

RHOADS, D. M. *Israel in Revolution, 6–74 C.E.: A Political History Based on the Writings of Josephus.* Philadelphia: Fortress Press, 1976.

RIVKIN, ELLIS. *A Hidden Revolution.* Nashville: Abingdon Press, 1978.

SANDERS, J. A. "The Dead Sea Scrolls—A Quarter Century of Study." *Biblical Archaeologist* 36 (1973): 110–148.

SCHALIT, A. "A Clash of Ideologies: Palestine Under the Seleucids and the Romans." In *The Crucible of Christianity; Judaism, Hellenism, and the Historical Background to the Christian Faith.* New York: World Publishing, 1969.

SCHÜRER, EMIL. *History of the Jewish People in the Age of Jesus Christ.* Vols. 1 and 2. Revised and edited by Geza Vermes and Fergus Millar. Edinburgh: T. & T. Clark, 1973.

SMITH, MORTON. "Palestinian Judaism in the First Century." In *Israel: Its Role in Civilization.* Edited by M. Davis. New York: Seminary Israel Institute of the Jewish Theological Seminary of America (distributed by Harper), 1976.

TCHERIKOVER, VICTOR. *Hellenistic Civilization and the Jews.* Translated by S. Applebaum. Philadelphia: Jewish Publication Society of America, 1959.

———. *World History of the Jewish People.* Vol. 6. New Brunswick, NJ: Rutgers University Press, 1964.

DE VAUX, ROLAND. *Archeology and the Dead Sea Scrolls.* London: Oxford University Press, 1973.

WRIGHT, GEORGE E. *Shechem, the Biography of a Biblical City.* New York: McGraw-Hill, 1965.

YADIN, Y. "Temple Scroll." In *Encyclopoedia Judaica Yearbook, 1977/8.* Jerusalem: Encyclopoedia Judaica, Keter Publishing House, 1979.

Chapter 4: A Narrative of Christian Beginnings, Acts 1–12.

BARRETT, CHARLES KINGSLEY. *New Testament Essays.* London: S.P.C.K., 1972.

BICKERMAN, ELIAS J. "The Name of Christians." *Harvard Theological Review* 42 (1949): 109–124.

BRUCE, FREDERICK FYVIE. *Commentary on the Book of Acts.* Grand Rapids: Eerdmans, 1956.

———. *Second Thoughts on the Dead Sea Scrolls.* Grand Rapids: Eerdmans, 1961.

BULTMANN, RUDOLF. *Theology of the New Testament.* Vols. 1 and 2. Translated by K. Grobel. New York: Charles Scribner's Sons, 1951, 1955.

CADBURY, H. J. "We and I Passages In Luke-Acts." *NT Studies* 3 (1956): 128–132.

CHARLES, ROBERT HENRY. *Religious Development Between the Old and New Testaments.* New York: H. Holt & Co., 1914.

CHARLESWORTH, JAMES H. "The Messiah in the Pseudepigrapha," *Aufstieg und Niedergang der römischen Welt.* New York: W. Gruyter, 1979.

DIBELIUS, MARTIN. "The Speeches in Acts and Ancient Historiography." In *Studies in the Acts of the Apostles.* Translated by M. Ling. Edited by H. Greeven. New York: Charles Scribners Sons, 1956.

DODD, CHARLES HAROLD. *The Apostolic Preaching and Its Developments.* 2nd ed. London: Hodder and Stoughton, 1951.

DUPONT, JACQUES. *The Salvation of the Gentiles: Essays on the Acts of the Apostles.* Translated by J. R. Keating. New York: Paulist Press, 1979.

———. *The Sources of Acts.* Translated by K. Pond. London: Darton, Longman, & Todd, 1964.

FITZMYER, JOSEPH A. The Gospel According to Luke, I–IX: Introduction, Translation, and Notes. *Anchor Bible Commentary*, 28, Garden City, NY: Doubleday, 1981.

———. *The Gospel According to Luke, X–XXIV: Introduction, Translation, and Notes.* Anchor Bible Commentary, 29, Garden City, NY: Doubleday, 1985.

FITZMYER, JOSEPH A., and RICHARD J. DILLON. "Acts of the Apostles." *Jerome Bible Commentary* (1968) 45:1–119.

FULLER, R. H. *The Foundations of New Testament Christology.* New York: Charles Scribner's Sons, 1965.

GEALY, F. D. "Stephen." *Interpreter's Dictionary of the Bible* (1962) 4:441–442.

GOGUEL, MAURICE. *The Birth of Christianity.* Translated by H. C. Snape. London: George Allen & Unwin Ltd., 1953.

HAENCHEN, ERNST. *The Acts of the Apostles.* Translated by R. McL. Wilson *et al.* Philadelphia: Westminster Press, 1971.

HANSON, PAUL. *The Dawn of Apocalyptic: The Historical and Sociological Roots of Jewish Apocalyptic Eschatology.* Rev. ed. Philadelphia: Fortress Press, 1979.

———. "Apocalypticism." *Interpreter's Dictionary of the Bible, Supplementary Volume* (1976): 28–34.

HENGEL, MARTIN. *Acts and the History of Earliest Christianity.* Translated by J. Bowden. Philadelphia: Fortress Press, 1980.

HIGGINS, A. J. B. "The Preface to Luke and the Kerygma in Acts." In *Apostolic History and the Gospels: Biblical and Historical Essays Presented to F. F. Bruce on his 60th Birthday.* Edited by W. W. Gasque and R. P. Martin. Exeter: Paternoster, 1970.

MACGREGOR, G. H. C. "The Acts of the Apostles." *Interpreter's Bible* (1954) 9:3–352.

JERVELL, J. "The Problem of Traditions in Acts." *Luke and the People of God.* Minneapolis: Augsburg, 1972.

KECK, LEANDER, and J. LOUIS MARTYN, eds. *Studies in Luke-Acts.* Philadelphia: Fortress Press, 1980.

KEE, HOWARD CLARK. *The Community of the New Age: Studies in Mark's Gospel.* Philadelphia: Fortress Press, 1977.

KLAUSNER, JOSEPH. *Messianic Idea in Israel: From Its Beginning to the Completion of the Mishnah.* Translated by W. F. Stinespring. New York: Macmillan, 1955.

KNOX, WILFRED LAWRENCE. *The Acts of the Apostles.* Cambridge: At the University Press, 1948.

MANSON, THOMAS WALTER. *The Servant-Messiah: A Study of the Public Ministry of Jesus.* Cambridge: At the University Press, 1953.

MANSON, WILLIAM. "Stephen and the World Mission of Christianity." *Epistle to the Hebrews: An Historical and Theological Reconsideration.* London: Hodder & Stoughton, 1951.

MILIK, JÓZEF TADEUSZ. *Ten Years of Discovery in the Wilderness of Judaea.* Translated by J. Strugnell. London: SCM Press, 1959.

MOORE, GEORGE FOOT. *Judaism in the First Centuries of the Christian Era, the Age of the Tannaim.* Vols. 1–3. Cambridge, Mass.: Harvard University Press, 1927–1930.

REICKE, BO. *The New Testament Era: The World of the Bible from 500 B.C. to A. D. 100.* Translated by D. E. Green. Philadelphia: Fortress Press, 1968.

ROWLEY, HAROLD HENRY. *The Relevance of Apocalyptic: A Study of Jewish and Christian Apocalypses from Daniel to the Revelation.* Rev. ed. New York: Harper, 1955.

RUSSEL, DAVID SYME. *The Method and Message of Jewish Apocalyptic, 200 B.C.–A.D. 100.* Philadelphia: Westminster Press, 1964.

SIMON, MARCEL. *St. Stephen and the Hellenists in the Primitive Church.* London: Longmans, Green, 1958.

STANTON, G. N. *Jesus of Nazareth in New Testament Preaching.* New York: Cambridge University Press, 1974.

STENDAHL, KRISTER, ed. *The Scrolls and the New Testament.* New York: Harper & Row, 1957.

TALBERT, C. H. *Literary Patterns, Theological Themes, and the Genre of Luke-Acts.* Missoula, Mont.: Scholars Press, 1974.

———. ed. *Perspectives on Luke-Acts.* Edinburgh: T. & T. Clark, 1978.

WILDER, AMOS N. *Eschatology and Ethics in the Teaching of Jesus.* Rev. ed. New York: Harper & Bros., 1950.

WILLIAMS, CHARLES STEPHEN CONWAY. *A Commentary on the Acts of the Apostles.* Harper's NT Commentary. 2nd ed. New York: Harper & Row, 1964.

Chapter 5: Early Oral and Written Traditions Concerning Jesus

ANDERSON, HUGH. *The Gospel of Mark.* New Century Bible Commentary. London: Oliphants, 1976.

———. *Jesus and Christian Origins: A Commentary on Modern Viewpoints.* New York: Oxford University Press, 1964.

BENOIT, PIERRE. "Reflections on "Formgeschichtliche Methode." In *Jesus and the Gospel.* Vol. 1. Translated by B. Weatherhead. New York: Herder and Herder, 1973.

BROWN, JOHN P. "An Early Revision of the Gospel of Mark." *Journal of Biblical Literature* 78 (1959): 215–227.

BUCHANAN, GEORGE W. "Has the Griesbach Hypothesis Been Falsified?" *Journal of Biblical Literature* (1974): 550–572.

BULTMANN, RUDOLF. *The History of the Synoptic Tradition.* Translated by J. Marsh. New York: Harper & Row, 1963.

CAIRD, GEORGE B. "The Study of the Gospels: II, Form Criticism." *Expository Times* 87 (1976): 137–141.

———. "The Study of the Gospels: I, Source Criticism." *Expository Times* 87 (1974): 99–107.

DAHL, NILS A. "Memory and Commemoration in Early Christianity." *Jesus in the Memory of the Early Church.* Minneapolis: Augsburg Publishing House, 1976.

DODD, CHARLES HAROLD. *About the Gospels.* Cambridge: At the University Press, 1950.

———. "The Appearances of the Risen Christ." In *Studies in the Gospels: Essays in Memory of R. H. Lightfoot.* Edited by D. H. Nineham. Oxford: B. Blackwell, 1955.

———. *According to the Scriptures: The Sub-structure of New Testament Theology.* London: Nisbet & Co., 1952.

DONAHUE, J. R. "From Passion Tradition to Passion Narrative." In *The Passion in Mark: Studies on Mark 14–16.* Edited by W. H. Kelber. Philadelphia: Fortress Press, 1976.

DUNGAN, DAVID L. "Mark—The Abridgment of Matthew and Luke." *Perspectives in Religious Studies* 1 (1970): 51–97.

EDWARDS, RICHARD ALAN. *A Theology of Q: Eschatology, Prophecy and Wisdom.* Philadelphia: Fortress Press, 1976.

FARMER, WILLIAM R. "Jesus and the Gospels: A Form Critical and Theological Essay." *Perkins School of Theology Journal* 28 (1975): 1–62.

———. "Modern Developments of Griesbach's Hypothesis." *NT Studies* 23 (1977): 51–97.

———. *The Synoptic Problem: A Critical Analysis.* New York: Macmillan, 1964.

FITZMYER, JOSEPH A. "The Priority of Mark and the 'Q' Source in Luke." *Perspectives in Religious Studies* 2 (1970): 130–170.

FULLER, REGINALD H., et al. "The Synoptic Problem: After Ten Years." *Perkins School of Theology Journal* 28 (1975): 63ff.

GOGUEL, MAURICE. *The Birth of Christianity.* Translated by H. C. Snape. London: George Allen and Unwin Ltd., 1953.

GRANT, FREDERICK CLIFTON. *The Gospels: Their Origin and Their Growth.* New York: Harper & Row, 1957.

HARNACK, ADOLF. *The Sayings of Jesus: The Second Source of St. Matthew and St. Luke.* Translated by J. R. Wilkinson. New York: G. P. Putnam, 1908.

HARVEY, V. A. *Jesus and the Constraints of History.* Philadelphia: Westminster, Wolthart, 1982.

KEE, HOWARD CLARK. *Jesus in History: An Approach to the Study of the Gospels.* 2nd ed. New York: Harcourt Brace Jovanovich, Inc., 1970.

KUNDSIN, KARL. "Primitive Christianity in the Light of Gospel Research." In *Form Criticism: Two Essays on NT Research.* Edited and translated by R. C. Grant. New York: Harper & Row, 1962.

LIGHTFOOT, R. H. *The Gospel Message of St. Mark.* Oxford: At the University Press, 1952.

MANSON, WILLIAM. *Jesus, the Messiah: The Synoptic Tradition of the Revelation of God in Christ; with Special Reference to Form-Criticism.* Philadelphia: Westminster Press, 1946.

MINEAR, PAUL S. "Form Criticism and Faith." *Religion in Life* 15 (1945): 46–56.

ORCHARD, BERNARD, and THOMAS R. W. LONGSTAFF. *J. J. Griesbach: Synoptic and Text-Critical Studies, 1776–1976.* New York: Cambridge University Press, 1978.

PANNENBERG, WOLFHART. *Jesus—God and Man.* Translated by L. L. Wilkins and D. A. Priesbe. Philadelphia: Westminster Press, 1968.

PERRIN, NORMAN. *Rediscovering the Teaching of Jesus.* New York: Harper & Row, 1976.

PERRY, ALFRED M. "The Growth of the Gospels." *Interpreter's Bible* (1951) 7: 60–74.

SANDERS, EDWARD P. "The Argument from Order and the Relationship Between Matthew and Luke." *NT Studies* (1968): 249–261.

STANTON, G. "On the Christology of Q." In *Christ and Spirit in the New Testament.* Edited by B. Lindars and S. Smalley. Cambridge: At the University Press, 1973.

STREETER, B. H. *The Four Gospels: A Study of Origins.* London: Macmillan & Co., 1924.

STYLER, G. M. "Excursus IV: The Priority of Mark." In *The Birth of the New Testament.* 3rd ed. Edited by C. F. D. Moule. New York: Harper & Row, 1982.

TALBERT, CHARLES H., and EDGAR V. MCKNIGHT. "Can the Griesbach Hypothesis be Falsified?" *Journal of Biblical Literature* 91 (1972): 338–368.

THROCKMORTON, BURTON H., JR., ed. *Gospel Parallels: A Synopsis of the First Three Gospels.* New York: Thomas Nelson Publishing, 1949.

WEISS, J. *The History of Primitive Christianity.* 2 vols. New York: Wilson-Erickson, Inc., 1937.

WINTER, PAUL. *On the Trial of Jesus.* Berlin: Walter de Gruyter, 1961.

WORDEN, R. D. "Redaction Criticism of Q: A Survey." *Journal of Biblical Literature* 94 (1975): 532–546.

Chapter 6: The Gospel of Mark

ACHTEMEIER, PAUL. "Mark as Interpreter of the Jesus Traditions." *Interpretation* 32 (1978): 339–352.

ANDERSON, HUGH. *The Gospel of Mark.* New Century Bible Commentary. London: Oliphants, 1976.

BEASLEY-MURRAY, GEORGE RAYMOND. *Jesus and the Future: An Examination of the Criticism of the Eschatological Discourse, Mk. 13, with Special Reference to the Little Apocalypse Theory.* New York: St. Martin's Press, 1954.

BEST, ERNEST. "The Role of the Disciples in Mark." *NT Studies* 23 (1977): 377ff.

BRANDON, S. G. F. "The Date of the Marcan Gospel." *NT Studies* 7 (1961): 126–141.

BROWN, SCHYLER. "The Secret of the Kingdom of God (Mark 4:11)." *Journal of Biblical Literature* 92 (1973): 60–74.

CULLMANN, OSCAR. *The Christology of the New Testament.* Rev. ed. Translated by S. C. Guthrie and C. A. M. Hall. London: SCM Press, 1963.

————. *Peter: Disciple, Apostle, Martyr: A Historical and Theological Study.* 2nd ed. Translated by F. V. Filson. Philadelphia: Westminster Press, 1962.

————. "Plurality of the Gospels as a Theological Problem." In *The Early Church: Studies in Early Christian History and Theology.* Edited by A. J. B. Higgins. Philadelphia: Westminster Press, 1956.

DONAHUE, JOHN E. *Are You the Christ? The Trial Narrative in the Gospel of Mark.* Missoula, Mont.: Society of Biblical Literature, 1973.

————. "Introduction: From Passion Tradition to Passion Narrative." In *The Passion in Mark: Studies on Mk. 14–16.* Edited by W. H. Kelber. Philadelphia: Fortress Press, 1976.

————. "Temple, Trial, and Royal Christology." In *The Passion in Mark: Studies on Mk. 14–16.* Edited by W. H. Kelber. Philadelphia: Fortress Press, 1976.

GASTON, LLOYD. *No Stone on Another: Studies in the Significance of the Fall of Jerusalem in the Synoptic Gospels.* Leiden: Brill, 1970.

HADAS, MOSES, and MORTON SMITH. *Heroes and Gods: Spiritual Biographies in Antiquity.* New York: Harper & Row, 1965.

HOOKER, MORNA D. *Jesus and the Servant: The Influence of the Servant Concept of Deutero-Isaiah in the New Testament.* London: S.P.C.K., 1959.

————. *The Son of Man in Mark: A Study of the Background of the Term "Son of Man" and Its Use in St. Mark's Gospel.* Montreal: McGill University Press, 1967.

JEREMIAS, JOACHIM. *The Eucharistic Words of Jesus.* Translated by A. Ehrhart. New York: Macmillan, 1955.

KEE, HOWARD CLARK. *Community of the New Age: Studies in Mark's Gospel.* Philadelphia: Westminster Press, 1977.

————. *Jesus in History: An Approach to the Study of the Gospels.* 2nd ed. New York: Harcourt Brace Jovanovich, Inc., 1970.

————. "Mark's Gospel in Recent Research." *Interpretation* 32 (1978): 353–368.

KELBER, W. H. *The Kingdom in Mark: A New Place and a New Time.* Philadelphia: Fortress Press, 1974.

————. *Mark's Story of Jesus.* Philadelphia: Fortress Press, 1979.

KINGSBURY, JACK DEAN. *The Christology of Mark.* Philadelphia: Fortress Press, 1983.

KNOX, WILFRED LAWRENCE. *The Sources of the Synoptic Gospels.* Edited by H. Chadwick. Cambridge: At the University Press, 1953.

LIGHTFOOT, R. H. *History and Interpretation in the Gospels.* London: Hodder & Stoughton, 1934.

————. *The Gospel Message of St. Mark.* London: Oxford University Press, 1949.

MALLY, EDWARD J. "The Gospel According to Mark." *Jerome Bible Commentary* (1964) 42:1–100.

MANSON, T. W. "The Cleansing of the Temple." *Bulletin of the John Rylands University Library, Manchester* 33 (1951): 271–282.

MARTIN, RALPH P. *Mark, Evangelist and Theologian.* Exeter: Paternoster Press, 1972.

NINEHAM, DENNIS ERIC. *The Gospel of St. Mark.* Pelican NT Commentary. Baltimore: Penguin Books, 1963.

PERRIN, NORMAN. "The Interpretation of the Gospel of Mark." *Interpretation* 30 (1976): 115–124.

————. *What is Redaction Criticism?* Philadelphia: Fortress Press, 1969.

RHOADS, D. M. *Mark as Story: An Introduction to the Narrative of a Gospel.* Philadelphia: Fortress Press, 1982.

ROBBINS, VERNON. "Last Meal: Preparation, Betrayal, and Absence." In *The Passion in*

Mark: Studies on Mark 14–16. Edited by W. H. Kelber. Philadelphia: Fortress Press, 1976.

ROBINSON, JAMES M. *The Problem of History in Mark.* Naperville, Ill.: Alec R. Allenson, 1957.

ROBINSON, JOHN ARTHUR THOMAS. *Redating the New Testament.* London: SCM Press, 1976.

ROBINSON, WILLIAM C., Jr. "The Quest for Wrede's Secret Messiah." *Interpretation* 27 (1973): 10–30.

STEIN, ROBERT H. "Is the Transfiguration (Mark 9:2–8) a Misplaced Resurrection Account?" *Journal of Biblical Literature* 95 (1976): 79–96.

———. "The Proper Methodology for Ascertaining a Markan Redaction History." *Novum Testamentum* 13 (1971): 181–198.

———. "What is Redaktionsgeschichte?" *Journal of Biblical Literature* 88 (1969): 45–56.

STRECKER, GEORG. "The Passion and Resurrection Predictions in Mark's Gospel." *Interpretation* 22 (1968): 421–442.

TANNEHILL, R. C. "The Disciples in Mark: The Function of a Narrative Role." *Journal of Religion* 57 (1977): 386–404.

TAYLOR, VINCENT. *The Gospel According to St. Mark. The Greek Text with Introduction, Notes, and Indexes.* London: Macmillan & Co., 1952.

TROCME, ÈTIENNE. *The Formation of the Gospel According to Mark.* Translated by Pamela Gaughan. Philadelphia: Westminster Press, 1975.

VIA, DAN OTTO. *Kerygma and Comedy in the New Testament: a Structuralist Approach to Hermeneutic.* Philadelphia: Fortress Press, 1975.

WEEDEN, THEODORE J. *Mark—Traditions in Conflict.* Philadelphia: Fortress Press, 1971.

WREDE, WILLIAM. *The Messianic Secret.* Translated by J. C. G. Greig. Cambridge: J. Clarke, 1971.

Chapter 7: The Gospel of Luke

BETZ, OTTO. "The Kerygma of Luke." *Interpretation* 22 (1968): 131–146.

CADBURY, HENRY JOEL. *The Making of Luke-Acts.* London: S.P.C.K. 1968.

———. *The Style and Literary Method of Luke.* Cambridge, Mass.: Harvard University Press, 1920.

CAIRD, G. B. *The Gospel of St. Luke.* Pelican NT Commentary. Baltimore: Penguin Books, 1963.

CONZELMANN, HANS. *Theology of St. Luke.* Translated by G. Buswell. London: Faber and Faber, 1960.

CREED, JOHN MARTIN. *The Gospel According to St. Luke: The Greek Text with Introduction, Notes, and Indices.* London: Macmillan & Co., 1942.

FITZMYER, JOSEPH A. "The Gospel According to Luke, Vol. I: Luke I–IX; Vol. II: Luke X–XXIV: Introductions, Translations, Notes." *Anchor Bible Commentary* 28, 28A, Garden City, NY: Doubleday, 1981, 1985.

GILMOUR, S. McL. "A Critical Examination of Proto-Luke." *Journal of Biblical Literature* 67 (1948): 143–152.

HULTGREN, ARLAND J. "Interpreting the Gospel of Luke." *Interpretation* 30 (1976): 353–365.

LEANEY, ALFRED ROBERT CLARE. *A Commentary on the Gospel According to St. Luke.* 2nd ed. *Harper's NT Commentary.* London: Black, 1966.

MANSON, THOMAS WALTER. *The Sayings of Jesus as Recorded in the Gospels According to St. Matthew and St. Luke.* London: SCM Press, 1950.

MARSHALL, I. HOWARD. *Luke: Historian and Theologian.* Grand Rapids, Mich.: Zondevan, 1970.

OLIVER, H. H. "The Lucan Birth Stories and the Purpose of Luke-Acts." *NT Studies* 10 (1963): 224f.

PERRY, ALFRED MORRIS. *The Sources of Luke's Passion Narrative.* Chicago: University of Chicago Press, 1920.

ROBINSON, WILLIAM CHILDS, JR. "Luke, Gospel of" *Interpreter's Dictionary of the Bible, Supplementary Volume* (1976), 558–560.

———. "The Theological Context of Luke's Travel Narrative (9:51ff)." *Journal of Biblical Literature* 79 (1960): 20–31.

TALBERT, CHARLES H. "The Redaction Critical Quest for Luke the Theologian." In D. Miller (ed.), *Jesus and Man's Hope I.* Pittsburgh: Pittsburgh Theological Seminary, 1970.

———. "Shifting Sands: The Recent Study of the Gospel of Luke." *Interpretation* 30 (1976): 381–395.

———, ed. *Luke-Acts, New Perspectives from the Society of Biblical Literature Seminar.* New York: Crossroads Publishers, 1984.

TAYLOR, VINCENT. *Behind the Third Gospel: A Study of the Proto-Luke Hypothesis.* Oxford: The Clarendon Press, 1926.

Chapter 8: *The Gospel of Matthew*

BACON, BENJAMIN WISNER. *Studies in Matthew.* New York: H. Holt & Co. 1930.

BANKS, ROBERT. *Jesus and the Law in the Synoptic Tradition.* Society for NT Studies Monograph Series 28. Cambridge: At the University Press, 1975.

BORNKAMM, GUNTHER, G. BARTH, and J. J. HELD. *Tradition and Interpretation in Matthew.* Translated by P. Scott. Philadelphia: Westminster Press, 1963.

BROWN, RAYMOND. *The Birth of the Messiah: A Commentary on the Infancy Narratives in Matthew and Luke.* Garden City, NY: Doubleday, 1977.

DAVIES, WILLIAM DAVID. *The Sermon on the Mount.* Cambridge: At the University Press, 1966.

———. *The Setting of the Sermon on the Mount.* Cambridge: At the University Press, 1964.

GUNDRY, R. H. *Matthew: A Commentary on His Literary and Theological Art.* Grand Rapids, Mich.: Eerdmans, 1982.

HARE, D. R. A. *The Theme of Jewish Persecution of Christians in the Gospel According to St. Matthew.* Society for NT Studies Monograph Series 6. Cambridge: At the University Press, 1967.

HILL, DAVID. *The Gospel of Matthew: Based on the RSV.* New Century Bible Commentary. Grand Rapids, Mich.: Eerdmans, 1972.

KINGSBURY, JACK DEAN. *Matthew: Structure, Christology, Kingdom.* Philadelphia: Fortress Press, 1975.

MEIER, J. P. *The Vision of Matthew: Christ, Church and Morality in the First Gospel. Theological Inquiries.* New York: Paulist Press, 1979.

PRZYBYLSKI, B. *Righteousness in Matthew and His World of Thought.* Society for NT Studies Monograph Series 41. Cambridge: At the University Press, 1980.

SCHWEIZER, EDUARD. *The Good News According to Matthew.* Translated by D. Green. Atlanta: John Knox Press, 1975.

SENIOR, DONALD P. *The Passion Narrative According to Matthew: A Redactional Study.* Louvain: Leuven University Press, 1975.

———. *What Are They Saying About Matthew?* New York: Paulist Press, 1983.

STENDAHL, KRISTER. *The School of St. Matthew and Its Use of the Old Testament.* Philadelphia: Fortress Press, 1968.

WINK, WALTER. *John the Baptist in the Gospel Tradition.* London: Cambridge University Press, 1968.

Chapter 9: The Historical Jesus

ANDERSON, HUGH. *Jesus and Christian Origins: A Commentary on Modern Viewpoints.* New York: Oxford University Press, 1964.

BARRETT, CHARLES KINGSLEY. "New Testament Eschatology." *Scottish Journal of Theology* 6 (1953): 136–155.

———. *Jesus and the Gospel Tradition.* London: S.P.C.K. 1967.

BETZ, OTTO. *What Do We Know About Jesus?* Translated by M. Kohl. London: SCM Press, 1968.

BORNKAMM, GÜNTHER. *Jesus of Nazareth.* Translated by I. McLuskey and F. McLuskey, with J. M. Robinson. New York: Harper & Row, 1960.

BRAATEN, C. E., and R. A. HARRISVILLE, eds. *The Historical Jesus and the Kerygmatic Christ: Essays on the New Quest of the Historical Jesus.* Translated by C. E. Braaten and R. A. Harrisville. New York: Abingdon Press, 1964.

CAIRD, G. B. "Chronology of the New Testament." *Interpreter's Dictionary of the Bible* (1962) 1:599–607.

CULLMANN, OSCAR. "The Gospel of Thomas and the Problem of the Age of the Tradition Contained Therein." Translated by B. H. Kelly. *Interpretation* 16 (1962): 418–438.

———. *Salvation in History.* Translated by S. Sowers and SCM Press. London: SCM Press, 1967.

DAHL, NILS A. "The Problem of the Historical Jesus." In *Kerygma and History: A Symposium on the Theology of R. Bultmann.* Edited by C. Braaten and R. Harrisville. New York: Abingdon Press, 1962.

DAVIES, WILLIAM DAVID. *Invitation to the New Testament: A Guide to Its Main Witnesses.* Garden City, NY: Doubleday, 1966.

DODD, CHARLES HAROLD. *Historical Tradition in the Fourth Gospel.* Cambridge: At the University Press, 1963.

———. *History and the Gospel.* New York: Charles Scribner's Sons, 1938.

———. "Life and Teachings of Jesus." In *A Companion to the Bible.* Edited by T. W. Manson. Edinburgh: T. & T. Clark, 1956.

———. *The Founder of Christianity.* New York: Macmillan, 1970.

DUNKERLEY, RODERIC. *Beyond the Gospels.* Harmondsworth: Penguin Books, 1957.

GOGUEL, MAURICE. *The Life of Jesus.* Translated by O. Wyon. New York: Macmillan, 1933.

GRANT, FREDERICK CLIFTON. *The Gospel of the Kingdom.* New York: Macmillan, 1940.

HARVEY, VAN A. "The Historical Jesus, the Kerygma, and Christian Faith." *Religion in Life* 33 (1964): 430–450.

HENNECKE, EDGAR, and WILHELM SCHNEEMELCHER, eds. *New Testament Apocrypha.* Vols. 1 and 2. Translated by A. J. B. Higgins, *et al.* Edited by R. McL. Wilson. Philadelphia: Westminster Press, 1963.

HOOKER, MORNA D. "Christology and Methodology." *NT Studies* 17 (1971): 480–487.

HUNTER, ARCHIBALD MACBRIDE. *The Work and Words of Jesus.* Philadelphia: Westminster Press, 1950.

JEREMIAS, JOACHIM. *Unknown Sayings of Jesus.* 2nd ed. Translated by R. H. Fuller. London: S.P.C.K., 1964.

KÄSEMANN, ERNST. *New Testament Questions of Today.* Translated by W. J. Montague. Philadelphia: Fortress Press, 1969.

KLAUSNER, JOSEPH. *Jesus of Nazareth: His Life, Times and Teaching.* Translated by H. Danby. New York: Macmillan, 1925.

LUNDSTRÖM, GÖSTRA. *The Kingdom of God in the Teaching of Jesus: A History of Interpretation from the Last Decades of the Nineteenth Century to the Present.* Translated by J. Bulman. Richmond: John Knox Press, 1963.

MARSHALL, IAN HOWARD. *The Gospel of Luke: A Commentary on the Greek Text.* Grand Rapids, Mich.: Eerdmans, 1978.

―――. *I Believe in the Historical Jesus.* Grand Rapids, Mich.: Eerdmans, 1977.

McARTHUR, HARVEY K. "The Dependence of the Gospel of Thomas on the Synoptics." *Expository Times* 71 (1960): 286–287.

―――. "Survey of Recent Gospel Research." *Interpretation* 18 (1964): 39–55.

O'COLLINS, GERALD, S. J. *The Resurrection of Jesus Christ.* Valley Forge, Penn.: Judson Press, 1973.

OGG, GEORGE. *The Chronology of the Public Ministry of Jesus.* Cambridge: At the University Press, 1940.

PERRIN, NORMAN. *The Kingdom of God in the Teaching of Jesus.* Philadelphia: Westminster Press, 1963.

PINES, SHLOMO. *An Arabic Version of the Testamonium Flavianum and its Implications.* Jerusalem: Israel Academy of Sciences and Humanities, 1971.

ROBINSON, JAMES M., ed. *The Nag Hammadi Library in English.* New York: Harper & Row, 1977.

SCHMIDT, K. L., K. G. HUHN, G. VON RAD, and H. KLEINKNECHT. "Basileus." *Theological Dictionary of the NT.* Vol. 1. Edited by G. Kittel. Translated and edited by G. W. Bromiley. Grand Rapids, Mich.: Eerdmans, 1964.

SCHWEITZER, ALBERT. *The Mystery of the Kingdom of God: The Secret of Jesus' Messiahship and Passion.* Translated by W. Lowrie. New York: Macmillan, 1950.

―――. *The Quest of the Historical Jesus: A Critical Study of its Progress from Reimarus to Wrede.* Translated by W. Montgomery. New York: Macmillan, 1968.

SHARMAN, HENRY BURTON. *Son of Man, and Kingdom of God: A Critical Study.* New York: Harper & Bros., 1943.

WERNER, M. *The Formation of Christian Dogma: An Historical Study of Its Problem.* Rev. ed. Translated by S. G. F. Brandon. New York: Harper & Row, 1957.

WILDER, AMOS. *New Testament Faith for Today.* London: SCM Press, 1955.

WINTER, P. "Josephus on Jesus." *Journal of Historical Studies* 1 (1968): 289–302.

Chapter 10: *The Ministry of Jesus: In Galilee*

ALON, GEDALYAHU. "The Attitude of the Pharisees to Roman Rule and the House of Herod." *Jews, Judaism and the Classical World: Studies in Jewish History in the Times of the Second Temple and Talmud.* Translated by I. Abrahams. Jerusalem: Magnes Press, 1977.

BANKS, ROBERT. *Jesus and the Law in the Synoptic Tradition.* Cambridge: At the University Press, 1975.

BEARE, F. W. "The Sabbath Was Made For Man?" *Journal of Biblical Literature* 79 (1960): 130–136.

BOWKER, JOHN WESTERDALE. *Jesus and the Pharisees.* Cambridge: At the University Press, 1973.

―――. *The Targums and Rabbinic Literature: An Introduction to Jewish Interpretations of Scripture.* London: Cambridge University Press, 1969.

BROWN, RAYMOND E. "Parable and Allegory Reconsidered." In *New Testament Essays.* Milwaukee: Bruce Publishing Co., 1965.

BUNDY, WALTER ERNEST. *Jesus and the First Three Gospels: An Introduction to the Synoptic Tradition.* Cambridge, Mass.: Harvard University Press, 1955.

BURROWS, MILLAR. *More Light on the Dead Sea Scrolls: New Scrolls and New Interpretations, with Translations of Important Recent Discoveries.* New York: Viking Press, 1958.

CADBURY, HENRY JOEL. *Jesus: What Manner of Man.* New York: Macmillan, 1947.

CRAIG, CLARENCE TUCKER. *The Beginning of Christianity.* Nashville: Abingdon-Cokesbury Press, 1943.

DAUBE, DAVID. *The New Testament and Rabbinic Judaism.* London: University Press, Athlone Press, 1956.

DAVIES, WILLIAM DAVID. *The Setting of the Sermon on the Mount.* Cambridge: At the University Press, 1964.

DODD, CHARLES HAROLD. *The Founder of Christianity.* New York: Macmillan, 1971.

————. *The Parables of the Kingdom.* Rev. ed. New York: Charles Scribner's Sons, 1961.

ENSLIN, MORTON. "Once Again: John the Baptist." *Religion in Life* 27 (1958): 557–566.

FERRIS, THEODORE. *The Story of Jesus.* New York: Oxford University Press, 1953.

FULLER, REGINALD HORACE. *Interpreting the Miracles.* London: SCM Press, 1963.

————. *The Mission and Achievements of Jesus: An Examination of the Presuppositions of NT Theology.* London: SCM Press, 1954.

GOGUEL, MAURICE. *The Life of Jesus.* Translated by O. Wyon. New York: Macmillan, 1933.

HIGGINS, A. J. B. *New Testament Essays. Studies in Memory of T. W. Manson, 1893–1958.* Manchester: Manchester University Press, 1959.

HULTGREN, ARLAND J. "The Formation of the Sabbath Pericope in Mark 2:23–28." *Journal of Biblical Literature* 91 (1972): 38–43.

JEREMIAS, JOACHIM. *Parables of Jesus.* Rev. ed. Translated by S. H. Hooke. New York: Charles Scribner's Sons, 1963.

KÄSEMANN, ERNST. "The Problem of the Historical Jesus." In *Essays on NT Themes.* Translated by W. J. Montague. London: SCM Press, 1964.

KLAUSNER, JOSEPH. *Jesus of Nazareth: His Life, Times and Teaching.* Translated by H. Danby. New York: Macmillan, 1925.

KRAELING, CARL HERMANN. *John the Baptist.* New York: Charles Scribner's Sons, 1951.

MANSON, T. W. *Servant-Messiah: A Study of the Public Ministry of Jesus.* Cambridge: At the University Press, 1953.

————. *The Teaching of Jesus: Studies of Its Form and Content.* Cambridge: At the University Press, 1945.

MANSON, W. *The Gospel of Luke. Moffatt NT Commentary.* New York: Harper & Bros., 1930.

MARSHALL, IAN HOWARD. *Commentary on Luke. New International Greek Commentary.* Grand Rapids, Mich.: Eerdmans, 1978.

MOULE, C. F. D. "Mark 4:1–20 Yet Once More." In *Neotestamentica Et Semitica: Studies in Honor of Matthew Black.* Edited by E. E. Ellis and M. Wilcox. Edinburgh: T. & T. Clark, 1969.

NEUSNER, JACOB. *From Politics to Piety: The Emergence of Pharisaic Judaism.* Englewood Cliffs, NJ: Prentice-Hall, 1973.

PANNENBERG, WOLFHART. *Jesus—God and Man.* Translated by L. L. Wilkins and D. A. Priebe. Philadelphia: Westminster Press, 1968.

PERRIN, NORMAN. *Kingdom of God in the Teaching of Jesus.* Philadelphia: Westminster Press, 1963.

————. *Rediscovering the Teaching of Jesus.* New York: Harper & Row, 1976.

RICHARDSON, ALAN. *The Miracle Stories of the Gospels.* New York: Harper & Bros., 1942.

RIVKIN, ELLIS. *A Hidden Revolution.* Nashville: Abingdon Press, 1978.

ROBINSON, JOHN A. T. "Elijah, John and Jesus: An Essay In Detection." *NT Studies* 4 (1958): 263–281.

SAFRAI, SAMUEL. "Jewish Self-government." In S. Safrai and M. Stern (eds.), *The Jew-*

ish People in the First Century: Historical Geography, Political History, Social Cultural and Religious Life and Institutions. Assen, Netherlands: Van Gorcum, 1974.

SAUNDERS, ERNEST WILLIAM. *Jesus in the Gospels.* Englewood Cliffs, NJ: Prentice-Hall, 1967.

SCHUBERT, KURT. *The Dead Sea Community: Its Origin and Teaching.* Translated by J. W. Doberstein. London: Adam & Charles Black, 1959.

SCHÜRER, EMIL. *A History of the Jewish People in the Age of Jesus Christ, 175 B.C.– A.D. 135.* Revised and edited by G. Vermes and F. Millar. Edinburgh: T. & T. Clark, 1973.

SCOBIE, CHARLES HUGH HOPE. *John the Baptist.* London: SCM Press, 1964.

STENDAHL, KRISTER. *The Scrolls and the New Testament.* New York: Harper & Row, 1957.

TALMON, SHEMARYAHU. "Ezra and Nehemiah." *Interpreter's Dictionary of the Bible, Supplementary Volume* (1976) 317–328.

———. *Scripture and Tradition in Judaism. Haggadic Studies.* 2nd rev. ed. Leiden: Brill, 1973.

VERMES, GÉZA. "Bible and Midrash." In C. F. Evans and P. Ackroyd (eds.), *The Cambridge History of the Bible I.* Cambridge: At the University Press, 1970.

Chapter 11: The Ministry of Jesus: Beyond Galilee and in Judea

ANDERSON, HUGH. *Jesus.* Englewood Cliffs, NJ: Prentice-Hall, 1967.

BARRETT, CHARLES KINGSLEY. *Jesus and the Gospel Tradition.* London: S.P.C.K., 1967.

BENOIT, PIERRE. *The Passion and Resurrection of Jesus Christ.* Translated by B. Weatherhead. New York: Herder & Herder, 1969.

BETZ, OTTO. *What Do We Know About Jesus?* Translated by M. Kohl. London: SCM Press, 1968.

BLINZLER, JOSEF. *The Trial of Jesus: The Jewish and Roman Proceedings Against Jesus Christ Described and Assessed from the Oldest Accounts.* Translated by I. McHugh and F. McHugh. Westminster, Md.: Newman Press, 1959.

BORNKAMM, GUNTHER. *Jesus of Nazareth.* Translated by I. McLuskey and F. McLuskey with James M. Robinson. New York: Harper & Row, 1960.

BORSCH, FREDERICK HOUK. *The Son of Man in Myth and History.* Philadelphia: Westminster Press, 1967.

BOWKER, JOHN WESTERDALE. *Jesus and the Pharisees.* Cambridge: At the University Press, 1973.

BROWN, RAYMOND EDWARD. *The Birth of the Messiah: A Commentary on the Infancy Narratives in Matthew and Luke.* Garden City, NY: Doubleday, 1977.

———. "Historical Reconstruction of the Arrest and Trial of Jesus." In "The Gospel According to John: Introduction, Translation, and Notes." Anchor Bible Commentary, Vol. 29A. Garden City, NY: Doubleday, 1966.

BULTMANN, RUDOLF. *History of the Synoptic Tradition.* 2nd ed. Translated by J. Marsh. Oxford: B. Blackwell, 1968.

———. *Theology of the New Testament.* Vol. 1. Translated by K. Grobel. New York: Charles Scribner's Sons, 1951.

CONZELMANN, HANS. *Jesus: The Classic Article from RGG Expanded and Updated.* Translated by J. R. Lord. Edited by J. Reumann. Philadelphia: Fortress Press, 1973.

DAHL, NILS. *The Crucified Messiah and other Essays.* Minneapolis: Augsburg Publishing House, 1974.

DAVIES, WILLIAM DAVID. *The Gospel and the Land: Early Christianity and Jewish Territorial Doctrine.* Berkeley: University of California Press, 1974.

DODD, CHARLES HAROLD. *The Founder of Christianity.* New York: Macmillan, 1970.

FILSON, FLOYD VIVIAN. *A New Testament History: The Story of the Emerging Church.* Philadelphia: Westminster Press, 1964.

FITZMYER, JOSEPH A. *A Wandering Aramean: Collected Aramaic Essays.* Missoula, Mont.: Scholars Press, 1979.

FULLER, REGINALD HORACE. *The Formation of the Resurrection Narratives.* New York: Macmillan, 1971.

———. *The Foundation of New Testament Christology.* New York: Charles Scribner's Sons, 1965.

———. "The Virgin Birth: Historical Fact or Kerygmatic Truth." *Biblical Research* 1 (1956): 1–8.

HAHN, FERDINAND. *The Titles of Jesus in Christology: Their History in Early Christianity.* Translated by H. Knight and G. Off. New York: World Publishing, 1969.

HIGGINS, ANGUS JOHN BROCKHURST. *Jesus and the Son of Man.* London: Lutterworth Press, 1964.

HOOKER, MORNA. *Jesus and the Servant: The Influence of the Servant Concept of Deutero-Isaiah in the New Testament.* London: S.P.C.K., 1959.

———. *The Son of Man in Mark: A Study of the Background of the Term 'Son of Man' and its Use in St. Mark's Gospel.* Montreal: McGill University Press, 1967.

HUNTER, ARCHIBALD MACBRIDE. *The Work and Words of Jesus.* Philadelphia: Westminster Press, 1950.

JEREMIAS, JOACHIM. *The Eucharistic Words of Jesus.* Translated by A. Ehrhardt. New York: Macmillan, 1955.

———. *Jesus' Promise to the Nations.* London: SCM Press, 1958.

———. *New Testament Theology.* New York: Charles Scribner's Sons, 1971.

JOHNSON, SHERMAN. *Jesus in His Homeland.* New York: Charles Scribner's Sons, 1957.

KÜMMEL, WERNER GEORG. *Promise and Fulfilment: The Eschatological Message of Jesus.* London: SCM Press, 1957.

———. *The Theology of the New Testament.* Translated by John E. Steely. New York: Abingdon Press, 1973.

MANSON, WILLIAM. *Jesus the Messiah: The Synoptic Tradition of the Revelation of God in Christ; with Special Reference to Form-Criticism.* Philadelphia: Westminster Press, 1946.

MARXSEN, WILLI, GERHARD DELLING, ULRICH WILCKENS, and HANS-GEORG GEYER. *The Significance of the Message of the Resurrection for Faith in Jesus Christ.* Translated by D. M. Barton and R. A. Wilson. Edited by C. F. D. Moule. London: SCM Press, 1968.

MINEAR, PAUL S. "The Interpreter and the Nativity Stories." *Theology Today* 7 (1950): 358ff.

MORGAN, R. "Nothing more Negative . . . A Concluding Unscientific Postscript to Historical Research on the Trial of Jesus." In *The Trial of Jesus.* Edited by E. Bammel. London: SCM Press, 1970.

NINEHAM, DENNIS ERIC. *Studies in the Gospels: Essays in Memory of R. H. Lightfoot.* Oxford: B. Blackwell, 1955.

REID, J. K. S. "Virgin (Birth)." In *Theological Word Book of the Bible.* Edited by Alan Richardson. New York: Macmillan, 1967.

ROBINSON, H. WHEELER. "Essay on Prophetic Symbolism." In *Old Testament Essays: Papers Read Before the Society for Old Testament Study at its Eighteenth Meeting, held at Keble College, Oxford.* Edited by David C. Simpson. 1927.

SAUNDERS, ERNEST WILLIAM. *Jesus in the Gospels.* Englewood Cliffs, NJ: Prentice-Hall, 1967.

SCHWEIZER, EDUARD. "The Son of Man." *Journal of Biblical Literature* 79 (1960): 119–129.

STRECKER, GEORG. "The Passion and Resurrection Traditions in Mark's Gospel." *Interpretation* 22 (1968): 421–442.

STEIN, R. H. "Is the Transfiguration (Mark 9:2–8) a Misplaced Resurrection-Account?" *Journal of Biblical Literature* 95 (1976): 79–96.

TAYLOR, VINCENT. "The Life and Ministry of Jesus." *Interpreter's Bible* 7: 114–144.

TÖDT, HEINZ EDUARD. *The Son of Man in the Synoptic Tradition.* Translated by D. M. Barton. London: SCM Press, 1965.

VERMES, GÉZA. *Jesus the Jew: A Historian's Reading of the Gospels.* London: Collins, 1973.

———. "The Use of *bar nash/bar nasha* in Jewish Aramaic." Appendix in M. Black, *An Aramaic Approach to the Gospels and Acts.* 2nd ed. Oxford: Clarendon Press, 1954.

ZIMMERLI, W., and J. JEREMIAS. *The Servant of God. Essays in Memory of R. H. Lightfoot.* Naperville, Ill.: A. R. Allenson, 1957.

Chapter 12: The Environment of Gentile Christianity

BEARE, F. W. "Greek Religion and Philosophy." *Interpreter's Dictionary of the Bible* 2: 487–500.

BEVAN, EDWYN R. *Later Greek Religion.* Boston: Beacon Press, 1950.

BULTMANN, RUDOLF. *Primitive Christianity in its Contemporary Setting.* Translated by R. H. Fuller. New York: Thomas & Hudson, 1956.

CASEY, R. P. "Gnosis, Gnosticism and the New Testament." In W. D. Davies and D. Daube, *The Background of the New Testament and its Eschatology.* Cambridge: At the University Press, 1956.

CULLMANN, OSCAR. *The Early Church: Studies in Early Christian History and Theology.* Edited A. J. Higgins. Philadelphia: Westminster Press, 1956.

CUMONT, FRANZ V. M. *The Oriental Religions in Roman Paganism.* Chicago: Open Court Publishing, 1911, 1957.

DAVIES, WILLIAM DAVID. *Paul and Rabbinic Judaism.* London: S. P. C. K., 1948.

DODD, CHARLES HAROLD. *The Interpretation of the Fourth Gospel.* Cambridge: At the University Press, 1953.

FESTUGIÈRE, ANDRÉ MARIE JEAN. *Personal Religion Among the Greeks.* Berkeley: University of California Press, 1954.

GRANT, FREDERICK CLIFTON. *Ancient Roman Religion.* New York: Liberal Arts Press, 1957.

———. *Hellenistic Religion: The Age of Syncretism.* New York: Liberal Arts Press, 1953.

———. "Gnosticism." *Interpreter's Dictionary of the Bible* (1962) 2: 404–406.

JONAS, HANS. *The Gnostic Religion: The Message of the Alien God and the Beginnings of Christianity.* Boston: Beacon Press, 1958.

LOHSE, EDUARD. *The New Testament Environment.* Translated by John E. Steely. Nashville: Abingdon Press, 1976.

MORRISON, CLINTON D. *The Powers that Be: Earthly Rulers and Demonic Powers in Rom. 13:1–7.* London: SCM Press, 1960.

NILSSON, M. P. *The Dionysiac Mysteries of the Hellenistic and Roman Age.* Lund: C. W. K. Gleerup, 1957.

———. *Greek Piety.* Translated by Herbert Jennings Rose. Oxford: Clarendon Press, 1968.

NOCK, ARTHUR DARBY. *Conversion: The Old and the New in Religion from Alexander the Great to Augustine of Hippo.* London: Oxford University Press, 1933.

PAGELS, ELAINE. "Gnosticism." *Interpreter's Dictionary of the Bible, Supplementary Volume,* 364–368.

PFEIFFER, ROBERT HENRY. *History of New Testament Times, with an Introduction to the Apocrypha.* Westport, Conn.: Greenwood Press, 1976.

ROBINSON, JAMES M., ed. *The Nag Hammadi Library in English.* New York: Harper & Row, 1977.

ROSE, HERBERT JENNINGS. *Religion in Greece and Rome.* New York: Harper & Row, 1959.

SAFRAI, S., and M. STERN, eds. *The Jewish People in the First Century: Historical Geography, Political History, Social, Cultural and Religious Life and Institutions.* Assen, Netherlands: Van Gorcum, 1974–1976.

SCHOEPS, HANS JOACHIM. *Paul: The Theology of the Apostle in the Light of Jewish Religious History.* Philadelphia: Westminster Press, 1961.

TARN, WILLIAM WOODTHROPE, and G. T. GRIFFITH. *Hellenistic Civilization.* 3rd ed. London: E. Arnold, 1952.

TCHERIKOVER, V. *Hellenistic Civilization and the Jews.* Translated by S. Applebaum. Philadelphia: Jewish Publication Society of America, 1959.

VAN UNNIK, WILLEM CORNELIS. *Newly Discovered Gnostic Writings: A Preliminary Survey of the Nag Hammadi Find.* London: SCM Press, 1960.

WILSON, ROBERT McL. *Gnosis and the New Testament.* Philadelphia: Fortress Press, 1968.

WINSLOW, D. "Religion and the Early Roman Empire." In *The Catacombs and the Colosseum: The Roman Empire as the Setting of Primitive Christianity.* Edited by S. Benko and J. J. O'Rourke. Valley Forge: Judson Press, 1971.

Chapter 13: The Acts Narrative of Paul's Missions

BARRETT, CHARLES KINGSLEY. "Acts and the Pauline Corpus." *Expository Times* 88 (1976–77): 2–5.

BORNKAMM, GUNTHER. *Paul.* New York:: Harper & Row, 1971.

BRUCE, FREDERICK FYVIE. *Paul: Apostle of the Heart Set Free.* Exeter: Paternoster, 1977.

CADBURY, H. J. *The Book of Acts in History.* New York: Harper & Bros., 1955.

CAIRD, C. B. "Chronology of the New Testament." *Interpreter's Dictionary of the Bible,* 599–607.

DIBELIUS, MARTIN. *Studies in the Acts of the Apostles.* Translated by M. Ling. Edited by H. Greeven. New York: Charles Scribner's Sons, 1956.

DUPONT, JACQUES. *The Salvation of the Gentiles: Essays on the Acts of the Apostles.* Translated by J. Keating. New York: Paulist Press, 1979.

FLENDER, HELMUT. *St. Luke: Theologian of Redemptive History.* Translated by I. Fuller and R. H. Fuller. Philadelphia: Fortress Press, 1967.

GÄRTNER, BERTIL EDGAR. *The Areopagus Speech and Natural Revelation.* Translated by C. H. King. Uppsala: C. W. K. Gleerup, 1955.

HAENCHEN, ERNST. "We in Acts and the Intinerary." *Journal For Theology and Church* 1 (1965): 65ff.

HULTGREN, ARLAND. "Paul's Pre-Christian Persecutions of the Church: their Purpose, Locale and Nature." *Journal of Biblical Literature* 95 (1976): 97–111.

JERVELL, J. *Luke and the People of God.* Minneapolis: Augsburg Publishing House, 1972.

JEWETT, ROBERT. *A Chronology of Paul's Life.* Philadelphia: Fortress Press, 1979.

KNOX, JOHN. *Chapters in a Life of Paul.* Nashville: Abingdon-Cokesbury Press, 1950.

KNOX, WILFRED LAWRENCE. *The Acts of the Apostles.* Cambridge: At the University Press, 1948.

LUEDEMANN, GERD. *Paul Apostle to the Gentiles. Studies in Chronology.* Translated by F. S. Jones. Philadelphia: Fortress Press, 1984.

NICKLE, KEITH FULLERTON. *The Collection: A Study in Paul's Strategy.* London: SCM Press, 1966.

OGG, G. *The Chronology of the Life of Paul*. London: Epworth Press, 1968.

UNNIK, WILLEM CORNELIUS VAN. *Tarsus or Jerusalem: The City of Paul's Youth*. Translated by G. Ogg. London: Epworth Press, 1962.

WILLIAMS, CHARLES STEPHEN CONWAY. *A Commentary on the Acts of the Apostles*. New York: Harper & Row, 1957.

Chapter 14: Paul's Letters to Thessalonica and Corinth

BAIRD, WILLIAM. "Among the Mature." *Interpretation* 13 (1959): 425–432.

BARRETT, CHARLES KINGSLEY, ed. *The New Testament Background: Selected Documents*. New York: Macmillan, 1957.

———. *A Commentary on the First Epistle to the Corinthians*. Harper's NT Commentary. New York: Harper & Row, 1968.

———. *A Commentary on the Second Epistle to the Corinthians*. Harper's NT Commentary. New York: Harper & Row, 1973.

BEARE, FRANCIS WRIGHT. *St. Paul and His Letters*. Nashville: Abingdon Press, 1962.

BEST, ERNEST. *A Commentary on the First and Second Epistles to the Thessalonians*. New York: Harper & Row, 1972.

BETZ, HANS DIETER. "2 Cor. 6:14–7:1: An Anti-Pauline Fragment." *Journal of Biblical Literature* 92 (1973): 88–108.

BOERS, H. W. "Apocalyptic Eschatology in I Corinthians 15." *Interpretation* 21 (1967): 50–65.

BORNKAMM, GUNTHER. *Paul*. New York: Harper & Row, 1971.

BRADLEY, D. G. "The Typos as a Form in Pauline Paraenesis." *Journal of Biblical Literature* 72 (1953): 238ff.

BRUCE, FREDERICK FYVIE. *I and II Corinthians*. London: Oliphants, 1971.

———. *Paul: Apostle of the Heart Set Free*. Exeter: Paternoster, 1977.

CHADWICK, HENRY. "All Things to All Men." *NT Studies* 1 (1955): 261–275.

———. "The Missionary Stance of Paul in I Corinthians and Acts." In *Studies in Luke-Acts*. Edited by L. Keck and J. Louis Martyn. Philadelphia: Fortress Press, 1966.

CONZELMANN, HANS. *I Corinthians: A Commentary on the First Epistle to the Corinthians*. Translated by J. W. Leitch. Philadelphia: Fortress Press, 1975.

CRAIG, CLARENCE. T. "I Corinthians." *Interpreter's Bible* (1954) 10: 3–262.

CULLMANN, OSCAR. *Christ and Time: The Primitive Christian Conception of Time and History*. Philadelphia: Westminster Press, 1950.

DAHL, NILS. "The Church at Corinth." In *Studies in Paul: Theology for the Early Christian Mission*. Translated by N. Dahl. Minneapolis: Augsburg Publishing House, 1977.

DEISSMANN, GUSTAV ADOLF. *Paul: A Study in Social and Religious History*. Translated by W. E. Wilson. London: Holder, 1926. 2nd ed.

DODD, CHARLES HAROLD. *Gospel and Law: The Relation of Faith and Ethics in Early Christianity*. New York: Columbia University Press, 1951.

FEE, GORDON D. "*Eidolothuta* Once Again: An Interpretation of I Cor. 8–10." *Biblica* 61 (1980): 172–197.

FITZMYER, JOSEPH. "A Feature of Qumran Angelology And The Angels of I Cor. 11:10." *NT Studies* (1957): 49–58.

———. "Qumran and the Interpolated Paragraph in 2 Cor. 6:14–7:1." In *Essays on the Semitic Background of the New Testament*. London: G. Chapman, 1971.

FILSON, FLOYD V. "The Second Epistle to the Corinthians." *Interpreter's Bible* 10: 265–425.

FUNK, ROBERT. *Language, Hermeneutic, and the Word of God: The Problem of Language in the NT and Contemporary Theology*. New York: Harper & Row, 1966.

FURNISH, VICTOR PAUL. *Second Corinthians.* Anchor Bible Commentary. Garden City, NY: Doubleday, 1984.

GEORGI, DIETER. "Second Letter to the Corinthians." *Interpreter's Dictionary of the Bible, Supplementary Volume,* 183–186.

HÉRING, JEAN. *The First Epistle of St. Paul to the Corinthians.* Translated by A. W. Heathcote and P. J. Allcock. London: Epworth Press, 1962.

HOOKER, MORNA D. "Authority on Her Head: An Examination of I Cor. 11:10." *NT Studies* 10 (1963): 410–416.

HURD, JOHN COOLIDGE. *The Origin of I Corinthians.* New York: Seabury Press, 1965.

JEWETT, ROBERT. *A Chronology of Paul's Life.* Philadelphia: Fortress Press, 1979.

KÄSEMANN, ERNST. "The Pauline Doctrine of the Lord's Supper." In *Essays on New Testament Themes.* Translated by W. J. Montague. London: SCM Press, 1964.

KECK, LEANDER. "The First Letter of Paul to the Thessalonians." In Charles M. Laymon (ed.), *Interpreter's Bible One-Volume Commentary.* Nashville: Abingdon Press, 1971.

MUNCK, JOHANNES. *Paul and the Salvation of Mankind.* Richmond: John Knox Press, 1959.

MURPHY-O'CONNOR, JEROME. *St. Paul's Corinth: Text and Archeology.* Wilmington, Del.: Michael Glazier, 1983.

PRICE, JAMES LIGON. "Aspects of Paul's Theology and Their Bearing on Literary Problems of 2 Corinthians." In *Studies and Documents.* Vol. 39. Edited by J. Geerlings. Salt Lake City: University of Utah, 1968.

REICKE, BO. "The Law and This World According to Paul; Some Thoughts Concerning Gal. 4:1–11." *Journal of Biblical Literature* 70 (1951): 261–276.

SCHMITHALS, WALTER. *Gnosticism in Corinth: An Investigation of the Letters to the Corinthians.* Translated by John Steely. Nashville: Abingdon Press, 1971.

SCROGGS, ROBIN. "Paul and the Eschatological Woman." *Journal of the American Academy of Religion* 40 (1972): 283–303; 42 (1974): 532–537.

WEISS, JOHANNES. *The History of Primitive Christianity.* Vols. 1–2. New York: Wilson-Erickson, Inc., 1937.

Chapter 15: The Galatian and Roman Letters

ACHTEMIER, ELIZABETH R. "Righteousness in the OT." *Interpreter's Dictionary of the Bible* 4: 80–85.

BARRETT, CHARLES KINGSLEY. *A Commentary on the Epistle to the Romans.* Harper's NT Commentary. New York: Harper & Row, 1957.

BARTH, KARL. *A Shorter Commentary on Romans.* Richmond: John Knox Press, 1959.

BARTH, MARKUS. "The Kerygma of Galatians." *Interpretation* 21 (1967): 131–146.

BEST, ERNEST. *One Body in Christ: A Study in the Relationship of the Church to Christ in the Epistles of the Apostle Paul.* London: S.P.C.K., 1955.

BETZ, HANS DIETER. *A Commentary on Paul's Letter to the Churches in Galatia.* Hermeneia Commentary. Philadelphia: Fortress Press, 1979.

BRAUCH, M. T. "Perspectives on God's Righteousness in Recent German Discussion." Appendix in Sanders, Ed Parish. *Paul and Palestinian Judaism: A Comparison of Patterns of Religion.* Philadelphia: Fortress Press, 1977.

BRUNNER, EMIL. *The Letter to the Romans, a Commentary.* Philadelphia: Westminster Press, 1959.

BURTON, ERNEST DE WITT. *A Critical and Exegetical Commentary on the Epistle to the Galatians.* International Critical Commentary. New York: Charles Scribner's Sons, 1920.

DAUBE, DAVID. "The Interpretation of a Generic Singular in Galatians 3:16." *Jewish Quarterly Review* 35 (1944): 227–230.

DODD, CHARLES H. *The Epistle of Paul to the Romans.* Moffatt NT Commentary. New York: Harper & Bros., 1932.

DONFRIED, KARL P., ed. *The Romans Debate.* Minneapolis: Augsburg Publishing House, 1977.

DUNCAN, GEORGE S. *The Epistle of Paul to the Galatians.* Moffatt NT Commentary. London: Hodder & Stoughton, 1934.

FITZMYER, JOSEPH AUGUSTINE. *Pauline Theology: A Brief Sketch.* Englewood Cliffs, NJ: Prentice-Hall, 1967.

GAGER, J. "Some Notes on Paul's Conversion." *NT Studies* 27 (1981): 697–704.

GAMBLE, HARRY, JR. "The Textual History of the Letter to the Romans." In *Studies and Documents* 42. Edited by I. A. Sparks. Grand Rapids, Mich.: Eerdmans, 1977.

HOWARD, GEORGE. "On the Faith of Christ." *Harvard Theological Review* 60 (1967): 459ff.

KÄSEMANN, ERNST. *New Testament Questions of Today.* Philadelphia: Fortress Press, 1969.

KNOX, JOHN. "The Epistle to the Romans." *Interpreter's Bible* 9: 355–668.

LEENHARDT, FRANZ J. *The Epistle to the Romans: a Commentary.* Translated by H. Knight. London: Butterworth Press, 1961.

LIGHTFOOT, JOSEPH BARBER. *St. Paul's Epistle to the Galatians.* London: Macmillan, 1905.

Manson, T. W. "St. Paul's Letter to the Romans—And Others." *Bulletin of the John Rylands University Library, Manchester* 31 (1948): 224–240.

MANSON, W. "Notes on the Argument of Romans 1–8." In *New Testament Essays: Studies in Memory of Thomas W. Manson.* Edited by A. J. B. Higgins. Manchester: Manchester University Press, 1959.

MARXSEN, WILLI. *Introduction to the New Testament: An Approach to its Problems.* Oxford: Blackwell, 1968.

MINEAR, PAUL SEVIER. *The Obedience of Faith: The Purposes of Paul in the Epistle to the Romans.* London: SCM Press, 1971.

MITTON, L. "Romans 7 Reconsidered." *Expository Times* 65 (1953–54): 78ff., 99ff., 132ff..

MORRISON, CLINTON D. *The Powers That Be: Earthly Rulers and Demonic Powers in Rom. 13:1–7.* London: SCM Press, 1960.

NYGREN, ANDERS. *Commentary on Romans.* Translated by D. C. Rasmussen. Philadelphia: Muhlenberg Press, 1949.

PRICE, JAMES LIGON. "God's Righteousness Shall Prevail." *Interpretation* 28 (1974): 249–280.

RAMSAY, WILLIAM M. *A Historical Commentary on St. Paul's Epistle to the Galatians.* London: Hodder & Stoughton, 1899.

———. *St. Paul the Traveller and Roman Citizen.* New York: G. P. Putnam's Sons, 1896.

REUMANN, JOHN. "The Gospel of the Righteousness of God." *Interpretation* 20 (1966): 432–452.

SANDERS, J. T. "Paul's Autobiographical Statements in Galatians 1–2." *Journal of Biblical Literature* 85 (1966): 335ff.

SCOTT, CHARLES ARCHIBALD ANDERSON. *Christianity According to St. Paul.* Cambridge: At the University Press, 1927.

TANNEHILL, R. C. *Dying and Rising with Christ. A Study in Pauline Theology.* Berlin: Topelmann, 1967.

TAYLOR, G. M. "The Function of Pistis Christou in Galatians." *Journal of Biblical Literature* 85 (1966): 58ff.

WAGNER, GÜNTER. *Pauline Baptism and the Pagan Mysteries: The Problem of the Pauline Doctrine of Baptism in Rom. 6:1–11, in the Light of its Religio-Historical "Parallels."* Translated by J. P. Smith. Edinburgh: Oliver & Boyd, 1967.

WILLIAMS, S. K. "The Righteousness of God in Romans." *Journal of Biblical Literature* 99 (1980): 241–290.

Chapter 16: Letters from Prison

BARTCHY, S. SCOTT. *Mallon Chrēsai: First-Century Slavery and 1 Corinthians 7:21.* Missoula, Mont.: Society of Biblical Literature, 1973.

BEARE, FRANCIS WRIGHT. *A Commentary on the Epistle to the Philippians.* Harper's NT Commentary, London: A. & C. Black, 1959.

CAIRD, GEORGE BRADFORD. *Paul's Letters from Prison: Ephesians, Philippians, Colossians, Philemon, in the Revised Standard Version: Introduction and Commentary.* New Clarendon Bible Commentary. Oxford: At the University Press, 1976.

COLEMAN-NORTON, P. R. "The Apostle Paul and the Roman Law of Slavery." In *Studies in Roman Economic and Social History in Honor of A. C. Johnson.* Edited by P. R. Coleman-Norton, et al. Princeton: Princeton University Press, 1951.

DUNCAN, GEORGE STEWART. *St. Paul's Ephesian Ministry: A Reconstruction with Special Reference to the Ephesian Origin of the Imprisonment Epistles.* London: Hodder & Stoughton, Ltd., 1929.

GOODSPEED, EDGAR J. *New Solutions of New Testament Problems.* Chicago: University of Chicago Press, 1927.

HAWTHORNE, GERALD F. *Philippians. Word Biblical Commentary* 43. Waco, Tex.: Word Books, 1983.

KÄSEMANN, ERNST. "A Critical Analysis of Philippians 2:5–11." Translated by A. F. Carse. *Journal for Theology and Church* 5 (1968): 45–88.

KNOX, JOHN. "The Epistle to Philemon." *Interpreter's Bible* 11: 555–573.

MARTIN, RALPH P. *Carmen Christi; Philippians 2:5–11 in Recent Interpretation and in the Setting of Early Christian Worship.* London: Cambridge University Press, 1967.

MOULE, CHARLES FRANCIS DIGBY. *The Epistles of Paul the Apostle to the Colossians and Philemon.* Cambridge: At the University Press, 1957.

REICKE, BO. "The Historical Setting of Colossians." *Review and Expositor* 70 (1973): 429–438.

SANDERS, ED PARISH. "Literary Dependence in Colossians." *Journal of Biblical Literature* 85 (1966): 28ff.

SCHWEIZER, EDUARD. "Christ in the Letter to the Colossians." *Review and Expositor* 70 (1973): 455–459.

Chapter 17: Writings from the Pauline Circle

BARRETT, CHARLES KINGSLEY. *The Pastoral Epistles in the New English Bible.* New Clarendon Bible Commentary. Oxford: Clarendon Press, 1963.

BARTH, MARKUS. *Ephesians: Introduction, Translation and Commentary.* 2 Vols. Anchor Bible Commentary. New York: Doubleday, 1974.

BEARE, FREDERICK FYVIE. *Paul: Apostle of the Heart Set Free.* Exeter: Paternoster, 1977.

CADBURY, HENRY J. "The Dilemma of Ephesians." *NT Studies* 5 (1958–1959): 91–102.

———. "The New Testament and Early Christian Literature." *Interpreter's Bible* 7: 32–42.

CROSS, FRANK LESLIE, ed. *Studies in Ephesians.* London: A. R. Mowbray, 1956.

DAHL, NILS. "Ephesians." *Interpreter's Dictionary of the Bible, Supplementary Volume* (1976), 268f.

DIBELIUS, MARTIN, and HANS CONZELMANN. *A Commentary on the Pastoral Epistles.*

Hermeneia Commentary. Translated by P. Buttolph and A. Yarbro. Philadelphia: Fortress Press, 1972.

DUNCAN, GEORGE. *St. Paul's Ephesian Ministry: A Reconstruction with Special Reference to the Ephesian Origin of the Imprisonment Epistles.* London: Hodder & Stoughton, 1929.

EASTON, BURTON SCOTT. *The Pastoral Epistles: Introduction, Translation, Commentary and Word Studies.* New York: Charles Scribner's Sons, 1947.

GEALY, F. D. "I and II Timothy, Titus." *Interpreter's Bible* 11: 343–551.

GOODSPEED, EDGAR JOHNSON. *The Meaning of Ephesians.* Chicago: University of Chicago Press, 1933.

GUTHRIE, DONALD. *The Pastoral Epistles: An Introduction and Commentary.* Tyndale NT Commentary. Grand Rapids, Mich.: Eerdmans, 1957.

HARRISON, PERCY NEALE. *The Problem of the Pastoral Epistles.* London: Oxford University Press, 1921.

KÄSEMANN, ERNST. "Ephesians and Acts." In *Studies in Luke-Acts.* Edited by L. Keck and J. L. Martyn. Philadelphia: Fortress Press, 1966.

KELLY, JOHN NORMAN DAVIDSON. *A Commentary on the Pastoral Epistles; I Timothy, II Timothy, Titus.* Harper's NT Commentary. New York: Harper & Row, 1963.

MITTON, C. LESLIE. *The Epistle to the Ephesians: Its Authorship, Origin, and Purpose.* New Century Bible Commentary. Oxford: Clarendon Press, 1951.

MURPHY-O'CONNOR, JEROME. *Paul and Qumran: Studies in NT Exegesis.* Chicago: Priory Press, 1968.

ROBINSON, JOHN ARTHUR THOMAS. *Redating the New Testament.* London: SCM Press, 1976.

SCHWEIZER, EDUARD. *Lordship and Discipleship.* London: SCM Press, 1960.

SCOTT, ERNEST FINDLEY. *The Pastoral Epistles.* New York: Harper & Bros. 1937.

SHEPHERD, M. H., Jr. "The Post-Apostolic Age." *Interpreter's Bible* 7: 214–227.

WILSON, ROBERT McL. *Gnosis and the New Testament.* Philadelphia: Fortress Press, 1968.

Chapter 18: Five "Open Letters" to Christians

BARRETT, CHARLES KINGSLEY. "The Eschatology of the Epistle to the Hebrews." In *The Background of the New Testament and Its Eschatology.* Edited by W. D. Davies and D. Daube. Cambridge: At the University Press, 1956.

BEARE, FRANCIS WRIGHT. *The First Epistle of Peter. The Greek Text with Introduction and Notes.* 3rd ed. Oxford: Blackwell, 1970.

BEKER, J. CHRISTIAAN. "Peter, Second Letter of." *Interpreter's Dictionary of the Bible* 3: 767–771.

BEST, ERNEST. *I Peter.* London: Oliphants, 1971.

———. "I Peter and the Gospel Tradition." *NT Studies* 16 (1969–1970): 95–113.

BROWN, RAYMOND E., K. DONFRIED and J. REUMANN, eds. *Peter in the New Testament; A Collaborative Assessment by Protestant and Roman Catholic Scholars.* Minneapolis: Augsburg Publishing House, 1973.

CROSS, FRANK LESLIE. *I Peter: a Paschal Liturgy.* London: A. R. Mowbray & Co., 1954.

DALTON, WILLIAM J. *Christ's Proclamation to the Spirits: A Study of 1 Peter 3:18–4:6.* Rome: Pontifical Biblical Institute, 1965.

DIBELIUS, MARTIN, and HEINRICH GREEVEN. *A Commentary on the Epistle of James.* Hermeneia Commentary. Translated by M. A. Williams. Philadelphia: Fortress Press, 1976.

ELLIOTT, JOHN H. *A Home for the Homeless: A Sociological Exegesis of I Peter, Its Situation and Strategy.* Philadelphia: Fortress Press, 1981.

———. "The Rehabilitation of an Exegetical Step-Child: I Peter in Recent Research." *Journal of Biblical Literature* 95 (1976): 243–254.

FITZMYER, JOSEPH. "The First Epistle of Peter." *Jerome Bible Commentary* 58: 1–27.

FULLER, REGINALD H., et al. *The Letter to the Hebrews, James, 1 and 2 Peter, Jude, Revelation.* Proclamation Commentaries. Edited by Gerhard Krodel. Philadelphia: Fortress Press, 1977.

GRANT, ROBERT McQUEEN. *A Historical Introduction to the New Testament.* New York: Harper & Row, 1963.

GUNDRY, ROBERT H. "Verba Christi in I Peter." *NT Studies* 13 (1966–67): 336–350.

JAMES, MONTAGUE RHODES. *The Apocryphal New Testament, being the Apocryphal Gospels, Acts, Epistles, and Apocalypses, with Other Narratives and Fragments.* Oxford: Clarendon Press, 1924.

KÄSEMANN, ERNST. "An Apologia for Primitive Christian Eschatology." In *Essays on New Testament Themes.* Translated by W. J. Montague. London: SCM Press, 1964.

KELLY, JOHN NORMAN DAVIDSON. *A Commentary on the Epistles of Peter and Jude.* Harper's NT Commentary. London: A. & C. Black, 1969.

KNOX, JOHN. "Pliny and I Peter." *Journal of Biblical Literature* 72 (1953): 187–189.

LAWS, SOPHIE. *A Commentary on the Epistle of James.* Harper's NT Commentary. San Francisco: Harper & Row, 1980.

McRAE, G. "Heavenly Temple and Eschatology in the Letter to the Hebrews." *Semeia* 12 (1978): 179ff.

MOFFATT, J. *A Critical and Exegetical Commentary on the Epistle to the Hebrews.* International Critical Commentary. New York: Charles Scribner's Sons, 1924.

MOULE, C. F. D. "The Nature and Purpose of I Peter." *NT Studies* 3 (1956): 1–11.

REICKE, BO. The Epistles of James, Peter and Jude. *Anchor Bible Commentary*, 37, Garden City, NY: Doubleday, 1964.

SELWYN, EDWARD GORDON. *The First Epistle of St. Peter.* London: Macmillan, 1947.

STREETER, BURNETT HILLMAN. *The Primitive Church. Studied With Special Reference to the Origins of the Christian Ministry.* London: Macmillan, 1929.

TALBERT, C. H. "II Peter and the Delay of the Parousia." *Vigilae Christianae* 20 (1966): 137–145.

TASKER, RANDOLPH VINCENT GREENWOOD. *The General Epistle of James: An Introduction and Commentary.* Tyndale NT Commentary. Grand Rapids, Mich.: Eerdmans, 1956.

THOMPSON, J. W. "That Which Cannot Be Shaken; Some Metaphysical Assumptions in Heb. 12:27." *Journal of Biblical Literature* 94 (1975): 580–587.

UNNIK, W. C. VAN. "Peter, First Letter of." *Interpreter's Dictionary of the Bible, 3,* (1962), 758–766.

WAND, JOHN WILLIAM CHARLES. *The General Epistles of St. Peter and St. Jude.* Westminster Commentaries. London: Methuen & Co., Ltd. 1934.

Chapter 19: *The Apocalypse from the Johannine Circle*

BOWMAN, JOHN W. "Revelation, Book of." *Interpreter's Dictionary of the Bible* (1962) 4:58–71.

CHARLES, ROBERT HENRY. *A Critical and Exegetical Commentary on the Revelation of St. John.* Vols. 1 and 2. International Critical Commentary. New York: Charles Scribner's Sons, 1920.

CAIRD, GEORGE BRADFORD. *A Commentary on the Revelation of St. John the Divine.* London: Black, 1966.

FULLER, REGINALD H., and G. ERNEST WRIGHT. *The Book of the Acts of God: Christian Scholarship Interprets the Bible.* Garden City, NY: Doubleday, 1960.

KALLAS, JAMES. "The Apocalypse—An Apocalyptic Book?" *Journal of Biblical Literature* 86 (1967): 69–80.

KLASSEN, WILLIAM. "Vengeance in the Apocalypse of John." *Catholic Biblical Quarterly* 28 (1966): 300–311.

MCNEILE, ALAN HUGH, and C. S. C. Williams. *An Introduction to the Study of the New Testament.* Oxford: Clarendon Press, 1953.

MOWRY, LUCETTA. "Revelation 4–5 and Early Christian Liturgical Usage." *Journal of Biblical Literature* 71 (1952): 75–84.

PRESTON, RONALD H., and ANTHONY T. HANSON. *The Revelation of St. John the Divine.* London: SCM Press, 1949.

RIST, MARTIN. "The Book of Revelation." *Interpreter's Bible* 12: 347–613.

SCOTT, ERNEST FINDLAY. *The Book of Revelation.* London: Student Christian Movement Press, 1941.

Chapter 20: *The Gospel and Letters of John*

ALBRIGHT, W. F. "Discoveries in Palestine and the Gospel of John." In *The Background of the New Testament and Its Eschatology.* Edited by W. D. Davies and D. Daube. Cambridge: At the University Press, 1956.

BARRETT, CHARLES KINGSLEY. *The Gospel According to St. John. An Introduction with Commentary and Notes on the Greek Text.* 2nd ed. Philadelphia: Westminster Press, 1978.

———. "The Theological Vocabulary of the Fourth Gospel and of the Gospel of Truth." In *Current Issues in New Testament Interpretation. Essays in Honor of Otto A. Piper.* Edited by W. Klassen and G. F. Snyder. New York: Harper & Row, 1962.

BROWN, RAYMOND E. *The Community of the Beloved Disciple.* New York: Paulist Press, 1979.

———. *The Epistles of John.* Anchor Bible Commentary, Vol. 30. Garden City, NY: Doubleday, 1982.

———. *The Gospel According to John. Introduction, Translation, and Notes. Vol. 1, chs. 1–12.* Anchor Bible Commentary, Vol. 29. Garden City, NY: Doubleday, 1966.

———. *The Gospel According to John. Introduction, Translation, and Notes. Vol. 2, chs. 13–21.* Vol. 29A. Garden City, NY: Doubleday, 1970.

CAIRD, GEORGE B. "John, Letters of." *Interpreter's Dictionary of the Bible* 2: 946–952.

CULPEPPER, R. ALAN. *Anatomy of Fourth Gospel: A study in Literary Design.* Philadelphia: Fortress Press, 1983.

DAHL, NILS. "The Johannine Church and History." In *Current Issues in New Testament Interpretation. Essays in Honor of Otto A. Piper.* Edited by W. Klassen and G. F. Snyder. New York: Harper & Row, 1962.

DODD, CHARLES HAROLD. *Historical Tradition in the Fourth Gospel.* Cambridge: At the University Press, 1963.

———. *The Interpretation of the Fourth Gospel.* Cambridge: At the University Press, 1953.

———. *The Johannine Epistles.* New York: Harper & Bros., 1946.

GARDNER-SMITH, PERCIVAL N. *St. John and the Synoptics.* Cambridge: At the University Press, 1938.

HAENCHEN, ERNST. *A Commentary on the Gospel of John.* 2 Vols. Hermeneia Commentary. Translated by R. W. Funk. Philadelphia: Fortress Press, 1984.

HOWARD, WILBERT FRANCIS. *The Fourth Gospel in Recent Criticism and Interpretation.* 4th ed. Revised by C. K. Barrett. London: Epworth Press, 1955.

———. "The Gospel According to St. John." *Interpreter's Bible* 8: 437–811.

KÄSEMANN, ERNST. *The Testament of Jesus: A Study of the Gospel of John in the Light of Chapter 17.* Translated by G. Krodel. Philadelphia: Fortress Press, 1968.

NEILL, STEPHEN CHARLES. *Interpretation of the New Testament, 1861–1961.* London: Oxford University Press, 1964.

ROBERTS, C. H. *An Unpublished Fragment of the Fourth Gospel in the John Rylands Library*. Manchester: Manchester University Press, 1935.

SCHNACKENBURG, RUDOLF. *The Gospel According to John. Vol. 1, Introduction and Commentary on Chapters 1–4*. Translated by K. Smyth. New York: Seabury Press, 1980.

————. *The Gospel According to John. Vol. 2, Commentary on Chapters 5–12*. Translated by Cecily Hastings, F. McDonagh, D. Smith, and R. Foley. New York: Seabury Press, 1980.

————. *The Gospel According to John. Vol. 3, Commentary on Chapters 13–21*. Translated by D. Smith and G. A. Kon. New York: Crossroads, 1982.

SMITH, D. MOODY. *The Composition and Order of the Fourth Gospel: Bultmann's Literary Theory*. New Haven and London: Yale University Press, 1965.

————. "John, Gospel of." *Interpreter's Dictionary of the Bible*, Supplementary Volume (1976), 482–486.

STRACHAN, ROBERT HARVEY. *The Fourth Gospel, its Significance and Environment*. 3rd ed. London: SCM Press, 1941.

Index